Discourses

CONCERNING GOVERNMENT

Algernon Sidney

Discourses

CONCERNING GOVERNMENT

by Algernon Sidney

EDITED BY THOMAS G. WEST

Liberty Fund

This book is published by Liberty Fund, Inc., a foundation established to encourage study of the ideal of a society of free and responsible individuals.

The cuneiform inscription that serves as the design motif for our end-papers is the earliest-known written appearance of the word "freedom" (*ama-gi*), or "liberty." It is taken from a clay document written about 2300 B.C. in the Sumerian city-state of Lagash.

Frontispiece portrait of Sidney by Justus Versus of Egmond reproduced by permission of Viscount De L'Isle VC.KG., from his private collection.

Library of Congress Cataloging-in-Publication Data

Sidney, Algernon, 1622–1683.
  Discourses concerning government / by Algernon Sidney ; edited by Thomas G. West.—Rev. ed.
    p.   cm.
  Includes bibliographical references and index.
  ISBN 0-86597-141-2 (hc).—ISBN 0-86597-142-0 (pbk.)
  1. Political science—Early works to 1800. 2. Monarchy.
3. Republics. I. West, Thomas G., 1945– . II. Title.
JC153.S5   1996b   95-46031
320.1—dc20

          22 23 24 25 26 C 7 6 5 4 3
          22 23 24 25 26 P 9 8 7 6 5

libertyfund.org

CONTENTS

FOREWORD, XV

BIBLIOGRAPHY, XXXVII

EDITOR'S NOTE, XLI

CHAPTER ONE

SECTION 1. *Introduction*   5

SECTION 2. *The common notions of Liberty are not from School Divines, but from Nature.*   8

SECTION 3. *Implicit Faith belongs to Fools, and Truth is comprehended by examining Principles.*   12

SECTION 4. *The Rights of particular Nations cannot subsist, if General Principles contrary to them are received as true.*   16

SECTION 5. *To depend upon the Will of a Man is Slavery.*   17

SECTION 6. *God leaves to man the choice of Forms in Government; and those who constitute one Form, may abrogate it.*   20

SECTION 7. *Abraham and the Patriarchs were not Kings.*   24

SECTION 8. *Nimrod was the first King, during the life of Cush, Ham, Shem, and Noah.*   25

Contents

Section 9. *The Power of a Father belongs only to a Father.*   29

Section 10. *Such as enter into Society, must in some degree diminish their Liberty.*   30

Section 11. *No Man comes to command many, unless by Consent or by Force.*   32

Section 12. *The pretended paternal Right is divisible or indivisible: if divisible, 'tis extinguished; if indivisible, universal.*   33

Section 13. *There was no shadow of a paternal Kingdom amongst the Hebrews, nor precept for it.*   36

Section 14. *If the paternal Right had included Dominion, and was to be transferred to a single Heir, it must perish if he were not known; and could be applied to no other person.*   39

[Section 15.]

Section 16. *The Ancients chose those to be Kings, who excelled in the Virtues that are most beneficial to Civil Socities.*   46

Section 17. *God having given the Government of the World to no one Man, nor declared how it should be divided, left it to the Will of Man.*   53

Section 18. *If a right of Dominion were esteemed Hereditary according to the Law of Nature, a multitude of destructive and inextricable Controversies would thereupon arise.*   57

Section 19. *Kings cannot confer the Right of Father upon Princes, nor Princes upon Kings.*   62

Section 20. *All just Magistratical Power is from the People.*   69

CHAPTER TWO

Section 1. *That 'tis natural for Nations to govern, or to chuse Governors; and that Virtue only gives a natural preference of one man above another, or reason why one should be chosen rather than another.*   77

Section 2. *Every Man that hath Children, hath the right of a Father, and is capable of preferment in a Society composed of many.*   88

Section 3. *Government is not instituted for the good of the Governor, but of the Governed; and Power is not an Advantage, but a Burden.*   91

Section 4. *The Paternal Right devolves to, and is inherited by all the Children.*   92

Section 5. *Freemen join together, and frame greater or lesser Societies, and give such Forms to them as best please themselves.*   97

Section 6. *They who have a right of chusing a King, have the right of making a King.*   108

Contents

SECTION 7. *The Laws of every Nation are the measure of Magistratical Power.* 113

SECTION 8. *There is no natural propensity in Man or Beast to Monarchy.* 121

SECTION 9. *The Government instituted by God over the Israelites was Aristocratical.* 124

SECTION 10. *Aristotle was not simply for Monarchy, or against Popular Government, but approved or disapproved of either according to circumstances.* 132

SECTION 11. *Liberty produceth Virtue, Order and Stability: Slavery is accompanied with Vice, Weakness and Misery.* 134

SECTION 12. *The Glory, Virtue, and Power of the Romans, began and ended with their Liberty.* 144

SECTION 13. *There is no disorder or prejudice in changing the name or number of Magistrates, whilst the root and principle of their Power continues entire.* 149

SECTION 14. *No Sedition was hurtful to Rome, til through their Prosperity some men gained a Power above the Laws.* 153

SECTION 15. *The Empire of Rome perpetually decay'd when it fell into the hands of one Man.* 157

SECTION 16. *The best Governments of the World have been composed of Monarchy, Aristocracy, and Democracy.* 166

SECTION 17. *Good Governments admit of Changes in the Superstructures, whilst the Foundations remain unchangeable.* 170

SECTION 18. *Xenophon in blaming the Disorders of Democracies, favours Aristocracies, not Monarchies.* 175

SECTION 19. *That Corruption and Venality which is natural to Courts, is seldom found in Popular Governments.* 184

SECTION 20. *Man's natural love to Liberty is temper'd by Reason, which originally is his Nature.* 191

SECTION 21. *Mixed and Popular Governments preserve Peace, and manage Wars better than Absolute Monarchies.* 195

SECTION 22. *Commonwealths seek Peace or War, according to the Variety of their Constitutions.* 202

SECTION 23. *That is the best Government, which best provides for War.* 209

SECTION 24. *Popular Governments are less subject to Civil Disorders than Monarchies; manage them more ably, and more easily recover out of them.* 217

Contents

SECTION 25. *Courts are more subject to Venality and Corruption than Popular Governments.* 251

SECTION 26. *Civil Tumults and Wars are not the greatest Evils that befall Nations.* 259

SECTION 27. *The Mischiefs and Cruelties proceeding from Tyranny are greater than any that can come from Popular or mixed Governments.* 263

SECTION 28. *Men living under Popular or Mix'd Governments, are more careful of the publick Good, than in Absolute Monarchies.* 270

SECTION 29. *There is no assurance that the Distempers of a State shall be cured by the Wisdom of a Prince.* 279

SECTION 30. *A Monarchy cannot be well regulated, unless the Powers of the Monarch are limited by Law.* 287

SECTION 31. *The Liberties of Nations are from God and Nature, not from Kings.* 303

SECTION 32. *The Contracts made between Magistrates, and the Nations that created them, were real, solemn, and obligtory.* 309

CHAPTER THREE

SECTION 1. *Kings not being fathers of their People, nor excelling all others in Virtue, can have no other just Power than what the Laws give; nor any title to the privileges of the Lord's Anointed.* 319

SECTION 2. *The Kings of Israel and Judah were under a Law not safely to be transgress'd.* 334

SECTION 3. *Samuel did not describe to the Israelites the glory of a free Monarchy; but the Evils the People should suffer, that he might divert them from desiring a King.* 336

SECTION 4. *No People can be obliged to suffer from their Kings what they have not a right to do.* 339

SECTION 5. *The Mischiefs suffer'd from wicked Kings are such as render it both reasonable and just for all Nations that have virtue and Power, to exert both in repelling them.* 344

SECTION 6. *'Tis not good for such Nations as will have Kings, to suffer them to be glorious, powerful, or abounding in Riches.* 348

SECTION 7. *When the Israelites asked for such a King as the Nations about them had, they asked for a Tyrant tho they did not call him so.* 353

SECTION 8. *Under the name of Tribute no more is understood than what the Law of each Nation gives to the Supreme Magistrate for the*

Contents

defraying of publick Charges; to which the customs of the Romans, or sufferings of the Jews have no relation.   359

SECTION 9. *Our own Laws confirm to us the enjoyment of our native Rights.*   366

SECTION 10. *The words of St. Paul enjoining obedience to higher Powers, favour all sorts of Governments no less than Monarchy.*   370

SECTION 11. *That which is not just, is not Law; and that which is not Law ought not to be obeyed.*   380

SECTION 12. *The Right and Power of a Magistrate depends upon his Institution, not upon his Name.*   383

SECTION 13. *Laws were made to direct and instruct Magistrates, and, if they will not be directed, to restrain them.*   387

SECTION 14. *Laws are not made by Kings, not because they are busied in greater matters than doing Justice, but because Nations will be governed by Rule, and not Arbitrarily.*   392

SECTION 15. *A general presumption that Kings will govern well, is not a sufficient security to the People.*   398

SECTION 16. *The observation of the Laws of Nature is absurdly expected from Tyrants, who set themselves up against all Laws: and he that subjects Kings to no other Law than what is common to Tyrants, destroys their being.*   402

SECTION 17. *Kings cannot be the Interpreters of the Oaths they take.*   408

SECTION 18. *The next in blood to deceased Kings cannot generally be said to be Kings till they are crowned.*   417

SECTION 19. *The greatest Enemy of a just Magistrate is he who endeavours to invalidate the Contract between him and the People, or to corrupt their Manners.*   431

SECTION 20. *Unjust Commands are not to be obey'd; and no man is obliged to suffer for not obeying such as are against Law.*   436

SECTION 21. *It cannot be for the good of the People that the Magistrate have a power above the Law: And he is not a Magistrate who has not his power by Law.*   439

SECTION 22. *The rigour of the Law is to be temper'd by men of known integrity and judgment, and not by the Prince, who may be ignorant or vicious.*   447

SECTION 23. *Aristotle proves, that no man is to be entrusted with an absolute power, by showing that no one knows how to execute it, but such a man as is not to be found.*   452

SECTION 24. *The power of Augustus Caesar was not given, but usurped.*   454

[XI]

Contents

SECTION 25. *The Regal Power was not the first in this Nation; nor necessarily to be continued, tho it had been the first.*   456

SECTION 26. *Tho the King may be entrusted with the power of chusing Judges, yet that by which they act is from the Law.*   465

SECTION 27. *Magna Charta was not the Original, but a Declaration of the English Liberties. The King's Power is not restrained, but created by that and other Laws: and the Nation that made them can only correct the defects of them.*   474

SECTION 28. *The English Nation has always been governed by itself or its Representatives.*   478

SECTION 29. *The King was never Master of the Soil.*   493

SECTION 30. *Henry the First was King of England by as good a Title as any of his Predecessors or Successors.*   497

SECTION 31. *Free Nations have a right of meeting, when and where they please, unless they deprive themselves of it.*   502

SECTION 32. *The powers of Kings are so various according to the Constitutions of several States, that no consequence can be drawn to the prejudice or advantage of any one, merely from the name.*   508

SECTION 33. *The Liberty of a People is the gift of God and Nature.*   510

SECTION 34. *No Veneration paid, or Honor conferr'd upon a just and lawful Magistrate, can diminish the Liberty of a Nation.*   514

SECTION 35. *The Authority given by our Law to the Acts performed by a King* de facto, *detract nothing from the people's right of creating whom they please.*   516

SECTION 36. *The general revolt of a Nation cannot be called a Rebellion.*   519

SECTION 37. *The English Government was not ill constituted, the defects more lately observed proceeding from the change of manners, and corruption of the times.*   524

SECTION 38. *The Power of calling and dissolving Parliaments is not simply in the King. The variety of Customs in chusing Parliament men, and the Errors a people may commit, neither prove that Kings are or ought to be Absolute.*   528

SECTION 39. *Those Kings only are heads of the People, who are good, wise, and seek to advance no Interest but that of the Publick.*   535

SECTION 40. *Good Laws prescribe easy and safe Remedies against the Evils proceeding from the vices or infirmities of the Magistrate; and when they fail, they must be supplied.*   542

SECTION 41. *The People for whom and by whom the Magistrate is created, can only judge whether he rightly perform his Office or not.*   547

Contents

SECTION 42. *The Person that wears the Crown cannot determine the Affairs which the Law refers to the King.*   552

SECTION 43. *Proclamations are not Laws.*   558

SECTION 44. *No People that is not free can substitute Delegates.*   563

SECTION 45. *The Legislative Power is always Arbitrary, and not to be trusted in the hands of any who are not bound to obey the Laws they make.*   569

SECTION 46. *The coercive power of the Law proceeds from the Authority of Parliament.*   572

INDEX,   579

FOREWORD

THOMAS JEFFERSON regarded John Locke and Algernon Sidney as the two leading sources for the American understanding of the principles of political liberty and the rights of humanity.[1] Locke's *Second Treatise* is readily available, but since 1805 only one major reprint of Sidney's *Discourses Concerning Government* has appeared until now.[2] This neglect is as undeserved today as it was when John Adams wrote to Jefferson in 1823:

> I have lately undertaken to read Algernon Sidney on government. . . . As often as I have read it, and fumbled it over, it now excites fresh admiration [i.e., wonder] that this work has excited so little interest in the literary world. As splendid an edition of it as the art of printing can produce—as well for the intrinsic merit of the work, as for the proof it brings of the bitter sufferings of the advocates of liberty from that time to this, and to show the slow progress of moral, philosophical, and political illumination in the world—ought to be now published in America.[3]

[1] "From the Minutes of the Board of Visitors, University of Virginia," March 4, 1825, in Thomas Jefferson, *Writings* (New York: Library of America, 1984), p. 479.

[2] New York: Arno, 1979. This is a hard-to-read facsimile reprint of the 1698 edition. A limited reprint of the 1751 edition appeared in 1968 (see Bibliography).

[3] Letter of September 17, 1823, in Lester J. Cappon, ed., *The Adams-Jefferson Letters* (New York: Simon & Schuster, 1971), p. 598.

Foreword

Sidney (or Sydney, as it was sometimes spelled) was once a popular hero. Like Socrates, he was famous for his controversial doctrines on government and for a nobility of character displayed during a dramatic trial and execution that was widely regarded as judicial murder. Unlike Socrates, Sidney was emphatically a political man and a partisan of republicanism. For a century and more he was celebrated as a martyr to free government, as Socrates is still celebrated as a martyr to the philosophic way of life. Socrates died the defiant inquirer, who knew only that he did not know the most important things. Sidney, in contrast, the defiant republican, kept getting into trouble for his democratic political views and projects. Asked to sign an inscription in the visitor's book at the University of Copenhagen, Sidney wrote, with typical spirit,

Manus haec inimica tyrannis
Einse petit placidam cum libertate quietem.
(This hand, enemy to tyrants,
By the sword seeks calm peacefulness with liberty.)

Eighteenth-century editors of Sidney's *Discourses* printed this beneath the frontispiece, and it remains the official motto of the state of Massachusetts to this day.

Sidney fell out of fashion during the nineteenth century. The educated began to favor statesmen like Cromwell and Napoleon, who relished the exercise of unrestrained power for grand projects in the service of mankind. Scholars have recently shown renewed interest in Sidney as an object of research. But in spite of twentieth-century tyrannies more terrible than any Sidney experienced or read about, he still fails to satisfy the taste of most contemporary intellectuals. This new edition of *Discourses Concerning Government* may provide an occasion for students of political liberty to reassess Sidney's eclipse.

The Argument of Sidney's Discourses

Sidney wrote *Discourses Concerning Government* in response to a book by Sir Robert Filmer defending the divine and natural right of kings to absolute rule. Filmer's book, *Patriarcha: A Defence of the Natural Power of Kings against the Unnatural Liberty of the People*, was first published in 1680, though it had been written much earlier.

[XVI]

Foreword

Sidney appears to have written the *Discourses* between 1681 and 1683. The manuscript was first published in 1698, fifteen years after Sidney's death. The *Discourses* as we have it is a nearly complete draft of a chapter-by-chapter refutation of Filmer. It is therefore helpful to know something of Filmer's argument and its context before reading Sidney.

FILMER'S POSITION ON POLITICAL POWER

Why should one obey the law? In pre-Christian times, the answer most often given was: The gods gave us our laws. The gods of the ancient polis were the gods of a particular political community. As a religion for all mankind, however, the Christian faith endorsed no particular legal code. The things of Caesar were not the things of God. As a practical matter, Roman Catholicism did support governments by giving them its sanction. But the universal claim of the Church undercut the authority of politics and, consequently, there was endless rivalry between priests and kings.

The Protestant Reformation solved that problem by overthrowing the political pretensions not only of the Pope but of all clergy. But if the Church no longer sanctified country and law, what did? England wrestled with this question for a century and a half after Henry VIII declared his religious independence from Rome in 1532. The question was theoretical, but the consequences were bloody. Men of good will sought a principled answer in authoritative books, practical experience, and through their own reasonings. In the end it was settled by force of arms.

Most of Protestant England believed unquestioning obedience to the king was not only the old but the best way. The view that the king has a divine right to rule that comes directly from God seemed to provide "the only means, which could preserve the civil, from being swallowed by the ecclesiastical powers."[4] In its traditional, pre-Filmer form, the divine right claim was qualified by the requirement that the king must obey the laws and customs of the kingdom.

But the logic of divine right did not stop there. If the king alone has his authority from God, why should there be any limit on what he might do? This radical conclusion was drawn by Sir Robert Filmer, whose *Patriarcha* defends absolute monarchical power, no matter how lawless, cruel, or tyrannical it might be. Like other royalists, Filmer argued on the basis of the Bible as well as of experience and reason unassisted by

---

[4] *The Works of James Wilson*, ed. Robert Green McCloskey (Cambridge: Harvard University Press, 1967), vol. 1, p. 120, from Wilson's 1790–91 lectures on Law.

faith. Unlike other royalists, Filmer liberated his king from all earthly restraint.[5]

Filmer maintained in *Patriarcha* that kings rule by right of birth. They inherit this right ultimately from Adam, to whom God gave sovereign power over the world. Men are born neither free nor equal. He thought monarchy the most natural form of government because it is based on the most natural of all relations, the family, in which the father rules. Both the natural law and the Bible, Filmer says, teach us to obey our parents. A king is a father writ large, *patriarch* of his country. Therefore, the king is not subject to any human law, including even the English common law. He is himself the source of law.

Filmer's radicalization of the theory of royalism might have been harmless enough had practical developments in England not made the threat of absolute monarchy quite real. The old nobility had entirely lost its former armed strength.[6] There was evidence that King Charles II and his brother, the future James II, were trying to impose upon England a government modeled on Louis XIV's France: state Catholicism with no Parliament. (Filmer himself, an Anglican, was strongly anti-Catholic, to be sure.) Unchecked by the nobles or by Parliament, the government threatened to become more absolute than any medieval monarchy.

A revolutionary ferment was occasioned by this threat, and in the early 1680s three Whig writers wrote books attacking Filmer: James Tyrrell's *Patriarcha non Monarcha* was published in 1681; John Locke's *Two Treatises of Government* appeared in 1689 and Algernon Sidney's *Discourses Concerning Government* in 1698.

SIDNEY'S RESPONSE

Filmer's *Patriarcha* was divided, in the 1680 edition that Sidney read, into three chapters with these titles:

    I. That the first Kings were Fathers of Families.
    II. It is unnatural for the People to Govern, or Choose Governours.
    III. Positive Laws do not infringe the Natural and Fatherly Power of Kings.

---

[5] On pre- and post-Christian political obligation, Harry V. Jaffa, *Original Intent and the Framers of the U.S. Constitution* (Washington: Regnery Gateway, 1994), pp. 313–317. On Filmer and English royalist writing, Alan Craig Houston, *Algernon Sidney and the Republican Heritage in England and America* (Princeton: Princeton University Press, 1991), ch. 2, and Nathan Tarcov, *Locke's Education for Liberty* (Chicago: University of Chicago Press, 1984), ch. 1.

[6] Addressed in *Discourses Concerning Government*, ch. 3, section 37.

Accordingly, Sidney's reply in the *Discourses* is also divided into three (untitled) chapters, which argue that:

    I. Paternal power is entirely different from political power.
   II. The people choose their governors by virtue of their natural right to liberty, and that government with a strong popular element is the best.
  III. Kings are entirely subject to the law, which in England means the Parliament.

Sidney sarcastically summed up Filmer's argument in this way: God "caused some to be born with crowns upon their heads, and all others with saddles upon their backs." Sidney (and Tyrrell and Locke) argued the opposite, that "men are naturally free," equal liberty being "the gift of God and nature." However, "Man cannot continue in the . . . liberty that God hath given him. The liberty of one is thwarted by that of another; and whilst they are all equal, none will yield to any, otherwise than by a general consent. This is the ground of all just government." Not birth but free choice determines men's rightful rulers (I.10, III.33).

But in Sidney *liberty* can be an equivocal term. In one sense it means the complete absence of external restraint: "liberty solely consists in an independency upon the will of another" (I.5). "Liberty without restraint," however, is undesirable, "being inconsistent with any government, and the good which man naturally desires for himself, children, and friends" (II.20).

Sidney alludes to a different understanding of liberty when he speaks of "one who is transported by his own passions or follies, a slave to his lusts and vices" (III.25 end). Following Aristotle, Sidney calls human beings who are incapable of self-control "slaves by nature" (I.2). In this sense liberty is acting in accord with reason, not passion.

Rational liberty, in either sense, involves some restraint. Liberty needs virtue as its support. More important, men need virtue if they are going to be masters of themselves. The purpose of government therefore goes beyond the protection of mere liberty; it must reward excellence and punish vice (I.20). "If the publick safety be provided, liberty and propriety secured, justice administered, virtue encouraged, vice suppressed, and the true interest of the nation advanced, the ends of government are accomplished," Sidney wrote (III.21).

Of course, the purpose of government, discovered by reason, is to protect the people in their natural liberty as far as that is prudent. In the ordinary course of providing for their families and subsistence, the people ought to be left alone (III.41). Government therefore must protect the people's rights to their "lands, goods, lives, and liberties" (III.16).

Governments are first formed when the people make an agreement with each other to give up some of their natural liberty. They contract to obey their rulers on condition that their rulers contract with them to rule for the sake of the ends for which government is constituted (II.32). Therefore all government should be limited to those ends.

The ends of government are determined by the *natural law*, by which Sidney meant something simple: the rules of conduct that common sense derives from reflecting on the nature of man. In Sidney's view, natural law teaches us, among other things, that human beings are born free, that fathers are to be obeyed, that injuries are to be repelled and avenged, that those best qualified ought to rule, and that one ought not to be a slave to one's passions. "Nothing but the plain and certain dictates of reason can be generally applicable to all men as the law of their nature; and they who, according to the best of their understanding, provide for the good of themselves and their posterity, do all equally observe it" (II.20).

Just government being instituted by the consent of the governed and for ends limited by the natural law and by the original contract, it follows that the people have a right to overthrow their government when it violates these limits. This right to revolution was the most controversial part of Sidney's teaching. It was denounced at his trial and led directly to his conviction and execution.

Since all human beings are subject to passion and inclined to self-interest, the good of the people is best secured through the rule of law. In a passage that John Adams liked to quote, Sidney says law is "void of desire and fear, lust and anger. 'Tis *mens sine affectu* [mind without passion], written reason, retaining some measure of the divine perfection" (III.15, paraphrasing Aristotle). In Sidney's strict use here, the term *law* excludes that which serves the private interest of the ruler. For "That which is not just is not law, and that which is not law ought not to be obeyed" (III.11 section title).

Of the several forms of government, Sidney unsurprisingly likes monarchy least. But it is not immediately evident whether his principles provide clear guidance as to the best form of government. (The question also arises in regard to the American Declaration of Independence.) It might seem that the people may consent to any form of government they please. However, it becomes clear as Sidney proceeds that partly or wholly democratic governments are his preference. They are most consistent with the liberty we are born to and provide the greatest opportunity for merit to receive its due reward and for wisdom to prevail in the public business (II.20, 21, III.16).

Prudence dictates that political constitutions are to some extent relative to the particular circumstances of a people (II.17). Rome became so corrupt that "the best men found it . . . impossible to restore liberty to the city" (II.19). But Sidney was not a relativist. The principles of government are eternally true; only their application varies with the times.

Sidney opposed hereditary monarchy not only because it denies liberty, but because it denies equal opportunity for merit. Unlike some other writers whose political theories were based upon man's natural liberty, Sidney accepted the principle, taught by Plato and Aristotle, that the most virtuous ought to rule. "*Detur digniori* [let it be given to the worthier] is the voice of nature; all her most sacred laws are perverted, if this be not observed in the disposition of the governments of mankind" (I.16). Sidney was even willing to admit, with Aristotle, the right of a godlike prince to rule without the consent of the governed. "When such a man is found, he is by nature a king." But Sidney went on to deny, in Aristotle's name, that any such being could be found among imperfect human beings. Thus the apparently aristocratic Aristotle turns out to be a teacher of republicanism (III.23). From this argument we may better understand why Thomas Jefferson said the Declaration of Independence was based on "the elementary books of public right, as Aristotle, Cicero, Locke, Sidney, &c." and why the monarchical philosopher Thomas Hobbes complained that the ancient Greek and Roman authors taught Englishmen that democracy was the best form of government.[7]

A leading difficulty in Sidney's argument lies in his simultaneous assertion that the right to rule derives from consent (from man's natural liberty) and that it derives from merit (from the sacred law of *detur digniori*). As a practical matter Sidney was confident that the people—if they are not corrupt—would recognize and elevate those most deserving of political power. For in a republic no accidents of birth can stand in the way of the people's honoring whoever is best. Further, Sidney was sure that corruption and absolute monarchy always go together in practice. But what if the people err and place fools or villains in power? Do we abandon democracy or merit? Which is more fundamental *in principle*: consent or virtue?

A similar question may be asked of his twofold conception of liberty. If one must choose, which form of liberty counts most: freedom from dependence on the will of a ruler one has not consented to, or freedom from enslavement to one's base passions? For practical purposes, experi-

---

[7] Thomas Jefferson to Henry Lee, May 8, 1825 in *Writings*, p. 1501. Hobbes makes this assertion in *Behemoth, or the Long Parliament*, ed. Ferdinand Tönnies (New York: Barnes and Noble, 1969), pp. 43, 56, 158.

ence solves the question for Sidney. A people unable to control its passions will not long retain its political freedom. But in principle the question may remain unresolved.

One characteristic feature of Sidney's book associates him with Machiavelli. That is his celebration of warlike virtue and foreign conquest. Like Machiavelli, Sidney prefers imperialist Rome to nonexpansionist Sparta. He asserts that "That is the best government, which best provides for war." Popular governments do this best, for their citizens are hardy and spirited, and there is a mutual rivalry for the honor that anyone may earn (II.15, II.22–23). But unlike Machiavelli, Sidney qualifies his imperialism with the requirement that a war of acquisition be a just war, carried on for a just cause and by just means.

The *Discourses* includes a vast amount of historical material. Some of Sidney's readers have inferred that his republicanism rests more on the prescriptive lessons of English history than on principles discovered by reason. That is not so. Sidney did believe that "the English nation has always been governed by itself or its representatives."[8] But in the end such evidence cannot be decisive: "time can make nothing lawful or just, that is not so of itself. . . . therefore in matters of the greatest importance, wise and good men do not so much inquire what has been, as what is good and ought to be" (III.28). So "there can be no reason, why a polite people should not relinquish the errors committed by their ancestors in the time of their barbarism and ignorance" (III.25).

Scholars have wondered about the religious dimension of Sidney's thought. The *Discourses* teems with Biblical references. But Sidney invokes the authority of divine revelation to vindicate conclusions reached by reason. At one point, quoting Ecclesiastes, Sidney notes that it "perfectly agrees with what we learn from Plato, and plainly shews, that true philosophy is perfectly conformable with what is taught us by those who were divinely inspired" (II.1). For Sidney, Biblical events are sometimes better explained by man's unaided reason than by religious doctrines. In the traditional view God in his wrath punished the Hebrews for their idolatry after Solomon's death by subjecting them to the rule of absolute monarchs. In Sidney's view the Hebrew "tragedy" actually proceeded "from such causes as are applicable to other nations. . . . [C]husing rather to subject themselves to the will of a man, than to the law of God, they

---

[8] Sidney's account of the English past has been much criticized by J. G. A. Pocock in *The Ancient Constitution and the Feudal Law* (Cambridge: Cambridge University Press, 1957), ch. 2 and 3, and others, but defended persuasively in James Conniff, "Reason and History in Early Whig Thought: The Case of Algernon Sidney," *Journal of the History of Ideas* 43 (1982), pp. 397–416.

deservedly suffer'd the evils that naturally follow the worst counsels" (II.24).

Similarly, Sidney meets the objection that his argument, which praises armed resistance to evil, is anti-Christian. "We shall be told, that prayers and tears were the only arms of the first Christians, and that Christ commanded his disciples to pray for those that persecuted them." Sidney responds "that those precepts were merely temporary, and directed to the persons of the apostles, who were armed only with the sword of the spirit; that the primitive Christians used prayers and tears only no longer than whilst they had no other arms" (III.7). Sidney sums up the sturdy spirit of his Christianity in a remark that later became famous: "God helps those who help themselves" (II.23). In this way Sidney defends Christianity against the Machiavellian charge that it celebrates feminine qualities at the expense of manliness and spiritedness and leads to the triumph of bad men over good by teaching nonresistance to evil.

Sidney's (and Locke's) overall argument gave to political obligation a new basis consistent with Christianity's universal claim but independent of any particular religious sect. The God of all mankind could now be the God of a particular political community. For if natural liberty and natural law come from God, only one kind of community will satisfy God's law: a consent-based republic protecting the equal liberty of all. The final stanza of "America" shows that this argument is no mere logical inference but a tenet of faith for the political community that established a representative democracy dedicated to the proposition that all men are created equal:

> Our fathers' God, to thee,
> Author of liberty,
> To thee we sing.
> Long may our land be bright
> With freedom's holy light;
> Protect us by thy might,
> Great God our king.

Citizens can fight for their country in good conscience, knowing that the cause of liberty is the cause of God, but free of the fanaticism so often associated with religious sectarianism.[9] The argument was new, but as expressed by Sidney it preserved the heart of the political teaching of the ancients. Politics and life are still understood in light of man's natural purpose: virtue and happiness.

[9] Jaffa, *Original Intent*, pp. 315–316.

Foreword

SIDNEY AND LOCKE

John Locke wrote *Two Treatises of Government* at the same time Sidney was working on the *Discourses*. Since Locke's book is much better known today, it is worth comparing to Sidney's.

While some scholars have assigned Locke to an emerging bourgeois or liberal tradition of natural rights, especially property rights, Sidney is said to belong to a supposed tradition of "classical republicanism" stemming from Machiavelli and ultimately the ancients. But other scholars have noted that Sidney does not fit this paradigm very well.[10] Sidney is as much a natural rights and contract man as Locke. Both advocate government by elected representatives.[11] Both maintain that natural liberty is governed by the natural law. Both argue for limited government and the people's right to revolution. Both are spirited proponents of liberty. Sidney and Locke are "republicans" as well as "liberals."

Notwithstanding these similarities, there are differences, and they are important. Sidney proves to be closer to the Greek and Roman classics than Locke is. It is characteristic that Sidney quotes frequently from the ancients while Locke hardly ever does. But the ancients were not "classical republicans" in a Machiavellian sense. Their political thought always began or ended with the individual human being, not in the sense of an isolated unit, but as a being oriented by human nature to a life in accord with reason. What follow are particular illustrations of this broad difference between Sidney and Locke.

While both men agree that government should be based on consent, Sidney also insists that superior men ought to rule, and he defends popular government for placing such men in power. In this he follows Plato and Aristotle, for whom excellence is a title to rule. Locke generally denies the right of virtue to govern.

Similarly, political liberty in Locke is merely a "fence" (Locke's term) protecting a man's life, liberty, and property. Sidney's broader conception includes the classical view of liberty as freedom from domination by one's passions. Accordingly, one purpose of government for Sidney, as it was for the ancients, is to foster virtue and suppress vice. It was not for Locke.

---

[10] Richard Ashcraft, *Revolutionary Politics and Locke's Two Treatises of Government* (Princeton: Princeton University Press, 1986), p. 212; and Houston, *Algernon Sidney*, Introduction. The leading proponent of the "classical republican" thesis is J. G. A. Pocock, *The Machiavellian Moment* (Princeton: Princeton University Press, 1975).

[11] This is sometimes denied, but Locke, *Second Treatise*, ch. 11 (end), affirms not only "no taxation without representation," but implies "no legislation without representation" (since "property" in Locke's view comprises life and liberty). Not one of America's founders doubted that Locke was a republican.

Characteristically, Sidney never calls the pre-civil state the "state of nature" as Locke does even when it degenerates into a state of war. Lockean man exists naturally in this state, which is one of poverty, danger, and insecurity. He becomes political by escaping nature, not by following it. Reason, for Locke, is the device by which man escapes and conquers nature, by constructing government and by engaging in capitalist industry. For Sidney, man's nature *is* reason, as he constantly repeats. Sidney calls the Hobbesian state of nature—the war of all against all— "epidemical madness," which men would fall into only if God abandoned the world (I.17). Man is born free, but Sidney does not think it natural for man to live without law. Without using Aristotle's formula, Sidney continues to think of man as a political and rational animal by nature.

Sidney's law of nature goes beyond the conditions of self-preservation and includes the several virtues that the rational life comprises. This conception continues the natural law tradition stemming from the ancients. However, Locke's doctrine of natural law breaks with the tradition in its being grounded in the individual's fundamental right to life and liberty. In Locke's moral universe the center is no longer man's end, but man or man's freedom. In this he follows Hobbes.[12]

The two men view commerce quite differently. For Locke, commerce is a principal means by which man escapes the privation that unimproved nature condemns him to. Sidney too praises wealth as an end of statesmanship, but only because of its contribution to a nation's fighting strength (a consideration similar to Hamilton's in *Federalist* 11); money-making he otherwise rejects as corrupting (II.22, 23).

Sidney never questions the right of the father to rule in the family. But Locke speaks of *honoring*, not obeying, the father *and mother*. Civil society for Sidney is still an association of fathers as heads of families (II.4). Locke's more radical individualism throws into question the traditional family, which is based on the different purposes, by nature, of male and female.

In sum, Locke's thought, although expressed with great caution, rests on premises more radically modern than Sidney's. Locke's republicanism ultimately stands on a view of human nature that doubts or denies the older view that man is oriented *by nature* to a life of decency and reason. Sidney's republicanism still adheres to a view of life that is recognizably at home within the ancient and medieval tradition of political philosophy.

---

[12] This point is controversial. The strongest argument on its behalf is that of Leo Strauss in *Natural Right and History* (Chicago: University of Chicago Press, 1953), pp. 202–251, and in *What Is Political Philosophy?* (New York: Free Press, 1959), ch. 8. For the opposing view, see John W. Yolton, "Locke on the Law of Nature," *Philosophical Review* 67 (1958), pp. 477–498.

Foreword

Sidney's argument might seem to have been vindicated five years after his death by the Glorious Revolution of 1688. The forced abdication of King James II broke up the last attempt to impose absolute monarchy on England. Yet Sidney would hardly have been satisfied by the Revolution settlement. He had been a long-time opponent of William III of Holland, who had been invited by Parliament to accept the English throne in 1689. And although the Revolution did restrain the royal power, it also postponed the day when a true republic could be established in England.

One of the early acts of Parliament in 1689 was formally to reverse Sidney's conviction, which was declared wrongful and unjust. Post-1689 Whigs hurried to assimilate Sidney to their cause. But in order to make him fit the new order, they had to distort him. His democratic principles were de-emphasized. His revolutionary schemes and his willingness to intrigue with the French were denied. He became altogether more respectable and less radical. As the myths accumulated, the real man receded from sight.[13]

But in the American colonies of the mid-1700s, where politics was not complicated by a surviving king and aristocracy, Sidney could be accepted without reservation. The men who made the Revolution of 1776 warmly admired Sidney's principles and fighting republican spirit. His death as a martyr to liberty provided them with a model in their own risky enterprise against the force of British arms. Among those who cited Sidney prominently in their writings, besides Jefferson and Adams, were Jonathan Mayhew, the spirited patriot preacher of Massachusetts, and Arthur Lee, a leading revolutionary politician of Virginia.

Why then was Locke and not Sidney cited most often by the American revolutionaries?[14] For one thing, the immediate dispute with Britain was over taxation (property), and here Locke's argument was simple and clear: no taxation without representation. For another, Locke's book is as concise and well-ordered as Sidney's is wordy and diffuse. But whenever he does appear, Sidney is always cited as an authority who agrees with Locke. In fact Sidney and Locke did agree on the most urgent principles of the American Revolution: that all men are created equal, that just government rests on the consent of the governed, that government is instituted to secure the rights of human nature, and that there is a right to revolution against despotism.

[13] Jonathan Scott, *Algernon Sidney and the English Republic, 1623–1677* (Cambridge: Cambridge University Press, 1988), Introduction.

[14] Donald S. Lutz, *The Origins of American Constitutionalism* (Baton Rouge: Louisiana State University Press, 1988), p. 143.

Nevertheless, although Locke was more often quoted, the core of Sidney's thought probably represents better than Locke's the spirit of American republicanism. Confident of the eternal moral order of the world, Sidney never thought of man as the enemy and conqueror of nature, as Locke did in his chapter on property.[15] Rather, nature was man's friend, providing him with his reason and an inclination to live together with others in society. Sidney's understanding of liberty was inseparable from the attachment to honor and decency especially visible in his taste for the classics.

Perhaps the leading defect in Sidney from the point of view of the Framers of the United States Constitution of 1787 is his tremendous confidence in the common people and their representatives. Sidney barely acknowledges the possibility of a popular assembly abusing its power—a leading theme of *The Federalist* (and of Locke and Montesquieu). Sidney is vulnerable to the criticism leveled by Madison against the authors of America's early state constitutions: "They seem never to have turned their eyes from the danger, to liberty, from the overgrown and all-grasping prerogative of an hereditary magistrate. . . . They seem never to have recollected the danger from legislative usurpations, which, by assembling all power in the same hands, must lead to the same tyranny as is threatened by executive usurpation" (*Federalist* 48). Accordingly, although Sidney was often mentioned by Americans as an authority on first principles of government, he was hardly ever appealed to as an authority on its proper structure.

Locke's greater sobriety regarding the people may have been responsible for his doctrine of the separation of powers, which differs from Sidney's account of mixed government. The latter restates a classical teaching shared by Aristotle, Cicero, and others. In the classical scheme the division of powers is based on social classes (the poor and the wealthy, for example, or warrior aristocrats and commoners). Locke's separation of powers, in contrast, represents a new approach to the problem of checking the abuse of power and designing competent government. Separating parts of government by function rather than by class origin made possible the American polity, in which each branch of government could be based directly or indirectly on democratic elections.

In *these* respects, at any rate, Locke was more judicious than Sidney and therefore closer to the spirit of the classics. In his enthusiastic anticipation of monarchy overthrown, Sidney may have been charmed, ever so slightly, by that "deceitful dream of a golden age" of a "happy

---

[15] Locke, *Second Treatise*, ch. 5.

empire of perfect wisdom and perfect virtue" that popular government seemed to promise. Hamilton's stern warning against this delusion in *Federalist* 6 was not anti-democratic; the Americans' hard-headed appraisal of the weaknesses of popular government made possible the success of democracy under the Constitution.

Yet modern republics have also benefited from writers like Sidney, who helped to domesticate the rights-and-consent vocabulary of modern individualism and to give it a home in the classical tradition of natural right. Thus did government based on the rights of man become safe for political practice.

Sidney's Life

Two old English aristocratic families were united in Algernon Sidney's birth in 1623. His mother was a Percy, the family of Northumberland earls famous for its spirited devotion to honor and the military arts—and for rebelling against kings. In *Richard II* and *Henry IV* Shakespeare portrays Sidney's ancestor Harry Percy, called Hotspur (referred to in the *Discourses*), who overthrew one king and warred against another.

The Sidney side of the family was more learned and scholarly, but it too had its fighting spirit. Today the Sidney name is best known through Algernon's great-uncle, the poet and courtier Sir Philip, who died thirty-seven years before Algernon was born. Algernon Sidney admired and emulated his famous forebear for his intellectual attainments as well as for his soldiership on behalf of Protestantism, in which cause he lost his life in battle.

Sidney spent his early childhood at Penshurst, the family estate in Kent.[16] In his teens he lived for six years in France with his father, the Earl of Leicester, who served as ambassador there. At home and abroad, Sidney was given the liberal education, grounded in the classics, that was characteristic of the age at its best.

Sidney's father was a scholar in his own right. His extraordinary library contained thousands of volumes, including philosophical, political, historical, and religious writings, ancient and modern. In France he was a

---

[16] For the facts of Sidney's life, see Houston, *Algernon Sidney*; Scott, *Algernon Sidney and the English Republic, 1623–1677*; Scott, *Algernon Sidney and the Restoration Crisis, 1677–1683* (Cambridge: Cambridge University Press, 1991); Blair Worden, "The Commonwealth Kidney of Algernon Sidney," *Journal of British Studies* 24 (January 1985), pp. 1–40; "Algernon Sidney," *Concise Dictionary of National Biography* (Oxford: Oxford University Press, 1992), vol. 3, p. 2742; and George W. Meadley, *Memoirs of Algernon Sydney* (London: Cradock and Joy, 1813). Unless otherwise noted, quotations are from these sources.

close acquaintance of Hugo Grotius, the Swedish ambassador and political philosopher whose views figured prominently in the earl's notes, along with those of Roman and English political writers. Their names appear frequently in Sidney's *Discourses*. Years later Sidney was reported to have called Grotius's *Law of War and Peace* the most important of all books in political theory.

Sidney's quarrel with Filmer in the *Discourses* was about whether men deserve to be rulers merely by being eldest born. Sidney argued for merit, not birth, as the title to rule, and he thought republics most likely to honor merit. Although he was himself a hereditary aristocrat, Sidney experienced the question personally in his own household. His older brother, the future Earl of Leicester, was as dull, lazy, and immoral as Algernon was precocious, energetic, and honorable. Their father acknowledged the difference by substantially disinheriting the brother and giving as much as he could to Algernon. The latter successfully defended his father's will in a lawsuit using many of the same arguments against favoring the eldest born that he used against Filmer on the political plane.

Sidney entered the military, served in Ireland, and returned to England in 1642. The country was agitated by civil war. For eleven years King Charles I had been governing without Parliament. He had raised taxes without any Parliament's consent. The king was finally compelled in 1640 to convene Parliament, which attempted, in response to Charles's usurpations, to subordinate the king in crucial respects to the nation's representatives. Sidney made his choice for Parliament—a choice to which he adhered throughout his life—and, as fighting broke out, took up arms against the king. In 1644 he fought in the battle of Marston Moor, where an eyewitness reported that "Colonel Sidney charged with much gallantry in the head of my Lord Manchester's regiment of horses, and came off with many wounds, the true badges of his honor." The wounds were severe.

In 1646 Sidney was elected to the famous Long Parliament. He firmly opposed compromise with the king, but he did not support the radicals' purge of parliamentary moderates in 1648, which created the Rump Parliament. Appointed one of the commissioners for the trial of Charles I, Sidney took little part in its proceedings. He had reservations about the lawfulness as well as the prudence of the trial, which was pushed forward by Cromwell and the army. But he never disputed the accusations against Charles. He later called his execution "the justest and bravest action that ever was done in England, or anywhere."

In Parliament Sidney was especially active in foreign affairs. By 1652, helping to direct the war against Holland, he had risen to a leading position. When Cromwell's army broke up the Rump of the Long Parliament in 1653, a bill was about to pass that would have made elections far freer than they had been. Cromwell entered Parliament with his soldiers, expelled the members, and locked the doors. Seated at the right hand of the speaker, Sidney refused to leave until hands were placed upon him threatening him with forcible removal. Thus began Cromwell's reign, which Sidney regarded as tyranny.

At some point during the next six years of forced retirement from politics, Sidney wrote his first surviving work, "Of Love." We do not know what events in his life may have provoked it. Sidney admits that love "hath with more violence transported me, than a man of understanding ought to suffer himself to be by any passion." Yet he celebrates the love of man and woman as "the fullest and most absolute happiness that our natures can be capable of, in comparison with which all other worldly pleasures are vain and empty shadows." His argument is built on a quite un-Machiavellian trust in the ordinary appearance of things. He is sure that beauty and goodness are "convertible terms," since "nature's works are not like hypocrites or sepulchers, beautiful without, and rottenness and corruption within."

> The glory of divine rays do show in faces, but much more in minds: Who can then without barbarity (I think I may say impiety) deny to suffer himself to be ravished with the admiration of such an excellence of a created beauty, as is an image of the uncreated?

This contrasts strongly with the bleak description of life by Sidney's contemporary Thomas Hobbes as "a perpetual and restless desire of power after power, that ceaseth only in death."[17]

In 1659 the army dissolved the Protectorate, threw out Cromwell's son Richard, and restored the Rump Parliament. Sidney resumed his seat and his position of prominence. He led an important delegation abroad to mediate peace between the kings of Denmark and Sweden. (One of Sidney's parliamentary colleagues who refused to join the delegation gives us a glimpse of his character: "I knew well the overruling temper and height of Colonel Sidney.") Sidney's diplomatic approach was to cut through the endless ceremony and prattle by the use of strong language and gunboat diplomacy to force a peace on English terms. His blunt style horrified the European diplomats, and his workable plan was scuttled by the English admiral on the spot, who sailed away with his fleet. In the

---

[17] Thomas Hobbes, *Leviathan*, ch. 11. Quotations from "Of Love" are taken from *A Collection of Scarce and Valuable Tracts . . . of the Late Lord Somers*, ed. Sir Walter Scott (London, 1809–16), vol. 8, pp. 612–619.

end a treaty was signed on terms favorable to England, for which Sidney deserves some credit.

While Sidney was concluding the treaty in 1660, the English Commonwealth collapsed and Charles II was restored to the throne. Sidney was willing to follow the authority of Parliament and obey the king. But the king demanded more: Sidney must condemn his own actions under the republic and beg forgiveness. He could not bring himself to do it. He wrote to his father:

> When I call to my remembrance all my actions relating to our civil distempers, I cannot find one that I can look upon as a breach of the rules of justice or honor; this is my strength, and, I thank God, by this I enjoy very serene thoughts. If I lose this by vile and unworthy submissions, acknowledgement of errors, asking of pardon, or the like, I shall from that moment be the miserablest man alive, and the scorn of all men.

Sensing how this momentous choice of voluntary exile would be viewed by his father and others, Sidney continued in a vein that shows his self-knowledge and his stubborn sense of honor:

> I know the titles that are given me of fierce, violent, seditious, mutinous, turbulent. . . . I know people will say, I strain at gnats, and swallow camels; that it is a strange conscience, that lets a man run violently on, till he is deep in civil blood, and then stays at a few words and compliments. . . . I cannot help if I judge amiss; I did not make myself, nor can I correct the defects of my own creation. I walk in the light that God hath given me; if it be dim or uncertain, I must bear the penalty of my errors. I hope to do it with patience, and that no burden shall be very grievous to me, except sin and shame.

Sidney wandered about Europe for almost twenty years "as a vagabond through the world, forsaken of my friends, poor, and known only to be a broken limb of a shipwrecked faction." Charles's agents and assassins pursued Sidney for years. He survived two serious attempts on his life.

Yet exile was not entirely grim. At first he lived in Italy, where he was kindly given access to a beautiful country villa whose description, he said, "would look more like poetry than truth." He lived there for a time "as a hermit in a palace," flirting with the solitary and contemplative life praised by the ancient philosophers:

> Here are walks and fountains in the greatest perfection. . . . My conversation is with birds, trees, and books: in these last months that I have had no business at all, I have applied myself to study a little more than I have done formerly; and though one who begins at my

age cannot hope to make any considerable progress that way, I find so much satisfaction in it, that for the future I shall very unwillingly, though I had the opportunity, put myself into any way of living that shall deprive me of that entertainment.

During this idyllic interlude Sidney no doubt undertook some of the wide philosophical and historical reading that is manifest in his *Discourses*. But anger at events in England gradually led him back into political activity.

> In the end I found that it was an ill-grounded peace that I enjoyed, and could have no rest in my own spirit, because I lived only to myself, and was in no ways useful to God's people, my country, and the world. This consideration, joined with those dispensations of providence which I observed and judged favorable unto the designs of good people, brought me out of my retirement.

Plunging back into the political life, Sidney worked vigorously, through both conspiracy and writing, to restore the English republic. An inscription he wrote in the visitor's book at the Calvinist Academy in Geneva plainly reveals his mood: SIT SANGUINIS ULTOR JUSTORUM ("Let there be an avenger of the blood of the just").

Of all the republican exiles, Sidney was the most determined to act and the least delicate about the means to be employed. Religious scruples did not hinder him as they did some of his colleagues. First he tried to organize them to undertake an invasion of England to be led by Holland, then at war with England. Partly to promote this enterprise, Sidney wrote the book-length *Court Maxims, Discussed and Refelled*, recently discovered in England but still unpublished. This work, an imaginary dialogue between an English monarchist and a republican, is a vigorous attack on the regime of Charles II, with strong encouragement to resistance against the tyrant. Many of its arguments reappeared later in the *Discourses*.

Turned down by the Dutch republican leader De Witt, Sidney approached Louis XIV of France, who was also at war with England. Louis reports in his memoirs that he offered Sidney a small sum, with the promise of more only if Sidney could show "that he was really capable of doing what he promised." Louis's aim was to keep England weak by keeping it divided, not to build up an English republic. Quarrels among the exiles, inflamed by Sidney's overbearing manner, prevented action in any event.

In the wake of this second failure, Louis granted Sidney permission to settle in the south of France, where he spent eleven years, until his return to England. Living as an aristocrat, he was known as "Le Compte de Sidney." He seems to have fathered an illegitimate daughter there.

Sidney was finally given permission to return to England in 1677, for personal purposes. Not long after his arrival he was detained by unexpected financial troubles, spending several months in debtor's prison. He pursued his lengthy but finally successful lawsuit to obtain the inheritance left to him by his recently deceased father.

Sidney soon found himself back in the thick of politics. In 1679 he and William Penn cooperated on a project to secure greater freedom of religion in England. Sidney discussed with Penn the constitution of Pennsylvania, although Sidney ended by arguing that Penn's frame of government, "worse than the Turk," was "not to be endured or lived under." Sidney also worked closely with Whigs sympathetic to republicanism, such as Henry Neville. With their help and Penn's, he tried to get into Parliament, standing unsuccessfully for election several times.

On the basis of considerable evidence Sidney and many other Whigs believed that Charles II, urged on by his Catholic brother, the future James II, intended to convert England into a monarchy on the model of Louis XIV's France. Catholicism would become the state religion, and Parliament would be dispensed with.[18] (In an early stage of this quarrel, Parliament impeached one of Charles's ministers, the Earl of Danby, who worked to expand the king's prerogative and to make him financially independent of Parliament. Sidney alludes to this event in the *Discourses*, III.42.)

In the late 1670s and early '80s the Whigs pursued a legal strategy to check the monarchy. They mobilized the electorate all the way down to the common people. They wrote books and pamphlets exposing the crisis. They captured a majority in Parliament and attempted to exclude by law Charles's brother James from the succession to the throne. In 1680, at the height of the exclusion crisis, Filmer's *Patriarcha* was published.[19]

Historians have sometimes been inclined to discount the republicanism of Sidney and other Whigs. The contest between Parliament and king has been portrayed as a quarrel among rival elites from which the people were largely excluded. However, the Whigs really did have strong roots among the common people. In many parliamentary electoral districts there was virtually unlimited manhood suffrage—a condition that disappeared from post-1689 Britain until the late nineteenth century. The Whigs strongly supported this increasingly democratic electoral politics,

---

[18] Richard Ashcraft has persuasively revived the case against Charles II in *Revolutionary Politics and John Locke's Two Treatises of Government* (Princeton: Princeton University Press, 1986), ch. 1.

[19] Ibid., ch. 4 and 6.

and their arguments for equality and liberty gave it a theoretical foundation.

At this time Sidney (and many other Whigs and Tories) received money from France's ambassador, Barillon. The French were secretly providing monetary support to Charles II, but also to leading opposition politicians. Their policy was to keep England weak by playing Parliament and king off each other. Sidney's honor in this affair has been impugned by many, including most notably Sir Winston Churchill. In Sidney's defense it must be said that he was willing to take French money only to the extent that doing so coincided with his own ends, which were entirely honorable. The French knew well what they were supporting: Barillon called him "a man of great views and high designs, which tend to the establishment of a republic."[20]

In 1681 Charles II defeated the Whigs' exclusion strategy by dismissing the last Parliament of his reign. He let it be known that he intended to rule thenceforth without it. At this time Sidney may have co-authored *Just and Modest Vindication of the Proceedings of the Last Two Parliaments.*

Sidney and his fellow Whigs believed the situation was desperate. Legal opposition had failed. To borrow the language of the American Declaration of Independence, here was "a long train of abuses and usurpations" evincing a design to reduce England "under absolute despotism." The leading Whigs, Sidney among them, began to plan a revolution. There was to be an armed insurrection, supported by an uprising in Scotland. The assassination of King Charles, definitely planned, may have been approved by Sidney. Parliament would then settle the affairs of the realm. Organizing the plot took time, and before the conspirators were ready to strike, Sidney and many of the other principals were betrayed. (The political philosopher John Locke never worked closely with Sidney, but he was part of the same conspiracy. Locke saved himself by fleeing England the moment the conspiracy was discovered.) On June 26, 1683, Sidney was arrested on a charge of treason.[21]

Sidney resolved to do nothing at his trial "which doth not agree with the character of a gentleman and a Christian." The trial was conducted by the brutal Lord Chief Justice Jeffreys, who did not conceal his intention to convict, within the law or without. The indictment itself contained important errors and alleged many things against Sidney irrelevant to the

---

[20] Winston Churchill, *Marlborough: His Life and Times* (London: Harrap, 1947), vol. 1, pp. 149–150.

[21] Ashcraft in *Revolutionary Politics*, ch. 7 and 8, refutes the older view that there was no significant Whig conspiracy. He argues that killing the king was part of the overall plan.

law, which said treason was "to design, intend, or endeavor" any action that might tend toward the king's death or "any restraint of his liberty"; the jury was not composed of Sidney's peers (fellow freeholders); Sidney was unlawfully denied permission even to examine the indictment. The most egregious wrong was in the want of legal evidence. Two witnesses were required for conviction. The prosecution produced but one, Lord Howard, who could only testify to having heard Sidney and others discussing arrangements to contact Whigs in Scotland; he could not report definite plans to make war on the king, as the indictment alleged. Sidney was also able to discredit this testimony by exposing Howard's treacherous character and showing that he had contradicted himself. The other "witness" produced was a few manuscript pages, seized when he was arrested, of Sidney's *Discourses*, "fixing the power in the people," as Jeffreys summarized it. The general and theoretical argument of the part of the *Discourses* read at his trial, privately written and never published, was of course no proof of a design tending toward the king's death or deprivation of his liberty. Sidney was well prepared for the trial, and he forcefully pointed out these and other defects in the prosecution's case, but to no effect. He was convicted and condemned to death.

While he was confined in the Tower, "some propositions" were made "for the saving of my life, but I did not think them reasonable or decent." Here again we are reminded of Socrates's honorable conduct in prison. But unlike Socrates, Sidney did request permission to go into exile. This was denied. In his last letter, privately written to a friend, Sidney faced death calmly and courageously, without any flourishes. One who attended his execution reported:

> When he came on the scaffold, instead of a speech, he told them only that he had made his peace with God, that he came not thither to talk, but to die; put a paper into the sheriffs' hand, and another into a friend's, said one prayer as short as a grace, laid down his neck, and bid the executioner do his office.

He died on December 7, 1683.

In the paper that he gave to the sheriffs, intended for publication, Sidney set forth the injustice of the trial and strongly affirmed his political principles. The paper concluded with this prayer, expressive of his spirited and political Christianity:

> The Lord forgive these practices, and avert the evils that threaten the nation from them! The Lord sanctify these my sufferings unto me, and, though I fall as a sacrifice to idols, suffer not idolatry to be established in this land! Bless thy people, and save them. Defend thy

own cause, and defend those that defend it. Stir up such as are faint; direct those that are willing; confirm those that waver; give wisdom and integrity unto all. Order all things so, as may most redound to thine own glory. Grant that I may die glorifying thee for all thy mercies; and that, at the last, thou hast permitted me to be singled out as a witness of thy truth; and even by the confession of my opposers, for that OLD CAUSE in which I was from my youth engaged and for which thou hast often and wonderfully declared thyself.[22]

We allow Sidney the final word, from his *Apology in the Day of His Death*:

I had from my youth endeavored to uphold the common rights of mankind, the laws of this land, and the true Protestant religion, against corrupt principles, arbitrary power, and Popery, and I do now willingly lay down my life for the same.[23]

Sidney's *Discourses* was the theoretical counterpart to his practical schemes. If those schemes had succeeded, the book might have served as a manifesto for the revolution. They failed, and the book remained unfinished.

There is no doubt that Sidney was guilty of treason, just as Socrates was guilty of impiety and of corrupting the young—as those crimes were understood by the governments who executed the two heroes. Socrates was vindicated when readers of his *Apology* were persuaded that Athenian law was defective in light of a higher standard of justice.[24] Likewise, Sidney's real vindication does not come from the exposure of the trial's many illegalities. Rather, it lies in his implicit appeal to a higher standard of justice, one that regards rebellion against tyranny not as a crime but as a benefaction. This is the argument of the *Discourses*.

THOMAS G. WEST
University of Dallas
August 1989

---

[22] Sidney, *Discourses Concerning Government*, 3rd ed. (London: Millar, 1751), p. xxvii. The "old cause" was the cause of the English republic.

[23] Ibid., p. xxx.

[24] Thomas G. West, *Plato's Apology of Socrates* (Ithaca: Cornell University Press, 1979), p. 150.

BIBLIOGRAPHY

Works by Sidney

A full listing of Sidney's writings, both published and unpublished and including letters, is provided in the works by Alan Craig Houston and Jonathan Scott (in the second volume of Scott's biography of Sidney) included in the Secondary Sources below.

Discourses Concerning Government. London, Printed, and are to be sold by the Booksellers, of London and Westminster, 1698.
[Published and edited by John Toland, this has been made available in a facsimile reprint (New York: Arno Press, 1979). It is the basis of the present edition.]

Discourses Concerning Government. The Second Edition carefully corrected. To which is Added, The Paper He delivered to the Sheriffs immediately before his Death. London: J. Darby, 1704.

Discourses Concerning Government. To which are added, Memoirs of his Life, and An Apology for Himself, Both Now first published, And the latter from his Original Manuscript. The Third Edition. London: A. Millar, 1751.
[Reprinted in a facsimile edition (Farnborough, England: Gregg International, 1968).]

Bibliography

Discourses Concerning Government. With his Letters, Trial, Apology, and Some Memoirs of his Life. London: A. Millar, 1763.

[Thomas Jefferson's personal copy is in the Library of Congress.]

Other editions of the *Discourses* were published in London, 1705; Edinburgh, 1750 (in two volumes); London, 1795; Philadelphia, 1805 (published for Washington's biographer, the Rev. M. L. Weems, in two volumes); New York, 1805 (three volumes). French translations, 1702 (repr. The Hague, 1755); and Paris, 1794. German translations, Erfurt, 1705; and Leipzig, 1793.

The Works of Algernon Sidney: A New Edition. London: W. Strahan, 1772. Edited by J. Robertson.

[Besides the *Discourses*, this edition contains the paper Sidney delivered to the sheriffs upon the scaffold; letters, taken from Thurloe's State Papers, including letters to his father; letters to Henry Savile, ambassador in France; the record of his trial; his *Apology in the Day of His Death.* The text of the *Discourses* in this edition was extensively corrected, and to some extent rewritten, by the editor.]

"The Character of Sir Henry Vane." Appendix F of *Sir Henry Vane the Younger: A Study in Political and Administrative History*, by Violet A. Rowe. London: Athlone Press, 1970.

Court Maxims, Discussed and Refelled. Cambridge: Cambridge University Press, forthcoming. Edited by Hans Blom et al.

[Sidney's only other book-length work, never previously published, was written about 1665. It is an attack on the Restoration regime of Charles II, with encouragement to rebellion.]

"Of Love." In *A Collection of Scarce and Valuable Tracts . . . of the Late Lord Somers*, ed. Sir Walter Scott. 13 vols. London, 1809–16. Vol. 8, pp. 612–619. Also printed in *The Essence of Algernon Sydney's Work on Government. To which is annexed, his Essay on Love.* London: J. Johnson, 1795.

A Just and Modest Vindication of the Proceedings of the Two Last Parliaments of K. Charles the Second. London, 1681. Printed in *State Tracts . . . in the Reign of K. Charles II.* London, 1689. Pp. 165–187.

[The published author is Sidney's friend Sir William Jones, but there is evidence that Sidney was the principal author.]

Trial Records

The earliest account of Sidney's trial is *An Exact Account of the Tryal & Condemnation of Algernon Sidney, esq.* London: E. Mallet, 1683. Next appeared *The Arraignment, Tryal, & Condemnation of Algernon Sidney, Esq; for High-Treason. For Conspiring the Death of the KING, and Intending to Raise a Rebellion in this KINGDOM.* London: Benj. Tooke, 1684. The trial record was reprinted in *Cobbett's Complete Collection of State Trials.* London: Bagshaw, 1811. Vol. 9, pp. 817–1022. See also the version published in the 1763 and 1772 editions of the *Discourses,* which was extensively corrected by an editor.

Secondary Sources

Ashcraft, Richard. *Revolutionary Politics and Locke's Two Treatises of Government.* Princeton: Princeton University Press, 1986.
[Contains a new and persuasive history of the Whig conspiracy in the early 1680s to overthrow Charles II, for which Sidney was beheaded.]

Carswell, John. *The Porcupine: The Life of Algernon Sidney.* London: John Murray Publishers, 1989.
[A reliable and very readable retelling of the story of Sidney's life, with a sympathetic view of Sidney's character. Written for educated readers interested in history, rather than for professional historians.]

Conniff, James. "Reason and History in Early Whig Thought: The Case of Algernon Sidney." *Journal of the History of Ideas* 43 (1982).
[Shows that Sidney's use of early Anglo-Saxon history to support his case against absolute monarchy is more defensible than scholars today generally acknowledge, and that the argument from history is not the heart of Sidney's book.]

Fink, Zera S. *The Classical Republicans: An Essay in the Recovery of a Pattern of Thought in Seventeenth-Century England.* 2d ed. Evanston, Ill.: Northwestern University Press, 1962.
[Briefly discusses Sidney's political thought.]

Firth, Charles H. "Sidney." *Dictionary of National Biography.* London: Oxford University Press, 1917–. Vol. 18, pp. 202–210.

Houston, Alan Craig. *Algernon Sidney and the Republican Heritage in England and America.* Princeton: Princeton University Press, 1991.
[Contains a good account of Sidney's life and a lengthy treatment of his political thought. The discussion of Filmer and English royalist thought is particularly helpful.]

Karsten, Peter. *Patriot Heroes in England and America.* Madison: University of Wisconsin Press, 1978.
[Chronicles Sidney's rise and decline as a popular hero.]

Meadley, George W. *Memoirs of Algernon Sydney.* London: Cradock and Joy, 1813.

[A well-written biography by a warm admirer of Sidney's character and principles, but not always accurate in its repetition of Whig myths about Sidney.]

Robbins, Caroline, *The Eighteenth-Century Commonwealthman*. Cambridge: Harvard University Press, 1959.
[Discusses Sidney's influence and reputation among leading eighteenth-century English republicans.]

————. "Algernon Sidney's *Discourses Concerning Government*: Textbook of Revolution." In *Absolute Liberty: A Selection from the Articles and Papers of Caroline Robbins*, ed. Barbara Taft. Hamden, Conn.: Archon Books, 1982.
[Reprinted from *William and Mary Quarterly* 4 (1947), 267–296. Discusses Sidney's reception in America during the Revolutionary era.]

Scott, Jonathan. *Algernon Sidney and the English Republic, 1623–1677*. Cambridge: Cambridge University Press, 1988.
[The first twentieth-century biography, it is the most thorough account, based on good historical detective-work. The parts on Sidney's political thought are helpful but sometimes misleading—for example, the frequently repeated assertion that Sidney was a "relativist."]

————. *Algernon Sidney and the Restoration Crisis, 1677–1683*. Cambridge: Cambridge University Press, 1991.
[The second volume of Scott's biography.]

Worden, Blair. "The Commonwealth Kidney of Algernon Sidney." *Journal of British Studies* 24 (January 1985).
[A competent scholarly overview of Sidney's career and a brief account of his thought.]

Additional Items, Second Printing.

Carrive, Paulette. *La Pensée politique d'Algernon Sidney: 1622–1683*. Paris: Mérediens-Klincksieck, 1989.

Dumbauld, Edward. "Algernon Sidney on Public Right." *University of Arkansas Law Journal* 10 (1987–88), 317–338.

Nelson, Scott A. *The Discourses of Algernon Sidney*. Rutherford, N.J.: Fairleigh Dickinson University Press, 1993.

EDITOR'S NOTE

Reading the Discourses

THE style of Sidney's *Discourses* is old-fashioned but quite readable. The main difficulty for the reader stems from the nature of the book. First, since it is a page-by-page commentary on Filmer's *Patriarcha*, Sidney constantly refers to Filmer's argument without always quoting it. He is thus not always easy to follow without having Filmer at one's elbow. There have been at least two modern editions of *Patriarcha*,[1] and it is a fairly short work, so a side-by-side reading is actually quite practicable.

Second, Sidney rarely gives his complete account of a theme or topic in one place. Instead, he repeats himself often, on each occasion giving a brief and partial version of the argument. Thus his understanding of, say, equality has to be culled from the many occasions on which he touches the subject.

Readers who do not have time or energy for the whole book may wish to look at these sections, which contain the meat of Sidney's argument:

Chapter One, sections 1, 3, 5, 10, 13, 16, 20.

[1] Besides the Laslett edition of Filmer already mentioned (reprinted in 1985 by Garland Publishers), *Patriarcha* is printed in John Locke, *Two Treatises of Government*, ed. Thomas I. Cook (New York: Hafner, 1947). At this writing both are still in print.

Chapter Two, sections 1, 4, 8, 9, first eight paragraphs of 11, 13, 16, 19, 20, 22, 23, 26, 28, 32.

Chapter Three, last three paragraphs of section 7, and sections 10, 11, 14, 15, 16, 19, 23, 25, 28, 33, 36, 37, 38, 41, 45.

The Text

Although Sidney did not live to finish the *Discourses*, the book as we have it appears to be a nearly complete draft; all but the final chapter of Filmer's *Patriarcha* are covered. Shortly before his arrest in 1683 he told a friend that it was "not like to be finished in a long time." He may have planned a thorough revision, removing repetitions and tightening a long, sometimes rambling argument. He said he had no "other thoughts concerning it, than when I had finished and examined it, if I was satisfied with it, to show it to some prudent friends, and then either to publish it, keep, or burn it, as they should advise."

The text of this edition is based on the first edition of 1698, published fifteen years after Sidney's death by John Toland, whose editor's note reports that the manuscript was "put into the hands of a person of eminent quality and integrity by the author himself," and from that person Toland, presumably, got it. Toland's was the only edition of the *Discourses* that claimed to be based on the original manuscript. The later editions appear to be founded on his. Accordingly, the 1698 text seems to be the closest we have to what Sidney wrote, and that is what is printed here.

Unfortunately, John Toland is not entirely trustworthy. For example, his edition of the political philosopher James Harrington, published one year after his Sidney, frequently changes what Harrington wrote, according to S. B. Liljegren: "In matters of spelling and punctuation, Toland obviously did not feel under any obligation towards the original edition. But he also made free with the sense intended by Harrington. . . ."[2] Still, the instances where Toland changed Harrington are relatively minor.

The same cannot be said for Toland's edition of Edmund Ludlow's autobiography, which Blair Worden pronounces "radically unfaithful." However, Worden gives "two grounds for reassurance" that Toland's Sidney is reasonably faithful to the original:

> First, besides the passages read out by the prosecution from Sidney's text, a part of his table of contents was presented to the court [when

[2] James Harrington, *Oceana*, ed. S. B. Liljegren (1924; repr. Westport, Conn.: Hyperion Press, 1979), p. xiii.

Sidney was tried for treason]. It is (with one probably trivial exception) encouragingly consistent with the chapter headings of the *Discourses*. Second, if the editor changed Sidney's text, why did he not change it more radically? Ludlow's manuscript was very long and repetitive, qualities that its editor ruthlessly removed. He did not remove these characteristics from the *Discourses*. . . . the title of the published work may well have been bestowed by its editor.[3]

We may conclude that the 1698 edition is fairly close to what Sidney actually wrote.

The present edition departs from the 1698 text in one place. At the end of Chapter Two we print the excerpt from the *Discourses* that was read at Sidney's trial. Worden explains:

> The passages produced as evidence against Sidney at his trial belong to the end of Chapter II, where we learn from the printed version that "the rest of this chapter is wanting in the original manuscript." We can see this by reading Sidney alongside Filmer. The fragments produced by the prosecution attack page 94 (in Laslett's edition) of *Patriarcha*. The part of the *Discourses* that surrounds the end of Chapter II attacks pages 93–97 of *Patriarcha*.[4]

The passage printed at the end of Chapter Two is taken from the 1684 trial record, *The Arraignment, Tryal, & Condemnation of Algernon Sidney, Esq; for High-Treason*.

MODERNIZATION OF THE TEXT

Our intention has been to print an edition of the *Discourses* that is accurate yet easily accessible to today's readers. To this end it has been modernized in several minor respects.

Capitalization in the 1698 *Discourses* is generally consistent with surviving manuscripts of letters in Sidney's own hand. By today's standards it looks haphazard. The section titles, which Sidney wrote as complete sentences, were not capitalized differently from the body of the text. In the body of the text we have changed capitalization to conform to today's usage, but we have set the section titles with their original capitalization.

Italics in the 1698 edition were used for proper names, foreign language phrases, and terms under discussion, such as *aristocracy*. Quotations and paraphrases from other works were also generally given in italics. In Sidney's surviving letters proper names are *not* underlined. Therefore we

[3] Worden, "The Commonwealth Kidney of Algernon Sidney," p. 39.

[4] Ibid.

have retained all italics except for proper names. (A few of Sidney's quotations were placed, inconsistently, in quotation marks. We did not change these.) We did not *add* italics except when proper names within italic quotations and book titles had been set in Roman type.

Spelling. Sidney's irregular spelling in his letters was typical of his day. The same words, including names, were sometimes spelled differently even within the same sentence. The 1698 editor, it appears, regularized Sidney's spelling, but according to standards no longer in use today. Spelling in this edition was determined as follows:

Except for King *Lewis* of France, we modernized proper names: *Hobbs* became *Hobbes*, King *Ralph* became *Rudolph*, in a radical instance. For Greek and Latin names we used the *Oxford Classical Dictionary*; for Biblical names, the King James Bible. For British and other names we followed accepted modern usage, with an occasional reliance upon spellings appearing in Webster's *Second International Dictionary*. This prompted us to retain Sidney's *Britains*, though *Britons* is preferred today. We let stand *Switzers* to refer to the Swiss.

A number of old, often familiar, spellings were retained: *chuse, compleat, shew, publick* (and other *-ck* endings), *compell'd* (and other contracted *-ed* endings, but *rendred* became *rendered*, and so on). *Tho*, without an apostrophe, seems quite contemporary, but it is Sidney's, and we let it stand.

Other old spellings, although easy to guess at, are unfamiliar today and were modernized: *bin* is *been*, *alledge* is *allege*, *sute* is *suit*, and so on. *Expresly*, which could be taken for a contemporary typographical error, became *expressly*. And finally, we modernized constructions like *no where* and *every thing*, making them one word, according to today's usage.

In the Latin, the *-que* endings that Sidney represented by *-q;* are spelled out.

Other changes. We retained Sidney's use of the ampersand (&) in the text and in his notes. Obvious typographical errors were silently corrected. We changed Sidney's (or Toland's) punctuation in a *very* few instances where the sense was unclear. Sidney's nouns in the possessive did not always have apostrophes; we have added them, so that *mens affairs* became *men's affairs*. Sidney also used, and we retained, the old-fashioned possessive *Brutus his sons* where we would write *Brutus's sons*. An occasional word has been added where Sidney or the first typesetter seems to have slipped. These are placed in brackets.

Editor's Note

FOOTNOTES

The notes that Sidney wrote were printed in the first edition either in the margins or as unnumbered footnotes. In our edition all his original notes are printed, without corrections, as *unbracketed* footnotes.

There are quite a few errors in Sidney's notes, which are often too brief to track down easily. Many of his notes may have been written from memory. With the help of later editions, and with reference to the original texts, the notes have been supplemented with corrected versions wherever possible. But any and all such editorial additions, which appear in the footnotes, are printed *within brackets*.

For easily accessible authors, such as Livy, Tacitus, and Aristotle, passages have been cited in the notes according to standard book, chapter, and (sometimes) page divisions as they appear in most modern translations. For more obscure authors, additional information is given where known. In the first footnote reference to an author, a relatively full citation on the work is given if available. Later citations will be abbreviated. The index will help the reader locate full citations.

The bracketed footnotes also include translations, by the editor or his assistants, of Sidney's foreign language quotations wherever Sidney has not provided a translation himself.

As is common in seventeenth-century writing, and as implied above, Sidney's quotations are rarely exact, and they are often better described as paraphrases. Occasionally there are outright errors. Again, no attempt has been made to correct these.

Classical references, Biblical names, regal names, and contemporary names and events are not generally identified unless they are necessary to understand the text. Readers who want further help may consult standard reference works located in most libraries, such as the *Oxford Classical Dictionary* and the *New Century Cyclopedia of Names*.

Acknowledgments

For research assistance with the notes, translations, and proper names, I thank J. Jackson Barlow, Daniel McCarthy, and Michael Cusick. Grace West helped with the proofreading and the Latin. William C. Dennis and Charles H. Hamilton, two successive Directors of Publications at Liberty Fund, Inc., gave excellent editorial advice. Thanks also to The Heritage Foundation, where I was able to finish this book during my year there as Bradley Resident Scholar.

Finally, the generosity of the late Pierre F. Goodrich of Indianapolis, founder of Liberty Fund, has made possible the publication, in inexpensive and handsome volumes, of this and other classics in the history of thought on political liberty.

T.G.W.

Discourses

CONCERNING GOVERNMENT

CHAPTER ONE

SECTION I

Introduction.

HAVING lately seen a book entitled *Patriarcha*,[1] written by Sir Robert Filmer, concerning the universal and undistinguished right of all kings, I thought a time of leisure might be well employed in examining his doctrine, and the questions arising from it; which seem so far to concern all mankind, that, besides the influence upon our future life, they may be said to comprehend all that in this world deserves to be cared for. If he say true, there is but one government in the world that can have anything of justice in it: and those who have hitherto been esteemed the best and wisest of men, for having constituted common-

---

[1] [The notes to the present edition refer to *Patriarcha and Other Political Writings*, edited by Peter Laslett (Oxford: Basil Blackwell, 1949), based on one of the two surviving early manuscripts.

Filmer's *Patriarcha* was first published in 1680, eleven years after its author's death. It was probably written around 1630. The book was divided into three chapters and 46 numbered sections. Sidney's *Discourses* accordingly has three chapters, but 98 sections.

A more recent edition, *Patriarcha and Other* *Writings*, edited by Johann P. Sommerville (Cambridge: Cambridge University Press, 1991), is based on a manuscript thought to be earlier than the one Laslett followed. This *Patriarcha* is very close to the 1680 edition.

Unlike the 1680 edition used by Sidney, Laslett's *Patriarcha* has 32 chapters with titles. The 1680 and 1991 editions' chapters correspond to Laslett's as follows: ch. 1 is 1–7; ch. 2 is 11–21; ch. 3 is 22–32. The 1680 edition omits Laslett's 8–10. —T.G.W., 1995]

wealths or kingdoms; and taken much pains so to proportion the powers of several magistracies, that they might all concur in procuring the publick good; or so to divide the powers between the magistrates and people, that a well-regulated harmony might be preserved in the whole, were the most unjust and foolish of all men. They were not builders, but overthrowers of governments: Their business was to set up aristocratical, democratical or mixed governments, in opposition to that monarchy which by the immutable laws of God and nature is imposed upon mankind; or presumptuously to put shackles upon the monarch, who by the same laws is to be absolute and uncontrolled: They were rebellious and disobedient sons, who rose up against their father; and not only refused to hearken to his voice, but made him bend to their will. In their opinion, such only deserved to be called good men, who endeavoured to be good to mankind; or to that country to which they were more particularly related: and in as much as that good consists in a felicity of estate, and perfection of person, they highly valued such as had endeavoured to make men better, wiser and happier. This they understood to be the end for which men enter'd into societies: And, tho Cicero says, that common-wealths were instituted for the obtaining of justice, he contradicts them not, but comprehends all in that word; because 'tis just that whosoever receives a power, should employ it wholly for the accomplishment of the ends for which it was given. This work could be performed only by such as excelled in virtue; but lest they should deflect from it, no government was thought to be well constituted, unless the laws prevailed above the commands of men;[2] and they were accounted as the worst of beasts, who did not prefer such a condition before a subjection to the fluctuating and irregular will of a man.

If we believe Sir Robert, all this is mistaken. Nothing of this kind was ever left to the choice of men. They are not to enquire what conduces to their own good: God and nature have put us into a way from which we are not to swerve: We are not to live to him, nor to ourselves, but to the master that he hath set over us. One government is established over all, and no limits can be set to the power of the person that manages it. This is the prerogative, or, as another author of the same stamp calls it, the *Royal Charter* granted to kings by God. They all have an equal right to it; women and children are patriarchs; and the next in blood, without any regard to age, sex, or other qualities of the mind or body, are fathers

---

[2] Potentiora legum quam hominum imperia. Tacit. ["The rule of laws is more powerful than that of men." Actually in Livy, *History of Rome*, 14 vols. (Cambridge: Harvard University Press, Loeb Classical Library, 1922–1959), bk. 2, ch. 1. Subsequent citations will refer to these standard editions as "Loeb."]

of as many nations as fall under their power. We are not to examine, whether he or she be young or old, virtuous or vicious, sober minded or stark mad; the right and power is the same in all. Whether virtue be exalted or suppressed; whether he that bears the sword be a praise to those that do well, and a terror to those that do evil; or a praise to those that do evil, and a terror to such as do well, it concerns us not; for the king must not lose his right, nor have his power diminished on any account. I have been sometimes apt to wonder, how things of this nature could enter into the head of any man: Or, if no wickedness or folly be so great, but some may fall into it, I could not well conceive why they should publish it to the world. But these thoughts ceased, when I considered that a people from all ages in love with liberty, and desirous to maintain their own privileges, could never be brought to resign them, unless they were made to believe that in conscience they ought to do it; which could not be, unless they were also persuaded to believe, that there was a law set to all mankind which none might transgress, and which put the examination of all those matters out of their power. This is our author's work. By this it will appear whose throne he seeks to advance, and whose servant he is, whilst he pretends to serve the king. And that it may be evident he hath made use of means suitable to the ends proposed for the service of his great master, I hope to shew that he hath not used one argument that is not false, nor cited one author whom he hath not perverted and abused. Whilst my work is so to lay open these snares that the most simple may not be taken in them, I shall not examine how Sir Robert came to think himself a man fit to undertake so great a work, as to destroy the principles, which from the beginning seem to have been common to all mankind; but only weighing the positions and arguments that he allegeth, will, if there be either truth or strength in them, confess the discovery comes from him that gave us least reason to expect it, and that in spite of the ancients, there is not in the world a piece of wood out of which a Mercury may not be made.[3]

---

[3] [According to a proverb, not every block of wood is good enough to make a statue of the god Mercury.]

SECTION 2

The common Notions of Liberty are not from School Divines, but from Nature.

In the first lines of his book he seems to denounce war against mankind, endeavouring to overthrow the principle of liberty in which God created us, and which includes the chief advantages of the life we enjoy, as well as the greatest helps towards the felicity, that is the end of our hopes in the other. To this end he absurdly imputes to the School divines that which was taken up by them as a common notion, written in the heart of every man, denied by none, but such as were degenerated into beasts, from whence they might prove such points as of themselves were less evident.[1] Thus did Euclid lay down certain axioms, which none could deny that did not renounce common sense, from whence he drew the proofs of such propositions as were less obvious to the understanding; and they may with as much reason be accused of paganism, who say that the whole is greater than a part, that two halfs make the whole, or that a straight line is the shortest way from point to point, as to say, that they who in politicks lay such foundations, as have been taken up by Schoolmen and others as undeniable truths, do therefore follow them, or have any regard to their authority. Tho the Schoolmen were corrupt, they were neither stupid nor unlearned: They could not but see that which all men saw, nor lay more approved foundations, than, that man is naturally free; that he cannot justly be deprived of that liberty without cause, and that he doth not resign it, or any part of it, unless it be in consideration of a greater good, which he proposes to himself. But if he doth unjustly impute the invention of this to School divines, he in some measure repairs his fault in saying, *This hath been fostered by all succeeding papists for good divinity: The divines of the reformed churches have entertained it, and the common people everywhere tenderly embrace it.* That is to say, all Christian divines, whether reformed or unreformed, do approve it, and the people everywhere magnify it, as the height of human felicity. But Filmer and such as are like to him, being neither reformed nor unreformed Christians, nor of the people, can have no title to Christianity; and, in as much as they set themselves against that which is the height of human felicity, they declare themselves enemies to all that are concern'd in it, that is, to all mankind.

But, says he, *They do not remember that the desire of liberty was the first*

[1] [Sidney's quotations from Filmer in this section are from *Patriarcha*, ch. 1 ("The Natural Freedom of Mankind, a New, Plausible, and Dangerous Opinion"), pp. 53–54 of Laslett's edition.]

cause of the fall of man: and I desire it may not be forgotten, that the liberty asserted is not a licentiousness of doing what is pleasing to everyone against the command of God; but an exemption from all human laws, to which they have not given their assent. If he would make us believe there was anything of this in Adam's sin, he ought to have proved, that the law which he transgressed was imposed upon him by man, and consequently that there was a man to impose it; for it will easily appear that neither the reformed or unreformed divines, nor the people following them, do place the felicity of man in an exemption from the laws of God, but in a most perfect conformity to them. Our Saviour taught us *not to fear such as could kill the body, but him that could kill and cast into hell:* And the Apostle tells us that we should obey God rather than man.[2] It hath been ever hereupon observed, that they who most precisely adhere to the laws of God, are least solicitous concerning the commands of men, unless they are well grounded; and those who most delight in the glorious liberty of the sons of God, do not only subject themselves to him, but are most regular observers of the just ordinances of man, made by the consent of such as are concerned according to the will of God.

The error of not observing this may perhaps deserve to be pardoned in a man that had read no books, as proceeding from ignorance; if such as are grossly ignorant can be excused, when they take upon them to write of such matters as require the highest knowledge: But in Sir Robert 'tis prevarication and fraud to impute to Schoolmen and Puritans that which in his first page he acknowledged to be the doctrine of all reformed and unreformed Christian churches, and that he knows to have been the principle in which the Grecians, Italians, Spaniards, Gauls, Germans, and Britains, and all other generous nations ever lived, before the name of Christ was known in the world; insomuch that the base effeminate Asiaticks and Africans, for being careless of their liberty, or unable to govern themselves, were by Aristotle and other wise men called *slaves by nature,*[3] and looked upon as little different from beasts.

This which hath its root in common sense, not being to be overthrown by reason, he spares his pains of seeking any; but thinks it enough to render his doctrine plausible to his own party, by joining the Jesuits to Geneva, and coupling Buchanan to Doleman,[4] as both maintaining the

---

[2] [Luke 12:4; Acts 5:29.]

[3] [Aristotle, *Politics* (Loeb, 1932), bk. 1, 1255a.]

[4] [In Sidney's day the Jesuits were the most extreme advocates of Catholic political power; Geneva was the home of the Protestant political writer John Calvin. The Protestant George Buchanan (in *De jure regni apud Scotos,* 1579) and the Jesuit R. Doleman (in *A* *Conference about the Next Succession to the Crowne of Ingland,* 1594) both defended the people's right to choose their form of government and to overthrow tyrannical kings. But Doleman (pseudonym for Robert Parsons) was abhorred in England as a treasonous advocate of Catholic Spain's pretensions to the British throne.]

same doctrine; tho he might as well have joined the Puritans with the Turks, because they all think that one and one makes two. But whoever marks the proceedings of Filmer and his masters, as well as his disciples, will rather believe that they have learn'd from Rome and the Jesuits to hate Geneva, than that Geneva and Rome can agree in anything farther than as they are obliged to submit to the evidence of truth; or that Geneva and Rome can concur in any design or interest that is not common to mankind.

These men allowed to the people a liberty of deposing their princes. This is a desperate opinion. Bellarmine and Calvin look asquint at it. [5] But why is this a desperate opinion? If disagreements happen between king and people, why is it a more desperate opinion to think the king should be subject to the censures of the people, than the people subject to the will of the king? Did the people make the king, or the king make the people? Is the king for the people, or the people for the king? Did God create the Hebrews that Saul might reign over them? or did they, from an opinion of procuring their own good, ask a king, that might judge them, and fight their battles? If God's interposition, which shall be hereafter explained, do alter the case; did the Romans make Romulus, Numa, Tullus Hostilius, and Tarquinius Priscus kings? or did they make or beget the Romans? If they were made kings by the Romans, 'tis certain they that made them sought their own good in so doing; and if they were made by and for the city and people, I desire to know if it was not better, that when their successors departed from the end of their institution, by endeavouring to destroy it, or all that was good in it, they should be censured and ejected, than be permitted to ruin that people for whose good they were created? Was it more just that Caligula or Nero should be suffered to destroy the poor remains of the Roman nobility and people, with the nations subject to that empire, than that the race of such monsters should be extinguished, and a great part of mankind, especially the best, against whom they were most fierce, preserved by their deaths?

I presume our author thought these questions might be easily decided; and that no more was required to shew the forementioned assertions were not at all desperate, than to examine the grounds of them; but he seeks to divert us from this enquiry by proposing the dreadful consequences of subjecting kings to the censures of their people: whereas no consequence can destroy any truth; and the worst of this is, that if it were received, some princes might be restrained from doing evil, or punished if they

[5] [Filmer cited the Jesuit Cardinal Robert Bellarmine, *De Laicis*, bk. 3, ch. 6, and Calvin's *Institutes*, bk. 4, ch. 10.]

will not be restrained. We are therefore only to consider whether the people, senate, or any magistracy made by and for the people, have, or can have such a right; for if they have, whatsoever the consequences may be, it must stand: And as the one tends to the good of mankind in restraining the lusts of wicked kings; the other exposes them without remedy to the fury of the most savage of all beasts. I am not ashamed in this to concur with Buchanan, Calvin, or Bellarmine, and without envy leave to Filmer and his associates the glory of maintaining the contrary.

But notwithstanding our author's aversion to truth, he confesses, *That Hayward, Blackwood, Barclay,*[6] *and others who have bravely vindicated the right of kings in this point, do with one consent admit, as an unquestionable truth, and assent unto the natural liberty and equality of mankind, not so much as once questioning or opposing it.* And indeed I believe, that tho since the sin of our first parents the earth hath brought forth briars and brambles, and the nature of man hath been fruitful only in vice and wickedness; neither the authors he mentions, nor any others have had impudence enough to deny such evident truth as seems to be planted in the hearts of all men; or to publish doctrines so contrary to common sense, virtue, and humanity, till these times. The production of Laud, Manwaring, Sybthorpe, Hobbes, Filmer, and Heylyn[7] seems to have been reserved as an additional curse to compleat the shame and misery of our age and country. Those who had wit and learning, with something of ingenuity and modesty, tho they believed that nations might possibly make an ill use of their power, and were very desirous to maintain the cause of kings, as far as they could

[6] [John Hayward answered Doleman (previous note) in *An Answer* . . .(London, 1603), attacking Doleman's defense of the people's right to choose their government and upholding the naturalness of monarchy. Hayward does not in fact argue for natural freedom and equality, as Filmer claimed (although he conceded for the sake of argument that even if there were natural freedom and equality, hereditary monarchy and passive obedience would still follow).

William Barclay, in *De regno et regali potestate* . . . (1600), asserted the sacredness of kings, but, unlike Hayward, he grounded kingly authority in popular consent.

Adam Blackwood attacked Buchanan in *Apologia pro regibus* (Paris, 1588), an ardent defense of absolute monarchy.]

[7] [These men were leading 17th-century defenders of absolute monarchy. William Laud, Archbishop of Canterbury under Charles I,

sought to eliminate Puritanism in England and Presbyterianism in Scotland. Parliament impeached him for high treason, and he was executed in 1645.

Anglicans Roger Manwaring and Robert Sybthorpe defended the full scope of royal prerogative under Charles I in sermons preached in 1627 (*Religion and Allegiance* and *Apostolike Obedience*, respectively). Manwaring was impeached but pardoned by the king.

Thomas Hobbes developed a theoretical defense of absolutism, but on grounds entirely opposed to Filmer's: the natural freedom and equality of all men.

Anglican clergyman Peter Heylyn wrote defenses of episcopacy and monarchy. A close friend of Filmer's, he contributed an introductory letter to the first edition of *Patriarcha*.]

put any good colour upon it; yet never denied that some had suffered justly (which could not be, if there were no power of judging them) nor ever asserted anything that might arm them with an irresistible power of doing mischief, animate them to persist in the most flagitious courses, with assurance of perpetual impunity, or engage nations in an inevitable necessity of suffering all manner of outrages. They knew that the actions of those princes who were not altogether detestable, might be defended by particular reasons drawn from them, or the laws of their country; and would neither undertake the defence of such as were abominable, nor bring princes, to whom they wished well, into the odious extremity of justifying themselves by arguments that favoured Caligula and Nero, as well as themselves, and that must be taken for a confession, that they were as bad as could be imagined; since nothing could be said for them that might not as well be applied to the worst that had been, or could be. But Filmer, Heylyn, and their associates scorning to be restrained by such considerations, boldly lay the ax to the root of the tree, and rightly enough affirm, *That the whole fabrick of that which they call popular sedition would fall to the ground, if the principle of natural liberty were removed.* And on the other hand it must be acknowledged that the whole fabrick of tyranny will be much weakened, if we prove, that nations have a right to make their own laws, constitute their own magistrats; and that such as are so constituted owe an account of their actions to those by whom, and for whom they are appointed.

SECTION 3

Implicit Faith belongs to Fools, and Truth is comprehended by examining Principles.

W HILST Filmer's business is to overthrow liberty and truth, he, in his passage, modestly professeth *not to meddle with mysteries of state*,[1] or *arcana imperii*.[2] He renounces those inquiries through an implicit faith, which never enter'd into the head of any but fools, and such, as through a carelessness of the point in question, acted as if they were so. This is the foundation of the papal power, and it can stand no longer

---

[1] [Quotations from Filmer in this section are from *Patriarcha*, ch. 1, pp. 54–55.]   [2] [Or: mysteries of government.]

than those that compose the Roman church can be persuaded to submit their consciences to the word of the priests, and esteem themselves discharged from the necessity of searching the Scriptures in order to know whether the things that are told them are true or false. This may shew whether our author or those of Geneva do best agree with the Roman doctrine: But his instance is yet more sottish than his profession. *An implicit faith*, says he, *is given to the meanest artificer.* I wonder by whom! Who will wear a shoe that hurts him, because the shoe-maker tells him 'tis well made? or who will live in a house that yields no defence against the extremities of weather, because the mason or carpenter assures him 'tis a very good house? Such as have reason, understanding, or common sense, will, and ought to make use of it in those things that concern themselves and their posterity, and suspect the words of such as are interested in deceiving or persuading them not to see with their own eyes, that they may be more easily deceived. This rule obliges us so far to search into matters of state, as to examine the original principles of government in general, and of our own in particular. We cannot distinguish truth from falsehood, right from wrong, or know what obedience we owe to the magistrate, or what we may justly expect from him, unless we know what he is, why he is, and by whom he is made to be what he is. These perhaps may be called *mysteries of state*, and some would persuade us they are to be esteemed *arcana;* but whosoever confesses himself to be ignorant of them, must acknowledge that he is incapable of giving any judgment upon things relating to the superstructure, and in so doing evidently shews to others, that they ought not at all to hearken to what he says.

His argument to prove this is more admirable. *If an implicit faith*, says he, *is given to the meanest artificer in his craft, much more to a prince in the profound secrets of government.* But where is the consequence? If I trust to the judgment of an artificer, or one of a more ingenuous profession, 'tis not because he is of it, but because I am persuaded he does well understand it, and that he will be faithful to me in things relating to his art. I do not send for Lower or Micklethwait when I am sick, nor ask the advice of Mainard or Jones in a suit of law, because the first are physicians, and the other lawyers; but because I think them wise, learned, diligent, and faithful, there being a multitude of others who go under the same name, whose opinion I would never ask. Therefore if any conclusion can be drawn from thence in favour of princes, it must be of such as have all the qualities of ability and integrity, that should create this confidence in me; or it must be proved that all princes, in as much as they are princes, have such qualities. No general conclusion can be drawn from the first

[13]

case, because it must depend upon the circumstances, which ought to be particularly proved: And if the other be asserted, I desire to know whether Caligula, Claudius, Nero, Vitellius, Domitian, Commodus, Heliogabalus, and others not unlike to them, had those admirable endowments, upon which an implicit faith ought to have been grounded; how they came by them; and whether we have any promise from God, that all princes should forever excel in those virtues, or whether we by experience find that they do so. If they are or have been wanting in any, the whole falls to the ground; for no man enjoys as a prince that which is not common to all princes: And if every prince have not wisdom to understand these profound secrets, integrity to direct him, according to what he knows to be good, and a sufficient measure of industry and valour to protect me, he is not the artificer, to whom the implicit faith is due. His eyes are as subject to dazzle as my own. But 'tis a shame to insist on such a point as this. We see princes of all sorts; they are born as other men: The vilest flatterer dares not deny that they are wise or foolish, good or bad, valiant or cowardly like other men: and the crown doth neither bestow extraordinary qualities, ripen such as are found in princes sooner than in the meanest, nor preserve them from the decays of age, sickness, or other accidents, to which all men are subject: And if the greatest king in the world fall into them, he is as incapable of that mysterious knowledge, and his judgment is as little to be relied on, as that of the poorest peasant.

This matter is not mended by sending us to seek those virtues in the ministers, which are wanting in the prince. The ill effects of Rehoboam's folly could not be corrected by the wisdom of Solomon's counsellors: He rejected them; and such as are like to him will always do the same thing.[3] Nero advised with none but musicians, players, chariot-drivers, or the abominable ministers of his pleasures and cruelties. Arcadius his senate was chiefly composed of buffoons and cooks, influenced by an old rascally eunuch. And 'tis an eternal truth, that a weak or wicked prince can never have a wise council, nor receive any benefit by one that is imposed upon him, unless they have a power of acting without him, which would render the government in effect aristocratical, and would probably displease our author as much as if it were so in name also. Good and wise counsellors do not grow up like mushrooms; great judgment is required in chusing and preparing them. If a weak or vicious prince should be so happy to find them chosen to his hand, they would avail him nothing. There will ever be variety of opinions amongst them; and he that is of a perverted judgment will always chuse the worst of those that are proposed, and

[3] [1 Kings 12.]

favour the worst men, as most like to himself. Therefore if this implicit faith be grounded upon a supposition of profound wisdom in the prince, the foundation is overthrown, and it cannot stand; for to repose confidence in the judgment and integrity of one that has none, is the most brutish of all follies. So that if a prince may have or want the qualities, upon which my faith in him can be rationally grounded, I cannot yield the obedience he requires, unless I search into the secrets relating to his person and commands, which he forbids. I cannot know how to obey, unless I know in what, and to whom: Nor in what, unless I know what ought to be commanded: Nor what ought to be commanded, unless I understand the original right of the commander, which is the great *arcanum*. Our author finding himself involved in many difficulties, proposes an expedient as ridiculous as anything that had gone before, being nothing more than an absurd begging the main question, and determining it without any shadow of proof. He enjoins an active or passive obedience before he shews what should oblige or persuade us to it. This indeed were a compendious way of obviating that which he calls popular sedition, and of exposing all nations, that fall under the power of tyrants, to be destroyed utterly by them. Nero or Domitian would have desired no more than that those who would not execute their wicked commands, should patiently have suffered their throats to be cut by such as were less scrupulous: and the world that had suffered those monsters for some years, must have continued under their fury, till all that was good and virtuous had been abolished. But in those ages and parts of the world, where there hath been anything of virtue and goodness, we may observe a third sort of men, who would neither do villainies, nor suffer more than the laws did permit, or the consideration of the publick peace did require. Whilst tyrants with their slaves, and the instruments of their cruelties, were accounted the dregs of mankind, and made the objects of detestation and scorn, these men who delivered their countries from such plagues were thought to have something of divine in them, and have been famous above all the rest of mankind to this day. Of this sort were Pelopidas, Epaminondas, Thrasybulus, Harmodius, Aristogiton, Philopoemen, Lucius Brutus, Publius Valerius, Marcus Brutus, C. Cassius, M. Cato, with a multitude of others amongst the ancient heathens. Such as were instruments of the like deliverances amongst the Hebrews, as Moses, Othniel, Ehud, Barak, Gideon, Samson, Jephthah, Samuel, David, Jehu, the Maccabees and others, have from the Scriptures a certain testimony of the righteousness of their proceedings, when they neither would act what was evil, nor suffer more than was reasonable. But lest we should learn by their examples, and the praises given to them, our

[15]

author confines the subject's choice to acting or suffering, that is, doing what is commanded, or lying down to have his throat cut, or to see his family and country made desolate. This he calls giving to Caesar that which is Caesar's; whereas he ought to have considered that the question is not whether that which is Caesar's should be rendered to him, for that is to be done to all men; but who is Caesar, and what doth of right belong to him, which he no way indicates to us: so that the question remains entire, as if he had never mentioned it, unless we do in a compendious way take his word for the whole.

SECTION 4

The Rights of particular Nations
cannot subsist, if General Principles contrary
to them are received as true.

NOTWITHSTANDING this our author, if we will believe him, *doth not question or quarrel at the rights or liberties of this or any other nation.*[1] He only denies they can have any such, in subjecting them necessarily and universally to the will of one man; and says not a word that is not applicable to every nation in the world as well as to our own. But as the bitterness of his malice seems to be most especially directed against England, I am inclined to believe he hurts other countries only by accident, as the famous French lady[2] intended only to poison her father, husband, brother, and some more of her nearest relations; but rather than they should escape, destroyed many other persons of quality, who at several times dined with them: and if that ought to excuse her, I am content he also should pass uncensured, tho his crimes are incomparably greater than those for which she was condemned, or than any can be which are not of a publick extent.

---

[1] [*Patriarcha*, ch. 1, p. 55.]

[2] The Marchioness of Brinvilliers. [She was executed for her many poisonings in Paris in 1676.]

SECTION 5

To depend upon the Will of a Man is Slavery.

THIS, as he thinks, is farther sweetened, by asserting, that he doth not inquire what the rights of a people are, but from whence; not considering, that whilst he denies they can proceed from the laws of natural liberty, or any other root than the grace and bounty of the prince, he declares they can have none at all. For as liberty solely consists in an independency upon the will of another, and by the name of slave we understand a man, who can neither dispose of his person nor goods, but enjoys all at the will of his master; there is no such thing in nature as a slave, if those men or nations are not slaves, who have no other title to what they enjoy, than the grace of the prince, which he may revoke whensoever he pleaseth. But there is more than ordinary extravagance in his assertion, that *the greatest liberty in the world is for a people to live under a monarch,*[1] when his whole book is to prove, that this monarch hath his right from God and nature, is endowed with an unlimited power of doing what he pleaseth, and can be restrained by no law. If it be liberty to live under such a government, I desire to know what is slavery. It has been hitherto believed in the world, that the Assyrians, Medes, Arabs, Egyptians, Turks, and others like them, lived in slavery, because their princes were masters of their lives and goods: Whereas the Grecians, Italians, Gauls, Germans, Spaniards, and Carthaginians, as long as they had any strength, virtue or courage amongst them, were esteemed free nations, because they abhorred such a subjection. They were, and would be governed only by laws of their own making: *Potentiora erant legum quam hominum imperia.*[2] Even their princes had the authority or credit of persuading, rather than the power of commanding. But all this was mistaken: These men were slaves, and the Asiaticks were freemen. By the same rule the Venetians, Switsers, Grisons, and Hollanders, are not free nations: but liberty in its perfection is enjoyed in France, and Turkey. The intention of our ancestors was, without doubt, to establish this amongst us by *Magna Charta*, and other preceding or subsequent laws; but they ought to have added one clause, That the contents of them should be in force only so long as it should please the king. King Alfred, upon whose laws *Magna Charta* was grounded, when he said the English nation was as free as the internal thoughts of a man, did only mean, that

[1] [*Patriarcha*, ch. 1, p. 55.]
[2] C. Tacit. ["The rule of laws was more powerful than that of men." Actually in Livy, *History of Rome*, bk. 2, ch. 1.]

[17]

it should be so as long as it pleased their master. This it seems was the end of our law, and we who are born under it, and are descended from such as have so valiantly defended their rights against the encroachments of kings, have followed after vain shadows, and without the expence of sweat, treasure, or blood, might have secured their beloved liberty, by casting all into the king's hands.

We owe the discovery of these secrets to our author, who after having so gravely declared them, thinks no offence ought to be taken at the freedom he assumes of examining things relating to the liberty of mankind, because he hath the right which is common to all: But he ought to have considered, that in asserting that right to himself, he allows it to all mankind. And as the temporal good of all men consists in the preservation of it, he declares himself to be a mortal enemy to those who endeavour to destroy it. If he were alive, this would deserve to be answered with stones rather than words. He that oppugns the publick liberty, overthrows his own, and is guilty of the most brutish of all follies, whilst he arrogates to himself that which he denies to all men.

I cannot but commend his modesty and care *not to detract from the worth of learned men;*[3] but it seems they were all subject to error, except himself, who is rendered infallible through pride, ignorance, and impudence. But if Hooker[4] and Aristotle were wrong in their fundamentals concerning natural liberty, how could they be in the right when they built upon it? Or if they did mistake, how can they deserve to be cited? or rather, why is such care taken to pervert their sense? It seems our author is by their errors brought to the knowledge of the truth. *Men have heard of a dwarf standing upon the shoulders of a giant, who saw farther than the giant;* but now that the dwarf standing on the ground sees that which the giant did overlook, we must learn from him. If there be sense in this, the giant must be blind, or have such eyes only as are of no use to him. He minded only the things that were far from him: These great and learned men mistook the very principle and foundation of all their doctrine. If we will believe our author, this misfortune befell them because they too much trusted to the Schoolmen. He names Aristotle, and I presume intends to comprehend Plato, Plutarch, Thucydides, Xenophon, Polybius, and all the ancient Grecians, Italians, and others, who asserted the natural freedom of mankind, only in imitation of the Schoolmen, to advance the power of the pope; and would have compassed their design, if Filmer

---

[3] [The quotations in this paragraph are from *Patriarcha*, ch. 1, p. 55.]

[4] [The Anglican political thinker Richard Hooker, like Barclay, defended the mon- archy but affirmed the basis of government in the consent of the governed. Sidney quotes Hooker in ch. II, sec. 6.]

and his associates had not opposed them. These men had taught us to make the unnatural distinction between *royalist* and *patriot*, and kept us from seeing, *that the relation between king and people is so great, that their well being is reciprocal.* If this be true, how came Tarquin to think it good for him to continue king at Rome, when the people would turn him out? or the people to think it good for them to turn him out, when he desired to continue in? Why did the Syracusians destroy the tyranny of Dionysius, which he was not willing to leave, till he was pulled out by the heels? How could Nero think of burning Rome? Or why did Caligula wish the people had but one neck, that he might strike it off at one blow, if their welfare was thus reciprocal? 'Tis not enough to say, these were wicked or mad men; for other princes may be so also, and there may be the same reason of differing from them. For if the proposition be not universally true, 'tis not to be received as true in relation to any, till it be particularly proved; and then 'tis not to be imputed to the quality of prince, but to the personal virtue of the man.

I do not find any great matters in the passages taken out of Bellarmine, which our author says, comprehend the strength of all that ever he had heard, read, or seen produced for the natural liberty of the subject:[5] but he not mentioning where they are to be found, I do not think myself obliged to examine all his works, to see whether they are rightly cited or not; however there is certainly nothing new in them: We see the same, as to the substance, in those who wrote many ages before him, as well as in many that have lived since his time, who neither minded him, nor what he had written. I dare not take upon me to give an account of his works, having read few of them; but as he seems to have laid the foundation of his discourses in such common notions as were assented to by all mankind, those who follow the same method have no more regard to Jesuitism and popery, tho he was a Jesuit and a cardinal, than they who agree with Faber[6] and other Jesuits in the principles of geometry which no sober man did ever deny.

[5] [*Patriarcha*, ch. 2 ("The Question Stated out of Bellarmine: And Some Contradictions of His Noted"), p. 56.]

[6] [Johannes Faber, German Roman Catholic Bishop, opponent of the Reformation, and author of *Malleus in Haeresin Lutheranam* (Hammer against the Lutheran Heresy), 1524.]

SECTION 6

God leaves to Man the choice of
Forms in Government; and those who constitute
one Form, may abrogate it.

BUT Sir Robert *desires to make observations on Bellarmine's words, before he examines or refutes them;*[1] and indeed it were not possible to make such stuff of his doctrine as he does, if he had examined or did understand it. First, he very wittily concludes, *That if by the law of God, the power be immediately in the people, God is the author of a democracy:* And why not as well as of a tyranny? Is there anything in it repugnant to the being of God? Is there more reason to impute to God Caligula's monarchy, than the democracy of Athens? Or is it more for the glory of God, to assert his presence with the Ottoman or French monarchs, than with the popular governments of the Switsers and Grisons? Is pride, malice, luxury and violence so suitable to his being, that they who exercise them are to be reputed his ministers? And is modesty, humility, equality and justice so contrary to his nature, that they who live in them should be thought his enemies? Is there any absurdity in saying, that since God in goodness and mercy to mankind, hath with an equal hand given to all the benefit of liberty, with some measure of understanding how to employ it, 'tis lawful for any nation, as occasion shall require, to give the exercise of that power to one or more men, under certain limitations or conditions; or to retain it in themselves, if they thought it good for them? If this may be done, we are at end of all controversies concerning one form of government, established by God, to which all mankind must submit; and we may safely conclude, that having given to all men in some degree a capacity of judging what is good for themselves, he hath granted to all likewise a liberty of inventing such forms as please them best, without favouring one more than another.

His second observation is grounded upon a falsity in matter of fact. Bellarmine does not say, that democracy is an ordinance of God more than any other government: nor that the people have no power to make use of their right; but that they do, that is to say ordinarily, transmit the exercise of it to one or more. And 'tis certain they do sometimes, especially in small cities, retain it in themselves: But whether that were observed

---

[1] [*Patriarcha*, ch. 2, p. 56.]

or not by Bellarmine, makes nothing to our cause, which we defend, and not him.

The next point is subtle, and he thinks thereby to have brought Bellarmine, and such as agree with his principle, to a nonplus. He doubts who shall judge of the lawful cause of changing the government, and says, It is a *pestilent conclusion to place that power in the multitude.*[2] But why should this be esteemed pestilent? or to whom? If the allowance of such a power to the senate was pestilent to Nero, it was beneficial to mankind; and the denial of it, which would have given to Nero an opportunity of continuing in his villainies, would have been pestilent to the best men, whom he endeavoured to destroy, and to all others that received benefit from them. But this question depends upon another; for if governments are constituted for the pleasure, greatness or profit of one man, he must not be interrupted; for the opposing of his will, is to overthrow the institution. On the other side, if the good of the governed be sought, care must be taken that the end be accomplished, tho it be with the prejudice of the governor: If the power be originally in the multitude, and one or more men, to whom the exercise of it, or a part of it was committed, had no more than their brethren, till it was conferred on him or them, it cannot be believed that rational creatures would advance one or a few of their equals above themselves, unless in consideration of their own good; and then I find no inconvenience in leaving to them a right of judging, whether this be duly performed or not. We say in general, he that institutes, may also abrogate,[3] most especially when the institution is not only by, but for himself. If the multitude therefore do institute, the multitude may abrogate; and they themselves, or those who succeed in the same right, can only be fit judges of the performance of the ends of the institution. Our author may perhaps say, the publick peace may be hereby disturbed; but he ought to know, there can be no peace, where there is no justice; nor any justice, if the government instituted for the good of a nation be turned to its ruin. But in plain English, the inconvenience with which such as he endeavour to affright us, is no more than that he or they, to whom the power is given, may be restrained or chastised, if they betray their trust; which I presume will displease none, but such as would rather submit Rome, with the best part of the world depending upon it, to the will of Caligula or Nero, than Caligula or Nero to the judgment of the senate and people; that is, rather to expose many

---

[2] [*Patriarcha*, ch. 2, p. 57.]

[3] Cujus est instituere, ejus est abrogare.

great and brave nations to be destroyed by the rage of a savage beast, than subject that beast to the judgment of all, or the choicest men of them, who can have no interest to pervert them, or other reason to be severe to him, than to prevent the mischiefs he would commit, and to save the people from ruin.

In the next place he recites an argument of Bellarmine, that *'tis evident in Scripture God hath ordained powers; but God hath given them to no particular person, because by nature all men are equal; therefore he hath given power to the people or multitude.*[4] I leave him to untie that knot if he can; but, as 'tis usual with impostors, he goes about by surmises to elude the force of his argument, pretending that in some other place he had contradicted himself, and acknowledged that every man was prince of his posterity; *because that if many men had been created together, they ought all to have been princes of their posterity.* But 'tis not necessary to argue upon passages cited from authors, when he that cites them may be justly suspected of fraud, and neither indicates the place nor treatise, lest it should be detected; most especially when we are no way concerned in the author's credit. I take Bellarmine's first argument to be strong; and if he in some place did contradict it, the hurt is only to himself: but in this particular I should not think he did it, tho I were sure our author had faithfully repeated his words; for in allowing every man to be prince of his posterity, he only says, every man should be chief in his own family, and have a power over his children, which no man denies: But he does not understand Latin, who thinks that the word *princeps* doth in any degree signify an absolute power, or a right of transmitting it to his heirs and successors, upon which the doctrine of our author wholly depends. On the contrary, the same law that gave to my father a power over me, gives me the like over my children; and if I had a thousand brothers, each of them would have the same over their children. Bellarmine's first argument therefore being no way enervated by the alleged passage, I may justly insist upon it, and add, that God hath not only declared in Scripture, but written on the heart of every man, that as it is better to be clothed, than to go naked; to live in a house, than to lie in the fields; to be defended by the united force of a multitude, than to place the hopes of his security solely in his own strength; and to prefer the benefits of society, before a savage and barbarous solitude; he also taught them to frame such societies, and to establish such laws as were necessary to preserve them. And we may as reasonably affirm, that mankind is forever obliged to use no other

---

[4] [The quotations in this paragraph are from *Patriarcha*, ch. 3 ("The Argument of Bellarmine Answered out of Bellarmine Himself: And of the Regal Authority of the Patriarchs after the Flood"), p. 57.]

clothes than leather breeches, like Adam; to live in hollow trees, and eat acorns, or to seek after the model of his house for a habitation, and to use no arms except such as were known to the patriarchs, as to think all nations forever obliged to be governed as they governed their families. This I take to be the genuine sense of the Scripture, and the most respectful way of interpreting the places relating to our purpose. 'Tis hard to imagine, that God who hath left all things to our choice, that are not evil in themselves, should tie us up in this; and utterly incredible that he should impose upon us a necessity of following his will, without declaring it to us. Instead of constituting a government over his people, consisting of many parts, which we take to be a model fit to be imitated by others, he might have declared in a word, that the eldest man of the eldest line should be king; and that his will ought to be their law. This had been more suitable to the goodness and mercy of God, than to leave us in a dark labyrinth, full of precipices; or rather, to make the government given to his own people, a false light to lead us to destruction. This could not be avoided, if there were such a thing as our author calls a *lord paramount over his children's children to all generations.* We see nothing in Scripture, of precept or example, that is not utterly abhorrent to this chimera. The only sort of kings mentioned there with approbation, is such a one *as may not raise his heart above his brethren.*[5] If God had constituted a lord paramount with an absolute power, and multitudes of nations were to labour and fight for his greatness and pleasure, this were to raise his heart to a height, that would make him forget he was a man. Such as are versed in Scripture, not only know that it neither agrees with the letter or spirit of that book; but that it is unreasonable in itself, unless he were of a species different from the rest of mankind. His exaltation would not agree with God's indulgence to his creatures, tho he were the better for it; much less when probably he would be made more unhappy, and worse, by the pride, luxury and other vices, that always attend the highest fortunes. 'Tis no less incredible that God, who disposes all things in wisdom and goodness, and appoints a due place for all, should, without distinction, ordain such a power, to everyone succeeding in such a line, as cannot be executed; the wise would refuse, and fools cannot take upon them the burden of it, without ruin to themselves, and such as are under them: or expose mankind to a multitude of other absurdities and mischiefs; subjecting the aged to be governed by children; the wise, to depend on the will of fools; the strong and valiant, to expect defence from the weak or cowardly; and all in general to receive justice from him, who neither knows nor cares for it.

[5] Deut. 17.

SECTION 7

Abraham and the Patriarchs were not kings.

I F any man say, that we are not to seek into the depth of God's
counsels; I answer, that if he had, for reasons known only to himself,
affixed such a right to any one line, he would have set a mark upon those
who come of it, that nations might know to whom they owe subjection;
or given some testimony of his presence with Filmer and Heylyn, if he
had sent them to reveal so great a mystery. Till that be done, we may
safely look upon them as the worst of men, and teachers only of lies and
follies. This persuades me little, to examine what would have been, if
God had at once created many men, or the conclusions that can be drawn
from Adam's having been alone. For nothing can be more evident, than
that if many had been created, they had been all equal, unless God had
given a preference to one. All their sons had inherited the same right
after their death; and no dream was ever more empty, than his whimsey
of Adam's kingdom, or that of the ensuing patriarchs. To say the truth,
'tis hard to speak seriously of Abraham's kingdom, or to think any man
to be in earnest who mentions it. He was a stranger, and a pilgrim in the
land where he lived, and pretended to no authority beyond his own
family, which consisted only of a wife and slaves. He lived with Lot as
with his equal, and would have no contest with him, because they were
brethren. His wife and servants could neither make up, nor be any part
of a kingdom, in as much as the despotical government, both in practice
and principle, differs from the regal. If his kingdom was to be grounded
on the paternal right, it vanished away of itself; he had no child: Eliezer
of Damascus, for want of a better, was to be his heir: Lot, tho his
nephew, was excluded: He durst not own his own wife: He had not one
foot of land, till he bought a field for a burying place: His three hundred
and eighteen men were servants (bought according to the custom of those
days), or their children;[1] and the war he made with them, was like to
Gideon's enterprize; which shews only that God can save by a few as
well as by many, but makes nothing to our author's purpose. For if they
had been as many in number as the army of Semiramis, they could have
no relation to the regal, much less to the paternal power; for a father
doth not buy, but beget children.

Notwithstanding this, our author bestows the proud title of lord
paramount upon him, and transmits it to Isaac, who was indeed a king

---

[1] [Genesis 13–15.]

like his father, great, admirable, and glorious in wisdom and holiness, but utterly void of all worldly splendor or power. This spiritual kingdom was inherited by Jacob, whose title to it was not founded on prerogative of birth, but election and peculiar grace; but he never enjoyed any other worldly inheritance, than the field and cave which Abraham had bought for a burying place, and the goods he had gained in Laban's service.

The example of Judah his sentence upon Thamar[2] is yet farther from the purpose, if it be possible; for he was then a member of a private family, the fourth son of a father then living; neither in possession, nor under the promise of the privileges of primogeniture, tho Reuben, Simeon and Levi fell from it by their sins. Whatsoever therefore the right was, which belonged to the head of the family, it must have been in Jacob; but as he professed himself a keeper of sheep, as his fathers had been, the exercise of that employment was so far from regal, that it deserves no explication. If that act of Judah is to be imputed to a royal power, I have as much as I ask: He, tho living with his father, and elder brothers, when he came to be of age to have children, had the same power over such, as were of, or came into his family, as his father had over him; for none can go beyond the power of life and death: The same in the utmost extent, cannot at the same time equally belong to many. If it be divided equally, it is no more than that universal liberty which God hath given to mankind; and every man is a king till he divest himself of his right, in consideration of something that he thinks better for him.

SECTION 8

Nimrod was the first King, during the life of Cush, Ham, Shem, and Noah.

T HE Creation is exactly described in the Scripture; but we know so little of what passed between the finishing of it and the Flood, that our author may say what he pleases, and I may leave him to seek his proofs where he can find them.[1] In the meantime I utterly deny, that any power did remain in the heads of families after the flood, that does in the least degree resemble the regal in principle or practice. If in this I

---

[2] [Genesis 38.]

[1] [*Patriarcha*, ch. 4 ("The Dispersion of Nations after the Flood Was by Entire Families over Which the Fathers Were Kings, and from Those Kings, all Kings are Descended"), pp. 58–60.]

am mistaken, such power must have been in Noah, and transmitted to one of his sons. The Scripture says only, that he built an altar, sacrificed to the Lord, was a husbandman, planted a vineyard, and performed such offices as bear nothing of the image of a king, for the space of three hundred and fifty years. We have reason to believe, that his sons after his death, continued in the same manner of life, and the equality properly belonging to brethren. 'Tis not easy to determine, whether Shem or Japheth were the elder;[2] but Ham is declared to be the younger; and Noah's blessing to Shem seems to be purely prophetical and spiritual, of what should be accomplished in his posterity; with which Japheth should be persuaded to join. If it had been worldly, the whole earth must have been brought under him, and have forever continued in his race, which never was accomplished, otherwise than in the spiritual kingdom of Christ, which relates not to our author's lord paramount.

As to earthly kings, the first of them was Nimrod, the sixth son of Cush the son of Ham, Noah's younger and accursed son. This kingdom was set up about a hundred and thirty years after the Flood, whilst Cush, Ham, Shem and Noah were yet living; whereas if there were anything of truth in our author's proposition, all mankind must have continued under the government of Noah whilst he lived; and that power must have been transmitted to Shem, who lived about three hundred and seventy years after the erection of Nimrod's kingdom; and must have come to Japheth if he was the elder, but could never come to Ham, who is declared to have been certainly the younger, and condemned to be a servant to them both; much less to the younger son of his son, whilst he, and those to whom he and his posterity were to be subjects, were still living.

This rule therefore, which the partizans of absolute monarchy fancy to be universal and perpetual, falling out in its first beginning, directly contrary to what they assert; and being never known to have been recovered, were enough to silence them, if they had anything of modesty or regard to truth. But the matter may be carried farther: For the Scripture doth not only testify, that this kingdom of Nimrod was an usurpation, void of all right, proceeding from the most violent and mischievous vices, but exercised with the utmost fury, that the most wicked man of the accursed race, who set himself up against God, and all that is good, could be capable of. The progress of this kingdom was suitable to its institution: that which was begun in wickedness, was carried on with madness, and produced confusion. The mighty hunter, whom the best interpreters call a *cruel tyrant*, receding from the simplicity and innocence of the patriarchs,

---

[2] Gen. 9.

who were husbandmen or shepherds, arrogating to himself a dominion over Shem, to whom he and his fathers were to be servants, did thereby so peculiarly become the heir of God's curse, that whatsoever hath been said to this day, of the power that did most directly set itself against God and his people, hath related literally to the Babel that he built, or figuratively to that which resembles it in pride, cruelty, injustice and madness.[3]

But the shameless rage of some of these writers is such, that they rather chuse to ascribe the beginning of their idol to this odious violence, than to own it from the consent of a willing people; as if they thought, that as all action must be suitable to its principle, so that which is unjust in its practice, ought to scorn to be derived from that which is not detestable in its principle. 'Tis hardly worth our pains to examine whether the nations, that went from Babel after the confusion of languages, were more or less than seventy two, for they seem not to have gone according to families, but every one to have associated himself to those that understood his speech; and the chief of the fathers, as Noah and his sons, were not there, or were subject to Nimrod; each of which points doth destroy, even in the root, all pretence to paternal government. Besides, 'tis evident in Scripture, that Noah lived three hundred and fifty years after the Flood; Shem five hundred; Abraham was born about two hundred and ninety years after the Flood, and lived one hundred seventy five years: He was therefore born under the government of Noah, and died under that of Shem: He could not therefore exercise a regal power whilst he lived, for that was in Shem: So that in leaving his country, and setting up a family for himself, that never acknowledged any superior, and never pretending to reign over any other, he fully shewed he thought himself free, and to owe subjection to none: And being as far from arrogating to himself any power upon the title of paternity, as from acknowledging it in any other, left every one to the same liberty.

The punctual enumeration of the years, that the fathers of the holy seed lived, gives us ground of making a more than probable conjecture, that they of the collateral lines were, in number of days, not unequal to them; and if that be true, Ham and Cush were alive when Nimrod set himself up to be king. He must therefore have usurped this power over his father, grandfather, and great grandfather; or, which is more probable, he turned into violence and oppression the power given to him by a multitude; which, like a flock without a shepherd, not knowing whom to obey, set him up to be their chief. I leave to our author the liberty of

---

[3] [Genesis 10–11.]

chusing which of these two doth best suit with his paternal monarchy; but as far as I can understand, the first is directly against it, as well as against the laws of God and man; the other being from the consent of the multitude, cannot be extended farther than they would have it, nor turned to their prejudice, without the most abominable ingratitude and treachery, from whence no right can be derived, nor any justifiable example taken.

Nevertheless, if our author resolve that Abraham was also a king, he must presume that Shem did emancipate him, before he went to seek his fortune. This was not a kingly posture; but I will not contradict him, if I may know over whom he reigned. Paternal monarchy is exercised by the father of the family over his descendants, or such as had been under the dominion of him, whose heir he is. But Abraham had neither of these: Those of his nearest kindred continued in Mesopotamia, as appears by what is said of Bethuel and Laban. He had only Lot with him, over whom he pretended no right: He had no children till he was a hundred years old (that is to say, he was a king without a subject), and then he had but one. I have heard that sovereigns do impatiently bear competitors;[4] but now I find subjection also doth admit of none. Abraham's kingdom was too great when he had two children, and to disburthen it, Ishmael must be expelled soon after the birth of Isaac. He observed the same method after the death of Sarah: He had children by Keturah; but he gave them gifts and sent them away, leaving Isaac like a stoical king reigning in and over himself, without any other subject till the birth of Jacob and Esau. But his kingdom was not to be of a larger extent than that of his father: The two twins could not agree: Jacob was sent away by his mother; he reigned over Esau only, and 'tis not easy to determine who was the heir of his worldly kingdom; for tho Jacob had the birthright, we do not find he had any other goods, than what he had gotten in Laban's service. If our author say true, the right of primogeniture, with the dominion perpetually annexed by the laws of God and nature, must go to the eldest: Isaac therefore, tho he had not been deceived, could not have conferred it upon the younger; for man cannot overthrow what God and nature have instituted. Jacob, in the court language, had been a double rebel, in beguiling his father, and supplanting his brother. The blessing of being lord over his brethren, could not have taken place. Or if Isaac had power, and his act was good, the prerogative of the elder is not rooted in the law of God or nature, but a matter of conveniency only,

---

[4] Omnisque potestas impatiens consortis erit.
Lucan. [Lucan, *Pharsalia*, also called *The Civil War* (Loeb, 1928), bk. 1, li. 92–93.]

which may be changed at the will of the father, whether he know what he do or not. But if this paternal right to dominion were of any value, or dominion over men were a thing to be desired, why did Abraham, Isaac and Jacob, content themselves with such a narrow territory, when after the death of their ancestors, they ought, according to that rule, to have been lords of the world? All authors conclude that Shem was the eldest by birth, or preferred by the appointment of God, so as the right must have been in him, and from him transmitted to Abraham and Isaac; but if they were so possessed with the contemplation of a heavenly kingdom, as not to care for the greatest on earth; 'tis strange that Esau, whose modesty is not much commended, should so far forget his interest, as neither to lay claim to the empire of the world, nor dispute with his brother the possession of the field and cave bought by Abraham, but rather to fight for a dwelling on Mount Seir, that was neither possessed by, nor promised to his fathers. If he was fallen from his right, Jacob might have claimed it; but God was his inheritance, and being assured of his blessing, he contented himself with what he could gain by his industry, in a way that was not at all suitable to the pomp and majesty of a king. Which way soever therefore the business be turned, whether, according to Isaac's blessing, Esau should serve Jacob, or our author's opinion, Jacob must serve Esau, neither of the two was effected in their persons: And the kingdom of two being divided into two, each of them remained lord of himself.

SECTION 9
The Power of a Father belongs only to a Father.

THIS leads us to an easy determination of the question, which our author thinks insoluble; *If Adam was lord of his children, he doth not see how any can be free from the subjection of his parents.*[1] For as no good man will ever desire to be free from the respect that is due to his father, who did beget and educate him, no wise man will ever think the like to be due to his brother or nephew that did neither. If Esau and Jacob were equally free; if Noah, as our author affirms, divided Europe, Asia and Africa, amongst his three sons, tho he cannot prove it; and if seventy two nations under so many heads or kings went from Babylon to people

---

[1] [*Patriarcha*, ch. 3, p. 57.]

the earth, about a hundred and thirty years after the Flood, I know not why, according to the same rule and proportion, it may not be safely concluded, that in four thousand years kings are so multiplied, as to be in number equal to the men that are in the world; that is to say, they are, according to the laws of God and nature, all free, and independent upon each other, as Shem, Ham and Japheth were. And therefore, tho Adam and Noah had reigned alone when there were no men in the world except such as issued from them, that is no reason why any other should reign over those that he hath not begotten. As the right of Noah was divided amongst the children he left, and when he was dead, no one of them depended on the other, because no one of them was father of the other; and the right of a father can only belong to him that is so, the like must forever attend every other father in the world. This paternal power must necessarily accrue to every father: He is a king by the same right as the sons of Noah; and how numerous soever families may be upon the increase of mankind, they are all free, till they agree to recede from their own right, and join together in, or under one government, according to such laws as best please themselves.

SECTION 10

Such as enter into Society, must in some degree diminish their Liberty.

REASON leads them to this: No one man or family is able to provide that which is requisite for their convenience or security, whilst everyone has an equal right to everything, and none acknowledges a superior to determine the controversies, that upon such occasions must continually arise, and will probably be so many and great, that mankind cannot bear them. Therefore tho I do not believe that Bellarmine said, a commonwealth could not exercise its power;[1] for he could not be ignorant, that Rome and Athens did exercise theirs, and that all the regular kingdoms in the world are commonwealths; yet there is nothing of absurdity in saying, that man cannot continue in the perpetual and entire fruition of the liberty that God hath given him. The liberty of one is thwarted by that of another; and whilst they are all equal, none will yield to any, otherwise than by a general consent. This is the ground of all

---

[1] [*Patriarcha*, ch. 2, p. 56.]

just governments; for violence or fraud can create no right; and the same consent gives the form to them all, how much soever they differ from each other. Some small numbers of men, living within the precincts of one city, have, as it were, cast into a common stock, the right which they had of governing themselves and children, and by common consent joining in one body, exercised such power over every single person as seemed beneficial to the whole; and this men call perfect *democracy*. Others chose rather to be governed by a select number of such as most excelled in wisdom and virtue; and this, according to the signification of the word, was called *aristocracy:* Or when one man excelled all others, the government was put into his hands under the name of *monarchy*. But the wisest, best, and far the greatest part of mankind, rejecting these simple species, did form governments mixed or composed of the three, as shall be proved hereafter, which commonly received their respective denomination from the part that prevailed, and did deserve praise or blame, as they were well or ill proportioned.

It were a folly hereupon to say, that the liberty for which we contend, is of no use to us, since we cannot endure the solitude, barbarity, weakness, want, misery and dangers that accompany it whilst we live alone, nor can enter into a society without resigning it; for the choice of that society, and the liberty of framing it according to our own wills, for our own good, is all we seek. This remains to us whilst we form governments, that we ourselves are judges how far 'tis good for us to recede from our natural liberty; which is of so great importance, that from thence only we can know whether we are freemen or slaves; and the difference between the best government and the worst, doth wholly depend upon a right or wrong exercise of that power. If men are naturally free, such as have wisdom and understanding will always frame good governments: But if they are born under the necessity of perpetual slavery, no wisdom can be of use to them; but all must forever depend on the will of their lords, how cruel, mad, proud or wicked soever they be.

SECTION 11

No Man comes to command many,
unless by Consent or by Force.

BUT because I cannot believe God hath created man in such a state of misery and slavery as I just now mentioned; by discovering the vanity of our author's whimsical patriarchical kingdom, I am led to a certain conclusion, that every father of a family is free and exempt from the domination of any other, as the seventy two that went from Babel were. 'Tis hard to comprehend how one man can come to be master of many, equal to himself in right, unless it be by consent or by force. If by consent, we are at an end of our controversies: Governments, and the magistrates that execute them, are created by man. They who give a being to them, cannot but have a right of regulating, limiting and directing them as best pleaseth themselves; and all our author's assertions concerning the absolute power of one man, fall to the ground: If by force, we are to examine how it can be possible or justifiable. This subduing by force we call conquest; but as he that forceth must be stronger than those that are forced, to talk of one man who in strength exceeds many millions of men, is to go beyond the extravagance of fables and romances. This wound is not cured by saying, that he first conquers one, and then more, and with their help others; for as to matter of fact, the first news we hear of Nimrod is, that he reigned over a great multitude, and built vast cities; and we know of no kingdom in the world, that did not begin with a greater number than any one man could possibly subdue. If they who chuse one to be their head, did under his conduct subdue others, they were fellow-conquerors with him; and nothing can be more brutish, than to think, that by their virtue and valour they had purchased perpetual slavery to themselves and their posterity. But if it were possible, it could not be justifiable; and whilst our dispute is concerning right, that which ought not to be is no more to be received, than if it could not be. No right can come by conquest, unless there were a right of making that conquest, which, by reason of the equality that our author confesses to have been amongst the heads of families, and as I have proved goes into infinity, can never be on the aggressor's side. No man can justly impose anything upon those who owe him nothing. Our author therefore, who *ascribes the enlargement of Nimrod's kingdom to usurpation and tyranny*, might as well have acknowledged the same in the beginning, as he says all other authors have done.[1] However, he ought not to have imputed to Sir Walter Raleigh an approbation of his right, as lord or king over his family; for he could never think him to be a lord by the right of a father, who by that rule must have lived and died a slave to his fathers that overlived him. Whosoever therefore like Nimrod grounds his pretensions of right upon usurpation and tyranny, declares himself to be, like Nimrod, a usurper and a tyrant, that is an enemy to God and man, and to have no right at all. That which was unjust in its beginning, can of itself never change its nature. *Tempus in se*, saith Grotius, *nullam habet vim effectricem.*[2] He that persists in doing injustice, aggravates it, and takes upon himself all the guilt of his predecessors. But if there be a king in the world, that claims a right by conquest, and would justify it, he might do well to tell whom he conquered, when, with what assistance, and upon what reason he undertook the war; for he can ground no title upon the obscurity of an unsearchable antiquity; and if he does it not, he ought to be looked upon as a usurping Nimrod.

SECTION 12

The pretended paternal Right is divisible or indivisible: if divisible, 'tis extinguished; if indivisible, universal.

THIS paternal right to regality, if there be anything in it, is divisible or indivisible; if indivisible, as Adam hath but one heir, one man is rightly lord of the whole world, and neither Nimrod nor any of his successors could ever have been kings, nor the seventy two that went from Babylon: Noah survived him near two hundred years: Shem continued one hundred and fifty years longer. The dominion must have been in him, and by him transmitted to his posterity forever. Those that call themselves kings in all other nations, set themselves up against the law of God and nature: This is the man we are to seek out, that we may yield obedience to him. I know not where to find him; but he must be of the race of Abraham. Shem was preferred before his brethren: The

---

[1] [*Patriarcha*, ch. 4, pp. 58–60.]

[2] ["Time in itself has no power as a cause." Hugo Grotius, *De jure belli ac pacis libri tres*, bk. 2, ch. 4, sec. 1. Trans. (in vol. 2) as *The Law of War and Peace* (New York: Oceana, 1964).]

inheritance that could not be divided must come to him, and from him to Isaac, who was the first of his descendants that outlived him. 'Tis pity that Jacob did not know this, and that the lord of all the earth, through ignorance of his title, should be forced to keep one of his subject's sheep for wages; and strange, that he who had wit enough to supplant his brother, did so little understand his own bargain, as not to know that he had bought the perpetual empire of the world. If in conscience he could not take such a price for a dish of pottage, it must remain in Esau: However our lord paramount must come from Isaac. If the deed of sale made by Esau be good, we must seek him amongst the Jews; if he could not so easily divest himself of his right, it must remain amongst his descendants, who are Turks. We need not scruple the reception of either, since the late Scots Act tells us, *That kings derive their royal power from God alone; and no difference of religion, &c. can divert the right of succession.*[1] But I know not what we shall do, if we cannot find this man; for *de non apparentibus & non existentibus eadem est ratio.*[2] The right must fall if there be none to inherit: If we do not know who he is that hath the right, we do not know who is near to him: All mankind must inherit the right, to which everyone hath an equal title; and that which is dominion, if in one, when 'tis equally divided among all men, is that universal liberty which I assert. Wherefore I leave it to the choice of such as have inherited our author's opinions, to produce this Jew or Turk that ought to be lord of the whole earth, or to prove a better title in some other person, and to persuade all the princes and nations of the world to submit: If this be not done, it must be confessed this paternal right is a mere whimsical fiction, and that no man by birth hath a right above another, or can have any, unless by the concession of those who are concerned.

If this right to an universal empire be divisible, Noah did actually divide it among his three sons: Seventy and two absolute monarchs did at once arise out of the multitude that had assembled at Babel: Noah, nor his sons, nor any of the holy seed, nor probably any elder than Nimrod having been there, many other monarchs must necessarily have arisen from them. Abraham, as our author says, was a king: Lot must have been so also; for they were equals: his sons Ammon and Moab had no dependence upon the descendants of Abraham. Ishmael and Esau set up for themselves, and great nations came of them: Abraham's sons by

---

[1] [A right established by the Parliament of Scotland in 1681.]

[2] [Concerning things which do not appear and things which do not exist the reasoning is the same.]

Keturah did so also; that is to say, every one as soon as he came to be of age to provide for himself, did so, without retaining any dependence upon the stock from whence he came: Those of that stock, or the head of it, pretended to no right over those who went from them. Nay, nearness in blood was so little regarded, that tho Lot was Abraham's brother's son, Eliezer his servant had been his heir, if he had died childless. The like continued amongst Jacob's sons; no jurisdiction was given to one above the rest: an equal division of land was made amongst them: Their judges and magistrates were of several tribes and families, without any other preference of one before another, than what did arise from the advantages God had given to any particular person. This I take to be a proof of the utmost extent and certainty, that the equality amongst mankind was then perfect: He therefore that will deny it to be so now, ought to prove that neither the prophets, patriarchs, or any other men did ever understand or regard the law delivered by God and nature to mankind; or that having been common and free at the first, and so continued for many hundreds of years after the Flood, it was afterwards abolished, and a new one introduced. He that asserts this must prove it; but till it does appear to us, when, where, how, and by whom this was done, we may safely believe there is no such thing; and that no man is or can be a lord amongst us, till we make him so; and that by nature we are all brethren.

Our author, by endeavouring farther to illustrate the patriarchical power, destroys it, and cannot deny to any man the right which he acknowledges to have been in Ishmael and Esau. But if every man hath a right of setting up for himself with his family, or before he has any, he cannot but have a right of joining with others if he pleases. As his joining or not joining with others, and the choice of those others depends upon his own will, he cannot but have a right of judging upon what conditions 'tis good for him to enter into such a society, as must necessarily hinder him from exercising the right which he has originally in himself. But as it cannot be imagined that men should generally put such fetters upon themselves, unless it were in expectation of a greater good that was thereby to accrue to them, no more can be required to prove that they do voluntarily enter into these societies, institute them for their own good, and prescribe such rules and forms to them as best please themselves, without giving account to any. But if every man be free, till he enter into such a society as he chuseth for his own good, and those societies may regulate themselves as they think fit; no more can be required to prove the natural equality in which all men are born, and continue, till they resign it as into a common stock, in such measure as they think fit for the constituting of societies for their own good, which I assert, and our author denies.

SECTION 13

There was no shadow of a paternal Kingdom amongst the Hebrews, nor precept for it.

OUR author is so modest to confess, that Jacob's kingdom consisting of seventy two persons, was swallowed up by the power of the greater monarch Pharaoh:[1] But if this was an act of tyranny, 'tis strange that the sacred and eternal right, grounded upon the immutable laws of God and nature, should not be restored to God's chosen people, when he delivered them from that tyranny. Why was not Jacob's monarchy conferred upon his right heir? How came the people to neglect a point of such importance? Or if they did forget it, why did not Moses put them in mind of it? Why did not Jacob declare to whom it did belong? Or if he is understood to have declared it, in saying the scepter should not depart from Judah, why was it not delivered into his hands, or into his heirs'? If he was hard to be found in a people of one kindred, but four degrees removed from Jacob their head, who were exact in observing genealogies, how can we hope to find him after so many thousand years, when we do not so much as know from whom we are derived? Or rather how comes that right, which is eternal and universal, to have been nipp'd in the bud, and so abolished before it could take any effect in the world, as never to have been heard of amongst the gentiles, nor the people of God, either before or after the Captivity, from the death of Jacob to this day? This I assert, and I give up the cause if I do not prove it. To this end I begin with Moses and Aaron the first rulers of the people, who were neither of the eldest tribe according to birth, nor the disposition of Jacob, if he did, or could give it to any; nor were they of the eldest line of their own tribe; and even between them the superiority was given to Moses, who was the younger, as 'tis said, *I have made thee a God to Pharaoh, and Aaron thy brother shall be thy Prophet.*[2] If Moses was a king, as our author says, but I deny, and shall hereafter prove, the matter is worse:

---

[1] [*Patriarcha*, ch. 4, p. 60.]   [2] [Exodus 7:1.]

He must have been an usurper of a most unjust dominion over his brethren; and this patriarchical power, which by the law of God was to be perpetually fixed in his descendants, perished with him, and his sons continued in an obscure rank amongst the Levites. Joshua of the tribe of Ephraim succeeded him; Othniel was of Judah, Ehud of Benjamin, Barak of Naphtali, and Gideon of Manasseh. The other judges were of several tribes; and they being dead, their children lay hid amongst the common people, and we hear no more of them. The first king was taken out of the least family of the least and youngest tribe. The second, whilst the children of the first king were yet alive, was the youngest of eight sons of an obscure man in the tribe of Judah: Solomon one of his youngest sons succeeded him: Ten tribes deserted Rehoboam, and by the command of God set up Jeroboam to be their king. The kingdom of Israel by the destruction of one family passed into another: That of Judah by God's peculiar promise continued in David's race till the Captivity; but we know not that the eldest son was ever preferred, and have no reason to presume it. David their most reverenced king left no precept for it, and gave an example to the contrary: he did not set up the eldest, but the wisest. After the Captivity they who had most wisdom or valour to defend the people, were thought most fit to command; and the kingdom at the last came to the Hasmonean race, whilst the posterity of David was buried in the mass of the common people, and utterly deprived of all worldly rule or glory. If the judges had not a regal power, or the regal were only just, as instituted by God, and eternally annexed to paternity, all that they did was evil: There could be nothing of justice in the powers exercised by Moses, Joshua, Gideon, Samuel, and the rest of the judges. If the power was regal and just, it must have continued in the descendants of the first: Saul, David, and Solomon could never have been kings: The right failing in them, their descendants could inherit none from them; and the others after the Captivity were guilty of the like injustice.

Now as the rule is not general, to which there is any one just exception, there is not one of these examples that would not overthrow our author's doctrine: If one deviation from it were lawful, another might be, and so to infinity. But the utmost degree of impudent madness to which perhaps any man in the world hath ever arrived, is to assert that to be universal and perpetual, which cannot be verified by any one example to have been in any place of the world, nor justified by any precept.

If it be objected, that all these things were done by God's immediate disposition: I answer, that it were an impious madness to believe that God did perpetually send his prophets to overthrow what he had ordained from the beginning, and as it were in spite to bring the minds of men into inextricable confusion and darkness; and by particular commands to overthrow his universal and eternal law. But to render this point more clear, I desire it may be considered, that we have but three ways of distinguishing between good and evil.

1. When God by his word reveals it to us.

2. When by his deeds he declareth it; because that which he does is good, as that which he says is true.

3. By the light of reason, which is good, in as much as it is from God.

And first; It cannot be said we have an explicit word for that continuance of the power in the eldest; for it appears not, and having none, we might conclude it to be left to our liberty: For it agrees not with the goodness of God to leave us in a perpetual ignorance of his will in a matter of so great importance, nor to have suffered his own people, or any other to persist, without the least reproof or admonition, in a perpetual opposition to it, if it had displeased him.

To the 2d. The dispensations of his providence, which are the emanations of his will, have gone contrary to this pretended law: There can therefore be no such thing; for God is constant to himself: his works do not contradict his word, and both of them do equally declare to us that which is good.

Thirdly; If there be any precept that by the light of nature we can in matters of this kind look upon as certain, 'tis that the government of a people should be given to him that can best perform the duties of it: No man has it for himself, or from himself; but for and from those who before he had it were his equals, that he may do good to them. If there were a man, who in wisdom, valour, justice and purity, surpassed all others, he might be called a king by nature, because he is best able to bear the weight of so great a charge; and like a good shepherd to lead the people to good. *Detur digniori*[3] is the voice of reason; and that we may be sure *detur seniori*[4] is not so, Solomon tells us, *That a wise child is better than an old and foolish king.*[5] But if this pretended right do not belong to him that is truly the eldest, nothing can be more absurd than a fantastical pretence to a right deduced from him that is not so. Now lest I should be thought to follow my own inventions, and call them reason, or the light of God in us, I desire it may be observed that God himself has ever taken this method. When he raised up Moses to be the leader of his

---

[3] [Let it be given to the worthier.]   [5] [Ecclesiastes 4:13.]
[4] [Let it be given to the elder.]

people, he endowed him with the most admirable gifts of his spirit that ever he bestowed upon a man: When he chose seventy men to assist him, he endowed them with the same spirit. Joshua had no other title to succeed him than the like evidence of God's presence with him. When the people through sin fell into misery, he did not seek out their descendants, nor such as boasted in a prerogative of birth; but shewed whom he designed for their deliverer, by bestowing such gifts upon him as were required for the performance of his work; and never fail'd of doing this, till that miserable sinful people rejecting God and his government, desired that which was in use among their accursed neighbours, that they might be as like to them in the most shameful slavery to man, as in the worship of idols set up against God.

But if this pretended right be grounded upon no word or work of God, nor the reason of man, 'tis to be accounted a mere figment, that hath nothing of truth in it.

SECTION 14

If the paternal Right had included Dominion,
and was to be transferred to a single Heir, it must perish
if he were not known;
and could be applied to no other person.

HAVING shewed that the first kings were not fathers, nor the first fathers kings; that all the kings of the Jews and gentiles mentioned in Scripture came in upon titles different from, and inconsistent with that of paternity; and that we are not led by the word nor the works of God, nor the reason of man, or light of nature to believe there is any such thing, we may safely conclude there never was any such thing, or that it never had any effect, which to us is the same. 'Tis as ridiculous to think of retrieving that, which from the beginning of the world was lost, as to create that which never was. But I may go farther, and affirm, that tho there had been such a right in the first fathers of mankind exercised by them, and for some ages individually transmitted to their eldest sons, it must necessarily perish, since the generations of men are so confused, that no man knows his own original, and consequently this heir is nowhere to be found; for 'tis a folly for a man to pretend to an inheritance, who cannot prove himself to be the right heir. If this be not true, I desire to know from which of Noah's sons the kings of England, France, or Spain do deduce their original, or what reason they can give why the title to dominion, which is fancied to be in Noah, did rather belong to the first of their respective races, that attained to the crowns they now enjoy, than to the meanest peasant of their kingdoms; or how that can be transmitted to them, which was not in the first. We know that no man can give what he hath not; that if there be no giver, there is no gift; if there be no root, there can be no branch; and that the first point failing, all that should be derived from it must necessarily fail.

Our author, who is good at resolving difficulties, shews us an easy way out of this strait. *'Tis true*, says he, *all kings are not natural parents of their subjects; yet they either are, or are to be reputed the next heirs to those first progenitors, who were at first the natural parents of the whole people, and in their right succeed to the exercise of the supreme jurisdiction; and such heirs are not only lords of their own children, but also of their brethren, and all those that were subject to their father, &c. By this means it comes to pass, that many a child succeeding a king hath the right of a father over many a grey-headed multitude, and hath the title of* pater patriae.[1]

An assertion comprehending so many points, upon which the most important rights of all mankind do depend, might deserve some proof: But he being of opinion we ought to take it upon his credit, doth not vouchsafe to give us so much as the shadow of any. Nevertheless being unwilling either crudely to receive, or rashly to reject it, I shall take the liberty of examining the proposition, and hope I may be pardoned, if I dwell a little more than ordinarily upon that which is the foundation of his work.

We are beholden to him for confessing modestly that all kings are not the natural fathers of their people, and sparing us the pains of proving, that the kings of Persia, who reigned from the Indies to the Hellespont, did not beget all the men that lived in those countries; or that the kings of France and Spain, who began to reign before they were five years old, were not the natural fathers of the nations under them. But if all kings are not fathers, none are, as they are kings: If any one is, or ever was, the rights of paternity belong to him, and to no other who is not so also. This must be made evident; for matters of such importance require proof, and ought not to be taken upon supposition. If Filmer therefore will pretend that the right of father belongs to any one king, he must prove that he is the father of his people; for otherwise it doth not appertain to him; he is not the man we seek.

[1] ["Father of his country." *Patriarcha*, ch. 5 ("Kings Are Either Fathers of Their People, or Heirs of Such Fathers, or the Usurpers of the Rights of Such Fathers"), pp. 60–61.]

'Tis no less absurd to say he is to be reputed heir to the first progenitor: for it must be first proved, that the nation did descend from one single progenitor without mixture of other races: that this progenitor was the man, to whom Noah (according to Filmer's whimsical division of Asia, Europe, and Africa among his sons) did give the land now inhabited by that people: That this division so made was not capable of subdivisions; and that this man is by a true and uninterrupted succession descended from the first and eldest line of that progenitor; and all fails, if every one of these points be not made good. If there never was any such man who had that right, it cannot be inherited from him. If by the same rule that a parcel of the world was allotted to him, that parcel might be subdivided amongst his children as they increased, the subdivisions may be infinite, and the right of dominion thereby destroyed. If several nations inhabit the same land, they owe obedience to several fathers: that which is due to their true father, cannot be rendered to him that is not so; for he would by that means be deprived of the right which is inseparably annexed to his person: And lastly, whatsoever the right of an heir may be, it can belong only to him that is heir.

Lest any should be seduced from these plain truths by frivolous suggestions, 'tis good to consider that the title of *pater patriae*, with which our author would cheat us, hath no relation to the matters of right, upon which we dispute. 'Tis a figurative speech, that may have been rightly enough applied to some excellent princes on account of their care and love to their people, resembling that of a father to his children; and can relate to none but those who had it. No man that had common sense, or valued truth, did ever call Phalaris, Dionysius, Nabis, Nero, or Caligula, fathers of their countries; but monsters, that to the utmost of their power endeavoured their destruction: which is enough to prove, that sacred name cannot be given to all, and in consequence to none but such, as by their virtue, piety, and good government do deserve it.

These matters will yet appear more evident, if it be considered, that tho Noah had reigned as a king; that Zoroaster, as some suppose, was Ham, who reigned over his children, and that thereby some right might perhaps be derived to such as succeeded them; yet this can have no influence upon such as have not the like original; and no man is to be presumed to have it, till it be proved, since we have proved that many had it not. If Nimrod set himself up against his grandfather, and Ninus, who was descended from him in the fifth generation, slew him; they ill deserved the name and rights of fathers; and none, but those who have renounced all humanity, virtue, and common sense, can give it to them, or their successors. If therefore Noah and Shem had not so much as the shadow of regal power, and the actions of Nimrod, Ninus, and others who were kings in their times, shew they did not reign in the right of fathers, but were set up in a direct opposition to it, the titles of the first kings were not from paternity, nor consistent with it.

Our author therefore, who should have proved every point, doth neither prove any one, nor assert that which is agreeable to divine or human story, as to matter of fact; and as little conformable to common sense. It does not only appear contrary to his general proposition, that all governments have not begun with the paternal power; but we do not find that any ever did. They who according to his rules should have been lords of the whole earth, lived and died private men, whilst the wildest and most boisterous of their children commanded the greatest part of the then inhabited world, not excepting even those countries where they spent and ended their days; and instead of entering upon the government by the right of fathers, or managing it as fathers, they did by the most outrageous injustice usurp a violent domination over their brethren and fathers.

It may easily be imagined what the right is that could be thus acquired, and transmitted to their successors. Nevertheless our author says, *All kings either are, or ought to be reputed next heirs*, &c. But why reputed, if they were not? How could any of the accursed race of Ham be reputed father of Noah or Shem, to whom he was to be a servant? How could Nimrod and Ninus be reputed fathers of Ham, and of those whom they ought to have obeyed? Can reason oblige me to believe that which I know to be false? Can a lie, that is hateful to God and good men, not only be excused, but enjoined, when (as he will perhaps say) it is for the king's service? Can I serve two masters, or without the most unpardonable injustice, repute him to be my father, who is not my father; and pay the obedience that is due to him who did beget and educate me, to one from whom I never received any good? If this be so absurd, that no man dares affirm it in the person of any, 'tis as preposterous in relation to his heirs: For Nimrod the first king could be heir to no man as king, and could transmit to no man a right which he had not. If it was ridiculous and abominable to say that he was father of Cush, Ham, Shem and Noah; 'tis as ridiculous to say, he had the right of father, if he was not their father; or that his successors inherited it from him, if he never had it. If there be any way through this, it must have accrued to him by the extirpation of all his elders, and their races; so as he who will assert this pretended right to have been in the Babylonian kings, must assert, that Noah, Shem, Japheth, Ham, Cush, and all Nimrod's elder brothers, with all their descendents, were utterly extirpated before he began to reign, and all mankind to be descended from him.

This must be, if Nimrod, as the Scripture says, was the first that became mighty in the earth; unless men might be kings, without having more power than others; for Cush, Ham and Noah were his elders and progenitors in the direct line, and all the sons of Shem and Japheth, and their descendants in the collaterals, were to be preferred before him; and he could have no right at all, that was not directly contrary to those principles which, our author says, are grounded upon the eternal and indispensable laws of God and nature. The like may be said of the seventy two heads of colonies, which (following, as I suppose, Sir Walter Raleigh)[2] he says, went out to people the earth, and whom he calls kings: for, according to the same rule, Noah, Shem and Japheth, with their descendants, could not be of the number; so that neither Nimrod, nor the others that established the kingdoms of the world, and from whence he thinks all the rest to be derived, could have anything of justice in them, unless it were from a root altogether inconsistent with his principles. They are therefore false, or the establishments before mentioned could have no right. If they had none, they cannot be reputed to have any; for no man can think that to be true, which he knows to be false: having none, they could transmit none to their heirs and successors. And if we are to believe, that all the kingdoms of the earth are established upon this paternal right; it must be proved that all those, who in birth ought to have been preferred before Nimrod, and the seventy two were extirpated; or that the first and true heir of Noah did afterwards abolish all these unjust usurpations; and making himself master of the whole, left it to his heirs, in whom it continues to this day. When this is done, I will acknowledge the foundation to be well laid, and admit of all that can be rightly built upon it; but if this fails, all fails: The poison of the root continues in the branches. If the right heir be not in possession, he is not the right who is in possession: If the true heir be known, he ought to be restored to his right: If he be not known, the right must perish: That cannot be said to belong to any man, if no man knows to whom it belongs, and can have no more effect than if it were not. This conclusion will continue unmoveable, tho the division into seventy two kingdoms were allowed; which cannot be without destroying the paternal power, or subjecting it to be subdivided into as many parcels as there are men,

---

[2] [Filmer refers to the seventy-two in *Patriarcha*, ch. 4, p. 58, and on the next page (in another connection) cites Sir Walter Raleigh, *History of the World*, in *Works* (Oxford: Oxford University Press, 1829), vol. 2, p. 353.]

which destroys regality; for the same thing may be required in every one of the distinct kingdoms, and others derived from them. We must know who was that true heir of Noah, that recovered all: How, when, and to whom he gave the several portions; and that every one of them do continue in the possession of those, who by this prerogative of birth are raised above the rest of mankind; and if they are not, 'tis an impious folly to repute them so, to the prejudice of those that are; and if they do not appear, to the prejudice of all mankind; who being equal, are thereby made subject to them. For as truth is the rule of justice; there can be none, when he is reputed superior to all who is certainly inferior to

[*In this place two pages are wanting in the original manuscript.*][3]

[SECTION 15][1]

—degenerated from that reason which distinguisheth men from beasts. Tho it may be fit to use some ceremonies, before a man be admitted to practice physick, or set up a trade, 'tis his own skill that makes him a doctor or an artificer, and others do but declare it. An ass will not leave his stupidity, tho he be covered with scarlet; and he that is by nature a slave, will be so still, tho a crown be put upon his head: and 'tis hard to imagine a more violent inversion of the laws of God and nature, than to raise him to the throne, whom nature intended for the chain; or to make them slaves to slaves, whom God hath endowed with the virtues required in kings. Nothing can be more preposterous, than to impute to God the frantick domination, which is often exercised by wicked, foolish and vile persons, over the wise, valiant, just and good; or to subject the best to the rage of the worst. If there be any family therefore in the world, that can by the law of God and nature, distinct from the ordinance of man, pretend to an hereditary right of dominion over any people, it must be one that never did, and never can produce any person that is not free

[3] [This is the first of three gaps in the manuscript that are noted by the editor of the first edition.]

[1] [The first edition of the *Discourses* does not indicate that a new section begins here, but the running head on the next page of that edition reads "Section 15," and the next new section is Section 16. Unless the first editor misnumbered the remaining sections in Chapter I, it appears that Sidney began a new section on the missing pages.]

from all the infirmities and vices that render him unable to exercise the sovereign power; and is endowed with all the virtues required to that end; or at least a promise from God, verified by experience, that the next in blood shall ever be able and fit for that work. But since we do not know that any such hath yet appeared in the world, we have no reason to believe that there is, or ever was any such; and consequently none upon whom God hath conferred the rights that cannot be exercised without them.

If there was no shadow of a paternal right in the institution of the kingdoms of Saul and David, there could be none in those that succeeded. Rehoboam could have no other, than from Solomon: When he reigned over two tribes, and Jeroboam over ten, 'tis not possible that both of them could be the next heir of their last common father Jacob; and 'tis absurd to say, that ought to be reputed, which is impossible: for our thoughts are ever to be guided by truth, or such an appearance of it, as doth persuade or convince us.

The same title of father is yet more ridiculously or odiously applied to the succeeding kings. Baasha had no other title to the crown, than by killing Nadab the son of Jeroboam, and destroying his family. Zimri purchased the same honour by the slaughter of Elah when he was drunk; and dealing with the house of Baasha, as he had done with that of Jeroboam. Zimri burning himself, transferred the same to Omri, as a reward for bringing him to that extremity. As Jehu was more fierce than these, he seems to have gained a more excellent recompence than any since Jeroboam, even a conditional promise of a perpetual kingdom; but falling from these glorious privileges, purchased by his zeal in killing two wicked kings, and above one hundred of their brethren, Shallum inherited them, by destroying Zechariah and all that remained of his race. This in plain English is no less than to say, that whosoever kills a king, and invades a crown, tho the act and means of accomplishing it be never so detestable, does thereby become father of his country, and heir of all the divine privileges annexed to that glorious inheritance. And tho I cannot tell whether such a doctrine be more sottish, monstrous or impious, I dare affirm, that if it were received, no king in the world could think himself safe in his throne for one day: They are already encompassed with many dangers; but lest pride, avarice, ambition, lust, rage, and all the vices that usually reign in the hearts of worldly men, should not be sufficient to invite them perpetually to disturb mankind, through the desire of gaining the power, riches and splendor that accompanies a crown, our author proposes to them the most sacred privileges, as a reward of the most execrable crimes. He that was stirred up only by the violence of his own nature, thought that a kingdom could never be bought at too dear a rate;

> *Pro regno velim*
> *Patriam, penates, conjugem flammis dare:*
> *Imperia precio quolibet constant bene.*
> Senec. Theb.[2]

But if the sacred character of God's anointed or vicegerent, and father of a country, were added to the other advantages that follow the highest fortunes; the most modest and just men would be filled with fury, that they might attain to them. Nay, it may be, even the best would be the most forward in conspiring against such as reigned: They who could not be tempted with external pleasures, would be most in love with divine privileges; and since they should become the sacred ministers of God, if they succeeded, and traitors or rogues only if they miscarried, their only care would be so to lay their designs, that they might be surely executed. This is a doctrine worthy of Filmer's invention, and Heylyn's approbation; which being well weighed, will shew to all good and just kings how far they are obliged to those, who under pretence of advancing their authority, fill the minds of men with such notions as are so desperately pernicious to them.

SECTION 16

The ancients chose those to be Kings, who excelled in the Virtues that are most beneficial to Civil Societies.

IF the Israelites, whose lawgiver was God, had no king in the first institution of their government, 'tis no wonder that other nations should not think themselves obliged to set up any: if they who came all of one stock, and knew their genealogies, when they did institute kings, had no regard to our author's chimerical right of inheritance, nor were taught by God or his prophets to have any; 'tis not strange that nations, who did not know their own original, and who probably, if not certainly,

[2] ["For a kingdom I would give country, household gods, and wife to the flames: Imperial power is well purchased at any price." These are the last verses of the surviving fragment of Seneca's *Thebaid*, widely known today as *Phoenissae*, in *Tragedies*, 2 vols. (Loeb, 1917).]

came of several stocks, never put themselves to the trouble of seeking one, who by his birth deserved to be preferred before others; and if the various changes happening in all kingdoms (whereby in process of time the crowns were transported into divers families, to which the right of inheritance could not without the utmost impiety and madness be imputed) such a fancy certainly could only enter into the heads of fools; and we know of none so foolish to have harbour'd it.

The Grecians, amongst others who followed the light of reason, knew no other original title to the government of a nation, than that wisdom, valour and justice, which was beneficial to the people. These qualities gave beginning to those governments, which we call *heroum regna*;[1] and the veneration paid to such as enjoyed them, proceeded from a grateful sense of the good received from them: They were thought to be descended from the gods, who in virtue and beneficence surpassed other men: The same attended their descendants, till they came to abuse their power, and by their vices shewed themselves like to, or worse than others. Those nations did not seek the most ancient, but the most worthy; and thought such only worthy to be preferred before others, who could best perform their duty. The Spartans knew that Hercules and Achilles were not their fathers, for they were a nation before either of them were born; but thinking their children might be like to them in valour, they brought them from Thebes and Epirus to be their kings. If our author is of another opinion, I desire to know, whether the Heraclidae, or the Aeacidae were, or ought to be reputed fathers of the Lacedemonians; for if the one was, the other was not.

The same method was followed in Italy; and they who esteemed themselves *Aborigines*,

> . . . *qui rupto robore nati*
> *Compositive luto, nullos habuere parentes.*
> Juven. Sat. 6.[2]

could not set up one to govern them under the title of *parent*. They could pay no veneration to any man under the name of a common father, who thought they had none; and they who esteemed themselves equal, could have no reason to prefer any one; unless he were distinguished from others by the virtues that were beneficial to all. This may be illustrated by matters of fact. Romulus and Remus, the sons of a nun, constuprated,

---

[1] [Kingdoms of heroes.]

[2] ["Natives, . . . who were born of split oaks, made of clay, having no parents." Juvenal, *Satire* 6, li. 12–13, in Juvenal and Perseus, *Satires* (rev. ed.; Loeb, 1940).]

as is probable, by a lusty soldier, who was said to be Mars, for their vigour and valour were made heads of a gathered people. We know not that ever they had any children; but we are sure they could not be fathers of the people that flocked to them from several places, nor in any manner be reputed heirs of him or them that were so; for they never knew who was their own father; and when their mother came to be discovered, they ought to have been subjects to Amulius or Numitor, when they had slain him. They could not be his heirs whilst he lived, and were not when he died: The government of the Latins continued at Alba, and Romulus reigned over those who joined with him in building Rome. The power not coming to him by inheritance, must have been gained by force, or conferred upon him by consent: It could not be acquired by force; for one man could not force a multitude of fierce and valiant men, as they appear to have been. It must therefore have been by consent: And when he aimed at more authority than they were willing to allow, they slew him. He being dead, they fetched Numa from among the Sabines: He was not their father, nor heir to their father, but a stranger; not a conqueror, but an unarmed philosopher. Tullus Hostilius had no other title: Ancus Marcius was no way related to such as had reigned. The first Tarquin was the son of a banished Corinthian. Servius Tullius came to Rome in the belly of his captive mother, and could inherit nothing but chains from his vanquished father. Tarquin the Proud murdered him, and first took upon himself the title of king, *sine jussu populi*.[3] If this murder and usurpation be called a conquest, and thought to create a right, the effect will be but small: The conqueror was soon conquered, banished, and his sons slain, after which we hear no more of him or his descendants. Whatsoever he gained from Servius, or the people, was soon lost, and did accrue to those that conquered and ejected him; and they might retain what was their own, or confer it upon one or more, in such manner and measure as best pleased themselves. If the regal power, which our author says was in the consuls, could be divided into two parts, limited to a year, and suffer such restrictions as the people pleased to lay upon it, they might have divided it into as many parcels, and put it into such form, as best suited with their inclinations; and the several magistracies which they did create for the exercise of the kingly, and all other powers, shews that they were to give account to none but themselves.

The Israelites, Spartans, Romans and others, who thus framed their governments according to their own will, did it not by any peculiar

[3] T. Liv. ["Without the command of the people." Livy, *History of Rome*, bk. 1, ch. 49.]

privilege, but by a universal right conferred upon them by God and nature: They were made of no better clay than others: They had no right, that does not as well belong to other nations; that is to say, the constitution of every government is referred to those who are concerned in it, and no other has anything to do with it.

Yet if it be asserted, that the government of Rome was paternal, or they had none at all; I desire to know, how they came to have six fathers of several families, whilst they lived under kings; and two or more new ones every year afterwards: Or how they came to be so excellent in virtue and fortune, as to conquer the best part of the world, if they had no government. Hobbes indeed doth scurrilously deride Cicero, Plato and Aristotle, *caeterosque Romanae & Graecae anarchiae fautores.*[4] But 'tis strange that this anarchy, which he resembles to a chaos, full of darkness and confusion, that can have no strength or regular action, should overthrow all the monarchies that came within their reach, *If* (as our author says) *the best order, greatest strength, and most stability be in them.*[5] It must therefore be confessed, that these governments are in their various forms, rightly instituted by several nations, without any regard to inheritance; or that these nations have had no governments, and were more strong, virtuous and happy without government, than under it, which is most absurd.

But if governments arise from the consent of men, and are instituted by men according to their own inclinations, they did therein seek their own good; for the will is ever drawn by some real good, or the appearance of it. This is that which man seeks by all the regular or irregular motions of his mind. Reason and passion, virtue and vice do herein concur, tho they differ vastly in the objects, in which each of them thinks this good to consist. A people therefore that sets up kings, dictators, consuls, praetors or emperors, does it not, that they may be great, glorious, rich or happy, but that it may be well with themselves and their posterity. This is not accomplished simply by setting one, a few, or more men in the administration of powers, but by placing the authority in those who may rightly perform their office. This is not every man's work: valour, integrity, wisdom, industry, experience and skill, are required for the management of those military and civil affairs that necessarily fall under the care of the chief magistrates. He or they therefore may reasonably be advanced above their equals, who are most fit to perform the duties belonging to their stations, in order to the publick good, for which they were instituted.

---

[4] ["And the other patrons of Greek and Roman anarchy." Thomas Hobbes, *On the Citizen*, ch. 12, sec. 3.]

[5] [*Patriarcha*, ch. 15, p. 86.]

Marius, Sulla, Catiline, Julius or Octavius Caesar, and all those who by force or fraud usurped a dominion over their brethren, could have no title to this right; much less could they become fathers of the people, by using all the most wicked means that could well be imagined to destroy them; and not being regularly chosen for their virtues, or the opinion of them, nor preferred on account of any prerogative that had been from the beginning annexed to their families, they could have no other right than occupation could confer upon them. If this can confer a right, there is an end of all disputes concerning the laws of God or man. If Julius and Octavius Caesar did successively become lords and fathers of their country, by slaughtering almost all the senate, and such persons as were eminent for nobility or virtue, together with the major part of the people, it cannot be denied, that a thief, who breaks into his neighbour's house, and kills him, is justly master of his estate; and may exact the same obedience from his children, that they render to their father. If this right could be transferred to Tiberius, either through the malice of Octavius, or the fraud of his wife; a wet blanket laid over his face, and a few corrupted soldiers could invest Caligula with the same. A vile rascal pulling Claudius out by the heels from behind the hangings where he had hid himself, could give it to him. A dish of mushrooms well seasoned by the infamous strumpet his wife, and a potion prepared for Britannicus by Locusta, could transfer it to her son, who was a stranger to his blood. Galba became heir to it, by driving Nero to despair and death. Two common soldiers by exciting his guards to kill him, could give a just title to the empire of the world to Otho, who was thought to be the worst man in it. If a company of villains in the German army, thinking it as fit for them as others, to create a father of mankind, could confer the dignity upon Vitellius; and if Vespasian, causing him to be killed, and thrown into a jakes less impure than his life, did inherit all the glorious and sacred privileges belonging to that title, 'tis in vain to inquire after any man's right to anything.

If there be such a thing as right or wrong to be examined by men, and any rules set, whereby the one may be distinguished from the other; these extravagancies can have no effect of right. Such as commit them, are not to be looked upon as fathers; but as the most mortal enemies of their respective countries. No right is to be acknowledged in any, but such as is conferred upon them by those who have the right of conferring, and are concerned in the exercise of the power, upon such conditions as best please themselves. No obedience can be due to him or them, who have not a right of commanding. This cannot reasonably be conferred upon any, that are not esteemed willing and able rightly to execute it.

This ability to perform the highest works that come within the reach of men; and integrity of will not to be diverted from it by any temptation, or consideration of private advantages, comprehending all that is most commendable in man; we may easily see, that whensoever men act according to the law of their own nature, which is reason, they can have no other rule to direct them in advancing one above another, than the opinion of a man's virtue and ability, best to perform the duty incumbent upon him; that is, by all means to procure the good of the people committed to his charge. He is only fit to conduct a ship, who understands the art of a pilot: When we are sick, we seek the assistance of such as are best skill'd in physick: The command of an army is prudently conferred upon him that hath most industry, skill, experience and valour: In like manner, he only can, according to the rules of nature, be advanced to the dignities of the world, who excels in the virtues required for the performance of the duties annexed to them; for he only can answer the end of his institution. The law of every instituted power, is to accomplish the end of its institution, as creatures are to do the will of their creator, and in deflecting from it, overthrow their own being. Magistrates are distinguished from other men, by the power with which the law invests them for the publick good: He that cannot or will not procure that good, destroys his own being, and becomes like to other men. In matters of the greatest importance, *detur digniori*[6] is the voice of nature; all her most sacred laws are perverted, if this be not observed in the disposition of the governments of mankind: But all is neglected and violated, if they are not put into the hands of such as excel in all manner of virtues; for they only are worthy of them, and they only can have a right who are worthy, because they only can perform the end for which they are instituted. This may seem strange to those, who have their heads infected with Filmer's whimseys; but to others, so certainly grounded upon truth, that Bartholomew de Las Casas Bishop of Chiapa, in a treatise written by him, and dedicated to the Emperor Charles the 5th, concerning the Indies, makes it the foundation of all his discourse, that notwithstanding his grant of all those countries from the pope, and his pretentions to conquest, he could have no right over any of those nations, unless he did in the first place, as the principal end, regard their good: *The reason*, says he, *is, that regard is to be had to the principal end and cause, for which a supreme or universal lord is set over them, which is their good and profit, and not that it should turn to their destruction and ruin; for if that should be, there is no doubt but from thence forward, that power would be tyrannical and unjust, as tending*

---

[6] ["Let it be given to the worthier."]

more to the interest and profit of that lord, than to the publick good and profit of the subjects; which, according to natural reason, and the laws of God and man, is abhorred, and deserves to be abhorred.[7] And in another place speaking of the governors, who, abusing their power, brought many troubles and vexations upon the Indians; he says, *They had rendered his majesty's government intolerable, and his yoke insupportable, tyrannical, and most justly abhorred.*[8] I do not allege this through an opinion, that a Spanish bishop is of more authority than another man; but to shew, that these are common notions agreed by all mankind; and that the greatest monarchs do neither refuse to hear them, or to regulate themselves according to them, till they renounce common sense, and degenerate into beasts.

But if that government be unreasonable, and abhorred by the laws of God and man, which is not instituted for the good of those that live under it; and an empire, grounded upon the donation of the pope, which amongst those of the Roman religion is of great importance, and an entire conquest of the people, with whom there had been no former compact, do degenerate into a most unjust and detestable tyranny, so soon as the supreme lord begins to prefer his own interest or profit, before the good of his subjects; what shall we say of those who pretend to a right of dominion over free nations, as inseparably united to their persons, without distinction of age or sex, or the least consideration of their infirmities and vices; as if they were not placed in the throne for the good of their people, but to enjoy the honours and pleasures that attend the highest fortune? What name can be fit for those, who have no other title to the places they possess, than the most unjust and violent usurpation, or being descended from those, who for their virtues were, by the people's consent, duly advanced to the exercise of a legitimate power; and having sworn to administer it, according to the conditions upon which it was given, for the good of those who gave it, turn all to their own pleasure and profit, without any care of the publick? These may be liable to hard censures;

---

[7] La razon es porque siempre se ha de tener respeto al fin y causa final, por el qual, el tal supremo y universal sennor se los pone, que es su bien y utilidad; y a que no se le convierte el tal supremo sennorio in danno, pernicie y destruycion. Porque si assi fuesse, no ay que dudar, que non desde entonees inclusivamente seria injusto, tyrannico y iniquo tal sennorio, come mas se enderezasse al proprio interesse y provecho del sennor, que al bien y utilidad comun de los subditos; lo qual de la razon natural y de todas las leyes humanas y divinas es abhorrecido y abhorrexible. Bar. de las Casas. destr. de las Indias, pag. 111. [Bartolomé de Las Casas, *Brevísima Relación de la Destrucción de las Indias* (1552), actually on p. 115. The quotation is from a dispute between Casas and Sepulveda, Twelfth Reply.]

[8] El yugo y governacion de Vuestra Magestad importable, tirannico y degno de todo abhorrecimento. Pag. 167. [Ibid. The quotation is from a section called *Entre los Remedios . . .* , Fourth Reason.]

but those who use them most gently, must confess, that such an extreme deviation from the end of their institution, annuls it; and the wound thereby given to the natural and original rights of those nations cannot be cured, unless they resume the liberties, of which they have been deprived, and return to the ancient custom of chusing those to be magistrates, who for their virtues best deserve to be preferred before their brethren, and are endowed with those qualities that best enable men to perform the great end of providing for the publick safety.

SECTION 17

God having given the Government of the World to no one Man, nor declared how it should be divided, left it to the Will of Man.

OUR author's next inquiry is, *What becomes of the right of fatherhood, in case the crown should escheat for want of an heir? Whether it doth not escheat to the people?* His answer is, *'Tis but the negligence or ignorance of the people, to lose the knowledge of the true heir,* &c. And a little below, *The power is not devolved to the multitude: No; the kingly power escheats on independent heads of families: All such prime heads have power to consent in the uniting, or conferring their fatherly right of sovereign authority on whom they please; and he that is so elected, claims not his power as a donative from the people, but as being substituted by God, from whom he receives his royal charter of universal father,* &c.[1]

In my opinion, before he had asked, What should be done in case the crown should escheat for want of an heir? he ought to have proved, there had been a man in the world, who had the right in himself, and telling who he was, have shewed how it had been transmitted for some generations, that we might know where to seek his heir; and before he accused the multitude of ignorance or negligence, in not knowing this heir, he ought to have informed us, how it may be possible to know him, or what it would avail us if we did know him, for 'tis in vain to know to whom a right belongs, that never was, and never can be executed. But we may go farther, and affirm, that as the universal right must have been in Noah and Shem (if in any) who never exercised it; we have reason to

---

[1] [*Patriarcha*, ch. 6 ("Of the Escheating of Kingdoms"), pp. 61–62.]

believe there never was any such thing: And having proved from Scripture and human history, that the first kingdoms were set up in a direct opposition to this right, by Nimrod and others, he that should seek and find their heirs, would only find those, who by a most accursed wickedness, had usurped and continued a dominion over their fathers, contrary to the laws of God and nature; and we should neither be more wise, nor more happy than we are, tho our author should furnish us with certain and authentick genealogies, by which we might know the true heirs of Nimrod, and the seventy two kings that went from Babylon, who, as he supposes, gave beginning to all the kingdoms of the earth.

Moreover, if the right be universal, it must be in one; for the universe being but one, the whole right of commanding it cannot at the same time be in many, and proceed from the ordinance of God, or of man. It cannot proceed from the ordinance of God; for he doth nothing in vain: He never gave a right that could not be executed: No man can govern that which he does not so much as know: No man did ever know all the world; no man therefore did or could govern it: and none could be appointed by God to do that which is absolutely impossible to be done; for it could not consist with his wisdom. We find this in ourselves. It were a shame for one of us poor, weak, shortsighted creatures, in the disposal of our affairs, to appoint such a method, as were utterly ineffectual for the preservation of our families, or destructive to them; and the blasphemy of imputing to God such an ordinance, as would be a reproach to one of us, can suit only with the wicked and impudent fury of such as our author, who delights in monsters. This also shews us that it cannot be from men: One, or a few, may commit follies, but mankind does not universally commit, and perpetually persist in any: They cannot therefore, by a general and permanent authority, enact that which is utterly absurd and impossible; or if they do, they destroy their own nature, and can no longer deserve the name of reasonable creatures. There can be therefore no such man, and the folly of seeking him, or his heir that never was, may be left to the disciples of Filmer.

The difficulties are as great, if it be said, the world might be divided into parcels, and we are to seek the heirs of the first possessors; for besides that no man can be obliged to seek that which cannot be found (all men knowing that *caliginosa nocte haec premit Deus*[2]), and that the genealogies of mankind are so confused, that, unless possibly among the Jews, we have reason to believe there is not a man in the world, who knows his own

[2] ["God obscures these things in the mists
of night." Horace, *Odes*, bk. 3, Ode 29, li.
30, *The Odes and Epodes* (rev. ed.; Loeb, 1927).]

original, it could be of no advantage to us tho we knew that of everyone; for the division would be of no value, unless it were at the first rightly made by him who had all the authority in himself (which does nowhere appear), and rightly deduced to him, who, according to that division, claims a right to the parcel he enjoys; and I fear our author would terribly shake the crowns, in which the nations of Europe are concerned, if they should be persuaded to search into the genealogies of their princes, and to judge of their rights according to the proofs they should give of titles rightly deduced by succession of blood from the seventy two first kings, from whom our author fancies all the kingdoms of the world to be derived.

Besides, tho this were done, it would be to no purpose: for the seventy two were not sent out by Noah, nor was he or his sons of that number; but they went or were sent from Babylon where Nimrod reigned, who, as has been already proved, neither had, nor could have any right at all; but was a mighty hunter, even a proud and cruel tyrant, usurping a power to which he had no right, and which was perpetually exercised by him and his successors against God and his people, from whence I may safely conclude, that no right can ever be derived; and may justly presume it will be denied by none who are of better morals, and of more sound principles in matters of law and religion than Filmer and Heylyn; since 'tis no less absurd to deduce a right from him that had none, than to expect pure and wholesome waters from a filthy, polluted, and poisonous fountain.

If it be pretended that some other man since Noah had this universal right, it must either remain in one single person, as his right heir, or be divided. If in one, I desire to know who he is, and where we may find him, that the empire of the world may be delivered to him: But if he cannot be found, the business is at an end; for every man in the world may pretend himself to be the person; and the infinite controversies arising thereupon can never be decided, unless either the genealogies of everyone from Noah were extant and proved, or we had a word from heaven, with a sufficient testimony of his mission who announceth it. When this is done, 'twill be time to consider what kind of obedience is due to this wonderfully happy and glorious person. But whilst the first appears to be absolutely impossible, and we have no promise or reason to expect the other, the proposition is to be esteemed one of our author's empty whimseys, which cannot be received by mankind, unless they come all to be possessed with an epidemical madness, which would cast them into that which Hobbes calls *bellum omnium contra omnes;*[3] when

[3] ["A war of all against all." Thomas Hobbes,
Leviathan, ch. 14.]

every man's sword would be drawn against every man, and every man's against him, if God should so abandon the world to suffer them to fall into such misery.

If this pretended right be divided, it concerns us to know by whom, when, how, and to whom: for the division cannot be of any value, unless the right was originally in one; that he did exercise this right in making the division; that the parcels into which the world is divided are according to the allotment that was made; and that the persons claiming them by virtue of it are the true heirs of those to whom they were first granted. Many other difficulties may be alleged no less inextricable than these; but this seeming sufficient for the present, I shall not trouble myself with more, promising that when they shall be removed I will propose others, or confessing my errors, yield up the cause.

But if the dominion of the whole world cannot belong to any one man, and every one have an equal title to that which should give it; or if it did belong to one, none did ever exercise it in governing the whole, or dividing it; or if he did divide it, no man knows how, when, and to whom; so that they who lay claim to any parcels can give no testimony of that division, nor shew any better title than other men derived from his first progenitor, to whom 'tis said to have been granted; and that we have neither a word, nor the promise of a word from God to decide the controversies arising thereupon, nor any prophet giving testimony of his mission that takes upon him to do it, the whole fabrick of our author's patriarchical dominion falls to the ground; and they who propose these doctrines, which (if they were received) would be a root of perpetual and irreconcilable hatred in every man against every man, can be accounted no less than ministers of the Devil, tho they want the abilities he has sometimes infused into those who have been employ'd upon the like occasions. And we may justly conclude that God having never given the whole world to be governed by one man, nor prescribed any rule for the division of it; nor declared where the right of dividing or subdividing that which every man has should terminate; we may safely affirm that the whole is forever left to the will and discretion of man: We may enter into, form, and continue in greater or lesser societies, as best pleases ourselves: The right of paternity as to dominion is at an end, and no more remains, but the love, veneration, and obedience, which proceeding from a due sense of the benefits of birth and education, have their root in gratitude, and are esteemed sacred and inviolable by all that are sober and virtuous. And as 'tis impossible to transfer these benefits by inheritance, so 'tis impossible to transfer the rights arising from them. No man can be my father but he that did beget me; and 'tis as absurd to say I owe that duty to one who is not my father, which I owe to my father, as to say, he did beget me, who did not beget me; for the obligation that arises from benefits can only be to him that conferred them. 'Tis in vain to say the same is due to his heir; for that can take place only when he has but one, which in this case signifies nothing: For if I being the only son of my father, inherit his right, and have the same power over my children as he had over me; if I had one hundred brothers, they must all inherit the same; and the law of England, which acknowledges one only heir, is not general, but municipal, and is so far from being general, as the precept of God and nature, that I doubt whether it was ever known or used in any nation of the world beyond our island. The words of the Apostle, *If we are children, we are therefore heirs and co-heirs with Christ*,[4] are the voice of God and nature; and as the universal law of God and nature is always the same, every one of us who have children have the same right over them, as Abraham, Isaac, and Jacob had over theirs; and that right which was not devolved to any one of them, but inherited by them all (I mean the right of father as father) not the peculiar promises, which were not according to the law of nature, but the election of grace, is also inherited by every one of us, and ours, that is, by all mankind. But if that which could be inherited was inherited by all, and it be impossible that a right of dominion over all can be due to everyone, then all that is or can be inherited by everyone is that exemption from the dominion of another, which we call liberty, and is the gift of God and nature.

SECTION 18

If a right of Dominion were esteemed Hereditary according to the Law of Nature, a multitude of destructive and inextricable Controversies would thereupon arise.

THERE being no such thing therefore, according to the law of nature, as an hereditary right to the dominion of the world, or any part of it; nor one man that can derive to himself a title from the first fathers of mankind, by which he can rightly pretend to be preferred before others to that command, or a part of it, and none can be derived from Nimrod, or other usurpers, who had none in themselves; we may justly spare our

---

[4] [Romans 8:17.]

pains of seeking farther into that matter. But as things of the highest importance can never be too fully explained; it may not be amiss to observe, that if mankind could be brought to believe that such a right of dominion were by the law of God and nature hereditary, a great number of the most destructive and inextricable controversies must thereupon arise, which the wisdom and goodness of God can never enjoin, and nature, which is reason, can never intend; but at present I shall only mention two, from whence others must perpetually spring. First if there be such a law, no human constitution can alter it: No length of time can be a defence against it: All governments that are not conformable to it are vicious and void even in their root, and must be so forever: That which is originally unjust may be justly overthrown. We do not know of any (at least in that part of the world in which we are most concerned) that is established, or exercised with an absolute power, as by the authors of those opinions is esteemed inseparable from it: Many, as the empire, and other states, are directly contrary; and on that account can have no justice in them. It being certain therefore that he or they who exercise those governments have no right: that there is a man to whom it doth belong, and no man knowing who he is, there is no one man who has not as good a title to it as any other: There is not therefore one who hath not a right, as well as any, to overthrow that which hath none at all. He that hath no part in the government may destroy it as well as he that has the greatest; for he neither has that which God ordained he should have, nor can shew a title to that which he enjoys from that original prerogative of birth, from whence it can only be derived.

If it be said, that some governments are arbitrary, as they ought to be, and France, Turkey, and the like be alleged as instances, the matter is not mended: for we do not only know when those, who deserve to be regarded by us, were not absolute, and how they came to be so; but also, that those very families which are now in possession are not of very long continuance, had no more title to the original right we speak of than any other men, and consequently can have none to this day. And tho we cannot perhaps say that the governments of the barbarous Eastern nations were ever other than they are, yet the known original of them deprives them of all pretence to the patriarchical inheritance, and they may be as justly as any other deprived of the power to which they have no title.

In the second place, tho all men's genealogies were extant, and fully verified, and it were allowed that the dominion of the world, or every part of it did belong to the right heir of the first progenitor, or any other to whom the first did rightly assign the parcel, which is under question; yet it were impossible for us to know who should be esteemed the true heir, or according to what rule he should be judged so to be: for God hath not by a precise word determined it, and men cannot agree about it, as appears by the various laws and customs of several nations, disposing severally of hereditary dominions.

'Tis a folly to say, they ought to go to the next in blood; for 'tis not known who is that next. Some give the preference to him who amongst many competitors is the fewest degrees removed from their common progenitor who first obtained the crown: Others look only upon the last that possessed it. Some admit of representation, by which means the grandchild of a king by his eldest son, is preferred before his second son, he being said to represent his dead father, who was the eldest: Others exclude these, and advance the younger son, who is nearer by one degree to the common progenitor that last enjoyed the crown than the grandchild. According to the first rule, Richard the second was advanced to the crown of England, as son of the eldest son of Edward the third, before his uncles, who by one degree were nearer to the last possessor: And in pursuance of the second, Sancho surnamed the Brave, second son of Alfonso the Wise, King of Castile, was preferred before Alfonso son of Ferdinand his elder brother, according to the law of tanistry, which was in force in Spain ever since we have had any knowledge of that country, as appears by the contest between Corbis and Orsua, decided by combat before Scipio Africanus; continued in full force as long as the kingdom of the Goths lasted, and was ever highly valued, till the House of Austria got possession of that country, and introduced laws and customs formerly unknown to the inhabitants.

The histories of all nations furnish us with innumerable examples of both sorts; and whosoever takes upon him to determine which side is in the right, ought to shew by what authority he undertakes to be the judge of mankind, and how the infinite breaches thereby made upon the rights of the governing families shall be cured, without the overthrow of those that he shall condemn, and of the nations where such laws have been in force as he dislikes: and till that be done, in my opinion, no place will afford a better lodging for him that shall impudently assume such a power, than the new buildings in Moor-Fields.

'Tis no less hard to decide whether this next heir is to be sought in the male line only, or whether females also be admitted. If we follow the first as the law of God and nature, the title of our English kings is wholly abolished; for not one of them since Henry the 1st has had the least pretence to an inheritance by the masculine line; and if it were necessary, we have enough to say of those that were before them.

If it be said, that the same right belongs to females, it ought to be proved that women are as fit as men to perform the office of a king, that is, as the Israelites said to Samuel, to go in and out before us, to judge us, and to fight our battles; for it were an impious folly to say that God had ordained those for the offices on which the good of mankind so much depends, who by nature are unable to perform the duties of them. If on the other side, the sweetness, gentleness, delicacy, and tenderness of the sex render them so unfit for manly exercises, that they are accounted utterly repugnant to, and inconsistent with that modesty which does so eminently shine in all those that are good amongst them; that law of nature which should advance them to the government of men, would overthrow its own work, and make those to be the heads of nations, which cannot be the heads of private families; for, as the Apostle says, *The woman is not the head of the man, but the man is the head of the woman.*[1] This were no less than to oblige mankind to lay aside the name of reasonable creature: for if reason be his nature, it cannot enjoin that which is contrary to itself; if it be not, the definition *homo est animal rationale,*[2] is false, and ought no longer to be assumed.

If any man think these arguments to be mistaken or misapplied, I desire him to enquire of the French nation on what account they have always excluded females, and such as descended from them? How comes the house of Bourbon to be advanced to the throne before a great number of families that come from the daughters of the house of Valois? Or what title those could have before the daughters of the other lines, descended from Hugh Capet, Pepin, Meroveus, or Pharamond? I know not how such questions would be received; but I am inclined to think that the wickedness and folly of those who should thereby endeavour to overthrow the most ancient and most venerated constitutions of the greatest nations, and by that means to involve them in the most inextricable difficulties, would be requited only with stones.

It cannot be denied that the most valiant, wise, learned, and best polished nations have always followed the same rule, tho the weak and barbarous acted otherwise;[3] and no man ever heard of a queen, or a man deriving his title from a female among the ancient civilized nations: but if this be not enough, the law of God, that wholly omits females, is sufficient to shew that nature, which is his handmaid, cannot advance them. When God describes who should be the king of his people (if they

---

[1] [Ephesians 5:23.]

[2] [Man is the rational animal.]

[3] reginarumque sub armis / Barbariae pars magna jacet. Lucan. *Phars.* ["And a great part of the barbarians is subjected to the arms of queens." Actually in Claudian, *Against Eutropius,* bk. 1, li. 322, *Poems,* vol. 1 (Loeb, 1922).]

would have one) and how he should govern; no mention is made of daughters.[4] The Israelites offer'd the kingdom to Gideon, and to his sons: God promised, and gave it to Saul, David, Jeroboam, Jehu and their sons. When all of them, save David, by their crimes fell from the kingdom, the males only were extirpated, and the females who had no part in the promises, did not fall under the penalties, or the vengeance that was executed upon those families: and we do not in the word of God, or in the history of the Jews, hear of any feminine reign, except that which was usurped by Athaliah; nor that any consideration was had of their descendants in relation to the kingdom: which is enough to shew that it is not according to the law of God, nor to the law of nature, which cannot differ from it. So that females, or such as derive their right by inheritance from females, must have it from some other law, or they can have none at all.

But tho this question were authentically decided, and concluded that females might or might not succeed, we should not be at the end of our contests: for if they were excluded, it would not from thence follow, as in France, that their descendants should be so also; for the privilege which is denied to them, because they cannot, without receding from the modesty and gentleness of the sex, take upon them to execute all the duties required, may be transferred to their children, as Henry the second and Henry the seventh were admitted, tho their mothers were rejected.

If it be said that every nation ought in this to follow their own constitutions, we are at an end of our controversies; for they ought not to be followed, unless they are rightly made: They cannot be rightly made, if they are contrary to the universal law of God and nature. If there be a general rule, 'tis impossible, but some of them being directly contrary to each other, must be contrary to it. If therefore all of them are to be followed, there can be no general law given to all; but every people is by God and nature left to the liberty of regulating these matters relating to themselves according to their own prudence or convenience: and this seems to be so certainly true, that whosoever does, as our author, propose doctrines to the contrary, must either be thought rashly to utter that which he does not understand, or maliciously to cast balls of division among all nations, whereby every man's sword would be drawn against every man, to the total subversion of all order and government.

---

[4] Deut. 17.

Algernon Sidney

SECTION 19
Kings cannot confer the right of Father upon Princes, nor Princes upon Kings.

L EST what has been said before by our author should not be sufficient to accomplish his design of bringing confusion upon mankind, and some may yet lie still for want of knowing at whose command he should cut his brother's throat, if he has not power or courage to set up a title for himself, he has a new project that would certainly do his work, if it were received. Not content with the absurdities and untruths already uttered in giving the incommunicable right of fathers, not only to those who, as is manifestly testified by sacred and profane histories, did usurp a power over their fathers, or such as owed no manner of obedience to them: and justifying those usurpations, which are most odious to God and all good men, he now fancies a kingdom so gotten may escheat for want of an heir; whereas there is no need of seeking any, if usurpation can confer a right; and that he who gets the power into his hands ought to be reputed the right heir of the first progenitor; for such a one will be seldom wanting, if violence and fraud be justified by the command of God, and nations stand obliged to render obedience, till a stronger or more successful villain throws him from the throne he had invaded. But if it should come to pass that no man would step into the vacant place, he has a new way of depriving the people of their right to provide for the government of themselves. *Because*, says he, *the dependency of ancient families is oft obscure, and worn out of knowledge; therefore the wisdom of all or most princes hath thought fit many times to adopt those for heads of families and princes of provinces, whose merits, abilities, or fortunes have ennobled them, and made them fit and capable of such royal favours: All such prime heads and fathers have power to consent to the uniting and conferring of their fatherly right and sovereignty on whom they please,* &c.[1]

I may justly ask how any one or more families come to be esteemed more ancient than others, if all are descended from one common father, as the Scriptures testify; or to what purpose it were to enquire what families were the most ancient, if there were any such, when the youngest and most mean by usurpation gets an absolute right of dominion over the eldest, tho his own progenitors, as Nimrod did: but I may certainly conclude, that whatever the right be that belongs to those ancient families,

[1] [*Patriarcha*, ch. 6, p. 62.]

it is inherent in them, and cannot be conferred on any other by any human power; for it proceeds from nature only. The duty I owe to my father does not arise from an usurped or delegated power, but from my birth derived from him; and 'tis as impossible for any man to usurp or receive by the grant of another the right of a father over me, as for him to become, or pretend to be made my father by another who did not beget me. But if he say true, this right of father does not arise from nature; nor the obedience that I owe to him that begot, from the benefits which I have received, but is merely an artificial thing depending upon the will of another: and that we may be sure there can be no error in this, our author attributes it to the wisdom of princes. But before this comes to be authentick, we must at the least be sure that all princes have this great and profound wisdom, which our author acknowledges to be in them, and which is certainly necessary for the doing of such great things, if they were referred to them. They seem to us to be born like other men, and to be generally no wiser than other men. We are not obliged to believe that Nebuchadnezzar was wise, till God had given him the heart of a man; or that his grandson Belshazzar, who being laid in the balance was found too light, had any such profound wisdom. Ahasuerus shewed it not in appointing all the people of God to be slain, upon a lie told to him by a rascal; and the matter was not very much mended, when being informed of the truth, he gave them leave to kill as many of their enemies as they pleased. The hardness of Pharaoh's heart, and the overthrow thereby brought upon himself and people, does not argue so profound a judgment as our author presumes every prince must have: And 'tis not probable that Samuel would have told Saul, *He had done foolishly*, if kings had always been so exceeding wise: Nay, if wisdom had been annexed to the character, Solomon might have spared the pains of asking it from God, and Rehoboam must have had it. Not to multiply examples out of Scripture, 'tis believed that Xerxes had not inflicted stripes upon the sea for breaking his navy in pieces, if he had been so very wise. Caligula for the same reason might have saved the labour of making love to the moon, or have chosen a fitter subject to advance to the consulate than his horse Incitatus: Nero had not endeavoured to make a woman of a man, nor married a man as a woman.[2] Many other examples might be alleged to shew that kings are not always wise: and not only

[2] Sueton. [Suetonius, *Life of Caligula*, ch. 22, 55, and *Life of Nero*, ch. 28–29, in *Lives of the Caesars*, 2 vols. (Loeb, 1913–1914). Xerxes, named in the preceding sentence, ordered the Hellespont to suffer three hundred lashes and to have a pair of fetters thrown into it; see Herodotus, bk. 7, ch. 35, in *Histories*, 4 vols. (Loeb, 1920–1925).]

the Roman satyrist, who says *quicquid delirant reges*, &c.[3] shews that he did not believe them to be generally wiser than other men; but Solomon himself judges them to be as liable to infirmities, when he prefers a wise child before an old and foolish king.[4] If therefore the strength of our author's argument lies in the certainty of the wisdom of kings, it can be of no value, till he proves it to be more universal in them than history or experience will permit us to believe. Nay, if there be truth or wisdom in the Scripture, which frequently represents the wicked man as a fool, we cannot think that all kings are wise, unless it be proved that none of them have been wicked; and when this is performed by Filmer's disciples, I shall confess my error.

Men give testimony of their wisdom, when they undertake that which they ought to do, and rightly perform that which they undertake; both which points do utterly fail in the subject of our discourse. We have often heard of such as have adopted those to be their sons who were not so, and some civil laws approve it. This signifies no more, than that such a man, either through affection to one who is not his son, or to his parents, or for some other reason, takes him into his family, and shews kindness to him, as to his son; but the adoption of fathers is a whimsical piece of nonsense. If this be capable of an aggravation, I think none can be greater, than not to leave it to my own discretion, who having no father, may resolve to pay the duty I owed to my father to one who may have shewed kindness to me; but for another to impose a father upon a man, or a people composed of fathers, or such as have fathers, whereby they should be deprived of that natural honour and right, which he makes the foundation of his discourse, is the utmost of all absurdities. If any prince therefore have ever undertaken to appoint fathers of his people, he cannot be accounted a man of profound wisdom, but a fool or a madman; and his acts can be of no value. But if the thing were consonant to nature, and referred to the will of princes (which I absolutely deny) the frequent extravagancies committed by them in the elevation of their favourites, shews that they intend not to make them fathers of the people, or know not what they do when they do it.

To chuse or institute a father is nonsense in the very term; but if any were to be chosen to perform the office of fathers to such as have none, and are not of age to provide for themselves (as men do tutors or guardians for orphans) none could be capable of being elected, but such as in kindness to the person they were to take under their care, did most

[3] Horat. ["Whatever kings rave at." Horace, *Epistles*, bk. 1, Ep. 2, li. 14. The full line is "Whatever kings rave at, the people suffer from." Horace, *Satires, Epistles, and Ars Poetica* (rev. ed.; Loeb, 1929).]
[4] [Ecclesiastes 4:13.]

resemble his true father, and had the virtues and abilities required rightly to provide for his good. If this fails, all right ceases; and such a corruption is introduced as we saw in our court of wards, which the nation could not bear, when the institution was perverted, and the king, who ought to have taken a tender care of the wards and their estates, delivered them as a prey to those whom he favoured.[5]

Our author ridiculously attributes the title and authority of father to the word *prince;* for it hath none in it, and signifies no more than a man, who in some kind is more eminent than the vulgar. In this sense Mucius Scaevola told Porsenna, that *three hundred princes of the Roman youth had conspired against him:*[6] by which he could not mean that three hundred fathers of the Roman youth, but three hundred Roman young men had conspired: and they could not be fathers of the city, unless they had been fathers of their own fathers. *Princeps senatus*[7] was understood in the same sense; and T. Sempronius the censor chusing Q. Fabius Maximus to that honour, gave for a reason, *Se lecturum Q. Fabium Maximum, quem tum principem Romanae civitatis esse, vel Annibale judice, dicturus esset;*[8] which could not be understood that Hannibal thought him to be the father or lord of the city (for he knew he was not) but the man, who for wisdom and valour was the most eminent in it.

The like are and ought to be the princes of every nation; and tho something of honour may justly be attributed to the descendants of such as have done great services to their country, yet they who degenerate from them cannot be esteemed princes; much less can such honours or rights be conferred upon court-creatures or favourites. Tiberius, Caligula, Claudius, Nero, Galba, and others, could advance Macro, Pallas, Narcissus, Tigellinus, Vinius, Laco, and the like, to the highest degrees of riches and power; but they still continued to be villains, and so they died.

No wise or good man ever thought otherwise of those who through the folly of princes have been advanced to the highest places in several countries. The madness of attributing to them a paternal power, seems to have been peculiarly reserved to compleat the infamy of our author; for he only could acknowledge a cooptitious father, or give to another

---

[5] [Parliament's attempt to reform these abuses in 1604 was vetoed by James I. It was the first of many occasions under the Stuart monarchs when Parliament stated its liberties in opposition to the king.]

[6] Trecenti Romanae juventutis principes. T. Liv. [Livy, *History of Rome*, bk. 2, ch. 12.]

[7] [Prince (i.e., leading man) of the senate.]

[8] T. Liv. 1. 7. ["He would choose Q. Fabius Maximus, whom he could prove, even with Hannibal as a judge, to be at that time the prince (i.e., first citizen) of the city of Rome." Livy, *History of Rome*, bk. 27, ch. 11.]

man the power of chusing him. I confess that a man in his infancy may have been exposed, like Moses, Cyrus, Oedipus, Romulus: He may have been taken in war; or by the charity of some good person saved from the teeth of wild beasts, or from the sword by which his parents fell, and may have been educated with that care which fathers usually have of their children: 'tis reasonable that such a one in the whole course of his life should pay that veneration and obedience to him, who gave him as it were a second birth, which was due to his natural father; and this, tho improperly, may be called an adoption. But to think that any man can assume it to himself, or confer it upon another, and thereby arrogate to himself the service and obedience, which, by the most tender and sacred laws of nature, we owe to those from whom we receive birth and education, is the most preposterous folly that hitherto has ever entered into the heart of man.

Our author nevertheless is not ashamed of it, and gives reasons no way unsuitable to the proposition. *Men are*, says he, *adopted fathers of provinces for their abilities, merits, or fortunes.*[9] But these abilities can simply deserve nothing; for if they are ill employed, they are the worst of vices, and the most powerful instruments of mischief. Merits, in regard of another, are nothing, unless they be to him; and he alone can merit from me the respect due to a father, who hath conferred benefits upon me, in some measure proportionable to those which we usually receive from our fathers: and the world may judge, whether all the court-ministers and favorites that we have known, do upon this account deserve to be esteemed fathers of nations. But to allow this on account of their fortunes, is, if possible, more extravagant than anything that hath been yet utter'd. By this account Mazarin must have been father of the French nation: The same right was inherited by his chaste niece, and remained in her, till she and her silly husband dissipated the treasures which her uncle had torn from the bowels of that people. The partizans may generally claim the same right over the provinces they have pillaged: Old Audley, Dog Smith, Bp. Duppa, Brownlow, Child, Dashwood, Fox, &c.[10] are to be esteemed fathers of the people of England. This doctrine is perfectly canonical, if Filmer and Heylyn were good divines; and legal, if they judged more rightly touching matters of law. But if it be absurd and detestable, they are to be reputed men, who, by attributing the highest honours to the vilest wretches of the world, for what they had gain'd by

[9] [*Patriarcha*, ch. 6, p. 62.]

[10] [These men acquired large fortunes as government officials.]

the most abominable means, endeavour to increase those vices, which are already come to such a height, that they can by no other way be brought to a greater. Daily experience too plainly shews, with what rage avarice usually fills the hearts of men. There are not many destructive villainies committed in the world, that do not proceed from it. In this respect 'tis called *idolatry*, and *the root of all evil*. Solomon warns us to beware of such as make haste to grow rich, and says, they shall not be innocent. But 'tis no matter what the prophets, the apostles, or the wisest of men say of riches, and the ways of gaining them; for our author tells us, that men of the greatest fortunes, without examining how they came to them, or what use they make of them, deserve to be made fathers of provinces.

But this is not his only quarrel with all that is just and good: His whole book goes directly against the letter and spirit of the Scripture. The work of all those, whom God in several ages has raised up to announce his word, was to abate the lusts and passions that arise in the hearts of men; to shew the vanity of worldly enjoyments, with the dangers that accompany riches and honours, and to raise our hearts to the love of those treasures that perish not. Honest and wise men following the light of nature, have in some measure imitated this. Such as lived private lives, as Plato, Socrates, Epictetus, and others, made it their business to abate men's lusts, by shewing the folly of seeking vain honours, useless riches, or unsatisfying pleasures; and those who were like to them, if they were raised to supreme magistracies, have endeavoured by the severest punishments to restrain men from committing the crimes by which riches are most commonly gained: but Filmer and Heylyn lead us into a new way. If they deserve credit, whosoever would become supreme lord and father of his country, absolute, sacred and inviolable, is only to kill him that is in the head of the government: Usurpation confers an equal right with election or inheritance: We are to look upon the power, not the ways by which it is obtained: Possession only is to be regarded; and men must venerate the present power, as set up by God, tho gained by violence, treachery or poison: Children must not impose laws upon, nor examine the actions of their father. Those who are a little more modest, and would content themselves with the honour of being fathers and lords only of provinces, if they get riches by the favour of the king, or the favour of the king by riches, may receive that honour from him: The lord paramount may make them peculiar lords of each province as sacred as himself; and by that means every man shall have an immediate and a subaltern father. This would be a spur to excite even the most sleeping lusts; and a poison that would fill the gentlest spirits with the most violent furies. If men should believe this, there would hardly be found one of whom it might not be said, *hac spe, minanti fulmen, occurret Jovi.*[11] No more is required to fill the world with fire and blood, than the reception of these precepts: No man can look upon that as a wickedness, which shall render him sacred; nor fear to attempt that which shall make him God's vicegerent. And I doubt, whether the wickedness of filling men's heads with such notions was ever equalled, unless by him who said, *Ye shall not die, but be as gods.*

But since our author is pleased to teach us these strange things, I wish he would also have told us, how many men in every nation ought to be look'd upon as adopted fathers: What proportion of riches, ability or merit, is naturally or divinely required to make them capable of this sublime character: Whether the right of this chimerical father does not destroy that of the natural; or whether both continue in force, and men thereby stand obliged, in despite of what Christ said, to serve two masters. For if the right of my artificial father arise from any act of the king, in favour of his riches, abilities or merit, I ought to know whether he is to excel in all, or any one of these points: How far, and which of them gives the preference; since 'tis impossible for me to determine whether my father, who may be wise, tho not rich, is thereby divested of his right, and it comes to be transferr'd to another, who may be rich tho not wise, nor of any personal merit at all, till that point be decided; or, so much as to guess, when I am emancipated from the duty I owe to him, by whom I was begotten and educated, unless I know whether he be fallen from his right, through want of merit, wisdom or estate: and that can never be, till it be determined that he hath forfeited his right, by being defective in all, or any of the three; and what proportion of merit, wisdom or estate is required in him, for the enjoyment of his right, or in another that would acquire it: for no man can succeed to the right of another, unless the first possessor be rightly deprived of it; and it cannot belong to them both, because common sense universally teaches, that two distinct persons cannot, at the same time, and in the same degree, have an equal right to the same individual thing.

The right of father cannot therefore be conferred upon princes by kings, but must forever follow the rule of nature. The character of a father is indelible, and incommunicable: The duty of children arising from benefits received is perpetual, because they can never not have received them; and can be due only to him from whom they are received. For these reasons, we see, that such as our author calls princes, cannot

[11] Senec. Theb. ["With this hope he will (even) attack Jupiter, who threatens with his lightning bolt." Actually in Seneca, *Thyestes*, li. 290.]

confer it upon a king; for they cannot give what they have not in themselves: They who have nothing, can give nothing: They who are only supposititious, cannot make another to be real; and the whimsey of kings making princes to be fathers, and princes conferring that right on kings, comes to nothing.

SECTION 20

All just Magistratical Power is from the People.

HAVING proved that the right of a father proceeds from the generation and education of his children: That no man can have that right over those, whom he hath not begotten and educated: That every man hath it over those, who owe their birth and education to him: That all the sons of Noah, Abraham, Isaac, Jacob, and others, did equally inherit it: That by the same reasons, it doth forever belong to every man that begets children; it plainly appears, that no father can have a right over others, unless it be by them granted to him, and that he receive his right from those who granted it. But our author, with an admirable sagacity peculiar to himself, discovers, and with equal confidence tells us, that that which is from the people, or the chief heads of them, is not from the people: *He that is so elected*, says he, *claims not his right from the people as a donative, but from God.*[1] That is, if I mistake not, Romulus was not made king of the Romans by that people, but by God: Those men being newly gathered together, had two fathers, tho neither of them had any children; and no man knew who was their father, nor which of them was the elder: But Romulus by the slaughter of his brother decided all questions, and purchased to himself a royal charter from God; and the act of the people which conferred the power on him, was the act of God. We had formerly learnt, that whatsoever was done by monarchs, was to be imputed to God; and that whosoever murdered the father of a people, acquired the same right to himself: but now it seems, that nations also have the same privilege, and that God doth, what they do. Now I understand why it was said of old, *vox populi est vox Dei:*[2] But if it was so in regard of Romulus, the same must be confessed of Tullus Hostilius,

---

[1] [*Patriarcha*, ch. 6, p. 62.]

[2] [The voice of the people is the voice of God.]

Ancus Marcius, Tarquinius Priscus, and Servius Tullius; who being all strangers to each other, and most of them aliens also, were successively advanced by the same people, without any respect to the children, relations or heirs of their predecessors. And I cannot comprehend, why the act of the same people should not have the same virtue, and be equally attributed to God, when they gave the same or more power to consuls, military tribunes, decemviri, or dictators; or why the same divine character should not be in the same manner conferred upon any magistracies, that by any people have been, are, or shall be at any time erected for the same ends.

Upon the same grounds we may conclude, that no privilege is peculiarly annexed to any form of government; but that all magistrates are equally the ministers of God, who perform the work for which they were instituted; and that the people which institutes them, may proportion, regulate and terminate their power, as to time, measure, and number of persons, as seems most convenient to themselves, which can be no other than their own good. For it cannot be imagined that a multitude of people should send for Numa, or any other person to whom they owed nothing, to reign over them, that he might live in glory and pleasure; or for any other reason, than that it might be good for them and their posterity. This shews the work of all magistrates to be always and everywhere the same, even the doing of justice, and procuring the welfare of those that create them. This we learn from common sense: Plato, Aristotle, Cicero, and the best human authors lay it as an unmoveable foundation, upon which they build their arguments relating to matters of that nature: And the Apostle from better authority declares, *That rulers are not a terror to good works, but to evil: Wilt thou then not be afraid of the power? do that which is good, and thou shalt have praise of the same; for he is the minister of God unto thee for good: But if thou do that which is evil, be afraid; for he beareth not the sword in vain; for he is the minister of God, a revenger to execute wrath upon him that doth evil.*[3] And the reason he gives *for praying for kings, and all that are in authority,* is, *that we may live a quiet and peaceable life, in all godliness and honesty.*[4] But if this be the work of the magistrate, and the glorious name of God's minister be given to him for the performance of it, we may easily see to whom that title belongs. *His children and servants ye are, whose works ye do.* He therefore, and he only, is the servant of God, who does the work of God; who is a terror to those that do evil, and a praise to those that do well; who beareth the sword for the punishment of wickedness and vice, and so governs, that the people may live quietly

[3] Rom. 13.   [4] 1 Tim. 2.

in all godliness and honesty. The order of his institution is inverted, and the institution vacated, if the power be turned to the praise of those that do evil, and becomes a terror to such as do well; and that none who live honestly and justly can be quiet under it. If God be the fountain of justice, mercy and truth, and those his servants who walk in them, no exercise of violence, fraud, cruelty, pride, or avarice, is patronized by him: and they who are the authors of those villainies, cannot but be the ministers of him, who sets himself up against God; because 'tis impossible that truth and falsehood, mercy and cruelty, justice and the most violent oppression can proceed from the same root. It was a folly and a lie in those Jews, to call themselves the children of Abraham, who did not the works of Abraham; and Christ declared them to be the children of the Devil, whose works they did:[5] which words proceeding from the eternal truth, do as well indicate to us, whose child and servant every man is to be accounted, as to those who first heard them.

If our author's former assertions were void of judgment and truth, his next clause shews a great defect in his memory, and contradicts the former: *The judgments of God*, says he, *who hath power to give and take away kingdoms, are most just; yet the ministry of men, who execute God's judgments without commission, is sinful and damnable.*[6] If it be true, as he says, that we are to look at the power, not the ways by which it is gained; and that he who hath it, whether it be by usurpation, conquest, or any other means, is to be accounted as father, or right heir to the father of the people, to which title the most sublime and divine privileges are annexed, a man, who by the most wicked and unjust actions advances himself to the power, becomes immediately the father of the people, and the minister of God; which I take to be a piece of divinity worthy our author and his disciples.

It may be doubted what he means by a commission from God; for we know of none but what is outwardly by his word, or inwardly by his spirit; and I am apt to think, that neither he nor his abettors allowing of either, as to the point in question, he doth fouly prevaricate, in alleging that which he thinks cannot be of any effect. If any man should say, that the word of God to Moses, Joshua, Ehud, Gideon, Samuel, Jeroboam and Jehu, or any others, are, in the like cases, rules to be observed by all; because that which was from God was good; that which was good, is good; and he that does good, is justified by it: He would probably tell us, that what was good in them, is not good in others; and that the word of God doth justify those only to whom it is spoken: That is to say, no man can execute the just judgments of God, to the benefit of mankind, according to the example of those servants of God, without damnable sin, unless he have a precise word particularly directed to him for it, as Moses had. But if any man should pretend that such a word was come to him, he would be accounted an enthusiast, and obtain no credit. So that, which way soever the clause be taken, it appears to be full of fraud, confessing only in the theory, that which he thinks can never be brought into practice; that his beloved villainies may be thereby secured, and that the glorious examples of the most heroick actions, performed by the best and wisest men that ever were in the world for the benefit of mankind, may never be imitated.

The next clause shews, that I did our author no wrong in saying, that he gave a right to usurpation; for he plainly says, *That whether the prince be the supreme father of his people, or the true heir of such a father; or whether he come to the crown by usurpation, or election of the nobles or people, or by any other way whatsoever, &c. it is the only right and authority of the natural father.*[7] In the 3d chap. sect. 8. *It skills not which way the king comes by his power, whether by election, donation, succession, or by any other means.*[8] And in another place, *That we are to regard the power, not the means by which it is gained.* To which I need say no more, than that I cannot sufficiently admire the ingeniously invented title of father by usurpation; and confess, that since there is such a thing in the world, to which not only private men, but whole nations owe obedience, whatsoever has been said anciently (as was thought to express the highest excess of fury and injustice), as, *jus datum sceleri; jus omne in ferro est situm; jus licet in jugulos nostros sibi fecerit ense Sylla potens Mariusque; ferox & Cinna cruentus, Caesareaeque domus series,*[9] were solid truths, good law and divinity; which did not only signify the actual exercise of the power, but induced a conscientious obligation of obeying it. The powers so gained, did carry in themselves the most sacred and inviolable rights; and the actors of the most detestable villainies thereby became the ministers of God, and the fathers of their subdued people. Or if this be not true, it cannot be denied, that Filmer and his followers, in the most impudent and outrageous blasphemy, have surpassed all that have gone before them.

---

[7] [Ibid.]

[8] [Chapter 26, p. 106 in the Laslett edition, which is based on Filmer's manuscript. Sidney used the 1680 edition of Filmer, which had three chapters subdivided into 46 numbered sections.]

[9] Lucan, &c. ["Right is ascribed to crime"; "all right is located in the sword"; "it is granted that powerful Sulla, fierce Marius, bloody Cinna, and the whole line of Caesar's house made right for themselves by the sword at our throats." The third quotation is from Lucan, *Pharsalia*, bk. 4, li. 821.]

To confirm his assertions, he gives us a wonderful explanation of the fifth commandment; which, he says, enjoins obedience to princes, under the terms of, *Honour thy father and thy mother;* drawing this inference, *That as all power is in the father, the prince who hath it, cannot be restrained by any law; which being grounded upon the perfect likeness between kings and fathers, no man can deny it to be true.* But if Claudius was the father of the Roman people, I suppose the chaste Messalina was the mother, and to be honoured by virtue of the same commandment: But then I fear that such as met her in the most obscene places, were not only guilty of adultery, but of incest. The same honour must needs belong to Nero and his virtuous Poppaea, unless it were transferred to his new-made woman Sporus; or perhaps he himself was the mother, and the glorious title of *pater patriae* belonged to the rascal, who married him as a woman. The like may be said of Agathocles, Dionysius, Phalaris, Busiris, Machanidas, Peter the Cruel of Castile, Christian of Denmark, the last princes of the house of Valois in France, and Philip the Second of Spain. Those actions of theirs, which men have ever esteemed most detestable, and the whole course of their abominable government, did not proceed from pride, avarice, cruelty, madness and lust, but from the tender care of most pious fathers. Tacitus sadly describes the state of his country, *urbs incendiis vastata, consumptis antiquissimis delubris, ipso Capitolio civium manibus incenso; pollutae ceremoniae; magna adulteria; plenum exiliis mare; infecti caedibus scopuli; atrocius in urbe saevitum; nobilitas, opes, omissi vel gesti honores pro crimine, & ob virtutes certissimum exitium;*[10] but he was to blame: All this proceeded from the ardency of a paternal affection. When Nero, by the death of Helvidius Priscus and Thrasea, endeavoured to cut up virtue by the roots, *ipsam exscindere virtutem,*[11] he did it, because he knew it was good for the world that there should be no virtuous man in it. When he fired the city, and when Caligula wished the people had but one neck, that he might strike it off at one blow, they did it through a prudent care of their children's good, knowing that it would be for their advantage to be destroyed; and that the empty desolated world would be no more troubled with popular seditions. By the same rule Pharaoh, Eglon, Nebuchadnezzar, Antiochus, Herod, and the like, were fathers of the Hebrews. And without looking far backward, or depending upon the faith of history, we may enumerate

---

[10] ["The city was devastated by conflagrations, in which her most ancient shrines were consumed and the very Capitol fired by citizens' hands; the rites were polluted; there were great adulteries; the sea was filled with exiles, the cliffs stained with their blood; in the city there was more awful savagery; nobility, wealth, the refusal or acceptance of office, were grounds for accusation, and virtues ensured ruin." Tacitus, *Histories*, bk. 1, ch. 2, in *The Histories and The Annals*, 4 vols. (Loeb, 1925–1937).]

[11] [Tacitus, *Annals*, bk. 16, ch. 21.]

many princes, who in a paternal care of their people, have not yielded to Nero or Caligula. If our author say true, all those actions of theirs, which we have ever attributed to the utmost excess of pride, cruelty, avarice and perfidiousness, proceeded from their princely wisdom and fatherly kindness to the nations under them: and we are beholden to him for the discovery of so great a mystery which hath been hid from mankind, from the beginning of the world to this day; if not, we may still look upon them as children of the Devil; and continue to believe, that princes as well as other magistrates were set up by the people for the publick good; that the praises given to such as are wise, just and good, are purely personal, and can belong only to those, who by a due exercise of their power do deserve it, and to no others.

CHAPTER TWO

*That 'tis natural for Nations to govern,
or to chuse Governors; and that Virtue only gives a
natural preference of one man above another, or reason
why one should be chosen rather than another.*

I N this chapter our author fights valiantly against Bellarmine and
Suarez, seeming to think himself victorious, if he can shew that either
of them hath contradicted the other, or himself;[1] but being no way
concerned in them, I shall leave their followers to defend their quarrel:
My work is to seek after truth; and, tho they may have said some things,
in matters not concerning their beloved cause of popery, that are agreeable
to reason, law or Scripture, I have little hope of finding it among those

---

[1] [Chapter II of the 1680 edition of Filmer
was entitled, "It is unnatural for the People
to Govern, or Choose Governours" and
comprised chapters 11–21 of Filmer's manuscript. Sidney's Chapter II thus answers
that part of *Patriarcha*. (Filmer's chapters 8–
10, in which Grotius, Selden, and the civil
law are treated, were not printed in the 1680
edition, which may have been based on an
early manuscript revised later by Filmer.
Therefore Sidney does not discuss these
chapters.)

Suarez and Bellarmine, as well-known
Catholic writers, had no prestige in Protestant England. Filmer's chapter 11 is "Suarez'
Dispute against the Regality of Adam. Families Diversely Defined, Suarez Contradicting Bellarmine" (pp. 74–78).]

who apply themselves chiefly to School-sophistry, as the best means to support idolatry. That which I maintain, is the cause of mankind; which ought not to suffer, tho champions of corrupt principles have weakly defended, or maliciously betrayed it: and therefore not at all relying on their authority, I intend to reject whatsoever they say that agrees not with reason, Scripture, or the approved examples of the best polished nations. He also attacks Plato and Aristotle, upon whose opinions I set a far greater value, in as much as they seem to have penetrated more deeply into the secrets of human nature;[2] and not only to have judged more rightly of the interests of mankind, but also to have comprehended in their writings the wisdom of the Grecians, with all that they had learnt from the Phoenicians, Egyptians and Hebrews; which may lead us to the discovery of the truth we seek. If this be our work, the question is not, whether it be a *paradox*, or a *received opinion*, *that people naturally govern, or chuse governors*, but whether it be true or not; for many paradoxes are true, and the most gross errors have often been most common. Tho I hope to prove, that what he calls a paradox, is not only true; but a truth planted in the hearts of men, and acknowledged so to be by all that have hearkened to the voice of nature, and disapproved by none, but such as through wickedness, stupidity, or baseness of spirit, seem to have degenerated into the worst of beasts, and to have retained nothing of men, but the outward shape, or the ability of doing those mischiefs which they have learnt from their master the Devil.

We have already seen, that the patriarchical power resembles not the regal in principle or practice: that the beginning and continuance of regal power was contrary to, and inconsistent with the patriarchical: that the first fathers of mankind left all their children independent on each other, and in an equal liberty of providing for themselves: that every man continued in this liberty, till the number so increased, that they became troublesome and dangerous to each other; and finding no other remedy to the disorders growing, or like to grow among them, joined many families into one civil body, that they might the better provide for the conveniency, safety, and defence of themselves and their children. This was a collation of every man's private right into a publick stock; and no one having any other right than what was common to all, except it were that of fathers over their children, they were all equally free when their fathers were dead; and nothing could induce them to join, and lessen that natural liberty by joining in societies, but the hopes of a publick advantage.

[2] [*Patriarcha*, ch. 12 ("Aristotle Agrees with the Scripture, Deducing Royal Authority from the Fatherhood"), pp. 78–80.]

Such as were wise and valiant procured it, by setting up regular governments, and placing the best men in the administration; whilst the weakest and basest fell under the power of the most boisterous and violent of their neighbours. Those of the first sort had their root in wisdom and justice, and are called lawful kingdoms or commonwealths; and the rules by which they are governed, are known by the name of laws. These governments have ever been the nurses of virtue: The nations living under them have flourished in peace and happiness, or made wars with glory and advantage: whereas the other sort springing from violence and wrong, have ever gone under the odious title of tyrannies; and by fomenting vices, like to those from whence they grew, have brought shame and misery upon those who were subject to them. This appears so plainly in Scripture, that the assertors of liberty want no other patron than God himself; and his word so fully justifies what we contend for, that it were not necessary to make use of human authority, if our adversaries did not oblige us to examine such as are cited by them. This, in our present case, would be an easy work, if our author had rightly marked the passages he would make use of, or had been faithful in his interpretation or explication of such as he truly cites; but failing grossly in both, 'tis hard to trace him.

He cites the 16th chapter of the third book of Aristotle's *Politicks*, and I do not find there is more than twelve;[3] or tho that wound might be cured, by saying the words are in the twelfth, his fraud in perverting the sense were unpardonable, tho the other mistake be passed over. 'Tis true that Aristotle doth there seem to doubt whether there be any such thing as one man naturally a lord over many citizens, since a city consists of equals: but in the whole scope of that chapter, book, and his other writings, he fully shews his doubt did not arise from an imagination that one man could naturally inherit a right of dominion over many not descended from him; or that they were born under a necessity of being slaves to him (for such fancies can proceed only from distemper'd brains) but that civil societies aiming at the publick good, those who by nature were endowed with such virtues or talents as were most beneficial to them, ought to be preferred. And nothing can be more contrary to the frantick whimsy of our author, who fancies an hereditary prerogative of dominion inherent in a person as father of a people, or heir, or to be reputed heir of the first father, when 'tis certain he is not, but that either

[3] [*Patriarcha*, ch. 12, p. 79. Filmer and Sidney are both correct. Book 3 of Aristotle's *Politics* is sometimes divided into 12, sometimes into 18 chapters. The quotation used by Filmer is at 1287a.]

he or his predecessor came in by election or usurpation, than to shew that 'tis only wisdom, justice, valour, and other commendable virtues, which are not hereditary, that can give the preference; and that the only reason why it should be given, is, that men so qualified can better than others accomplish the ends for which societies are constituted: For tho, says he, all are equally free, all are not equally endowed with those virtues that render liberty safe, prosperous, and happy. That equality which is just among equals, is just only among equals; but such as are base, ignorant, vicious, slothful, or cowardly, are not equal in natural or acquired virtues, to the generous, wise, valiant, and industrious; nor equally useful to the societies in which they live: they cannot therefore have an equal part in the government of them; they cannot equally provide for the common good; and 'tis not a personal, but a publick benefit that is sought in their constitution and continuance. There may be a hundred thousand men in an army, who are all equally free; but they only are naturally most fit to be commanders or leaders, who most excel in the virtues required for the right performance of those offices; and that, not because 'tis good for them to be raised above their brethren, but because 'tis good for their brethren to be guided by them, as 'tis ever good to be governed by the wisest and the best. If the nature of man be reason, *detur digniori*, in matters of this kind, is the voice of nature; and it were not only a deviation from reason, but a most desperate and mischievous madness, for a company going to the Indies, to give the guidance of their ship to the son of the best pilot in the world, if he want the skill required to that employment, or to one who was maliciously set to destroy them; and he only can have a right grounded upon the dictates of nature, to be advanced to the helm, who best knows how to govern it, and has given the best testimonies of his integrity and intentions to employ his skill for the good of those that are embarked. But as the work of a magistrate, especially if he be the supreme, is the highest, noblest, and most difficult that can be committed to the charge of a man, a more excellent virtue is required in the person who is to be advanced to it, than for any other; and he that is most excellent in that virtue, is reasonably and naturally to be preferred before any other. Aristotle having this in his view, seems to think, that those who believed it not to be natural for one man to be lord of all the citizens, since a city consists of equals, had not observed that inequality of endowments, virtues and abilities in men, which render some more fit than others, for the performance of their duties, and the work intended; but it will not be found, as I suppose, that he did ever dream of a natural superiority, that any man could ever have in a civil society, unless it be such a superiority in virtue, as most conduces to the publick good.[4]

He confirms this in proceeding to examine the different sorts of governments, according to the different dispositions of nations; and is so bold to say, that a popular government is the best for a people, who are naturally generous and warlike: that the government of a few suits best with those, among whom a few men are found to excel others in those virtues that are profitable to societies; and that the government of one is good, when that one does so far surpass all others in those virtues, that he hath more of them than all the rest of the people together: and for the same reason that induced him to believe that equality is just amongst equals, he concludes inequality of power to be most unjust, unless there be inequality of merit; and equality of power to be so also, when there is inequality of virtue, that being the only rule by which every man's part ought to be regulated.[5]

But if it be neither reasonable nor just that those who are not equal in virtue should be made equal in power, or that such as are equal in virtue should be unequal in power, the most brutal and abominable of all extravagancies is to make one or a few, who in virtue and abilities to perform civil functions are inferior to others, superior to all in power; and the miseries suffered by those nations, who inverting the laws of nature and reason, have placed children, or men of no virtue in the government, when men that excelled in all virtues were not wanting, do so far manifest this truth, that the pains of proving it may be spared.

'Tis not necessary for me to inquire, whether it be possible to find such a man as Aristotle calls *naturâ regem*,[6] or whether he intended to recommend Alexander to the world, for the man designed by God and nature to be king over all, because no man was equal to him in the virtues that were beneficial to all. For pursuing my position, that virtue only can give a just and natural preference, I ingenuously confess, that when such a man, or race of men as he describes, shall appear in the world, they carry the true marks of sovereignty upon them: We ought to believe, that God has raised them above all, whom he has made to excel all: It were an impious folly to think of reducing him into the ordinary level of mankind, whom God has placed above it. 'Twere better for us to be guided by him, than to follow our own judgment; nay, I could almost say, 'twere better to serve such a master, than to be free. But this will

[4] [Aristotle, *Politics*, bk. 3, 1282B–1283a.]   [6] [King by nature.]
[5] [Aristotle, *Politics*, bk. 3, 1288a.]

be nothing to the purpose, till such a man, or succession of men do appear; and if our author would persuade us, that all mankind, or every particular, is obliged to a perpetual subjection to one man or family, upon any other condition, he must do it by the credit of those who favour his design more than Aristotle.

I know not who that will be, but am confident he will find no help from Plato: for if his principles be examined, by which a grave author's sense is best comprehended, it will appear, that all his books of laws, and of a commonwealth,[7] are chiefly grounded upon this, that magistrates are chosen by societies, seeking their own good; and that the best men ought to be chosen for the attaining of it: whereas his whole design of seeking which is the best form of government, or what laws do most conduce to its perfection and permanency (if one rule were by nature appointed for all, and none could justly transgress it; if God had designed an universal lord over the whole world, or a particular one over every nation, who could be bound by no law), were utterly absurd; and they who write books concerning political matters, and take upon them to instruct nations how to govern themselves, would be found either foolishly to misspend their time, or impiously to incite people to rebel against the ordinance of God. If this can justly be imputed to Plato, he is not the wise man he is supposed to have been; and can less deserve the title of divine, which our author gives him: but if he remain justly free from such censures, it must be confessed, that whilst he seeks what is good for a people, and to convince them by reason that it is so, he takes it for granted, that they have a liberty of chusing that which appears to be the best to them. He first says, that this good consists in the obtaining of justice; but farther explaining himself, he shews that under the name of justice, he comprehends all that tends to their perfection and felicity; in as much as every people, by joining in a civil society, and creating magistrates, doth seek its own good; and 'tis just, that he or they who are created, should, to the utmost of their power, accomplish the end of their creation, and lead the people to justice, without which there is neither perfection nor happiness: That the proper act of justice is to give to everyone his due; to man that which belongs to man, and to God that which is God's. But as no man can be just, or desire to be so, unless he know that justice is good; nor know that it is good, unless he know that original justice and goodness, through which all that is just is just, and all that is good is good, 'tis impossible for any man to perform the part of a good magistrate, unless he have the knowledge of God; or to bring

[7] Plato de Leg. & de Republ. [Plato, *Laws*
and *Republic*.]

a people to justice, unless he bring them to the knowledge of God, who is the root of all justice and goodness.[8] If Plato therefore deserve credit, he only can duly perform the part of a good magistrate, whose moral virtues are ripened and heightened by a superinduction of divine knowledge. The misery of man proceeds from his being separated from God: This separation is wrought by corruption; his restitution therefore to felicity and integrity, can only be brought about by his reunion to the good from which he is fallen. Plato looks upon this as the only worthy object of man's desire; and in his *Laws* and *Politicks* he intends not to teach us how to erect manufactures, and to increase trade or riches; but how magistrates may be helpful to nations in the manner before-mentioned, and consequently what men are fit to be magistrates. If our author therefore would make use of Plato's doctrine to his end, he ought to have proved that there is a family in every nation, to the chief of which, and successively to the next in blood, God does ever reveal and infuse such a knowledge of himself, as may render him a light to others; and failing in this, all that he says is to no purpose.

The weakness in which we are born, renders us unable to attain this good of ourselves: we want help in all things, especially in the greatest. The fierce barbarity of a loose multitude, bound by no law, and regulated by no discipline, is wholly repugnant to it: Whilst every man fears his neighbour, and has no other defence than his own strength, he must live in that perpetual anxiety which is equally contrary to that happiness, and that sedate temper of mind which is required for the search of it. The first step towards the cure of this pestilent evil, is for many to join in one body, that everyone may be protected by the united force of all; and the various talents that men possess, may by good discipline be rendered useful to the whole; as the meanest piece of wood or stone being placed by a wise architect, conduces to the beauty of the most glorious building. But every man bearing in his own breast affections, passions, and vices that are repugnant to this end, and no man owing any submission to his neighbour; none will subject the correction or restriction of themselves to another, unless he also submit to the same rule. They are rough pieces of timber or stone, which 'tis necessary to cleave, saw, or cut: This is the work of a skillful builder, and he only is capable of erecting a great fabrick, who is so: Magistrates are political architects; and they only can perform the work incumbent on them, who excel in political virtues. Nature, in variously framing the minds of men, according to the variety

---

[8] Plato de Leg. [Several of these points are made in *Laws*, bk. 4.]

of uses in which they may be employ'd, in order to the institution and preservation of civil societies, must be our guide, in allotting to every one his proper work. And Plato observing this variety, affirms, that the laws of nature cannot be more absurdly violated, than by giving the government of a people to such, as do not excel others in those arts and virtues that tend to the ultimate ends for which governments are instituted. By this means those who are slaves by nature, or rendered so by their vices, are often set above those that God and nature had fitted for the highest commands; and societies which subsist only by order, fall into corruption, when all order is so preposterously inverted, and the most extreme confusion introduced. This is an evil that Solomon detested: *Folly is set in great dignity, and the rich sit in low places: I have seen servants upon horses, and princes walking as servants upon the earth.*[9] They who understand Solomon's language, will easily see, that the rich, and the princes he means, are such only who are rich in virtue and wisdom, and who ought to be preferred for those qualities: And when he says, a servant that reigneth is one of the *three things the earth cannot bear*, he can only mean such as deserve to be servants; for when they reign, they do not serve, but are served by others: which perfectly agrees with what we learn from Plato, and plainly shews, that true philosophy is perfectly conformable with what is taught us by those who were divinely inspired. Therefore tho I should allow to our author, that Aristotle, in those words, *It seems to some, not to be natural for one man to be lord of all the citizens, since the city consists of equals,*[10] did speak the opinion of others rather than his own; and should confess that he and his master Plato, did acknowledge a natural inequality among men, it would be nothing to his purpose: for the inequality, and the rational superiority due to some, or to one, by reason of that inequality, did not proceed from blood or extraction, and had nothing patriarchical in it; but consisted solely in the virtues of the persons, by which they were rendered more able than others to perform their duty, for the good of the society. Therefore if these authors are to be trusted, whatsoever place a man is advanced to in a city, 'tis not for his own sake, but for that of the city; and we are not to ask who was his father, but what are his virtues in relation to it. This induces a necessity of distinguishing between a simple and a relative inequality; for if it were possible for a man to have great virtues, and yet no way beneficial to the society of which he is, or to have some one vice that renders them useless, he could have no pretence to a magistratical power more than any other. They who are equally free, may equally enjoy their freedom; but the

[9] Eccl. 10.7.   [10] [Aristotle, *Politics*, bk. 3, 1287a.]

powers that can only be executed by such as are endowed with great wisdom, justice and valour, can belong to none, nor be rightly conferred upon any, except such as excel in those virtues. And if no such can be found, all are equally by turns to participate of the honours annexed to magistracy; and law, which is said to be written reason, cannot justly exalt those, whom nature, which is reason, hath depressed, nor depress those whom nature hath exalted. It cannot make kings slaves, nor slaves kings, without introducing that evil, which, if we believe Solomon, and the spirit by which he spoke, *the earth cannot bear.*[11] This may discover what lawgivers deserve to be reputed wise or just; and what decrees or sanctions ought to be reputed laws. Aristotle proceeding by this rule, rather tells us, who is naturally a king, than where we should find him; and after having given the highest praises to this true natural king and his government, he sticks not to declare that of one man, in virtue equal or inferior to others, to be a mere tyranny, even the worst of all, as it is the corruption of the best (or, as our author calls it, the most divine), and such as can be fit only for those barbarous and stupid nations, which, tho bearing the shape of men, are little different from beasts. Whoever therefore will from Aristotle's words infer, that nature has designed one man, or succession of men, to be lords of every country, must shew that man to be endowed with all the virtues, that render him fit for so great an office, which he does not bear for his own pleasure, glory or profit, but for the good of those that are under him; and if that be not done, he must look after other patrons than Aristotle for his opinion.

Plato does more explicitly say, that the civil or politick man, the shepherd, father, or king of a people, is the same, designed for the same work, enabled to perform it by the excellency of the same virtues, and made perfect by the infusion of the divine wisdom. This is Plato's monarch, and I confess, that wheresoever he does appear in the world, he ought to be accounted as sent from God for the good of that people. His government is the best that can be set up among men; and if assurance can be given, that his children, heirs or successors, shall forever be equal to him in the above-mentioned virtues, it were a folly and a sin to bring him under the government of any other, or to an equality with them, since God had made him to excel them all; and 'tis better for them to be ruled by him, than to follow their own judgment. This is that which gives him the preference: *He is wise through the knowledge of the truth, and thereby becomes good, happy, pure, beautiful and perfect. The divine light shining forth in him, is a guide to others; and he is a fit leader of a people to the good*

[11] [Proverbs 30:21–22.]

that he enjoys.[12] If this can be expressed by words in fashion, this is his prerogative; this is the *royal charter* given to him by God; and to him only, who is so adapted for the performance of his office. He that should pretend to the same privileges, without the same abilities to perform the works for which they are granted, would exceed the folly of a child, that takes upon him a burden which can only be borne by a giant; or the madness of one who presumes to give physick, and understands not the art of a physician, thereby drawing guilt upon himself, and death upon his patient. It were as vain to expect that a child should carry the giant's burden, and that an ignorant man should give wholsome physick, as that one who lives void of all knowledge of good, should conduct men to it. Whensoever therefore such a man, as is above-described, does not appear, nature and reason instruct us to seek him or them who are most like to him; and to lay such burdens upon them as are proportionable to their strength; which is as much as to say, to prefer every man according to his merit, and assign to every one such works as he seems able to accomplish.

But that Plato and Aristotle may neither be thought unreasonably addicted to monarchy; nor, wholly rejecting it, to have talked in vain of a monarch, that is not to be found; 'tis good to consider that this is not a fiction. Moses, Joshua, Samuel, and others, were such as they define; and were made to be such, by that communion with God which Plato requires: And he in all his writings, intending the institution of such a discipline as should render men happy, wise and good, could take no better way to bring his countrymen to it, than by shewing them that wisdom, virtue, and purity only could make a natural difference among men.

'Tis not my work to justify these opinions of Plato and his scholar Aristotle: They were men, and, tho wise and learned, subject to error. If they erred in these points, it hurts not me, nor the cause I maintain, since I make no other use of their books, than to shew the impudence and prevarication of those, who gather small scraps out of good books, to justify their assertions concerning such kings as are known amongst us; which being examined, are found to be wholly against them; and if they were followed, would destroy their persons and power.

But our author's intention being only to cavil, or to cheat such as are not versed in the writings of the ancients, or at least to cause those who do not make truth their guide, to waver and fluctuate in their discourses,

---

[12] Plato in Alcib. 1. 1, 2. [Sidney paraphrases such passages as *Alcibiades I*, 133e–134e, and *Alcibiades II*, 145e–147b and 150a, in Plato, *Charmides, Alcibiades I, II* . . . (Loeb, 1927).]

he does in one page say, *That without doubt Moses his history of the Creation guided these philosophers in finding out this lineal subjection:* And in the next affirms, *That the ignorance of the Creation, occasioned several amongst the heathen philosophers to think that men met together as herds of cattle:*[13] Whereas they could not have been ignorant of the Creation, if they had read the books that Moses writ; and having that knowledge, they could not think that men met together as herds of cattle. However, I deny that any of them did ever dream of that lineal subjection, derived from the first parents of mankind, or that any such thing was to be learnt from Moses. Tho they did not perhaps justly know the beginning of mankind, they did know the beginnings and progress of the governments under which they lived; and being assured that the first kingdoms had been those, which they called *heroum regna*, that is, of those who had been most beneficial to mankind; that their descendants in many places degenerating from their virtues, had given nations occasion to set up *aristocracies;* and they also falling into corruption, to institute *democracies*, or mixed governments; did rightly conclude, that every nation might justly order their own affairs according to their own pleasure, and could have neither obligation nor reason to set up one man or a few above others, unless it did appear to them that they had more of those virtues, which conduce to the good of civil societies, than the rest of their brethren.

Our author's cavil upon Aristotle's opinion, *That those who are wise in mind are by nature fitted to be lords, and those who are strong of body ordained to obey,*[14] deserves no answer; for he plainly falsifies the text: Aristotle speaks only of those qualities which are required for every purpose; and means no more, than that such as are eminent in the virtues of the mind deserve to govern, tho they do not excel in bodily strength; and that they who are strong of body, tho of little understanding, and incapable of commanding, may be useful in executing the commands of others: But is so far from denying that one man may excel in all the perfections of mind and body, that he acknowledges him only to be a king by nature who does so, both being required for the full performance of his duty. And if this be not true, I suppose that one who is like Agrippa Posthumus, *corporis viribus stolidé ferox,*[15] may be fit to govern many nations; and Moses or Samuel, if they naturally wanted bodily strength, or that it decayed by age, might justly be made slaves, which is a discovery worthy our author's invention.

---

[13] [*Patriarcha*, ch. 12, p. 80.]

[14] [*Patriarcha*, p. 80; Aristotle, *Politics*, bk. 1, 1252a.]

[15] ["Stupidly daring in his bodily strength." Tacitus, *Annals*, bk. 1, ch. 3.]

SECTION 2

Every Man that hath Children,
hath the right of a Father, and is capable of preferment
in a Society composed of many.

I AM not concerned in making good what Suarez says: A Jesuit may speak that which is true; but it ought to be received, as from the Devil, cautiously, lest mischief be hid under it: and Sir Robert's frequent prevarications upon the Scripture, and many good authors, give reason to suspect he may have falsified one, that few Protestants read, if it served to his purpose; and not mentioning the place, his fraud cannot easily be discovered, unless it be by one who has leisure to examine all his vastly voluminous writings. But as to the point in question, that pains may be saved; there is nothing that can be imputed to the invention of Suarez; for, *that Adam had only an oeconomical, not a political power,*[1] is not the voice of a Jesuit, but of nature and common sense: for politick signifying no more in Greek, than civil in Latin, 'tis evident there could be no civil power, where there was no civil society; and there could be none between him and his children, because a civil society is composed of equals, and fortified by mutual compacts, which could not be between him and his children, at least, if there be anything of truth in our author's doctrine, *That all children do perpetually and absolutely depend upon the will of their father.*[2] Suarez seems to have been of another opinion; and observing the benefits we receive from parents, and the veneration we owe to them to be reciprocal, he could not think any duty could extend farther than the knowledge of the relation upon which it was grounded; and makes a difference between the power of a father, before and after his children are made free; that is in truth, before and after they are able to provide for themselves, and to deliver their parents from the burden of taking care of them: which will appear rational to any who are able to distinguish between what a man of fifty years old, subsisting by himself, and having a family of his own, or a child of eight doth owe to his father: The same reason that obliges a child to submit entirely to the will of his parents, when he is utterly ignorant of all things, does permit, and often enjoin men of ripe age to examine the commands they receive before they obey

---

[1] [*Patriarcha*, ch. 11, p. 78. "Oeconomical" means "household-governing," the root meaning of "economic."]

[2] [*Patriarcha*, ch. 11, pp. 75–77. Filmer attacks Suarez' *Tractatus de Legibus*, bk. 3, ch. 2.]

them; and 'tis not more plain that I owe all manner of duty, affection, and respect to him that did beget and educate me, than that I can owe nothing on any such account to one that did neither.

This may have been the opinion of Suarez: but I can hardly believe such a notion, as, *that Adam in process of time might have servants,*[3] could proceed from any other brain than our author's; for if he had lived to this day, he could have had none under him but his own children; and if a family be not compleat without servants, his must always have been defective; and his kingdom must have been so too, if that has such a resemblance to a family as our author fancies. This is evident, that a hard father may use his children as servants, or a rebellious, stubborn son may deserve to be so used; and a gentle and good master may shew that kindness to faithful and well-deserving servants, which resembles the sweetness of a fatherly rule: but neither of them can change their nature; a son can never grow to be a servant, nor a servant to be a son. If a family therefore be not compleat, unless it consist of children and servants, it cannot be like to a kingdom or city, which is composed of freemen and equals: Servants may be in it, but are not members of it. As truth can never be repugnant to justice, 'tis impossible this should be a prejudice to the paternal rule, which is most just; especially when a grateful remembrance of the benefits received, doth still remain, with a necessary and perpetual obligation of repaying them in all affection and duty: whereas the care of ever providing for their families, as they did probably increase in the time of our first long living fathers, would have been an insupportable burden to parents, if it had been incumbent on them. We do not find that Adam exercised any such power over Cain, when he had slain Abel, as our author fancies to be regal: The murderer went out, and built a city for himself, and called it by the name of his first-born. And we have not the least reason to believe, that after Adam's death Cain had any dominion over his brethren, or their posterity; or any one of them over him and his. He feared that whosoever saw him would kill him, which language does not agree with the rights belonging to the haughty title of heir apparent to the dominion of the whole earth. The like was practiced by Noah and his sons, who set up colonies for themselves: but lived as private men in obscure places, whilst their children of the fourth or fifth generation, especially of the youngest and accursed son, were great and powerful kings, as is fully proved in the first chapter.

Tho this had been otherwise, it would have no effect upon us; for no

---

[3] [*Patriarcha*, ch. 11, p. 74.]

argument drawn from the examples of Shem, Ham, and Japheth, if they and their children had continued under the dominion of Noah as long as he lived, can oblige me to resign myself and all my concernments absolutely into the hands of one who is not my father. But when the contrary is evidently true in them, and their next ensuing generations, 'tis an admirable boldness in our author to think of imposing upon us for an eternal and universal law (when the knowledge of our first progenitors is utterly extinguished) that which was not at all regarded by those, who could not be ignorant of their own original, or the duty thereby incumbent upon them, or their immediate fathers then living, to whom the rights must have belonged, if there had been any such thing in nature, or that they had been of any advantage to them: whereas in truth, if there had been such a law in the beginning, it must have vanished of itself, for want of being exercised in the beginning, and could not possibly be revived after four thousand years, when no man in the world can possibly know to whom the universal right of dominion over the whole world or particular nations does belong; for 'tis in vain to speak of a right, when no one man can have a better title to it than any other. But there being no precept in the Scripture for it, and the examples directed or approved by God himself and his most faithful servants, being inconsistent with, and contrary to it, we may be sure there never was any such thing; and that men being left to the free use of their own understanding, may order and dispose of their own affairs as they think fit. No man can have a better title than another, unless for his personal virtues; every man that in the judgment of those concerned excels in them, may be advanced: and those nations that through mistake set up such as are unworthy, or do not take right measures in providing for a succession of men worthy, and other things necessary to their welfare, may be guilty of great folly, to their own shame and misery; but can do no injustice to any people, in relation to an hereditary right, which can be naturally in none.

SECTION 3

Government is not instituted for the good of the Governor, but of the Governed; and Power is not an Advantage, but a Burden.

THE follies with which our author endeavours to corrupt and trouble the world, seem to proceed from his fundamental mistakes of the ends for which governments are constituted; and from an opinion, that an excessive power is good for the governor, or the diminution of it a prejudice: whereas common sense teaches, and all good men acknowledge, that governments are not set up for the advantage, profit, pleasure or glory of one or a few men, but for the good of the society. For this reason Plato and Aristotle find no more certain way of distinguishing between a lawful king and a tyrant, than that the first seeks to procure the common good, and the other his own pleasure or profit; and doubt not to declare, that he who according to his institution was the first, destroys his own being, and degenerates into the latter, if he deflect from that rule: He that was the best of men, becomes the worst; and the father or shepherd of the people makes himself their enemy. And we may from hence collect, that in all controversies concerning the power of magistrates, we are not to examine what conduces to their profit or glory, but what is good for the publick.

His second error is no less gross and mischievous than the first; and that absolute power to which he would exalt the chief magistrate, would be burdensome, and desperately dangerous if he had it. The highest places are always slippery: Men's eyes dazzle when they are carried up to them; and all falls from them are mortal. Few kings or tyrants, says Juvenal, go down to the grave in peace;[1] and he did not imprudently couple them together, because in his time few or no kings were known who were not tyrants. Dionysius thought no man left a tyranny, till he was drawn out by the heels. But Tacitus says, *Nescit quam grave & intolerandum sit cuncta regendi onus.*[2] Moses could not bear it: Gideon would not accept of any resemblance of it. The moral sense of Jotham's wise

---

[1] Sine caede & sanguine pauci/Descendunt reges, & sicca morte tyranni. Juven. Sat. ["Without slaughter and blood few kings descend (into Hades), and few tyrants die a dry (i.e., bloodless) death." Juvenal, *Satire* 10, li. 112.]

[2] ["He did not know how difficult and insupportable the burden of universal rule is." Tacitus, *Annals*, bk. 1, ch. 11.]

parable is eternal: The bramble coveted the power, which the vine, olive and fig tree refused.[3] The worst and basest of men are ambitious of the highest places, which the best and wisest reject; or if some, who may be otherwise well qualified—

[In this place two pages are wanting in the original manuscript.]

—as the fittest to be followed by mankind. If these philosophers and divines deserve credit, Nimrod, Ninus, Pharaoh, and the rest of that accursed crew, did not commit such excesses as were condemned by God, and abhorred by good men; but gaining to themselves the glorious character of his vicegerents, left their practices as a perpetual law to all succeeding generations; whereby the world, and every part of it, would be forever exposed to the violence, cruelty and madness of the most wicked men that it should produce. But if these opinions comprehend an extravagancy of wickedness and madness, that was not known among men, till some of these wretches presumed to attempt the increase of that corruption under which mankind groans, by adding fuel to the worst of all vices; we may safely return to our propositions, that God having established no such authority as our author fancies, nations are left to the use of their own judgment, in making provision for their own welfare: That there is no lawful magistrate over any of them, but such as they have set up; that in creating them, they do not seek the advantage of their magistrate, but their own: and having found that an absolute power over a people, is a burden which no man can bear; and that no wise or good man ever desired it; from thence conclude, that it is not good for any to have it, nor just for any to affect it, tho it were personally good for himself; because he is not exalted to seek his own good, but that of the publick.

SECTION 4

The Paternal Right devolves to, and is inherited by all the Children.

THO the perversity of our author's judgment and nature may have driven him into the most gross errors, 'tis not amiss to observe, that many of those delivered by him, proceed from his ignorance of the most important differences between father and lord, king and tyrant;

[3] [Judges 9:7–15.]

which are so evident and irreconcilable, that one would have thought no man could be so stupid, as not to see it impossible for one and the same man, at the same time, to be father and master, king and tyrant, over the same persons. But lest he should think me too scrupulous, or too strict in inquiring after truth, I intend for the present to waive that inquiry, and to seek what was good for Adam or Noah: What we have reason to believe they desired to transmit to their posterity, and to take it for a perpetual law in its utmost extent; which I think will be of no advantage to our author: for this authority, which was universal during their lives, must necessarily after their decease be divided, as an inheritance, into as many parcels as they had children. The Apostle says, *If children, then heirs, heirs of God, and joint heirs with Christ;*[1] which alluding to the laws and customs of nations, could have been of no force, unless it had been true and known to be so. But if children are heirs, or joint heirs, whatsoever authority Adam or Noah had, is inherited by every man in the world; and that title of heir which our author so much magnifies, as if it were annexed to one single person, vanishes into nothing; or else the words of the Apostle could have neither strength nor truth in them, but would be built upon a false foundation, which may perhaps agree with our author's divinity.

Yet if the Apostle had not declared himself so fully in this point, we might easily have seen that Adam and Noah did leave their children in that equality; for fathers are ever understood to embrace all their children with equal affection, till the discovery of personal virtues or vices make a difference. But the personal virtues, that give a reasonable preference of one before another, or make him more fit to govern than the others, cannot appear before he is, nor can be annexed to any one line: Therefore the father cannot be thought to have given to one man, or his descendants, the government of his brethren and their descendants.

Besides, tho the law of England may make one man to be sole heir of his father, yet the laws of God and nature do not so. All the children of Noah were his heirs: The land promised to Abraham, Isaac and Jacob, was equally divided among their children. If the children of Joseph made two tribes, it was not as the first born, but by the will of Jacob, who adopted Ephraim and Manasseh; and they thereby became his sons, and obtained an inheritance equal to that of the other tribes. The law allowed a double portion to the first-begotten; but this made a difference between brothers only in *proportion*, whereas that between lord and servant, is in *specie*, not in degree. And if our author's opinion might take place, instead

[1] Rom. 8.19. [Actually Romans 8:17.]

of such a division of the common inheritance between brothers, as was made between the children of Jacob, all must continue forever slaves to one lord; which would establish a difference in *specie* between brethren, which nature abhors.

If nature does not make one man lord over his brethren, he can never come to be their lord, unless they make him so, or he subdue them. If he subdue them, it is an act of violence, contrary to right, which may consequently be recovered: If they make him lord, 'tis for their own sakes, not for his; and he must seek their good, not his own, lest, as Aristotle says, he degenerate from a king into a tyrant. He therefore who would persuade us, that the dominion over every nation, does naturally belong to one man, woman or child, at a venture; or to the heir, whatsoever he or she be, as to age, sex, or other qualifications, must prove it good for all nations to be under them. But as reason is our nature, that can never be natural to us that is not rational. Reason gives *paria paribus*,[2] equal power to those who have equal abilities and merit: It allots to everyone the part he is most fit to perform; and this fitness must be equally lasting with the law that allots it. But as it can never be good for great nations, having men amongst them of virtue, experience, wisdom and goodness, to be governed by children, fools, or vicious and wicked persons; and we neither find that the virtues required in such as deserve to govern them, did ever continue in any race of men, nor have reason to believe they ever will, it can never be reasonable to annex the dominion of a nation to any one line. We may take this upon Solomon's word, *Woe to thee, O land, when thy king is a child, and thy princes eat in the morning:*[3] And I wish the experience of all ages, did not make this truth too evident to us. This therefore can never be the work, much less the law of nature; and if there be any such thing in the world, as the dominion over a nation, inseparably united to a man and his family, it can have no other root, than a civil or municipal law, which is not the subject of our discourse.

Moreover, every father's right must cease, when he ceases to be, or be transmitted to those, who being also fathers, have the same title to it. And tho the contrary method of annexing the whole inheritance to one person, or exposing all his brethren to be destroyed by his rage, if they will not submit, may conduce to the enlargement of a proud and violent empire, as in Turkey; where he that gains the power, usually begins his reign with the slaughter of his brothers and nephews: yet it can never

---

[2] [Equal things to equals.]　　　　　　　　[3] Eccl. 10.16.

agree with the piety, gentleness and wisdom of the patriarchs, or the laws of God and nature.

These things being agreed, we need not trouble ourselves with the limits or definition of a family, and as little with the titles given to the head of it: 'Tis all one to us, whether it be confined to one roof and fire, or extended farther; and none but such as are strangers to the practice of mankind, can think that titles of civility have a power to create a right of dominion. Every man in Latin is called *dominus*, unless such as are of the vilest condition, or in a great subjection to those who speak to them; and yet the word strictly taken, relates only to *servus*, for a man is lord only of his servant or slave. The Italians are not less liberal of the titles of *signore* and *padrone*, and the Spaniards of *señor*; but he would be ridiculous in those countries, who thereupon should arrogate to himself a right of dominion over those who are so civil. The vanity of our age seems to carry this point a little higher, especially among the French, who put a great weight upon the word *prince*; but they cannot change the true signification of it; and even in their sense, *prince du sang* signifies no more than a chief man of the royal blood, to whom they pay much respect, because he may come to the crown; as they at Rome do to cardinals, who have the power of chusing popes, and out of whose number, for some ages, they have been chosen. In this sense did Scaevola, when he was apprehended by Porsenna, say, *Trecenti conjuravimus Romanae juventutis principes;*[4] which was never otherwise understood, than of such young citizens as were remarkable amongst their companions. And nothing can be more absurd than to think, if the name of prince had carried an absolute and despotical power with it, that it could belong to three hundred in a city, that possessed no more than a ten miles territory; or that it could have been given to them, whilst they were young, and the most part of their fathers, as is most probable, still living.

I should, like our author, run round in a circle, if I should refute what he says of a regal power in our first parents; or shew, that the regal, where it is, is not absolute as often as he does assert it. But having already proved, that Adam, Noah, Abraham, Isaac, Jacob, &c. enjoyed no such power; transmitted to every one of their sons that which they had, and they became fathers of many great nations, who always continued independent on each other, I leave to our author to prove, when and by what law the right of subdividing the paternal power was stopped, and

---

[4] T. Liv. l. 2. ["Three hundred *principes* (prominent ones) of the Roman youth had con-spired against him." Livy, *History of Rome*, bk. 2, ch. 12.]

how any one or more of their descendants came to have that power over their brethren, which none of their immediate children had over theirs.

His question to Suarez, how and when sons become free, savours more of Jesuitical sophistry, than anything said by the Jesuit;[5] but the solution is easy: for if he mean the respect, veneration and kindness proceeding from gratitude, it ceases only with the life of the father to whom it is due, and the memory of it must last as long as that of the son; and if they had been possessed of such an absolute power as he fancies, it must have ceased with the reasons upon which it was grounded.

First, because the power, of which a father would probably have made a wise and gentle use, could not be rightly trusted in the hands of one who is not a father; and that which tended only to the preservation of all the children, could not be turned to the increase of the pride, luxury and violence of one, to the oppression of others who are equally heirs.

In the second place, societies cannot be instituted, unless the heads of the families that are to compose them, resign so much of their right as seems convenient into the publick stock, to which everyone becomes subject: But that the same power should, at the same time, continue in the true father, and the figurative father, the magistrate; and that the children should owe entire obedience to the commands of both, which may often cross each other, is absurd.

Thirdly, it ceases when it cannot be executed; as when men live to see four or five generations, as many do at this day; because the son cannot tell whether he should obey his father, grandfather, or great-grandfather, and cannot be equally subject to them all; most especially, when they live in divers places, and set up families of their own, as the sons of the patriarchs did: which being observed, I know no place where this paternal power could have any effect, unless in the fabulous Island of Pines; and even there it must have ceased, when he died, who by the inventor of the story, is said to have seen above ten thousand persons issued of his body.[6]

And if it be said, that Noah, Shem, Abraham, &c. consented that their children should go where they thought fit, and provide for themselves; I answer, that the like has been done in all ages, and must be done forever. 'Tis the voice of nature, obeyed, not only by mankind, but by all living creatures; and there is none so stupid as not to understand it. A hen leaves her chickens, when they can seek their own nourishment: A cow looks after her calf no longer, than till it is able to feed: A lion gives over

[5] [*Patriarcha*, ch. 11, p. 77.]

[6] [Henry Neville, *The Isle of Pines* (London, 1668). A strong republican who worked closely with his friend Sidney in Parliament, Neville translated Machiavelli into English and authored republican political tracts.]

hunting for his whelps, when they are able to seek their own prey, and have strength enough to provide what is sufficient for themselves. And the contrary would be an insupportable burden to all living creatures, but especially to men; for the good order that the rational nature delights in, would be overthrown, and civil societies, by which it is best preserved, would never be established.

We are not concerned to examine, whether the political and oeconomical powers be entirely the same, or in what they differ: for that absolute power which he contends for, is purely despotical, different from both, or rather inconsistent with either as to the same subject; and that which the patriarchs exercised, having been equally inherited by their children, and consequently by every one of their posterity, 'tis as much as is required for my purpose of proving the natural, universal liberty of mankind; and I am no way concerned in the question, whether the first parents of mankind had a power of life and death over their children, or not.

SECTION 5

Freemen join together and frame greater or lesser Societies,
and give such Forms to them as best please themselves.

THIS being established, I shall leave Filmer to fight against Suarez or Bellarmine; or to turn one of them against the other, without any concernment in the combat, or the success of it. But since he thereupon raises a question, *Whether the supreme power be so in the people, that there is but one and the same power in all the people of the world; so that no power can be granted, unless all men upon the earth meet, and agree to chuse a governor:*[1] I think it deserves to be answered, and might do it by proposing a question to him; Whether in his opinion, the empire of the whole world doth, by the laws of God and nature, belong to one man, and who that man is? Or, how it came so to be divided, as we have ever known it to have been, without such an injury to the universal monarch, as can never be repaired? But intending to proceed more candidly, and not to trouble myself with Bellarmine or Suarez, I say, that they who place the power in a multitude, understand a multitude composed of

[1] [*Patriarcha*, ch. 13 ("Of Election of Kings
by the Major Part of the People, by Proxy,
by Silent Acceptation"), p. 81.]

freemen, who think it for their convenience to join together, and to establish such laws and rules as they oblige themselves to observe: which multitude, whether it be great or small, has the same right, because ten men are as free as ten millions of men; and tho it may be more prudent in some cases to join with the greater than the smaller number, because there is more strength, it is not so always: But however every man must therein be his own judge, since if he mistake, the hurt is only to himself; and the ten may as justly resolve to live together, frame a civil society, and oblige themselves to laws, as the greatest number of men that ever met together in the world.

Thus we find that a few men assembling together upon the banks of the Tiber, resolved to build a city, and set up a government among themselves: And the multitude that met at Babylon, when their design of building a tower that should reach up to heaven failed, and their language was confounded, divided themselves, as our author says, into seventy two parcels, and by the same right might have divided into more, as their descendants did, into almost an infinite number before the death of their common father Noah. But we cannot find a more perfect picture of freemen, living according to their own will, than in Abraham and Lot; they went together into Canaan, continued together as long as was convenient for them, and parted when their substance did so increase, that they became troublesome to each other. In the like manner Ishmael, Isaac, and Abraham's six sons by Keturah, might have continued together and made one nation; Isaac and Esau, Moab and Ammon might have done so too; or all of them that came of the same stock might have united together; but they did not; and their descendants by the same rule might have subdivided perpetually, if they had thought it expedient for themselves: and if the sons of Jacob did not do the like, 'tis probable they were kept together by the hope of an inheritance promised to them by God, in which we find no shadow of a despotical dominion, affected by one as father or heir to the first father, or reputed to be the heir; but all continued in that fraternal equality, which according to Abraham's words to Lot they ought to do.[2] There was no lord, slave or vassal; no strife was to be among them: They were brethren; they might live together, or separate, as they found it convenient for themselves. By the same law that Abraham and Lot, Moab and Ammon, Ishmael, Isaac, and the sons of Keturah, Jacob, Esau, and their descendants, did divide and set up several governments, every one of their children might have done the like: and the same right remained to their issue, till they had by agreement

---

[2] Gen. 13.

engaged themselves to each other. But if they had no dependence upon each other, and might live together in that fraternal equality which was between Abraham and Lot; or separate, and continue in that separation, or reunite; they could not but have a right of framing such conditions of their reunion as best pleased themselves. By this means every number of men, agreeing together and framing a society, became a compleat body, having all power in themselves over themselves, subject to no other human law than their own. All those that compose the society, being equally free to enter into it or not, no man could have any prerogative above others, unless it were granted by the consent of the whole; and nothing obliging them to enter into this society, but the consideration of their own good; that good, or the opinion of it, must have been the rule, motive and end of all that they did ordain. 'Tis lawful therefore for any such bodies to set up one, or a few men to govern them, or to retain the power in themselves; and he or they who are set up, having no other power but what is so conferred upon them by that multitude, whether great or small, are truly by them made what they are; and by the law of their own creation, are to exercise those powers according to the proportion, and to the ends for which they were given.

These rights, in several nations and ages, have been variously executed, in the establishment of *monarchies, aristocracies, democracies,* or *mixed governments,* according to the variety of circumstances; and the governments have been good or evil, according to the rectitude or pravity of their institution, and the virtue and wisdom, or the folly and vices of those to whom the power was committed: but the end which was ever proposed, being the good of the publick, they only performed their duty, who procured it according to the laws of the society, which were equally valid as to their own magistrates, whether they were few or many.

This might suffice to answer our author's question; but he endeavours further to perplex it, by a fiction of his own brain, *That God gave this power to the whole multitude met, and not to every particular assembly of men:* And expects a proof, *That the whole multitude met, and divided this power which God gave them in gross, by breaking it into parcels, and by appointing a distinct power to each commonwealth.* He also fathers it upon the assertors of liberty; *and does not see,* as he says, *how there can be an election of a magistrate by any commonwealth, that is not an usurpation upon the privilege of the whole world, unless all mankind had met together, and divided the power into parcels which God had given them in gross.*[3] But before I put myself to the trouble of answering that which is but an appendix to a whimsy of his

---

[3] [*Patriarcha,* ch. 13, p. 81.]

own, I may justly ask, what hurt he finds in usurpation, who asserts, that the same obedience is due to all monarchs, whether they come in by inheritance, election or usurpation? If usurpation can give a right to a monarch, why does it not confer the same upon a people? Or rather, if God did in gross confer such a right upon all mankind, and they neither did, nor can meet together by consent to dispose of it for the good of the whole; why should not those who can, and do consent to meet together, agree upon that which seems most expedient to them for the government of themselves? Did God create man under the necessity of wanting government, and all the good that proceeds from it; because at the first all did not, and afterwards all could not meet to agree upon rules? Or did he ever declare, that unless they should use the first opportunity of dividing themselves into such parcels as were to remain unalterable, the right of reigning over everyone shall fall to the first villain that should dare to attempt it? Is it not more consonant to the wisdom and goodness of God, to leave to every nation a liberty of repairing the mischiefs fallen upon them through the omission of their first parents, by setting up governments among themselves, than to lay them under a necessity of submitting to any that should insolently aspire to a domination over them? Is it not more just and reasonable to believe, that the universal right not being executed, devolves upon particular nations, as members of the great body, than that it should become the reward of violence or fraud? Or is it possible that any one man can make himself lord of a people, or parcel of that body, to whom God had given the liberty of governing themselves, by any other means than violence or fraud, unless they did willingly submit to him? If this right be not devolved upon any one man, is not the invasion of it the most outrageous injury that can be done to all mankind, and most particularly to the nation that is enslaved by it? Or if the justice of every government depends necessarily upon an original grant, and a succession certainly deduced from our first fathers, does not he by his own principles condemn all the monarchies of the world, as the most detestable usurpations, since not one of them that we know do any way pretend to it? Or, tho I, who deny any power to be just that is not founded upon consent, may boldly blame usurpation, is it not an absurd and unpardonable impudence in Filmer, to condemn usurpation in a people, when he has declared that the right and power of a father may be gained by usurpation; and that nations in their obedience are to regard the power, not the means by which it was gained? But not to lose more time upon a most frivolous fiction, I affirm, that the liberty which we contend for is granted by God to every man in his own person, in such a manner as may be useful to him and his posterity, and as it was exercised by Noah, Shem, Abraham, Isaac, Jacob, &c. and their children, as has been proved, and not to the vast body of all mankind, which never did meet together since the first age after the Flood, and never could meet to receive any benefit by it.

His next question deserves scorn and hatred, with all the effects of either, if it proceed from malice; tho perhaps he may deserve compassion, if his crime proceed from ignorance: *Was a general meeting of a whole kingdom*, says he, *ever known for the election of a prince?*[4] But if there never was any general meetings of whole nations, or of such as they did delegate and entrust with the power of the whole, how did any man that was elected come to have a power over the whole? Why may not a people meet to chuse a prince, as well as any other magistrate? Why might not the Athenians, Romans, or Carthaginians, have chosen princes as well as archons, consuls, dictators or suffetes, if it had pleased them? Who chose all the Roman kings, except Tarquin the Proud, if the people did not; since their histories testify, that he was the first who took upon him to reign *sine jussu populi?*[5] Who ever heard of a king of the Goths in Spain, that was not chosen by the nobility and people? Or, how could they chuse him, if they did not meet in their persons, or by their deputies, which is the same thing, when a people has agreed it should be so? How did the kings of Sweden come by their power, unless by the like election, till the crown was made hereditary, in the time of Gustavus the First, as a reward of his virtue and service, in delivering that country from the tyranny of the Danes? How did Charles Gustavus come to be king, unless it was by the election of the nobility? He acknowledged by the act of his election, and upon all occasions, that he had no other right to the crown than what they had conferred on him. Did not the like custom prevail in Hungary and Bohemia, till those countries fell under the power of the House of Austria? and in Denmark till the year 1660? Do not the kings of Poland derive their authority from this popular election, which he derides? Does not the style of the oath of allegiance used in the kingdom of Aragon, as it is related by Antonio Perez secretary of state to Philip 2d, shew, that their kings were of their own making? Could they say, *We who are as good as you, make you our king, on condition that you keep and observe our privileges and liberties; and if not, not;*[6] if he did not come in by their election? Were not the Roman emperors in disorderly times chosen

---

[4] [Ibid.]

[5] T. Liv. l. 1. ["Without the order of the people." Livy, *History of Rome*, bk. 1, ch. 49.]

[6] Nos que valemos tanto come vos, os ha-zemos nuestro Rey, con tal que nos guardeys nuestros fueros y libertades, y sino, no. *Relacion. de Ant. Perez.* [*Relaciones de Antonio Pérez* (Leon, Spain, 1592). Pérez was Secretary of State under King Philip II of Spain.]

by the soldiers; and in such as were more regular, by the senate, with the consent of the people?

Our author may say, the whole body of these nations did not meet at their elections; tho that is not always true, for in the infancy of Rome, when the whole people dwelt within the walls of a small city, they did meet for the choice of their kings, as afterwards for the choice of other magistrates. Whilst the Goths, Franks, Vandals and Saxons, lived within the precincts of a camp, they frequently met for the election of a king, and raised upon a target the person they had chosen: but finding that to be inconvenient, or rather impossible, when they were vastly increased in number, and dispersed over all the countries they had conquered, no better way was found, than to institute gemotes, parliaments, diets, cortes, assemblies of estates, or the like, to do that which formerly had been performed by themselves; and when a people is, by mutual compact, joined together in a civil society, there is no difference as to right, between that which is done by them all in their own persons, or by some deputed by all, and acting according to the powers received from all.

If our author was ignorant of these things, which are the most common in all histories, he might have spared the pains of writing upon more abstruse points; but 'tis a stupendous folly in him, to presume to raise doctrines depending upon the universal law of God and nature, without examining the only law that ever God did in a publick manner give to man. If he had looked into it, he might have learnt, that all Israel was, by the command of God, assembled at Mizpeh to chuse a king, and did chuse Saul:[7] He being slain, all Judah came to Hebron, and made David their king;[8] after the death of Ishbosheth, all the tribes went to Hebron, and anointed him king over them, and he made a covenant with them before the Lord.[9] When Solomon was dead, all Israel met together in Shechem, and ten tribes disliking the proceedings of Rehoboam, rejected him, and made Jeroboam their king.[10] The same people in the time of the judges, had general assemblies, as often as occasion did require, to set up a judge, make war, or the like: and the several tribes had their assemblies to treat of businesses relating to themselves. The histories of all nations, especially of those that have peopled the best parts of Europe, are so full of examples in this kind, that no man can question them, unless he be brutally ignorant, or maliciously contentious. The great matters among the Germans were transacted *omnium consensu. De minoribus*

[7] 1 Sam. 10.
[8] 2 Sam. 2.
[9] 2 Sam. 5.
[10] 1 King. 12.

consultant principes; de majoribus omnes.[11] The *mickelgemote* among the Saxons was an assembly of the whole people: The *baronagium* is truly said to be the same, in as much as it comprehended all the freemen, that is, all the people; for the difference between *civis* and *servus* is irreconcilable; and no man, whilst he is a servant, can be a member of a commonwealth; for he that is not in his own power, cannot have a part in the government of others. All the forementioned northern nations had the like customs among them: The governments they had were so instituted. The utmost that any now remaining pretends to, is, to derive their right from them: If, according to Filmer, these first assemblies could not confer it upon the first, they had none: Such as claim under them, can inherit none from those that had none; and there can be no right in all the governments we so much venerate; and nothing can tend more to their overthrow than the reception of our author's doctrine.

Tho any one instance would be sufficient to overthrow his general negative proposition (for a rule is not generally true, if there be any just exception against it) I have alleged many, and find it so easy to increase the number, that there is no nation, whose original we know, out of whose histories I will not undertake to produce the like: but I have not been solicitous precisely to distinguish, which nations have acted in their own persons, and which have made use of delegates; nor in what times they have changed from one way to the other: for if any have acted by themselves, the thing is possible; and whatsoever is done by delegated powers, must be referred to their principals; for none can give to any a power which they have not in themselves.

He is graciously pleased to confess, That *when men are assembled by a human power, that power that doth assemble them, may also limit the manner of the execution of that power, &c. But in assemblies that take their authority from the law of nature, it is not so; for what liberty or freedom is due to any man by the law of nature, no inferior power can alter, limit or diminish: No one man, or multitude of men, can give away the natural right of another, &c.*[12] These are strong lines, and such as, if there be any sense in them, utterly overthrow all our author's doctrine; for if any assembly of men did ever take their authority from the law of nature, it must be of such, as remaining in the entire fruition of their natural liberty, and restrained by no contract, meet together to deliberate of such matters as concern

[11] C. Tacit. de mor. Germ. [". . . by the consent of all. Concerning minor things, they consult the leading men; concerning major things, everyone." Tacitus, *De origine et moribus Germanorum,* also known as *Germania,* ch. 11, in Tacitus, *Agricola, Germania, Dialogus* (Loeb, 1970).]

[12] [*Patriarcha,* ch. 13, p. 82.]

themselves; and if they can be restrained by no one man, or number of men, they may dispose of their own affairs as they think fit. But because no one of them is obliged to enter into the society that the rest may constitute, he cannot enjoy the benefit of that society unless he enter into it: He may be gone, and set up for himself, or set up another with such as will agree with him. But if he enter into the society, he is obliged by the laws of it; and if one of those laws be, that all things should be determined by the plurality of voices, his assent is afterwards comprehended in all the resolutions of that plurality. Reuben or Simeon might, according to the laws of nature, have divided themselves from their brethren, as well as Lot from Abraham, or Ishmael and the sons of Keturah from Isaac; but when they, in hopes of having a part in the inheritance promised to their fathers, had joined with their brethren, a few of their descendants could not have a right, by their dissent, to hinder the resolutions of the whole body, or such a part of it as by the first agreement was to pass for an act of the whole. And the Scripture teaches us, that when the lot was fallen upon Saul, they who despised him were styled *men of Belial;*[13] and the rest, after his victory over the Ammonites, would have slain them if he had permitted. In the like manner, when a number of men met together to build Rome, any man who had disliked the design, might justly have refused to join in it; but when he had entered into the society, he could not by his vote invalidate the acts of the whole, nor destroy the rights of Romulus, Numa, and the others, who by the senate and people were made kings; nor those of the other magistrates, who after their expulsion were legally created.

This is as much as is required to establish the natural liberty of mankind in its utmost extent, and cannot be shaken by our author's surmise, *That a gap is thereby opened for every seditious multitude to raise a new commonwealth:*[14] For till the commonwealth be established, no multitude can be seditious, because they are not subject to any humane law; and sedition implies an unjust and disorderly opposition of that power which is legally established; which cannot be when there is none, nor by him who is not a member of the society that makes it; and when it is made, such as entered into it, are obliged to the laws of it.

This shewing the root and foundation of civil powers, we may judge of the use and extent of them, according to the letter of the law, or the true intentional meaning of it; both which declare them to be purely human ordinances, proceeding from the will of those who seek their own good; and may certainly infer, that since all multitudes are composed of

---

[13] 1 Sam. 10.   [14] [*Patriarcha*, ch. 13, p. 81.]

such as are under some contract, or free from all, no man is obliged to enter into those contracts against his own will, nor obliged by any to which he does not assent: Those multitudes that enter into such contracts, and thereupon form civil societies, act according to their own will: Those that are engaged in none, take their authority from the law of nature; their rights cannot be limited or diminished by any one man, or number of men; and consequently whoever does it, or attempts the doing of it, violates the most sacred laws of God and nature.

His cavils concerning proxies, and the way of using them, deserve no answer, as relating only to one sort of men amongst us, and can have no influence upon the laws of nature, or the proceedings of assemblies, acting according to such rules as they set to themselves. In some places they have voted all together in their own persons, as in Athens: In others by tribes, as in Rome: Sometimes by delegates, when the number of the whole people is so great, that no one place can contain them, as in the parliaments, diets, general assemblies of estates, long used in the great kingdoms of Europe. In other parts many cities are joined together in leagues, as anciently the Achaeans, Aetolians, Samnites, Tuscans; and in these times the states of Holland, and cantons of Switzerland: but our author not regarding such matters, in pursuance of his folly, with an ignorance as admirable as his stupidity, repeats his challenge, *I ask*, says he, *but one example out of the history of the whole world; let the commonwealth be named, wherever the multitude, or so much as the major part of it, consented either by voice or procuration to the election of a prince;*[15] not observing, that if an answer could not be given, he did overthrow the rights of all the princes that are, or ever have been in the world: for if the liberty of one man cannot be limited or diminished by one, or any number of men, and none can give away the right of another, 'tis plain that the ambition of one man, or of many a faction of citizens, or the mutiny of an army, cannot give a right to any over the liberties of a whole nation. Those who are so set up, have their root in violence or fraud, and are rather to be accounted robbers and pirates, than magistrates. Leo Africanus observing in his history, that since the extinction of Mahomet's race (to whom his countrymen thought God had given the empire of the world) their princes did not come in by the consent of those nations which they governed, says, that they are esteemed thieves; and that on this account, the most honourable men among the Arabians and Moors, scorn to eat, drink, or make alliances with them:[16] and if the case were as general as

[15] [Ibid., p. 82.]

[16] Leonis Afr. hist. Africae. [Johannes Leo, the African, *A Geographical History of Africa* (orig. in Arabic; trans. London: G. Bishop, 1600).]

that author makes it, no better rule could be anywhere followed by honourable and worthy men. But a good cause must not be lost by the fault of an ill advocate; the rights of kings must not perish, because Filmer knows not how to defend, or does maliciously betray them. I have already proved that David, and divers of the judges, were chosen by all Israel; Jeroboam by ten tribes; all the kings of Rome, except Tarquin the Proud, by the whole city. I may add many examples of the Saxons in our own country: Ine and Offa were made kings, *omnium consensu:*[17] These *all* are expressed plainly by the words, *archiepiscopis, episcopis, abbatibus, senatoribus, ducibus & populo terrae.*[18] Egbert and Ethelward came to the crown by the same authority, *omnium consensu rex creatur.*[19] Ethelwolf the Monk, *necessitate cogente factus est rex, & consensus publicus in regem dari petiit.* Ethelstan, tho a bastard, *electus est magno consensu optimatum, & a populo consalutatus.*[20] In the like manner Edwin's government being disliked, they chose Edgar, *unanimi omnium conspiratione; Edwino dejecto, eligerunt Deo dictante Edgarum in regem, & annuente populo;*[21] And in another place, *Edgarus ab omni Anglorum populo electus est.*[22] Ironside being dead, Canute was received by the general consent of all; *Juraverunt illi, quod eum regem sibi eligere vellent: foedus etiam cum principibus & omni populo ipse, & illi cum ipso percusserunt.*[23]

[17] Mat. Paris. ["By the consent of all." Found in reference to Offa in Roger of Wendover, *Flowers of History*, 2 vols. (written early 1400s; the 1849 trans. repr. New York: AMS Press, 1968), vol. 1, p. 382. Sidney found this passage in his edition of Matthew Paris, who had copied it directly from Roger of Wendover's *Flowers*. (See note 22 below.)]

[18] ["By the archbishops, bishops, abbots, elders, dukes, and people of the land." Sir Henry Spelman, *Concilia, decreta, leges, constitutiones, in re ecclesiarum orbis Britannici* (London: Warren, 1664), p. 300, from the Council of Calchuth of 787.]

[19] Guil. Malms. Polid. ["By the consent of all he was made king." William of Malmesbury, *Chronicle of the Kings of England* (written early 1100s; the 1847 trans. repr. New York: AMS Press, 1968), p. 95. Polydorus Vergilius, *English History* (Basil, 1534; the 1846 trans. repr. New York: AMS Press, 1968), bk. 5, p. 189. See p. 376, n. 16.]

[20] Polid. Huntingd. ["Under compulsion of necessity he was made king, and popular consent demanded that he assume the kingship." The first part of this quotation is from Henry of Huntingdon, *Chronicle* (written mid-1100s; the 1853 trans. repr. New York: AMS Press, 1968), p. 151. The second part

of the quotation was not located. "Polid." is quoted in the next sentence.]

[21] ["Was chosen by overwhelming agreement of the nobles, and hailed (as king) by the people." William of Malmesbury, *Chronicle*, bk. 2, ch. 6, p. 128; Polydorus Vergilius, *English History*, bk. 6, p. 231.]

[22] Mat. West. ["By the agreement of all, without exception, Edwin having been removed, they elected Edgar as king at the command of God, and, with the consent of the people. . . ." The passage goes on to tell how the realm was divided among Edgar's brothers. "Edgar was elected by all the English people." Roger of Wendover, *Flowers of History*, in Sidney's day ascribed to "Matthew Westminster," vol. 1 (the years 957 and 959).]

[23] Hoveden. Florent. ["They swore an oath that they desired to choose him their king: he also struck an agreement with the leaders and the whole people; and they struck one with him." Roger de Hoveden, *Annals*, 2 vols. (written late 1100s; the 1853 trans. repr. New York: AMS Press, 1968), vol. 1, p. 103. Florence of Worcester, *Chronicle* (written c. 1100; the 1854 trans. repr. New York: AMS Press, 1968), pp. 132–133.]

Whereupon, *omnium consensu super totam Angliam Canutus coronatur.*[24] *Hardicanutus gaudenter ab omnibus suscipitur & electus est.*[25] The same author says that Edward the Confessor *electus est in regem ab omni populo:*[26] And another, *omnium electione in Edwardum concordatur.*[27] Tho the name of Conqueror be odiously given to William the Norman, he had the same title to the crown with his predecessors, *in magna exultatione a clero & populo susceptus, & ab omnibus rex acclamatus.*[28] I cannot recite all the examples of this kind, that the history of almost all nations furnishes, unless I should make a volume in bulk not inferior to the book of martyrs: But those which I have mentioned out of the sacred, Roman, and English history, being more than sufficient to answer our author's challenge, I take liberty to add, that tho there could not be one example produced of a prince, or any other magistrate, chosen by the general consent of the people, or by the major part of them, it could be of no advantage to the cause he has undertaken to maintain: For when a people hath either indefinitely, or under certain conditions and limitations, resigned their power into the hands of a certain number of men; or agreed upon rules, according to which persons should, from time to time, be deputed for the management of their affairs, the acts of those persons, if their power be without restrictions, are of the same value as the acts of the whole nation, and the assent of every individual man is comprehended in them. If the power be limited, whatsoever is done according to that limitation, has the same authority. If it do therefore appear (as is testified by the laws and histories of all our northern nations) that the power of every people is either wholly, or to such a degree as is necessary for creating kings, granted to their several gemotes, diets, cortes, assemblies of estates, parliaments, and the like, all the kings that they have anywhere, or at any time chosen, do reign by the same authority, and have the same right, as if every individual man of those nations had assented to their election. But that these gemotes, diets, and other assemblies of state, have everywhere had such powers, and executed them by rejecting or setting up kings; and that the kings now in being among us have received their beginning from such acts, has been fully proved, and is so plain in

---

[24] Abbas Croyl. Huntingd. ["By the consent of all Canute was crowned (king) over all England." Abbot Ingulf, *Chronicle of the Abbey of Croyland* (1854; repr. New York: AMS Press, 1968), p. 116.]

[25] ["Hardicanute was gladly accepted by all and was elected." Roger de Hoveden, *Annals,* vol. 1, p. 109.]

[26] ["Was chosen king by all the people." Henry of Huntingdon, *Chronicle*, p. 202.]

[27] ["The choice of Edward was agreed to by all." Ingulf, *Chronicle*, p. 125.]

[28] ["In great exultation he was accepted by the clergy and people, and was acclaimed king by all." Roger of Wendover, *Flowers of History*, vol. 1, p. 333. Several of the old Anglo-Saxon chroniclers cited by Sidney in this section were available to him in a collection published by Henry Savile, *Rerum Anglicarum scriptores post Bedam* (London, 1596).]

itself, that none but those who are grossly stupid or impudent can deny it: which is enough to shew that all kings are not set up by violence, deceit, faction of a few powerful men, or the mutinies of armies; but from the consent of such multitudes, as joining together, frame civil societies; and either in their own persons at general assemblies, or by their delegates, confer a just and legal power upon them; which our author rejecting, he does, as far as in him lies, prove them all to be usurpers and tyrants.

SECTION 6

They who have a right of chusing a King, have the right
of making a King.

THO the right of magistrates do essentially depend upon the consent of those they govern, it is hardly worth our pains to examine, *Whether the silent acceptation of a governor by part of the people be an argument of their concurring in the election of him; or by the same reason the tacit consent of the whole commonwealth may be maintained:*[1] for when the question is concerning right, fraudulent surmises are of no value; much less will it from thence follow, *that a prince commanding by succession, conquest, or usurpation, may be said to be elected by the people;*[2] for evident marks of dissent are often given: Some declare their hatred; others murmur more privately; many oppose the governour or government, and succeed according to the measure of their strength, virtue, or fortune. Many would resist, but cannot; and it were ridiculous to say, that the inhabitants of Greece, the kingdom of Naples, or duchy of Tuscany, do tacitly assent to the government of the Great Turk, king of Spain, or duke of Florence; when nothing is more certain than that those miserable nations abhor the tyrannies they are under; and if they were not mastered by a power that is much too great for them, they would soon free themselves. And those who are under such governments do no more assent to them, tho they may be silent, than a man approves of being robbed, when, without saying a word, he delivers his purse to a thief that he knows to be too strong for him.

'Tis not therefore the bare sufferance of a government when a disgust

[1] [*Patriarcha*, ch. 13, p. 82.]   [2] [Ibid.]

is declared, nor a silent submission when the power of opposing is wanting, that can imply an assent, or election, and create a right; but an explicit act of approbation, when men have ability and courage to resist or deny. Which being agreed, 'tis evident that our author's distinction between *eligere* and *instituere*[3] signifies nothing: tho, if the power of instituting were only left to nations, it would be sufficient; for he is in vain elected who is not instituted; and he that is instituted is certainly elected; for his institution is an election. As the Romans who chose Romulus, Numa, and Hostilius to be kings; and Brutus, Valerius, or Lucretius to be consuls, did make them so, and their right was solely grounded upon their election. The text brought by our author against this doth fully prove it, *Him shalt thou set king over thee whom the Lord shall chuse;*[4] for God did not only make the institution of a king to be purely an act of the people, but left it to them to institute one or not, as should best please themselves; and the words, *whom the Lord shall chuse*, can have no other signification, than that the people resolving to have a king, and following the rules prescribed by his servant Moses, he would direct them in their choice; which relates only to that particular people in covenant with God, and immediately under his government, which no other was. But this pains might have been saved, if God by a universal law had given a rule to all. The Israelites could not have been three hundred years without a king, and then left to the liberty of making one, or not, if he by a perpetual law had ordained that every nation should have one; and it had been as well impertinent as unjust to deliberate who should be king, if the dominion had by right of inheritance belonged to one: They must have submitted to him whether they would or not: No care was to be taken in the election or institution of him, who by his birth had a right annexed to his person that could not be altered: He could not have been forbidden *to multiply silver or gold*, who by the law of his creation might do what he pleased: It had been ridiculous to say, *he should not raise his heart above his brethren*, who had no brethren, that is, no equals; but was raised above all by God, who had imposed upon all others a necessity of obeying him.[5] But God, who does nothing in vain, did neither constitute or elect any till they desired it, nor command them to do it themselves, unless it so pleased themselves; nor appoint them to take him out of any one line: Every Israelite might be chosen: None but

---

[3] ["Elect" and "institute." Filmer makes this distinction in *Patriarcha*, ch. 14 ("No Example in Scripture of the People's Choosing Their King. Mr. Hooker's Judgment Therein"), p. 83.]

[4] Deut. 17.

[5] [Deuteronomy 17:17, 20.]

strangers were excluded; and the people were left to the liberty of chusing and instituting any one of their brethren.

Our author endeavouring by Hooker's authority to establish his distinction between *eligere* and *instituere*, destroys it, and the paternal right, which he makes the foundation of his doctrine. *Heaps of Scripture are alleged*, says he, *concerning the solemn coronation and inauguration of Saul, David, Solomon and others, by nobles, ancients, and people of the commonwealth of Israel:*[6] which is enough to prove that the whole work was theirs; that no other had any title more than what they bestowed upon him: They were set up by the nobles, ancients, and people: Even God did no otherwise intervene than by such a secret disposition of the lots by his Providence, as is exercised in the government of all the things in the world; and we cannot have a more certain evidence, that a paternal right to dominion is a mere whimsy, than that God did not cause the lot to fall upon the eldest, of the eldest line, of the eldest tribe; but upon Saul, a young man, of the youngest tribe: and afterwards, tho he had designed David, Solomon, Jeroboam, and others, who had no pretence to the paternal right to be kings, he left both the election and institution of them to the elders and people.

But Hooker being well examined, it will appear that his opinions were as contrary to the doctrine of our author, as those we have mentioned out of Plato and Aristotle. He plainly says, *It is impossible that any should have a compleat lawful power over a multitude consisting of so many families, as every politick society doth, but by consent of men, or immediate appointment from God: Because not having the natural superiority of fathers, their power must needs be usurped, and then unlawful; or if lawful, then either granted or consented unto by them over whom they exercise the same, or else given extraordinarily by God.* And tho he thinks kings to have been the first governors so constituted, he adds, *That this is not the only regiment that hath been received in the world. The inconveniences of one kind have caused sundry others to be devised. So that in a word, all publick regiment, of what kind soever, seemeth evidently to have risen from deliberate advice, consultation and composition between men, judging it convenient and behoofeful.* And a little below, *Man's nature standing therefore as it doth, some kind of regiment the law of nature doth require; yet the kinds thereof being many, nature tyeth not to any one, but leaveth the choice as a thing arbitrary.* And again, *To live by one man's will, became all men's misery: This constrained them to come unto laws, &c.* But as those laws do not only teach that which is good, but enjoin it, they have in them a constraining force. To constrain men to anything inconvenient seemeth unreasonable: Most requisite therefore it is

[6] [*Patriarcha*, ch. 14, p. 83.]

that to devise laws, which all men should be forced to obey, none but wise men should be admitted. Moreover that which we say concerning the power of government must here be applied unto the power of making laws, whereby to govern; which power God hath over all; and by the natural law, whereunto he hath made all subject, the lawful power of making laws to command whole politick societies of men, belongeth so properly unto the same entire societies, that for any prince or potentate, of what kind soever upon earth, to exercise the same of himself, and not either by express commission immediately from God, or else by authority derived at the first from their consent, upon whose persons they impose laws, it is no better than mere tyranny. Laws therefore they are not, which publick consent hath not made so.[7] The humour of our age considered, I should not have dared to say so much; but if Hooker be a man of such great authority, I cannot offend in transcribing his words, and shewing how vilely he is abused by Filmer; concluding, that if he be in the right, the choice and constitution of government, the making of laws, coronation, inauguration, and all that belongs to the chusing and making of kings, or other magistrates, is merely from the people; and that all power exercised over them, which is not so, is usurpation and tyranny, unless it be by an immediate commission from God; which if any man has, let him give testimony of it, and I will confess he comes not within the reach of our reasonings, but ought to be obeyed by those to whom he is sent, or over whom he is placed.

Nevertheless, our author is of another opinion; but scorning to give us a reason, he adds to Hooker's words, *As if these solemnities were a kind of deed, whereby the right of dominion is given; which strange, untrue, and unnatural conceits are set abroad by seedsmen of rebellion;* and a little farther, *Unless we will openly proclaim defiance unto all law, equity, and reason, we must say (for there is no remedy) that in kingdoms hereditary, birthright giveth a right unto sovereign dominion, &c. Those solemnities do either serve for an open testification of the inheritor's right, or belong to the form of inducing him into the possession.*[8] These are bold censures, and do not only reach Mr. Hooker, whose modesty and peaceableness of spirit is no less esteemed than his learning; but the Scriptures also, and the best of human authors, upon which he founded his opinions. But why should it be thought a strange, untrue,

---

[7] Hooker, *Eccl. Pol.* l. 1. c. 10. [Richard Hooker, *Of the Laws of Ecclesiastical Polity*, 3 vols. (1593–) (Cambridge: Harvard University Press, 1977), bk. 1, ch. 10.]

[8] [*Patriarcha*, ch. 14, p. 83. These words are in fact Hooker's. Sidney was deceived by the 1680 edition of Filmer, which neglected to put this part of the Hooker quotation in italics. Sidney's 1772 editor comments that Sidney probably would not have objected to the quotation if he had known that Hooker says immediately afterward "that kings, even inheritors, do hold their right to the power of dominion with dependency upon the whole body politic over which they rule as kings."]

or unnatural conceit, to believe that when the Scriptures say Nimrod was the first that grew powerful in the earth long before the death of his fathers, and could consequently neither have a right of dominion over the multitude met together at Babylon, nor subdue them by his own strength, he was set up by their consent; or that they who made him their governor, might prescribe rules by which he should govern? Nothing seems to me less strange, than that a multitude of reasonable creatures, in the performance of acts of the greatest importance, should consider why they do them. And the infinite variety which is observed in the constitution, mixture, and regulation of governments, does not only shew that the several nations of the world have considered them; but clearly prove that all nations have perpetually continued in the exercise of that right. Nothing is more natural than to follow the voice of mankind: The wisest and best have ever employed their studies in forming kingdoms and commonwealths, or in adding to the perfections of such as were already constituted; which had been contrary to the laws of God and nature, if a general rule had been set, which had obliged all to be forever subject to the will of one; and they had not been the best, but the worst of men who had departed from it. Nay, I may say, that the law given by God to his peculiar people, and the commands delivered by his servants in order to it, or the prosecution of it, had been contrary to his own eternal and universal law; which is impossible. A law therefore having been given by God, which had no relation to, or consistency with the absolute paternal power; judges and kings created, who had no pretence to any preference before their brethren, till they were created, and commanded not to raise their hearts above them when they should be created; the wisdom and virtue of the best men in all ages shewn in the constitution or reformation of governments; and nations in variously framing them, preserving the possession of their natural right, to be governed by none, and in no other way than they should appoint: The opinions of Hooker, *That all publick regiment, of what kind soever, ariseth from the deliberate advice of men seeking their own good, and that all other is mere tyranny,* are not *untrue and unnatural conceits set abroad* by the seedsmen of *rebellion;*[9] but real truths grounded upon the laws of God and nature, acknowledged and practiced by mankind. And no nation being justly subject to any, but such as they set up, nor in any other manner than according to such laws as they ordain, the right of chusing and making those that are to govern them, must wholly depend upon their will.

---

[9] [Hooker, bk. 1, ch. 10; bk. 8, ch. 3.]

SECTION 7

The Laws of every Nation are the measure of Magistratical Power.

OUR author lays much weight upon the word hereditary; but the question is, what is inherited in an hereditary kingdom, and how it comes to be hereditary. 'Tis in vain to say *the kingdom;* for we do not know what he means by the kingdom: 'tis one thing in one place, and very different in others; and I think it not easy to find two in the world that in power are exactly the same. If he understand all that is comprehended within the precincts over which it reaches, I deny that any such is to be found in the world: If he refer to what preceding kings enjoyed, no determination can be made, till the first original of that kingdom be examined, that it may be known what that first king had, and from whence he had it.

If this variety be denied, I desire to know whether the kings of Sparta and Persia had the same power over their subjects; if the same, whether both were absolute, or both limited; if limited, how came the decrees of the Persian kings to pass for laws? if absolute, how could the Spartan kings be subject to fines, imprisonment, or the sentence of death; and not to have power to send for their own supper out of the common hall? Why did Xenophon call Agesilaus a good and faithful king, obedient to the laws of his country, when upon the command of the *ephori*,[1] he left the war that he had with so much glory begun in Asia, if he was subject to none? How came the *ephori* to be established to restrain the power of kings, if it could no way be restrained, if all owed obedience to them, and they to none? Why did Theopompus his wife reprove him for suffering his power to be diminished by their creation, if it could not be diminished? Or why did he say he had made the power more permanent in making it less odious, if it was perpetual and unalterable? We may go farther, and taking Xenophon and Plutarch for our guides, assert that the kings of Sparta never had the powers of war or peace, life and death, which our author esteems inseparable from regality, and conclude either that no king has them, or that all kings are not alike in power. If they are not in all places the same, kings do not reign by an universal law, but by the particular laws of each country; which give to every one so much power, as in the opinion of the givers conduces to the end of their institution, which is the publick good.

[1] [Annually elected Spartan magistrates.]

It may be also worth our inquiry how this inherited power came to be hereditary. We know that the sons of Vespasian and Constantine inherited the Roman empire, tho their fathers had no such title; but gaining the empire by violence, which Hooker says is mere tyranny that can create no right, they could devolve none to their children. The kings of France of the three races have inherited the crown; but Meroveus, Pepin, and Hugh Capet could neither pretend title nor conquest, or any other right than what was conferred upon them by the clergy, nobility, and people; and consequently whatsoever is inherited from them can have no other original; for that is the gift of the people which is bestowed upon the first, under whom the successors claim, as if it had been by a peculiar act given to every one of them. It will be more hard to shew how the crown of England is become hereditary, unless it be by the will of the people; for tho it were granted that some of the Saxon kings came in by inheritance (which I do not, having, as I think, proved them to have been absolutely elective) yet William the Norman did not, for he was a bastard, and could inherit nothing. William Rufus and Henry did not; for their elder brother Robert by right of inheritance ought to have been preferred before them: Stephen and Henry the second did not; for Maude the only heiress of Henry the first was living when both were crowned: Richard, John, and those who followed, did not, for they were bastards born in adultery. They must therefore have received their right from the people, or they could have none at all; and their successors fall under the same condition.

Moreover, I find great variety in the deduction of this hereditary right. In Sparta there were two kings of different families, endowed with an equal power. If the Heraclidae did reign as fathers of the people, the Aeacidae did not; if the right was in the Aeacidae, the Heraclidae could have none; for 'tis equally impossible to have two fathers as two thousand. 'Tis in vain to say that two families joined, and agreed to reign jointly: for 'tis evident the Spartans had kings before the time of Hercules or Achilles, who were the fathers of the two races. If it be said that the regal power with which they were invested did entitle them to the right of fathers, it must in like manner have belonged to the Roman consuls, military tribunes, dictators, and praetors; for they had more power than the Spartan kings; and that glorious nation might change their fathers every year, and multiply or diminish the number of them as they pleased. If this be most ridiculous and absurd, 'tis certain that the name and office of king, consul, dictator, or the like, does not confer any determined right upon the person that hath it: Everyone has a right to that which is allotted to him by the laws of the country by which he is created.

As the Persians, Spartans, Romans or Germans, might make such magistrates, and under such names as best pleased themselves, and accordingly enlarge or diminish their power; the same right belongs to all nations, and the rights due unto, as well as the duties incumbent upon everyone, are to be known only by the laws of that place. This may seem strange to those who know neither books nor things, histories nor laws, but is well explain'd by Grotius; who denying the sovereign power to be annexed to any man, speaks of divers magistrates under several names that had, and others that under the same names had it not; and distinguishes those who have the *summum imperium summo modo*, from those who have it *modo non summo:*[2] and tho probably he looked upon the first sort as a thing merely speculative, if by that *summo modo*, a right of doing what one pleases be understood; yet he gives many examples of the other, and among those who had *liberrimum imperium*,[3] if any had it, he names the kings of the Sabaeans; who nevertheless were under such a condition, that tho they were, as Agatharchides reports, obeyed in all things, whilst they continued within the walls of their palace, might be stoned by any that met them without it. He finds also another obstacle to the absolute power, *cum rex partem habeat summi imperii, partem senatus, sive populus;*[4] which parts are proportioned according to the laws of each kingdom, whether hereditary or elective, both being equally regulated by them.

The law that gives and measures the power, prescribes rules how it should be transmitted. In some places the supreme magistrates are annually elected, in others their power is for life; in some they are merely elective, in others hereditary under certain rules or limitations. The ancient kingdoms and lordships of Spain were hereditary; but the succession went ordinarily to the eldest of the reigning family, not to the nearest in blood. This was the ground of the quarrel between Corbis the brother, and Orsua the son of the last prince, decided by combat before Scipio.[5] I know not whether the Goths brought that custom with them when they conquered Spain, or whether they learnt it from the inhabitants; but certain it is, that keeping themselves to the families of the Balthi, and Amalthi, they had more regard to age than proximity; and almost ever preferred the brother, or eldest kinsman of the last king before his son.[6]

---

[2] Grot. de Jur. bel. et pac. l. 1. c. 1. ["The supreme power in the supreme manner" . . . "not in the supreme manner." Grotius, *De jure*, bk. 1, ch. 3, sec. 14.]

[3] [The most unlimited power.]

[4] ["When the king holds part of the supreme power, and the senate or the people holds part." Agatharchides, Greek historian and geographer of the second century B.C., is quoted by Grotius in bk. 1, ch. 3, sec. 16 end.]

[5] T. Liv. l. 28. [Livy, *History of Rome*, bk. 28, ch. 21.]

[6] Saavedra corona Gothica. [Diego de Saavedra y Fajardo, *Corona gothica, castellana, y austriaca*, 1677.]

The like custom was in use among the Moors in Spain and Africa, who according to the several changes that happened among the families of Almohades, Almoravides, and Benemerini, did always take one of the reigning blood; but in the choice of him had most respect to age and capacity.[7] This is usually called the law of *tanistry;* and, as in many other places, prevailed also in Ireland, till that country fell under the English government.

In France and Turkey the male that is nearest in blood, succeeds; and I do not know of any deviation from that rule in France, since Henry the First was preferred before Robert his elder brother, grandchild to Hugh Capet: but notwithstanding the great veneration they have for the royal blood, they utterly exclude females, lest the crown should fall to a stranger; or a woman that is seldom able to govern herself, should come to govern so great a people. Some nations admit females, either simply, as well as males; or under a condition of not marrying out of their country, or without the consent of the estates, with an absolute exclusion of them and their children if they do; according to which law, now in force among the Swedes, Charles Gustavus was chosen king upon the resignation of Queen Christina, as having no title; and the crown settled upon the heirs of his body, to the utter exclusion of his brother Adolphus, their mother having married a German. Tho divers nations have differently disposed their affairs; all those that are not naturally slaves, and like to beasts, have preferred their own good before the personal interests of him that expects the crown, so as upon no pretence whatever to admit of one, who is evidently guilty of such vices as are prejudicial to the state. For this reason the French, tho much addicted to their kings, rejected the vile remainders of Meroveus his race, and made Pepin the son of Charles Martel king: And when his descendants fell into the like vices, they were often deposed, till at last they were wholly rejected, and the crown given to Capet and to his heirs male as formerly. Yet for all this Henry his grandchild, being esteemed more fit to govern than his elder brother Robert, was, as is said before, made king, and that crown still remains in his descendants; no consideration being had of the children of Robert, who continued dukes of Burgundy during the reigns of ten kings. And in the memory of our fathers, Henry of Navarre was rejected by two assemblies of the estates, because he differed in religion from the body of the nation, and could never be received as king, till he had renounced his own, tho he was certainly the next in blood; and that in all other respects he excelled in those virtues which they most esteem.

[7] Marian. Hist. Hispan. [Juan de Mariana, *Historia General de España* (Toledo: P. Rod-riguez, 1601), bk. 11, ch. 1, and bk. 13, ch. 7.]

We have already proved, that our own history is full of the like examples, and might enumerate a multitude of others, if it were not too tedious: and as the various rules, according to which all the hereditary crowns of the world are inherited, shew, that none is set by nature, but that every people proceeds according to their own will; the frequent deviations from those rules do evidently testify, that *salus populi est lex suprema;*[8] and that no crown is granted otherwise, than in submission to it.

But tho there were a rule, which in no case ought to be transgressed, there must be a power of judging to whom it ought to be applied. 'Tis perhaps hard to conceive one more precise than that of France, where the eldest legitimate male in the direct line is preferred; and yet that alone is not sufficient. There may be bastardy in the case: Bastards may be thought legitimate, and legitimate sons bastards. The children born of Isabel of Portugal during her marriage with John the Third of Castile were declared bastards; and the title of the house of Austria to that crown, depends upon that declaration. We often see that marriages which have been contracted, and for a long time taken to be good, have been declared null; and the legitimation of the present king of France, is founded solely upon the abolition of the marriage of Henry the Fourth with Marguerite of Valois, which for the space of twenty seven years was thought to have been good. Whilst Spain was divided into five or six kingdoms, and the several kings linked to each other by mutual alliances, incestuous marriages were often contracted, and upon better consideration annulled; many have been utterly void, through the preengagement of one of the parties. These are not feigned cases, but such as happen frequently; and the diversity of accidents, as well as the humours of men, may produce many others, which would involve nations in the most fatal disorders, if everyone should think himself obliged to follow such a one who pretended a title, that to him might seem plausible, when another should set up one as pleasing to others, and there were no power to terminate those disputes to which both must submit, but the decision must be left to the sword.

This is that which I call the application of the rule, when it is as plain and certain as humane wisdom can make it; but if it be left more at large, as where females inherit, the difficulties are inextricable: and he that says, the next heir is really king when one is dead, before he be so declared by a power that may judge of his title, does, as far as in him lies, expose nations to be split into the most desperate factions, and every man to fight for the title which he fancies to be good, till he destroy those of the

[8] [The welfare (or: safety) of the people is the supreme law.]

contrary party, or be destroyed by them. This is the blessed way proposed by our author to prevent sedition:[9] But, God be thanked, our ancestors found a better. They did not look upon Robert the Norman as king of England after the death of his father; and when he did proudly endeavour, on pretence of inheritance, to impose himself upon the nation, that thought fit to prefer his younger brothers before him, he paid the penalty of his folly, by the loss of his eyes and liberty. The French did not think the grandchild of Pharamond to be king after the death of his father, nor seek who was the next heir of the Merovingian line, when Childeric the third was dead; nor regard the title of Charles of Lorraine after the death of his brother Lothair, or of Robert of Burgundy eldest son of King Robert; but advanced Meroveus, Pepin, Capet and Henry the first, who had no other right than what the nobility and people bestowed upon them. And if such acts do not destroy the pretences of all who lay claim to crowns by inheritance, and do not create a right, I think it will be hard to find a lawful king in the world, or that there ever have been any; since the first did plainly come in like Nimrod, and those who have been everywhere since histories are known to us, owed their exaltation to the consent of nations, armed or unarmed, by the deposition or exclusion of the heirs of such as had reigned before them.

Our author not troubling himself with these things, or any other relating to the matter in question, is pleased to slight Hooker's opinions concerning coronation and inauguration, with *the heaps of Scripture* upon which he grounds them; whereas those solemnities would not only have been foolish and impertinent, but profane and impious, if they were not deeds by which the right of dominion is really conferred.[10] What could be more wickedly superstitious, than to call all Israel together before the Lord, and to cast lots upon every tribe, family and person, for the election of a king, if it had been known to whom the crown did belong by a natural and unalterable right? Or if there had been such a thing in nature, how could God have caused that lot to fall upon one of the youngest tribe forever to discountenance his own law, and divert nations from taking any notice of it? It had been absurd for the tribe of Judah to chuse and anoint David, and for the other tribes to follow their example after the death of Ishbosheth, if he had been king by a right not depending on their will. David did worse in slaying the sons of Rimmon, saying, they had killed a righteous man lying upon his bed, if Ishbosheth, whose head they presented, had most unrighteously detained from him, as long as he lived, the dominion of the ten tribes: The king, elders and people, had

[9] [*Patriarcha*, ch. 14, p. 83.] [10] [Ibid.]

most scornfully abused the most sacred things, by using such ceremonies in making him king, and compleating their work in a covenant made between him and them before the Lord, if he had been already king, and if those acts had been empty ceremonies conferring no right at all.[11]

I dare not say that a league does imply an absolute equality between both parties; for there is a *foedus inequale*,[12] wherein the weaker, as Grotius says, does usually obtain protection, and the stronger honour; but there can be none at all, unless both parties are equally free to make it, or not to make it. David therefore was not king, till he was elected, and those covenants made; and he was made king by that election and covenants.

This is not shaken by our author's supposition, *that the people would not have taken Joash, Manasseh or Josiah, if they had had a right of chusing a king;*[13] since Solomon says, *Woe unto the kingdom whose king is a child.* For, first, they who at the first had a right of chusing whom they pleased to be king, by the covenant made with him whom they did chuse, may have deprived themselves of the farther execution of it, and rendered the crown hereditary even to children, unless the conditions were violated upon which it was granted. In the second place, if the infancy of a king brings woe upon a people, the government of such a one cannot be according to the laws of God and nature; for governments are not instituted by either for the pleasure of a man, but for the good of nations; and their weal, not their woe, is sought by both: and if children are anywhere admitted to rule, 'tis by the particular law of the place, grounded perhaps upon an opinion, that it is the best way to prevent dangerous contests; or that other ways may be found to prevent the inconveniences that may proceed from their weakness. Thirdly, It cannot be concluded that they might not reject children, because they did not: such matters require positive proofs, suppositions are of no value in relation to them, and the whole matter may be altered by particular circumstances. The Jews might reasonably have a great veneration for the house of David: they knew what was promised to that family; and whatever respect was paid, or privilege granted on that account, can be of no advantage to any other in the world. They might be farther induced to set up Joash, in hope the defects of his age might be supplied by the virtue, experience and wisdom of Jehoiada. We do not know what good opinion may have been conceived of Manasseh when he was twelve years old; but much might be hoped from one that had been virtuously educated, and was probably under the

[11] [2 Samuel 4.]

[12] ["Unequal treaty." Grotius, *De jure*, bk. 1, ch. 3, sec. 21.]

[13] [*Patriarcha*, ch. 14, pp. 83–84.]

care of such as had been chosen by Hezekiah: and tho the contrary did fall out, the mischiefs brought upon the people by his wicked reign, proceeded not from the weakness of his childhood, but from the malice of his riper years. And both the examples of Joash and Josiah prove, that neither of them came in by their own right, but by the choice of the people. *Jehoiada gathered the Levites out of all the cities of Judah, and the chief of the fathers of Israel, and they came to Jerusalem: And all the congregation made a covenant with the king in the house of God, and brought out the king's son, and put upon him the crown, and gave him the testimony, and made him king;* whereupon they slew *Athaliah.*[14] *And when Ammon was slain, the people of the land slew them that had conspired against King Ammon; and the people of the land made Josiah his son king in his stead:*[15] which had been most impertinent, if he was of himself king before they made him so. Besides, tho infancy may be a just cause of excepting against, and rejecting the next heir to a crown, 'tis not the greatest or strongest. 'Tis far more easy to find a remedy against the folly of a child (if the state be well regulated) than the more rooted vices of grown men. The English, who willingly received Henry the sixth, Edward the fifth and sixth, tho children, resolutely opposed Robert the Norman: And the French, who willingly submitted to Charles the ninth, Lewis the thirteenth and fourteenth in their infancy, rejected the lewd remainders of Meroveus his race; Charles of Lorraine with his kindred descended from Pepin, Robert duke of Burgundy with his descendants, and Henry of Navarre, till he had satisfied the nobility and people in the point of religion. And tho I do not know that the letter upon the words, *Vae regno cujus rex puer est,* recited by Lambarde[16] was written by Eleutherius bishop of Rome; yet the authority given to it by the Saxons, who made it a law, is much more to be valued than what it could receive from the writer; and whoever he was, he seems rightly to have understood Solomon's meaning, who did not look upon him as a child that wanted years, or was superannuated, but him only who was guilty of insolence, luxury, folly and madness: and he that said, *A wise child was better than an old and foolish king,*[17] could have no other meaning, unless he should say, it was worse to be governed by a wise person than a fool; which may agree with the judgment of our author, but could never enter into the heart of Solomon.

---

[14] 2 Chron. [2 Chronicles 23:2–3, 11–15.]

[15] 2 Chron. [2 Chronicles 33:25.]

[16] Lamb. leg. Saxon. ["Woe to the kingdom whose king is a child." William Lambarde, *Archaionomia, sive, De priscis Anglorum legibus* (compiled late 14th century; Cambridge: Roger Daniel, 1644) contained the Anglo-Saxon laws from Ine to Canute.]

[17] [Ecclesiastes 4:13.]

Lastly, tho the practice of one or more nations may indicate what laws, covenants or customs were in force among them, yet they cannot bind others: The diversity of them proceeds from the variety of men's judgments, and declares, that the direction of all such affairs depends upon their own will; according to which every people for themselves forms and measures the magistracy, and magistratical power; which, as it is directed solely for the good, hath its exercises and extent proportionable to the command of those that institute it; and such ordinances being good for men, God makes them his own.

SECTION 8

There is no natural propensity in Man or Beast to Monarchy.

I SEE no reason to believe that God did approve the government of one over many, because he created but one; but to the contrary, in as much as he did endow him, and those that came from him, as well the youngest as the eldest line, with understanding to provide for themselves, and by the invention of arts and sciences, to be beneficial to each other; he shewed, that they ought to make use of that understanding in forming governments according to their own convenience, and such occasions as should arise, as well as in other matters: and it might as well be inferr'd, that it is unlawful for us to build, clothe, arm, defend, or nourish ourselves, otherwise than as our first parents did, before, or soon after the Flood, as to take from us the liberty of instituting governments that were not known to them. If they did not find out all that conduces to the use of man, but a faculty as well as a liberty was left to everyone, and will be to the end of the world, to make use of his wit, industry, and experience, according to present exigencies, to invent and practise such things as seem convenient to himself and others in matters of the least importance; it were absurd to imagine, that the political science, which of all others is the most abstruse and variable according to accidents and circumstances, should have been perfectly known to them who had no use of it; and that their descendants are obliged to add nothing to what they practiced. But the reason given by our author to prove this extravagant fancy, is yet more ridiculous than the thing itself; *God*, saith he, *shewed his opinion*, viz. that all should be governed by one, *when he endowed not only men, but beasts with a natural propensity to monarchy: Neither* can it be doubted, but a natural propensity is referred to God who is the author of nature:[1] Which I suppose may appear if it be considered.

Nevertheless I cannot but commend him in the first place for introducing God speaking so modestly, not declaring his will, but his opinion. He puts haughty and majestick language into the mouth of kings. They command and decide, as if they were subject to no error, and their wills ought to be taken for perpetual laws; but to God he ascribes an humble delivery of his opinion only, as if he feared to be mistaken. In the second place, I deny that there is any such general propensity in man or beast, or that monarchy would thereby be justified tho it were found in them. It cannot be in beasts, for they know not what government is; and being incapable of it, cannot distinguish the several sorts, nor consequently incline to one more than another. Salmasius his story of bees[2] is only fit for old women to prate of in chimney corners; and they who represent lions and eagles as kings of birds and beasts, do it only to show, that their power is nothing but brutish violence, exercised in the destruction of all that are not able to oppose it, and that hath nothing of goodness or justice in it: which similitude (tho it should prove to be in all respects adequate to the matter in question) could only shew, that those who have no sense of right, reason or religion, have a natural propensity to make use of their strength, to the destruction of such as are weaker than they; and not that any are willing to submit, or not to resist it if they can, which I think will be of no great advantage to monarchy. But whatever propensity may be in beasts, it cannot be attributed generally to men; for if it were, they never could have deviated from it, unless they were violently put out of their natural course; which in this case cannot be, for there is no power to force them. But that they have most frequently deviated, appears by the various forms of government established by them. There is therefore no natural propensity to anyone, but they chuse that which in their judgment seems best for them. Or, if he would have that inconsiderate impulse, by which brutish and ignorant men may be swayed when they know no better, to pass for a propensity; others are no more obliged to follow it, than to live upon acorns, or inhabit hollow trees, because their fathers did it when they had no better dwellings, and found no better nourishment in the uncultivated world. And he that exhibits such examples, as far as in him lies, endeavours to take from us

[1] [*Patriarcha*, ch. 15 ("God Governed Always by Monarchy. Bellarmine's and Aristotle's Judgment of Monarchy"), p. 84.]

[2] [Claudius Salmasius, a French classical scholar, argued in his *Royal Defense of Charles I* (1649) that since bees are organized monarchically, so also should men be. John Milton, the republican poet, discussed the bees in his widely read *Defense of the People of England Against Salmasius* (1651).]

the use of reason, and extinguishing the light of it, to make us live like the worst of beasts, that we may be fit subjects to absolute monarchy. This may perhaps be our author's intention, having learnt from Aristotle, that such a government is only suitable to the nature of the most bestial men, who being incapable of governing themselves, fall under the power of such as will take the conduct of them: but he ought withal to have remembered, that according to Aristotle's opinion, this conductor must be in nature different from those he takes the charge of; and if he be not, there can be no government, nor order, by which it subsists: Beasts follow beasts, and the blind lead the blind to destruction.

But tho I should grant this propensity to be general, it could not be imputed to God, since man by sin is fallen from the law of his creation. *The wickedness of man* (even in the first ages) *was great in the world: All the imaginations of his heart are evil, and that continually. All men are liars: There is none that doth good, no not one. Out of the heart proceed evil thoughts, murders, adulteries, fornications, thefts, false testimonies, &c.* [3] These are the fruits of our corrupted nature, which the Apostle observing, does not only make a difference between the natural and the spiritual man, whose proceeding only can be referred to God, and that only so far as he is guided by his spirit; but shews, that the natural man is in a perpetual enmity against God, without any possibility of being reconciled to him, unless by the destruction of the old man, and the regenerating or renewing him through the spirit of grace. There being no footsteps of this in our author's book, he and his master Heylyn may have differed from the Apostle, referring that propensity of nature to God, which he declares to be utter enmity against him; and we may conclude, that this propensity, however general it may be, cannot be attributed to God as the author of nature, since it cannot be more general than the corruptions into which we are fallen.

[3] [The first quotation is from Genesis 6:5; the second, Psalms 116:11 and 14:3; the third, Matthew 15:19.]

SECTION 9

The Government instituted by God over the Israelites was Aristocratical.

NOTWITHSTANDING all this, our author is resolved that monarchy must be from God: *What form of government*, says he, *God ordained by his authority, may be gathered by that commonwealth which he instituted amongst the Hebrews; which was not aristocratical, as Calvin saith, but plainly monarchical.*[1] I may in as few words deny the government set up by God to have been monarchical, as he asserts it; but finding such language ordinarily to proceed from a mixture of folly, impudence and pride, I chuse rather to shew upon what I ground my opinions, than nakedly to deliver them; most especially, when by insisting upon the government instituted by God over his people, he refers us to the Scripture. And I do this the more boldly, since I follow Calvin's exposition, and believe that he having been highly esteemed for his wit, judgment and learning, by such as were endowed with the like, and reverenced as a glorious servant of God, might, if he were now alive, comfort himself, tho he had the misfortune to fall under the censures of Filmer and his followers. 'Tis probable he gave some reasons for his opinions; but our author having maliciously concealed them, and I not having leisure at present to examine all his writings to find them, must content myself with such as my small understanding may suggest, and such as I have found in approved authors.

In the first place I may safely say, he was not alone of that opinion: Josephus, Philo, and Moses Maimonides, with all the best of the Jewish and Christian authors, had long before delivered the same. Josephus says, that Saul's first sin by which he fell, was, *that he took away the aristocracy;*[2] which he could not do if it had never been established. Philo imputes the institution of kingly government, as it was in Israel, neither to God nor his word, but to the fury of the sinful people. Abravanel says, it proceeded from their delight in the idolatry to which their neighbours were addicted, and which could be upheld only by a government, in practice and principle contrary to that which God had instituted.[3] Maimonides frequently says the same thing, grounded upon the words of Hosea, *I gave them kings in my wrath;*[4] and whosoever will call that a divine institution, may give the

---

[1] [*Patriarcha*, ch. 15, p. 84.]

[2] Jos. Ant. Jud. [Josephus, *Jewish Antiquities*, 6 vols. (Loeb, 1930–1965), bk. 6, ch. 5, sec. 4–6.]

[3] Abar. in 1 Sam. 8. [Isaac Abravanel, Com-

mentary on the Prior Prophets (late 1400s), on 1 Samuel 8.]

[4] Maim. More-Nevochim. [Moses Maimonides, *More-Nevochim* translated as *The Guide of the Perplexed*.]

same name to plagues or famines, and induce a necessity incumbent upon all men to go and search the one where they may find it, and to leave their lands forever uncultivated that they may be sure of the other: which being too bestial to be asserted by a man, I may safely say, the Hebrew kings were not instituted by God, but given as a punishment of their sin, who despised the government that he had instituted: and the above-mentioned authors agree in the same thing, calling the people's desire to have a king, furious, mad, wicked, and proceeding from their love to the idolatry of their neighbours, which was suited to their government; both which were inconsistent with what God had established over his own people.

But waiving the opinions of men, 'tis good to see what we can learn from the Scripture, and enquire if there be any precept there expressly commanding them to make a king; or any example that they did so whilst they continued obedient to the word of God; or anything from whence we may reasonably infer they ought to have done it: all which, if I mistake not, will be found directly contrary.

The only precept that we find in the law concerning kings, is that of Deuteron. 17. already mentioned; and that is not a command to the people to make, but instructions what manner of king they should make if they desired to have one: There was therefore none at all.

Examples do as little favour our author's assertions. Moses, Joshua, and the other judges, had not the name or power of kings: They were not of the tribe to which the scepter was promised: They did not transmit the power they had to their children, which in our adversary's opinion is a right inseparable from kings; and their power was not continued by any kind of succession, but created occasionally, as need required, according to the virtues discovered in those who were raised by God to deliver the nation in the time of their distress; which being done, their children lay hid among the rest of the people. Thus were Ehud, Gideon, Jephthah, and others set up: *Whosoever will give battle* (say the princes and people of Gilead) *to the children of Ammon, shall be head over the inheritance of Gilead:* and finding Jephthah to be such a man as they sought, they made him their chief, and all Israel followed them.[5] When Othniel had shew'd his valour in taking Kirjath-Sepher, and delivering his brethren from Cushan-Rishathaim, he was made judge: When Ehud had killed Eglon; when Shamgar and Samson had destroyed great numbers of the Philistines; and when Gideon had defeated the Midianites, they were fit to be advanced above their brethren.[6] These dignities were not inherent

---

[5] Judg. 10. [6] [Judges 1:12; 3:9–10; 36:12–26; 15:20.]

in their persons or families, but conferred upon them; nor conferred, that they might be exalted in riches and glory, but that they might be ministers of good to the people. This may justify Plato's opinion, that if one man be found incomparably to excel all others in the virtues that are beneficial to civil societies, he ought to be advanced above all: but I think it will be hard from thence to deduce an argument in favour of such a monarchy as is necessarily to descend to the next in blood, whether man, woman, or child, without any consideration of virtue, age, sex, or ability; and that failing, it can be of no use to our author. But whatever the dignity of a Hebrew judge was, and howsoever he was raised to that office, it certainly differ'd from that of a king. Gideon could not have refused to be a king when the people would have made him so, if he had been a king already; or that God from the beginning had appointed that they should have one:[7] The elders and people could not have asked a king of Samuel, if he had been king; and he could not without impiety have been displeased with them for asking for such a one as God had appointed; neither would God have said to him, *They have not rejected thee, but they have rejected me that I should not reign over them*, if he had ordained what they desired.[8]

They did not indeed reject God with their mouths: They pretended to use the liberty he had given them to make a king; but would have such a one as he had forbidden: They drew near to him with their lips, but their hearts were far from him; and he seeing their hypocrisy, severely chastised them in granting their ill conceived request; and foretold the miseries that should thereupon befall them, from which he would not deliver them, tho they should cry to him by reason of what they suffered from their king: He was their creature, and the mischiefs thereby brought upon them were the fruits of their own labour.

This is that which our author calls God's institution of kings; but the prophet explains the matter much better, *I gave them kings in my anger, and took them away in my wrath:*[9] in destroying them God brought desolation upon the people that had sinned in asking for them, and following their example in all kind of wickedness. This is all our author has to boast of: but God who acknowledges those works only to be his own, which proceed from his goodness and mercy to his people, disowns this; *Israel hath cast off the thing that is good* (even the government that he had established) *the enemy shall pursue him: They have set up kings, but not by me; and princes, but I know them not.*[10] As if he sought to justify the

---

[7] [Judges 8:22–23.]

[8] 1 Sam. 8.

[9] Hos. 13.

[10] Hos. 8.

severity of his judgments brought upon them by the wickedness of their kings, that they, not he, had ordained.

Having seen what government God did not ordain, it may be seasonable to examine the nature of the government which he did ordain; and we shall easily find that it consisted of three parts, besides the magistrates of the several tribes and cities. They had a chief magistrate, who was called judge or captain, as Joshua, Gideon, and others, a council of seventy chosen men, and the general assemblies of the people.[11]

The first was merely occasional, like to the dictators of Rome; and as the Romans in times of danger frequently chose such a man as was much esteemed for valour and wisdom, God's peculiar people had a peculiar regard to that wisdom and valour which was accompanied with his presence, hoping for deliverance only from him.

The second is known by the name of the great Sanhedrin, which being instituted by Moses according to the command of God, continued, till they were all save one slain by Herod. And the third part, which is the assembly of the people, was so common, that none can be ignorant of it, but such as never looked into the Scripture. When the tribes of Reuben, Gad, and half that of Manasseh had built an altar on the side of Jordan, *The whole congregation of the children of Israel gathered together at Shiloh to go up to war against them, and sent Phineas the son of Eliezer, and with him ten princes, &c.*[12] This was the highest and most important action that could concern a people, even war or peace, and that not with strangers, but their own brethren. Joshua was then alive: The elders never failed; but this was not transacted by him or them, but by the collected body of the people; *for they sent Phineas.* This democratical embassy was democratically received: It was not directed to one man, but to all the children of Reuben, Gad, and Manasseh, and the answer was sent by them all; which being pleasing to Phineas, and the ten that were with him, they made their report to the congregation, and all was quiet.

The last eminent act performed by Joshua was the calling of a like assembly to Shechem, composed of elders, heads of families, judges, officers, and all the people, to whom he proposed, and they agreeing made a covenant before the Lord.[13]

Joshua being dead, the proceedings of every tribe were grounded upon counsels taken at such assemblies among themselves for their own concernments, as appears by the actions of Judah, Simeon, &c. against the Canaanites;[14] and when the Levite complained that his wife had been

[11] Numb. 11.

[12] Josh. 22.

[13] Jos. 24.

[14] Judg. 1.

forced by those of Gibeah, the whole congregation of Israel met together at Mizpah from all parts, *even from Dan to Beersheba*, as one man, and there resolved upon that terrible war which they made against the tribe of Benjamin.[15] The like assembly was gathered together for the election of Saul, every man was there: and tho the elders only are said to have asked a king of Samuel, they seem to have been deputed from the whole congregation; for God said, *Hearken to the voice of the people.*[16] In the same manner the tribe of Judah, and after that the rest chose and anointed David to be their king. After the death of Solomon all Israel met together to treat with Rehoboam; and not receiving satisfaction from him, ten of the tribes abrogated his kingdom.[17]

If these actions were considered singly by themselves, Calvin might have given the name of a democracy to the Hebrew government, as well as to that of Athens; for without doubt they evidently manifest the supreme power to have been in the supreme manner in these general assemblies; but the government (as to its outward order) consisting of those three parts, which comprehend the three simple *species*, tho in truth it was a *theocracy;* and no times having been appointed, nor occasions specified, upon which judges should be chosen, or these assemblies called; whereas the Sanhedrin, which was the aristocratical part, was permanent, the whole might rightly be called an aristocracy, that part prevailing above the others: and tho Josephus calls it a theocracy, by reason of God's presence with his people;[18] yet in relation to man he calls it an aristocracy, and says that Saul's first sin by which he fell from the kingdom was, that *gubernationem optimatum sustulit;*[19] which could not be, if they were governed by a monarch before he was chosen.

Our author taking no notice of these matters, first endeavours to prove the excellency of monarchy from natural instinct; and then begging the question, says, that God did always govern his people by monarchy; whereas he ought in the first place to have observed that this instinct (if there be any such thing) is only an irrational appetite, attributed to beasts, that know not why they do anything; and is to be followed only by those men who being equally irrational, live in the same ignorance: and the second being proved to be absolutely false by the express words of the Scripture, *There was then no king in Israel,*[20] several times repeated, and the whole series of the history, he hath no other evasion than to say,

---

[15] [Judges 20:1–2.]

[16] 1 Sam. 8.

[17] [2 Samuel 21:7; 1 Kings 12:1–20.]

[18] [Josephus, *Against Apion*, bk. 2, sec. 165, in *The Life, Against Apion* (Loeb, 1926).]

[19] ["He took away the government of the nobles." Josephus, *Jewish Antiquities*, bk. 6, ch. 5, sec. 4–6.]

[20] Judg. 18.

That even then the Israelites were under the kingly government of the fathers of particular families.[21]

It appears by the forementioned text cited also by our author, that in the assembly of the people, gathered together to take counsel concerning the war against Benjamin, were four hundred thousand footmen that drew sword: They all arose together, saying, Not a man of us shall go to his tent. *So all the men of Israel were gathered together against the city.* This is repeated several times in the relation. The Benjaminites proceeded in the like manner in preparing for their defence; and if all these who did so meet to consult and determine were monarchs, there were then in Israel and Benjamin four hundred and twenty six thousand, seven hundred monarchs or kings, tho the Scriptures say there was not one.[22]

If yet our author insist upon his notion of kingly government, I desire to know who were the subjects, if all these were kings; for the text says, that the *whole congregation was gathered together as one man from Dan to Beersheba.* If there can be so many kings without one subject, what becomes of the right of Abraham, Isaac and Jacob, that was to have been devolved upon one man as heir to them, and thereby lord of all? If every man had an equal part in that inheritance, and by virtue of it became a king, why is not the same eternally subdivided to as many men as are in the world, who are also kings? If this be their natural condition, how comes it to be altered, till they do unthrone themselves by consent to set up one or more to have a power over them all? Why should they divest themselves of their natural right to set up one above themselves, unless in consideration of their own good? If the 426,700 kings might retain the power in themselves, or give it to one, why might they not give it to any such number of men as should best please themselves, or retain it in their own hands, as they did till the days of Saul; or frame, limit, and direct it according to their own pleasure? If this be true, God is the author of democracy; and no asserter of human liberty did ever claim more than the people of God did enjoy and exercise at the time when our author says they were under the kingly government; which liberty being not granted by any peculiar concession or institution, the same must belong to all mankind.

'Tis in vain to say the 426,700 men were heads of families; for the Scripture only says, *They were footmen that drew the sword,* or rather all the men of Israel from Dan to Beersheba, who were able to make war. When six hundred Benjaminites did only remain of the 26,700, 'tis plain that no more were left of that tribe, their women and children having

[21] [*Patriarcha*, ch. 15, p. 84.]   [22] [Judges 20:2, 8, 11.]

been destroyed in the cities after their defeat. The next chapter makes the matter yet more plain; for when all that were at the congregation in Mizpah were found to have sworn, they would not give their daughters to any of the tribe of Benjamin, no Israelite was free from the oath, but the men of Jabesh-Gilead, who had not been at the assembly: All the rest of Israel was therefore comprehended; and they continuing to govern in a popular way with absolute power, sent twelve thousand of their most valiant men to destroy all the males of Jabesh-Gilead, and the women that had lain by man, reserving the virgins for the Benjaminites.[23] This is enough for my purpose: for the question is not concerning the power that every householder in London hath over his wife, children, and servants; but whether they are all perpetually subject to one man and family; and I intend not to set up their wives, prentices, and children against them, or to diminish their rights, but to assert them, as the gift of God and nature, no otherwise to be restrained than by laws made with their consent.

Reason failing, our author pleases himself with terms of his own invention: *When the people begged a king of Samuel, they were governed by a kingly power: God out of a special love and care to the house of Israel, did chuse to be their king himself, and did govern them at that time by his viceroy Samuel and his sons.*[24] The behaviour of the Israelites towards Samuel has been thought proud, perverse, and obstinate; but the fine court word *begging* was never before applied to them; and their insolent fury was not only seen against Samuel, but against God; *They have not rejected thee, but they have rejected me.*[25] And I think Filmer is the first who ever found that beggars in begging did reject him of whom they begged: Or if they were beggars, they were such as would not be denied; for after all that Samuel had said to dissuade them from their wicked design, they said, *nay, but we will have a king.*[26]

But lest I should be thought too much inclined to contradict our author, I confess that once he hath happened to be in the right. *God out of a special love to the house of Israel chose to be their king: He gave them laws, prescribed a form of government, raised up men in a wonderful manner to execute it, filled them with his spirit, was ever present when they called upon him: He gave them counsel in their doubts, and assistance in all their extremities: He made a covenant with them, and would be exalted by them.*[27] But what is this to an earthly monarch? Who can from hence derive a right to any one man to play the

[23] Judg. 21.
[24] [*Patriarcha*, ch. 15, p. 85.]
[25] 1 Sam. 8.

[26] Ver. 19.
[27] [*Patriarcha*, ch. 15, p. 85.]

lord over his brethren, or a reason why any nation should set him up? God is our lord by right of creation, and our only lord, because he only hath created us. If any other were equal to him in wisdom, power, goodness, and beneficence to us, he might challenge the same duty from us. If growing out of ourselves, receiving being from none, depending on no providence, we were offered the protection of a wisdom subject to no error, a goodness that could never fail, and a power that nothing could resist; it were reasonable for us to enter into a covenant, submit ourselves to him, and with all the faculties of our minds to addict ourselves to his service. But what right can from hence accrue to a mortal creature like to one of us, from whom we have received nothing, and who stands in need of help as much as we? Who can from hence deduce an argument to persuade us to depend upon his wisdom, who has as little as other men? To submit to his will who is subject to the same frailties, passions, and vices with the rest of mankind? Or to expect protection and defence from him whose life depends upon as slender threads as our own; and who can have no power but that which we confer upon him? If this cannot be done, but is of all things the most contrary to common sense, no man can in himself have any right over us; we are all as free as the four hundred twenty six thousand seven hundred Hebrew kings: We can naturally owe allegiance to none; and I doubt whether all the lusts that have reigned amongst men since the beginning of the world, have brought more guilt and misery upon them than that preposterous and impudent pretence of imitating what God had instituted. When Saul set himself most violently to oppose the command of God, he pretended to fulfill it:[28] When the Jews grew weary of God's government, and resolved to reject him, that he should not reign over them, they used some of Moses his words, and asked that king of God, whom they intended to set up against him: But this king had not been set up against God, the people had not rejected God, and sinned in asking for him, if every nation by a general law ought to have one, or by a particular law one had been appointed by him over them. There was therefore no king amongst them, nor any law of God or nature, particular or general, according to which they ought to have one.

---

[28] [1 Samuel 15:31.]

Algernon Sidney

SECTION 10

Aristotle was not simply for Monarchy
or against Popular Government; but approved or disapproved
of either according to circumstances.

OUR author well observes that Aristotle is hardly brought to give a general opinion in favour of Monarchy, as if it were the best form of government, or to say true, never does it. He uses much caution, proposes conditions, and limitations, and makes no decision but according to circumstances. Men of wisdom and learning are subject to such doubts; but none ought to wonder if stupidity and ignorance defend Filmer and his followers from them; or that their hatred to the ancient virtue should give them an aversion to the learning that was the nurse of it. Those who neither understand the several species of government, nor the various tempers of nations, may without fear or shame give their opinions in favour of that which best pleaseth them; but wise men will always proportion their praises to the merit of the subject, and never commend that simply which is good only according to circumstances. Aristotle highly applauds monarchy, when the monarch has more of those virtues that tend to the good of a commonwealth than all they who compose it. This is the king mentioned in his *Ethicks*, and extolled in his *Politicks*:[1] He is above all by nature, and ought not by a municipal law to be made equal to others in power: He ought to govern, because 'tis better for a people to be governed by him, than to enjoy their liberty; or rather they do enjoy their liberty, which is never more safe, than when it is defended by one who is a living law to himself and others. Wheresoever such a man appears, he ought to reign: He bears in his person the divine character of a sovereign: God has raised him above all; and such as will not submit to him, ought to be accounted sons of Belial, brought forth and slain. But he does withal confess, that if no such man be found, there is no natural king: All the prerogatives belonging to him vanish, for want of one who is capable of enjoying them. He lays severe censures upon those who not being thus qualified take upon them to govern men, equal to or better than themselves; and judges the assumption of such powers by persons who are not naturally adapted to the administration of them, as barbarous usurpations, which no law or reason can justify; and is not so much transported with the excellency of this true king, as not to confess

[1] [Aristotle, *Nicomachean Ethics*, bk. 8, 1160b; *Politics*, bk. 3, 1288b.]

he ought to be limited by law: *Qui legem praeesse jubet, videtur jubere praeesse Deum & leges: qui autem hominem praeesse jubet, adjungit & bestiam; libido quippe talis est, atque obliquos agit, etiam viros optimos qui sunt in potestate, ex quo mens atque appetitus lex est.*[2] This agrees with the words of the best king that is known to have been in the world, proceeding, as is most probable, from a sense of the passions that reigned in his own breast; *Man being in honour, hath no understanding, but is like to the beast that perisheth.*[3] This shews that such as deny that kings do reign by law, or that laws may be put upon kings, do equally set themselves against the opinions of wise men, and the word of God: and our author having found that learning made the Grecians seditious, may reasonably doubt that religion may make others worse; so as none will be fit subjects of his applauded government, but those who have neither religion nor learning; and that it cannot be introduced till both be extinguished.

Aristotle having declared his mind concerning government, in the books expressly written on that subject, whatsoever is said by the by in his moral discourses, must be referred to and interpreted by the other: And if he said (which I do not find) that monarchy is the best form of government, and a popular state the worst, he cannot be thought to have meant otherwise, than that those nations were the most happy, who had such a man as he thinks fit to be made a monarch; and those the most unhappy, who neither had such a one, nor a few, that any way excelled the rest; but all being equally brutish, must take upon them the government they were unable to manage: for he does nowhere admit any other end of just and civil government, than the good of the governed; nor any advantage due to one or a few persons, unless for such virtues as conduce to the common good of the society. And as our author thinks learning makes men seditious, Aristotle also acknowledges, that those who have understanding and courage, which may be taken for learning, or the effect of it, will never endure the government of one or a few that do not excel them in virtue: but nowhere dispraises a popular government, unless the multitude be composed of such as are barbarous, stupid, lewd, vicious, and incapable of the happiness for which governments are instituted; who cannot live to themselves, but like a herd of beasts must be brought under the dominion of another; or who, having amongst themselves such an

---

[2] Arist. Polit. l. 3. c. 12. ["He who commands the law to rule seems to command God and the laws to rule; he, however, who commands man to rule adds also the beast: for desire is such, and it drives astray even the best men who are in power; therefore the law is mind and appetite." Aristotle, *Politics*, bk. 3, 1287a. Sidney or the typesetter slipped; the last words should read "mind *without* appetite." The same text is given correctly at sec. 30, n. 4 below.]

[3] [Psalms 49:12.]

excellent person as is above described, will not submit to him, but either kill, banish, or bring him to be equal with others, whom God had made to excel all. I do not trouble myself, or the reader, with citing here or there a line out of his books, but refer myself to those who have perused his moral and political writings, submitting to the severest censures, if this be not the true sense of them; and that virtue alone, in his opinion, ought to give the preeminence. And as Aristotle following the wise men of those times, shews us how far reason, improved by meditation, can advance in the knowledge and love of that which is truly good; so we may in Filmer, guided by Heylyn, see an example of corrupted Christians, extinguishing the light of religion by their vices, and degenerating into beasts, whilst they endeavour to support the personal interest of some men, who being raised to dignities by the consent of nations, or by unwarrantable ways and means, would cast all the power into the hands of such as happen to be born in their families; as if governments had not been instituted for the common good of nations, but only to increase their pride, and foment their vices; or that the care and direction of a great people were so easy a work, that every man, woman, or child, how young, weak, foolish or wicked soever, may be worthy of it, and able to manage it.

SECTION I I

Liberty produceth Virtue, Order and Stability: Slavery is accompanied with Vice, Weakness and Misery.

OUR author's judgment, as well as inclinations to virtue, are manifested in the preference he gives to the manners of the Assyrians and other Eastern nations, before the Grecians and Romans: Whereas the first were never remarkable for anything, but pride, lewdness, treachery, cruelty, cowardice, madness, and hatred to all that is good; whilst the others excelled in wisdom, valour, and all the virtues that deserve imitation. This was so well observed by St. Augustine, that he brings no stronger argument to prove, that God leaves nothing that is good in man unrewarded, than that he gave the dominion of the best part of the world to the Romans, who in moral virtues excelled all other nations.[1] And I

[1] De Civ. Dei. [Augustine, *City of God*, 7 vols. (Loeb, 1957), bk. 5, ch. 19.]

think no example can be alleged of a free people that has ever been conquer'd by an absolute monarch, unless he did incomparably surpass them in riches and strength; whereas many great kings have been overthrown by small republicks: and the success being constantly the same, it cannot be attributed to fortune, but must necessarily be the production of virtue and good order. Machiavelli discoursing of these matters, finds virtue to be so essentially necessary to the establishment and preservation of liberty, that he thinks it impossible for a corrupted people to set up a good government, or for a tyranny to be introduced if they be virtuous; and makes this conclusion, *That where the matter* (that is, the body of the people) *is not corrupted, tumults and disorders do no hurt; and where it is corrupted, good laws do no good:*[2] Which being confirmed by reason and experience, I think no wise man has ever contradicted him.

But I do not more wonder that Filmer should look upon absolute monarchy to be the nurse of virtue, tho we see they did never subsist together, than that he should attribute order and stability to it; whereas order doth principally consist in appointing to everyone his right place, office, or work; and this lays the whole weight of the government upon one person, who very often does neither deserve, nor is able to bear the least part of it. Plato, Aristotle, Hooker, and (I may say in short) all wise men have held, that order required that the wisest, best, and most valiant men, should be placed in the offices where wisdom, virtue and valour are requisite. If common sense did not teach us this, we might learn it from the Scripture. When God gave the conduct of his people to Moses, Joshua, Samuel, and others, he endowed them with all the virtues and graces that were required for the right performance of their duty. When the Israelites were oppressed by the Midianites, Philistines and Ammonites, they expected help from the most wise and valiant. When Hannibal was at the gates of Rome, and had filled Italy with fire and blood; or when the Gauls overwhelmed that country with their multitudes and fury, the senate and people of Rome put themselves under the conduct of Camillus, Manlius, Fabius, Scipio, and the like; and when they failed to chuse such as were fit for the work to be done, they received such defeats as convinced them of their error. But if our author say true, order did require that the power of defending the country should have been annexed as an inheritance to one family, or left to him that could get it, and the exercise of all authority committed to the next in blood, tho the weakest of women, or the basest of men.

[2] Si puo far questa conclusione, che dove la materia non e corrotta, i tumulti ed altri scandali non nuocono: là dove la e corrotta le buone leggi non giovano. Machiav. Disc. sopra T. Livio, lib. 1. [Niccolo Machiavelli, *Discourses on Livy*, bk. 1, ch. 17.]

The like may be said of judging, or doing of justice; and 'tis absurd to pretend that either is expected from the power, not the person of the monarch; for experience doth too well shew how much all things halt in relation to justice or defence, when there is a defect in him that ought to judge us, and to fight our battles. But of all things this ought least to be alleged by the advocates for absolute monarchy, who deny that the authority can be separated from the person, and lay it as a fundamental principle, that whosoever hath it may do what he pleases, and be accountable to no man.

Our author's next work is to shew, that stability is the effect of this good order; but he ought to have known, that stability is then only worthy of praise, when it is in that which is good. No man delights in sickness or pain, because it is long, or incurable; nor in slavery and misery, because it is perpetual: much less will any man in his senses commend a permanency in vice and wickedness. He must therefore prove, that the stability he boasts of is in things that are good, or all that he says of it signifies nothing.

I might leave him here with as little fear, that any man who shall espouse his quarrel, shall ever be able to remove this obstacle, as that he himself should rise out of his grave and do it: but I hope to prove, that of all things under the sun, there is none more mutable or unstable than absolute monarchy; which is all that I dispute against, professing much veneration for that which is mixed, regulated by law, and directed to the publick good.

This might be proved by many arguments, but I shall confine myself to two; the one drawn from reason, the other from matters of fact.

Nothing can be called stable, that is not so in principle and practice, in which respect human nature is not well capable of stability; but the utmost deviation from it that can be imagined, is, when such an error is laid for a foundation as can never be corrected. All will confess, that if there be any stability in man, it must be in wisdom and virtue, and in those actions that are thereby directed; for in weakness, folly and madness there can be none. The stability therefore that we seek, in relation to the exercise of civil and military powers, can never be found, unless care be taken that such as shall exercise those powers, be endowed with the qualities that should make them stable. This is utterly repugnant to our author's doctrine: He lays for a foundation, that the succession goes to the next in blood, without distinction of age, sex, or personal qualities; whereas even he himself could not have the impudence to say, that children, and women (where they are admitted) or fools, madmen, and such as are full of all wickedness, do not come to be the heirs of reigning families, as well as of the meanest.[3] The stability therefore that can be expected from such a government, either depends upon those who have none in themselves, or is referred wholly to chance, which is directly opposite to stability.

This would be the case, tho it were (as we say) an even wager, whether the person would be fit or unfit, and that there were as many men in the world able, as unable to perform the duty of a king; but experience shewing that among many millions of men, there is hardly one that possesses the qualities required in a king, 'tis so many to one, that he upon whom the lot shall fall, will not be the man we seek, in whose person and government there can be such a stability as is asserted. And that failing, all must necessarily fail; for there can be no stability in his will, laws or actions, who has none in his person.

That we may see whether this be verified by experience, we need not search into the dark relations of the Babylonian and Assyrian monarchies: Those rude ages afford us little instruction; and tho the fragments of history remaining do sufficiently show, that all things there were in perpetual fluctuation, by reason of the madness of their kings, and the violence of those who transported the empire from one place or family to another, I will not much rely upon them, but slightly touching some of their stories, pass to those that are better known to us.

The kings of those ages seem to have lived rather like beasts in a forest than men joined in civil society: they followed the example of Nimrod the mighty hunter; force was the only law that prevailed, the stronger devoured the weaker, and continued in power till he was ejected by one of more strength or better fortune.[4] By this means the race of Ninus was destroy'd by Belochus: Arbaces rent the kingdom asunder, and took Media to himself. Morodach extinguished the race of Belochus, and was made king: Nebuchadnezzar like a flood overwhelmed all for a time, destroy'd the kingdoms of Jerusalem and Egypt, with many others, and found no obstacle, till his rage and pride turned to a most bestial madness: And the Assyrian empire was wholly abolish'd at the death of his grandchild Belshazzar;[5] and no stability can be found in the reigns of those great kings, unless that name be given to the pride, idolatry, cruelty and wickedness in which they remained constant. If we examine things more distinctly, we shall find that all things varied according to the humour of the prince. Whilst Pharaoh lived, who had received such signal

[3] [Filmer discusses succession as an inherited right in *Patriarcha*, ch. 5–6, pp. 60–63.]

[5] [Daniel 1–5.]

[4] [Genesis 10:8–12.]

services from Joseph, the Israelites were well used: but when another rose up who knew him not, they were persecuted with all the extremities of injustice and cruelty, till the furious king persisting in his design of exterminating them, brought destruction upon himself and the nation.[6] Where the like power hath prevailed, it has ever produced the like effects. When some great men of Persia had persuaded Darius, that it was a fine thing to command, that no man for the space of thirty days should make any petition to God or man, but to the king only, Daniel the most wise and holy man then in the world must be thrown to the lions. When God had miraculously saved him, the same sentence was passed against the princes of the nation.[7] When Haman had filled Ahasuerus his ears with lies, all the Jews were appointed to be slain; and when the fraud of that villain was detected, leave was given them, with the like precipitancy, to kill whom they pleased.[8] When the Israelites came to have kings, they were made subject to the same storms, and always with their blood suffer'd the penalty of their prince's madness. When one kind of fury possessed Saul, he slew the priests, persecuted David, and would have killed his brave son Jonathan: When he fell under another, he took upon him to do the priest's office, pretended to understand the word of God better than Samuel, and spared those that God had commanded him to destroy: Upon another whimsy he killed the Gibeonites, and never rested from finding new inventions to vex the people, till he had brought many thousands of them to perish with himself and his sons on Mount Gilboa.[9] We do not find any king, in wisdom, valour and holiness, equal to David; and yet he falling under the temptations that attend the greatest fortunes, brought civil wars and a plague upon the nation. When Solomon's heart was drawn away by strange women, he filled the land with idols, and oppressed the people with intolerable tributes.[10] Rehoboam's folly made that rent in the kingdom which could never be made up.[11] Under his successors the people served God, Baal or Ashtaroth, as best pleased him who had the power; and no other marks of stability can be alleged to have been in that kingdom, than the constancy of their kings in the practice of idolatry, their cruelty to the prophets, hatred to the Jews, and civil wars producing such slaughters as are reported in few other stories: The kingdom was in the space of about two hundred years possessed by nine several families, not one of them getting possession otherwise than

[6] [Exodus 1–11.]

[7] Dan. 6.

[8] [Esther 3–10.]

[9] [The reign of Saul is described in 1 Samuel 8–31.]

[10] [2 Samuel 11, 12.]

[11] [1 Kings 11.]

by the slaughter of his predecessor, and the extinction of his race; and ended in the bondage of the ten tribes, which continues to this day.[12]

He that desires farther proofs of this point, may seek them in the histories of Alexander of Macedon, and his successors: He seems to have been endow'd with all the virtues that nature improved by discipline did ever attain, so that he is believed to be the man meant by Aristotle, who on account of the excellency of his virtues was by nature framed for a king; and Plutarch ascribes his conquests rather to those, than to his fortune: But even that virtue was overthrown by the successes that accompanied it: He burnt the most magnificent palace of the world, in a frolick, to please a mad drunken whore: Upon the most frivolous suggestions of eunuchs and rascals, he kill'd the best and bravest of his friends; and his valour, which had no equal, not subsisting without his other virtues, perished when he became lewd, proud, cruel and superstitious; so as it may be truly said, he died a coward.[13] His successors did not differ from him: When they had killed his mother, wife and children, they exercised their fury against one another; and tearing the kingdom to pieces, the survivors left the sword as an inheritance to their families, who perished by it, or under the weight of the Roman chains.

When the Romans had lost that liberty which had been the nurse of their virtue, and gained the empire in lieu of it, they attained to our author's applauded stability. Julius being slain in the senate, the first question was, whether it could be restored, or not? And that being decided by the battle of Philippi, the conquerors set themselves to destroy all the eminent men in the city, as the best means to establish the monarchy. Augustus gained it by the death of Antonius, and the corruption of the soldiers; and he dying naturally, or by the fraud of his wife, the empire was transferred to her son Tiberius; under whom the miserable people suffer'd the worst effects of the most impure lust and inhuman cruelty: He being stifled, the government went on with much uniformity and stability; Caligula, Claudius, Nero, Galba, Otho, Vitellius regularly and constantly did all the mischief they could, and were not more like to each other in the villainies they committed, than in the deaths they suffered. Vespasian's more gentle reign did no way compensate the blood he spilt to attain the empire: And the benefits received from Titus his short-liv'd virtue, were infinitely overbalanced by the detestable vices of his brother Domitian, who turned all things into the old channel of cruelty, lust, rapine and perfidiousness. His slaughter gave

---

[12] [1 Kings 12.]

[13] Plut. in Vit. Alex. [Plutarch, *Life of Alexander.*]

a little breath to the gasping perishing world; and men might be virtuous under the government of Nerva, Trajan, Antoninus, Aurelius, and a few more; tho even in their time religion was always dangerous. But when the power fell into the hands of Commodus, Heliogabalus, Caracalla, and others of that sort, nothing was safe but obscurity, or the utmost excesses of lewdness and baseness. However, whilst the will of the governor passed for a law, and the power did usually fall into the hands of such as were most bold and violent, the utmost security that any man could have for his person or estate, depended upon his temper; and princes themselves, whether good or bad, had no longer leases of their lives, than the furious and corrupted soldiers would give them; and the empire of the world was changeable, according to the success of a battle.

Matters were not much mended when the emperors became Christians: Some favour'd those who were called Orthodox, and gave great revenues to corrupt the clergy. Others supported Arianism, and persecuted the Orthodox with as much asperity as the pagans had done. Some revolted, and shewed themselves more fierce against the professors of Christianity, than they that had never had any knowledge of it. The world was torn in pieces amongst them, and often suffered as great miseries by their sloth, ignorance and cowardice, as by their fury and madness, till the empire was totally dissolved and lost. That which under the weakness and irregularity of a popular government, had conquer'd all from the Euphrates to Britain, and destroyed the kingdoms of Asia, Egypt, Macedon, Numidia, and a multitude of others, was made a prey to unknown barbarous nations, and rent into as many pieces as it had been composed of, when it enjoy'd the stability that accompanies divine and absolute monarchy.

The like may be said of all the kingdoms in the world; they may have their ebbings and flowings according to the virtues or vices of princes or their favorites; but can never have any stability, because there is, and can be none in them: Or if any exception may be brought against this rule, it must be of those monarchies only which are mixed and regulated by laws, where diets, parliaments, assemblies of estates or senates, may supply the defects of a prince, restrain him if he prove extravagant, and reject such as are found to be unworthy of their office, which are as odious to our author and his followers, as the most popular governments, and can be of no advantage to his cause.

There is another ground of perpetual fluctuation in absolute monarchies; or such as are grown so strong, that they cannot be restrained by law, tho according to their institution they ought to be, distinct from, but in some measure relating to the inclinations of the monarch, that is, the impulse of ministers, favorites, wives or whores, who frequently govern all things according to their own passions or interests. And tho we cannot say who were the favorites of every one of the Assyrian or Egyptian kings, yet the examples before-mentioned of the different method follow'd in Egypt before, and after the death of Joseph, and in Persia whilst the idolatrous princes, and Haman, or Daniel, Esther and Mordecai were in credit; the violent changes happening thereupon, give us reason to believe the like were in the times of other kings: and if we examine the histories of later ages, and the lives of princes that are more exactly known, we shall find that kingdoms are more frequently swayed by those who have power with the prince, than by his own judgment: So that whosoever hath to deal with princes concerning foreign or domestick affairs, is obliged more to regard the humour of those persons, than the most important interests of a prince or people.

I might draw too much envy upon myself, if I should take upon me to cite all the examples of this kind that are found in modern histories, or the memoirs that do more precisely shew the temper of princes, and the secret springs by which they were moved. But as those who have well observed the management of affairs in France during the reigns of Francis the First, Henry the Second, Francis the Second, Charles the Ninth, Henry the Third, Henry the Fourth, and Lewis the Thirteenth, will confess, that the interests of the dukes of Montmorency and Guise, Queen Catherine de Medici, the duke of Epernon, La Fosseuse, Madame de Guiche, de Gabriele, d'Entragues, the Marechal d'Ancre, the Constable de Luines, and the Cardinal de Richelieu,[14] were more to be consider'd by those who had any private or publick business to treat at court, than the opinions of those princes, or the most weighty concernments of the state; so it cannot be denied, that other kingdoms where princes legally have, or wrongfully usurp the like power, are governed in the like manner; or if it be, there is hardly any prince's reign that will not furnish abundant proof of what I have asserted.

I agree with our author, that *good order and stability produce strength.* If monarchy therefore excel in them, absolute monarchies should be of more strength than those that are limited according to the proportion of their riches, extent of territory, and number of people that they govern; and those limited monarchies in the like proportion more strong than popular governments or commonwealths. If this be so, I wonder how a few of *those giddy Greeks who,* according to our author, *had learning enough only to make them seditious,*[15] came to overthrow those vast armies of the

[14] [These royal favorites held great sway over their respective monarchs in France.]

[15] [*Patriarcha*, ch. 15, pp. 85–86.]

Persians as often as they met with them; and seldom found any other difficulty than what did arise from their own countrymen, who sometimes sided with the barbarians. Seditions are often raised by a little prating; but when one man was to fight against fifty, or a hundred, as at the battles of Salamis, Plataea, Marathon, and others, then industry, wisdom, skill and valour was required; and if their learning had not made them to excel in those virtues, they must have been overwhelmed by the prodigious multitudes of their enemies. This was so well known to the Persians, that when Cyrus the younger prepar'd to invade his brother Artaxerxes, he brought together indeed a vast army of Asiaticks; but chiefly relied upon the counsel and valour of ten thousand Grecians, whom he had engaged to serve him. These giddy heads, accompanied with good hands, in the great battle near Babylon, found no resistance from Artaxerxes his army; and when Cyrus was killed by accident in the pursuit of the victory they had gained, and their own officers treacherously murder'd, they made good their retreat into Greece under the conduct of Xenophon, in despite of above four hundred thousand horse and foot, who endeavour'd to oppose them. They were destitute of horse, money, provisions, friends and all other help, except what their wisdom and valour furnished them; and thereupon relying, they passed over the bellies of all the enemies that ventur'd to appear against them in a march of a thousand miles. These things were performed in the weakness of popular confusion; but Agesilaus not being sensible of so great defects, accompanied only with six and thirty Spartans, and such other forces as he could raise upon his personal credit, adventured without authority or money to undertake a war against that great king Artaxerxes; and having often beaten Pharnabazus and Tissaphernes his lieutenants, was preparing to assault him in the heart of his kingdom, when he was commanded by the *ephori* to return for the defence of his own country.[16]

It may in like manner appear strange, that Alexander with the forces of Greece, much diminished by the Phocaean, Peloponnesian, Theban, and other intestine wars, could overthrow all the powers of the East, and conquer more provinces than any other army ever saw; if so much order and stability were to be found in absolute monarchies, and if the liberty in which the Grecians were educated did only fit them for seditions: and it would seem no less astonishing, that Rome and Greece, whilst they were free, should furnish such numbers of men excelling in all moral virtues, to the admiration of all succeeding ages; and thereby become so powerful that no monarchs were able to resist them; and that the same

16 Plut. vit. Artax. [Plutarch, *Life of Artaxerxes.*]

countries since the loss of their liberty, have always been weak, base, cowardly and vicious, if the same liberty had not been the mother and nurse of their virtue, as well as the root of their power.

It cannot be said that Alexander was a monarch in our author's sense; for the power of the Macedonian kings was small. Philip confessed the people were freemen, and his son found them to be so, when his fortune had overthrown his virtue, and he fell to hate and fear that generosity of spirit which it creates. He made his conquests by it, and lov'd it as long as he deserved to be lov'd. His successors had the same fortune: When their hearts came to be filled with barbarick pride, and to delight only in rendering men slaves, they became weak and base, and were easily overthrown by the Romans, whose virtue and fortune did also perish with their liberty. All the nations they had to deal with, had the same fate. They never conquer'd a free people without extreme difficulty: They received many great defeats, and were often necessitated to fight for their lives against the Latins, Sabines, Tuscans, Samnites, Carthaginians, Spaniards; and in the height of their power found it a hard work to subdue a few poor Aetolians: But the greatest kings were easily overcome. When Antiochus had insolently boasted that he would cover Greece and Italy with the multitude of his troops, Quintus Flaminius ingeniously compared his army of Persians, Chaldeans, Syrians, Mesopotamians, Cappadocians, Arabians, and other base Asiatic slaves, to a supper set before him by a Grecian friend, which seeming to be of several sorts of venison, was all cut out of one hog, variously dress'd; and not long after was as easily slaughter'd as the hog had been.[17] The greatest danger of the war with Mithridates was to avoid his poisons and treacheries; and to follow him through the deserts where he fled. When Lucullus with less than twenty thousand men had put Tigranes with two hundred thousand to flight, the Roman soldiers who for a while had pursued the chase, stood still on a sudden, and fell into loud laughter at themselves for using their arms against such wretched cowardly slaves.[18] If this be not enough to prove the falsehood of our author's proposition, I desire it may be consider'd whether good order or stability be wanting in Venice: Whether Tuscany be in a better condition to defend itself since it fell under the power of the Medicis, or when it was full of free cities: Whether it were an easy work to conquer Switzerland: Whether the Hollanders are of greater strength since the recovery of their liberty, or when they groaned under the yoke of Spain: And lastly, whether the entire conquest of Scotland and Ireland, the victories obtained against the Hollanders

---

[17] Plut. in vit. Q. Flamin. [Plutarch, *Life of Quintus Flaminius*, ch. 17.]

[18] Plut. in vit. Lucul. [Plutarch, *Life of Lucullus*, ch. 28.]

when they were in the height of their power, and the reputation to which England did rise in less than five years after 1648,[19] be good marks of the instability, disorder, and weakness of free nations: And if the contrary be true, nothing can be more absurdly false than our author's assertion.

SECTION 12

The Glory, Virtue, and Power of the Romans began and ended with their Liberty.

AMONG many fine things proposed by our author, I see none more to be admired, or that better declares the soundness of his judgment, than that he is only pleased with the beginning and end of the Roman empire; and says, *that their time of liberty* (between those two extremes) *had nothing of good in it, but that it was of short continuance:*[1] whereas I dare affirm that all that was ever desirable, or worthy of praise and imitation in Rome, did proceed from its liberty, grow up and perish with it: which I think will not be contradicted by any, but those who prefer the most sordid vices before the most eminent virtues; who believe the people to have been more worthily employ'd by the Tarquins in cleaning jakes and common shores, than in acquiring the dominion of the best part of mankind; and account it better for a people to be oppressed with hard labour under a proud master in a sterile, unhealthy ten-mile territory, than to command all the countries that lie between the Euphrates and Britain. Such opinions will hardly find any better patrons than Filmer and his disciples, nor the matters of fact, as they are represented, be denied by any that know the histories of those times. Many Romans may have had seeds of virtue in them, whilst in the infancy of that city they lived under kings; but they brought forth little fruit. Tarquin, surnamed the Proud, being a Grecian by extraction, had perhaps observed that the virtue of that nation had rendered them averse to the divine government he desir'd to set up; and having by his well-natur'd Tullia poison'd his own brother her husband, and his own wife her sister, married her, killed her father, and spared none that he thought able to oppose his designs,

---

[19] [Charles I was executed in early 1649, from which time Parliament governed England unchallenged until 1653.]

[1] [*Patriarcha*, ch. 16 ("Imperfections of De-mocracies. Rome Began Her Empire under Kings and Perfected It under Emperors. The People of Rome in Danger Oft Fled to Monarchy"), p. 87.]

to finish the work, he butcher'd the senate, with such as seemed most eminent among the people, and like a most pious father endeavour'd to render the city desolate: during that time they who would not be made instruments of those villainies were obliged for their own safety to conceal their virtues; but he being removed, they shined in their glory. Whilst he reign'd, Brutus, Valerius, Horatius, Herminius, Larcius, and Coriolanus, lay hid and unregarded; but when they came to fight for themselves, and to employ their valour for the good of their country, they gave such testimonies of bravery, as have been admired by all succeeding ages, and settled such a discipline, as produced others like to them, or more excellent than they, as long as their liberty lasted. In two hundred and sixty years that they remained under the government of kings, tho all of them, the last only excepted, were chosen by the senate and people, and did as much to advance the publick service as could reasonably be expected from them, their dominion hardly extended so far as from London to Hownslow: But in little more than three hundred years after they recovered their liberty, they had subdued all the warlike nations of Italy, destroy'd vast armies of the Gauls, Cimbri, and Germans, overthrown the formidable power of Carthage, conquer'd the Cisalpine and Transalpine Gauls, with all the nations of Spain, notwithstanding the ferocity of the one, and the more constant valour of the other, and the prodigious multitudes of both: They had brought all Greece into subjection, and by the conquest of Macedon the spoils of the world to adorn their city; and found so little difficulty in all the wars that happened between them and the greatest king after the death of Alexander of Epirus and Pyrrhus, that the defeats of Syphax, Perseus, Antiochus, Prusias, Tigranes, Ptolemy, and many others, did hardly deserve to be numbered amongst their victories.

It were ridiculous to impute this to chance, or to think that fortune, which of all things is the most variable, could for so many ages continue the same course, unless supported by virtue; or to suppose that all these monarchies which are so much extoll'd, could have been destroyed by that commonwealth, if it had wanted strength, stability, virtue, or good order. The secret counsels of God are impenetrable; but the ways by which he accomplishes his designs are often evident: When he intends to exalt a people, he fills both them and their leaders with the virtues suitable to the accomplishment of his end; and takes away all wisdom and virtue from those he resolves to destroy. The pride of the Babylonians and Assyrians fell through the baseness of Sardanapalus; and the great city was taken while Belshazzar lay drunk amongst his whores: The empire was transported to the Persians and Grecians by the valor of Cyrus,

Alexander, and the brave armies that follow'd them. Histories furnish us with innumerable examples of this kind: But I think none can be found of a cowardly, weak, effeminate, foolish, ill disciplin'd people, that have ever subdued such as were eminent in strength, wisdom, valor, and good discipline; or that these qualities have been found or subsisted anywhere, unless they were cultivated and nourished by a well order'd government. If this therefore was found among the Romans, and not in the kingdoms they overthrew, they had the order and stability which the monarchies had not; and the strength and virtue by which they obtained such success was the product of them. But if this virtue and the glorious effects of it did begin with liberty, it did also expire with the same. The best men that had not fallen in battle were gleaned up by the proscriptions, or circumvented for the most part by false and frivolous accusations. Mankind is inclin'd to vice, and the way to virtue is so hard, that it wants encouragement; but when all honours, advantages and preferments are given to vice, and despised virtue finds no other reward than hatred, persecution, and death, there are few who will follow it. Tacitus well describes the state of the empire, when the power was absolutely fallen into the hands of one: *Italia novis cladibus, vel post longam seculorum seriem repetitis, afflicta; urbs incendiis vastata, consumptis antiquissimis delubris, ipso Capitolio civium manibus incenso; pollutae ceremoniae; magna adulteria; plenum exiliis mare; infecti caedibus scopuli; atrocius in urbe saevitum; nobilitas, opes, omissi vel gesti honores pro crimine, & ob virtutes certissimum exitium.*[2] His following words shew, that the rewards of these abominations were not less odious than the things themselves: The highest dignities were bestowed upon the *delatores*, who were a kind of rogues like to our Irish witnesses, or those that by a new coin'd word we call *trepanners*. This is not a picture drawn by a vulgar hand, but by one of the best painters in the world; and being a model that so much pleases our author, 'tis good to see what it produced. The first fruit was such an entire degeneracy from all good, that Rome may be justly said never to have produced a brave man since the first age of her slavery. Germanicus and Corbulo were born *expirante libertate;*[3] and the recompence they received did so little encourage others to follow their example, that none have been found in any degree like to

[2] C. Tacit. Hist. l. 1. ["Italy was afflicted with new disasters or ones that recurred after a long series of ages; the city was devastated by conflagrations, in which her most ancient shrines were consumed and the very Capitol fired by citizens' hands; the rites were polluted; there were great adulteries; the sea was filled with exiles, the cliffs stained with their blood; in the city there was more awful savagery; nobility, wealth, the refusal or acceptance of office, were grounds for accusations, and virtues ensured ruin." Tacitus, *Histories*, bk. 1, ch. 2.]

[3] ["When liberty was dying."]

them; and those of the most noble families applied themselves to sleep, laziness, and luxury, that they might not be suspected to be better than their masters. Thrasea, Soranus, and Helvidius were worthy men, who resolved to persist in their integrity, tho they should die for it; but that was the only thing that made them eminent; for they were of unknown families, not Romans by birth, nor ever employ'd in war: And those emperors who did arrive to any degree of virtue, were Spaniards, Gauls, Africans, Thracians, and of all nations, except Romans. The patrician and plebeian families, which for many ages had fill'd the world with great commanders, and such as excelled in all virtues, being thus extinguished or corrupted, the common people fell into the lowest degree of baseness: *Plebs sordida circo & theatris sueta.*[4] That people which in magnanimity surpassed all that have been known in the world; who never found any enterprize above their spirit to undertake, and power to accomplish, with their liberty lost all their vigour and virtue. They who by their votes had disposed of kingdoms and provinces, fell to desire nothing but to live and see plays.

> *Duas tantum res anxius optat,*
> *Panem & circenses.*[5]

Whether their emperors were good or bad, they usually rejoic'd at their death, in hopes of getting a little money or victuals from the successor. Tho the empire was by this means grown weak and bloodless, yet it could not fall on a sudden: So vast a body could not die in a moment: All the neighbouring nations had been so much broken by their power, that none was able to take advantage of their weakness; and life was preserved by the strength of hungry barbarians, allured by the greatness of the pay they received to defend those, who had no power left to defend themselves. This precarious and accidental help could not be durable. They who for a while had been contented with their wages, soon began to think it fit for them rather to fight for themselves, than for their weak masters; and thereupon fell to set up emperors depending on themselves, or to seize upon the naked provinces, where they found no other difficulty than to contend with other strangers, who might have the like design upon the same. Thus did the armies of the East and West set up emperors at their pleasure; and tho the Goths, Vandals, Huns, Sueves, Alans, and others had cruel wars among themselves, yet they feared and suffered

[4] C. Tacit. ["The degraded common people frequented the circus and theaters." Tacitus, *Histories*, bk. 1, ch. 4.]

[5] Juven. Sat. ["Anxiously the people desire only two things, bread and circuses." Juvenal, *Satire* 10, li. 80.]

little or nothing from the Romans. This state of things was so soon observed, that in the beginning of Tiberius his reign they who endeavoured to excite the Gauls to take arms, used no other arguments than such as were drawn from the extreme weakness of the Romans, *Quam inops Italia, plebs urbana imbellis, nihil in exercitibus validum praeter externum.*[6] It was evident that after the battles of Philippi and Actium, the strength of the Roman armies consisted of strangers; and even the victories that went under their name were gained by those nations which in the time of their liberty they had subdued. They had nothing left but riches gather'd out of their vast dominions; and they learnt by their ruin, that an empire acquir'd by virtue could not long be supported by money. They who by their valour had arrived at such a height of glory, power, greatness, and happiness as was never equalled, and who in all appearance had nothing to fear from any foreign power, could never have fallen, unless their virtue and discipline had decay'd, and the corruption of their manners had excited them to turn their victorious swords into their own bowels. Whilst they were in that flourishing condition, they thought they had nothing more to desire than continuance: but if our author's judgment is to be followed, there was *nothing of good in it, except the shortness of its continuance;* they were beholden to those who wrought the change, they were the better for the battles of Pharsalia, Philippi, Munda, and Actium; the destruction of two thirds of the people, with the slaughter of all the most eminent men among them was for their advantage: The proscriptions were wholesome remedies: Tacitus did not understand the state of his own country, when he seems to be ashamed to write the history of it, *Nobis in arcto & inglorius labor;*[7] when instead of such glorious things as had been achieved by the Romans, whilst either the senate, or the common people prevailed, he had nothing left to relate, but *saeva jussa, continuas accusationes, fallaces amicitias, perniciem innocentium.*[8] They enjoy'd nothing that was good from the expulsion of the Tarquins to the reestablishment of divine absolute monarchy in the persons of those pious fathers of the people, Tiberius, Caligula, Claudius, Nero, Galba, Otho, Vitellius, &c. There was no virtue in the Junii, Horatii, Cornelii, Quintii, Decii, Manlii; but the generous and tender-hearted princes before-mentioned were perfect examples of it: Whilst annual magistrates governed, there was no stability; Sejanus, Macro, and Tigellinus introduced good order: Virtue

---

[6] C. Tacit. An. l. 3. ["How weak is Italy, how unwarlike the common people of the city; there is no strength in the armies except the foreign element." Tacitus, *Annals*, bk. 3, ch. 4.]

[7] Annal. l. 4. ["My labor is restricted and inglorious." Ibid., bk. 4, ch. 32.]

[8] ["Savage commands, endless accusations, false friendships, destruction of the innocent." Ibid., ch. 33.]

was not esteemed by the ancient senate and people; Messalina, Agrippina, Poppaea, Narcissus, Pallas, Vinius, and Laco knew how to put a just value upon it: The irregularities of popular assemblies, and want of prudence in the senate, was repaired by the temperate proceedings of the German, Pannonian and Eastern armies, or the modest discretion of the Praetorian bands: The city was delivered by them from the burden of governing the world, and for its own good frequently plunder'd, fired; and at last, with the rest of desolated Italy, and the noblest provinces of Europe, Asia, and Africa, brought under the yoke of the most barbarous and cruel nations. By the same light we may see that those who endeavour'd to perpetuate the misery of liberty to Rome, or lost their lives in the defence of it, were the worst, or the most foolish of men, and that they were the best who did overthrow it. This rectifies all our errors; and if the highest praises are due to him that did the work, the next are well deserved by those who perished in attempting it: and if the sons of Brutus, with their companions the Vitellii and Aquilii; Claudius Appius the decemvir; those that would have betrayed the city to Porsenna; Spurius Maelius, Spur. Cassius, Manlius Capitolinus, Saturninus, Catiline, Cethegus, Lentulus, had been as fortunate as Julius Caesar, they might as well have deserved an apotheosis. But if all this be false, absurd, bestial, and abominable, the principles that necessarily lead us to such conclusions are so also; which is enough to shew, that the strength, virtue, glory, wealth, power, and happiness of Rome proceeding from liberty, did rise, grow, and perish with it.

SECTION 13

*There is no disorder or prejudice in changing
the name or number of Magistrates, whilst the root and principle
of their Power continues entire.*

I N the next place our author would persuade us that the Romans were inconstant, because of their changes from annual consuls to military tribunes, decemviri, and dictators; and gives the name of sedition to the complaints made against usury, or the contests concerning marriages or magistracy: but I affirm,

   1. That no change of magistracy, as to the name, number, or form, doth testify irregularity, or bring any manner of prejudice, as long as it

is done by those who have a right of doing it, and he or they who are created continue within the power of the law to accomplish the end of their institution; many forms being in themselves equally good, and may be used as well one as another, according to times and other circumstances.

2. In the second place, 'tis a rare thing for a city at the first to be rightly constituted: Men can hardly at once foresee all that may happen in many ages, and the changes that accompany them ought to be provided for. Rome in its foundation was subject to these defects, and the inconveniences arising from them were by degrees discover'd and remedi'd. They did not think of regulating usury, till they saw the mischiefs proceeding from the cruelty of usurers; or setting limits to the proportion of land that one man might enjoy, till the avarice of a few had so far succeeded, that their riches were grown formidable, and many by the poverty to which they were reduced became useless to the city. It was not time to make a law that the plebeians might marry with the patricians, till the distinction had raised the patricians to such pride, as to look upon themselves to have something of divine, and the others to be *inauspicati* or profane, and brought the city into danger by that division; nor to make the plebeians capable of being elected to the chief magistracies, till they had men able to perform the duties of them. But these things being observed, remedies were seasonably applied without any bloodshed or mischief, tho not without noise and wrangling.

3. All human constitutions are subject to corruption, and must perish, unless they are timely renewed, and reduced to their first principles: This was chiefly done by means of those tumults which our author ignorantly blames: The whole people by whom the magistracy had been at first created, executed their power in those things which comprehend sovereignty in the highest degree, and brought everyone to acknowledge it: There was nothing that they could not do, who first conferr'd the supreme honours upon the patricians, and then made the plebeians equal to them. Yet their modesty was not less than their power or courage to defend it: and therefore when by the law they might have made a plebeian consul, they did not chuse one in forty years; and when they did make use of their right in advancing men of their own order, they were so prudent, that they cannot be said to have been mistaken in their elections three times, whilst their votes were free: whereas, of all the emperors that came in by usurpation, pretence of blood from those who had usurped, or that were set up by the soldiers, or a few electors, hardly three can be named who deserved that honour, and most of them were such as seemed to be born for plagues to mankind.

4. He manifests his fraud or ignorance in attributing the legislative

power sometimes to the senate, and sometimes to the people; for the senate never had it. The style of *senatus censuit, populus jussit,*[1] was never alter'd; but the right of advising continuing in the senate, that of enacting ever continued in the people.

5. An occasion of commending absolute power, in order to the establishment of hereditary monarchy, is absurdly drawn from their custom of creating a dictator in time of danger; for no man was ever created, but such as seemed able to bear so great a burden, which in hereditary governments is wholly left to chance. Tho his power was great, it did arise from the law; and being confin'd to six months, 'twas almost impossible for any man to abuse it, or to corrupt so many of those who had enjoy'd the same honour, or might aspire to it, as to bring them for his pleasure to betray their country: and as no man was ever chosen who had not given great testimonies of his virtues, so no one did ever forfeit the good opinion conceived of him. Virtue was then honour'd, and thought so necessarily to comprehend a sincere love and fidelity to the commonwealth, that without it the most eminent qualities were reputed vile and odious; and the memory of former services could no way expiate the guilt of conspiring against it. This seeming severity was in truth the greatest clemency: for tho our author has the impudence to say, that during the *Roman liberty the best men thrived worst, and the worst best,*[2] he cannot allege one example of any eminent Roman put to death (except Manlius Capitolinus) from the expulsion of the Tarquins to the time of the Gracchi, and the Civil Wars not long after ensuing; and of very few who were banished. By these means crimes were prevented; and the temptations to evil being removed, treachery was destroy'd in the root; and such as might be naturally ambitious, were made to see there was no other way to honour and power than by acting virtuously.

But lest this should not be sufficient to restrain aspiring men, what power soever was granted to any magistrate, the sovereignty still remained in the people, and all without exception were subject to them. This may seem strange to those who think the dictators were absolute, because they are said to have been *sine provocatione;*[3] but that is to be only understood in relation to other magistrates, and not to the people, as is clearly proved in the case of Q. Fabius, whom Papirius the dictator would have put to death: *Tribunos plebis appello,* says Fabius Maximus his father, *& provoco ad populum, eumque tibi fugienti exercitus tui, fugienti senatus judicium, judicem fero; qui certe unus plusquam tua dictatura potest polletque: videro, cessurusne sis*

---

[1] [The senate advises, the people command.]   [3] [Without appeal.]

[2] [*Patriarcha*, ch. 18, p. 89.]

provocationi, cui Tullus Hostilius cessit.[4] And tho the people did rather intercede for Fabius than command his deliverance, that modesty did evidently proceed from an opinion that Papirius was in the right; and tho they desired to save Fabius, who seems to have been one of the greatest and best men that ever the city produced, they would not enervate that military discipline, to which they owed, not only their greatness, but their subsistence; most especially when their sovereign authority was acknowledged by all, and the dictator himself had submitted. This right of appeals to the people was the foundation of the Roman commonwealth, laid in the days of Romulus, submitted to by Hostilius in the case of Horatius,[5] and never violated, till the laws and the liberty which they supported were overthrown by the power of the sword. This is confirmed by the speech of Metellus the tribune, who in the time of the second Carthaginian War, causelessly disliking the proceedings of Q. Fabius Maximus then dictator, in a publick assembly of the people said, *Quod si antiquus animus plebi Romanae esset, se audacter laturum de abrogando Q. Fabii imperio; nunc modicam rogationem promulgaturum, de aequando magistri equitum & dictatoris jure:*[6] which was done, and that action, which had no precedent, shews that the people needed none, and that their power being eminently above that of all magistrates was obliged to no other rule than that of their own will. Tho I do therefore grant that a power like to the dictatorian, limited in time, circumscribed by law, and kept perpetually under the supreme authority of the people, may, by virtuous and well-disciplin'd nations, upon some occasions, be prudently granted to a virtuous man, it can have no relation to our author's monarch, whose power is in himself, subject to no law, perpetually exercised by himself, and for his own sake, whether he have any of the abilities required for the due performance of so great a work, or be entirely destitute of them; nothing being more unreasonable than to deduce consequences from cases, which in substance and circumstances are altogether unlike: but to the contrary, these examples shewing that the Romans, even in the time of such magistrates as seemed to be most absolute, did retain and exercise

[4] T. Liv. l. 8. ["I will call upon the tribunes of the people, and I will appeal to the people and bring them as judge to you who avoid the judgment of your army and the senate; the people, who alone are more capable and powerful than your dictatorship: I will see whether you intend to yield to the appeal to which Tullus Hostilius yielded." Livy, *History of Rome*, bk. 8, ch. 33.]

[5] T. Liv. l. 1. [Ibid., bk. 1, ch. 26.]

[6] T. Liv. l. 22. ["But if the Roman plebs had their ancient spirit, they would boldly assert themselves concerning the removal of Quintus Fabius' power; now they intend to publish a modest request concerning the equalization of the right of the master of the cavalry and the dictator." Ibid., bk. 22, ch. 25.]

the sovereign power, do most evidently prove that the government was ever the same remaining in the people, who without prejudice might give the administration to one or more men as best pleased themselves, and the success shews that they did it prudently.

SECTION 14

No Sedition was hurtful to Rome,
till through their Prosperity some men gained
a Power above the Laws.

LITTLE pains is required to confute our author, who imputes much bloodshed to the popular government of Rome; for he cannot prove that one man was unjustly put to death, or slain in any sedition before Publius Gracchus: The foundations of the commonwealth were then so shaken, that the laws could not be executed; and whatsoever did then fall out ought to be attributed to the monarchy for which the great men began to contend. Whilst they had no other wars than with neighbouring nations, they had a strict eye upon their commanders, and could preserve discipline among the soldiers: but when by the excellence of their valour and conduct the greatest powers of the world were subdued, and for the better carrying on of foreign wars, armies were suffered to continue in the same hands longer than the law did direct, soldiery came to be accounted a trade, and those who had the worst designs against the commonwealth, began to favour all manner of licentiousness and rapine, that they might gain the favour of the legions, who by that means became unruly and seditious; 'twas hard, if not impossible, to preserve a civil equality, when the spoils of the greatest kingdoms were brought to adorn the houses of private men; and they who had the greatest cities and nations to be their dependents and clients, were apt to scorn the power of the law. This was a most dangerous disease, like those to which human bodies are subject when they are arrived to that which physicians call the athletick habit, proceeding from the highest perfection of health, activity and strength, that the best constitution by diet and exercise can attain. Whosoever falls into them shews that he had attain'd that perfection; and he who blames that which brings a state into the like condition, condemns that which is most perfect among men. Whilst the Romans were in the way to this, no sedition did them any hurt: they were composed without blood; and those that seemed to be the most dangerous, produced the best laws. But when they were arrived to that condition, no order could do them good; the fatal period set to human things was come, they could go no higher,

Summisque negatum
Stare diu;[1]

and all that our author blames, is not to be imputed to their constitution, but their departing from it. All men were ever subject to error, and it may be said that the mistaken people in the space of about three hundred years did unjustly fine or banish five or six men; but those mistakes were so frankly acknowledged, and carefully repair'd by honours bestow'd upon the injured persons, as appears by the examples of Camillus, Livius Salinator, Aemilius Paulus, and others, that they deserve more praise than if they had not failed.

If for the above-mentioned time seditions were harmless or profitable, they were also absolutely exempted from civil wars. Those of Apulia and Greece were revolts of conquer'd nations, and can no way fall under that name: But 'tis most absurdly applied to the servile and gladiatorian wars; for the gladiators were slaves also, and civil wars can be made only by those who are members of the civil society, which slaves are not. Those that made the *bellum sociale*,[2] were freemen, but not citizens; and the war they made could not be called civil. The Romans had three ways of dealing with conquered nations.

1. Some were received into the body of the city, *civitate donati*,[3] as the Latins by Romulus; the Albans by Hostilius; the Privernates when their ambassador declared, that no peace could be durable unless it were just and easy; and the Senate said, *se viri & liberi vocem audivisse, talesque dignos esse ut Romani fiant;*[4] and the like favour was shewn to many others.

2. By making leagues with them, as Livy says, *populum Romanum devictos bello populos, malle societate & amicitia habere conjunctos, quam tristi subjectos servitio:*[5] Of which sort were the Samnites, who not liking their condition, joined with Hannibal; and afterwards, under the conduct of the brave Telesinus, with other nations that lived under the condition of *socii*, made an unprosperous attempt to deliver themselves.

---

[1] Lucan. l. 1. ["To those who are highest it is denied that they stand long." Lucan, *Pharsalia*, bk. 1, li. 70.]

[2] [Social War.]

[3] [Presented with citizenship.]

[4] ["That they had heard the voice of a man, indeed a free man, and that such are worthy to become Romans." Livy, *History of Rome*, bk. 8, ch. 21.]

[5] ["The Roman people prefer to hold those peoples conquered in war in joint alliance and friendship, rather than subdued in sad slavery." Ibid., bk. 26, ch. 49.]

3. Those who after many rebellions were *in provinciam redacti*,[6] as the Capuans, when their city was taken by Appius Claudius, and Q. Fulvius Flaccus.

We often hear of wars made by those of the two latter sorts; but of none that can be called civil, till the times of Marius, Sulla, and Catiline: and as they are to be esteemed the last strugglings of expiring liberty, when the laws, by which it had subsisted, were enervated: so those that happened between Caesar and Pompey, Octavius and Antonius, with the proscriptions, triumvirate, and all the mischiefs that accompanied them, are to be imputed wholly to the monarchy for which they contended, as well as those between Nero, Galba, Otho, Vitellius, and Vespasian, that hardly ever ceased till the empire was abolished; for the name of a commonwealth continued to the end; and I know not why Tiberius or Nero might not use it as well as Sulla or Marius.

Yet if our author be resolved to impute to popular government all that passed before Caesar made himself perpetual dictator, he will find no more than is seen in all places. We have known few small states, and no great one free from revolts of subjects or allies; and the greatest empire of the East was overthrown by the rebellion of the Mamelukes their slaves. If there is any difference to be observed between what happened at Rome, 'tis chiefly, that whilst there was any shadow of liberty, the slaves, gladiators, subjects or allies, were always beaten and suppressed; whereas in the time of the emperors, the revolt of a province was sufficient to give a new master to the best part of mankind; and he having no more power than was required for a present mischief, was for the most part, in a short time, destroy'd by another. But to please our author, I will acknowledge a second defect, even that wantonness to which he ascribes all their disorders; tho I must withal desire him to consider from whence wantonness doth proceed. If the people of Turkey or France did rebel, I should think they were driven to it by misery, beggary, or despair; and could lay wantonness only to the charge of those who enjoy'd much prosperity. Nations that are oppress'd and made miserable, may fall into rage, but can never grow wanton. In the time of the Roman emperors, the praetorian cohorts, or the armies that had the liberty of ravaging the richest provinces, might be proud of their strength, or grow wanton through the abundance of their enjoyments: The Janizaries in later ages may, for the same reasons, have fallen into the like excesses; but such as have lost their liberty are in no danger of them. When all the nobility of Rome was destroyed, and those who excelled in reputation or virtue,

---

[6] [Reduced to a province.]

were fallen in the wars, or by the proscriptions; when two thirds of the people were slain, the best cities and colonies burnt, the provinces exhausted, and the small remains left in them oppressed with a most miserable slavery, they may have revolted, and sometimes did, as the Britains, Batavians, and others mentioned in the Roman history: But they were driven to those revolts by fury and necessity, arising from the miseries and indignities they suffer'd under an insupportable tyranny; and wantonness had no part in them. The people of Rome, when they were a little freed from the terror of the soldiers, did sometimes for the same reasons conspire against the emperors; and when they could do no more, expressed their hatred by breaking their statues: But after the battles of Pharsalia, Philippi, and the proscriptions, they never committed any folly through wantonness. In the like manner Naples and Sicily have revolted within these few years; and some who are well acquainted with the state of those kingdoms, think them ready again to do the like; but if it should so happen, no man of understanding would impute it to wantonness. The pressures under which they groan, have cured them of all such diseases: and the Romans since the loss of their liberty could never fall into them. They may have grown wanton when their authority was reverenced, their virtue admired, their power irresistible, and the riches of the world were flowing in upon them, as it were, to corrupt their manners, by enticing them to pleasure: But when all that was lost, and they found their persons expos'd to all manner of violence from the basest of men; their riches exhausted by tributes and rapine, whilst the treasures of the empire were not sufficient to supply the luxury of their masters; the misery they suffer'd, and the shame of suffering it, with the contemptible weakness to which they were reduc'd, did too strongly admonish them, that the vices of wantonness belonged only to those who enjoy'd a condition far different from theirs; and the memory of what they had lost, sharpened the sense of what they felt. This is the state of things which pleases our author; and, by praising that government, which depriv'd those who were under it of all that is most desirable in the world, and introduc'd all that ought to be detested, he sufficiently shews, that he delights only in that which is most abominable, and would introduce his admir'd absolute monarchy, only as an instrument of bringing vice, misery, devastation and infamy upon mankind.

SECTION 15

The Empire of Rome perpetually decay'd when it fell into the hands of one Man.

I N pursuance of his design our author, with as much judgment as truth, denies that Rome became mistress of the world under the popular government: *It is not so,* says he, *for Rome began her empire under kings, and did perfect it under emperors: It did only increase under that popularity: Her greatest exaltation was under Trajan, and longest peace under Augustus.*[1] For the illustration of which, I desire these few things may be consider'd.

1. That the first monarchy of Rome was not absolute: The kings were made by the people without regard to any man's title, or other reason than the common good, chusing him that seemed most likely to procure it; setting up at the same time a senate consisting of a hundred of the most eminent men among them; and, after the reception of the Sabines into the city, adding as many more to them, and committing the principal part of the government to their care, retaining the power of making those laws to which the kings who reigned by their command were subject, and reserving to themselves the judgment of all great matters upon appeal. If any of their kings deserved to be called a monarch, according to Filmer's definition, it was the last Tarquin; for he alone of all their kings reigned not *jussu populi,*[2] but came in by treachery and murder. If he had continued, he had cured the people of all vices proceeding from wantonness; but his farthest conquest was of the small town of Gabii ten miles distant from Rome, which he effected by the fraud of his detestable son; and that being then the utmost limit of the Roman empire, must deserve to be called the world, or the empire of it was not gained by their kings.

2. The extent of conquests is not the only, nor the chief thing that ought to be consider'd in them; regard is to be had to the means whereby they are made, and the valour or force that was employ'd by the enemy. In these respects not only the overthrow of Carthage, and the conquests of Spain, but the victories gained against the Sabines, Latins, Tuscans, Samnites, and other valiant nations of Italy, who most obstinately defended their liberty, when the Romans had no forces but their own, shew more virtue, and deserve incomparably more praise, than the defeats of any nations whatsoever, when they were increased in number, riches, reputation and power, and had many other warlike people instructed in their

[1] [*Patriarcha*, ch. 16, p. 87.]
[2] T. Liv. l. 2. ["By the command of the people." Livy, *History of Rome*, bk. 1, ch. 48–49.]

discipline, and fighting under their ensigns. But I deny that the Romans did ever make any considerable acquisition after the loss of their liberty. They had already subdued all Italy, Greece, Macedon, the islands of the Mediterranean Sea, Thracia, Illyrium, Asia the Less, Pontus, Armenia, Syria, Egypt, Africa, Gaul and Spain. The forces of Germany were broken; a bridge laid over the Rhine, and all the countries on this side subdued. This was all that was ever gained by the valour of their own forces, and that could bring either honour or profit. But I know of no conquest made after that time, unless the name of conquest be given to Caligula's expedition, when he said he had subdued the sea, in making an useless bridge from Puteoli to Baiae; or that of the other fool, who entered Rome in triumph, for having gathered shells on the sea-shore.[3] Trajan's expedition into the East, was rather a journey than a war: He rambled over the provinces that Augustus had abandoned as not worth keeping, and others that had nothing to defend them, but ill-armed and unwarlike barbarians: Upon the whole matter, he seems to have been led only by curiosity; and the vanity of looking upon them as conquests, appears in their being relinquish'd as soon as gained. Britain was easily taken from a naked and unskillful, tho a brave people; hardly kept, and shamefully lost. But tho the emperors had made greater wars than the commonwealth, vanquished nations of more valour and skill than their Italian neighbours, the Grecians or Carthaginians; subdued and slaughter'd those that in numbers and ferocity had exceeded the Cimbri, Gauls and Teutons, encountered captains more formidable than Pyrrhus and Hannibal, it might indeed increase the glory of him that should have done it, but could add nothing of honour or advantage to the Roman name: The nobility was extirpated long before, the people corrupted and enslaved, Italy lay desolate, so as a Roman was hardly to be found in a Roman army, which was generally composed of such, as fighting for themselves or their commander, never thought of anything less than the interest of Rome: And as it is impossible that what is so neglected and betray'd, should be durable, that empire which was acquired by the valour and conduct of the bravest and best disciplin'd people of the world, decay'd and perished in the hands of those absolute monarchs, who ought to have preserved it.

3. Peace is desirable by a state that is constituted for it, who contenting themselves with their own territories, have no desires of enlarging them: Or perhaps it might simply deserve praise, if mankind were so framed, that a people intending hurt to none, could preserve themselves; but the

[3] [Suetonius, *Life of Caligula*, ch. 19, 46.
"The other fool" was also Caligula.]

world being so far of another temper, that no nation can be safe without valour and strength, those governments only deserve to be commended, which by discipline and exercise increase both, and the Roman above all, that excelled in both. Peace therefore may be good in its season, and was so in Numa's reign; yet two or three such kings would have encouraged some active neighbours to put an end to that aspiring city, before its territory had extended beyond Fidenae. But the discipline that best agreed with the temper and designs of a warlike people, being renew'd by his brave successors, the dangers were put on their enemies; and all of them, the last only excepted, persisting in the same way, did reasonably well perform their duty. When they were removed, and the affairs of the city depended no longer upon the temper or capacity of one man, the ends for which the city was constituted were vigorously pursued, and such magistrates annually chosen, as would not long continue in a universal peace, till they had gotten the empire to which they aspir'd, or were by ill fortune brought to such weakness, as to be no longer able to make war. Both of these happened in the so much magnified reign of Augustus. He found the empire so great, that all additions might rationally be rejected as useless or prejudicial; and Italy so exhausted, that wars could only be carried on by the strength of strangers: It was time to lie still when they had no power to act; and they might do it safely, whilst the reputation gained by former victories preserved them from foreign invasions. When Crassus, Pompey, and Caesar, who had torn the commonwealth into three monarchies, were kill'd, and the flower of the Roman nobility and people destroyed with them, or by them: When Cato's virtue had prov'd too weak to support a falling state, and Brutus with Cassius had perished in their noble attempt to restore the liberty: When the best part of the senate had been exposed for a prey to the vultures and wolves of Thessaly, and one hundred and thirty of those who deserved the hatred of tyrants, and had escaped the fury of war, had been destroy'd by the proscriptions: When neither captains nor soldiers remained in the desolate city; when the tyrant abhorr'd and fear'd all those who had either reputation or virtue, and by the most subtle arts endeavoured so to corrupt or break the spirits of the remaining people, that they might not think of their former greatness, or the ways of recovering it, we ought not to wonder that they ceased from war. But such a peace is no more to be commended, than that which men have in the grave; as in the epitaph of the Marquess Trivultio seen at Milan, *Qui nunquam quievit, quiescit, tace.*[4] This peace is in every wilderness: The

---

[4] [He who never rested, rests: be silent.]

Turks have established it in the empty provinces of Asia and Greece. Where there are no men, or if those men have no courage, there can be no war. Our ancestors the Britains observed, that the peace which in that age the Romans established in the provinces, consisted in the most wretched slavery and solitude: *Miserrimam servitutem pacem appellant.* And in another place, *solitudinem faciunt, pacem vocant.*[5] This is the peace the Spaniards settled in their dominions of the West-Indies, by the destruction of forty millions of souls.[6] The countries were very quiet, when wild beasts only were left to fight in them, or a few miserable wretches, who had neither strength nor courage to resist their violence. This was the peace the Romans enjoyed under Augustus: A few of those who made themselves subservient to his pleasure, and ministers of the publick calamities, were put into a flourishing condition; but the rest pined, withered, and never recovered. If yet our author will have us to think the liberty and people of Rome obliged to Augustus, who procured such a peace for them, he ought to remember, that besides what they suffered in settling it, they paid dear for it even in the future; for Italy was thereby so weakened, as never to recover any strength or virtue to defend itself; but depending absolutely upon barbarous nations, or armies composed of them, was ravaged and torn in pieces by every invader.

4. That peace is only to be valued which is accompanied with justice; and those governments only deserve praise, who put the power into the hands of the best men. This was wholly wanting during the reigns of Augustus and his successors. The worst of men gained the sovereignty by alliance, fraud or violence, and advanced such as most resembled themselves. Augustus was worse in the beginning than in the latter end of his reign; but his bloody and impure successor, grew every day more wicked as long as he lived: Whilst he sat upon the rocks at Capri with his Chaldeans, he meditated nothing but lust or mischief, and had Sejanus and Macro always ready to execute his detestable designs. Caligula could find none equal to himself in all manner of villainies; but favour'd those most who were likest to him. Claudius his stupidity, drunkenness, and subjection to the fury of two impudent strumpets and manumised slaves, proved as hurtful to the empire, as the savage fury of his predecessor. Tho Nero was a monster that the world could not bear, yet the raging soldiers kill'd Galba, and gave the empire to Otho for no other reason,

---

[5] C. Tacit. ["They call the most wretched servitude peace"; "They make a wasteland and call it peace." Tacitus, *Histories,* bk. 4, ch. 17; *Life of Agricola,* ch. 20.]
[6] Barth. de las Casas, destruyc. de las Indias.

[Bartolomé de Las Casas, *Brevísima Relación de la Destrucción de las Indias,* translated as *Tears of the Indians* (Williamstown, Mass.: Lilburne, 1970), p. 9.]

than that he had been the companion of his debauches, and of all men was thought most to resemble him: With them all evils came in like a flood; and their successors finding none so bad as themselves, but the favourites, whores and slaves that governed them, would suffer no virtue to grow up; and filled the city with a base, lewd, and miserable rabble, that cared for nothing beyond stage-plays and bread. Such a people could not be seditious; but Rome had been desolate, if they had not thus filled it. And tho this temper and condition of a people may please our author; yet it was an incurable wound to the state, and in consequence to the best part of the world.

When the city had been burnt by the Gauls, it was soon restored: The defeats of Ticinum, Trebia, Trasimene, and Cannae were repair'd with equal or greater victories: The war of the allies ended in their overthrow: The fury of the gladiators was extinguished with their blood: The commonwealth lost battles, but was never conquer'd in any war; and in the end triumphed over all that had contended with them. Whilst liberty continued, it was the nurse of virtue; and all the losses suffered in foreign or civil wars, were easily recovered: but when liberty was lost, valour and virtue was torn up by the roots, and the Roman power proceeding from it, perished.

I have not dwelt so long upon this point to expose the folly of our author, but to show that the above mention'd evils did proceed from a permanent cause, which will always produce the like effects; and histories testify, that it has done the same in all places. Carthage was rebuilt, after it had been destroy'd by Scipio, and continued to be a rich city for almost a thousand years, but produced no such men as Hamilcar, Hasdrubal and Hannibal: Cleomenes and Euclidas were the last that deserved to be called Spartans: Athens never had an eminent man, after it felt the weight of the Macedonian yoke; and Philopoemen was the last of the Achaeans. Tho the commonwealths of Italy in later ages, having too much applied themselves to the acquisition of money, and wanted that greatness of spirit which had reigned in their ancestors, yet they have not been without valour and virtue. That of Pisa was famous for power at sea, till the Genoese overthrew them. Florence had a brave nobility, and a stout people. Arezzo, Pistoia, Cortona, Siena, and other small towns of Tuscany, were not without strength, tho for the most part unhappily exercised in the factions of Ghibellines and Guelphs, Neri and Bianchi, that divided all Italy; but since the introduction of Filmer's divine absolute monarchy, all power, virtue, reputation and strength, is utterly perished from among them, and no man dares to oppose the publick mischiefs. They usually decide private quarrels by assassination or poison; and in other respects they enjoy the happiness of that peace which is always found within empty walls and desolated countries: And if this be according to the laws of God and nature, it cannot be denied, that weakness, baseness, cowardice, destruction and desolation are so likewise. These are the blessings our well-natur'd author would confer upon us; but if they were to be esteemed so, I cannot tell why those that felt them, complained so much of them. Tacitus reciting what passed in his time, and somewhat before (for want of a Christian spirit) in the bitterness of his soul says, *nec unquam atrocioribus populi Romani cladibus, magisque; justis indiciis probatum est, non esse curae deis securitatem nostram, esse ultionem.*[7] Some thought that no punishments could be justly deserved by a people that had so much favour'd virtue; others, that even the gods they ador'd, envied their felicity and glory; but all confess'd they were fallen from the highest pitch of human happiness into the lowest degree of infamy and misery: And our author being the first that ever found they had gained by the change, we are to attribute the discovery of so great a secret to the excellency of his wisdom. If, suspending my judgment in this point, till it be proved by better authority than his word, I in the meantime follow the opinion of those who think slavery doth naturally produce meanness of spirit, with its worst effect, flattery, which Tacitus calls *foedum servitutis crimen;*[8] I must believe, that the impudence of carrying it to such a height, as to commend nothing in the most glorious liberty, that made the most virtuous people in the world, but the shortness of its continuance, and to prefer the tyranny of the basest of men, or worst of monsters, is peculiar to Filmer; and that their wickedness, which had never been equalled, is surpassed by him, who recommends as the ordinance of God, the principles that certainly produce them.

But, says our author, *tho Rome was for a while miraculously upheld in glory by a greater prudence than its own, yet in a short time, after manifold alterations, she was ruined by her own hand.*[9] But 'tis absurd to say, that the overthrow of a government, which had nothing of good in it, can be a ruin; or that the glory in which it continued, had nothing of good in it; and most of all, that it could be ruin'd by no hands but its own, if that glory had not been gained, and immediately or instrumentally supported by such virtue and strength as is worthily to be preferr'd before all other temporal

---

[7] C. Tacit. l. 1. ["Never by more terrible disasters to the Roman people and by more just indictments has it been proved that the concern of the gods is vengeance, not our security." Tacitus, *Histories*, bk. 1, ch. 3.]

[8] ["The foul reproach of slavery." Ibid., bk. 1, ch. 1.]

[9] [*Patriarcha*, ch. 16, p. 87.]

happiness, and does ever produce it. This shews that liars ought to have good memories. But passing over such foolish contradictions, I desire to know, how that *prudence, greater than its own* (which till I am better inform'd, I must think to be inseparably united to justice and goodness) came miraculously to support a government, which was not only evil in itself, as contrary to the laws of God and nature; but so perpetually bent against that monarchy, which he says is according to them, as to hate all monarchs, despite all that would live under them, destroy as many of them as came within their reach; and make a law by which any man was authorised to kill him, who should endeavour to set up this divine power among them. Moreover, no human prudence preserved the Roman glory but their own: the others directly set themselves to oppose it, and the most eminent fell under it. We know of no prudence surpassing the human, unless it be the divine: But the divine prudence did never miraculously exert itself, except to bear witness to the truth, and to give authority to those that announced it. If therefore the glory of this popular government was miraculously supported by a more than human prudence, it was good in itself; the miracles done in favour of it did testify it, and all that our author says against it is false and abominable.

If I lay aside the word *miraculous*, as put in by chance, 'twill be hard to know how God (who in the usual course of his providence guides all things by such a gentle and undiscerned power, that they seem to go on of themselves) should give such virtue to this popular government, and the magistrates bred up under it, that the greatest monarchs of the earth were as dust before them, unless there had been an excellency in their discipline, far surpassing that of their enemies; or how that can be called ill in its principle, and said to comprehend no good, which God did so gloriously support, and no man was ever able to resist. This cannot be better answer'd than by our author's citation, *suis & ipsa Roma viribus ruit;*[10] That city which had overthrown the greatest powers of the world must, in all appearance, have lasted forever, if their virtue and discipline had not decay'd, or their forces been turned against themselves. If our author therefore say true, the greatest good that ever befell the Romans, was the decay of their virtue and discipline; and the turning of their own arms against themselves, was not their ruin but their preservation.

When they had brought the warlike nations of Italy into subjection, or association; often repressed the fury of the Gauls, Cimbri and Teutons;

[10] ["Rome ruins herself by her own strength." *Patriarcha*, p. 87, quoting Horace, *Epodes*, 16, li. 2.]

overthrown the wealth, power and wit of Carthage supported by the skill, industry, and valour of Hannibal and his brave relations; almost extirpated the valiant Spaniards, who would no other way be subdued; defeated Philip, Perseus, Antiochus, Gentius, Syphax and Jugurtha; struck an awe into Ptolemy; avoided the snares and poisons of Mithridates; followed him in his flights, reveng'd his treacheries, and carried their victorious arms beyond his conquer'd kingdoms to the banks of Tigris: When neither the revolt of their Italian associates, nor the rebellion of their slaves led by Spartacus (who in skill seems to have been equal to Hannibal, and above him in courage) could put a stop to their victories: When Greece had been reduced to yield to a virtue rather than a power greater than their own, we may well say that government was supported by a more than human prudence, which led them through virtue to a height of glory, power and happiness, that till that day had been unknown to the world, and could never have been ruined, if by the decay of that virtue they had not turned their victorious arms against themselves. That city was a giant that could die by no other hand than his own; like Hercules poison'd and driven into madness, after he had destroy'd thieves, monsters and tyrants, and found nothing on the earth able to resist him.[11] The wisest of men in ancient times, looking upon this as a point of more than human perfection, thought or feigned to think, that he was descended from the gods, and at his death received into their number, tho perhaps Filmer would prefer a weak, base and effeminate slave before him. The matter will not be much different, if we adhere to the foremention'd similitude of the *athletick habit;* for the danger proceeds only from the perfection of it, and he who dislikes it, must commend that weakness and vice which may perish, but can never be changed into anything worse than itself, as those that lie upon the ground can never fall. However this fall of the Romans, which our author, speaking truth against his will, calls their ruin, was into that which he recommends as the ordinance of God: Which is as much as to say, that they were ruin'd when they fell from their own unnatural inventions to follow the law of God and of nature; that luxury also through which they fell, was the product of their felicity; and that the nations that had been subdued by them, had no other way of avenging their defeats, than by alluring their masters to their own vices: This was the root of their civil wars. When that proud city found no more resistance, it grew wanton.

[11] [See Chapter III, Section 39, n. 1, below.]

Saevior armis
Luxuria incubuit, victumque; ulciscitur orbem
Lucan[12]

Honest poverty became uneasy, when honours were given to ill-gotten riches. This was so monarchical, that a people infected with such a custom must needs fall by it. They who by vice had exhausted their fortunes, could repair them only by bringing their country under a government that would give impunity to rapine; and such as had not virtues to deserve advancement from the senate and people, would always endeavour to set up a man that would bestow the honours that were due to virtue, upon those who would be most abjectly subservient to his will and interests. When men's minds are filled with this fury, they sacrifice the common good to the advancement of their private concernments. This was the temper of Catiline expressed by Sallust, *luxuria principi gravis, paupertas vix à privato toleranda;* and this put him upon that desperate extremity to say, *incendium meum ruinâ extinguam.*[13] Others in the same manner being filled with the same rage, he could not want companions in his most villainous designs. 'Tis not long since a person of the highest quality, and no less famous for learning and wit, having observed the state of England, as it stood not many years ago, and that to which it has been reduc'd since the year sixty,[14] as is thought very much by the advice and example of France, said, that they now were taking a most cruel vengeance upon us for all the overthrows received from our ancestors, by introducing their most damnable maxims, and teaching us the worst of their vices. 'Tis not for me to determine whether this judgment was rightly made or not; for I intend not to speak of our affairs: but all historians agreeing, that the change of the Roman government was wrought by such means as I have mentioned; and our author acknowledging that change to have been their ruin, as in truth it was, I may justly conclude, that the overthrow of that government could not have been a ruin to them, but good for them, unless it had been good; and that the power which did ruin it, and was set up in the room of it, cannot

---

[12] ["Luxury, more savage than arms, has oppressed (Rome), and avenges a conquered world." Actually in Juvenal, *Satires*, 6, li. 292.]

[13] Sallust. bel. Catilin. ["Luxury too heavy for a prince, poverty hardly to be endured by a private man." This is actually Tacitus's description of what motivated Otho in a similar situation. Tacitus, *Histories*, bk. 1, ch. 21. "I will extinguish my fire (of passion) with destruction." Sallust, *Catilinarian War* (rev. ed.; Loeb, 1931), ch. 31.]

[14] [That is, 1660, the year of the restoration of the English monarchy with Charles II.]

have been according to the laws of God or nature, for they confer only that which is good, and destroy nothing that is so; but must have been most contrary to that good which was overthrown by it.

SECTION 16

The best Governments of the World have been composed of Monarchy, Aristocracy, and Democracy.

OUR author's cavils concerning I know not what vulgar opinions that democracies were introduc'd to curb tyranny, deserve no answer; for our question is, whether one form of government be prescribed to us by God and nature, or we are left according to our own understanding, to constitute such as seem best to ourselves. As for democracy he may say what pleases him of it; and I believe it can suit only with the convenience of a small town, accompanied with such circumstances as are seldom found. But this no way obliges men to run into the other extreme, in as much as the variety of forms between mere democracy and absolute monarchy is almost infinite: And if I should undertake to say, there never was a good government in the world, that did not consist of the three simple species of monarchy, aristocracy and democracy, I think I might make it good. This at the least is certain, that the government of the Hebrews instituted by God, had a judge, the great Sanhedrin, and general assemblies of the people: Sparta had two kings, a senate of twenty eight chosen men, and the like assemblies: All the Dorian cities had a chief magistrate, a senate, and occasional assemblies: The Ionian, Athens, and others, had an archon, the areopagi; and all judgments concerning matters of the greatest importance, as well as the election of magistrates, were referr'd to the people. Rome in the beginning had a king and a senate, whilst the election of kings, and judgments upon appeals remained in the people; afterwards consuls representing kings, and vested with equal power, a more numerous senate, and more frequent meetings of the people. Venice has at this day a duke, the senate of the *pregadi*, and the great assembly of the nobility, which is the whole city, the rest of the inhabitants being only *incolae*, not *cives*;[1] and those of the other cities or countries are their subjects, and do not participate of the government. Genoa is governed in like manner: Lucca not unlike to them.

[1] [*Incolae* are inhabitants; *cives* are citizens.]

Germany is at this day governed by an emperor, the princes or great lords in their several precincts, the cities by their own magistrates, and by general diets, in which the whole power of the nation resides, and where the emperor, princes, nobility, and cities have their places in person, or by their deputies. All the northern nations, which upon the dissolution of the Roman empire possessed the best provinces that had composed it, were under that form which is usually called the Gothick polity: They had king, lords, commons, diets, assemblies of estates, cortes, and parliaments, in which the sovereign powers of those nations did reside, and by which they were exercised. The like was practised in Hungary, Bohemia, Sweden, Denmark, Poland; and if things are changed in some of these places within few years, they must give better proofs of having gained by the change than are yet seen in the world, before I think myself obliged to change my opinion.

Some nations not liking the name of king, have given such a power as kings enjoy'd in other places to one or more magistrates, either limited to a certain time, or left to be perpetual, as best pleased themselves: Others approving the name, made the dignity purely elective. Some have in their elections principally regarded one family as long as it lasted: Others consider'd nothing but the fitness of the person, and reserved to themselves a liberty of taking where they pleased. Some have permitted the crown to be hereditary as to its ordinary course; but restrained the power, and instituted officers to inspect the proceedings of kings, and to take care that the laws were not violated: Of this sort were the *ephori* of Sparta, the *maires du palais*,[2] and afterwards the constable of France; the *justicia* in Aragon; *Rijckshofmeister* in Denmark; the high steward in England; and in all places such assemblies as are before-mentioned under several names, who had the power of the whole nation. Some have continued long, and it may be always in the same form; others have changed it: Some being incensed against their kings, as the Romans exasperated by the villainies of Tarquin, and the Tuscans by the cruelties of Mezentius, abolished the name of king: Others, as Athens, Sicyon, Argos, Corinth, Thebes, and the Latins, did not stay for such extremities; but set up other governments when they thought it best for themselves, and by this conduct prevented the evils that usually fall upon nations, when their kings degenerate into tyrants, and a nation is brought to enter into a war by which all may be lost, and nothing can be gained which was not their own before. The Romans took not this salutary course; the mischief was grown up before they perceived, or set themselves against it; and when

---

[2] [Mayors of the palace.]

the effects of pride, avarice, cruelty and lust were grown to such a height, that they could no longer be endured, they could not free themselves without a war: and whereas upon other occasions their victories had brought them increase of strength, territory, and glory; the only reward of their virtue in this was, to be delivered from a plague they had unadvisedly suffered to grow up among them. I confess this was most of all to be esteemed; for if they had been overthrown, their condition under Tarquin would have been more intolerable than if they had fallen under the power of Pyrrhus or Hannibal; and all their following prosperity was the fruit of their recover'd liberty: But it had been much better to have reformed the state after the death of one of their good kings, than to be brought to fight for their lives against that abominable tyrant. Our author in pursuance of his aversion to all that is good, disapproves this; and wanting reasons to justify his dislike, according to the custom of impostors and cheats, hath recourse to the ugly terms of a *back-door, sedition* and *faction:*[3] as if it were not as just for a people to lay aside their kings when they receive nothing but evil, and can rationally hope for no benefit by them, as for others to set them up in expectation of good from them. But if the truth be examin'd, nothing will be found more orderly than the changes of government, or of the persons and races of those that govern'd, which have been made by many nations. When Pharamond's grandson seemed not to deserve the crown he had worn, the French gave it to Meroveus, who more resembled him in virtue: In process of time when this race also degenerated, they were rejected, and Pepin advanced to the throne; and the most remote in blood of his descendants having often been preferred before the nearest, and bastards before the legitimate issue, they were at last all laid aside; and the crown remains to this day in the family of Hugh Capet, on whom it was bestow'd upon the rejection of Charles of Lorraine. In like manner the Castilians took Don Sancho surnamed the Brave, second son to Alfonso the Wise, before Alfonso el Desheredado, son of the elder brother Ferdinand. The states of Aragon preferred Martin, brother to John the first, before Mary his daughter married to the Count de Foix, tho females were not excluded from the succession; and the house of Austria now enjoys that crown from Joan daughter to Ferdinand. In that and many other kingdoms, bastards have been advanced before their legitimate brothers. Henry Count of Trasta-mara, bastard to Alfonso the II king of Castile, received the crown as a reward of the good service he had done to his country against his brother

[3] [*Patriarcha*, ch. 17 ("Democracies Not Invented to Bridle Tyrants, but Came In by
Stealth"), p. 88.]

Peter the Cruel, without any regard had to the house of La Cerda descended from Alfonso el Desheredado, which to this day never enjoy'd any greater honour than that of duke de Medina Celi. Not long after the Portuguese conceiving a dislike of their King Ferdinand, and his daughter married to John king of Castile, rejected her and her uncle by the father's side, and gave the crown to John a knight of Calatrava, and bastard to an uncle of Ferdinand their king. About the beginning of this age the Swedes deposed their King Sigismund for being a papist, and made Charles his uncle king. Divers examples of the like nature in England have been already mentioned. All these transportations of crowns were acts performed by assemblies of the three estates in the several kingdoms, and these crowns are to this day enjoy'd under titles derived from such as were thus brought in by the deposition or rejection of those, who according to descent of blood had better titles than the present possessors. The acts therefore were lawful and good, or they can have no title at all; and they who made them, had a just power so to do.

If our author can draw any advantage from the resemblance of regality that he finds in the Roman consuls and Athenian archons, I shall without envy leave him the enjoyment of it; but I am much mistaken if that do not prove my assertion, that those governments *were composed of the three simple species:* for if the monarchical part was in them, it cannot be denied that the aristocratical was in the senate or *areopagi*, and the democratical in the people. But he ought to have remembered that if there was something of monarchical in those governments when they are said to have been popular, there was something of aristocratical and democratical in those that were called regal; which justifies my proposition on both sides, and shews that the denomination was taken from the part that prevail'd; and if this were not so, the governments of France, Spain, and Germany might be called democracies, and those of Rome and Athens monarchies, because the people have a part in the one, and an image of monarchy was preserved in the other.

If our author will not allow the cases to be altogether equal, I think he will find no other difference, than that the consuls and archons were regularly made by the votes of the consenting people, and orderly resign'd their power, when the time was expir'd for which it was given; whereas Tarquin, Dionysius, Agathocles, Nabis, Phalaris, Caesar, and almost all his successors, whom he takes for compleat monarchs, came in by violence, fraud, and corruption, by the help of the worst men, by the slaughter of the best, and most commonly (when the method was once establish'd) by that of his predecessor, who, if our author say true, was the father of his country and his also. This was the root and foundation of the only government that deserves praise: this is that which stamped the divine character upon Agathocles, Dionysius and Caesar, and that had bestow'd the same upon Manlius, Marius, or Catiline, if they had gain'd the monarchies they affected. But I suppose that such as God has bless'd with better judgment, and a due regard to justice and truth, will say, that all those who have attained to such greatness as destroys all manner of good in the places where they have set up themselves by the most detestable villainies, came in by a *back door;* and that such magistrates as were orderly chosen by a willing people, were the true shepherds who came in by the gate of the sheepfold, and might justly be called the ministers of God, so long as they performed their duty in providing for the good of the nations committed to their charge.

SECTION 17

Good Governments admit of Changes in the Superstructures, whilst the Foundations remain unchangeable.

IF I go a step farther, and confess the Romans made some changes in the outward form of their government, I may safely say they did well in it, and prosper'd by it. After the expulsion of the kings, the power was chiefly in the nobility, who had been leaders of the people; but it was necessary to humble them, when they began to presume too much upon the advantages of their birth; and the city could never have been great, unless the plebeians who were the body of it, and the main strength of their armies, had been admitted to a participation of honours. This could not be done at the first: They who had been so vilely oppressed by Tarquin, and harass'd with making or cleansing sinks, were not then fit for magistracies, or the command of armies; but they could not justly be excluded from them, when they had men who in courage and conduct were equal to the best of the patricians; and it had been absurd for any man to think it a disparagement to him to marry the daughter of one whom he had obey'd as dictator or consul, and perhaps follow'd in his triumph. Rome that was constituted for war, and sought its grandeur by that means, could never have arriv'd to any considerable height, if the people had not been exercised in arms, and their spirits raised to delight in conquests, and willing to expose themselves to the greatest fatigues and dangers to accomplish them. Such men as these were not to be used like slaves, or oppressed by the unmerciful hand of usurers. They who by their sweat and blood were to defend and enlarge the territories of the state, were to be convinced they fought for themselves; and they had reason to demand a magistracy of their own, vested with a power that none might offend, to maintain their rights, and to protect their families, whilst they were abroad in the armies. These were the tribunes of the people, made, as they called it, *sacrosancti* or inviolable; and the creation of them was the most considerable change that happened till the time of Marius, who brought all into disorder. The creation or abolition of military tribunes with consular power, ought to be accounted as nothing; for it imported little whether that authority were exercised by two, or by five: That of the decemviri was as little to be regarded, they were intended only for a year; and tho new ones were created for another, on pretence that the laws they were to frame could not be brought to perfection in so short a time, yet they were soon thrown down from the power they usurped, and endeavoured to retain contrary to law: The creation of dictators was no novelty, they were made occasionally from the beginning, and never otherwise than occasionally, till Julius Caesar subverted all order, and invading that supreme magistracy by force, usurped the right which belong'd to all.[1] This indeed was a mortal change even in root and principle. All other magistrates had been created by the people for the publick good, and always were within the power of those that had created them. But Caesar coming in by force, sought only the satisfaction of his own raging ambition, or that of the soldiers, whom he had corrupted to destroy their country; and his successors governing for themselves by the help of the like rascals, perpetually exposed the empire to be ravaged by them. But whatever opinion any man may have of the other changes, I dare affirm, there are few or no monarchies (whose histories are so well known to us as that of Rome) which have not suffer'd changes incomparably greater and more mischievous than those of Rome whilst it was free. The Macedonian monarchy fell into pieces immediately after the death of Alexander: 'Tis thought he perished by poison: His wives, children and mother, were destroyed by his own captains: The best of those who had escaped his fury, fell by the sword of each other. When the famous Argyraspides[2] might have expected some reward of their labours, and a little rest in old age, they were maliciously sent into the East by Antigonus to perish by hunger and misery, after he had corrupted them to betray Eumenes. No better fate attended the rest; all was in confusion, every one follow'd whom he pleased, and all of them

[1] Jura omnium in se traxit. Suet. [Actually in Tacitus, *Annals*, bk. 1, ch. 2.] [2] [The silver-shield corps of Alexander.]

seemed to be filled with such a rage that they never ceased from mutual slaughters till they were consumed; and their kingdoms continued in perpetual wars against each other, till they all fell under the Roman power. The fortune of Rome was the same after it became a monarchy: Treachery, murder and fury, reigned in every part; there was no law but force; he that could corrupt an army, thought he had a sufficient title to the empire: by this means there were frequently three or four, and at one time thirty several pretenders, who called themselves emperors; of which number he only reigned that had the happiness to destroy all his competitors; and he himself continued no longer than till another durst attempt the destruction of him and his posterity. In this state they remained, till the wasted and bloodless provinces were possess'd by a multitude of barbarous nations. The kingdoms established by them enjoy'd as little peace or justice; that of France was frequently divided into as many parts as the kings of Meroveus or Pepin's race had children, under the names of the kingdoms of Paris, Orleans, Soissons, Arles, Burgundy, Austrasia, and others: These were perpetually vexed by the unnatural fury of brothers or nearest relations, whilst the miserable nobility and people were obliged to fight upon their foolish quarrels, till all fell under the power of the strongest. This mischief was in some measure cured by a law made in the time of Hugh Capet, that the kingdom should no more be divided: But the *apanages*, as they call them, granted to the king's brothers, with the several dukedoms and earldoms erected to please them and other great lords, produced frequently almost as bad effects. This is testified by the desperate and mortal factions, that went under the names of Burgundy and Orleans, Armagnae and Orleans, Montmorency and Guise: These were followed by those of the League,[3] and the Wars of the Huguenots: They were no sooner finish'd by the taking of La Rochelle, but new ones began by the intrigues of the duke of Orleans, brother to Lewis the 13th, and his mother; and pursued with that animosity by them, that they put themselves under the protection of Spain: To which may be added, that the houses of Condé, Soissons, Montmorency, Guise, Vendôme, Angoulême, Bouillon, Rohan, Longueville, Rochefoucault, Eperne and I think I may say every one that is of great eminency in that kingdom, with the cities of Paris, Bourdeaux, and many others, in the space of these last fifty years, have sided with the perpetual enemies of their own country.

[3] [The League of the Public Weal was founded in the mid-15th century by the French nobility to oppose Louis XI.]

Again, other great alterations have happened within the same kingdom: The races of kings four times wholly changed: Five kings deposed in less than 150 years after the death of Charles the Great: The offices of *maire du palais*, and constable, erected and laid aside: The great dukedoms and earldoms, little inferior to sovereign principalities, establish'd and suppress'd: The decision of all causes, and the execution of the laws, placed absolutely in the hands of the nobility, their deputies, seneschals, or vice-seneschals, and taken from them again: Parliaments set up to receive appeals from the other courts, and to judge sovereignly in all cases, expressly to curb them: The power of these parliaments, after they had crushed the nobility, brought so low, that within the last twenty years they are made to register, and give the power of laws, to edicts, of which the titles only are read to them; and the general assemblies of estates, that from the time of Pepin had the power of the nation in their hands, are now brought to nothing, and almost forgotten.

Tho I mention these things, 'tis not with a design of blaming them, for some of them deserve it not; and it ought to be consider'd that the wisdom of man is imperfect, and unable to foresee the effects that may proceed from an infinite variety of accidents, which according to emergencies, necessarily require new constitutions, to prevent or cure the mischiefs arising from them, or to advance a good that at the first was not thought on: And as the noblest work in which the wit of man can be exercised, were (if it could be done) to constitute a government that should last forever, the next to that is to suit laws to present exigencies, and so much as is in the power of man to foresee: And he that should resolve to persist obstinately in the way he first entered upon, or to blame those who go out of that in which their fathers had walked, when they find it necessary, does as far as in him lies, render the worst of errors perpetual. Changes therefore are unavoidable, and the wit of man can go no farther than to institute such, as in relation to the forces, manners, nature, religion or interests of a people and their neighbours, are suitable and adequate to what is seen, or apprehended to be seen: And he who would oblige all nations at all times to take the same course, would prove as foolish as a physician who should apply the same medicine to all distempers, or an architect that would build the same kind of house for all persons, without considering their estates, dignities, the number of their children or servants, the time or climate in which they live, and many other circumstances; or, which is, if possible, more sottish, a general who should obstinately resolve always to make war in the same way, and to draw up his army in the same form, without examining the nature, number, and strength of his own and his enemies' forces, or the advantages and disadvantages of the ground. But as there may be some universal rules in physick, architecture and military discipline, from which men ought never to depart; so there are some in politicks also which ought always to be observed: and wise legislators adhering to them only, will be ready to change all others as occasion may require, in order to the publick good. This we may learn from Moses, who laying the foundation of the law given to the Israelites in that justice, charity and truth, which having its root in God is subject to no change, left them the liberty of having judges or no judges, kings or no kings, or to give the sovereign power to high priests or captains, as best pleased themselves; and the mischiefs they afterwards suffer'd, proceeded not simply from changing, but changing for the worse. The like judgment may be made of the alterations that have happen'd in other places. They who aim at the publick good, and wisely institute means proportionable and adequate to the attainment of it, deserve praise; and those only are to be dislik'd, who either foolishly or maliciously set up a corrupt private interest in one or a few men. Whosoever therefore would judge of the Roman changes, may see, that in expelling the Tarquins, creating consuls, abating the violence of usurers, admitting Plebeians to marry with the patricians, rendering them capable of magistracies, deducing colonies, dividing lands gained from their enemies, erecting tribunes to defend the rights of the commons, appointing the decemviri to regulate the law, and abrogating their power when they abused it, creating dictators and military tribunes with a consular power, as occasions requir'd; they acted in the face of the sun for the good of the public; and such acts having always produced effects suitable to the rectitude of their intentions, they consequently deserve praise. But when another principle began to govern, all things were changed in a very different manner: Evil designs, tending only to the advancement of private interests, were carried on in the dark by means as wicked as the end. If Tarquin when he had a mind to be king, poison'd his first wife and his brother, contracted an incestuous marriage with his second by the death of her first husband, murder'd her father and the best men in Rome, yet Caesar did worse: He favour'd Catiline and his villainous associates; bribed and corrupted magistrates; conspir'd with Crassus and Pompey; continued in the command of an army beyond the time prescribed by law, and turned the arms with which he had been entrusted for the service of the commonwealth, to the destruction of it; which was rightly represented by his dream, that he had constuprated his mother: In the like manner when Octavius, Antonius and Lepidus, divided the empire, and then quarrelled among themselves; and when

Galba, Otho, Vitellius and Vespasian set up parties in several provinces, all was managed with treachery, fraud and cruelty; nothing was intended but the advancement of one man, and the recompence of the villains that served him: And when the empire had suffered infinite calamities by pulling down or rejecting one, and setting up another, it was for the most part difficult to determine who was the worst of the two; or whether the prevailing side had gained or lost by their victory. The question therefore upon which a judgment may be made to the praise or dispraise of the Roman government, before or after the loss of their liberty, ought not to be, whether either were subject to changes, for neither they nor anything under the sun was ever exempted from them; but whether the changes that happened after the establishment of absolute power in the emperors, did not solely proceed from ambition, and tend to the publick ruin: whereas those alterations related by our author concerning consuls, dictators, decemviri, tribunes and laws, were far more rare, less violent, tending to, and procuring the publick good, and therefore deserving praise. The like having been proved by the examples of other kingdoms, and might be farther confirmed by many more, which on account of brevity I omit, is in my opinion sufficient to manifest, that whilst the foundation and principle of a government remains good, the superstructures may be changed according to occasions, without any prejudice to it.

SECTION 18
Xenophon in blaming the Disorders of Democracies, favours Aristocracies, not Monarchies.

I N the next place our author introduces Xenophon, *disallowing popular governments:* Cites Rome and Athens as places *where the best men thriv'd worst, and the worst best;* and condemns the Romans for making it capital to pass sentence *of death, banishment, loss of liberty, or stripes upon any citizen of Rome.*[1] But lest his fraud in this should be detected, he cites no precise passage of any author, alleges few examples, and those mistaken; never tells us what that law was, when made, or where to be found; whereas I hope to prove, that he has upon the whole matter abominably prevaricated, and advanced things that he knows to be either impertinent or false.

---

[1] [*Patriarcha*, ch. 18 ("Democracies Vilified by Their Own Historians"), pp. 88–89.]

1. To this end we are in the first place to consider, whether Xenophon speaks of popular governments simply, or comparatively: if simply, 'tis confess'd that a pure democracy can never be good, unless for a small town; if comparatively, we must examine to what he compares it: We are sure it was not to absolute monarchy; there was no such thing amongst the Greeks established by law: The little tyrants who had enslaved their own countries, as Jason, Phaereus, Phalaris, and the like, had no pretence to it, and were accounted as the worst of beasts: None but such as in all bestiality were like to them, did ever speak or think well of them: Xenophon's opinion in this point, may be easily found out by what pass'd between his master Plato and the Sicilian tyrant;[2] and the matter will not be mended by referring to his own experience: He had seen the vast monarchy of Persia torn in pieces by the fury of two brothers, and more than a million of men brought to fight upon their private quarrel: Instead of that order, stability and strength which our author ascribes to absolute monarchy as the effect of wisdom and justice, he knew, that by filling one man with pride and cruelty, it brought unspeakable miseries upon all others, and infected them with all the vices that accompany slavery: Men lived like fishes; the great ones devour'd the small; and as appeared by Tissaphernes, Pharnabazus, and others with whom he had to deal, the worst and basest were made to be the greatest: The satraps insulted over those of meaner rank, with an insolence and cruelty that equal'd the depth of their servile submission to their proud master.[3] Luxury and avarice reigned in all: many great nations were made to live for the service of one man, and to foment his vices. This produced weakness and cowardice; no number of those slaves were able to stand against a few free Grecians. No man knew this better than Xenophon, who after the death of Cyrus the younger, and the treacherous murder of Clearchus, and other officers that commanded the Greeks who had served him, made his retreat from Babylon to the Hellespont with ten thousand foot, and passed over the bellies of all that dared to oppose him.[4] He would never have spent his life in exciting his countrymen to attempt the conquest of Asia, nor persuaded Agesilaus to put himself at the head of the enterprize, if he had thought there was such admirable order, stability and strength in that monarchy, and in the Greeks nothing but *giddiness of spirit, and so much learning as made them seditious:*[5] Nor could

[2] [Xenophon's *Hiero* portrays an imaginary conversation, between the poet Simonides (not Plato) and Hiero, tyrant of Syracuse in Sicily, that denounces tyranny. Trans. in Leo Strauss, *On Tyranny* (rev. ed.; Ithaca: Cornell University Press, 1968).]

[3] [Satraps were Persian governors or overseers of parts of the Persian empire.]

[4] [Xenophon describes these events in his *Anabasis* (Loeb, 1922).]

[5] [*Patriarcha*, ch. 15, p. 85.]

he, being a wise man and an excellent captain, have conceived such a design, if he had not by experience found that liberty inspir'd his countrymen with such solid virtue, and produced such stability, good order and strength, that with small numbers of them he might hope to overthrow the vain pomp of the barbarians, and to possess himself of their riches, tho they could bring more than a hundred men to fight against one; which design being interrupted in his time by domestick wars, was soon after his death accomplished by Alexander.

But that Xenophon's meaning may be better understood, 'tis good to consider, that he spoke of such governments as were then in use among the Greeks; which tho mixed, yet took their denomination from the prevailing part: so that the Dorians, who placed the power chiefly in the hands of a few chosen men, were said to be governed aristocratically; and the Ionians giving more power to the common people, democratically:[6] And he, tho an Ionian, either through friendship to Agesilaus, conversation with the Spartans, or for other reasons best known to himself, preferr'd the government of Sparta, or some other which he thought he could frame, and desir'd to introduce, before that of Athens; as Cimon, Thucydides, and many other excellent men of that city are said to have done: And if I acknowledge they were in the right, and that Athens was more subject to disorder, and had less stability than Sparta, I think it will be of little advantage to absolute monarchy.

2. The Athenians did banish some worthy men, and put others to death; but our author, like the Devil, never speaking truth, unless to turn it into a lie, prevaricates in his report of them. The temporary banishment which they called *ostracism*, was without hurt or dishonour, never accounted as a punishment, nor intended for any other end, than to put a stop to the too eminent greatness of a man, that might prove dangerous to the city; and some excellent persons who fell under it, were soon recalled and brought home with glory. But I am not solicitous whether that reason be sufficient to justify it or not: We are upon a general *thesis* relating to the laws of God and nature; and if the Athenians, by a fancy of their own, did make an imprudent use of their liberty, it cannot prejudice the publick cause. They who make the worst of it can only say, that by such means they, for a time, deprived themselves of the benefits they might have received from the virtues of some excellent men, to the hurt of none but themselves; and the application of it as an injustice done to Themistocles is absolutely false: He was a man of great wit,

---

[6] [The Dorians and Ionians were two distinct ethnic stems of Greeks. Sparta was Doric, Athens Ionic.]

industry and valour, but of uncertain faith, too much addicted to his own interest, and held a most dangerous correspondence with the Persians, who then threatened the destruction of Greece.[7] Through envy and spite to Aristides, and to increase his own power, he raised dangerous factions in the city; and being summoned to render an account of his proceedings, he declined the judgment of his country, fled to their enemies, and justly deserved the sentence pronounc'd against him. Some among them were unjustly put to death, and above all Socrates; but the people, who, deceived by false witnesses (against whom neither the laws of God or man have ever prescrib'd a sufficient defence), had condemned him, did so much lament their crime, when the truth was discovered to them, that I doubt whether a more righteous judgment had given better testimony of their righteous intentions. But our author's impudence appears in the highest excess, in imputing the death of Phocion to the popular state of Athens: Their forces had been broken in the Sicilian War; the city taken, and the principal men slain by Lysander; the remains of the most worthy destroy'd by the thirty tyrants set up by him; their ill-recovered liberty overthrown by the Macedonians, and the death of Phocion compassed by Polyperchon, who with foreign soldiers, slaves, vagabonds, and outlaws, overpower'd the people.

The proceedings of Rome may be more compleatly justified: Coriolanus was duly condemn'd, he set too great a price upon his own valour, and arrogated to himself a power in Rome, which would hardly have been endur'd in Corioli: His violence and pride overbalanced his services; and he that would submit to no law, was justly driven out from the society which could subsist only by law. Quintius was not unlike him, and Manlius Capitolinus far worse than either. Their virtues were not to be consider'd when they departed from them. Consideration ought to be had of human frailty, and some indulgence may be extended to those who commit errors, after having done important services; but a state cannot subsist, which compensating evil actions with good, gives impunity to the most dangerous crimes, in remembrance of any services whatever. He that does well, performs his duty, and ought always to do so: Justice and prudence concur in this; and 'tis no less just than profitable, that every action be considered by itself, and such a reward or punishment allotted to it, as in nature and proportion it doth best deserve.

This, as I suppose, is enough for their cases; but relates not to those of Mamercus, Camillus, Livius Salinator, and Aemilius Paulus; their virtue was compleat, they were wrongfully sentenc'd. But the best

[7] Plut. in vita Themist. [Plutarch, *Life of Themistocles.*]

princes, senate or people that ever was in the world, by the deceit of evil men, may and have been drawn out of the way of justice: Yet of all the states that are known to us, none was ever so free from crimes of malice and wilful injustice; none was ever guilty of so few errors as that of Rome; and none did ever give better testimonies of repentance, when they were discovered, than the Romans did by the veneration they shew'd to those worthy persons, and the honours they conferr'd upon them afterwards. Mamercus was made dictator, to repair the unjust mark of infamy laid upon him by the censors. Camillus being recall'd from his banishment, often enjoyed the same honour, and died the most reverenced man that had ever been in that city. Livius Salinator was not only made consul after he had been fined, but the people (as it were to expiate the guilt of having condemn'd him) suffer'd that asperity of speech and manners, which might have persuaded such as had been less confident of his virtue and their own, that he desir'd to be reveng'd, tho it were with the ruin of the city. They dealt in the like manner with Aemilius Paulus, repairing the injury of a fine unduly impos'd. Their generosity in leaving the tribunes in the forum, with their accusation against Scipio Africanus, and following him to celebrate an annual sacrifice in the capitol, in commemoration of his victory against Hannibal, was no less admirable than the greatness of his mind, who thought his virtue should be so well known, that no account ought to be expected from him; which was an error proceeding from a noble root, but not to be borne in a well-govern'd commonwealth.[8] The laws that aim at the publick good, make no distinction of persons; and none can be exempted from the penalties of them, otherwise than by approved innocence, which cannot appear without a trial: He that will not bend his mind to them, shakes off the equality of a citizen, and usurps a power above the law, to which no man submits upon any other condition, than that none should be exempted from the power of it. And Scipio being the first Roman that thus disdained the power of the law, I do not know whether the prejudice brought upon the city by so dangerous an example, did not outweigh all the services he had done: Nevertheless the people contented with his retirement to his own house, and afterwards convinc'd of his innocence, would probably (if he had not died in a few months) have brought him back with the honours that fate reserved for his ashes.

I do not at present remember any other eminent men, who can be said in any respect to have *thrived ill*, whilst the people and senate of Rome acted freely; and if this be not sufficient to clear the point, I desire to

---

[8] T. Liv. [Livy, *History of Rome*, bk. 4, ch.   27, ch. 34 and bk. 29, ch. 37 (Salinator); bk. 31 (Mamercus); bk. 7, ch. 1 (Camillus); bk.   38, ch. 31 (Aemilius Paulus).]

know the names of those *worst men that thrived best*. If they may have been judged to thrive, who were frequently advanced to the supreme magistracies, and enjoy'd the chief honours; I find no men so eminent as Brutus, Publicola, Quinctius Cincinnatus, and Capitolinus, the two Fabii surnamed Maximi, Corvinus, Torquatus, Camillus, and the like: and if these were the worst men that Rome produced in those ages, valour, wisdom, industry in the service of their country, and a most entire love to it must have been the worst of qualities; and I presume our author may have thought them so, since they were invincible obstacles to the introduction of that divine monarchy which Appius Claudius the decemvir, Manlius Capitolinus, Spurius Cassius, Sp. Maelius, and some others may be thought to have affected.

However, these instances are not to be understood as they are simply in themselves, but comparatively with what has happen'd in other places under absolute monarchies: for our inquiry is not after that which is perfect, well knowing that no such thing is found among men; but we seek that human constitution which is attended with the least, or the most pardonable inconveniences. And if we find that in the space of three hundred years, whilst the senate, people, and legally created magistrates governed Rome, not one worthy man was put to death, not above five or six condemned to fines by the beguiled people, and those injuries repair'd by the most honourable satisfaction that could be given; so that virtue continued ever flourishing; the best men that could be found were put into the chief commands, and the city was filled with more excellent men than were ever known to be in any other place: And on the other side, if the emperors so soon as the government was changed, made it their business to destroy the best, and so far succeeded in their design, that they left none; and never failed to advance the worst, unless it fell out as to Queen Catherine de Medici, who is said never to have done any good but by mistake, and some few may have proved better than was intended; it will appear, that our author's assertions are in the utmost degree false. Of this we need no better witness than Tacitus. The civil wars, and the proscriptions upon which he touches, are justly to be attributed to that monarchy which was then setting up, the only question being who should be the monarch, when the liberty was already overthrown. And if any eminent men escaped, it was much against the will of those who had usurped the power: He acknowledges his histories to be a continued relation of the slaughter of the most illustrious persons, and that in the times of which he writes, virtue was attended with certain destruction. After the death of Germanicus and his eldest children, Valerius Asiaticus, Seneca, Corbulo, and an infinite number more who were thought most to resemble them, found this to be true at the expence of their lives: Nero, in pursuance of the same tyrannical design, murder'd Helvidius and Thrasea, that he might *tear up virtue by the roots:*[9] Domitian spared none willingly that had either virtue or reputation; and tho Trajan, with perhaps some other, might grow up under him in the remote provinces, yet no good man could escape who came under his eye, and was so eminent as to be observed by him. Whilst these, who were thought to be the best men that appear'd in the Roman empire, did *thrive* in this manner, Sejanus, Macro, Narcissus, Pallas, Tigellinus, Icetus, Vinius, Laco, and others like to them, had the power of the empire in their hands. Therefore, unless mankind has been mistaken to this day, and that these, who have hitherto been accounted the worst of villains, were indeed the best men in the world, and that those destroy'd by them, who are thought to have been the best, were truly the worst, it cannot be denied that the best men, during the liberty of Rome, *thrived* best; that good men suffer'd no indignity, unless by some fraud imposed upon the well-meaning people; and that so soon as the liberty was subverted, the worst men *thrived* best. The best men were exposed to so many calamities and snares, that it was thought a matter of great wonder to see a virtuous man die in his bed: and if the account were well made, I think it might appear, that every one of the emperors before Titus shed more noble and innocent blood than Rome and all the commonwealths in the world have done whilst they had the free enjoyment of their own liberty. But if any man in favour of our author seek to diminish this vast disproportion between the two differing sorts of government, and impute the disorders that happen'd in the time of the Gracchi, and others, whilst Rome was struggling for her liberty, to the government of a commonwealth, he will find them no more to be compar'd with those that fell out afterwards, than the railings of a turbulent tribune against the senate, to the villainies and cruelties that corrupted and dispeopled the provinces from Babylon to Scotland: And whereas the state never fail'd to recover from any disorders, as long as the root of liberty remain'd untouch'd, and became more powerful and glorious than ever, even after the wars of Marius and Sulla; when that was destroy'd, the city fell into a languishing condition, and grew weaker and weaker, till that and the whole empire was ruin'd by the barbarians.

   3. Our author, to shew that his memory is as good as his judgment, having represented Rome in the times of liberty as a publick slaughter-house, soon after blames the clemency of their laws; whereas 'tis impossible

[9] Ipsam exscindere virtutem. Tacit. [Tacitus, *Annals*, bk. 26, ch. 21.]

that the same city could at the same time be guilty of those contrary extremities; and no less certain, that it was perfectly free from them both. His assertion seems to be grounded upon Caesar's speech (related by Sallust) in favour of Lentulus and Cethegus companions of Catiline:[10] but tho he there endeavoured to put the best colour he could upon their cause, it signified only thus much, that a Roman citizen could not be put to death, without being heard in publick; which law will displease none that in understanding and integrity may not be compared to Filmer and his followers. 'Tis a folly to extend it farther; for 'tis easily proved that there was always a power of putting citizens to death, and that it was exercised when occasion required. The laws were the same in the time of the kings, and when that office was executed by consuls, excepting such changes as are already mention'd. The *lex perduellionis*[11] cited by Livy in the case of Horatius who had kill'd his sister, continued in force from the foundation to the end of that government: the condemnation was to death, the words of the sentence these, *caput obnubito, infelici arbore reste suspendito; verberato intra pomaerium vel extra pomaerium.*[12] He was tried by this law upon an appeal made to the people by his father, and absolved *admiratione magis virtutis quam jure causae;*[13] which could not have been, if by the law no citizen might be put to death. The sons of Brutus were condemn'd to death in publick, and executed with the Aquilii and Vitellii their companions in the same conspiracy: Manlius Capitolinus was put to death by the vote of the people: Titus Manlius by the command of his father Torquatus, for fighting without order: Two legions were decimated by Appius Claudius: Spurius Maelius refusing to appear before the dictator, was killed by Servilius Ahala general of the horse, and pronounced *jure caesum:*[14] Quintus Fabius was by Papirius the dictator condemn'd to die, and could not have been saved but by the intercession and authority of the people. If this be not so, I desire to be informed what the senate meant by condemning Nero to be put to death *more majorum,*[15] if *more majorum* no citizen might be put to death: Why the consuls, dictators, military tribunes, decemviri, caused rods and axes to be carried before them, as well within as without the city, if no use was to be made of them. Were they only vain badges of a power never to be

---

[10] Salust. Bell. Catilin. [Sallust, *Catilinarian War*, ch. 51.]

[11] [Law of treason.]

[12] T. Liv. l. 1. ["(The lictor) shall veil his head, shall hang him with rope from a barren tree; he shall whip (him) either inside the sacred wall or outside the sacred wall." Livy, *History of Rome*, bk. 1, ch. 26.]

[13] ["More from admiration of his courage than the law of the case." Ibid.]

[14] ["Killed lawfully." These examples are all taken from Livy.]

[15] ["In the custom of our ancestors." The defendant was in fact Antistius the praetor during the reign of Nero. Tacitus, *Annals*, bk. 14, ch. 48.]

executed; or upon whom was the supreme power signified by them, to be exercised within and without the city, if the citizens were not subject to it? 'Tis strange that a man who had ever read a book of matters relating to the affairs of Rome, should fancy these things; or hope to impose them upon the world, if he knew them to be foolish, false, and absurd. But of all the marks of a most supine stupidity that can be given by a man, I know no one equal to this of our author, who in the same clause wherein he says no citizen could be put to death or banished, adds, that the magistrates were upon pain of death forbidden to do it; for if a magistrate might be put to death for banishing a citizen, or causing him to be executed, a citizen might be put to death; for the magistrates were not strangers, but citizens. If this was not so, he must think that no crime was capital, but the punishment of capital crimes; or that no man was subject to the supreme power, but he that was created for the execution of it. Yet even this will not stop the gap; for the law that condemned the magistrate to die, could be of no effect, if there were no man to execute it; and there could be none if the law prohibited it, or that he who did it was to die for it: And this goes on to infinity. For if a magistrate could not put a citizen to death, I suppose a citizen could not put to death a magistrate; for he also is a citizen. So that upon the whole matter we may conclude, that malice is blind, and that wickedness is madness. 'Tis hard to say more in praise of popular governments than will result from what he says against them: his reproaches are praises, and his praises reproaches. As government is instituted for the preservation of the governed, the Romans were sparing of blood, and are wisely commended by Livy for it: *Nulli unquam populo mitiores placuere poenae;*[16] which gentleness will never be blamed, unless by those who are pleased with nothing so much as the fury of those monsters, who with the ruin of the best part of mankind, usurp'd the dominion of that glorious city. But if the Romans were gentle in punishing offences, they were also diligent in preventing them: the excellence of their discipline led the youth to virtue, and the honours they received for recompence confirmed them in it. By this means many of them became laws to themselves; and they who were not the most excellent, were yet taught so much of good, that they had a veneration for those they could not equal, which not only served to incite them to do well according to their talents, but kept them in such awe as to fear incurring their ill opinion by any bad action, as much as by the penalty of the law. This integrity of manners made the laws as it were

[16] ["No people was ever satisfied with milder punishments." Livy, *History of Rome*, bk. 1, ch. 28.]

useless; and whilst they seemed to sleep, ignorant persons thought there were none: But their discipline being corrupted by prosperity, those vices came in which made way for the monarchy; and wickedness being placed in the throne, there was no safety for any but such as would be of the same spirit, and the empire was ruined by it.

SECTION 19

That Corruption and Venality which is natural to Courts, is seldom found in Popular Governments.

OUR author's next work is, with that modesty and truth which is natural to him, to impute corruption and venality to commonwealths. He knows that monarchies are exempted from those evils, and has discovered this truth from the integrity observed in the modern courts of England, France, and Spain, or the more ancient of Rome and Persia: But after many falsehoods in matter of fact, and misrepresentations of that which is true, he shews that the corruption, venality, and violence he blames, were neither the effects of liberty, nor consistent with it. Gnaeus Manlius, who with his Asiatic army brought in the luxury that gave birth to those mischiefs, did probably follow the looseness of his own disposition; yet the best and wisest men of that time knew from the beginning that it would ruin the city, unless a stop might be put to the course of that evil: But they who had seen kings under their feet, and could no longer content themselves with that equality which is necessary among citizens, fomented it as the chief means to advance their ambitious designs. Tho Marius was rigid in his nature, and cared neither for money nor sensual pleasures, yet he favour'd those vices in others, and is said to be the first that made use of them to his advantage. Catiline was one of the lewdest men in the world, and had no other way of compassing his designs than by rendering others as bad as himself: and Caesar set up his tyranny by spreading that corruption farther than the others had been able to do; and tho he, Caligula, and some others were slain, yet the best men found it as impossible to restore liberty to the city when it was corrupted, as the worst had done to set up a tyranny whilst the integrity of their manners did continue. Men have a strange propensity to run into all manner of excesses, when plenty of means invite, and that there is no power to deter; of which the succeeding emperors took advantage, and knowing that even their subsistence depended upon it, they thought themselves obliged by interest as well as inclination to make honours and preferments the rewards of vice: and tho it be not always true in the utmost extent that all men follow the example of the king; yet it is of very great efficacy: Tho some are so good that they will not be perverted, and others so bad that they will not be corrected; yet a great number does always follow the course that is favour'd and rewarded by those that govern. There were idolaters doubtless among the Jews in the days of David and Hezekiah; but they prosper'd better under Jeroboam and Ahab: England was not without papists in the time of Queen Elizabeth; but they thrived much better during the reign of her furious sister. False witnesses and accusers had a better trade under Tiberius, who called them *custodes legum*,[1] than under Trajan who abhorred them; and whores, players, fiddlers, with other such vermin, abounded certainly more when encouraged by Nero than when despised by Antoninus and Marcus Aurelius. But as every one of these manifested what he was by those he favour'd or punish'd, and that a man can only be judged by his principles or practices, he that would know whether absolute monarchies or mixed governments do most foment or punish venality and corruption, ought to examine the principle and practice of both, and compare them one with the other.

As to the principle, the above-mentioned vices may be profitable to private men, but they can never be so to the government, if it be popular or mixed: No people was ever the better for that which renders them weak or base; and a duly created magistracy, governing a nation with their consent, can have no interest distinct from that of the publick, or desire to diminish the strength of the people, which is their own, and by which they subsist. On the other side, the absolute monarch who governs for himself, and chiefly seeks his own preservation, looks upon the strength and bravery of his subjects as the root of his greatest danger, and frequently desires to render them weak, base, corrupt, and unfaithful to each other, that they may neither dare to attempt the breaking of the yoke he lays upon them, nor trust one another in any generous design for the recovery of their liberty. So that the same corruption which preserves such a prince, if it were introduced by a people, would weaken, if not utterly destroy them.

Again, all things have their continuance from a principle in nature

---

[1] [Guardians of the laws.]

suitable to their original: all tyrannies have had their beginnings from corruption. The histories of Greece, Sicily, and Italy shew that all those who made themselves tyrants in several places, did it by the help of the worst, and the slaughter of the best: Men could not be made subservient to their lusts whilst they continued in their integrity; so as their business was to destroy those who would not be corrupted. They must therefore endeavour to maintain or increase the corruption by which they attain their greatness: If they fail in this point, they must fall as Tarquin, Pisistratus, and others have done; but if they succeed so far that the vicious part do much prevail, the government is secure, tho the prince may be in danger. And the same thing doth in a great measure accidentally conduce to the safety of his person: For they who for the most part are the authors of great revolutions, not being so much led by a particular hatred to the man, as by a desire to do good to the publick, seldom set themselves to conspire against the tyrant, unless he be altogether detestable and intolerable, if they do not hope to overthrow the tyranny.

The contrary is seen in all popular and well-mixed governments: they are ever established by wise and good men, and can never be upheld otherwise than by virtue: The worst men always conspiring against them, they must fall, if the best have not power to preserve them. Wheresoever therefore a people is so governed, the magistrates will obviate afar off the introduction of vices, which tend as much to the ruin of their persons and government, as to the preservation of the prince and his. This is evidenced by experience. 'Tis not easy to name a monarch that had so many good qualities as Julius Caesar, till they were extinguished by his ambition, which was inconsistent with them: He knew that his strength lay in the corruption of the people, and that he could not accomplish his designs without increasing it. He did not seek good men, but such as would be for him; and thought none sufficiently addicted to his interests, but such as stuck at the performance of no wickedness that he commanded: he was a soldier according to Caesar's heart who said,

> *Pectore si fratris gladium juguloque parentis*
> *Condere me jubeas, gravidaeve in viscera partu*
> *Conjugis, invita peragam tamen omnia dextra.*
> Lucan[2]

---

[2] ["If you should command me to bury my sword in the chest of a brother or the throat of a parent, or in the body of my wife heavy with child, I would perform it all, even if my right hand be unwilling." Lucan, *Pharsalia*, bk. 1, li. 376.]

And lest such as were devoted to him should grow faint in villainy, he industriously inflamed their fury:

> *Vult omnia Caesar*
> *A se saeva peti, vult praemia Martis amari.*
> Ib.[3]

Having spread this poison amongst the soldiers, his next work was by corrupting the tribunes to turn the power to the destruction of the people, which had been erected for their preservation; and pouring the treasures he had gained by rapine in Gaul into the bosom of Curio, made him an instrument of mischief, who had been a most eminent supporter of the laws. Tho he was thought to have affected the glory of sparing Cato, and with trouble to have found that he despised life when it was to be accounted his gift; yet in suspecting Brutus and Cassius, he shew'd he could not believe that virtuous men who loved their country could be his friends. Such as carry on the like designs with less valour, wit, and generosity of spirit, will always be more bitterly bent to destroy all that are good, knowing that the deformity of their own vices is rendered most manifest, when they are compared with the good qualities of those who are most unlike them; and that they can never defend themselves against the scorn and hatred they incur by their vices, unless such a number can be infected with the same, and made to delight in the recompences of iniquity that foment them, as may be able to keep the rest of the people in subjection.

The same thing happens even when the usurpation is not so violent as that of Agathocles, Dionysius, or the last king of Denmark, who in one day by the strength of a mercenary soldiery overthrew all the laws of his country: and a lawfully created magistrate is forced to follow the same ways as soon as he begins to affect a power which the laws do not confer upon him. I wish I could say there were few of these; but experience shews that such a proportion of wisdom, moderation of spirit, and justice is requir'd in a supreme magistrate, to render him content with a limited power, as is seldom found. Man is of an aspiring nature, and apt to put too high a value upon himself; they who are raised above their brethren, tho but a little, desire to go farther; and if they gain the name of king,

---

[3] ["(Caesar) wants all savage things to be asked of him; he wants war to be loved." Ibid., bk. 5, li. 307.]

they think themselves wronged and degraded, when they are not suffer'd
to do what they please.

Sanctitas, pietas, fides
Privata bona sunt: qua juvat reges eant.[4]

In these things they never want masters; and the nearer they come to a
power that is not easily restrained by law, the more passionately they
desire to abolish all that opposes it: and when their hearts are filled with
this fury, they never fail to chuse such ministers as will be subservient
to their will: and this is so well known, that those only approach them
who resolve to be so. Their interests as well as their inclinations incite
them to diffuse their own manners as far as they can, which is no less
than to bring those who are under their power to all that wickedness of
which the nature of man is capable; and no greater testimony can be
given of the efficacy of these means towards the utter corruption of
nations, than the accursed effects we see of them in our own and the
neighbouring countries.

It may be said that some princes are so full of virtue and goodness, as
not to desire more power than the laws allow, and are not obliged to
chuse ill men, because they desire nothing but what the best are willing
to do. This may be, and sometimes is: the nation is happy that has such
a king: but he is hard to find, and more than a human power is required
to keep him in so good a way. The strength of his own affections will
ever be against him: Wives, children, and servants will always join with
those enemies that arise in his own breast to pervert him: if he has any
weak side, any lust unsubdued, they will gain the victory. He has not
search'd into the nature of man, who thinks that anyone can resist when
he is thus on all sides assaulted: Nothing but the wonderful and immediate
power of God's spirit can preserve him; and to allege it will be nothing
to the purpose, unless it can be proved that all princes are blessed with
such an assistance, or that God hath promised it to them and their
successors forever, by what means soever they came to the crowns they
enjoy.

Nothing is farther from my intention than to speak irreverently of
kings; and I presume no wise man will think I do so, if I profess, that
having observed as well as I can what history and daily experience teach
us concerning the virtues and religions that are or have been from the

[4] Senec. Thyest. ["Sanctity, piety, faith are
private goods; let kings go where they please."
Seneca, *Thyestes*, li. 218.]

beginning of the world encouraged and supported by monarchs, the methods they have follow'd since they have gone under the name of Christians, their moral as well as their theological graces, together with what the Scriptures tell us of those who in the last days will principally support the throne of Antichrist; I cannot be confident that they are generally in an extraordinary manner preserved by the hand of God from the vices and frailties to which the rest of mankind is subject. If no man can shew that I am in this mistaken, I may conclude, that as they are more than any other men in the world exposed to temptations and snares, they are more than any in danger of being corrupted, and made instruments of corrupting others, if they are no otherwise defended than the rest of men.

This being the state of the matter on both sides, we may easily collect, that all governments are subject to corruption and decay; but with this difference, that absolute monarchy is by principle led unto, or rooted in it; whereas mixed or popular governments are only in a possibility of falling into it: As the first cannot subsist, unless the prevailing part of the people be corrupted; the other must certainly perish, unless they be preserved in a great measure free from vices: and I doubt whether any better reason can be given, why there have been and are more monarchies than popular governments in the world, than that nations are more easily drawn into corruption than defended from it; and I think that monarchy can be said to be natural in no other sense, than that our depraved nature is most inclined to that which is worst.

To avoid unnecessary disputes, I give the name of popular governments to those of Rome, Athens, Sparta, and the like, tho improperly, unless the same may also be given to many that are usually called monarchies, since there is nothing of violence in either; the power is conferr'd upon the chief magistrates of both by the free consent of a willing people, and such a part as they think fit is still retained and executed in their own assemblies; and in this sense it is that our author seems to speak against them. As to popular government in the strictest sense (that is pure democracy, where the people in themselves, and by themselves, perform all that belongs to government), I know of no such thing; and if it be in the world, have nothing to say for it. In asserting the liberty, generally, as I suppose, granted by God to all mankind, I neither deny, that so many as think fit to enter into a society, may give so much of their power as they please to one or more men, for a time or perpetually, to them and their heirs, according to such rules as they prescribe; nor approve the disorders that must arise if they keep it entirely in their own hands: And looking upon the several governments, which under different forms and names have been regularly constituted by nations, as so many undeniable testimonies, that they thought it good for themselves and their posterity so to do, I infer, that as there is no man who would not rather chuse to be governed by such as are just, industrious, valiant and wise, than by those that are wicked, slothful, cowardly and foolish; and to live in society with such as are qualified like those of the first sort, rather than with those who will be ever ready to commit all manner of villainies, or want experience, strength or courage, to join in repelling the injuries that are offer'd by others: So there are none who do not according to the measure of understanding they have, endeavour to set up those who seem to be best qualified, and to prevent the introduction of those vices, which render the faith of the magistrate suspected, or make him unable to perform his duty, in providing for the execution of justice, and the publick defence of the state against foreign or domestick enemies. For as no man who is not absolutely mad, will commit the care of a flock to a villain, that has neither skill, diligence, nor courage to defend them, or perhaps is maliciously set to destroy them, rather than to a stout, faithful, and wise shepherd; 'tis less to be imagined that any would commit the same error in relation to that society which comprehends himself with his children, friends, and all that is dear to him.

The same considerations are of equal force in relation to the body of every nation: For since the magistrate, tho the most perfect in his kind, cannot perform his duty, if the people be so base, vicious, effeminate and cowardly, as not to second his good intentions; those who expect good from him, cannot desire so to corrupt their companions that are to help him, as to render it impossible for him to accomplish it. Tho I believe there have been in all ages bad men in every nation, yet I doubt whether there was one in Rome, except a Catiline or a Caesar, who design'd to make themselves tyrants, that would not rather have wished the whole people as brave and virtuous as in the time of the Carthaginian Wars, than vile and base as in the days of Nero and Domitian. But 'tis madness to think, that the whole body would not rather wish to be as it was when virtue flourished, and nothing upon earth was able to resist their power, than weak, miserable, base, slavish, and trampled under foot by any that would invade them; and forced as a chattel to become a prey to those that were strongest. Which is sufficient to shew, that a people acting according to the liberty of their own will, never advance unworthy men, unless it be by mistake, nor willingly suffer the introduction of vices: Whereas the absolute monarch always prefers the worst of those who are addicted to him, and cannot subsist unless the prevailing part of the people be base and vicious.

If it be said, that those governments in which the democratical part governs most, do more frequently err in the choice of men or the means of preserving that purity of manners which is required for the well-being of a people, than those wherein aristocracy prevails; I confess it, and that in Rome and Athens the best and wisest men did for the most part incline to aristocracy. Xenophon, Plato, Aristotle, Thucydides, Livy, Tacitus, Cicero, and others, were of this sort: But if our author there seek patrons for his absolute monarchy, he will find none but Phalaris, Agathocles, Dionysius, Catiline, Cethegus, Lentulus, with the corrupted crew of mercenary rascals, who did, or endeavour'd to set them up. These are they *quibus ex honesto nulla est spes;*[5] they abhor the dominion of the law, because it curbs their vices, and make themselves subservient to the lusts of a man who may nourish them. Similitude of interests, manners, and designs, is a link of union between them: Both are enemies to popular and mixed government; and those governments are enemies to them, and by preserving virtue and integrity, oppose both; knowing, that if they do not, they and their governments must certainly perish.

SECTION 20

Man's natural love to Liberty is temper'd by Reason,
which originally is his Nature.

THAT our author's book may appear to be a heap of incongruities and contradictions, 'tis not amiss to add to what has already been observed, that having asserted absolute monarchy to be *the only natural government*, he now says, *that the nature of all people is to desire liberty without restraint.*[1] But if monarchy be that power which above all restrains liberty, and subjects all to the will of one; this is as much as to say, that all people naturally desire that which is against nature; and by a wonderful excess of extravagance and folly to assert contrary propositions, that on both sides are equally absurd and false. For as we have already proved that no government is imposed upon men by God or nature, 'tis no less evident, that man being a rational creature, nothing can be universally natural to him, that is not rational. But this liberty without restraint being inconsistent with any government, and the good which man naturally

[5] [For whom there is no hope from an honest man.]   [1] [*Patriarcha*, ch. 15, p. 84; ch. 18, p. 89.]

desires for himself, children and friends, we find no place in the world where the inhabitants do not enter into some kind of society or government to restrain it: and to say that all men desire liberty without restraint, and yet that all do restrain it, is ridiculous. The truth is, man is hereunto led by reason which is his nature. Everyone sees they cannot well live asunder, nor many together, without some rule to which all must submit. This submission is a restraint of liberty, but could be of no effect as to the good intended, unless it were general; nor general, unless it were natural. When all are born to the same freedom, some will not resign that which is their own, unless others do the like: This general consent of all to resign such a part of their liberty as seems to be for the good of all, is the voice of nature, and the act of men (according to natural reason) seeking their own good: And if all go not in the same way, according to the same form, 'tis an evident testimony that no one is directed by nature; but as a few or many may join together, and frame smaller or greater societies, so those societies may institute such an order or form of government as best pleases themselves; and if the ends of government are obtained, they all equally follow the voice of nature in constituting them.

Again, if man were by nature so tenacious of his liberty without restraint, he must be rationally so. The creation of absolute monarchies, which entirely extinguishes it, must necessarily be most contrary to it, tho the people were willing; for they thereby abjure their own nature. The usurpation of them can be no less than the most abominable and outrageous violation of the laws of nature that can be imagined: The laws of God must be in the like measure broken; and of all governments, democracy, in which every man's liberty is least restrained, because every man hath an equal part, would certainly prove to be the most just, rational and natural; whereas our author represents it as a perpetual spring of disorder, confusion and vice. This consequence would be unavoidable, if he said true; but it being my fate often to differ from him, I hope to be excused if I do so in this also, and affirm, that nothing but the plain and certain dictates of reason can be generally applicable to all men as the law of their nature; and they who, according to the best of their understanding, provide for the good of themselves and their posterity, do all equally observe it. He that enquires more exactly into the matter may find, that reason enjoins every man not to arrogate to himself more than he allows to others, nor to retain that liberty which will prove hurtful to him; or to expect that others will suffer themselves to be restrain'd, whilst he, to their prejudice, remains in the exercise of that freedom which nature allows. He who would be exempted from this common rule, must shew for what reason he should be raised above his brethren; and if he do it not, he is an enemy to them. This is not popularity, but tyranny; and tyrants are said *exuisse hominem*,[2] to throw off the nature of men, because they do unjustly and unreasonably assume to themselves that which agrees not with the frailty of human nature, and set up an interest in themselves contrary to that of their equals, which they ought to defend as their own. Such as favour them are like to them; and we know of no tyranny that was not set up by the worst, nor of any that have been destroy'd, unless by the best of men. The several tyrannies of Syracuse were introduced by Agathocles, Dionysius, Hieronymus, Hippocrates, Epicides, and others, by the help of lewd, dissolute mercenary villains; and overthrown by Timoleon, Dion, Theodorus and others, whose virtues will be remembered in all ages. These, and others like to them, never sought liberty without restraint, but such as was restrained by laws tending to the publick good; that all might concur in promoting it, and the unruly desires of those who affected power and honours which they did not deserve might be repressed.

The like was seen in Rome: When Brutus, Valerius, and other virtuous citizens had thrown out the lewd Tarquins, they trusted to their own innocence and reputation; and thinking them safe under the protection of the law, contented themselves with such honours as their countrymen thought they deserved. This would not satisfy the dissolute crew that us'd to be companions to the Tarquins. *Sodales adolescentium Tarquiniorum assueti more regio vivere, eam tum aequato jure omnium licentiam quaerentes libertatem aliorum in suam vertisse servitutem conquerebantur. Regem hominem esse, à quo impetres ubi jus, ubi injuria opus sit. Esse gratiae locum, esse beneficio: & irasci & ignoscere posse. Leges rem surdam esse & inexorabilem, salubriorem inopi quam potenti: nihil laxamenti nec veniae habere, si modum excesseris: periculosum esse in tot humanis erroribus sola innocentia vivere.*[3] I cannot say that either of these sought a liberty without restraint; for the virtuous were willing to be restrained by the law, and the vicious to submit to the will of a man, to gain impunity in offending. But if our author say true, the licentious fury of these lewd young men, who endeavour'd to subvert the constitution of their country, to procure the impunity of their own

---

[2] [To have laid aside the man.]

[3] T. Liv. l. 2. ["The companions of the young Tarquins, accustomed to live in regal fashion, sought that same license at the time when the rights of all were equal. They complained that the liberty of others had turned into their own servitude. A king, they said, was a man from whom you could request where a right, where a wrong, might be needed. There was a place for favors, for benefits: and he was able to grow angry and forgive. But laws are a deaf and severe thing, more wholesome to those in want than the powerful. They hold no respite or pardon if you are excessive in any way: it is dangerous to live among so many human errors relying on innocence alone." Livy, *History of Rome*, bk. 2, ch. 3.]

crimes would have been more natural, that is more reasonable than the orderly proceedings of the most virtuous, who desir'd that the law might be the rule of their actions, which is most absurd.

The like vicious wretches have in all times endeavour'd to put the power into the hands of one man, who might protect them in their villainies, and advance them to exorbitant riches or undeserved honours; whilst the best men trusting in their innocence, and desiring no other riches or preferments, than what they were by their equals thought to deserve, were contented with a due liberty, under the protection of a just law: and I must transcribe the histories of the world, or at least so much of them as concerns the tyrannies that have been set up or cast down, if I should here insert all the proofs that might be given of it. But I shall come nearer to the point, which is not to compare democracy with monarchy, but a regular mixed government with such an absolute monarchy, as leaves all to the will of that man, woman, or child, who happens to be born in the reigning family, how ill soever they may be qualified. I desire those who are lovers of truth to consider, whether the wisest, best, and bravest of men, are not naturally led to be pleased with a government that protects them from receiving wrong, when they have not the least inclination to do any? Whether they who desire no unjust advantage above their brethren, will not always desire that a people or senate constituted as that of Rome, from the expulsion of Tarquin to the setting up of Caesar, should rather judge of their merit, than Tarquin, Caesar, or his successors? Or whether the lewd or corrupted Praetorian bands, with Macro, Sejanus, Tigellinus, and the like, commanding them, will not ever, like Brutus his sons, abhor the inexorable power of the laws, with the necessity of living only by their innocence, and favour the interest of princes like to those that advanced them? If this be not sufficient, they may be pleased a little to reflect upon the affairs of our own country, and seriously consider whether H–de, Cl–f–d, F–lm–th, Arl–ng–n and D–nby,[4] could have pretended to the chief places, if the disposal of them had been in a free and well-regulated parliament? Whether they did most resemble Brutus, Publicola, and the rest of the Valerii, the Fabii, Quintii, Cornelii, &c. or Narcissus, Pallas, Icetus, Laco, Vinius, and the like? Whether all men, good and bad, do not favour that state of things, which favours them and such as they are?

---

[4] [Laurence Hyde, Earl of Rochester; Sir Thomas Clifford; Henry Bennet, Earl of Arlington; and Sir Thomas Osborne, Earl of Danby, leading ministers under Charles II, were believed by many to be promoting absolute monarchy. Charles Berkeley, reputed dissolute by his contemporaries, was made Earl of Falmouth by his personal friend the king.]

Whether Cl-v-l-d, P-rtsm-th,[5] and others of the same trade, have attained to the riches and honours they enjoy by services done to the common-wealth? And what places Chiffinch, F–x and Jenkins,[6] could probably have attained, if our affairs had been regulated as good men desire? Whether the old arts of begging, stealing and bawding, or the new ones of informing and trepanning, thrive best under one man who may be weak or vicious, and is always subject to be circumvented by flatterers, or under the severe scrutinies of a senate or people? In a word, whether they who live by such arts, and know no other, do not always endeavour to advance the government under which they enjoy, or may hope to obtain the highest honours, and abhor that, in which they are exposed to all manner of scorn and punishment? Which being determined, it will easily appear why the worst men have ever been for absolute monarchy, and the best against it; and which of the two in so doing can be said to desire an unrestrained liberty of doing that which is evil.

SECTION 21

Mixed and Popular Governments preserve Peace, and manage Wars, better than Absolute Monarchies.

B EING no way concerned in the defence of democracy; and having proved that Xenophon, Thucydides, and others of the ancients, in speaking against the over great power of the common people, intended to add reputation to the aristocratical party to which they were addicted, and not to set up absolute monarchy, which never fell under discourse among them, but as an object of scorn and hatred, evil in itself, and only to be endured by base and barbarous people, I may leave our knight, like Don Quixote, fighting against the phantasms of his own brain, and saying what he pleases against such governments as never were, unless in such a place as San Marino near Sinigaglia in Italy, where a hundred clowns govern a barbarous rock that no man invades, and relates nothing to our question. If his doctrine be true, the monarchy he extols is not only to

[5] [Barbara Villiers, Duchess of Cleveland, and Louise Renée de Kéroualle, Duchess of Portsmouth, were influential mistresses of Charles II.]

[6] [William Chiffinch, page to Charles II, was famous for his low character, intrigues, and extravagant self-indulgence. Sir Stephen Fox amassed a fortune as commissioner of the treasury under Charles. Sir Leoline Jenkins had mediocre talent but profited in the king's service.]

be preferred before unruly democracy, and mixed governments, but is the only one that, without a gross violation of the laws of God and nature, can be established over any nation. But having, as I hope, sufficiently proved, that God did neither institute, nor appoint any such to be instituted, nor approve those that were; that nature does not incline us to it, and that the best as well as the wisest men have always abhorr'd it; that it has been agreeable only to the most stupid and base nations; and if others have submitted to it, they have done so only as to the greatest of evils brought upon them by violence, corruption or fraud; I may now proceed to shew that the progress of it has been in all respects suitable to its beginning.

To this end 'twill not be amiss to examine our author's words: *Thus,* says he, *do they paint to the life this beast with many heads: Let me give the cypher of their form of government: as it is begot by sedition, so it is nourish'd by crimes: It can never stand without wars, either with an enemy abroad, or with friends at home;*[1] And in order to this I will not criticize upon the terms, tho the cypher of a form, and war with friends, may be justly called nonsense; but coming to his assertions, that popular or mixed governments have their birth in sedition, and are ever afterwards vexed with civil or foreign wars, I take liberty to say, that whereas there is no form appointed by God or nature, those governments only can be called just, which are established by the consent of nations. These nations may at the first set up popular or mixed governments, and without the guilt of sedition introduce them afterwards, if that which was first established prove unprofitable or hurtful to them; and those that have done so, have enjoy'd more justice in times of peace, and managed wars, when occasion requir'd, with more virtue and better success, than any absolute monarchies have done. And whereas he says, that *in popular governments each man hath a care of his particular, and thinks basely of the common good; They look upon approaching mischiefs as they do upon thunder, only every man wisheth it may not touch his own person:*[2] I say that men can no otherwise be engaged to take care of the publick, than by having such a part in it, as absolute monarchy does not allow; for they can neither obtain the good for themselves, posterity and friends, that they desire, nor prevent the mischiefs they fear, which are the principal arguments that persuade men to expose themselves to labours or dangers. 'Tis a folly to say, that the vigilance and wisdom of the monarch supplies the defect of care in others; for we know that no men under the sun were ever more void of both, and all manner of virtue requir'd to such a work, than very many monarchs

---

[1] [*Patriarcha*, ch. 18, p. 90.]   [2] [Ibid.]

have been: And, which is yet worse, the strength and happiness of the people being frequently dangerous to them, they have not so much as the will to promote it; nay, sometimes set themselves to destroy it. Ancient monarchies afford us frequent examples of this kind; and if we consider those of France and Turkey, which seem most to flourish in our age, the people will appear to be so miserable under both, that they cannot fear any change of governor or government; and all, except a few ministers, are kept so far from the knowledge of, or power in the management of affairs, that if any of them should fancy a possibility of something that might befall them worse than what they suffer, or hope for that which might alleviate their misery, they could do nothing towards the advancement of the one, or prevention of the other. Tacitus observes, that in his time no man was able to write what passed, *inscitia reipublicae ut alienae.*[3] They neglected the publick affairs in which they had no part. In the same age it was said, that the people, who whilst they fought for their own interests, had been invincible, being enslaved, were grown sordid, idle, base, running after stage-plays and shows; so as the whole strength of the Roman armies consisted of strangers. When their spirits were depressed by servitude, they had neither courage to defend themselves, nor will to fight for their wicked masters; and least of all to increase their power, which was destructive to themselves: The same thing is found in all places. Tho the Turk commands many vast provinces, that naturally produce as good soldiers as any, yet his greatest strength is in children that do not know their fathers; who not being very many in number, may perish in one battle, and the empire by that means be lost, the miserable nations that groan under that tyranny having neither courage, power, nor will to defend it. This was the fate of the Mamelukes. They had for the space of almost two hundred years domineer'd in Egypt, and a great part of Asia; but the people under them being weak and disaffected, they could never recover the defeat they received from Selim near Tripoli, who pursuing his victory, in a few months utterly abolished their kingdom.

Notwithstanding the present pride of France, the numbers and warlike inclinations of that people, the bravery of the nobility, extent of dominion, convenience of situation, and the vast revenues of their king, his greatest advantages have been gained by the mistaken counsels of England, the valour of our soldiers unhappily sent to serve him, and the strangers of whom the strength of his armies consists; which is so unsteady a support,

---

[3] Tacit. An. l. 1. ["Through ignorance of
public affairs, which were alien to them."
Tacitus, *Histories*, bk. 1, ch. 1.]

that many who are well versed in affairs of this nature, incline to think he subsists rather by little arts, and corrupting ministers in foreign courts, than by the power of his own armies; and that some reformation in the counsels of his neighbours might prove sufficient to overthrow that greatness which is grown formidable to Europe; the same misery to which he has reduced his people, rendering them as unable to defend him, upon any change of fortune, as to defend their own rights against him.

This proceeds not from any particular defect in the French government, but that which is common to all absolute monarchies. And no state can be said to stand upon a steady foundation, except those whose strength is in their own soldiery, and the body of their own people. Such as serve for wages, often betray their masters in distress, and always want the courage and industry which is found in those who fight for their own interests, and are to have a part in the victory. The business of mercenaries is so to perform their duty, as to keep their employments, and to draw profit from them; but that is not enough to support the spirits of men in extreme dangers. The shepherd who is a hireling, flies when the thief comes; and this adventitious help failing, all that a prince can reasonably expect from a disaffected and oppressed people is, that they should bear the yoke patiently in the time of his prosperity; but upon the change of his fortune, they leave him to shift for himself, or join with his enemies to avenge the injuries they had received. Thus did Alfonso and Ferdinand kings of Naples, and Lodovico Sforza duke of Milan fall, in the times of Charles the Eighth and Louis the Twelfth kings of France. The two first had been false, violent, and cruel; nothing within their kingdom could oppose their fury: but when they were invaded by a foreign power, they lost all, as Guicciardini says, without breaking one lance; and Sforza was by his own mercenary soldiers delivered into the hands of his enemies.[4]

I think it may be hard to find examples of such as proceeding in the same way have had better success: But if it should so fall out, that a people living under an absolute monarchy, should through custom, or fear of something worse (if that can be) not only suffer patiently, but desire to uphold the government; neither the nobility, nor commonalty can do anything towards it. They are strangers to all publick concernments: All things are govern'd by one or a few men, and others know nothing either of action or counsel. Filmer will tell us 'tis no matter; the profound wisdom of the prince provides for all. But what if this prince be a child, a fool, a superannuated dotard, or a madman? Or if he does not fall under

---

[4] [Francesco Guicciardini, *History of Italy* (published 1561/1564; Princeton: Princeton University Press, 1969), bk. 1, p. 75.]

any of these extremities, and possesses such a proportion of wit, industry, and courage as is ordinarily seen in men, how shall he supply the office that indeed requires profound wisdom, and an equal measure of experience and valour? 'Tis to no purpose to say a good council may supply his defects; for it does not appear how he should come by this council, nor who should oblige him to follow their advice: If he be left to his own will to do what he pleases, tho good advice be given to him; yet his judgment being perverted, he will always incline to the worst: If a necessity be imposed upon him of acting according to the advice of his council, he is not that absolute monarch of whom we speak, nor the government monarchical, but aristocratical. These are imperfect fig-leaf coverings of nakedness. It was in vain to give good counsel to Sardanapalus; and none could defend the Assyrian empire, when he lay wallowing amongst his whores without any other thought than of his lusts. None could preserve Rome, when Domitian's chief business was to kill flies, and that of Honorius to take care of his hens. The monarchy of France must have perished under the base kings they call *les roys faineants*,[5] if the scepter had not been wrested out of their unworthy hands. The world is full of examples in this kind: and when it pleases God to bestow a just, wise, and valiant king as a blessing upon a nation, 'tis only a momentary help, his virtues end with him; and there being neither any divine promise nor human reason moving us to believe that they shall always be renewed and continued in his successors, men cannot rely upon it; and to allege a possibility of such a thing is nothing to the purpose.

On the other side, in a popular or mixed government every man is concerned: Every one has a part according to his quality or merit; all changes are prejudicial to all: whatsoever any man conceives to be for the publick good, he may propose it in the magistracy, or to the magistrate: the body of the people is the publick defence, and every man is arm'd and disciplin'd: The advantages of good success are communicated to all, and everyone bears a part in the losses. This makes men generous and industrious; and fills their hearts with love to their country: This, and the desire of that praise which is the reward of virtue,[6] raised the Romans above the rest of mankind; and wheresoever the same ways are taken, they will in a great measure have the same effects. By this means they had as many soldiers to fight for their country as there were freemen in it. Whilst they had to deal with the free nations of Italy, Greece, Africa,

[5] ["The do-nothing kings" refers to the later kings of the Merovingian dynasty, who were replaced by the Mayors of the Palace, beginning with Pepin the Short.]

[6] Amor patriae laudisque immensa cupido. Virg. ["Love of fatherland and great desire of praise." Virgil, *Aeneid*, bk. 6, li. 823.]

or Spain, they never conquer'd a country, till the inhabitants were exhausted: But when they came to fight against kings, the success of a battle was enough to bring a kingdom under their power. Antiochus upon a ruffle received from Acilius at Thermopylae, left all that he possessed in Greece; and being defeated by Scipio Nasica, he quitted all the kingdoms and territories of Asia on this side Taurus. Aemilius Paulus became master of Macedon by one prosperous fight against Perseus. Syphax, Gentius, Tigranes, Ptolemy, and others were more easily subdued. The mercenary armies on which they relied being broken, the cities and countries not caring for their masters, submitted to those who had more virtue and better fortune. If the Roman power had not been built upon a more sure foundation, they could not have subsisted. Notwithstanding their valour, they were often beaten; but their losses were immediately repair'd by the excellence of their discipline. When Hannibal had gained the battles of Trebia, Ticinum, Trasimene, and Cannae; defeated the Romans in many other encounters, and slain above two hundred thousand of their men, with Aemilius Paulus, C. Servilius, Sempronius Gracchus, Quintius, Marcellus, and many other excellent commanders: When about the same time the two brave Scipio's had been cut off with their armies in Spain, and many great losses had been sustain'd in Sicily and by sea, one would have thought it impossible for the city to have resisted: But their virtue, love to their country, and good government was a strength that increased under all their calamities, and in the end overcame all. The nearer Hannibal came to the walls, the more obstinate was their resistance. Tho he had kill'd more great captains than any kingdom ever had, others daily stepp'd up in their place, who excell'd them in all manner of virtue. I know not, if at any time that conquering city could glory in a greater number of men fit for the highest enterprises, than at the end of that cruel war, which had consumed so many of them; but I think that the finishing victories by them obtained, are but ill proofs of our author's assertion, that they *thought basely of the common good, and sought only to save themselves.*[7] We know of none except Caecilius Metellus, who after the battle of Cannae had so base a thought as to design the withdrawing himself from the publick ruin; but Scipio (afterwards surnamed Africanus) threatening death to those who would not swear never to abandon their country, forced him to leave it. This may in general be imputed to good government and discipline, with which all were so seasoned from their infancy, that no affection was so rooted in them, as an ardent love to their country, and a resolution to

---

[7] [*Patriarcha*, ch. 18, p. 90.]

die for it, or with it; but the means by which they accomplished their great ends, so as after their defeats to have such men as carried on their noblest designs with more glory than ever, was their annual elections of magistrates, many being thereby advanc'd to the supreme commands, and every one by the honours they enjoy'd, fill'd with a desire of rendering himself worthy of them.

I should not much insist upon these things, if they had been seen only in Rome: but tho their discipline seems to have been more perfect, better observed, and to have produc'd a virtue that surpassed all others; the like has been found, tho perhaps not in the same degree, in all nations that have enjoyed their liberty, and were admitted to such a part of the government, as might give them a love to it. This was evident in all the nations of Italy. The Sabines, Volsci, Aequi, Tuscans, Samnites and others were never conquer'd, till they had no men left. The Samnites alone inhabiting a small and barren province, suffer'd more defeats before they were subdued, than all the kingdoms of Numidia, Egypt, Macedon, and Asia; and, as 'tis exprest in their embassy to Hannibal, never yielded, till they who had brought vast numbers of men into the field, and by them defeated some of the Roman armies, were reduced to such weakness, that they could not resist one legion. We hear of few Spartans who did not willingly expose their lives for the service of their country; and the women themselves were so far inflamed with the same affection, that they refused to mourn for their children and husbands who died in the defence of it. When the brave Brasidas was slain, some eminent men went to comfort his mother upon the news of his death; and telling her he was the most valiant man in the city, she answer'd, that he was indeed a valiant man, and died as he ought to do, but that through the goodness of the gods, many others were left as valiant as he.[8]

When Xerxes invaded Greece, there was not a citizen of Athens able to bear arms, who did not leave his wife and children to shift for themselves in the neighbouring cities, and their houses to be burnt when they embarked with Themistocles; and never thought of either till they had defeated the barbarians at Salamis by sea, and at Plataea by land. When men are thus spirited, some will ever prove excellent; and as none did ever surpass those who were bred under this discipline in all moral, military and civil virtues; those very countries where they flourished most, have not produced any eminent men since they lost that liberty which was the mother and nurse of them.

[8] Thucyd. de bel. Pelopon. [Thucydides,
Peloponnesian War, 4 vols. (Loeb, 1919–1923),
bk. 5, ch. 15.]

Tho I should fill a volume with examples of this kind (as I might easily do) such as our author will say, that in popular governments men look upon mischiefs as thunder, and only wish it may not touch themselves:[9] But leaving them to the scorn and hatred they deserve by their impudence and folly, I conclude this point with the answer, that Trajano Boccalini puts into the mouth of Apollo, to the princes who complained that their subjects had not that love to their countries, as had been, and was daily seen in those who lived under commonwealths; which did amount to no more than to tell them, that their ill government was the cause of that defect, and that the prejudices incurr'd by rapine, violence, and fraud were to be repaired only by liberality, justice, and such a care of their subjects, that they might live happily under them.[10]

SECTION 22

Commonwealths seek Peace or War according to the Variety of their Constitutions.

I F I have hitherto spoken in general of popular or mixed governments, as if they were all founded on the same principle, it was only because our author without distinction has generally blamed them all, and generally imputed to every one those faults, which perhaps never were in any; but most certainly are directly opposite to the temper and constitution of many among them. Malice and ignorance reign so equally in him, that 'tis not easy to determine from which of the two this false representation proceeds. But lest any man should thereby be imposed upon, 'tis time to observe, that the constitutions of commonwealths have been so various, according to the different temper of nations and times, that if some of them seem to have been principally constituted for war, others have as much delighted in peace; and many having taken the middle, and (as some think) the best way, have so moderated their love to peace, as not to suffer the spirits of the people to fall, but kept them in a perpetual readiness to make war when there was occasion: and every one of those having followed several ways and ends, deserve our particular consideration.

[9] [*Patriarcha*, ch. 18, p. 90.]

[10] Ragion. 99. [Trajano Boccalini, *I ragguagli di Parnasso*, or *Advertisements from Parnassus* (1612–13; trans. London: Dring, Starkey, and Basset, 1669); a strongly anti-Catholic, anti-monarchical satire on 17th-century politics, art, and literature.]

The cities of Rome, Sparta, Thebes, and all the associations of the Aetolians, Achaeans, Sabines, Latins, Samnites, and many others that anciently flourish'd in Greece and Italy, seem to have intended nothing but the just preservation of liberty at home, and making war abroad. All the nations of Spain, Germany, and Gaul sought the same things. Their principal work was to render their people valiant, obedient to their commanders, lovers of their country, and always ready to fight for it: And for this reason when the senators of Rome had kill'd Romulus, they persuaded Julius Proculus to affirm, that he had seen him in a most glorious form ascending to heaven, and promising great things to the city, *proinde rem militarem colant.*[1] The Athenians were not less inclined to war, but applied themselves to trade, as subservient to that end, by increasing the number of the people, and furnishing them with the means of carrying it on with more vigour and power. The Phoenician cities, of which Carthage was the most eminent, followed the same method; but knowing that riches do not defend themselves, or scorning slothfully to enjoy what was gained by commerce, they so far applied themselves to war, that they grew to a power, which Rome only was able to overthrow. Venice, Florence, Genoa, Lucca, and some other cities of Italy seem chiefly to have aimed at trade; and placing the hopes of their safety in the protection of more powerful states, unwillingly enter'd into wars, especially by land; and when they did, they made them by mercenary soldiers.

Again, some of those that intended war desir'd to enlarge their territories by conquest; others only to preserve their own, and to live with freedom and safety upon them. Rome was of the first sort; and knowing that such ends cannot be accomplished without great numbers of men, they freely admitted strangers into the city, senate, and magistracy. Numa was a Sabine: Tarquinius Priscus was the son of a Grecian: One hundred of those Sabines who came with Tatius were admitted into the senate: Appius Claudius of the same people came to Rome, was made a member of the senate, and created consul. They demolished several cities, and brought the inhabitants to their own; gave the right of citizens to many others (sometimes to whole cities and provinces) and cared not how many they received, so as they could engraft them upon the same interest with the old stock, and season them with the same principles, discipline, and manners. On the other side the Spartans desiring only to continue free, virtuous, and safe in the enjoyment of their own territory; and thinking themselves strong enough to defend it, framed a most severe discipline,

[1] ["Accordingly, let them cultivate warfare."
Livy, *History of Rome*, bk. 1, ch. 16.]

to which few strangers would submit. They banished all those curious arts, that are useful to trade; prohibited the importation of gold and silver; appointed the Helots to cultivate their lands, and to exercise such trades as are necessary to life; admitted few strangers to live amongst them; made none of them free of their city, and educated their youth in such exercises only as prepared them for war. I will not take upon me to judge whether this proceeded from such a moderation of spirit, as placed felicity rather in the fullness and stability of liberty, integrity, virtue, and the enjoyment of their own, than in riches, power, and dominion over others; nor which of these two different methods deserves most to be commended: But certain it is that both succeeded according to the intention of the founders.

Rome conquer'd the best part of the world, and never wanted men to defend what was gained: Sparta lived in such happiness and reputation, that till it was invaded by Epaminondas, an enemy's trumpet had not been heard by those within the town for the space of eight hundred years, and never suffer'd any great disaster, till receding from their own institutions, they were brought by prosperity to affect the principality of Greece, and to undertake such wars as could not be carried on without money, and greater numbers of men than a small city was able to furnish; by which means they were obliged to beg assistance from the barbarians, whom they scorned and hated, as appears by the stories of Callicratidas, Lysander, and Agesilaus, and fell into such straits as were never recovered.

The like variety has been observed in the constitutions of those northern nations that invaded the Roman empire; for tho all of them intended war, and looked upon those only to be members of their commonwealths, who used arms to defend them, yet some did immediately incorporate themselves with those of the conquer'd countries. Of this number were the Franks, who presently became one nation with the Gauls; others kept themselves in a distinct body, as the Saxons did from the Britains: And the Goths for more than three hundred years that they reigned in Spain, never contracted marriages, or otherwise mixed with the Spaniards, till their kingdom was overthrown by the Moors.

These things, and others of the like nature, being weighed, many have doubted whether it were better to constitute a commonwealth for war or for trade; and of such as intend war, whether those are most to be praised who prepare for defence only, or those who design by conquest to enlarge their dominions. Or, if they admit of trade, whether they should propose the acquisition of riches for their ultimate end, and depend upon foreign or mercenary forces to defend them; or to be as helps to enable their own people to carry on those wars, in which they may be frequently engaged.

These questions might perhaps be easily decided, if mankind were of a temper to suffer those to live in peace, who offer no injury to any; or that men who have money to hire soldiers when they stand in need of them, could find such as would valiantly and faithfully defend them, whilst they apply themselves to their trades. But experience teaching us that those only can be safe who are strong; and that no people was ever well defended, but those who fought for themselves; the best judges of these matters have always given the preference to those constitutions that principally intend war, and make use of trade as assisting to that end: and think it better to aim at conquest, rather than simply to stand upon their own defence; since he that loses all if he be overcome, fights upon very unequal terms; and if he obtain the victory, gains no other advantage, than for the present to repel the danger that threatened him.

These opinions are confirmed by the examples of the Romans, who prosper'd much more than the Spartans: And the Carthaginians, who made use of trade as a help to war, raised their city to be one of the most potent that ever was in the world: Whereas the Venetians having relied on trade and mercenary soldiers, are always forced too much to depend upon foreign potentates; very often to buy peace with ignominious and prejudicial conditions; and sometimes to fear the infidelity of their own commanders, no less than the violence of their enemies. But that which ought to be valued above all in point of wisdom as well as justice, is, the government given by God to the Hebrews, which chiefly fitted them for war, and to make conquests. Moses divided them under several captains, into thousands, hundreds, fifties, and tens: This was a perpetual ordinance amongst them: In numbering them, those only were counted, who were able to bear arms: Every man was obliged to go out to war, except such as had married a wife, or upon other special occasions were for a time excused; and the whole series of the sacred history shews that there were always as many soldiers to fight for their country as there were men able to fight. And if this be taken for a picture of a many-headed beast delighting in blood, begotten by sedition, and nourished by crimes,[2] God himself was the drawer of it.

In this variety of constitutions and effects proceeding from them, I can see nothing more justly and generally to be attributed to them all, than that love to their country, which our author impudently affirms to be wanting in all. In other matters their proceedings are not only different, but contrary to each other: yet it cannot be said that any nations have enjoyed so much peace as some republicks. The Venetians' too great

---

[2] [*Patriarcha*, ch. 18, p. 90.]

inclination to peace is accounted to be a mortal error in their constitution, and they have not been less free from domestick seditions than foreign wars; the conspiracies of the Falerii and Tiepoli were extinguished by their punishment, and that of La Cueva crushed before it was ripe. Genoa has not been altogether so happy: the factions of the Guelphs and Ghibellines that spread themselves over all Italy, infected that city; and the malice of the Spaniards and French raised others under the Fregosi and Adorni; but they being composed, they have for more than a hundred and fifty years rested in quiet.

There is another sort of commonwealth composed of many cities associated together, and living *aequo jure;*[3] every one retaining and exercising a sovereign power within itself, except in some cases expressed in the act of union, or league made between them. These I confess are more hardly preserved in peace. Disputes may arise among them concerning limits, jurisdiction, and the like. They cannot always be equally concerned in the same things. The injuries offer'd to one do not equally affect all. Their neighbours will sow divisions among them; and not having a mother city to decide their controversies by her authority, they may be apt to fall into quarrels, especially if they profess Christianity; which having been split into variety of opinions ever since it was preached, and the papists by their cruelty to such as dissent from them, shewing to all, that there is no other way of defending themselves against them, than by using the same, almost every man is come to think he ought (as far as in him lies) to impose his belief on others, and that he can give no better testimony of his zeal, than the excess of his violence on that account. Nevertheless the cantons of the Switzers, tho accompanied with all the most dangerous circumstances that can be imagined, being thirteen in number, independent on each other, governed in a high degree popularly, professing Christianity differing in most important points; eight of them much influenced by the Jesuits, and perpetually excited to war against their brethren by the powerful crowns of Spain and France, have ever since they cast off the insupportable yoke of the earls of Hapsburg, enjoy'd more peace than any other state of Europe, and from the most inconsiderable people, are grown to such a power, that the greatest monarchs do most solicitously seek their friendship; and none have dared to invade them, since Charles duke of Burgundy did it to his ruin: and he who for a long time had been a terror to the great, dangerous, and subtle king of France, gave by the loss of three armies and his own life a lasting testimony of his temerity in assaulting a free and valiant,

[3] [With equal right.]

tho a poor people, fighting in their own quarrel. Comines well relates that war; but a vast heap of bones remaining to this day at Muret with this inscription, *Caroli fortissimi Burgundiorum ducis exercitus Muretum obsidens ab Helvetiis caesus, hoc sui monumentum reliquit,*[4] best shews the success of it. Since that time their greatest wars have been for the defence of Milan; or such as they have undertaken for pay under the ensigns of France or Spain, that by the use of arms they may keep up that courage, reputation, and experience which is requir'd for the defence of their own country. No government was ever more free from popular seditions; the revolts of their subjects have been few, weak, and easily suppressed; the dissension raised by the Jesuits between the cantons of Zurich and Lucerne was as soon composed as the rebellion of the county of Vaux against the canton of Bern; and those few of the like nature that have happened among them have had the like success: So that Thuanus in the history of his time,[5] comprehending about fifty years, and relating the horrid domestick and foreign wars, that distracted Germany, France, Spain, Italy, Flanders, England, Scotland, Poland, Denmark, Sweden, Hungary, Transylvania, Muscovy, Turkey, Africa, and other places, has no more to say of them than to shew what arts had been in vain used to disturb their so much envied quiet. But if the modest temper of the people, together with the wisdom, justice, and strength of their government, could not be discomposed by the measures of Spain and France, by the industry of their ambassadors, or the malicious craft of the Jesuits, we may safely conclude that their state is as well settled as anything among men can be, and can hardly comprehend what is like to interrupt it. As much might be said of the cities of the Hanseatick Society, if they had an entire sovereignty in themselves: But the cities of the united provinces in the Low Countries being every one of them sovereign within themselves, and many in number, still continuing in their union in spite of all the endeavours that have been used to divide them, give us an example of such steadiness in practice and principle, as is hardly to be parellel'd in the world, and that undeniably prove a temper in their constitutions directly opposite to that which our author imputes to all popular governments: and if the death of Barneveldt and De Witt, or the preferment of some most unlike to them be taken for a testimony that the best men thrive worst, and the

---

[4] ["The army of Charles, bravest leader of the Burgundians, slaughtered by the Swiss while besieging Morat, has left this monument of itself." Philippe de Comines describes the battle in *Memoirs* (London: Bohn, 1855), bk. 5, ch. 3, pp. 313–316.]

[5] [Jacques-Auguste de Thou, *Historiae sui temporis, 1543–1607*, or *History of His Time,* (published 1604–1620 in 138 books; Arles: de la Rouiere, 1626–1630).]

worst best, I hope it may be consider'd that those violences proceeded from that which is most contrary to popularity, tho I am not very willing to explain it.

If these matters are not clear in themselves, I desire they may be compared with what has happen'd between any princes that from the beginning of the world have been joined in league to each other, whether they were of the same or of different nations. Let an example be brought of six, thirteen, or more princes or kings who enter'd into a league; and for the space of one or more ages, did neither break it, nor quarrel upon the explication of it. Let the states of the Switzers, Grisons, or Hollanders, be compared with that of France, when it was sometimes divided between two, three, or four brothers of Meroveus' or Pepin's races; with the heptarchy of England; the kingdoms of Leon, Aragon, Navarre, Castile and Portugal, under which the Christians in Spain were divided; or those of Cordoba, Seville, Malaga, Granada, and others under the power of the Moors; and if it be not evident, that the popular states have been remarkable for peace among themselves, constancy to their union and fidelity to the leagues made with their associates; whereas all the abovementioned kingdoms, and such others as are known among men to have been joined in the like leagues, were ever infested with domestick rebellions and quarrels arising from the ambition of princes, so as no confederacy could be so cautiously made, but they would find ways to elude it, or so solemn and sacred, but they would in far less time break through it: I will confess, that kingdoms have sometimes been as free from civil disturbances; and that leagues made between several princes, have been as constantly and religiously observed, as by commonwealths. But if no such thing do appear in the world, and no man who is not impudent or ignorant dare pretend it, I may justly conclude, that tho every commonwealth hath its action suitable to its constitution, and that many associated together are not so free from disturbances, as those that wholly depend upon the authority of a mother city; yet we know of none that have not been, and are more regular and quiet than any principalities; and as to foreign wars, they seek or avoid them according to their various constitutions.

SECTION 23

That is the best Government, which best provides for War.

Oᴜʀ author having huddled up all popular and mixed governments into one, has in some measure forced me to explain the various constitutions and principles upon which they are grounded: but as the wisdom of a father is seen, not only in providing bread for his family, or increasing his patrimonial estate, but in making all possible provision for the security of it; so that government is evidently the best, which, not relying upon what it does at first enjoy, seeks to increase the number, strength, and riches of the people; and by the best discipline to bring the power so improved into such order as may be of most use to the publick. This comprehends all things conducing to the administration of justice, the preservation of domestick peace, and the increase of commerce, that the people being pleased with their present condition, may be filled with love to their country, encouraged to fight boldly for the publick cause, which is their own; and as men do willingly join with that which prospers, that strangers may be invited to fix their habitations in such a city, and to espouse the principles that reign in it. This is necessary for several reasons; but I shall principally insist upon one, which is, that all things in their beginning are weak: The whelp of a lion newly born has neither strength nor fierceness. He that builds a city, and does not intend it should increase, commits as great an absurdity, as if he should desire his child might ever continue under the same weakness in which he is born. If it do not grow, it must pine and perish; for in this world nothing is permanent; that which does not grow better will grow worse. This increase also is useless, or perhaps hurtful, if it be not in strength, as well as in riches or number: for everyone is apt to seize upon ill guarded treasures; and the terror that the city of London was possessed with, when a few Dutch ships came to Chatham, shews that no numbers of men, tho naturally valiant, are able to defend themselves, unless they be well arm'd, disciplin'd and conducted. Their multitude brings confusion: their wealth, when 'tis like to be made a prey, increases the fears of the owners; and they, who if they were brought into good order, might conquer a great part of the world, being destitute of it, durst not think of defending themselves.

If it be said that the wise father mention'd by me endeavours to secure his patrimony by law, not by force; I answer, that all defence terminates in force; and if a private man does not prepare to defend his estate with his own force, 'tis because he lives under the protection of the law, and expects the force of the magistrate should be a security to him: but kingdoms and commonwealths acknowledging no superior, except God alone, can reasonably hope to be protected by him only; and by him, if with industry and courage they make use of the means he has given them for their own defence. God helps those who help themselves; and men are by several reasons (suppose to prevent the increase of a suspected power) induced to succour an industrious and brave people: But such as neglect the means of their own preservation, are ever left to perish with shame. Men cannot rely upon any league: The state that is defended by one potentate against another becomes a slave to their protector: Mercenary soldiers always want fidelity or courage, and most commonly both. If they are not corrupted or beaten by the invader, they make a prey of their masters. These are the followers of camps who have neither faith nor piety, but prefer gain before right.[1] They who expose their blood to sale, look where they can make the best bargain, and never fail of pretences for following their interests.

Moreover, private families may by several arts increase their wealth, as they increase in number; but when a people multiplies (as they will always do in a good climate under a good government) such an enlargement of territory as is necessary for their subsistence can be acquired only by war. This was known to the northern nations that invaded the Roman empire; but for want of such constitutions as might best improve their strength and valour, the numbers they sent out when they were over-burden'd, provided well for themselves, but were of no use to the countries they left; and whilst those Goths, Vandals, Franks, and Normans enjoyed the most opulent and delicious provinces of the world, their fathers languished obscurely in their frozen climates. For the like reasons, or through the same defect, the Switzers are obliged to serve other princes; and often to employ that valour in advancing the power of their neighbours, which might be used to increase their own. Genoa, Lucca, Geneva, and other small commonwealths, having no wars, are not able to nourish the men they breed; but sending many of their children to seek their fortunes abroad, scarce a third part of those that are born among them die in those cities; and if they did not take this course, they would have no better than the nations inhabiting near the River Niger, who sell their children as the increase of their flocks.

This does not less concern monarchies than commonwealths; nor the absolute less than the mixed: All of them have been prosperous or

---

[1] —Ibi fas ubi maxima merces. Lucan.
["Where the greatest reward is, there is the right." Lucan, *Pharsalia*, bk. 10, li. 408.]

miserable, glorious or contemptible, as they were better or worse arm'd, disciplin'd, or conducted. The Assyrian valour was irresistible under Nebuchadnezzar, but was brought to nothing under his base and luxurious grandson Belshazzar: The Persians who under Cyrus conquer'd Asia, were like swine exposed to slaughter when their discipline failed, and they were commanded by his proud, cruel, and cowardly successors. The Macedonian army overthrown by Aemilius Paulus was not less in number than that with which Alexander gained the empire of the East; and perhaps had not been inferior in valour, if it had been as well commanded. Many poor and almost unknown nations have been carried to such a height of glory by the bravery of their princes, that I might incline to think their government as fit as any other for disciplining a people to war, if their virtues continued in their families, or could be transmitted to their successors. The impossibility of this is a breach never to be repaired; and no account is to be made of the good that is always uncertain, and seldom enjoy'd. This disease is not only in absolute monarchies, but in those also where any regard is had to succession of blood, tho under the strictest limitations. The fruit of all the victories gained by Edward the first and third, or Henry the fifth of England, perished by the baseness of their successors: the glory of our arms was turned into shame; and we, by the loss of treasure, blood, and territory, suffer'd the punishment of their vices. The effects of these changes are not always equally violent; but they are frequent, and must fall out as often as occasion is presented. It was not possible for Lewis the 13th of France to pursue the great designs of Henry the Fourth: Christina of Sweden could not supply the place of her brave father; nor the present king in his infancy accomplish what the great Charles Gustavus had nobly undertaken: and no remedy can be found for this mortal infirmity, unless the power be put into the hands of those who are able to execute it, and not left to the blindness of fortune. When the regal power is committed to an annual or otherwise chosen magistracy, the virtues of excellent men are of use, but all does not depend upon their persons: One man finishes what another had begun; and when many are by practice rendered able to perform the same things, the loss of one is easily supplied by the election of another. When good principles are planted, they do not die with the person that introduced them; and good constitutions remain, tho the authors of them perish. Rome did not fall back into slavery when Brutus was killed, who had led them to recover their liberty: Others like to him pursued the same ends; and notwithstanding the loss of so many great commanders consumed in their almost continual wars, they never wanted such as were fit to execute whatever they could design. A well-governed state is as fruitful to all good purposes, as the seven-headed serpent is said to have been in evil; when one head is cut off, many rise up in the place of it. Good order being once established, makes good men; and as long as it lasts, such as are fit for the greatest employments will never be wanting. By this means the Romans could not be surprised: No king or captain ever invaded them, who did not find many excellent commanders to oppose him; whereas they themselves found it easy to overthrow kingdoms, tho they had been established by the bravest princes, through the baseness of their successors.

But if our author say true, 'tis of no advantage to a popular state to have excellent men; and therefore he imposes *a necessity upon every people to chuse the worst men for being the worst, and most like to themselves; lest that if virtuous and good men should come into power, they should be excluded for being vicious and wicked, &c. Wise men would seize upon the state, and take it from the people.*[2] For the understanding of these words, 'tis good to consider whether they are to be taken simply, as usually applied to the Devil and some of his instruments, or relatively, as to the thing in question: If simply, it must be concluded that Valerius, Brutus, Cincinnatus, Capitolinus, Mamercus, Aemilius Paulus, Nasica, and others like to them, were not only the worst men of the city; but that they were so often advanced to the supreme magistracies, because they were so: if in the other sense relating to magistracy and the command of armies, the worst are the most ignorant, unfaithful, slothful, or cowardly; and our author to make good his proposition, must prove, that when the people of Rome, Carthage, Athens, and other states had the power of chusing whom they pleased, they did chuse Camillus, Corvinus, Torquatus, Fabius, Rullus, Scipio, Hamilcar, Hannibal, Hasdrubal, Pelopidas, Epaminondas, Pericles, Aristides, Themistocles, Phocion, Alcibiades, and others like to them, for their ignorance, infidelity, sloth, and cowardice; and on account of those vices, most like to those who chose them. But if these were the worst, I desire to know what wit or eloquence can describe or comprehend the excellency of the best; or of the discipline that brings whole nations to such perfection, that worse than these could not be found among them? And if they were not so, but such as all succeeding ages have justly admir'd for their wisdom, virtue, industry, and valour, the impudence of so wicked and false an assertion ought to be rejected with scorn and hatred.

But if all governments whether monarchical or popular, absolute or limited, deserve praise or blame as they are well or ill constituted for

[2] [*Patriarcha*, ch. 18, p. 89.]

making war; and that the attainment of this end do entirely depend upon the qualifications of the commanders, and the strength, courage, number, affection, and temper of the people out of which the armies are drawn; those governments must necessarily be the best which take the best care that those armies may be well commanded; and so provide for the good of the people, that they may daily increase in number, courage, and strength, and be so satisfied with the present state of things, as to fear a change, and fight for the preservation or advancement of the publick interest as of their own. We have already found that in hereditary monarchies no care at all is taken of the commander: He is not chosen, but comes by chance; and does not only frequently prove defective, but for the most part utterly incapable of performing any part of his duty; whereas in popular governments excellent men are generally chosen; and there are so many of them, that if one or more perish, others are ready to supply their places. And this discourse having (if I mistake not) in the whole series, shewn, that the advantages of popular governments, in relation to the increase of courage, number, and strength in a people, out of which armies are to be formed, and bringing them to such a temper as prepares them bravely to perform their duty, are as much above those of monarchies, as the prudence of choice surpasses the accidents of birth, it cannot be denied that in both respects the part which relates to war is much better perform'd in popular governments than in monarchies.

That which we are by reason led to believe, is confirmed to us by experience. We everywhere see the difference between the courage of men fighting for themselves and their posterity, and those that serve a master who by good success is often render'd insupportable. This is of such efficacy, that no king could ever boast to have overthrown any considerable commonwealth, unless it were divided within itself, or weakened by wars made with such as were also free; which was the case of the Grecian commonwealths when the Macedonians fell in upon them. Whereas the greatest kingdoms have been easily destroy'd by commonwealths; and these also have lost all strength, valour, and spirit after the change of their government. The power and virtue of the Italians grew up, decayed and perished with their liberty. When they were divided into many commonwealths, every one of them was able to send out great armies, and to suffer many defeats before they were subdued; so that their cities were delivered up by the old men, women, and children, when all those who were able to bear arms had been slain: And when they were all brought under the Romans, either as associates or subjects, they made the greatest strength that ever was in the world.

Alexander of Epirus was in valour thought equal, and in power little inferior to Alexander of Macedon: but having the fortune to attack those who had been brought up in liberty, taught to hazard or suffer all things for it, and to think that God has given to men hands and swords only to defend it, he perished in his attempt; whilst the other encountering slavish nations, under the conduct of proud, cruel, and for the most part unwarlike tyrants, became master of Asia.

Pyrrhus seems to have been equal to either of them; but the victories he obtain'd by an admirable valour and conduct, cost him so dear, that he desir'd peace with those enemies who might be defeated, not subdued.

Hannibal wanting the prudence of Pyrrhus, lost the fruits of all his victories; and being torn out of Italy, where he had nested himself, fell under the sword of those whose fathers he had defeated or slain; and died a banish'd man from his ruin'd country.

The Gauls did once bring Rome, when it was small, to the brink of destruction; but they left their carcasses to pay for the mischiefs they had done; and in succeeding times their invasions were mention'd as tumults rather than wars.

The Germans did perhaps surpass them in numbers and strength, and were equal to them in fortune as long as Rome was free. They often enter'd Italy, but they continued not long there, unless under the weight of their chains. Whereas the same nations, and others like to them, assaulting that country, or other provinces under the emperors, found no other difficulty than what did arise upon contests among themselves who should be master of them. No manly virtue or discipline remain'd among the Italians: Those who govern'd them, relied upon tricks and shifts; they who could not defend themselves, hired some of those nations to undertake their quarrels against others. These trinklings could not last: The Goths scorning to depend upon those who in valour and strength were much inferior to themselves, seized upon the city that had commanded the world, whilst Honorius was so busy in providing for his hens, that he could not think of defending it. Arcadius had the luck not to lose his principal city; but passing his time among fiddlers, players, eunuchs, cooks, dancers, and buffoons, the provinces were securely plunder'd and ransack'd by nations, that are known only from their victories against him.

'Tis in vain to say that this proceeded from the fatal corruption of that age; for that corruption proceeded from the government, and the ensuing desolation was the effect of it. And as the like disorder in government has been ever since in Greece and the greatest part of Italy, those countries which for extent, riches, convenience of situation, and numbers of men, are equal to the best in the world, and for the wit, courage, and industry of the natives, perhaps justly preferable to any, have since that time been always exposed as a prey to the first invader. Charles the Eighth of France is by Guicciardini, and other writers, represented as a prince equally weak in body, mind, money, and forces; but as an ill hare is said to make a good dog, he conquer'd the best part of Italy without breaking a lance.[3] Ferdinand and Alfonso of Aragon, kings of Naples, had governed by trepanners, false witnesses, corrupt judges, mercenary soldiers, and other ministers of iniquity; but these could afford no help against an invader; and neither the oppressed nobility, nor people, concerning themselves in the quarrel, they who had been proud, fierce, and cruel against their poor subjects, never durst look an enemy in the face; and the father dying with anguish and fear, the son shamefully fled from his ill governed kingdom.

The same things are no less evident in Spain. No people ever defended themselves with more obstinacy and valour than the Spaniards did against the Carthaginians and Romans, who surpassed them in wealth and skill. Livy calls them *gentem ad bella gerenda & reparanda natam*,[4] and who generally kill'd themselves when they were master'd and disarm'd, *nullam sine armis vitam esse rati*.[5] But tho the mixture of Roman blood could not impair their race, and the conjunction of the Goths had improved their force; yet no more was requir'd for the overthrow of them all, than the weakness and baseness of the two lewd tyrants Witiza and Rodrigo, who disdained all laws, and resolved to govern according to their lust. They who for more than two hundred years had resisted the Romans, were entirely subdued by the vile, half naked Moors, in one slight skirmish; and do not to this day know what became of the king who brought the destruction upon them. That kingdom after many revolutions is with many others come to the house of Austria, and enjoys all the wealth of the Indies; whereupon they are thought to have affected an universal monarchy. *Sed ut sunt levia aulicorum ingenia*,[6] this was grounded upon nothing except their own vanity: They had money and craft; but wanting that solid virtue and strength which makes and preserves conquests, their kings have nothing but Milan that did not come to them by marriage: And tho they have not received any extraordinary disasters in war, yet they languish and consume through the defects of their own government, and are forced to beg assistance from their mortal and formerly despis'd enemies. These are the best hopes of defence that they have from abroad;

[3] [Guicciardini, *History of Italy*, bk. 1, p. 75.]

[4] ["A nation born for waging and preparing for wars." Livy, *History of Rome*, bk. 24, ch. 42.]

[5] ["They thought there was no life without arms." Ibid., bk. 34, ch. 17.]

[6] [But as the character of (princely) courts is slight.]

and the only enemy an invader ought to fear in their desolate territories is that want and famine which testifies the good order, strength and stability of our author's divine monarchy; the profound wisdom of their kings in subtly finding out so sure a way of defending the country; their paternal care in providing for the good of their subjects; and that whatsoever is defective in the prince, is assuredly supplied by the sedulity of a good council.

We have already said enough to obviate the objections that may be drawn from the prosperity of the French monarchy. The beauty of it is false and painted. There is a rich and haughty king, who is bless'd with such neighbours as are not likely to disturb him, and has nothing to fear from his miserable subjects; but the whole body of that state is full of boils, and wounds, and putrid sores: There is no real strength in it. The people is so unwilling to serve him, that he is said to have put to death above fourscore thousand of his own soldiers within the space of fifteen years, for flying from their colours; and if he were vigorously attack'd, little help could be expected from a discontented nobility, or a starving and despairing people. If to diminish the force of these arguments and examples, it be said that in two or three thousand years all things are changed; the ancient virtue of mankind is extinguished; and the love that everyone had to his country is turned into a care of his private interests: I answer, that time changes nothing, and the changes produced in this time proceed only from the change of governments. The nations which have been governed arbitrarily, have always suffer'd the same plagues, and been infected with the same vices; which is as natural, as for animals ever to generate according to their kinds, and fruits to be of the same nature with the roots and seeds from which they come. The same order that made men valiant and industrious in the service of their country during the first ages, would have the same effect, if it were now in being: Men would have the same love to the publick as the Spartans and Romans had, if there was the same reason for it. We need no other proof of this than what we have seen in our own country, where in a few years good discipline, and a just encouragement given to those who did well, produced more examples of pure, compleat, incorruptible, and invincible virtue than Rome or Greece could ever boast; or if more be wanting, they may easily be found among the Switzers, Hollanders and others: but 'tis not necessary to light a candle to the sun.

SECTION 24

Popular Governments are less subject to
Civil Disorders than Monarchies; manage them more ably,
and more easily recover out of them.

Tis in vain to seek a government in all points free from a possibility of civil wars, tumults, and seditions: that is a blessing denied to this life, and reserved to compleat the felicity of the next. But if these are to be accounted the greatest evils that can fall upon a people, the rectitude or defects of governments will best appear if we examine which *species* is more or less exposed to, or exempted from them.

This may be done two ways.

1. By searching into the causes from whence they may, or usually do arise.

2. Which kind has actually been most frequently and dangerously disturbed by them.

To the first: Seditions, tumults, and wars do arise from mistake, or from malice; from just occasions, or unjust: from mistake, when a people thinks an evil to be done or intended, which is not done nor intended, or takes that to be evil which is done, tho in truth it be not so. Well regulated cities may fall into these errors. The Romans being jealous of their newly recover'd liberty, thought that Valerius Publicola designed to make himself king, when he built a house in a place that seemed too strong and eminent for a private man. The Spartans were not less suspicious of Lycurgus; and a lewd young fellow in a sedition put out one of his eyes: but no people ever continued in a more constant affection to their best deserving citizens, than both the Romans and Spartans afterwards manifested to those virtuous and wrongfully suspected men.

Sometimes the fact is true, but otherwise understood than was intended. When the Tarquins were expelled from Rome, the patricians retained to themselves the principal magistracies; but never thought of bringing back kings, or of setting up a corrupt oligarchy among themselves, as the plebeians imagin'd: And this mistake being discover'd, the fury they had conceived, vanished; and they who seemed to intend nothing less than the extirpation of all the patrician families, grew quiet. Menenius Agrippa appeased one of the most violent seditions that ever happened amongst them (till civil interests were pursued by armed troops) with a fable of the several parts of the body that murmur'd against the belly: and the most dangerous of all was composed by creating tribunes to protect them. Some of the patrician young men had favour'd the decemviri, and others being unwilling to appear against them, the people believed they had all conspired with those new tyrants: but Valerius and Horatius putting themselves at the head of those who sought their destruction, they perceived their error, and looked upon the patricians as the best defenders of their liberties: *Et inde*, says Livy, *auram libertatis captare, unde servitutem timuissent.*[1] Democratical governments are most liable to these mistakes: In aristocracies they are seldom seen, and we hear of none in Sparta after the establishment of the laws by Lycurgus; but absolute monarchies seem to be totally exempted from them. The mischiefs design'd are often dissembled or denied, till they are past all possibility of being cured by any other way than force: and such as are by necessity driven to use that remedy, know they must perfect their work or perish. He that draws his sword against the prince, say the French, ought to throw away the scabbard; for tho the design be never so just, yet the authors are sure to be ruin'd if it miscarry. Peace is seldom made, and never kept, unless the subject retain such a power in his hands, as may oblige the prince to stand to what is agreed; and in time some trick is found to deprive them of that benefit.

Seditions proceeding from malice, are seldom or never seen in popular governments; for they are hurtful to the people, and none have ever willingly and knowingly hurt themselves. There may be, and often is malice in those who excite them; but the people is ever deceiv'd, and whatsoever is thereupon done, ought to be imputed to error, as I said before. If this be discovered in time, it usually turns to the destruction of the contriver; as in the cases of Manlius Capitolinus, Spurius Maelius, and Sp. Cassius: if not, for the most part it produces a tyranny, as in those of Agathocles, Dionysius, Pisistratus, and Caesar. But in absolute monarchies, almost all the troubles that arise, proceed from malice; they cannot be reformed, the extinction of them is exceeding difficult, if they have continued long enough to corrupt the people; and those who appear against them, seek only to set up themselves, or their friends. Thus we see that in the civil wars of the East, the question was, whether Artaxerxes or Cyrus, Phraates or Bardanes, should reign over the Persians and Parthians: The people suffer'd equally from both whilst the contests lasted; and the decision left them under the power of a proud and cruel master. The like is seen in all places. After the death of Brutus and

---

[1] ["And to catch the breath of freedom from where they had feared servitude." Livy, *History of Rome*, bk. 3, ch. 37.]

Cassius, no war was ever undertaken in the Roman empire upon a better account than one man's private concernments: The provinces suffer'd under all; and he, whom they had assisted to overthrow one wicked tyrant, very often proved worse than his predecessor. And the only ground of all the dissensions with which France was vexed under the princes of Meroveus's and Pepin's races, were, which of them should reign, the people remaining miserable under them all.

The case is not much different in mixed monarchies: Some wars may be undertaken upon a just and publick account, but the pretences are commonly false: a lasting reformation is hardly introduced, an entire change often disliked. And tho such kingdoms are frequently and terribly distracted, as appears by the beforemention'd examples of England, Spain, &c. the quarrels are for the most part begun upon personal titles, as between Henry the First and Robert; Stephen and Maude; or the houses of Lancaster and York: and the people who get nothing by the victory which way soever it fall, and might therefore prudently leave the competitors to decide their own quarrels, like Theorestes and Polynices,[2] with their own swords, become cruelly engaged in them.

It may seem strange to some that I mention seditions, tumults, and wars, upon just occasions; but I can find no reason to retract the term. God intending that men should live justly with one another, does certainly intend that he or they who do no wrong, should suffer none; and the law that forbids injuries, were of no use, if no penalty might be inflicted on those that will not obey it. If injustice therefore be evil, and injuries forbidden, they are also to be punished; and the law instituted for their prevention, must necessarily intend the avenging of such as cannot be prevented. The work of the magistracy is to execute this law; the sword of justice is put into their hands to restrain the fury of those within the society who will not be a law to themselves, and the sword of war to protect the people against the violence of foreigners. This is without exception, and would be in vain if it were not. But the magistrate who is to protect the people from injury, may, and is often known not to have done it: he sometimes renders his office useless by neglecting to do justice; sometimes mischievous by overthrowing it. This strikes at the root of God's general ordinance, that there should be laws; and the particular ordinances of all societies that appoint such as seem best to them. The magistrate therefore is comprehended under both, and subject to both, as well as private men.

[2] [Sidney seems to refer to Eteocles and Polynices, the sons of Oedipus who killed each other over the rule of Thebes.]

The ways of preventing or punishing injuries, are judicial or extra-judicial. Judicial proceedings are of force against those who submit or may be brought to trial, but are of no effect against those who resist, and are of such power that they cannot be constrained. It were absurd to cite a man to appear before a tribunal who can awe the judges, or has armies to defend him; and impious to think that he who has added treachery to his other crimes, and usurped a power above the law, should be protected by the enormity of his wickedness. Legal proceedings therefore are to be used when the delinquent submits to the law; and all are just, when he will not be kept in order by the legal.

The word sedition is generally applied to all numerous assemblies, without or against the authority of the magistrate, or of those who assume that power. Athaliah and Jezebel[3] were more ready to cry out treason than David; and examples of that sort are so frequent, that I need not allege them.

Tumult is from the disorderly manner of those assemblies, where things can seldom be done regularly; and war is that *decertatio per vim*, or trial by force, to which men come when other ways are ineffectual.

If the laws of God and men are therefore of no effect, when the magistracy is left at liberty to break them; and if the lusts of those who are too strong for the tribunals of justice, cannot be otherwise restrained than by sedition, tumults and war, those seditions, tumults, and wars, are justified by the laws of God and man.

I will not take upon me to enumerate all the cases in which this may be done, but content myself with three, which have most frequently given occasion for proceedings of this kind.

The first is, when one or more men take upon them the power and name of a magistracy, to which they are not justly called.

The second, when one or more being justly called, continue in their magistracy longer than the laws by which they are called do prescribe.

And the third, when he or they who are rightly called, do assume a power, tho within the time prescribed, that the law does not give; or turn that which the law does give, to an end different and contrary to that which is intended by it.

For the first; Filmer forbids us to examine titles: he tells us, we must submit to the power, whether acquired by usurpation or otherwise, not observing the mischievous absurdity of rewarding the most detestable villainies with the highest honours, and rendering the veneration due to the supreme magistrate as father of the people, to one who has no other

[3] [2 Kings 9, 11.]

advantage above his brethren, than what he has gained by injuriously dispossessing or murdering him that was so. Hobbes fearing the advantages that may be taken from such desperate nonsense, or not thinking it necessary to his end to carry the matter so far, has no regard at all to him who comes in without title or consent; and denying him to be either king or tyrant, gives him no other name than *hostis & latro,*[4] and allows all things to be lawful against him, that may be done to a publick enemy or pirate: which is as much as to say, any man may destroy him how he can. Whatever he may be guilty of in other respects, he does in this follow the voice of mankind, and the dictates of common sense: for no man can make himself a magistrate for himself, and no man can have the right of a magistrate, who is not a magistrate.[5] If he be justly accounted an enemy to all, who injures all; he above all must be the publick enemy of a nation, who by usurping a power over them, does the greatest and most publick injury that a people can suffer: For which reason, by an established law among the most virtuous nations, every man might kill a tyrant; and no names are recorded in history with more honour, than of those who did it.

These are by other authors called *tyranni sine titulo,*[6] and that name is given to all those who obtain the supreme power by illegal and unjust means. The laws which they overthrow can give them no protection; and every man is a soldier against him who is a publick enemy.

The same rule holds tho they are more in number, as the magi who usurped the dominion of Persia after the death of Cambyses; the thirty tyrants at Athens overthrown by Thrasybulus; those of Thebes slain by Pelopidas; the decemviri of Rome, and others: for tho the multitude of offenders may sometimes procure impunity, yet that act which is wicked in one, must be so in ten or twenty; and whatsoever is lawful against one usurper, is so against them all.

2. If those who were rightly created, continue beyond the time limited by the law, 'tis the same thing. That which is expir'd, is as if it had never been. He that was created consul for a year, or dictator for six months, was after that a private man; and if he had continued in the exercise of his magistracy, had been subject to the same punishment as if he had usurped it at the first. This was known to Epaminondas, who finding that his enterprize against Sparta could not be accomplished within the time for which he was made boeotarch, rather chose to trust his countrymen with his life than to desist, and was saved merely through

---

[4] [Enemy and pirate.]

[5] De Civ. l. 2. [Hobbes, *On the Citizen*, ch. 7, sec. 3.]

[6] [Tyrants without title.]

an admiration of his virtue, assurance of his good intentions, and the glory of the action.

The Roman decemviri, tho duly elected, were proceeded against as private men usurping the magistracy, when they continued beyond their time. Other magistrates had ceased; there was none that could regularly call the senate or people to an assembly: but when their ambition was manifest, and the people exasperated by the death of Virginia, they laid aside all ceremonies. The senate and people met, and exercising their authority in the same manner as if they had been regularly called by the magistrate appointed to that end, they abrogated the power of the decemviri, proceeded against them as enemies and tyrants, and by that means preserved themselves from utter ruin.

3. The same course is justly used against a legal magistrate, who takes upon him (tho within the time prescribed by the law) to exercise a power which the law does not give; for in that respect he is a private man, *Quia,* as Grotius says, *eatenus non habet imperium;*[7] and may be restrain'd as well as any other, because he is not set up to do what he lists, but what the law appoints for the good of the people; and as he has no other power than what the law allows, so the same law limits and directs the exercise of that which he has. This right naturally belonging to nations, is no way impair'd by the name of supreme given to their magistrates; for it signifies no more, than that they do act sovereignly in the matters committed to their charge. Thus are the parliaments of France called *cours souveraines;* for they judge of life and death, determine controversies concerning estates; and there is no appeal from their decrees: but no man ever thought, that it was therefore lawful for them to do what they pleased; or that they might not be opposed, if they should attempt to do that which they ought not. And tho the Roman dictators and consuls were supreme magistrates, they were subject to the people, and might be punished as well as others if they transgressed the law. Thuanus carries the word so far, that when Barlotta, Giustiniano, and others who were but colonels, were sent as commanders in chief of three or four thousand men upon an enterprize, he always says, *summum imperium ei delatum.*[8] Grotius explains this point, by distinguishing those who have the *summum imperium summo modo,* from those who have it *modo non summo.*[9] I know not where to find an example of this sovereign power, enjoy'd without restriction, under a better title than occupation; which relates not to our

---

[7] ["Since he does not so far have command." Grotius, *De jure,* bk. 1, ch. 4, sec. 13.]

[8] ["Highest command is conferred on him." De Thou, *History of His Time.*]

[9] ["The supreme power in the supreme manner" . . . "not in the supreme manner." Grotius, *De jure,* bk. 1, ch. 3, sec. 14.]

purpose, who seek only that which is legal and just. Therefore laying aside that point for the present, we may follow Grotius in examining the right of those who are certainly limited: *Ubi partem imperii habet rex, partem senatus sive populus;* in which case he says, *regi in partem non suam involanti, vis justa opponi potest,* in as much as they who have a part, cannot but have a right of defending that part. *Quia data facultate, datur jus facultatem tuendi,* without which it could be of no effect.[10]

The particular limits of the rights belonging to each, can only be judged by the precise letter, or general intention of the law. The dukes of Venice have certainly a part in the government, and could not be called magistrates if they had not. They are said to be supreme; all laws and publick acts bear their names. The ambassador of that state speaking to Pope Paul the 5th, denied that he acknowledged any other superior than God.[11] But they are so well known to be under the power of the law, that divers of them have been put to death for transgressing it; and a marble gallows is seen at the foot of the stairs in St. Mark's palace, upon which some of them, and no others, have been executed. But if they may be duly opposed, when they commit undue acts, no man of judgment will deny, that if one of them by an outrageous violence should endeavour to overthrow the law, he might by violence be suppressed and chastised.

Again, some magistrates are entrusted with a power of providing ships, arms, ammunition, and victuals for war; raising and disciplining soldiers, appointing officers to command in forts and garrisons, and making leagues with foreign princes and states. But if one of these should embezzle, sell, or give to an enemy those ships, arms, ammunition or provisions; betray the forts; employ only or principally, such men as will serve him in those wicked actions; and, contrary to the trust reposed in him, make such leagues with foreigners, as tend to the advancement of his personal interests, and to the detriment of the publick, he abrogates his own magistracy; and the right he had, perishes (as the lawyers say) *frustratione finis.*[12] He cannot be protected by the law which he has overthrown, nor obtain impunity for his crimes from the authority that was conferred upon him, only that he might do good with it. He was *singulis major* on account of the excellence of his office; but *universis minor,*[13] from the

---

[10] Grot. de jur. bel. et pac. l. 2. ["When the king holds part of the supreme power, and the senate or the people holds part" . . . "just force can be used against a king who encroaches upon the part which is not his own" . . . "since when power is given the right of protecting that power is given." Ibid., bk. 1, ch. 4, sec. 13.]

[11] Thuan. l. 137. [De Thou, *History of His Time*, bk. 137.]

[12] [Because the end (of his office) is frustrated.]

[13] [Greater than the individual (citizens) . . . less than the whole people.]

nature and end of his institution. The surest way of extinguishing his prerogative, was by turning it to the hurt of those who gave it. When matters are brought to this posture, the author of the mischief, or the nation must perish. A flock cannot subsist under a shepherd that seeks its ruin, nor a people under an unfaithful magistrate. Honour and riches are justly heaped upon the heads of those who rightly perform their duty, because the difficulty as well as the excellency of the work is great. It requires courage, experience, industry, fidelity and wisdom. The good shepherd, says our Saviour, lays down his life for his sheep: The hireling who flies in time of danger, is represented under an ill character; but he that sets himself to destroy his flock, is a wolf. His authority is incompatible with their subsistence; and whoever disapproves tumults, seditions or war, by which he may be removed from it, if gentler means are ineffectual, subverts the foundation of all law, exalts the fury of one man to the destruction of a nation; and giving an irresistible power to the most abominable iniquity, exposes all that are good to be destroy'd, and virtue to be utterly extinguished.

Few will allow such a preeminence to the dukes of Venice or Genoa the avoyers of Switzerland, or the burgomasters of Amsterdam. Many will say these are rascals if they prove false, and ought rather to be hang'd, than suffer'd to accomplish the villainies they design. But if this be confess'd in relation to the highest magistrates that are among those nations, why should not the same be in all others, by what name soever they are called? When did God confer upon those nations the extraordinary privilege of providing better for their own safety than others? Or was the gift universal, tho the benefit accrue only to those who have banished great titles from among them? If this be so, 'tis not their felicity, but their wisdom that we ought to admire and imitate. But why should any think their ancestors had not the same care? Have not they, who retain'd in themselves a power over a magistrate of one name, the like over another? Is there a charm in words, or any name of such efficacy, that he who receives it should immediately become master of those that created him, whereas all others do remain forever subject to them? Would the Venetian government change its nature, if they should give the name of king to their prince? Are the Polanders less free since the title of king is conferr'd upon their dukes; or are the Muscovites less slaves, because their chief magistrate has no other than that of duke? If we examine things but a little, 'twill appear that magistrates have enjoy'd large powers, who never had the name of kings; and none were ever more restrained by laws than those of Sparta, Aragon, the Goths in Spain, Hungary, Bohemia, Sweden, Denmark, Poland, and others, who had that title.

There is therefore no such thing as a right universally belonging to a name; but everyone enjoys that which the laws, by which he is, confer upon him. The law that gives the power, regulates it; and they who give no more than what they please, cannot be obliged to suffer him to whom they give it, to take more than they thought fit to give, or to go unpunished if he do. The agreements made are always confirmed by oath, and the treachery of violating them is consequently aggravated by perjury. They are good philosophers and able divines, who think this can create a right to those who had none; or that the laws can be a protection to such as overthrow them, and give opportunity of doing the mischiefs they design. If it do not, then he that was a magistrate, by such actions returns into the condition of a private man; and whatever is lawful against a thief who submits to no law, is lawful against him.

Men who delight in cavils may ask, who shall be the judge of these occasions? and whether I intend to give to the people the decision of their own cause? To which I answer, that when the contest is between the magistrate and the people, the party to which the determination is referred, must be the judge of his own case; and the question is only, whether the magistrate should depend upon the judgment of the people, or the people on that of the magistrate; and which is most to be suspected of injustice: That is, whether the people of Rome should judge Tarquin, or Tarquin judge the people. He that knew all good men abhorred him for the murder of his wife, brother, father-in-law, and the best of the senate, would certainly strike off the heads of the most eminent remaining poppies; and having incurr'd the general hatred of the people by the wickedness of his government, he feared revenge; and endeavouring to destroy those he feared (that is the city) he might easily have accomplish'd his work, if the judgment had been referred to him. If the people judge Tarquin, 'tis hard to imagine how they should be brought to give an unjust sentence: They loved their former kings, and hated him only for his villainies: They did not fancy, but know his cruelty. When the best were slain, no man that any way resembled them could think himself secure. Brutus did not pretend to be a fool, till by the murder of his brother he found how dangerous a thing it was to be thought wise. If the people, as our author says, be always lewd, foolish, mad, wicked, and desirous to put the power into the hands of such as are most like to themselves, he and his sons were such men as they sought, and he was sure to find favourable judges: If virtuous and good, no injustice was to be feared from them, and he could have no other reason to decline their judgment, than what was suggested by his own wickedness. Caligula, Nero, Domitian, and the like, had probably the same considerations: But no man of common sense ever thought that the senate and people of Rome did not better deserve to judge, whether such monsters should reign over the best part of mankind to their destruction, than they to determine whether their crimes should be punished or not.

If I mention some of these known cases, every man's experience will suggest others of the like nature; and whosoever condemns all seditions, tumults and wars raised against such princes, must say, that none are wicked, or seek the ruin of their people, which is absurd; for Caligula wish'd the people had but one neck, that he might cut it off at a blow: Nero set the city on fire, and we have known such as have been worse than either of them: They must either be suffer'd to continue in the free exercise of their rage, that is, to do all the mischief they design; or must be restrain'd by a legal, judicial, or extrajudicial way; and they who disallow the extrajudicial, do as little like the judicial. They will not hear of bringing a supreme magistrate before a tribunal, when it may be done. *They will*, says our author, *depose their kings.*[14] Why should they not be deposed, if they become enemies to their people, and set up an interest in their own persons inconsistent with the publick good, for the promoting of which they were erected? If they were created by the publick consent, for the publick good, shall they not be removed when they prove to be of publick damage? If they set up themselves, may they not be thrown down? Shall it be lawful for them to usurp a power over the liberty of others, and shall it not be lawful for an injur'd people to resume their own? If injustice exalt itself, must it be forever established? Shall great persons be rendered sacred by rapine, perjury and murder? Shall the crimes for which private men do justly suffer the most grievous punishments, exempt them from all, who commit them in the highest excess, with most power, and most to the prejudice of mankind? Shall the laws that solely aim at the prevention of crimes be made to patronize them, and become snares to the innocent whom they ought to protect? Has every man given up into the common store his right of avenging the injuries he may receive, that the publick power which ought to protect or avenge him, should be turned to the destruction of himself, his posterity, and the society into which they enter, without any possibility of redress? Shall the ordinance of God be rendered of no effect; or the powers he hath appointed to be set up for the distribution of justice, be made subservient to the lusts of one or a few men, and by impunity encourage them to commit all manner of crimes? Is the corruption of

[14] [*Patriarcha*, ch. 20, p. 94.]

man's nature so little known, that such as have common sense should expect justice from those, who fear no punishment if they do injustice; or that the modesty, integrity, and innocence, which is seldom found in one man, tho never so cautiously chosen, should be constantly found in all those who by any means attain to greatness, and continue forever in their successors; or that there can be any security under their government, if they have them not? Surely if this were the condition of men living under government, forests would be more safe than cities; and 'twere better for every man to stand in his own defence, than to enter into societies. He that lives alone might encounter such as should assault him upon equal terms, and stand or fall according to the measure of his courage and strength; but no valour can defend him, if the malice of his enemy be upheld by a publick power. There must therefore be a right of proceeding judicially or extrajudicially against all persons who transgress the laws; or else those laws, and the societies that should subsist by them, cannot stand; and the ends for which governments are constituted, together with the governments themselves, must be overthrown. Extrajudicial proceedings by sedition, tumult, or war, must take place, when the persons concern'd are of such power, that they cannot be brought under the judicial. They who deny this, deny all help against an usurping tyrant, or the perfidiousness of a lawfully created magistrate, who adds the crimes of ingratitude and treachery to usurpation. These of all men are the most dangerous enemies to supreme magistrates: for as no man desires indemnity for such crimes as are never committed, he that would exempt all from punishment, supposes they will be guilty of the worst; and by concluding that the people will depose them if they have the power, acknowledge that they pursue an interest annexed to their persons, contrary to that of their people, which they would not bear if they could deliver themselves from it. This shewing all those governments to be tyrannical, lays such a burden upon those who administer them, as must necessarily weigh them down to destruction.

If it be said that the word sedition implies that which is evil; I answer, that it ought not then to be applied to those who seek nothing but that which is just; and tho the ways of delivering an oppressed people from the violence of a wicked magistrate, who having armed a crew of lewd villains, and fatted them with the blood and confiscations of such as were most ready to oppose him, be extraordinary, the inward righteousness of the act doth fully justify the authors. He that has virtue and power to save a people, can never want a right of doing it. Valerius Asiaticus had no hand in the death of Caligula; but when the furious guards began tumultuously to enquire who had kill'd him, he appeased them with wishing he had been the man.[15] No wise man ever asked by what authority Thrasybulus, Harmodius, Aristogiton, Pelopidas, Epaminondas, Dion, Timoleon, Lucius Brutus, Publicola, Horatius, Valerius, Marcus Brutus, C. Cassius, and the like, delivered their countries from tyrants. Their actions carried in themselves their own justification, and their virtues will never be forgotten whilst the names of Greece and Rome are remembered in the world.

If this be not enough to declare the justice inherent in, and the glory that ought to accompany these works, the examples of Moses, Aaron, Othniel, Ehud, Barak, Gideon, Samuel, Jephthah, David, Jehu, Jehoiada, the Maccabees, and other holy men raised up by God for the deliverance of his people from their oppressors, decide the question. They are perpetually renowned for having led the people by extraordinary ways (which such as our author express under the names of sedition, tumult, and war) to recover their liberties, and avenge the injuries received from foreign or domestick tyrants. The work of the apostles was not in their time to set up or pull down any civil state; but they so behaved themselves in relation to all the powers of the earth, that they gained the name of pestilent, seditious fellows, disturbers of the people; and left it as an inheritance to those, who in succeeding ages by following their steps should deserve to be called their successors; whereby they were exposed to the hatred of corrupt magistrates, and brought under the necessity of perishing by them, or defending themselves against them: and he that denies them that right, does at once condemn the most glorious actions of the wisest, best, and holiest men that have been in the world, together with the laws of God and man, upon which they were founded.

Nevertheless, there is a sort of sedition, tumult, and war proceeding from malice, which is always detestable, aiming only at the satisfaction of private lust, without regard to the publick good. This cannot happen in a popular government, unless it be amongst the rabble; or when the body of the people is so corrupted, that it cannot stand; but is most frequent in, and natural to absolute monarchies. When Abimelech desir'd to make himself king, he raised a tumult among the basest of the people: He hired light and vain persons, some translations call them lewd vagabonds, kill'd his brethren, but perished in his design; the corrupt party that favour'd him not having strength enough to subdue the other,

[15] Utinam fecissem. Tacit. ["Would that I had done it." This reply is actually in Josephus, *Jewish Antiquities*, bk. 19, ch. 1, sec. 20.]

who were more sincere.[16] Sp. Maelius, Sp. Cassius, and Manlius attempted the like in Rome: they acted maliciously, their pretences to procure the publick good were false. 'Tis probable that some in the city were as bad as they, and knew that mischief was intended; but the body of the people not being corrupted, they were suppressed. It appear'd, says Livy, *nihil esse minus populare quam regnum:* they who had favour'd Manlius, condemned him to death when it was proved, that *egregias alioqui virtutes foeda regni cupidine maculasset.*[17] But when the people is generally corrupted, such designs seldom miscarry, and the success is always the erection of a tyranny. Nothing else can please vain and profligate persons, and no tyranny was ever set up by such as were better qualified. The ways of attaining it have always been by corrupting the manners of the people, bribing soldiers, entertaining mercenary strangers, opening prisons, giving liberty to slaves, alluring indigent persons with hopes of abolishing debts, coming to a new division of lands, and the like. Seditions raised by such men always tend to the ruin of popular governments; but when they happen under absolute monarchies, the hurt intended is only to the person, who being removed the promoters of them set up another; and he that is set up, subsisting only by the strength of those who made him, is obliged to foment the vices that drew them to serve him; tho another may perhaps make use of the same against him.

The consequence of this is, that those who uphold popular governments, look upon vice and indigence as mischiefs that naturally increase each other, and equally tend to the ruin of the state. When men are by vice brought into want, they are ready for mischief: there is no villainy that men of profligate lives, lost reputation, and desperate fortunes will not undertake. Popular equality is an enemy to these; and they who would preserve it must preserve integrity of manners, sobriety, and an honest contentedness with what the law allows. On the other side, the absolute monarch who will have no other law than his own will, desires to increase the number of those who through lewdness and beggary may incline to depend upon him; tho the same temper of mind, and condition of fortune prepare them also for such seditions as may bring him into danger; and the same corruption which led them to set him up, may invite them to sell him to another that will give them better wages.

I do not by this conclude that all monarchs are vicious men; but that whoever will set up an absolute power, must do it by these means; and

---

[16] Judg. 9.

[17] ["Nothing was less popular than a kingdom" . . . "he had stained otherwise outstanding virtues with the vile desire for a kingdom." Livy, *History of Rome*, bk. 6, ch. 19–20.]

that if such a power be already established, and should fall into the hands of a person, who by his virtue and the gentleness of his nature should endeavour to render the yoke so easy, that a better disciplin'd people might be contented to bear it; yet this method could last no longer than his life, and probably would be a means to shorten it; that which was at first established by evil arts always returning to the same: That which was vicious in the principle, can never be long upheld by virtue; and we see that the worst of the Roman emperors were not in greater danger from such good men as remained undestroy'd, than the best from the corrupt party that would not be corrected, and sought such a master as would lay no restriction upon their vices. Those few who escaped the rage of these villains, only gave a little breathing time to the afflicted world, which by their children or successors was again plunged into that extremity of misery, from which they intended to deliver it. An extraordinary virtue was required to keep a prince in a way contrary to the principles of his own government; which being rarely found, and never continuing long in a family or succession of men, the endeavours of the best became ineffectual, and either they themselves perished in them, or after their death all things returned into the old polluted channel.

Tho the power of the Hebrew kings was not unlimited, yet it exceeded the rules set by God, and was sufficient to increase the number of the worst of men, and to give them opportunities of raising perpetual disturbances. On the king's side there were flatterers and instruments of mischief: On the other side there were indebted and discontented persons. Notwithstanding the justice of David's cause, the wisdom, valour, and piety of his person, none would follow him, except a few of his own kindred (who knew what God had promised to him) and such as were uneasy in their worldly circumstances. After the death of Saul there was a long and bloody war between Ishbosheth and David. The former being killed, the slightest matters were sufficient to put the whole nation into blood. Absalom with a few fair words was able to raise all Israel against his father: Sheba the son of Bichri with as much ease raised a more dangerous tumult: David by wisdom, valour, and the blessing of God surmounted these difficulties, and prepared a peaceable reign for Solomon; but after his death they broke out into a flame that was never quenched till the nation was so dispersed that no man knew where to find his enemies. Solomon by his magnificence had reduced Israel to such poverty, as inclined them to revolt upon the first offer of an opportunity by Jeroboam. From that time forward Israel was perpetually vexed with civil seditions and conspiracies, or wars with their brethren of Judah. Nine kings with their families were destroyed by the first, and the latter brought such slaughters upon the miserable people as were never suffer'd by any who were not agitated by the like fury; and the course of these mischiefs was never interrupted, till they had brought the nation into captivity, and the country to desolation. Tho God according to his promise did preserve a light in the house of David, yet the tribe of Judah was not the more happy. Joash was slain by a private conspiracy, and Amaziah (as is most probable) by publick authority, for having foolishly brought a terrible slaughter upon Judah. Athaliah destroyed the king's race, and was killed herself by Jehoiada, who not having learnt from our author to regard the power only, and not the ways by which it was obtained, caused her to be dragg'd out of the Temple, and put to a well-deserved death. The whole story is a tragedy: and if it be pretended that this proceeded rather from the wrath of God against his people for their idolatry, than from such causes as are applicable to other nations; I answer, that this idolatry was the production of the government they had set up, and most suitable to it; and chusing rather to subject themselves to the will of a man, than to the law of God, they deservedly suffer'd the evils that naturally follow the worst counsels. We know of none who, taking the like course, have not suffer'd the like miseries. Notwithstanding the admirable virtue and success of Alexander, his reign was full of conspiracies, and his knowledge of them prompted him to destroy Parmenio, Philotas, Clitus, Callisthenes, Hermolaus, and many more of his best friends. If he escaped the sword, he fell by poison. The murder of his wives, mother, and children, by the rage of his own soldiers; the fury of his captains employed in mutual slaughters, till they were consumed; his paternal kingdom after many revolutions transferred to Cassander his most mortal enemy; the utter extinction of his conquering army, and particularly the famous Argyraspides, who being grown faithless and seditious, after the death of Eumenes were sent to perish in unknown parts of the East, abundantly testify the admirable stability, good order, peace, and quiet that is enjoy'd under absolute monarchy.[18] The next government of the like nature that appeared upon the stage of the world was that of Rome, introduced by wars that consumed two thirds of the people; confirmed by proscriptions, in which all that were eminent for nobility, riches, or virtue, perished. The peace they had under Augustus was like that which the Devil allow'd to the child in the Gospel, whom he rent sorely, and left as dead.[19] The miserable city was only cast into a swoon: after long and violent vexations by seditions, tumults, and wars, it lay as dead; and finding no helper like to him who

---

[18] [Plutarch, *Life of Alexander*, ch. 48–55.]   [19] Mar. 19.21.

cured the child, it was delivered to new devils to be tormented, till it was utterly destroy'd. Tiberius was appointed as a fit instrument for such a purpose. It was thought that those who should feel the effects of his pride, cruelty, and lust, would look upon the death of Augustus as a loss. He performed the work for which he was chosen; his reign was an uninterrupted series of murders, subornations, perjuries, and poisonings, intermixed with the most detestable impurities, the revolts of provinces, and mutinies of armies. The matter was not mended by his successors: Caligula was kill'd by his own guards: Claudius poison'd by his wife: Spain, Gaul, Germany, Pannonia, Moesia, Syria, and Egypt, revolted at once from Nero; the people and senate followed the example of the provinces. This I think was, in our author's sense, sedition with a witness. Nero being dead by the hand of a slave, or his own to prevent that of the hangman, Galba enter'd the city with blood and slaughter; but when his own soldiers found he would not give the money for which they intended to sell the empire, they killed him: and to shew the stability of absolute monarchy, it may be observed, that this was not done by the advice of the senate, or by a conspiracy of great men; *Suscepêre duo manipulares populi Romani imperium transferendum, & transtulerunt.*[20] Two rascals gave the empire to Otho, and the whole senate was like to be butcher'd for not being so ready to follow their venerable authority as they ought to have been, and hardly escaped the fury of their mad and drunken companions. As a farther testimony that these monarchies are not subject to seditions and tumults, he had at once only two competitors against whom he was to defend the well-acquired empire: His army was defeated at Brescia, he kill'd himself; and his successor Vitellius was soon after thrown into the common shore. The same method still continued: Rome was fill'd with blood and ashes; and to recite all the publick mischiefs would be to transcribe the history: For as Pyrrhus being asked who should succeed him, answered, he who has the sharpest sword;[21] that was the only law that governed in the following ages. Whoever could corrupt two or three legions, thought he had a good title to the empire; and unless he happen'd to be kill'd by treachery, or another tumult of his own soldiers, he seldom receded from it without a battle, wherein he that was most successful, had no other security than what the present temper of the soldiers afforded him; and the miserable provinces having neither virtue nor force, were obliged slavishly to follow the fury or

---

[20] C. Tacit. Hist. l. 1. ["Two soldiers undertook to transfer the empire of the Roman people, and they transferred it." Tacitus, *Histories*, bk. 1, ch. 25.]

[21] [Plutarch, *Life of Pyrrhus*, ch. 9.]

fortune of those villains. In this state did Rome dedicate to Constantine the triumphal arch that had been prepared for Maxentius; and those provinces which had set up Albinus and Niger submitted to Septimius Severus. In the vast variety of accidents that in those ages disturbed the world, no emperor had a better title than what he purchased by money or violence; and enjoyed it no longer than those helps continued, which of all things were the most uncertain. By this means most of the princes perished by the sword, Italy was made desolate, and Rome was several times sacked and burnt. The mistress of the world being made a slave, the provinces which had been acquir'd by the blood of her ancient virtuous citizens, became part of an usurper's patrimony, who without any regard to the publick good, distributed them to his children according to their number, or his passion. These either destroy'd one another, or fell under the sword of a third who had the fortune of their father, the greatest part most commonly falling to the share of the worst. If at any time the contrary happened, the government of the best was but a lucid interval. Well-wishing men grew more extremely to abhor the darkness that follow'd when they were gone. The best of them could do no more than suspend mischief for a while, but could not correct the corrupt principle of their government; and some of them were destroyed as soon as they were thought to intend it: And others who finished their days in peace, left the empire to such persons of their relations as were most unlike to them. Domitian came in as brother to Titus. Commodus and Heliogabalus were recommended by the memory of those virtues that had been found in Antoninus and Aurelius. Honorius and Arcadius, who by their baseness brought utter ruin upon the Western and Eastern empires, were the sons of the brave Theodosius. They who could keep their hands free from blood, and their hearts from malice, covetousness, and pride, could not transmit their virtues to their successors, nor correct the perverseness that lay at the root and foundation of their government. The whole mass of blood was vitiated: the body was but one vast sore, which no hand but that of the Almighty could heal; and he who from an abhorrence of iniquity had declared he would not hear the cries of his own people, when they had chosen the thing that was not good, would not shew mercy to strangers who had done the same thing.

I have insisted upon the Hebrew, Macedonian and Roman histories, because they are the most eminent and best known to us: We are in the dark concerning the Babylonian, Assyrian, Chaldean, Bactrian, and Egyptian monarchies: We know little more of them than the Scripture occasionally relates concerning their barbarous cruelty, bestial pride, and extravagant folly. Others have been like to them, and I know not where to find a peaceable monarchy unless it be in Peru, where the Inca Garcilaso de la Vega says, that a man and a woman, children of the sun and the moon, appearing amongst a barbarous people living without any religion or law, established a government amongst them, which continued in much peace and justice for twelve generations:[22] But this seeming to be as fabulous as their birth, we may pass it over, and fix upon those that are better known; of which there is not one that has not suffer'd more dangerous and mischievous seditions, than all the popular governments that have been in the world: And the condition of those kingdoms which are not absolute, and yet give a preference to birth, without consideration of merit or virtue, is not much better.

This is proved by the reasons of those seditions and tumults, as well as from the fact itself.

The reasons do arise from the violence of the passions that incite men to them, and the intricacy of the questions concerning succession.

Every man has passions; few know how to moderate, and no one can wholly extinguish them. As they are various in their nature, so they are governed by various objects; and men usually follow that which is predominant in them, whether it proceed from anger or desire, and whether it terminate in ambition, covetousness, lust, or any other more or less blamable appetite. Every manner of life furnishes something, that in some measure may foment these; but a crown comprehends all that can be grateful to the most violent and vicious. He who is covetous, has vast revenues, besides what he may get by fraud and rapine, to satisfy his appetite. If he be given to sensuality, the variety of pleasures, and the facility of accomplishing whatever he desires, tends farther to inflame that passion. Such as are ambitious, are incited by the greatness of their power to attempt great matters; and the most sottish or lazy may discharge themselves of cares, and hope that others will be easily hired to take the burden of business upon them whilst they lie at ease. They who naturally incline to pride and cruelty, are more violently tempted to usurp dominion; and the wicked advices of flatterers, always concurring with their passions, incite them to exercise the power they have gotten with the utmost rigor, to satiate their own rage, and to secure themselves against the effects of the publick hatred, which they know they have deserved. If there be, as our author says, no other rule than force and success, and that he must be taken for the father of a people who is in possession of a power over them; whoever has the one, may put the other to a trial. Nay, even those

[22] [Garcilaso de la Vega, El Inca, *Royal Commentaries of the Incas*, 2 vols. (written c. 1600; Austin: University of Texas Press, 1966), vol. 1, part 1, bk. 1.]

who have regard to justice, will seldom want reasons to persuade them that it is on their side. Something may be amiss in the state; injuries may be done to themselves and their friends. Such honours may be denied as they think they deserve; or others of less merit, as they suppose, may be preferred before them. Men do so rarely make a right estimate of their own merits, that those who mean well may be often deceived: and if nothing but success be requir'd to make a monarch, they may think it just to attempt whatever they can hope to accomplish. This was the case of Julius Caesar; he thought all things lawful, when the consulate, which he supposed he had deserved, was denied.

> *Viribus utendum est quas fecimus: arma tenenti*
> *Omnia dat qui justa negat.*
> Lucan.[23]

These enterprizes seem to belong to men of great spirits; but there are none so base not to be capable of undertaking, and (as things may stand) of bringing them to perfection. History represents no man under a more contemptible character of sottish laziness, cowardice, and drunkenness, than Vitellius; no one more impure and sordid than Galba: Otho was advanced for being in his manners like to Nero: Vespasian was scorned for his avarice; till the power fell into such hands as made the world believe none could be unworthy of the empire; and in the following ages the worst men by the worst means most frequently obtained it.

These wounds are not cured by saying, that the law of God and nature prevents this mischief, by annexing the succession of crowns to proximity of blood; for mankind had not been continually afflicted with them if there had been such a law, or that they could have been prevented by it: and tho there were such a law, yet more questions would arise about that proximity, than any wise man would dare to determine. The law can be of no effect, unless there be a power to decide the contests arising upon it: But the fundamental maxim of the great monarchies is, that there can be no *interregnum:* The heir of the crown is in possession, as soon as he who did enjoy it is dead. *Le mort,* as the French say, *saisit le vif:*[24] There can be therefore no such law, or it serves for nothing. If there be judges to interpret the law, no man is a king till judgment be given in his favour; and he is not king by his own title, but by the sentence given by them. If there be none, the law is merely imaginary, and every man may in his

[23] ["The strength which we have achieved must be used: he who refuses to give justice to the one who holds arms grants him everything." Lucan, *Pharsalia*, bk. 1, li. 348.]

[24] ["The dead man seizes the living." A legal expression meaning that the inheritor has possession of all the goods and rights due to him immediately upon the death of the original possessor.]

own case make it what he pleases. He who has a crown in his view, and arms in his hand, wants nothing but success to make him a king; and if he prosper, all men are obliged to obey him.

'Tis a folly to say the matter is clear, and needs no decision; for every man knows that no law concerning private inheritances can be so exactly drawn, but many controversies will arise upon it, that must be decided by a power to which both parties are subject: and the disputes concerning kingdoms are so much the more difficult, because this law is nowhere to be found; and the more dangerous, because the competitors are for the most part more powerful.

Again, this law must either be general to all mankind, or particular to each nation. If particular, a matter of such importance requires good proof, when, where, how, and by whom it was given to everyone. But the Scriptures testifying to the contrary, that God gave laws to the Jews only, and that no such thing as hereditary monarchy, according to proximity of blood, was prescribed by them, we may safely say, that God did never give any such law to every particular, nor to any nation. If he did not give it to any one, he did not give it to all, for every one is comprehended in all; and if no one has it, 'tis impossible that all can have it; or that it should be obligatory to all, when no man knows or can tell, when, where, and by what hand it was given, nor what is the sense of it: all which is evident by the various laws and customs of nations in the disposal of hereditary successions: And no one of them, that we know, has to this day been able to shew that the method follow'd by them, is more according to nature than that of others.

If our author pretend to be God's interpreter, and to give the solution of these doubts, I may ask which of the five following ways are appointed by God, and then we may examine cases resulting from them.

1. In France, Turkey, and other places, the succession comes to the next male, in the straight eldest line, according to which the son is preferr'd before the brother of him who last enjoy'd the crown (as the present king of France before his uncle the duke of Orleans), and the son of the eldest before the brothers of the eldest; as in the case of Richard the second of England, who was advanced preferably to all the brothers of the Black Prince his father.

2. Others keep to the males of the reigning family, yet have more regard to the eldest man than to the eldest line: and representation taking no place among them, the eldest man is thought to be nearest to the first king; and a second son of the person that last reigned, to be nearer to him than his grandchild by the eldest son: according to which rule, any

one of the sons of Edward the third remaining after his death, should have been preferr'd before Richard the second who was his grandchild.

3. In the two cases beforementioned, no manner of regard is had to females, who being thought naturally incapable of commanding men, or performing the functions of a magistrate, are, together with their descendants, utterly excluded from the supreme as well as from the inferior magistracies; and in Turkey, France, and other great kingdoms, have no pretence to any title: But in some places, and particularly in England, the advantages of proximity belong to them as well as to males; by which means our crown has been transported to several families and nations.

4. As in some places they are utterly rejected, and in others received simply without any condition; so those are not wanting, where that of not marrying out of the country, or without the consent of the estates, is imposed, of which Sweden is an example.

5. In some places proximity of blood is only regarded, whether the issue be legitimate or illegitimate; in others bastards are wholly excluded.

By this variety of judgments made by several nations upon this point, it may appear, that tho it were agreed by all that the next in blood ought to succeed, yet such contests would arise upon the interpretation and application of the general rule, as must necessarily be a perpetual spring of irreconcilable and mortal quarrels.

If any man say, the rule observed in England is that which God gave to mankind; I leave him first to dispute that point with the kings of France, and many others, who can have no right to the crowns they wear, if it be admitted; and in the next place to prove that our ancestors had a more immediate communication with God, and a more certain knowledge of his will than others, who for anything we know, may be of authority equal to them: but in the meantime we may rationally conclude, that if there be such a rule, we have had no king in England for the space of almost a thousand years, having not had one who did not come to the crown by a most manifest violation of it; as appears by the forecited examples of William the first and second; Henry the first, Henry the second and his children; John, Edward the third, Henry the fourth, Edward the fourth and his children; Henry the seventh, and all that claim under any of them. And if possession or success can give a right, it will I think follow, that Jack Straw, Wat Tyler, Perkin Warbeck,[25] or any

---

[25] [Wat Tyler and Jack Straw led a minor revolt of the peasants of Kent and Essex against Richard II in 1381. Tyler was killed. Perkin Warbeck, son of a Flemish merchant, claimed to be a son of Edward IV. Taking advantage of Henry VII's weak claim, he made several attempts as "Richard IV" to seize the throne. He was eventually captured and executed.]

other rascal, might have had it if he had been as happy as bold in his enterprize. This is no less than to expose crowns to the first that can seize them, to destroy all law and rule, and to render right a slave to fortune. If this be so, a late earl of Pembroke, whose understanding was not thought great, judged rightly when he said his grandfather was a wise man tho he could neither write nor read, in as much as he resolved to follow the crown, tho it were upon a coalstaff. But if this be sufficient to make a wise man, 'tis pity the secret was no sooner discovered, since many, who for want of it liv'd and died in all the infamy that justly accompanies knavery, cowardice and folly, might have gained the reputation of the most excellent men in their several ages. The bloody factions with which all nations subject to this sort of monarchy have been perpetually vexed, might have been prevented by throwing up cross or pile, or by battle between the competitors body to body, as was done by Corbis and Orsua, Cleorestes and Polynices, Ironside and Canute; it being most unreasonable, or rather impiously absurd for any to venture their lives and fortunes, when their consciences are not concern'd in the contest, and that they are to gain nothing by the victory.

If reason teaches, that till this expeditious way of ending controversies be received, the ambition of men will be apt to embroil nations in their quarrels, and others judging variously of those matters, which can be reduced to no certain rule, will think themselves in conscience obliged to follow the party that seems to them to be most just; experience manifests the same, and that ambition has produced more violent mischiefs than all the other desires and passions that have ever possessed the hearts of men. That this may appear, it will not be amiss to divide them into such as proceed from him who is in possession of the power, through jealousy of state, as they call it, to prevent the enterprizes of those who would dispossess him, and such as arise between competitors contending for it.

Tarquin's counsel concerning the poppies, and Periander's heads of corn, is of the first sort.[26] The most eminent are always most feared as the readiest to undertake, and most able to accomplish great designs. This eminence proceeds from birth, riches, virtue, or reputation, and is sometimes wrought up to the greatest height by a conjunction of all these. But I know not where to find an example of such a man, who could long subsist under absolute monarchy. If he be of high birth, he must, like Brutus, conceal his virtue, and gain no reputation, or resolve to perish,

---

[26] [Tarquin's son asked for advice through a messenger. Without speaking Tarquin went to his garden and knocked off the heads of the tallest poppies with his stick. Livy, *History of Rome*, bk. 1, ch. 54; Periander's advice was similar: Herodotus, *Histories*, bk. 5, ch. 92.]

if he do not prevent his own death by that of the tyrant: All other ways are ineffectual; the suspicions, fears, and hatred thereupon arising, are not to be removed: Personal respects are forgotten, and such services as cannot be sufficiently valued, must be blotted out by the death of those who did them. Various ways may be taken, and pretences used according to the temper of times and nations; but the thing must be done; and whether it be colour'd by a trick of law, or performed by a mute with a bowstring, imports little. Henry the fourth was made king by the Earl of Northumberland, and his brave son Hotspur; Edward the fourth by the valiant Earl of Warwick; Henry the seventh by Stanley: but neither of them could think himself safe, till his benefactor was dead. No continued fidelity, no testimonies of modesty and humility can prevent this. The modesty of Germanicus in rejecting the honours that were offer'd to him, and his industry in quieting the mutinied legions, accelerated his ruin: When 'twas evident he might be emperor if he pleased, he must be so, or die: There was no middle station between the throne and the grave. 'Tis probable that Caligula, Nero, and other beasts like to them, might hate virtue for the good which is in it; but I cannot think that either they, their predecessors or successors, would have put themselves upon the desperate design of extirpating it, if they had not found it to be inconsistent with their government; and that being once concluded, they spared none of their nearest relations. Artaxerxes killed his son Darius: Herod murder'd the best of his wives, and all his sons except the worst. Tiberius destroy'd Agrippa Posthumus, and Germanicus with his wife and two sons. How highly soever Constantine the Great be commended, he was polluted with the blood of his father-in-law, wife, and son. Philip the second of Spain did in the like manner deliver himself from his fears of Don Carlos; and 'tis not doubted that Philip the fourth, for the same reasons, dispatched his brother Don Carlos, and his son Balthasar. The like cases were so common in England, that all the Plantagenets, and the noble families allied to them being extinguish'd, our ancestors were sent to seek a king in one of the meanest in Wales.[27]

This method being known, those who are unwilling to die so tamely, endeavour to find out ways of defending themselves; and there being no other than the death of the person who is in the throne, they usually seek to compass it by secret conspiracy, or open violence; and the number of princes that have been destroy'd, and countries disturb'd by those who through fear have been driven to extremities, is not much less than of

[27] [The Plantagenets ruled England from Henry II in 1154 to Richard III in 1485, when the throne was given to Henry VII, son of the Welshman Owen Tudor. Henry did have some Plantagenet blood on his mother's side.]

those who have suffer'd the like from men following the impulse of their own ambition.

The disorders arising from contests between several competitors, before any one could be settled in the possession of kingdoms, have been no less frequent and bloody than those above-mention'd, and the miseries suffer'd by them, together with the ruin brought upon the empires of Macedon and Rome, may be sufficient to prove it; however to make the matter more clear, I shall allege others. But because it may be presumption in me to think I know all the histories of the world, or tedious to relate all those I know, I shall content myself with some of the most eminent and remarkable: And if it appear that they have all suffer'd the same mischiefs, we may believe they proceed not from accidents, but from the power of a permanent cause that always produces the same or the like effects.

To begin with France. The succession not being well settled in the time of Meroveus, who dispossess'd the grandchildren of Pharamond, he was no sooner dead than Gillon set up himself, and with much slaughter drove Chilperic his son out of the kingdom; and he after a little time returning with like fury, is said to have seen a vision, first of lions and leopards, then of bears and wolves, and lastly of dogs and cats, all tearing one another to pieces. This has been always accounted by the French to be a representation of the nature and fortune of the three races that were to command them, and has been too much verified by experience.[28] Clovis their first Christian and most renowned king, having by good means or evil exceedingly enlarged his territories, but chiefly by the murders of Alaric and Ragnacaire, with his children, and suborning Sigismond of Metz to kill his father Sigebert, left his kingdom to be torn in pieces by the rage of his four sons, each of them endeavouring to make himself master of the whole; and when, according to the usual fate of such contests, success had crown'd Clothaire, who was the worst of them all, by the slaughter of his brothers and nephews, with all the flower of the French and Gaulish nobility, the advantages of his fortune only resulted to his own person.[29] For after his death the miserable nations suffer'd as much from the madness of his sons, as they had done by himself and his brothers. They had learnt from their predecessors not to be slow in doing mischief, but were farther incited by the rage of two infamous strumpets, Fredegonde and Brunehaud, which is a sort of vermin that, I am inclin'd

[28] Hist. de France en la Vie de Chilperic 1. [Fredegarius, *Historiae Francorum* (Basil, 1558).]

[29] Mezeray and de Serres. [François Eudes de Mézeray, *Abregé chronologique de l'histoire de France* (1643–1651), trans. *A General Chronological History of France* (London: Bassett et al., 1683); Jean de Serres, *General History of France, to 1598* (1611).]

to think, has not usually govern'd senates or popular assemblies. Chilperic the second, who by the slaughter of many persons of the royal blood, with infinite numbers of the nobility and people, came to be master of so much of the country, as procured him the name of king of France, killed his eldest son on suspicion that he was excited against him by Brunehaud, and his second, lest he should revenge the death of his brother: he married Fredegonde, and was soon after kill'd by her adulterer Landry. The kingdom continued in the same misery through the rage of the surviving princes, and found no relief, tho most of them fell by the sword; and that Brunehaud who had been a principal cause of those tragedies, was tied to the tails of four wild horses, and suffer'd a death as foul as her life. These were lions and leopards. They involved the kingdom in desperate troubles; but being men of valour and industry, they kept up in some measure the reputation and power of the nation, and he who attain'd to the crown defended it. But they being fallen by the hands of each other, the poisonous root put forth another plague more mortal than their fury. The vigour was spent, and the succession becoming more settled, ten base and slothful kings, by the French called *les roys faineants*, succeeded. Some may say, They who do nothing, do no hurt; but the rule is false in relation to kings. He that takes upon him the government of a people, can do no greater evil than by doing nothing, nor be guilty of a more unpardonable crime, than by negligence, coward-ice, voluptuousness, and sloth, to desert his charge. Virtue and manhood perish under him; good discipline is forgotten; justice slighted; the laws perverted or rendered useless; the people corrupted; the publick treasures exhausted; and the power of the government always falling into the hands of flatterers, whores, favorites, bawds, and such base wretches as render it contemptible, a way is laid open for all manner of disorders. The greatest cruelty that has been known in the world, if accompanied with wit and courage, never did so much hurt as this slothful bestiality; or rather these slothful beasts have ever been most cruel. The reigns of Septimius Severus, Mahomet the second, or Selim the second, were cruel and bloody; but their fury was turned against foreigners, and some of their near relations, or against such as fell under the suspicion of making attempts against them: The condition of the people was tolerable; those who would be quiet might be safe; the laws kept their right course; the reputation of the empire was maintained, the limits defended, and the publick peace preserved. But when the sword passed into the hands of lewd, slothful, foolish, and cowardly princes, it was of no power against foreign enemies, or the disturbers of domestic peace, tho always sharp against the best of their own subjects. No man knew how to secure himself against them, unless by raising civil wars; which will always be frequent, when a crown defended by a weak hand is proposed as a prize to any that dare invade it. This is a perpetual spring of disorders; and no nation was ever quiet, when the most eminent men found less danger in the most violent attempts, than in submitting patiently to the will of a prince, that suffers his power to be managed by vile persons, who get credit by flattering him in his vices. But this is not all; such princes naturally hate and fear those who excel them in virtue and reputation, as much as they are inferior to them in fortune; and think their persons cannot be secured, nor their authority enlarged, except by their destruction. 'Tis ordinary for them, *inter scorta & ganeas principibus viris perniciem machinare,*[30] and to make cruelty a cover to ignorance and cowardice. Besides the mischiefs brought upon the publick by the loss of eminent men, who are the pillars of every state, such reigns are always accompanied with tumults and civil wars, the great men striving with no less violence who shall get the weak prince into his power, when such regard is had to succession, that they think it not fit to divest him of the title, than when with less respect they contend for the sovereignty itself. And whilst this sort of princes reigned, France was not less afflicted with the contests between Grimbauld, Ebroin, Grimoald, and others, for the mayoralty of the palace, than they had been before by the rage of those princes who had contested for the crown. The issue also was the same: After many revolutions, Charles Martel gained the power of the kingdom, which he had so bravely defended against the Saracens; and having transmitted it to his son Pepin, the general assembly of estates, with the approbation of mankind, conferred the title also upon him. This gave the nation ease for the present; but the deep-rooted evil could not be so cured; and the kingdom, that by the wisdom, valour, and reputation of Pepin, had been preserved from civil troubles during his life, fell as deeply as ever into them so soon as he was dead. His sons, Carloman and Charles, divided the dominions, but in a little time each of them would have all. Carloman fill'd the kingdom with tumult; raised the Lombards, and marched with a great army against his brother, till his course was interrupted by death, caused, as is supposed, by such helps as princes liberally afford to their aspiring relations. Charles[31] deprived his two sons of their inheritance, put them in prison, and we hear no more of them. His third brother Griffon was not more quiet, nor more successful; and there could be no peace in Gascony, Italy or Germany, till he was kill'd. But all the

[30] C. Tacit. ["To plot the destruction of the leading men among whores and in cheap taverns." Tacitus, *Annals,* bk. 6, ch. 4.]

[31] [Charlemagne.]

advantages which Charles, by an extraordinary virtue and fortune, had purchased for his country, ended with his life. He left his son Lewis the Gentle in possession of the empire, and kingdom of France, and his grandson Bernard king of Italy: But these two could not agree, and Bernard falling into the hands of Lewis, was deprived of his eyes, and some time after kill'd. This was not enough to preserve the peace: Lothair, Lewis and Pepin, all three sons to Lewis, rebelled against him; called a council at Lyons, deposed him, and divided the empire amongst themselves. After five years he escaped from the monastery where he had been kept, renew'd the war, and was again taken prisoner by Lothair. When he was dead, the war broke out more fiercely than ever between his children: Lothair the emperor assaulted Lewis king of Bavaria and Charles king of Rhaetia; was defeated by them, and confined to a monastery, where he died. New quarrels arose between the two brothers, upon the division of the countries taken from him, and Lorraine only was left to his son. Lewis died soon after, and Charles getting possession of the empire and kingdom, ended an inglorious reign in an unprosperous attempt to deprive Hermingrade, daughter to his brother Lewis, of the kingdom of Arles, and other places left to her by her father. Lewis his son, call'd the Stutterer, reigned two years in much trouble; and his only legitimate son, Charles the Simple, came not to the crown till after the death of his two bastards Lewis and Carloman, Charles le Gros, and Eudes duke of Anjou. Charles le Gros was deposed from the empire and kingdom, stripp'd of his goods, and left to perish through poverty in an obscure village. Charles the Simple, and the nations under him, thrived no better: Robert duke of Anjou raised war against him, and was crown'd at Rheims; but was himself slain soon after in a bloody battle near Soissons. His son-in-law, Hebert earl of Vermandois, gathered up the remains of his scatter'd party, got Charles into his power, and called a general assembly of estates, who deposed him, and gave the crown to Raoul duke of Burgundy; tho he was no otherwise related to the royal blood than by his mother, which in France is nothing at all. He being dead, Lewis son to the deposed Charles was made king; but his reign was as inglorious to him, as miserable to his subjects. This is the peace which the French enjoy'd for the space of five or six ages under their monarchy; and 'tis hard to determine whether they suffer'd most by the violence of those who possessed, or the ambition of others who aspired to the crown; and whether the fury of active, or the baseness of slothful princes was most pernicious to them: But upon the whole matter, through the defects of those of the latter sort, they lost all that they had gained by sweat and blood under the conduct of the former. Henry and Otto of

Saxony, by a virtue like that of Charlemagne, deprived them of the empire, and settled it in Germany, leaving France only to Lewis surnamed Outremer, and his son Lothair. These seemed to be equally composed of treachery, cruelty, ambition, and baseness: They were always muti- nous, and always beaten: Their frantick passions put them always upon unjust designs, and were such plagues to their subjects and neighbours, that they became equally detested and despised. These things extinguished the veneration due to the memory of Pepin and Charles; and obliged the whole nation rather to seek relief from a stranger, than to be ruin'd by their worthless descendants. They had tried all ways that were in their power, deposed four crowned kings within the space of a hundred and fifty years; crowned five who had no other title than the people conferred upon them, and restored the descendants of those they had rejected, but all was in vain: Their vices were incorrigible, the mischiefs produc'd by them intolerable; they never ceased from murdering one another in battle, or by treachery, and bringing the nation into civil wars upon their wicked or foolish quarrels, till the whole race was rejected, and the crown placed upon the head of Hugh Capet. These mischiefs raged not in the same extremity under him and his descendants, but the abatement proceeded from a cause no way advantageous to absolute monarchy. The French were by their calamities taught more strictly to limit the regal power; and by turning the dukedoms and earldoms into patrimonies, which had been offices, gave an authority to the chief of the nobility, by which that of kings was curbed; and tho by this means the commonalty was exposed to some pressures, yet they were small in comparison of what they had suffer'd in former times. When many great men had estates of their own that did not depend upon the will of kings, they grew to love their country; and tho they cheerfully served the crown in all cases of publick concernment, they were not easily engaged in the personal quarrels of those who possessed it, or had a mind to gain it. To preserve themselves in this condition, they were obliged to use their vassals gently; and this continuing in some measure till within the last fifty years, the monarchy was less tumultuous, than when the king's will had been less restrained. Nevertheless they had not much reason to boast; there was a root still remaining, that from time to time produced poisonous fruit: Civil wars were frequent among them, tho not carried on with such desperate madness as formerly; and many of them upon the account of disputes between competitors for the crown. All the wars with England, since Edward II married Isabella daughter, and, as he pretended, heir of Philip Le Bel, were of this nature. The defeats of Crecy, Poitiers, and Agincourt, with the slaughters and devastations suffer'd from Edward III the Black

Prince, and Henry V were merely upon contests for the crown, and for want of an interpreter of the law of succession, who might determine the question between the heir male, and the heir general. The factions of Orleans and Burgundy, Orleans and Armagnac, proceeded from the same spring; and the murders that seem to have been the immediate causes of those quarrels, were only the effects of the hatred growing from their competition. The more odious, tho less bloody contests between Lewis the 11th, and his father Charles the 7th, with the jealousy of the former against his son Charles the 8th, arose from the same principle. Charles of Bourbon prepared to fill France with fire and blood upon the like quarrel, when his designs were overthrown by his death in the assault of Rome. If the dukes of Guise had been more fortunate, they had soon turned the cause of religion into a claim to the crown, and repair'd the injury done, as they pretended, to Pepin's race, by destroying that of Capet: And Henry the third thinking to prevent this by the slaughter of Henry le Balafré, and his brother the cardinal de Guise, brought ruin upon himself, and cast the kingdom into a most horrid confusion. Our own age furnishes us with more than one attempt of the same kind attended with the like success. The duke of Orleans was several times in arms against Lewis the 13th his brother; the Queen-Mother drew the Spaniards to favour him; Montmorency perished in his quarrel; Fontrailles reviv'd it by a treaty with Spain, which struck at the king's head as well as the cardinal's, and was suppress'd by the death of Cinq Mars and de Thou. Those who understand the affairs of that kingdom, make no doubt that the count de Soissons would have set up for himself, and been follow'd by the best part of France, if he had not been kill'd in the pursuit of his victory at the battle of Sedan. Since that time the kingdom has suffer'd such disturbances as show, that more was intended than the removal of Mazarin: And the marechal de Turenne was often told, that the check he gave to the prince of Condé at Gien, after he had defeated Hocquincourt, had preserved the crown upon the king's head. And to testify the stability, good order, and domestick peace that accompanies absolute monarchy, we have in our own days seen the house of Bourbon often divided within itself; the duke of Orleans, the count de Soissons, the princes of Condé and Conti in war against the king; the dukes of Angoulême, Vendôme, Longueville, the count de Moret, and other bastards of the royal family following their example; the houses of Guise, D'Elbeuf, Bouillon, Nemours, Rochefoucault, and almost all the most eminent in France, with the parliaments of Paris, Bourdeaux, and some others, joining with them. I might allege many more examples, to shew that this monarchy, as well as all others, has from the first establishment been full of blood and slaughter, through the violence of those who possessed the crown, and the ambition of such as aspired to it; and that the end of one civil war has been the beginning of another: but I presume upon the whole these will be thought sufficient to prove, that it never enjoyed any permanent domestick quiet.

The kingdoms of Spain have been no less disturbed by the same means; but especially that of Castile, where the kings had more power than in other places. To cite all the examples, were to transcribe their histories; but whoever has leisure to examine them will find, that after many troubles, Alfonso the II, notwithstanding his glorious surname of Wise, was deposed by means of his ambitious son: Don Alfonso, surnamed El Desheredado, supplanted by his uncle Don Sancho el bravo: Peter the Cruel cast from the throne, and killed by his bastard brother the conde de Trastamara. From the time of the above-named Alfonso to that of Ferdinand and Isabella, containing about two hundred years, so few of them passed without civil wars, that I hardly remember two together that were free from them: And whosoever pretends that of late years that monarchy has been more quiet, must, if he be ingenuous, confess their peace is rather to be imputed to the dexterity of removing such persons as have been most likely to raise disturbances (of which number were Don John of Austria, Don Carlos son to Philip the second, another of the same name son to Philip the third, and Don Balthazar son to Philip the fourth) than to the rectitude of their constitutions.

He that is not convinced of these truths by what has been said, may come nearer home, and see what mischiefs were brought upon Scotland by the contests between Baliol and Bruce, with their consequences, till the crown came to the Stuart family; the quiet reigns and happy deaths of the five Jameses, together with the admirable stability and peace of the government under Queen Mary, and the perfect union in which she lived with her husband, son and people, as well as the happiness of the nation whilst it lasted.[32]

But the miseries of England, upon the like occasions, surpass all. William the Norman was no sooner dead, but the nation was rent in pieces by his son Robert, contesting with his sons William and Henry for the crown. They being all dead and their sons, the like happen'd between Stephen and Maud: Henry the second was made king to terminate all disputes, but it proved a fruitless expedient. Such as were more

---

[32] Buchan. de reb. Scot. Drummond. Melvil. [George Buchanan, *Rerum Scoticarum historia* (1582), trans. *The History of Scotland* (London: E. Jones, 1690); William Drummond, *The* *History of Scotland from the Year 1423 until the Year 1542* (London: Henry Hills, 1655); *The Memoires of Sir James Melville of Hal-Hill* (London: Robert Boulter, 1683).]

scandalous, and not less dangerous, did soon arise between him and his sons; who besides the evils brought upon the nation, vexed him to death by their rebellion. The reigns of John and Henry the third were yet more tempestuous. Edward the second's lewd, foolish, infamous and detestable government ended in his deposition and death, to which he was brought by his wife and son. Edward the third employ'd his own and his subjects' valour against the French and Scots; but whilst the foundations were out of order, the nation could never receive any advantage by their victories: All was calculated for the glory, and turned to the advantage of one man. He being dead, all that the English held in Scotland and in France was lost through the baseness of his successor, with more blood than it had been gained; and the civil wars raised by his wickedness and madness, ended as those of Edward the second had done. The peace of Henry the fourth's reign was interrupted by dangerous civil wars; and the victory obtained at Shrewsbury had not perhaps secured him in the throne, if his death had not prevented new troubles. Henry the fifth acquired such reputation by his virtue and victories, that none dared to invade the crown during his life; but immediately after his death the storms prepared against his family, broke out with the utmost violence. His son's weakness encouraged Richard duke of York to set up a new title, which produced such mischiefs as hardly any people has suffer'd, unless upon the like occasion: For besides the slaughter of many thousands of the people, and especially of those who had been accustom'd to arms, the devastation of the best parts of the kingdom, and the loss of all that our kings had inherited in France, or gained by the blood of their subjects, fourscore princes of the blood, as Philippe de Comines calls them, died in battle, or under the hand of the hangman.[33] Many of the most noble families were extinguished; others lost their most eminent men. Three kings and two presumptive heirs of the crown were murder'd, and the nation brought to that shameful exigence, to set up a young man to reign over them, who had no better cover for his sordid extraction than a Welsh pedigree, that might shew how a tailor was descended from Prince Arthur, Cadwallader and Brutus.[34] But the wounds of the nation were not to be healed with such a plaster. He could not rely upon a title made up of such stuff, and patch'd with a marriage to a princess of a very questionable birth. His own meanness inclin'd him to hate the nobility; and thinking it to be as easy for them to take the crown from him, as to give it to him,

[33] [Philippe de Comines, *Memoirs*, bk. 1, ch. 7.]

[34] [The Wars of the Roses (1455–1485) between the houses of Lancaster and York over the English throne ended in the establishment of the Tudor dynasty with Henry VII.]

he industriously applied himself to glean up the remainders of the house of York, from whence a competitor might arise, and by all means to crush those who were most able to oppose him. This exceedingly weakened the nobility, who held the balance between him and the commons, and was the first step towards the dissolution of our ancient government: but he was so far from settling the kingdom in peace, that such rascals as Perkin Warbeck and Simnel were able to disturb it. The reign of Henry the eighth was turbulent and bloody; that of Mary furious, and such as had brought us into subjection to the most powerful, proud and cruel nation at that time in the world, if God had not wonderfully protected us. Nay, Edward the sixth, and Queen Elizabeth, notwithstanding the natural excellency of their dispositions, and their knowledge of the truth in matters of religion, were forced by that which men call *jealousy of state*, to foul their hands so often with illustrious blood, that if their reigns deserve to be accounted amongst the most gentle of monarchies, they were more heavy than the government of any commonwealth in time of peace; and yet their lives were never secure against such as conspired against them upon the account of title.

Having in some measure shew'd what miseries have been usually, if not perpetually brought upon nations subject to monarchies by the violence of some princes, and the baseness, folly, and cowardice of others, together with what they have suffer'd in contests for the several crowns, whilst men divided into divers factions, strive with as much vehemency to advance the person they favour, as if they or their country were interested in the quarrel, and fight as fiercely for a master as they might reasonably do to have none, I am not able to determine which of the two evils is the most mortal. 'Tis evident the vices of princes result to the damage of the people; but whether pride and cruelty, or stupidity and sloth be the worst, I cannot tell. All monarchies are subject to be afflicted with civil wars; but whether the most frequent and bloody do arise from the quarrels of divers competitors for crowns before any one gain the possession of them, or afterwards through the fears of him that would keep what he has gained, or the rage of those who would wrest it from him, is not so easily decided. But commonwealths are less troubled with those distempers. Women, children, or such as are notoriously foolish or mad, are never advanced to the supreme power. Whilst the laws, and that discipline which nourishes virtue is in force, men of wisdom and valor are never wanting; and every man desires to give testimony of his virtue, when he knows 'twill be rewarded with honour and power. If unworthy persons creep into magistracies, or are by mistake any way preferr'd, their vices for the most part turn to their own hurt; and the state cannot easily receive any great damage by the incapacity of one who is not to continue in office above a year; and is usually encompassed with those who having born, or are aspiring to the same, are by their virtue able to supply his defects; cannot hope for a reward from one unable to corrupt them, and are sure of the favour of the senate and people to support them in the defence of the publick interest. As long as this good order continues, private quarrels are suppress'd by the authority of the magistrate, or prove to be of little effect. Such as arise between the nobles and commons frequently produce good laws for the maintenance of liberty, as they did in Rome for above three hundred years after the expulsion of Tarquin; and almost ever terminated with little or no blood. Sometimes the errors of one or both parties are discovered by the discourse of a wise and good man; and those who have most violently opposed one another become the best friends, everyone joining to remove the evil that causes the division. When the senate and people of Rome seemed to be most furiously incensed against each other, the creation of tribunes, communications of honours and marriages between the patrician and plebeian families, or the mitigation of usury composed all; and these were not only harmless things, but such as gave opportunities of correcting the defects that had been in the first constitution of the government, without which they could never have attained to the greatness, glory, and happiness they afterwards enjoy'd. Such as had seen that people meeting in tumult, running through the city, crying out against the kings, consuls, senate, or decemviri, might have thought they would have filled all with blood and slaughter; but no such thing happened. They desired no more than to take away the kingdom which Tarquin had wickedly usurped; and never went about so much as to punish one minister of the mischiefs he had done, or to take away his goods, till upon pretence of treating his ambassadors by a new treachery had cast the city into greater danger than ever. Tho the decemviri had by the like villainies equally provoked the people, they were used with the like gentleness: Appius Claudius and Oppius having by voluntary death substracted themselves from publick punishment, their colleagues were only banished, and the magistracies of the city reduced to the former order without the effusion of more blood.[35] They who contended for their just rights, were satisfied with the recovery of them; whereas such as follow the impulse of an unruly ambition never think themselves safe, till they have destroyed all that seem able to disturb them, and satiated their rage with the blood of

[35] T. Liv. 1. 3. [Livy, *History of Rome*, bk. 3, ch. 58.]

their adversaries. This makes, as well as shews the difference between the tumults of Rome, or the secession of the common people to Mount Aventine, and the battles of Towton, Tewkesbury, Eveshal, Lewes, Hexham, Barnet, St. Albans, and Bosworth.[36] 'Tis in vain to say these ought rather to be compared to those of Pharsalia, Actium, or Philippi; for when the laws of a commonwealth are abolish'd, the name also ceases. Whatever is done by force or fraud to set up the interests and lusts of one man in opposition to the laws of his country, is purely and absolutely monarchical. Whatsoever passed between Marius, Sulla, Cinna, Catiline, Caesar, Pompey, Crassus, Augustus, Antonius, and Lepidus, is to be imputed to the contests that arise between competitors for monarchy, as well as those that in the next age happened between Galba, Otho, Vitellius, and Vespasian: Or, which is worse, whereas those in commonwealths fight for themselves when there is occasion, and if they succeed, enjoy the fruits of their victory, so as even those who remain of the vanquished party, partake of the liberty thereby established, or the good laws thereupon made; such as follow'd the ensigns of these men who sought to set up themselves, did, rather like beasts than men, hazard and suffer many unspeakable evils to purchase misery to themselves and their posterity, and to make him their master, who increasing in pride, avarice, and cruelty, was to be thrown down again with as much blood as he had been set up.

These things, if I mistake not, being in the last degree evident, I may leave to our author all the advantages he can gain by his rhetorical description of the tumults of Rome, *when blood was in the marketplace sucked up with sponges, and the jakes stuffed with carcasses;*[37] to which he may add the crimes of Sulla's life, and the miseries of his death: but withal I desire to know what number of sponges were sufficient to suck up the blood of five hundred thousand men slain in one day, when the houses of David and Jeroboam contended for the crown of Israel, or of four hundred thousand who fell in one battle between Joash and Amaziah on the same occasion; what jakes were capacious enough to contain the carcasses of those that perished in the quarrels between the successors of Alexander, the several competitors for the Roman empire; or those which have happened in France, Spain, England, and other places upon the like occasions. If Sulla for some time acted as an absolute monarch, 'tis no wonder that he died like one, or that God punished him as Herod, Philip the second of Spain, and some others, because the hand of his fellow-

[36] [Battles of the Wars of the Roses; those in the next sentence were battles of the Roman civil wars.]

[37] [*Patriarcha*, ch. 18, p. 89.]

citizens had unjustly spar'd him. If when he was become detestable to God and man, he became also miserable, his example ought to deter others from the crimes that are avenged by a power which none can escape, and to encourage those who defend, or endeavour to recover their violated liberties, to act vigorously in a cause that God does evidently patronize.

SECTION 25

Courts are more subject to Venality and Corruption than Popular Governments.

Tho court-flatterers impute many evils to popular governments they no way deserve, I could not think any so impudent as to lay corruption and venality to their charge, till I found it in our author. They might in my opinion have taken those faults upon themselves, since they certainly abound most where bawds, whores, buffoons, players, slaves and other base people who are naturally mercenary, are most prevalent. And whosoever would know whether this does more frequently befall commonwealths than monarchies, especially if they are absolute, need only to inquire whether the Cornelii, Junii, Fabii, Valerii, Quintii, Curii, Fabricii, and others who most prevailed in Rome after the expulsion of the kings, or Sejanus, Macro, Narcissus, Pallas, Icetus, Tigellinus, Vinius, Laco, Agrippina, Messalina, Lollia, Poppaea, and the like, were most subject to those base vices: Whether it were more easy to corrupt one or two of those villains and strumpets, or the senates and people of Rome, Carthage, Athens, and Sparta; and whether that sort of rabble had more power over the princes they served, than such as most resembled them had whilst the popular government continued. 'Tis in vain to say those princes were wicked and vile, for many others are so likewise; and when the power is in the hands of one man, there can be no assurance he will not be like them. Nay, when the power is so placed, ill men will always find opportunities of compassing their desires: *Bonus, cautus, optimus imperator venditur,* said Diocletian;[1] and tho he was no unwise man, yet that which principally induced him to renounce the empire, was the

---

[1] ["The good, wary, best emperor is sold."
Pomponius Laetus, *Romanae historiae compen-dium* (Venice, 1500), ch. 17.]

impossibility he found of defending himself against those that were in credit with him, who daily betray'd and sold him. They see with the eyes of other men, and cannot resist the frauds that are perpetually put upon them. Antoninus Pius and Marcus Aurelius seem to have been the best and wisest of all the Roman emperors; but the two Faustinas had such an ascendent over them, as was most shameful to their persons, and mischievous to the empire and the best men in it. Such as these may gain too much upon the affections of one man in the best regulated government; but that could be of no great danger to the publick, when many others equal or not much inferior to him in authority, are ready to oppose whatever he should endeavour to promote by their impulse: but there is no remedy when all depends upon the will of a single person who is governed by them. There was more of acuteness and jest, than of truth in that saying of Themistocles, *that his little boy had more power than any man in Greece; for he governed his mother, she him, he Athens, and Athens Greece.*[2] For he himself was found to have little power, when for private passions and concernments he departed from the interest of the publick; and the like has been found in all places that have been governed in the like manner.

Again, corruption will always reign most where those who have the power do most favour it, where the rewards of such crimes are greatest, easiest, and most valued, and where the punishment of them is least feared.

1. For the first, we have already proved that liberty cannot be preserved, if the manners of the people are corrupted, nor absolute monarchy introduced where they are sincere; which is sufficient to shew that those who manage free governments ought always to the utmost of their power to oppose corruption, because otherwise both they and their government must inevitably perish; and that on the other hand, the absolute monarch must endeavour to introduce it, because he cannot subsist without it. 'Tis also so natural for all such monarchs to place men in power who pretend to love their persons, and will depend upon their pleasure, that possibly 'twould be hard to find one in the world who has not made it the rule of his government: And this is not only the way to corruption, but the most dangerous of all. For tho a good man may love a good monarch, he will obey him only when he commands that which is just; and no one can engage himself blindly to do whatever he is commanded, without renouncing all virtue and religion; because he knows not whether that which shall be commanded is consistent with either, or directly

[2] [Plutarch, *Life of Themistocles*, ch. 18, sec. 4.]

contrary to the laws of God and man. But if such a monarch be evil, and his actions such as they are too often found to be, whoever bears an affection to him, and seconds his designs, declares himself an enemy to all that is good; and the advancement of such men to power does not only introduce, foment, and increase corruption, but fortifies it in such a manner, that without an entire renovation of that state it cannot be removed. Ill men may possibly creep into any government; but when the worst are plac'd nearest to the throne, and raised to honors for being so, they will with that force endeavour to draw all men to a conformity of spirit with themselves, that it can no otherwise be prevented, than by destroying them and the principle in which they live.

2. To the second; man naturally follows that which is good, or seems to him to be so. Hence it is that in well-govern'd states, where a value is put upon virtue, and no one honoured unless for such qualities as are beneficial to the publick, men are from the tenderest years brought up in a belief, that nothing in this world deserves to be sought after, but such honors as are acquired by virtuous actions: By this means virtue itself becomes popular, as in Sparta, Rome, and other places, where riches (which with the vanity that follows them, and the honors men give to them, are the root of all evil) were either totally banished, or little regarded. When no other advantage attended the greatest riches than the opportunity of living more sumptuously or deliciously, men of great spirits slighted them. When Aristippus told Cleanthes, that if he would go to court and flatter the tyrant, he need not seek his supper under a hedge; the philosopher answer'd, that he who could content himself with such a supper, need not go to court, or flatter the tyrant.[3] Epaminondas, Aristides, Phocion, and even the Lacedaemonian kings, found no inconvenience in poverty, whilst their virtue was honour'd, and the richest princes in the world feared their valour and power. It was not difficult for Curius, Fabricius, Quintius Cincinnatus, or Aemilius Paulus, to content themselves with the narrowest fortune, when it was no obstacle to them in the pursuit of those honours which their virtues deserved. 'Twas in vain to think of bribing a man who supped upon the coleworts of his own garden. He could not be gained by gold, who did not think it necessary. He that could rise from the plow to the triumphal chariot, and contentedly return thither again, could not be corrupted; and he that left the sense of his poverty to his executors, who found not wherewith to bury him, might leave Macedon and Greece to the pillage of his

---

[3] [Diogenes Laertius, *Lives of Eminent Philosophers* (Loeb, 1925), bk. 2, ch. 8.]

soldiers, without taking to himself any part of the booty. But when luxury was brought into fashion, and they came to be honor'd who liv'd magnificently, tho they had in themselves no qualities to distinguish them from the basest of slaves, the most virtuous men were exposed to scorn if they were poor: and that poverty which had been the mother and nurse of their virtue, grew insupportable. The poet well understood what effect this change had upon the world, who said,

> *Nullum crimen abest facinusque libidinis, ex quo*
> *Paupertas Romana perit.*
>
> Juven.[4]

When riches grew to be necessary, the desire of them which is the spring of all mischief, follow'd. They who could not obtain honours by the noblest actions, were oblig'd to get wealth to purchase them from whores and villains, who exposed them to sale: and when they were once entered into this track, they soon learnt the vices of those from whom they had received their preferment, and to delight in the ways that had brought them to it. When they were come to this, nothing could stop them: All thought and remembrance of good was extinguish'd. They who had bought the commands of armies or provinces, from Icetus or Narcissus, sought only how to draw money from them, to enable them to purchase higher dignities, or gain a more assured protection from those patrons. This brought the government of the world under a most infamous traffick, and the treasures arising from it were, for the most part, dissipated by worse vices than the rapine, violence and fraud with which they had been gotten. The authors of those crimes had nothing left but their crimes, and the necessity of committing more, through the indigence into which they were plung'd by the extravagance of their expences. These things are inseparable from the life of a courtier; for as servile natures are guided rather by sense than reason, such as addict themselves to the service of courts, find no other consolation in their misery, than what they receive from sensual pleasures, or such vanities as they put a value upon; and have no other care, than to get money for their supply by begging, stealing, bribing, and other infamous practices. Their offices are more or less esteemed according to the opportunities they afford for the exercise of these virtues; and no man seeks them for any other end than for gain, nor takes any other way than that which conduces to it. The usual means

[4] ["No charge and crime of lust was absent from the time when Roman poverty perished." Juvenal, *Satire* 6, li. 294.]

of attaining them are, by observing the prince's humour, flattering his vices, serving him in his pleasures, fomenting his passions, and by advancing his worst designs, to create an opinion in him that they love his person, and are entirely addicted to his will. When valour, industry and wisdom advanced men to offices, it was no easy matter for a man to persuade the senate he had such qualities as were requir'd, if he had them not: But when princes seek only such as love them, and will do what they command, 'tis easy to impose upon them; and because none that are good will obey them when they command that which is not so, they are always encompassed by the worst. Those who follow them only for reward, are most liberal in professing affection to them, and by that means rise to places of authority and power. The fountain being thus corrupted, nothing that is pure can come from it. These mercenary wretches having the management of affairs, justice and honours are set at a price, and the most lucrative traffick in the world is thereby established. Eutropius when he was a slave, used to pick pockets and locks; but being made a minister, he sold cities, armies and provinces:[5] and some have undertaken to give probable reasons to believe, that Pallas, one of Claudius his manumised slaves, by these means brought together more wealth in six years, than all the Roman dictators and consuls had done from the expulsion of the kings to their passage into Asia. The rest walked in the same way, used the same arts, and many of them succeeded in the same manner. Their riches consisted not of spoils taken from enemies, but were the base product of their own corruption. They valued nothing but money, and those who could bribe them, were sure to be advanc'd to the highest offices; and whatever they did, feared no punishment. Like effects will ever proceed from the like causes. When vanity, luxury and prodigality are in fashion, the desire of riches must necessarily increase in proportion to them: And when the power is in the hands of base mercenary persons, they will always (to use the courtiers' phrase) make as much profit of their places as they can. Not only matters of favour, but of justice too, will be exposed to sale; and no way will be open to honours or magistracies, but by paying largely for them. He that gets an office by these means, will not execute it *gratis:* he thinks he may sell what he has bought; and would not have entered by corrupt ways, if he had not intended to deal corruptly. Nay, if a well-meaning man should suffer himself to be so far carried away by the stream of a prevailing custom, as to purchase honours of such villains, he would be obliged to continue in the same course, that he might gain riches to

---

[5] Nunc uberiore rapina/Peccat in orbe manus. Claud. ["Now by more fruitful pillaging his   hand sins in the world." Claudian, *Against Eutropius*, bk. 1, li. 191.]

procure the continuance of his benefactors' protection, or to obtain the favour of such as happen to succeed them: And the corruption thus beginning in the head, must necessarily diffuse itself into all the members of the commonwealth. Or, if anyone (which is not to be expected) after having been guilty of one villainy, should resolve to commit no more, it could have no other effect than to bring him to ruin; and he being taken away, all things would return to their former channel.

Besides this, whosoever desires to advance himself, must use such means as are suitable to the time in which he lives, and the humour of the persons with whom he is to deal. It had been as absurd for any man void of merit to set himself up against Junius Brutus, Cincinnatus, Papirius Cursor, Camillus, Fabius Maximus, or Scipio; and by bribing the senate and people of Rome, think to be chosen captain against the Tarquins, Tuscans, Latins, Samnites, Gauls or Carthaginians, as for the most virtuous men by the most certain proofs of their wisdom, experience, integrity and valour, to expect advancement from Caligula, Claudius, and Nero, or the lewd wretches that govern'd them. They hated and feared all those that excelled in virtue, and setting themselves to destroy the best for being the best, they placed the strength of the government in the hands of the worst, which produced the effects beforementioned. This seems to have been so well known, that no man pretended to be great at court, but those who had cast off all thoughts of honour and common honesty: *Revertar cum leno, meretrix, scurra, cinaedus ero,*[6] said one who saw what manners prevailed there; and wheresoever they do prevail, such as will rise, must render themselves conformable in all corruption and venality. And it may be observed, that a noble person now living amongst us, who is a great enemy to bribery, was turned out from a considerable office, as a scandal to the court; for, said the principal minister, he will make no profit of his place, and by that means casts a scandal upon those that do.

If any man say, this is not generally the fate of all courts, I confess it; and that if the prince be just, virtuous, wise, of great spirit, and not pretending to be absolute, he may chuse such men as are not mercenary, or take such a course as may render it hard for them to deserve bribes, or to preserve themselves from punishment, if they should deflect from his intention. And a prince of this age speaking familiarly with some great men about him, said, he had heard much of vast gains made by those who were near to princes, and asked if they made the like? One of them answer'd, that they were as willing as others to get something, but

[6] [I will return when I turn into a pimp, a whore, a dandy, a sodomite.]

that no man would give them a farthing; for everyone finding a free admittance to his majesty, no man needed a solicitor: And it was no less known that he did of himself grant those things that were just, than that none of them had so much credit as to promote such as were not so. I will not say such a king is a phoenix; perhaps more than one may be found in an age; but they are certainly rare, and all that is good in their government proceeding from the excellency of their personal virtues, it must fail when that virtue fails, which was the root of it. Experience shews how little we can rely upon such a help; for where crowns are hereditary, children seldom prove like to their fathers; and such as are elective have also their defects. Many seem to be modest and innocent in private fortunes, who prove corrupt and vicious when they are raised to power. The violence, pride and malice of Saul, was never discover'd till the people had placed him in the throne. But where the government is absolute, or the prince endeavours to make it so, this integrity can never be found: He will always seek such as are content to depend upon his will, which being always unruly, good men will never comply; ill men will be paid for it, and that opens a gap to all manner of corruption. Something like to this may befall regular monarchies, or popular governments. They who are placed in the principal offices of trust may be treacherous; and when they are so, they will always by these means seek to gain partizans and dependents upon themselves. Their designs being corrupt, they must be carried on by corruption; but such as would support monarchy in its regularity, or popular governments, must oppose it, or be destroy'd by it. And nothing can better manifest how far absolute monarchies are more subject to this venality and corruption than the regular and popular governments, than that they are rooted in the principle of the one, which cannot subsist without them; and are so contrary to the others, that they must certainly perish unless they defend themselves from them.

If any man be so far of another opinion, as to believe that Brutus, Camillus, Scipio, Fabius, Hannibal, Pericles, Aristides, Agesilaus, Epaminondas or Pelopidas, were as easily corrupted as Sejanus, Tigellinus, Vinius or Laco: That the senate and people of Rome, Carthage, Athens, Sparta or Thebes, were to be bought at as easy rates as one profligate villain, a slave, an eunuch or a whore; or tho it was not in former ages, yet it is so now: he may be pleased to consider by what means men now rise to places of judicature, church-preferment, or any offices of trust, honour or profit under those monarchies which we know, that either are or would be absolute. Let him examine how all the offices of justice are now disposed in France; how Mazarin came to be advanced; what traffick he made of abbies and bishopricks, and what treasures he gained by that means: Whether the like has not continued since his death, and as a laudable example been transmitted to us since his majesty's happy restoration: Whether bawds, whores, thieves, buffoons, parasites, and such vile wretches as are naturally mercenary, have not more power at Whitehall, Versailles, the Vatican, and the Escurial, than in Venice, Amsterdam, and Switzerland: Whether H-de, Arl-ng-t-n, D-nby, their Graces of Cleveland and Portsmouth, S-nd-rl-nd, Jenkins or Chiffinch,[7] could probably have attained such power as they have had amongst us, if it had been disposed by the suffrages of the parliament and people: Or lastly, whether such as know only how to work upon the personal vices of a man, have more influence upon one who happens to be born in a reigning family, or upon a senate consisting of men chosen for their virtues and quality, of the whole body of a nation.

But if he who possesses or affects an absolute power be by his interest led to introduce that corruption which the people, senate, and magistrates who uphold popular governments abhor, as that which threatens them with destruction: if the example, arts, and means used by him and his dependents be of wonderful efficacy towards the introduction of it: if nothing but an admirable virtue, which can hardly be in one that enjoys or desires such a power, can divert him from that design; and if such virtue never did, nor probably ever will continue long in any one family, we cannot rationally believe there ever was a race of men invested with, or possessing such a power, or that there will ever be any who have not, and will not endeavour to introduce that corruption, which is so necessary for the defence of their persons, and most important concernments, and certainly accomplish their great design, unless they are opposed or removed.

[7] [The names with letters missing are Hyde, Arlington, Danby, Sunderland. For Hyde, Arlington, and Danby, see Section 20, n. 4. Robert Spencer, Earl of Sunderland, was a talented, opportunistic English politician, prominent under Charles II during the early 1680s. He worked closely with the Duchess of Portsmouth, Charles's mistress in these years.]

SECTION 26
*Civil Tumults and Wars are not the greatest Evils
that befall Nations.*

BUT *skin for skin,* says our author, *and all that a man hath will he give for his life.*[1] And since it was necessary to grace his book with some Scripture phrases, none could be fitter for that purpose than those that were spoken by the Devil; but they will be of little use to him: For tho I should so far recede from truth, as to avow those words to be true, I might safely deny the conclusions he draws from them, *that those are the worst governments under which most men are slain; or, that more are slain in popular governments than in absolute monarchies.*[2] For having proved that all the wars and tumults that have happen'd in commonwealths, have never produced such slaughters as were brought upon the empires of Macedon and Rome, or the kingdoms of Israel, Judah, France, Spain, Scotland or England, by contests between several competitors for those crowns; if tumult, war, and slaughter, be the point in question, those are the worst of all governments where they have been most frequent and cruel. But tho these are terrible scourges, I deny that government to be simply the worst that has most of them. 'Tis ill that men should kill one another in seditions, tumults and wars; but 'tis worse to bring nations to such misery, weakness and baseness, as to have neither strength nor courage to contend for anything; to have nothing left worth defending, and to give the name of peace to desolation. I take Greece to have been happy and glorious, when it was full of populous cities, flourishing in all the arts that deserve praise among men: When they were courted and feared by the greatest kings, and never assaulted by any but to his own loss and confusion: When Babylon and Susa trembled at the motion of their arms; and their valour exercised in these wars and tumults, which our author looks upon as the greatest evils, was raised to such a power that nothing upon earth was found able to resist them: and I think it now miserable, when peace reigns within their empty walls, and the poor remains of those exhausted nations sheltering themselves under the ruins of the desolated cities, have neither anything that deserves to be disputed amongst them, nor spirit or force to repel the injuries they daily suffer from a proud and insupportable master.

[1] [*Patriarcha*, ch. 19 ("Popular Governments More Bloody than Tyranny"), p. 90, quoting Job 2:4.]

[2] [*Patriarcha*, ch. 19, pp. 90–92.]

The like may be said of Italy: Whilst it was inhabited by nations governing themselves by their own will, they fell sometimes into domestick seditions, and had frequent wars with their neighbours. When they were free, they loved their country, and were always ready to fight in its defence. Such as succeeded well, increased in vigor and power; and even those that were the most unfortunate in one age, found means to repair their greatest losses if their government continued. Whilst they had a propriety in their goods, they would not suffer the country to be invaded, since they knew they could have none if it were lost. This gave occasion to wars and tumults; but it sharpened their courage, kept up a good discipline, and the nations that were most exercised by them, always increased in power and number; so that no country seems ever to have been of greater strength than Italy was when Hannibal invaded it: and after his defeat, the rest of the world was not able to resist their valour and power. They sometimes killed one another; but their enemies never got anything but burying-places within their territories. All things are now brought into a very different method by the blessed governments they are under. The fatherly care of the king of Spain, the pope, and other princes, has established peace amongst them. We have not in many ages heard of any sedition among the Latins, Sabines, Volsci, Aequi, Samnites, or others. The thin, half-starv'd inhabitants of walls supported by ivy, fear neither popular tumults, nor foreign alarms; and their sleep is only interrupted by hunger, the cries of their children, or the howling of wolves. Instead of many turbulent, contentious cities, they have a few scatter'd silent cottages; and the fierceness of those nations is so temper'd, that every rascally collector of taxes extorts without fear from every man, that which should be the nourishment of his family. And if any of those countries are free from that pernicious vermin, 'tis through the extremity of their poverty. Even in Rome a man may be circumvented by the fraud of a priest, or poison'd by one who would have his estate, wife, whore, or child; but nothing is done that looks like tumult or violence. The governors do as little fear Gracchus as Hannibal; and instead of wearying their subjects in wars, they only seek, by perverted laws, corrupt judges, false witnesses, and vexatious suits, to cheat them of their money and inheritance. This is the best part of their condition. Where these arts are used, there are men, and they have something to lose; but for the most part the lands lie waste, and they who were formerly troubled with the disorders incident to populous cities, now enjoy the quiet and peaceable estate of a wilderness.

Again, there is a way of killing worse than that of the sword: for as

Tertullian says upon a different occasion, *prohibere nasci est occidere;*[3] those governments are in the highest degree guilty of blood, which by taking from men the means of living, bring some to perish through want, drive others out of the country, and generally dissuade men from marriage, by taking from them all ways of subsisting their families. Notwithstanding all the seditions of Florence, and other cities of Tuscany, the horrid factions of Guelphs and Ghibellines, Neri and Bianchi, nobles and commons, they continued populous, strong, and exceeding rich; but in the space of less than a hundred and fifty years, the peaceable reign of the Medicis is thought to have destroyed nine parts in ten of the people of that province. Amongst other things 'tis remarkable, that when Philip the second of Spain gave Siena to the duke of Florence, his ambassador then at Rome sent him word, that he had given away more than six hundred and fifty thousand subjects; and 'tis not believ'd there are now twenty thousand souls inhabiting that city and territory. Pisa, Pistoia, Arezzo, Cortona, and other towns that were then good and populous, are in the like proportion diminished, and Florence more than any. When that city had been long troubled with seditions, tumults, and wars, for the most part unprosperous, they still retain'd such strength, that when Charles the eighth of France being admitted as a friend with his whole army, which soon after conquer'd the kingdom of Naples, thought to master them, the people taking arms, struck such a terror into him, that he was glad to depart upon such conditions as they thought fit to impose.[4] Machiavelli reports, that in that time Florence alone, with the Val d'Arno, a small territory belonging to that city, could, in a few hours, by the sound of a bell, bring together a hundred and thirty five thousand well arm'd men;[5] whereas now that city, with all the others in that province, are brought to such despicable weakness, emptiness, poverty and baseness, that they can neither resist the oppressions of their own prince, nor defend him or themselves if they were assaulted by a foreign enemy. The people are dispers'd or destroy'd, and the best families sent to seek habitations in Venice, Genoa, Rome, Naples, and Lucca. This is not the effect of war or pestilence; they enjoy a perfect peace, and suffer no other plague than the government they are under. But he who has

---

[3] ["To prohibit from being born is to kill." Tertullian, *Against Marcion*, bk. 1 (at the end), in *The Ante-Nicene Fathers*, ed. Alexander Roberts and James Donaldson, vol. 3 (New York: Scribner's, 1926).]

[4] Guicciard. [Guicciardini, *History of Flor-*ence, ch. 12; *History of Italy*, bk. 1, pp. 64–65.]

[5] [Machiavelli, *History of Florence* (New York: Harper and Row, 1960), bk. 2.]

thus cured them of disorders and tumults, does, in my opinion, deserve no greater praise than a physician, who should boast there was not a sick person in a house committed to his care, when he had poison'd all that were in it. The Spaniards have established the like peace in the kingdoms of Naples and Sicily, the West-Indies, and other places. The Turks by the same means prevent tumults in their dominions. And they are of such efficacy in all places, that Mario Chigi brother to Pope Alexander the seventh, by one sordid cheat upon the sale of corn, is said within eight years to have destroy'd above a third part of the people in the Ecclesiastical State; and that country which was the strength of the Romans in the time of the Carthaginian Wars, suffer'd more by the covetousness and fraud of that villain, than by all the defeats receiv'd from Hannibal.

'Twere an endless work to mention all the places where this peaceable solitude has been introduc'd by absolute monarchy; but popular and regular governments have always applied themselves to increase the number, strength, power, riches, and courage of their people, by providing comfortable ways of subsistence for their own citizens, inviting strangers, and filling them all with such a love to their country, that every man might look upon the publick cause as his own, and be always ready to defend it. This may sometimes give occasion to tumults and wars, as the most vigorous bodies may fall into distempers: When everyone is solicitous for the publick, there may be difference of opinion, and some by mistaking the way may bring prejudice when they intend profit: But unless a tyrant do arise, and destroy the government which is the root of their felicity; or they be overwhelm'd by the irresistible power of a virtue or fortune greater than their own, they soon recover, and for the most part rise up in greater glory and prosperity than before. This was seen in the commonwealths of Greece and Italy, which for this reason were justly called nurseries of virtue, and their magistrates preservers of men; whereas our author's peace-making monarchs can deserve no better title than that of enemies and destroyers of mankind.

I cannot think him in earnest when he exaggerates Sulla's cruelties as a proof that the mischiefs suffer'd under free states are more universal than under kings and tyrants:[6] For there never was a tyrant in the world if he was not one, tho through weariness, infirmity of body, fear, or perhaps the horror of his own wickedness, he at length resigned his power; but the evil had taken root so deep, that it could not be removed: There was nothing of liberty remaining in Rome: The laws were

---

[6] [*Patriarcha*, ch. 19, p. 91.]

overthrown by the violence of the sword: the remaining contest was who should be lord; and there is no reason to believe that if Pompey had gained the battle of Pharsalia, he would have made a more modest use of his victory than Caesar did; or that Rome would have been more happy under him than under the other. His cause was more plausible because the senate follow'd him, and Caesar was the invader; but he was no better in his person, and his designs seem to have been the same. He had been long before *suarum legum auctor & eversor.*[7] He gave the beginning to the first triumvirate; and 'twere folly to think that he who had been insolent when he was not come to the highest pitch of fortune, would have proved moderate if success had put all into his hands. The proceedings of Marius, Cinna, Catiline, Octavius, and Antonius were all of the same nature. No laws were observ'd: No publick good intended; the ambition of private persons reigned; and whatsoever was done by them, or for their interests, can no more be applied to popular, aristocratical or mix'd governments, than the furies of Caligula and Nero.

SECTION 27

The Mischiefs and Cruelties proceeding from
Tyranny are greater than any that can come from
Popular or mixed Governments.

T IS now time to examine the reasons of our author's general maxims. *The cruelties*, says he, *of a tyrant extend ordinarily no farther than some particular men that offend him, and not to the whole kingdom. It is truly said of his late majesty King James, a king can never be so notoriously vicious, but he will generally favour justice, and maintain some order. Even cruel Domitian, Dionysius the tyrant, and many others are commended in histories as great observers of justice, except in particular cases, wherein his inordinate lusts may carry him away.*[1] This may be said of popular governments; for tho a people through error do sometimes hurt a private person, and that may possibly result to the publick damage, because the man that is offended or destroy'd, might have been useful to the society, they never do it otherwise than by error: For having the government in themselves, whatever is prejudicial to it, is so to them; and if they ruin it, they ruin themselves, which no

---

[7] ["The author and destroyer of his own laws." Tacitus, *Annals*, bk. 3, ch. 28.]

[1] [*Patriarcha*, ch. 19, p. 92.]

man ever did willingly and knowingly. In absolute monarchies the matter is quite otherwise. A prince that sets up an interest in himself, becomes an enemy to the publick: in following his own lusts he offends all, except a few of his corrupt creatures, by whose help he oppresses others with a yoke they are unwilling to bear, and thereby incurs the universal hatred. This hatred is always proportionable to the injuries received, which being extreme, that must be so too; and every people being powerful in comparison to the prince that governs, he will always fear those that hate him, and always hate those he fears. When Luigi Farnese first duke of Parma had by his tyranny incensed the people of that small city, their hatred was not less mortal to him than that of the whole empire had been to Nero; and as the one burn'd Rome, the other would have destroy'd Parma, if he had not been prevented. The like has been, and will be everywhere, in as much as every man endeavours to destroy those he hates and fears; and the greatness of the danger often drives this fear to rage and madness.[2] For this reason Caligula wish'd but one neck to all the people; and Nero triumphed over the burning city, thinking by that ruin he had prevented his own danger. I know not who the good authors are that commend Domitian for his justice; but Tacitus calls him *principem virtutibus infestum;*[3] and 'tis hard to find out how such a man can be an observer of justice, unless it be just, that whoever dares to be virtuous under a vicious and base prince should be destroy'd. Another author of the same time speaking of him, does not say he was unjust but gives us reason to think he was so,[4] unless it were just for him, who had a power over the best part of the world, to destroy it; and that he who by his cruelty had brought it to the last gasp, would have finish'd the work, if his rage had not been extinguished.

Many princes not having in themselves power to destroy their people, have stirred up foreign nations against them, and placed the only hopes of their safety in the publick calamity; and lawful kings when they have fallen into the first degree of madness, so as to assume a power above that which was allowed by the law, have in fury proved equal to the worst usurpers. Cleonymus of Sparta was of this sort: He became, says Plutarch, an enemy to the city, because they would not allow him the absolute power he affected; and brought Pyrrhus, the fiercest of their

---

[2] Cuncta ferit dum cuncta timet. Lucan. ["He strikes down everything while he fears everything." Claudian, *Against Eutropius*, bk. 1, li. 182.]

[3] Tacit. in vit. Agric. ["A prince hostile to virtues." Tacitus, *Life of Agricola*, ch. 41.]

[4] Cum jam semianimem laceraret Flavius orbem/Tertius, & calvo serviret Roma tyranno. Juvenal. ["When the third Flavian was torturing the already half-dead world, and Rome served a bald tyrant." Juvenal, *Satire* 4, li. 36.]

enemies, with a mighty and excellently well disciplin'd army to destroy them.[5] Vortigern the Britain call'd in the Saxons with the ruin of his own people, who were incensed against him for his lewdness, cruelty, and baseness.[6] King John for the like reasons offer'd the kingdom of England to the Moors, and to the pope. Peter the Cruel, and other kings of Castile brought vast armies of Moors into Spain to the ruin of their own people, who detested their vices, and would not part with their privileges. Many other examples of the like nature might be alleged; and I wish our own experience did not too well prove that such designs are common. Let him that doubts this, examine the causes of the wars with Scotland in the years 1639, 1640; the slaughters of the Protestants in Ireland 1641; the whole course of alliances and treaties for the space of fourscore years; the friendship contracted with the French; frequent quarrels with the Dutch, together with other circumstances that are already made too publick: if he be not convinced by this, he may soon see a man in the throne,[7] who had rather be a tributary to France than a lawful king of England, whilst either parliament or people shall dare to dispute his commands, insist upon their own rights, or defend a religion inconsistent with that which he has espoused; and then the truth will be so evident as to require no proof.

Grotius was never accused of dealing hardly with kings, or laying too much weight upon imaginary cases; nevertheless amongst other reasons that in his opinion justify subjects in taking arms against their princes, he alleges this, *propter immanem saevitiam*, and *quando rex in populi exitium fertur*; in as much as it is *contrary to, and inconsistent with the ends for which governments are instituted*;[8] which were most impertinent, if no such thing could be; for that which is not, can have no effect. There are therefore princes who seek the destruction of their people, or none could be justly opposed on that account.

If King James[9] was of another opinion, I could wish the course of his government had been suited to it. When he said that whilst he had the power of making judges and bishops, he would make that to be law and gospel which best pleased him, and filled those places with such as turned

---

[5] Plut. vit. Pyrrh. [Plutarch, *Life of Pyrrhus*, ch. 26.]

[6] Math. Westm. [Roger of Wendover, *Flowers of History* (formerly attributed to "Matthew Westminster"), vol. 1, p. 5 (the year 449).]

[7] [The future James II, a professed Catholic, who became king shortly after Sidney's execution.]

[8] ["On account of their great savagery" and "when the king hastens to the ruin of his people." Hugo Grotius, *De jure*, bk. 1, ch. 4, sec. 11.]

[9] [James I, author of several works on kingship referred to elsewhere by Sidney.]

both according to his will and interests, I must think that by overthrowing justice, which is the rule of civil and moral actions, and perverting the Gospel which is the light of the spiritual man, he left nothing unattempted that he durst attempt, by which he might bring the most extensive and universal evils upon our nation that any can suffer. This would stand good, tho princes never erred, unless they were *transported with some inordinate lusts;*[10] for 'tis hard to find one that does not live in the perpetual power of them. They are naturally subject to the impulse of such appetites as well as others, and whatever evil reigns in their nature is fomented by education. 'Tis the handle by which their flatterers lead them; and he that discovers to what vice a prince is most inclin'd, is sure to govern him by rendering himself subservient. In this consists the chief art of a courtier, and by this means it comes to pass that such lusts as in private men are curbed by fear, do not only rage as in a wild beast, but are perpetually inflamed by the malice of their own servants: their hatred to the laws of God or men that might restrain them, increases in proportion with their vices, or their fears of being punished for them. And when they are come to this, they can set no limits to their fury, and there is no extravagance into which they do not frequently fall. But many of them do not expect these violent motives: the perversity of their own nature carries them to the extremities of evil. They hate virtue for its own sake, and virtuous men for being most unlike to themselves. This virtue is the dictate of reason, or the remains of divine light, by which men are made beneficent and beneficial to each other. Religion proceeds from the same spring, and tends to the same end; and the good of mankind so entirely depends upon these two, that no people ever enjoyed anything worth desiring that was not the product of them; and whatsoever any have suffer'd that deserves to be abhorr'd and feared, has proceeded either from the defect of these, or the wrath of God against them. If any prince therefore has been an enemy to virtue and religion, he must also have been an enemy to mankind, and most especially to the people under him. Whatsoever he does against those that excel in virtue and religion, tends to the destruction of the people who subsist by them. I will not take upon me to define who they are, or to tell the number of those that do this: but 'tis certain there have been such; and I wish I could say they were few in number, or that they had liv'd only in past ages. Tacitus does not fix this upon one prince, but upon all that he writes of; and to give his readers a taste of what he was to write, he says, *that nobility and honours were dangerous, but that virtue brought most certain destruction;* and

[10] [*Patriarcha*, ch. 19, p. 92.]

in another place, that *after the slaughter of many excellent men, Nero resolved to cut down virtue itself, and therefore kill'd Thrasea Paetus and Barea Soranus.*[11] And whosoever examines the Christian or ecclesiastical histories, will find those princes to have been no less enemies to virtue and religion than their predecessors, and consequently enemies to the nations under them, unless religion and virtue be things prejudicial or indifferent to mankind.

But our author may say, these were particular cases; and so was the slaughter of the prophets and apostles, the crucifixion of Christ, and all the villainies that have ever been committed; yet they proceeded from a universal principle of hatred to all that is good, exerting itself as far as it could, to the ruin of mankind: And nothing but the over-ruling power of God, who resolved to preserve to himself a people, could set bounds to their rage, which in other respects had as full success as our author, or the Devil could have wished.

Dionysius (his other example of justice) deserves observation: More falsehood, lewdness, treachery, ingratitude, cruelty, baseness, avarice, impudence and hatred to all manner of good, was hardly ever known in a mortal creature. For this reason, Diogenes seeing him at Corinth, tho in a poor and contemptible condition, said, he rather deserved to have continued in the misery, fears and villainies of his tyranny, than to be suffer'd peaceably to converse with honest men.[12] And if such as these are to be called observers of justice, it must be concluded that the laws of God and of men, are either of no value, or contrary to it; and that the destruction of nations is a better work than their preservation. No faith is to be observed: temples may be justly sack'd; the best men slain for daring to be better than their masters; and the whole world, if it were in the power of one man, rightly torn in pieces and destroy'd.

His reasons for this are as good as his doctrine: *It is,* saith he, *the multitude of people and abundance of riches, that are the glory and strength of every prince: the bodies of his subjects do him service in war, and their goods supply his wants. Therefore if not out of affection to his people, yet out of natural love unto himself, every tyrant desires to preserve the lives and goods of his subjects.*[13] I should have thought that princes, tho tyrants, being God's vicegerents, and fathers of their people, would have sought their good, tho no advantage had thereby redounded to themselves, but it seems no such thing is to be expected from them. They consider nations, as grazers do their herds and flocks, according to the profit that can be made of

---

[11] C. Tacit. Hist. l. 1. Ann. l. 4. [Tacitus, *Histories*, bk. 1, ch. 3; *Annals*, bk. 16, ch. 21.]

[12] [Plutarch, *Precepts of Statecraft*, ch. 54, in Plutarch, *Moralia*, vol. 10 (Loeb, 1936).]

[13] [*Patriarcha*, ch. 19, p. 92.]

them: and if this be so, a people has no more security under a prince, than a herd or flock under their master. Tho he desire to be a good husband, yet they must be delivered up to the slaughter when he finds a good market, or a better way of improving his land; but they are often foolish, riotous, prodigal, and wantonly destroy their stock, tho to their own prejudice. We thought that all princes and magistrates had been set up, that under them we might live quietly and peaceably, in all godliness and honesty: but our author teaches us, that they only seek what they can make of our bodies and goods, and that they do not live and reign for us, but for themselves. If this be true, they look upon us not as children, but as beasts, nor do us any good for our own sakes, or because it is their duty, but only that we may be useful to them, as oxen are put into plentiful pastures that they may be strong for labour, or fit for slaughter. This is the divine model of government that he offers to the world. The just magistrate is the minister of God for our good: but this absolute monarch has no other care of us, than as our riches and multitude may increase his own glory and strength. We might easily judge what would be the issue of such a principle, when the being of nations depending upon his will, must also depend upon his opinion, whether the strength, multitude and riches of a people do conduce to the increase of glory and power, or not, tho histories were silent in the case; for these things speak of themselves. The judgment of a single man is not to be relied upon; the best and wisest do often err, the foolish and perverse always; and our discourse is not of what Moses or Samuel would do, but what may come into the fancy of a furious or wicked man who may usurp the supreme power, or a child, a woman, or a fool, that may inherit it. Besides, the proposition upon which he builds his conclusion, proves often false: for as the riches, power, number and courage of our friends is for our advantage, and that of our enemies threatens us with ruin; those princes only can reasonably believe the strength of their subjects beneficial to them, who govern so as to be assured of their affection, and that their strength will be employ'd for them: But those who know they are, or deserve to be hated, cannot but think it will be employ'd against them, and always seek to diminish that which creates their danger. This must certainly befall as many as are lewd, foolish, negligent, imprudent, cowardly, wicked, vicious, or any way unworthy the places they obtain; for their reign is a perpetual exercise of the most extreme and ruinous injustice: Every man that follows an honest interest, is prejudic'd: Every-one who finds the power that was ordained for his good, to be turned to his hurt, will be angry and hate him that does it: If the people be of uncorrupted manners, this hatred will be universal, because every one of them desires that which is just; if composed of good and evil, the first will always be averse to the evil government, and the others endeavouring to uphold it, the safety of the prince must depend upon the prevalence of either party. If the best prove to be the strongest, he must perish: and knowing himself to be supported only by the worst, he will always destroy as many of his enemies as he can; weaken those that remain; enrich his creatures with their spoils and confiscations; by fraud and rapine accumulate treasures to increase the number of his party, and advance them into all places of power and trust, that by their assistance he may crush his adversaries; and every man is accounted his adversary, who has either estate, honor, virtue or reputation. This naturally casts all the power into the hands of those who have no such dangerous qualities, nor anything to recommend them, but an absolute resignation of themselves to do whatever they are commanded. These men having neither will nor knowledge to do good, as soon as they come to be in power, justice is perverted, military discipline neglected, the publick treasures exhausted, new projects invented to raise more; and the prince's wants daily increasing, through their ignorance, negligence, or deceit, there is no end of their devices and tricks to gain supplies. To this end swarms of spies, informers and false witnesses are sent out to circumvent the richest and most eminent men: The tribunals are fill'd with court-parasites of profligate consciences, fortunes and reputation, that no man may escape who is brought before them. If crimes are wanting, the diligence of well-chosen officers and prosecutors, with the favour of the judges, supply all defects; the law is made a snare; virtue suppress'd, vice fomented, and in a short time honesty and knavery, sobriety and lewdness, virtue and vice, become badges of the several factions; and every man's conversation and manners shewing to what party he is addicted, the prince who makes himself head of the worst, must favour them to the overthrow of the best, which is so straight a way to an universal ruin, that no state can prevent it, unless that course be interrupted.

These things consider'd, no general judgment can be made of a magistrate's counsels, from his name or duty. He that is just, and become grateful to the people by doing good, will find his own honour and security in increasing their number, riches, virtue, and power: If on the other side, by doing evil, he has drawn upon himself the publick hatred, he will always endeavour to take from them the power of doing him any hurt, by bringing them into the utmost weakness, poverty, and baseness. And whoever would know whether any particular prince desires to increase or destroy the bodies and goods of his subjects, must examine whether his government be such as renders him grateful or odious to them; and whether he do pursue the publick interest, or for the advancement of his own authority set up one in himself contrary to that of his people; which can never befall a popular government, and consequently no mischief equal to it can be produced by any such, unless something can be imagined worse than corruption and destruction.

SECTION 28

Men living under Popular or Mix'd Governments, are more careful of the publick Good, than in Absolute Monarchies.

O UR author delighting in strange things, does in the next place, with an admirable sagacity, discover two faults in popular governments, that were never found by any man before him; and these are no less than ignorance and negligence. Speaking of the care of princes to preserve their subjects, he adds, *On the contrary in a popular state, every man knows the publick good doth not wholly depend upon his care, but the commonwealth may be well enough governed by others, tho he only tend his private business.* And a little below, *Nor are they much to be blamed for their negligence, since it is an even wager their ignorance may be as great. The magistrates amongst the people being for the most part annual, do always lay down their office before they understand it; so as a prince of a duller understanding must needs excel them.*[1] This is bravely determin'd, and the world is beholden to Filmer for the discovery of the errors that have hitherto been epidemical. Most men had believed, that such as live in free states, are usually pleas'd with their condition, desire to maintain it; and every man finding his own good comprehended in the publick, as those that sail in the same ship, employs the talent he has in endeavouring to preserve it, knowing that he must perish if that miscarry. This was an encouragement to industry; and the continual labours and dangers to which the Romans and other free nations exposed themselves, have been taken for testimonies that they thought themselves concerned in the businesses that passed among them, and that everyone did not neglect them through an opinion that they would be done well enough by others. It was also thought that free cities, by frequent elections of magistrates, became nurseries of great and able men,

---

[1] [*Patriarcha*, ch. 19, p. 92.]

every man endeavouring to excel others, that he might be advanced to the honor he had no other title to than what might arise from his merit or reputation; in which they succeeded so well, that one of them may be justly said to have produced more eminent men, than all the absolute monarchies that have been in the world. But these were mistakes. Perhaps Brutus, Valerius, and other Roman senators or magistrates, for the space of three hundred years, might have taken some care of the commonwealth, if they had thought it wholly depended upon one of them. But believing it would be well enough governed by others, they neglected it. Camillus, Cincinnatus, Papirius, Fabius, Rullus and Maximus, Scipio Africanus, Hamilcar, Hannibal, Pericles, Themistocles, Alcibiades, Epaminondas, Philopoemen, and others, might have proved able men in affairs of war or government; but they were removed from their offices before they understood them, and must needs be excelled in both by princes, tho of duller understanding. This may be enough to excuse them for performing their duty so slackly and meanly: But 'tis strange that Tacitus, and others, should so far overlook the reason, and so grossly mistake the matter of fact, as not only to say, that great and excellent spirits failed when liberty was lost, and all preferments given to those who were most propense to slavery; but that there wanted men even to write the history, *inscitia reipublicae ut alienae.*[2] They never applied themselves to understand affairs depending upon the will of one man, in whom they were no otherwise concern'd, than to avoid the effects of his rage; and that was chiefly to be done, by not falling under the suspicion of being virtuous. This was the study then in request; and the most cunning in this art were called *scientes temporum:*[3] No other wisdom was esteemed in that and the ensuing ages, and no more was requir'd, since the paternal care, deep wisdom, and profound judgment of the princes provided for all; and tho they were of duller understandings, they must needs excel other magistrates, who having been created only for a year, left their offices before they could understand the duties of them. This was evidenced by that tenderness and sincerity of heart, as well as the great purity of manners observed in Tiberius; the clemency, justice, solid judgment and frugality of Caligula; the industry, courage and sobriety of Claudius; the good nature and prudent government of Nero; the temperance, vivacity and diligence of Vitellius; the liberality of Galba and Vespasian; together with the encouragement given by Domitian, Commodus, Heliogabalus, and many

---

[2] Tacit. Annal. l. 1. ["Through ignorance of public affairs, which were alien to them." Tacitus, *Annals*, bk. 1, ch. 1, and *Histories*, bk. 1, ch. 1.]

[3] [Knowers of the times.]

others, to all manner of virtues and favours conferred upon those that excelled in them. Our author giving such infallible proof of his integrity and understanding, by teaching us these things that would never have come into our heads, ought to be credited, tho that which he proposes seem to be most absurd. But if we believe such as lived in those times, or those who in later ages have perused their writings, we cannot but think the princes beforementioned, and the greatest part of those who possessed the same place, not only to have been void of all virtue, and to have suffer'd none to grow up under them but in baseness, sottishness and malice, to have been equal to the worst of all beasts. Whilst one prince polluted with lust and blood, sat in his grotto at Capri,[4] surrounded with an infamous troop of astrologers, and others were govern'd by whores, bardashes, manumised slaves, and other villains, the empire was ruin'd through their negligence, incapacity and wickedness; and the city that had flourish'd in all manner of virtue, as much or more than any that has been yet known in the world, produced no more; the discipline was dissolved that nourish'd it; no man could hope to advance a publick good, or obviate an evil by his diligence and valour; and he who acquired reputation by either, could expect no other reward than a cruel death. If Germanicus and Corbulo, who were born when liberty was expiring, be brought for examples against the first part of my assertion, their ends will justify the latter; and no eminent Roman family is known to have brought forth a man that deserved to be named in history since their time. This is as probable in reason, as true in fact. Men are valiant and industrious, when they fight for themselves and their country; they prove excellent in all the arts of war and peace, when they are bred up in virtuous exercises, and taught by their fathers and masters to rejoice in the honors gained by them: they love their country, when the good of every particular man is comprehended in the publick prosperity, and the success of their achievements is improved to the general advantage: They undertake hazards and labours for the government, when 'tis justly administered; when innocence is safe, and virtue honour'd; when no man is distinguish'd from the vulgar, but such as have distinguish'd themselves by the bravery of their actions; when no honor is thought too great for those who do it eminently, unless it be such as cannot be communicated to others of equal merit: They do not spare their persons, purses, or friends, when the publick powers are employ'd for the publick benefit, and imprint the like affections in their children from their infancy. The discipline of obedience in which the Romans were bred, taught them to

[4] [Tiberius.]

command: and few were admitted to the magistracies of inferior rank, till they had given such proof of their virtue as might deserve the supreme. Cincinnatus, Camillus, Papirius, Mamercus, Fabius Maximus, were not made dictators, that they might learn the duties of the office; but because they were judged to be of such wisdom, valour, integrity and experience, that they might be safely trusted with the highest powers; and whilst the law reigned, not one was advanced to that honour, who did not fully answer what was expected from him. By this means the city was so replenished with men fit for the greatest employments, that even in its infancy, when three hundred and six of the Fabii, *Quorum neminem*, says Livy, *ducem sperneret quibuslibet temporibus senatus*,[5] were killed in one day, the city did lament the loss, but was not so weakened to give any advantage to their enemies: and when every one of those who had been eminent before the second Punic War, Fabius Maximus only excepted had perished in it, others arose in their places, who surpassed them in number, and were equal to them in virtue. The city was a perpetual spring of such men as long as liberty lasted; but that was no sooner overthrown, than virtue was torn up by the roots, the people became base and sordid, the small remains of the nobility slothful and effeminate, and their Italian associates becoming like to them, the empire whilst it stood, was only sustained by the strength of foreigners.

The Grecian virtue had the same fate, and expired with liberty: instead of such soldiers as in their time had no equals, and such generals of armies and fleets, legislators and governors, as all succeeding ages have justly admired, they sent out swarms of fiddlers, jesters, chariot-drivers, players, bawds, flatterers, ministers of the most impure lusts; or idle, babbling, hypocritical philosophers not much better than they. The emperors' courts were always crowded with this vermin; and notwithstanding the necessity our author imagines that princes must needs understand matters of government better than magistrates annually chosen, they did for the most part prove so brutish as to give themselves and the world to be governed by such as these, and that without any great prejudice, since none could be found more ignorant, lewd, and base than themselves.

'Tis absurd to impute this to the change of times; for time changes nothing; and nothing was changed in those times but the government, and that changed all things. This is not accidental, but according to the rules given to nature by God, imposing upon all things a necessity of perpetually following their causes. Fruits are always of the same nature

[5] ["None of whom the senate would have rejected as a leader at any period (of Roman history)." Livy, *History of Rome*, bk. 2, ch. 49.]

with the seeds and roots from which they come, and trees are known by the fruits they bear: As a man begets a man, and a beast a beast, that society of men which constitutes a government upon the foundation of justice, virtue, and the common good, will always have men to promote those ends; and that which intends the advancement of one man's desires and vanity, will abound in those that will foment them. All men follow that which seems advantageous to themselves. Such as are bred under a good discipline, and see that all benefits procured to their country by virtuous actions, redound to the honour and advantage of themselves, their children, friends, and relations, contract from their infancy a love to the publick, and look upon the common concernments as their own. When they have learnt to be virtuous, and see that virtue is in esteem, they seek no other preferments than such as may be obtained that way; and no country ever wanted great numbers of excellent men, where this method was established. On the other side, when 'tis evident that the best are despised, hated, or mark'd out for destruction; all things calculated to the humour or advantage of one man, who is often the worst, or govern'd by the worst; honours, riches, commands, and dignities disposed by his will, and his favour gained only by a most obsequious respect, or a pretended affection to his person, together with a servile obedience to his commands, all application to virtuous actions will cease; and no man caring to render himself or his children worthy of great employments, such as desire to have them will by little intrigues, corruption, scurrility and flattery endeavour to make way to them; by which means true merit in a short time comes to be abolish'd, as fell out in Rome as soon as the Caesars began to reign.

He who does not believe this, may see whether the like did not happen in all the other commonwealths of Italy and Greece; or if modern examples are thought to be of more value, let him examine whether the noblemen of Venice, who are born and bred in families that never knew a master, who act for themselves, and have a part in all the good or evil that befalls the commonwealth, and know that if it be destroy'd, they must perish, or at least that all changes are to their prejudice, do neglect the publick interests, as thinking that the whole not depending upon any one of them, things will be well enough governed, tho they attend only their private benefit. Let it be observed whether they do better understand the common concernments, than the great men of France or Spain, who never come to the knowledge of anything, unless they happen to be favour'd by the king or his ministers, and know themselves never to be more miserable than when their master is most prosperous. For my own part, I cannot think it necessary to allege any other proof of this point than that when Maximilian the emperor, Lewis the twelfth of France, the fierce Pope Julius the second, and Ferdinand the subtle, powerful, and bold king of Spain, had by the league of Cambray combin'd against the Venetians, gained the battle of La Ghirad'adda, taken Alviano their general prisoner, deprived them of all their dominion on the *terra firma*, and prepared to assault the city, it was, under God, solely preserved by the vigour and wisdom of their nobility, who tho no way educated to war, unless by sea, sparing neither persons nor purses, did with admirable industry and courage first recover Padua, and then many other cities, so as at the end of that terrible war they came off without any diminution of their territories.[6] Whereas Portugal having in our age revolted from the house of Austria, no one doubts that it had been immediately reduced, if the great men of Spain had not been pleased with such a lessening of their master's power, and resolved not to repair it by the recovery of that kingdom, or to deprive themselves of an easy retreat when they should be oppressed by him or his favourites. The like thought was more plainly express'd by the mareschal de Bassompierre, who seeing how hardly Rochelle was pressed by Lewis the 13th, said, he thought they should be such fools to take it:[7] but 'tis believ'd they would never have been such fools; and the treachery only of our countrymen did enable the Cardinal Richelieu to do it (as for his own glory, and the advancement of the popish cause he really intended) and nothing is to this day more common in the mouth of their wisest and best men, tho papists, than the acknowledgment of their own folly in suffering that place to fall, the king having by that means gotten power to proceed against them at his pleasure. The brave Monsieur de Turenne is said to have carried this to a greater height in his last discourse to the present king of France: "You think, said he, you have armies, but you have none; the one half of the officers are the bawdy-house companions of Monsieur de xxx, or the creatures of his whore Madam de xxx: the other half may be men of experience, and fit for their employments; but they are such as would be pleased with nothing more than to see you lose two or three battles, that coming to stand in need of them, you might cause them to be better used by your ministers than of late they have been." It may easily be imagin'd how men in such sentiments do serve their master; and nothing is more evident than that the French in this age have had so great advantages, that they might have brought Europe, and perhaps Asia, under their power, if the

[6] Paol. Paruta. hist. Venet. Guicciard. [Paolo Poruta, *Istoria Veneziana*, (1605); Guicciardini, *History of Italy*, bk. 8.]

[7] Je croy qu'enfin nous serons assez fous pour prendre la Rochelle. Mem. de Bassompierre. [François de Bassompierre, *Memoires du Mareschal de Bassompierre* (Cologne: Pierre du Marteau, 1666).]

interest of the nation had been united to that of the government, and the strength, vigour, and bravery of the nobility employ'd that way. But since it has pleased God to suffer us to fall into a condition of being little able to help ourselves, and that they are in so good terms with the Turk as not to attack him, 'tis our happiness that they do not know their own strength, or cannot without ruin to themselves turn it to our prejudice.

I could give yet more pregnant testimonies of the difference between men fighting for their own interests in the offices to which they had been advanced by the votes of numerous assemblies, and such as serve for pay, and get preferments by corruption or favour, if I were not unwilling to stir the spleen of some men by obliging them to reflect upon what has passed in our own age and country; to compare the justice of our tribunals within the time of our memory, and the integrity of those who for a while manag'd the publick treasure; the discipline, valour, and strength of our armies and fleets; the increase of our riches and trade; the success of our wars in Scotland, Ireland, and at sea, the glory and reputation not long since gained, with that condition into which we are of late fallen. But I think I shall offend no wise or good man, if I say, that as neither the Romans nor Grecians in the time of their liberty ever performed any actions more glorious than freeing the country from a civil war that had raged in every part, the conquest of two such kingdoms as Scotland and Ireland, and crushing the formidable power of the Hollanders by sea; nor ever produced more examples of valor, industry, integrity, and in all respects compleat, disinterested, unmoveable and incorruptible virtue, than were at that time seen in our nation: So neither of them upon the change of their affairs did exceed us in weakness, cowardice, baseness, venality, lewdness, and all manner of corruption. We have reason therefore not only to believe that all princes do not necessarily understand the affairs of their people, or provide better for them than those who are otherwise chosen; but that, as there is nothing of greatness, power, riches, strength, and happiness, which we might not reasonably have hoped for, if we had rightly improved the advantages we had, so there is nothing of shame and misery which we may not justly fear, since we have neglected them.

If any man think that this evil of advancing officers for personal respects, favour or corruption, is not of great extent, I desire him to consider, that the officers of state, courts of justice, church, armies, fleets and corporations, are of such number and power as wholly to corrupt a nation when they themselves are corrupted; and will ever be corrupt, when they attain to their offices by corruption. The good management of all affairs, civil, military, and ecclesiastical, necessarily depends upon good order and discipline; and 'tis not in the power of common men to reform abuses patronized by those in authority, nor to prevent the mischiefs thereupon ensuing; and not having power to direct publick actions to the publick good, they must consequently want the industry and affection that is required to bring them to a good issue. The Romans were easily beaten under the decemviri, tho immediately before the erection, and after the extinction of that power, none of their neighbours were able to resist them. The Goths who with much glory had reigned in Spain for about three hundred years, had neither strength nor courage under their lewd and odious King Rodrigo, and were in one day subdued with little loss of blood by the Saracens, and could not in less than eight hundred years free their country from them. That brave nation having of late fallen under as base a conduct, has now as little heart or power to defend itself: Court-parasites have rendered valour ridiculous; and they who have ever shew'd themselves as much inclin'd to arms as any people of the world, do now abhor them, and are sent to the wars by force, laid in carts, and bound like calves brought to the shambles, and left to starve in Flanders as soon as they arrive. It may easily be judged what service can be expected from such men, tho they should happen to be well commanded: but the great officers, by the corruption of the court, think only of enriching themselves; and increasing the misery of the soldiers by their frauds, both become equally useless to the state.

Notwithstanding the seeming prosperity of France, matters there are not much better managed. The warlike temper of that people is so worn out by the frauds and cruelties of corrupt officers, that few men list themselves willingly to be soldiers; and when they are engaged or forced, they are so little able to endure the miseries to which they are exposed, that they daily run away from their colours, tho they know not whither to go, and expect no mercy if they are taken. The king has in vain attempted to correct this humour by the severity of martial law; but mens' minds will not be forced, and tho his troops are perfectly well arm'd, cloth'd, and exercised, they have given many testimonies of little worth. When the prince of Condé had by his own valour, and the strength of the king's guards, broken the first line of the prince of Orange's army at the battle of Seneffe, and put the rest into disorder, he could not make the second and third line of his own army to advance and reinforce the first, by which means he lost all the fair hopes he had conceived of an entire victory.[8] Not long after, the marechal de Crequi was abandoned

---

[8] [The battle of Seneffe was fought in 1674 in the war between France and the Neth- erlands. Seneffe is a Belgian village near Brussels.]

by his whole army near Trier, who ran away, hardly striking a stroke, and left him with sixteen horse to shift for himself. When Monsieur de Turenne, by the excellency of his conduct and valour, had gain'd such a reputation amongst the soldiers, that they thought themselves secure under him, he did not suffer such disgraces; but he being kill'd, they return'd to the usual temper of forced and ill-used soldiers: half the army was lost in a retreat, little differing from a flight; and the rest, as they themselves confess, saved by the bravery of two English regiments. The prince of Condé was soon after sent to command; but he could not with all his courage, skill and reputation, raise their fallen spirits, nor preserve his army any other way, than by lodging them in a camp near Schlestadt, so fortified by art and nature that it could not be forc'd.

To these we may add some examples of our own. In our late war the Scots foot, whether friends or enemies, were much inferior to those of the parliament, and their horse esteemed as nothing. Yet in the year 1639 and 1640, the king's army, tho very numerous, excellently armed and mounted, and in appearance able to conquer many such kingdoms as Scotland, being under the conduct of courtiers, and affected as men usually are towards those that use them ill, and seek to destroy them, they could never resist a wretched army commanded by Leven; but were shamefully beaten at Newborn, and left the northern counties to be ravaged by them.[9]

When Van Tromp set upon Blake in Foleston-Bay,[10] the parliament had not above thirteen ships against threescore, and not a man that had ever seen any other fight at sea, than between a merchant ship and a pirate, to oppose the best captain in the world, attended with many others in valour and experience not much inferior to him. Many other difficulties were observ'd in the unsettled state: Few ships, want of money, several factions, and some who to advance particular interests betray'd the publick. But such was the power of wisdom and integrity in those that sat at the helm, and their diligence in chusing men only for their merit was blessed with such success, that in two years our fleets grew to be as famous as our land armies; the reputation and power of our nation rose to a greater height, than when we possessed the better half of France, and the kings of France and Scotland were our prisoners. All the states, kings and potentates of Europe, most respectfully, not to say submissively, sought our friendship; and Rome was more afraid of Blake and his fleet,

[9] [Alexander Leslie, Earl of Leven.]

[10] [Parliament was ruling without a king when Martin Tromp, admiral of the Dutch navy, was defeated in 1652 by the English admiral Robert Blake.]

than they had been of the great king of Sweden, when he was ready to invade Italy with a hundred thousand men. This was the work of those, who, if our author say true, *thought basely of the publick concernments;*[11] and believing things might be well enough managed by others, minded only their private affairs. These were the effects of the negligence and ignorance of those, who being suddenly advanced to offices, were removed before they understood the duties of them. These diseases which proceed from popular corruption and irregularity, were certainly cured by the restitution of that integrity, good order and stability that accompany divine monarchy. The justice of the war made against Holland in the year 1665; the probity of the gentleman, who without partiality or bribery, chose the most part of the officers that carried it on; the wisdom, diligence and valour manifested in the conduct, and the glory with which it was ended, justifies all that our author can say in its commendation. If any doubt remains, the subtlety of making the king of France desire that the Netherlands might be an accession to his crown; the ingenious ways taken by us to facilitate the conquest of them; the industry of our ambassadors in diverting the Spaniards from entering into the war till it was too late to recover the losses sustain'd;[12] the honourable design upon the Smyrna fleet, and our frankness in taking the quarrel upon ourselves; together with the important figure we now make in Europe, may wholly remove it; and in confirmation of our author's doctrine, shew, that princes do better perform the offices that require wisdom, industry and valour, than annual magistrates; and do more seldom err in the choice of officers, than senates and popular assemblies.

SECTION 29

There is no assurance that the Distempers of a State
shall be cured by the Wisdom of a Prince.

B UT, says our author, *the virtue and wisdom of a prince supplies all. Tho he were of a duller understanding, by use and experience he must needs excel all:*[1] Nature, age, or sex, are, as it seems, nothing to the case. A child as soon as he comes to be a king, has experience; the head of a fool is filled with wisdom, as soon as a crown is set upon it, and the most vicious do

[11] [*Patriarcha*, ch. 18, p. 90.]
[12] [The Thirty Years War.]   [1] [*Patriarcha*, ch. 19, p. 92.]

in a moment become virtuous. This is more strange than that an ass being train'd to a course, should outrun the best Arabian horse; or a hare bred up in an army, become more strong and fierce than a lion; for fortune does not only supply all natural defects in princes, and correct their vices, but gives them the benefit of use and experience, when they have none. Some reasons and examples might have been expected to prove this extraordinary proposition: But according to his laudable custom, he is pleased to trouble himself with neither; and thinks that the impudence of an assertion is sufficient to make that to pass, which is repugnant to experience and common sense, as may appear by the following discourse.

I will not insist upon terms; for tho *duller understanding* signifies nothing, in as much as no understanding is dull, and a man is said to be dull only because he wants it; but presuming he means little understanding, I shall so take it. This defect may possibly be repair'd in time; but to conclude it must be so, is absurd, for no one has this use and experience when he begins to reign. At that time many errors may be committed to the ruin of himself or people, and many have perish'd even in their beginning. Edward the fifth and sixth of England, Francis the second of France, and divers other kings have died in the beginning of their youth: Charles the ninth lived only to add the furies of youth to the follies of his childhood; and our Henry the second, Edward the second, Richard the second, and Henry the sixth, seem to have been little wiser in the last, than in the first year of their reign or life. The present kings of Spain, France, and Sweden, came to the crowns they wear before the sixth year of their age; and if they did then surpass all annual magistrates in wisdom and valour, it was by a peculiar gift of God, which, for anything we know, is not given to every king, and it was not use and experience that made them to excel. If it be pretended that this experience, with the wisdom that it gives, comes in time and by degrees; I may modestly ask, what time is requir'd to render a prince excellent in wisdom who is a child or a fool? and who will give security that he shall live to that time, or that the kingdom shall not be ruin'd in the time of his folly? I may also doubt how our author, who concludes that every king in time must needs become excellent in wisdom, can be reconciled to Solomon, who in preferring a wise child before an old and foolish king that will not be advised, shews that an old king may be a fool, and he that will not be advised is one. Some are so naturally brutish and stupid, that neither education nor time will mend them. 'Tis probable that Solomon took what care he could to instruct his only son Rehoboam; but he was certainly a fool at forty years of age, and we have no reason to believe that he deserved a better name. He seems to have been the very fool his father intended, who tho brayed in a mortar would never leave his folly: He would not be advised, tho the hand of God was against him; ten tribes revolted from him, and the city and temple was pillaged by the Egyptians. Neither experience nor afflictions could mend him, and he is called to this day by his own countrymen *stultitia gentium*.[2] I might offend tender ears, if I should allege all the examples of princes mentioned in history, or known in our own age, who have lived and died as foolish and incorrigible as he: but no man, I presume, will be scandalized, that the ten last kings of Meroveus his race, whom the French historians call *les roys faineants*, were so far from excelling other men in understanding, that they liv'd and died more like to beasts than men. Nay, the wisdom and valour of Charles Martel expired in his grandchild Charles the Great; and his posterity grew to be so sottish, that the French nation must have perished under their conduct, if the nobility and people had not rejected them, and placed the crown upon a more deserving head.

This is as much as is necessary to be said to the general proposition; for it is false, if it be not always true; and no conclusion can be made upon it. But I need not be so strict with our author, there being no one sound part in his assertion. Many children come to be kings when they have no experience, and die, or are depos'd before they can gain any. Many are by nature so sottish that they can learn nothing: Others falling under the power of women, or corrupt favorites and ministers, are persuaded and seduced from the good ways to which their own natural understanding or experience might lead them; the evils drawn upon themselves or their subjects, by the errors committed in the time of their ignorance, are often grievous, and sometimes irreparable, tho they should be made wise by time and experience. A person of royal birth and excellent wit, was so sensible of this as to tell me, "That the condition of kings was most miserable, in as much as they never heard truth till they were ruin'd by lies, and then everyone was ready to tell it to them, not by way of advice, but reproach, and rather to vent their own spite, than to seek a remedy to the evils brought upon them and the people." Others attain to crowns when they are of full age, and have experience as men, tho none as kings; and therefore are apt to commit as great mistakes as children: And upon the whole matter all the histories of the world shew, that instead of this profound judgment and incomparable wisdom which our author generally attributes to all kings, there is no sort of men that do more frequently and entirely want it.

But tho kings were always wise by nature, or made to be so by

---

[2] [Folly of nations.]

experience, it would be of little advantage to nations under them, unless their wisdom were pure, perfect, and accompanied with clemency, magnanimity, justice, valour and piety. Our author durst hardly have said, that these virtues or graces are gained by experience, or annexed by God to any rank of men or families. He gives them where he pleases without distinction. We sometimes see those upon thrones, who by God and nature seem to have been designed for the most sordid offices; and those have been known to pass their lives in meanness and poverty, who had all the qualities that could be desir'd in princes. There is likewise a kind of ability to dispatch some sort of affairs, that princes who continue long in a throne may to a degree acquire or increase. Some men take this for wisdom, but K. James more rightly called it by the name of *kingcraft;* and as it principally consists in dissimulation, and the arts of working upon mens' passions, vanities, private interests or vices, to make them for the most part instruments of mischief, it has the advancement or security of their own persons for object, is frequently exercised with all the excesses of pride, avarice, treachery and cruelty; and no men have been ever found more notoriously to deflect from all that deserves praise in a prince, or a gentleman, than those that have most excelled in it. Pharasmenes king of Iberia, is recorded by Tacitus to have been well vers'd in this science. His brother Mithridates king of Armenia had married his daughter, and given his own daughter to Rhadamistus son of Pharasmenes. He had some contests with Mithridates, but by the help of these mutual alliances, nearness of blood, the diligence of Rhadamistus, and an oath, strengthen'd with all the ceremonies that amongst those nations were esteemed most sacred, not to use arms or poison against him, all was compos'd; and by this means getting him into his power, he stifled him with a great weight of clothes thrown upon him, kill'd his children, and not long after his own son Rhadamistus also.[3] Louis the eleventh of France, James the third of Scotland, Henry the seventh of England, were great masters of these arts; and those who are acquainted with history, will easily judge how happy nations would be if all kings did in time certainly learn them.

Our author, as a farther testimony of his judgment, having said that kings must needs excel others in understanding, and grounded his doctrine upon their profound wisdom, imputes to them those *base and panick fears* which are inconsistent with it, or any royal virtue: and to carry the point higher, tells us, *There is no tyrant so barbarously wicked, but his own reason*

---

[3] Tacit. An. l. 11. 12. [Tacitus, *Annals*, bk. 12, ch. 44–48.]

and sense will tell him, that tho he be a god, yet he must die like a man; and that there is not the meanest of his subjects, but may find a means to revenge himself of the injuries offer'd him; and from thence concludes, that *there is no such tyranny as that of a multitude which is subject to no such fears.*[4] But if there be such a thing in the world, as a barbarous and wicked tyrant, he is something different from a king, or the same; and his wisdom is consistent or inconsistent with barbarity, wickedness, and tyranny. If there be no difference, the praises he gives, and the rights he ascribes to the one belong also to the other: and the excellency of wisdom may consist with barbarity, wickedness, tyranny, and the panick fears that accompany them; which hitherto have been thought to comprehend the utmost excesses of folly and madness: and I know no better testimony of the truth of that opinion, than that wisdom always distinguishing good from evil, and being seen only in the rectitude of that distinction, in following and adhering to the good, rejecting that which is evil, preferring safety before danger, happiness before misery, and in knowing rightly how to use the means of attaining or preserving the one, and preventing or avoiding the other, there cannot be a more extravagant deviation from reason, than for a man, who in a private condition might live safely and happily, to invade a principality: or if he be a prince, who by governing with justice and clemency might obtain the inward satisfaction of his own mind, hope for the blessing of God upon his just and virtuous actions, acquire the love and praises of men, and live in safety and happiness amongst his safe and happy subjects, to fall into that barbarity, wickedness, and tyranny, which brings upon him the displeasure of God, and detestation of men, and which is always attended with those base and panick fears, that comprehend all that is shameful and miserable. This being perceiv'd by Machiavelli, he could not think that any man in his senses would not rather be a Scipio than a Caesar; or if he came to be a prince, would not rather chuse to imitate Agesilaus, Timoleon, or Dion, than Nabis, Phalaris, or Dionysius; and imputes the contrary choice to madness.[5] Nevertheless 'tis too well known that many of our author's profound wise men in the depth of their judgment, made perfect by use and experience, have fallen into it.

If there be a difference between this barbarous wicked tyrant, and a king, we are to examine who is the tyrant, and who the king; for the name conferred or assumed cannot make a king, unless he be one. He

[4] [*Patriarcha*, ch. 19, p. 92.]

[5] Discors. sopra T. Liv. l. 1. c. 10. [Machiavelli, *Discourses on Livy*, bk. 1, ch. 10.]

who is not a king, can have no title to the rights belonging to him who is truly a king: so that a people who find themselves wickedly and barbarously oppressed by a tyrant, may destroy him and his tyranny without giving offence to any king.

But 'tis strange that Filmer should speak of the barbarity and wickedness of a tyrant, who looks upon the world to be the patrimony of one man; and for the foundation of his doctrine, asserts such a power in everyone that makes himself master of any part, as cannot be limited by any law. His title is not to be questioned; usurpation and violence confer an incontestable right: the exercise of his power is no more to be disputed than the acquisition: his will is a law to his subjects; and no law can be imposed by them upon his conduct. For if these things be true, I know not how any man could ever be called a tyrant, that name having never been given to any unless for usurping a power that did not belong to him, or an unjust exercise of that which had been conferred upon him, and violating the laws which ought to be a rule to him. 'Tis also hard to imagine how any man can be called barbarous and wicked, if he be obliged by no law but that of his own pleasure; for we have no other notion of wrong, than that it is a breach of the law which determines what is right. If the lives and goods of subjects depend upon the will of the prince, and he in his profound wisdom preserve them only to be beneficial to himself, they can have no other right than what he gives, and without injustice may retain when he thinks fit: If there be no wrong, there can be no just revenge; and he that pretends to seek it, is not a free man vindicating his right, but a perverse slave rising up against his master. But if there be such a thing as a barbarous and wicked tyrant, there must be a rule relating to the acquisition and exercise of the power, by which he may be distinguish'd from a just king; and a law superior to his will, by the violation of which he becomes barbarous and wicked.

Tho our author so far forgets himself, to confess this to be true, he seeks to destroy the fruits of it by such flattery as comprehends all that is most detestable in profaneness and blasphemy, and gives the name of gods to the most execrable of men. He may by such language deserve the name of Heylyn's disciple; but will find few among the heathens so basely servile, or so boldly impious. Tho Claudius Caesar was a drunken sot, and transported with the extravagance of his fortune, he detested the impudence of his predecessor Caligula (who affected that title), and in his rescript to the procurator of Judea, gives it no better name than *turpem Caii insaniam.*[6] For this reason it was rejected by all his pagan successors,

[6] ["Base insanity of Gaius." Josephus, *Jewish Antiquities*, bk. 19, ch. 5, sec. 2.]

who were not as furiously wicked as he: yet Filmer has thought fit to renew it, for the benefit of mankind, and the glory of the Christian religion.

I know not whether these extreme and barbarous errors of our author are to be imputed to wickedness or madness; or whether, to save the pains of a distinction, they may not rightly be said to be the same thing; but nothing less than the excess of both could induce him to attribute anything of good to the fears of a tyrant, since they are the chief causes of all the mischiefs he does. Tertullian says they are *metu quam furore saeviores;*[7] and Tacitus, speaking of a most wicked king, says, that he did *saevitiam ignaviae obtendere;*[8] and we do not more certainly find that cowards are the cruelest of men, than that wickedness makes them cowards; that every man's fears bear a proportion with his guilt, and with the number, virtue, and strength of those he has offended. He who usurps a power over all, or abuses a trust reposed in him by all, in the highest measure offends all; he fears and hates those he has offended, and to secure himself, aggravates the former injuries: When these are publick, they beget a universal hatred, and every man desires to extinguish a mischief that threatens ruin to all. This will always be terrible to one that knows he has deserved it; and when those he dreads are the body of the people, nothing but a publick destruction can satisfy his rage, and appease his fears.

I wish I could agree with Filmer, in exempting multitudes from fears; for they having seldom committed any injustice, unless through fear, would, as far as human fragility permits, be free from it. Tho the *Attick ostracism* was not an extreme punishment, I know nothing usually practised in any commonwealth, that did so much favour of injustice: but it proceeded solely from a fear that one man, tho in appearance virtuous, when he came to be raised too much above his fellow citizens, might be tempted to invade the publick liberty. We do not find that the Athenians, or any other free cities, ever injur'd any man, unless through such a jealousy, or the perjury of witnesses, by which the best tribunals that ever were, or can be establish'd in the world, may be misled; and no injustice could be apprehended from any, if they did not fall into such fears.

But tho multitudes may have fears as well as tyrants, the causes and effects of them are very different. A people, in relation to domestick affairs, can desire nothing but liberty, and neither hate or fear any but such as do, or would, as they suspect, deprive them of that happiness:

---

[7] ["More savage from fear than from madness."]

[8] ["Make savagery a cover for cowardice." Tacitus, *Annals*, bk. 12, ch. 10.]

Their endeavours to secure that seldom hurt any except such as invade their rights; and if they err, the mistake is for the most part discovered before it produce any mischief; and the greatest that ever came that way, was the death of one or a few men. Their hatred and desire of revenge can go no farther than the sense of the injury received or feared, and is extinguished by the death or banishment of the persons; as may be gathered from the examples of the Tarquins, decemviri, Cassius, Maelius, and Manlius Capitolinus. He therefore that would know whether the hatred and fear of a tyrant, or of a people, produces the greater mischiefs, needs only to consider, whether it be better that the tyrant destroy the people, or that the people destroy the tyrant: or at the worst, whether one that is suspected of affecting the tyranny should perish, or a whole people, amongst whom very many are certainly innocent; and experience shows that such are always first sought out to be destroy'd for being so: Popular furies or fears, how irregular or unjust soever they may be, can extend no farther; general calamities can only be brought upon a people by those who are enemies to the whole body, which can never be the multitude, for they are that body. In all other respects, the fears that render a tyrant cruel, render a people gentle and cautious; for every single man knowing himself to be of little power, not only fears to do injustice because it may be revenged upon his person, by him, or his friends, kindred and relations that suffers it; but because it tends to the overthrow of the government, which comprehends all publick and private concern-ments, and which every man knows cannot subsist unless it be so easy and gentle, as to be pleasing to those who are the best, and have the greatest power: and as the publick considerations divert them from doing those injuries that may bring immediate prejudice to the publick, so there are strict laws to restrain all such as would do private injuries. If neither the people nor the magistrates of Venice, Switzerland, and Holland, commit such extravagances as are usual in other places, it does not perhaps proceed from the temper of those nations different from others, but from a knowledge, that whosoever offers an injury to a private person, or attempts a publick mischief, is exposed to the impartial and inexorable power of the law; whereas the chief work of an absolute monarch is to place himself above the law, and thereby rendering himself the author of all the evils that the people suffer, 'tis absurd to expect that he should remove them.

SECTION 30

A *Monarchy cannot be well regulated, unless the Powers of the Monarch are limited by Law.*

Our author's next step is not only to reject popular governments, but all such monarchies as are not absolute: *for if the king*, says he, *admits the people to be his companions, he leaves to be a king.*[1] This is the language of French lackeys, valet de chambres, tailors, and others like them in wisdom, learning and policy, who when they fly to England for fear of a well-deserved galley, gibbet, or wheel, are ready to say, *Il faut que le roy soit absolu, autrement il n'est point roy.*[2] And finding no better men to agree with Filmer in this sublime philosophy, I may be pardoned if I do not follow them, till I am convinced in these ensuing points.

1. It seems absurd to speak of kings admitting the nobility or people to part of the government: for tho there may be, and are nations without kings, yet no man can conceive a king without a people. These must necessarily have all the power originally in themselves; and tho kings may and often have a power of granting honors, immunities, and privileges to private men or corporations, he does it only out of the publick stock, which he is entrusted to distribute; but can give nothing to the people, who give to him all that he can rightly have.

2. 'Tis strange that he who frequently cites Aristotle and Plato, should unluckily acknowledge such only to be kings as they call tyrants, and deny the name of king to those, who in their opinion are the only kings.

3. I cannot understand why the Scripture should call those kings whose powers were limited, if they only are kings who are absolute; or why Moses did appoint that the power of kings in Israel should be limited (if they resolved to have them) if that limitation destroy'd the being of a king.[3]

4. And lastly, how he knows that in the kingdoms which have a shew of popularity, the power is wholly in the king.

The first point was proved when we examined the beginning of monarchies, and found it impossible that there could be anything of justice in them, unless they were established by the common consent of those who were to live under them; or that they could make any such establishment, unless the right and power were in them.

---

[1] [*Patriarcha*, ch. 20 ("Of a Mixed Government of King and People: The People May Not Correct their King"), p. 93.]

[2] ["The king must be absolute, or he is no king at all."]

[3] Deut. 17.

Secondly, neither Plato nor Aristotle acknowledge either reason or justice in the power of a monarch, unless he has more of the virtues conducing to the good of the civil society than all those who compose it; and employ them for the publick advantage, and not to his own pleasure and profit, as being set up by those who seek their own good, for no other reason than that he should procure it. To this end a law is set as a rule to him, and the best men, that is such as are most like to himself, made to be his assistants, because, say they, *Lex est mens sine affectu, & quasi Deus;*[4] whereas the best of men have their affections and passions and are subject to be misled by them: Which shews, that as the monarch is not for himself nor by himself, he does not give, but receive power, nor admit others to the participation of it, but is by them admitted to what he has. Whereupon they conclude, that to prefer the absolute power of a man, as in those governments which they call *barbarorum regna,*[5] before the regular government of kings justly exercising a power instituted by law, and directed to the publick good, is to chuse rather to be subject to the lust of a beast than to be governed by a god. And because such a choice can only be made by a beast, I leave our author to find a description of himself in their books which he so often cites.

But if Aristotle deserve credit, the princes who reign for themselves and not for the people, preferring their own pleasure or profit before the publick, become tyrants; which in his language is enemies to God and man. On this account Boccalini introduces the princes of Europe raising a mutiny against him in Parnassus, for giving such definitions of tyrants as they said comprehended them all; and forcing the poor philosopher to declare by a new definition, that *Tyrants were certain men of ancient times whose race is now extinguished.*[6] But with all his wit and learning he could not give a reason why those who do the same things that rendered the ancient tyrants detestable, should not be so also in our days.

In the third place, the Scriptures declare the necessity of setting bounds to those who are placed in the highest dignities. Moses seems to have had as great abilities as any man that ever lived in the world; but he alone was not able to bear the weight of the government, and therefore God appointed seventy chosen men to be his assistants. This was a perpetual law to Israel; and as no king was to have more power than Moses, or more abilities to perform the duties of his office, none could

---

[4] Plat. de Leg. Arist. Polit. [Plato, *Laws*, bk. 9, 875a. The quotation, "law is mind without passion and is, as it were, God," is from Aristotle, *Politics*, bk. 3, 1287a.]

[5] [Kingdoms of barbarians.]

[6] Che i tiranni furono certi huomini del tempo antico de i quali hoggidi si e perduta la razza. Boccal. Rag. de Parn. [Boccalini, *Advertisements from Parnassus*, cent. 1, rag. 76.]

be exempted from the necessity of wanting the like helps. Our author therefore must confess that they are kings who have them, or that kingly government is contrary to the Scriptures. When God by Moses gave liberty to his people to make a king, he did it under these conditions. *He must be one of their brethren: They must chuse him: he must not multiply gold, silver, wives, or horses: he must not lift up his heart above his brethren.*[7] And Josephus paraphrasing upon the place, says, *He shall do nothing without the advice of the Sanhedrin; or if he do, they shall oppose him.*[8] This agrees with the confession of Zedekiah to the princes (which was the Sanhedrin) *The king can do nothing without you;*[9] and seems to have been in pursuance of the law of the kingdom, which was written in a book, and laid up before the Lord; and could not but agree with that of Moses, unless they spake by different spirits, or that the spirit by which they did speak was subject to error or change: and the whole series of God's law shews, that the pride, magnificence, pomp and glory usurped by their kings was utterly contrary to the will of God. They did lift up their hearts above their brethren, which was forbidden by the law. All the kings of Israel, and most of the kings of Judah utterly rejected it, and every one of them did very much depart from the observation of it. I will not deny that the people in their institution of a king intended they should do so: they had done it themselves, and would have a king that might uphold them in their disobedience; they were addicted to the idolatry of their accursed neighbours, and desired that government by which it was maintained amongst them. In doing this they did not reject Samuel; but they rejected God that he should not reign over them. They might perhaps believe that unless their king were such as the law did not permit, he would not perform what they intended; or that the name of king did not belong to him, unless he had a power that the law denied. But since God and his prophets give the name of king to the chief magistrate, endow'd with a power that was restrain'd within very narrow limits, whom they might without offence set up, we also may safely give the same to those of the same nature, whether it please Filmer or not.

4. The practice of most nations, and (I may truly say) of all that deserve imitation, has been as directly contrary to the absolute power of one man as their constitutions: or if the original of many governments lie hid in the impenetrable darkness of antiquity, their progress may serve to shew the intention of the founders. Aristotle seems to think that the first

---

[7] Deut. 17. [9] Jer. 38.

[8] Jos. Ant. Jud. [Josephus, *Jewish Antiquities*, bk. 4, ch. 8.]

monarchs having been chosen for their virtue, were little restrain'd in the exercise of their power; but that they or their children falling into corruption and pride, grew odious; and that nations did on that account either abolish their authority, or create senates and other magistrates, who having part of the power might keep them in order.[10] The Spartan kings were certainly of this nature; and the Persian, till they conquer'd Babylon. Nay, I may safely say, that neither the kings which the frantick people set up in opposition to the law of God, nor those of the bordering nations, whose example they chose to follow, had that absolute power which our author attributes to all kings as inseparable from the name. Achish the Philistine lov'd and admir'd David; he look'd upon him as an angel of God, and promised that he should be the keeper of his head forever; but when the princes suspected him, and said *he shall not go down with us to battle*, he was obliged to dismiss him.[11] This was not the language of slaves, but of those who had a great part in the government; and the king's submission to their will, shows that he was more like to the kings of Sparta, than to an absolute monarch who does whatever pleases him. I know not whether the Spartans were descended from the Hebrews, as some think; but their kings were under a regulation much like that of the 17 of Deut. tho they had two: Their senate of twenty eight, and the ephori, had a power like to that of the Sanhedrin; and by them kings were condemned to fines, imprisonment, banishment, and death, as appears by the examples of Pausanias, Cleonymus, Leonidas, Agis, and others. The Hebrew discipline was the same; *Reges Davidicae stirpis*, says Maimonides, *judicabant & judicabantur*.[12] They gave testimony in judgment when they were called, and testimony was given against them: Whereas the kings of Israel, as the same author says, were *superbi, corde elati, & spretores legis, nec judicabant, nec judicabantur;*[13] proud, insolent, and contemners of the law, who would neither judge, nor submit to judgment as the law commanded. The fruits they gathered were suitable to the seed they had sown: their crimes were not left unpunish'd: they who despised the law were destroy'd without law; and when no ordinary course could be taken against them for their excesses, they were overthrown by force, and the crown within the space of few years transported into nine several families, with the utter extirpation of those that had possess'd

---

[10] [Aristotle, *Politics*, bk. 3, 1286b.]

[11] 1 Sam. 29.

[12] More Nevochim. ["Kings of the line of David judged and were judged." *More Nevochim (Guide of the Perplexed)*, appears incorrect; the reference is to *The Code of Maimonides*

(Mishneh Torah), Book 14: The Book of Judges (New Haven: Yale University Press, 1949), Treatise One: Sanhedrin, ch. 2, p. 8.]

[13] Ibid. ["The proud, exalted in heart, and despisers of the law, did not judge nor were they judged."]

it. On the other hand, there never was any sedition against the Spartan kings; and after the moderate discipline according to which they liv'd, was established, none of them died by the hands of their subjects, except only two, who were put to death in a way of justice: the kingdom continued in the same races, till Cleomenes was defeated by Antigonus, and the government overthrown by the insolence of the Macedonians. This gave occasion to those bestial tyrants Nabis and Machanidas to set up such a government as our author recommends to the world, which immediately brought destruction upon themselves, and the whole city. The Germans who pretended to be descended from the Spartans, had the like government. Their princes according to their merit had the credit of persuading, not the power of commanding; and the question was not what part of the government their kings would allow to the nobility and people, but what they would give to their kings;[14] and 'tis not much material to our present dispute, whether they learnt this from some obscure knowledge of the law which God gave to his people, or whether led by the light of reason which is also from God, they discovered what was altogether conformable to that law. Whoever understands the affairs of Germany, knows that the present emperors, notwithstanding their haughty title, have a power limited as in the days of Tacitus. If they are good and wise, they may persuade; but they can command no farther than the law allows. They do not admit the princes, noblemen, and cities to the power which they all exercise in their general diets, and each of them within their own precincts; but they exercise that which has been by publick consent bestow'd upon them. All the kingdoms peopled from the north observed the same rules. In all of them the powers were divided between the kings, the nobility, clergy, and commons; and by the decrees of councils, diets, parliaments, cortes, and assemblies of estates, authority and liberty were so balanced, that such princes as assumed to themselves more than the law did permit, were severely punished; and those who did by force or fraud invade thrones, were by force thrown down from them.

This was equally beneficial to kings and people. The powers, as Theopompus king of Sparta said, were most safe when they were least envied and hated.[15] Lewis the 11th of France was one of the first that broke this golden chain; and by more subtle arts than had been formerly known, subverted the laws, by which the fury of those kings had been restrain'd, and taught others to do the like; tho all of them have not so

[14] Tacit. de morib. Germ. [Tacitus, *Germania*, ch. 11.] [15] [Plutarch, *Life of Lycurgus*, ch. 7.]

well saved themselves from punishment. James the third of Scotland was one of his most apt scholars; and Buchanan in his life says, *That he was precipitated into all manner of infamy by men of the most abject condition; that the corruption of those times, and the ill example of neighbouring princes, were considerable motives to pervert him: for Edward the fourth of England, Charles of Burgundy, Lewis the 11th of France, and John the second of Portugal, had already laid the foundations of tyranny in those countries; and Richard the third was then most cruelly exercising the same in the kingdom of England.*[16]

This could not have been, if all the power had always been in kings, and neither the people nor the nobility had ever had any: For no man can be said to gain that which he and his predecessors always possessed, or to take from others that which they never had; nor to set up any sort of government, if it had been always the same. But the foresaid Lewis the 11th did assume to himself a power above that of his predecessors; and Philippe de Comines shews the ways by which he acquir'd it, with the miserable effects of his acquisition both to himself and to his people: Modern authors observe that the change was made by him, and for that reason he is said by Mezeray, and others, *to have brought those kings out of guardianship:*[17] they were not therefore so till he did emancipate them. Nevertheless this emancipation had no resemblance to the unlimited power of which our author dreams. The general assemblies of estates were often held long after his death, and continued in the exercise of the sovereign power of the nation. Davila, speaking of the general assembly held at Orleans in the time of Francis the second, asserts the whole power of the nation to have been in them.[18] Monsieur de Thou says the same thing, and adds, that the king dying suddenly, the assembly continued, even at the desire of the council, in the exercise of that power, till they had settled the regency, and other affairs of the highest importance, according to their own judgment.[19] Hotman a lawyer of that time and nation, famous for his learning, judgment and integrity, having diligently examin'd the ancient laws and histories of that kingdom, distinctly proves that the French nation never had any kings but of their own chus-

---

[16] Ab hominibus infimae sortis in omnia simul vitia est praeceps datus: tempora etiam corrupta & vicinorum regum exempla non parum ad eum evertendum juverunt: nam & Edvardus in Anglia, Carolus in Burgundia, Ludovicus undecimus in Gallia, Joannes secundus in Lusitania, tyrannidis fundamenta jecerunt: Richardus tertius in Anglia eam immanissime exercuit. Hist. Scot. l. 12. [Buchanan, *History of Scotland*, bk. 12.]

[17] Davoir mis les roys hors de page. [Mézeray, *Life of Louis XI*, in *General Chronological History of France*, p. 481.]

[18] Hist. delle guerre Civ. [Enrico Caterino Davila, *Historia delle guerre civili di Francia* (1630). Translated as *The History of the Civil Wars of France* (London, 1647).]

[19] Thuan. Hist. l. 1. [de Thou, *History of His Time*, bk. 27 (the year 1560).]

ing; that their kings had no power except what was conferr'd upon them; and that they had been removed, when they excessively abused, or rendered themselves unworthy of that trust.[20] This is sufficiently clear by the forecited examples of Pharamond's grandchildren, and the degenerated races of Meroveus and Pepin; of which many were deposed, some of the nearest in blood excluded; and when their vices seemed to be incorrigible, they were wholly rejected. All this was done by virtue of that rule which they call the Salic Law: And tho some of our princes pretending to the inheritance of that crown by marrying the heirs general, denied that there was any such thing, no man can say that for the space of above twelve hundred years, females, or their descendants, who are by that law excluded, have ever been thought to have any right to the crown: And no law, unless it be explicitly given by God, can be of greater authority than one which has been in force for so many ages. What the beginning of it was is not known: But Charles the sixth receding from this law, and thinking to dispose of the succession otherwise than was ordained by it, was esteemed mad, and all his acts rescinded. And tho the reputation, strength and valour of the English, commanded by Henry the fifth, one of the bravest princes that have ever been in the world, was terrible to the French nation; yet they opposed him to the utmost of their power, rather than suffer that law to be broken. And tho our success under his conduct was great and admirable; yet soon after his death, with the expence of much blood and treasure, we lost all that we had on that side, and suffer'd the penalty of having unadvisedly entered into that quarrel.[21] By virtue of the same law, the agreement made by King John when he was prisoner at London, by which he had alienated part of that dominion, as well as that of Francis the first, concluded when he was under the same circumstances at Madrid, were reputed null; and upon all occasions that nation has given sufficient testimony, that the laws by which they live are their own, made by themselves, and not imposed upon them. And 'tis as impossible for them who made and deposed kings, exalted or depressed reigning families, and prescribed rules to the succession, to have received from their own creatures the power, or part of the government they had, as for a man to be begotten by his own son. Nay, tho their constitutions were much changed by Lewis the 11th, yet they retained so much of their ancient liberty, that in the last age, when the house of Valois was as much

---

[20] Hottom. Franco-Gallia. [François Hotman, *Francogallia* (Geneva, 1573), ch. 6. Trans. as *Franco-Gallia: Or, an Account of the Ancient Free State of France, and Most Other Parts of Europe, before the Loss of their Liberties* (London, 1711).]

[21] [The Hundred Years War, 1338–1453.]

depraved as those of Meroveus and Pepin had been, and Henry the third by his own lewdness, hypocrisy, cruelty and impurity, together with the baseness of his minions and favorites, had rendered himself odious and contemptible to the nobility and people; the great cities, parliaments, the greater and (in political matters) the sounder part of the nation declared him to be fallen from the crown, and pursued him to the death, tho the blow was given by the hand of a base and half-distracted monk.

Henry of Bourbon was without controversy the next heir; but neither the nobility nor the people, who thought themselves in the government, would admit him to the crown, till he had given them satisfaction that he would govern according to their laws, by abjuring his religion which they judged inconsistent with them.[22]

The later commotions in Paris, Bordeaux, and other places, together with the wars for religion, shew, that tho the French do not complain of every grievance, and cannot always agree in the defence and vindication of their violated liberties, yet they very well understand their rights; and that, as they do not live by, or for the king, but he reigns by, and for them; so their privileges are not from him, but that his crown is from them; and that, according to the true rule of their government, he can do nothing against their laws, or if he do, they may oppose him.

The institution of a kingdom is the act of a free nation; and whoever denies them to be free, denies that there can be anything of right in what they set up. That which was true in the beginning is so, and must be so forever. This is so far acknowledged by the highest monarchs, that in a treatise published in the year 1667, by authority of the present king of France, to justify his pretensions to some part of the Low-Countries, notwithstanding all the acts of himself, and the king of Spain to extinguish them, it is said, *That kings are under the happy inability to do anything against the laws of their country.*[23] And tho perhaps he may do things contrary to law, yet he grounds his power upon the law; and the most able and most trusted of his ministers declare the same. About the year 1660, the Count d' Aubijoux, a man of eminent quality in Languedoc, but averse to the court, and hated by Cardinal Mazarin, had been tried by the Parliament of Toulouse for a duel, in which a gentleman was kill'd; and it appearing to the court (then in that city) that he had been acquitted upon forged

---

[22] [Henry IV was forced to renounce Calvinism before ascending the throne of Catholic France in 1589.]

[23] Que les roys ont cette bienheureuse impuissance de ne pouvoir rien faire contre les loix de leur pays. *Traité des droits de la Reyne.*

[Antoin Bilain(?), *Traitté des droits de la reyne très chrestienne sur divers estats de la monarchie d'Espagne* (Paris, 1667). Trans. as *A Dialogue Concerning the Rights of Her Most Christian Majesty* (London: Thomas Newcomb, 1667).]

letters of grace, false witnesses, powerful friends, and other undue means, Mazarin desired to bring him to a new trial: but the chancellor Seguier told the Queen-Mother it could not be; for the law did not permit a man once acquitted to be again question'd for the same fact; and that if the course of the law were interrupted, neither the Salic Law, nor the succession of her children, or anything else could be secure in France.

This is farther proved by the histories of that nation. The kings of Meroveus and Pepin's races, were suffer'd to divide the kingdom amongst their sons; or, as Hotman says, the estates made the division, and allotted to each such a part as they thought fit.[24] But when this way was found to be prejudicial to the publick, an act of state was made in the time of Hugh Capet, by which it was ordain'd, that for the future the kingdom should not be dismembered; which constitution continuing in force to this day, the sons or brothers of their kings receive such an *apanage* (they call it) as is bestow'd on them, remaining subject to the crown as well as other men. And there has been no king of France since that time (except only Charles the sixth) who has not acknowledged that he cannot alienate any part of their dominion.

Whoever imputes the acknowledgment of this to kingcraft, and says, that they who avow this, when 'tis for their advantage, will deny it on a different occasion, is of all men their most dangerous enemy. In laying such fraud to their charge, he destroys the veneration by which they subsist, and teaches subjects not to keep faith with those, who by the most malicious deceits show, that they are tied by none. Human societies are maintained by mutual contracts, which are of no value if they are not observ'd. Laws are made, and magistrates created to cause them to be performed in publick and private matters, and to punish those who violate them. But none will ever be observed, if he who receives the greatest benefit by them, and is set up to oversee others, give the example to those who of themselves are too much inclin'd to break them. The first step that Pompey made to his own ruin was, by violating the laws he himself had proposed.[25] But it would be much worse for kings to break those that are established by the authority of a whole people, and confirmed by the succession of many ages.

I am far from laying any such blemishes on them, or thinking that they deserve them. I must believe the French king speaks sincerely, when he says he can do nothing against the laws of his country: And that our

---

[24] Hotom. Fran. Gall. [Hotman, *Francogallia.*]

[25] Suarum legum lator et eversor. Tacit.

["The author and destroyer of his own laws." Tacitus, *Annals*, bk. 3, ch. 28.]

King James did the like, when he acknowledged himself to be the servant of the commonwealth; and the rather, because 'tis true, and that he is placed in the throne to that end. Nothing is more essential and fundamental in the constitutions of kingdoms, than that diets, parliaments, and assemblies of estates should see this perform'd. 'Tis not the king that gives them a right to judge of matters of war or peace, to grant supplies of men and money, or to deny them; and to make or abrogate laws at their pleasure: All the powers rightly belonging to kings, or to them, proceed from the same root. The northern nations seeing what mischiefs were generally brought upon the eastern, by referring too much to the irregular will of a man; and what those who were more generous had suffer'd, when one man by the force of a corrupt mercenary soldiery had overthrown the laws by which they lived, feared they might fall into the same misery; and therefore retained the greater part of the power to be exercised by their general assemblies, or by delegates, when they grew so numerous that they could not meet. These are the kingdoms of which Grotius speaks, *where the king has his part, and the senate or people their part of the supreme authority;*[26] and where the law prescribes such limits, *that if the king attempt to seize that part which is not his, he may justly be opposed:*[27] Which is as much as to say, that the law upholds the power it gives, and turns against those who abuse it.

This doctrine may be displeasing to court-parasites; but no less profitable to such kings as follow better counsels, than to the nations that live under them: the wisdom and virtue of the best is always fortified by the concurrence of those who are placed in part of the power; they always do what they will, when they will nothing but that which is good; and 'tis a happy impotence in those, who through ignorance or malice desire to do evil, not to be able to effect it. The weakness of such as by defects of nature, sex, age or education, are not able of themselves to bear the weight of a kingdom, is thereby supported, and they together with the people under them preserved from ruin; the furious rashness of the insolent is restrained; the extravagance of those who are naturally lewd, is aw'd; and the bestial madness of the most violently wicked and outrageous, suppress'd. When the law provides for these matters, and prescribes ways by which they may be accomplished, every man who receives or fears an injury, seeks a remedy in a legal way, and vents his passions in such a manner as brings no prejudice to the commonwealth: If his complaints against a king may be heard, and redressed by courts

---

[26] De jur. bel. et pac. l. 2. [Grotius, *De jure,*   [27] Ibid.
bk. 1, ch. 4, sec. 13.]

of justice, parliaments, and diets, as well as against private men, he is
satisfied, and looks no farther for a remedy. But if kings, like those of
Israel, will neither judge nor be judged, and there be no power orderly
to redress private or publick injuries, every man has recourse to force, as
if he liv'd in a wood where there is no law; and that force is always
mortal to those who provoke it: No guards can preserve a hated prince
from the vengeance of one resolute hand; and they as often fall by the
swords of their own guards as of others: Wrongs will be done, and when
they that do them cannot or will not be judged publickly, the injur'd
persons become judges in their own case, and executioners of their own
sentence. If this be dangerous in matters of private concernment, 'tis
much more so in those relating to the publick. The lewd extravagancies
of Edward and Richard the second, whilst they acknowledged the power
of the law, were gently reproved and restrained with the removal of some
profligate favourites; but when they would admit of no other law than
their own will, no relief could be had but by their deposition. The lawful
Spartan kings, who were obedient to the laws of their country, liv'd in
safety, and died with glory; whereas 'twas a strange thing to see a lawless
tyrant die without such infamy and misery, as held a just proportion
with the wickedness of his life: They did, as Plutarch says of Dionysius,
many mischiefs, and suffer'd more.[28] This is confirmed by the examples
of the kingdom of Israel, and of the empires of Rome and Greece; they
who would submit to no law, were destroy'd without any. I know not
whether they thought themselves to be gods, as our author says they
were; but I am sure the most part of them died like dogs, and had the
burial of asses rather than of men.

This is the happiness to which our author would promote them all. *If
a king admit a people to be his companions, he ceaseth to be a king, and the state
becomes a democracy.* And a little farther, *If in such assemblies, the king,
nobility, and people, have equal shares in the sovereignty, then the king hath but
one voice, the nobility likewise one, and the people one; and then any two of these
voices should have power to overrule the third: Thus the nobility and commons
should have a power to make a law to bridle the king, which was never seen in
any kingdom.*[29] We have heard of nations that admitted a man to reign
over them (that is, made him king) but of no man that made a people.
The Hebrews made Saul, David, Jeroboam, and other kings: when they
returned from captivity, they conferred the same title upon the Asmonean
race, as a reward of their valour and virtue: the Romans chose Romulus,
Numa, Hostilius, and others to be their kings; the Spartans instituted

[28] Vit. Timoleon. [Plutarch, *Life of Timoleon.*]   [29] [*Patriarcha*, ch. 20, p. 93.]

two, one of the Heraclidae, the other of the Aeacidae. Other nations set up one, a few, or more magistrates to govern them: and all the world agrees, that *qui dat esse, dat modum esse;* he that makes him to be, makes him to be what he is: and nothing can be more absurd than to say, that he who has nothing but what is given, can have more than is given to him. If Saul and Romulus had no other title to be kings, than what the people conferred upon them, they could be no otherwise kings than as pleased the people: They therefore did not admit the people to be partakers of the government; but the people who had all in themselves, and could not have made a king if they had not had it, bestow'd upon him what they thought fit, and retained the rest in themselves. If this were not so, then instead of saying to the multitude, *Will ye have this man to reign?* they ought to say to the man, *Wilt thou have this multitude to be a people?* And whereas the nobles of Aragon used to say to their new made king, *We who are as good as you, make you our king, on condition you keep and maintain our rights and liberties, and if not, not;*[30] he should have said to them, I who am better than you, make you to be a people, and will govern you as I please. But I doubt whether he would have succeeded, till that kingdom was joined to others of far greater strength, from whence a power might be drawn to force them out of their usual method.

That which has been said of the governments of England, France, and other countries, shows them to be of the same nature; and if they do not deserve the name of kingdoms, and that their princes will by our author's arguments be persuaded to leave them, those nations perhaps will be so humble to content themselves without that magnificent title, rather than resign their own liberties to purchase it: and if this will not please him, he may seek his glorious sovereign monarchy among the wild Arabs, or in the island of Ceylon; for it will not be found among civiliz'd nations.

However more ignorance cannot be express'd, than by giving the name of *democracy* to those governments that are composed of the three simple species, as we have proved that all the good ones have ever been: for in a strict sense it can only suit with those, where the people retain to themselves the administration of the supreme power; and more largely, when the popular part, as in Athens, greatly overbalances the other two, and that the denomination is taken from the prevailing part. But our author, if I mistake not, is the first that ever took the ancient governments of Israel, Sparta and Rome, or those of England, France, Germany and Spain, to be *democracies*, only because every one of them had senates and assemblies of the people, who in their persons, or by their deputies, did

[30] [See Chapter II, Section 5, n. 6 for this quotation from *Relaciones de Antonio Pérez.*]

join with their chief magistrates in the exercise of the supreme power. That of Israel, to the time of Saul, is called by Josephus an *aristocracy*.[31] The same name is given to that of Sparta by all the Greek authors; and the great contest in the Peloponnesian War was between the two kinds of government; the cities that were governed aristocratically, or desired to be so, following the Lacedaemonians; and such as delighted in *democracy* taking part with the Athenians. In like manner Rome, England, and France, were said to be under monarchies; not that their kings might do what they pleased, but because one man had a preeminence above any other. Yet if the Romans could take Romulus, the son of a man that was never known, Numa a Sabine, Hostilius and Ancus Marcius private men, and Tarquinius Priscus the son of a banished Corinthian, who had no title to a preference before others till it was bestowed upon them; 'tis ridiculous to think, that they who gave them what they had, could not set what limits they pleased to their own gift.

But, says our author, *The nobility will then have one voice, and the people another, and they joining may overrule the third, which was never seen in any kingdom*.[32] This may perhaps be a way of regulating the monarchical power, but it is not necessary, nor the only one: There may be a senate, tho the people be excluded; that senate may be composed of men chosen for their virtue, as well as for the nobility of their birth: The government may consist of king and people without a senate; or the senate may be composed only of the people's delegates. But if I should grant his assertion to be true, the reasonableness of such a constitution cannot be destroy'd by the consequences he endeavours to draw from it; for he who would instruct the world in matters of state, must show what is, or ought to be, not what he fancies may thereupon ensue. Besides, it does not follow, that where there are three equal votes, laws should be always made by the plurality; for the consent of all the three is in many places required: and 'tis certain that in England, and other parts, the king and one of the estates cannot make a law without the concurrence of the other. But to please Filmer, I will avow, that where the nobles and commons have an equal vote, they may join and over-rule or limit the power of the king: and I leave any reasonable man to judge, whether it be more safe and fit, that those two estates comprehending the whole body of the nation in their persons, or by representation, should have a right to over-rule or limit the power of that man, woman, or child, who sits in the throne; or that he or she, young or old, wise or foolish, good or bad, should over-rule them, and by their vices, weakness, folly, impertinence, incapacity,

---

[31] [Josephus, *Jewish Antiquities*, bk. 6, ch. 5, sec. 4.]   [32] [*Patriarcha*, ch. 20, p. 93.]

or malice, put a stop to their proceedings; and whether the chief concernments of a nation may more safely and prudently be made to depend upon the votes of so many eminent persons, amongst whom many wise and good men will always be found if there be any in the nation, and who in all respects have the same interest with them, or upon the will of one, who may be, and often is as vile, ignorant, and wretched as the meanest slave; and either has, or is for the most part made to believe he has an interest so contrary to them, that their suppression is his advancement. Common sense so naturally leads us to the decision of this question, that I should not think it possible for mankind to have mistaken, tho we had no examples of it in history: and 'tis in vain to say, that all princes are not such as I represent; for if a right were annexed to the being of a prince, and that his single judgment should over-balance that of a whole nation, it must belong to him as a prince, and be enjoy'd by the worst and basest, as well as by the wisest and best, which would inevitably draw on the absurdities above-mention'd: But that many are, and have been such, no man can deny, or reasonably hope that they will not often prove to be such, as long as any preference is granted to those who have nothing to recommend them, but the families from whence they derive; a continual succession of those who excel in virtue, wisdom, and experience, being promised to none, nor reasonably to be expected from any. Such a right therefore cannot be claimed by all; and if not by all, then not by any, unless it proceed from a particular grant in consideration of personal virtue, ability, and integrity, which must be proved: and when anyone goes about to do it, I will either acknowledge him to be in the right, or give the reasons of my denial.

However this is nothing to the general proposition: nay, if a man were to be found, who had more of the qualities requir'd for making a right judgment in matters of the greatest importance, than a whole nation, or an assembly of the best men chosen out of it (which I have never heard to have been, unless in the persons of Moses, Joshua, or Samuel, who had the spirit of God for their guide) it would be nothing to our purpose; for even he might be biased by his personal interests, which governments are not established principally to promote.

I may go a step farther, and truly say, that as such vast powers cannot be generally granted to all who happen to succeed in any families, without evident danger of utter destruction, when they come to be executed by children, women, fools, vicious, incapable or wicked persons, they can be reasonably granted to none, because no man knows what anyone will prove till he be tried; and the importance of the affair requires such a trial as can be made of no man till he be dead. He that resists one temptation may fall under the power of another; and nothing is more common in the world, than to see those men fail grossly in the last actions of their lives, who had passed their former days without reproach: Wise and good men will with Moses say of themselves, *I cannot bear the burden*: and every man who is concern'd for the publick good, ought to let fools know they are not fit to undergo it, and by law to restrain the fury of such as will not be guided by reason. This could not be denied, tho governments were constituted for the good of the governor. 'Tis good for him that the law appoints helps for his infirmities, and restrains his vices: but all nations ought to do it tho it were not so, in as much as kingdoms are not established for the good of one man, but of the people; and that king who seeks his own good before that of the people, departs from the end of his institution.

This is so plain, that all nations who have acted freely, have some way or other endeavoured to supply the defects, or restrain the vices of their supreme magistrates; and those among them deserve most praise, who by appointing means adequate to so great a work, have taken care that it might be easily and safely accomplished: Such nations have always flourished in virtue, power, glory, and happiness, whilst those who wanted their wisdom, have suffer'd all manner of calamities by the weakness and injustice of their princes, or have had their hands perpetually in blood to preserve themselves from their fury. We need no better example of the first, than that of the Spartans, who by appointing such limits to the power of their kings as could hardly be transgress'd, continued many ages in great union with them, and were never troubled with civil tumults. The like may be said of the Romans from the expulsion of the Tarquins, till they overthrew their own orders, by continuing Marius for five years in the consulate, whereas the laws did not permit a man to hold the same office two years together; and when that rule was broken, their own magistrates grew too strong for them, and subverted the commonwealth. When this was done, and the power came to be in the hands of one man, all manner of evils and calamities broke in like a flood: 'Tis hard to judge, whether the mischiefs he did, or those he suffer'd were the greater: he who set up himself to be lord of the world, was like to a beast crowned for the slaughter, and his greatness was the forerunner of his ruin. By this means some of those who seem not to have been naturally prone to evil, were by their fears put upon such courses to preserve themselves, as being rightly estimated, were worse than the death they apprehended: and the so much celebrated Constantine the Great died no less polluted with the blood of his nearest relations and friends, than Nero himself. But no place can show a more lively picture of this, than the kingdoms of Granada, and others possessed by the Moors in Spain; where there being neither senate nor assemblies of the nobility and people, to restrain the violence and fury of their kings, they had no other way than to kill them when their vices became insupportable; which happening for the most part, they were almost all murder'd; and things were brought to such extremity, that no man would accept a crown, except he who had neither birth nor virtue to deserve it.[33]

If it be said that kings have now found out more easy ways of doing what they please, and securing themselves; I answer, that they have not proved so to them all, and it is not yet time for such as tread in the same steps to boast of their success: many have fallen when they thought their designs accomplished; and no man, as long as he lives, can reasonably assure himself the like shall not befall him. But if in this corrupted age, the treachery and perjury of princes be more common than formerly; and the number of those who are brought to delight in the rewards of injustice, be so increased, that their parties are stronger than formerly: this rather shows that the balance of power is broken, or hard to be kept up, than that there ought to be none; and 'tis difficult for any man, without the spirit of prophesy, to tell what this will produce. Whilst the ancient constitutions of our Northern kingdoms remain'd entire, such as contested with their princes sought only to reform the governments, and by redressing what was amiss, to reduce them to their first principles; but they may not perhaps be so modest, when they see the very nature of their government chang'd, and the foundations overthrown. I am not sure that they who were well pleased with a moderate monarchy, will submit to one that is absolute; and 'tis not improbable, that when men see there is no medium between tyranny and popularity, they who would have been contented with the reformation of their government, may proceed farther, and have recourse to force, when there is no help in the law. This will be a hard work in those places where virtue is wholly abolished; but the difficulty will lie on the other side, if any sparks of that remain: if vice and corruption prevail, liberty cannot subsist; but if virtue have the advantage, arbitrary power cannot be established. Those who boast of their *loyalty*, and think they give testimonies of it, when they addict themselves to the will of one man, tho contrary to the law from whence that quality is derived, may consider, that by putting their masters upon illegal courses they certainly make them the worst of men, and bring them into danger of being also the most miserable. Few or no

---

[33] Hist. de Espan. de Mariana. [Mariana, *General History of Spain.*]

good princes have fallen into disasters, unless through an extremity of corruption introduced by the most wicked; and cannot properly be called unhappy, if they perished in their innocence; since the bitterness of death is assuaged by the tears of a loving people, the assurance of a glorious memory, and the quiet of a well satisfied mind. But of those who have abandoned themselves to all manner of vice, followed the impulse of their own fury, and set themselves to destroy the best men for opposing their pernicious designs, very few have died in peace. Their lives have been miserable, death infamous, and memory detestable.

They therefore who place kings within the power of the law, and the law to be a guide to kings, equally provide for the good of king and people. Whereas they who admit of no participants in power, and acknowledge no rule but their own will, set up an interest in themselves against that of their people, lose their affections, which is their most important treasure, and incur their hatred, from whence results their greatest danger.

SECTION 3 I

The Liberties of Nations are from God and Nature, not from Kings.

WHATSOEVER is usually said in opposition to this, seems to proceed from a groundless conceit, that the liberties enjoy'd by nations arise from the concessions of princes. This point has been already treated: but being the foundation of the doctrine I oppose, it may not be amiss farther to examine how it can be possible for one man born under the same condition with the rest of mankind to have a right in himself that is not common to all others, till it be by them or a certain number of them conferred upon him; or how he can without the utmost absurdity be said to grant liberties and privileges to them who made him to be what he is.

If I had to do with a man that sought after truth, I should think he had been led into this extravagant opinion by the terms ordinarily used in patents and charters granted to particular men; and not distinguishing between the proprietor and the dispenser, might think kings had given, as their own, that which they only distribute out of the publick treasury, and could have had nothing to distribute by parcels, if it had not been given to them in gross by the publick. But I need not use our author so gently. The perversity of his judgment, and obstinate hatred to truth is sufficient to draw him into the most absurd errors without any other inducement; and it were not charity, but folly to think he could have attributed in general to all princes, without any regard to the ways by which they attain to their power, such an authority as never justly belonged to any.

This will be evident to all those who consider, that no man can confer upon others that which he has not in himself: If he be originally no more than they, he cannot grant to them or any of them more than they to him. In the 7th, 8th, 9th and subsequent sections of the first chapter, it has been proved that there is no resemblence between the paternal right, and the absolute power which he asserts in kings: that the right of a father, whatever it be, is only over his children; that this right is equally inherited by them all when he dies: that everyone cannot inherit dominion; for the right of one would be inconsistent with that of all others: that the right which is common to all is that which we call liberty, or exemption from dominion: that the first fathers of mankind after the Flood had not the exercise of regal power; and whatsoever they had was equally devolved to every one of their sons, as appears by the examples of Noah, Shem, Abraham, Isaac, Jacob, and their children: that the erection of Nimrod's kingdom was directly contrary to, and inconsistent with the paternal right, if there was any regality in it: that the other kingdoms of that time were of the same nature: that Nimrod not exceeding the age of threescore years when he built Babel, could not be the father of those that assisted him in that attempt: that if the seventy two kings, who, as our author says, went from Babylon upon the confusion of languages, were not the sons of Nimrod, he could not govern them by the right of a father; if they were, they must have been very young, and could not have children of their own to people the kingdoms they set up: that whose children soever they were, who out of a part of mankind did within a hundred and thirty two years after the flood, divide into so many kingdoms, they shewed that others in process of time might subdivide into as many as they pleased; and kingdoms multiplying in the space of four thousand years since the 72, in the same proportion they did in one hundred and thirty two years into seventy two, there would now be as many kings in the world as there are men; that is, no man could be subject to another: that this equality of right and exemption from the domination of any other is called liberty: that he who enjoys it cannot be deprived of it, unless by his own consent, or by force: that no one man can force a multitude, or if he did, it could confer no right upon him: that a multitude

consenting to be governed by one man, doth confer upon him the power
of governing them; the powers therefore that he has, are from them, and
they who have all in themselves can receive nothing from him, who has
no more than every one of them, till they do invest him with it. This is
proved by sacred and profane histories. The Hebrews in the creation of
judges, kings, or other magistrates, had no regard to paternity, or to any
who by extraction could in the least pretend to the right of fathers: God
did never direct them to do it, nor reprove them for neglecting it: If they
would chuse a king, he commanded them to take one of their brethren,
not one who called himself their father: When they did resolve to have
one, he commanded them to chuse him by lot, and caused the lot to fall
upon a young man of the youngest tribe: David and the other kings of
Israel or Judah had no more to say for themselves in that point than Saul:
All the kings of that nation before and after the Captivity, ordinarily or
extraordinarily set up, justly or unjustly, were raised without any regard
to any prerogative they could claim or arrogate to themselves on that
account. All that they had therefore was from their elevation, and their
elevation from those that elevated them: 'Twas impossible for them to
confer anything upon those from whom they received all they had; or
for the people to give power to kings, if they had not had it in themselves;
which power universally residing in everyone, is that which we call
liberty. The method of other nations was much like to this. They placed
those in the throne who seemed best to deserve so great an honour, and
most able to bear so great a burden: The kingdoms of the heroes were
nothing else but the government of those who were most beneficent to
the nations amongst whom they lived, and whose virtues were thought
fit to be raised above the ordinary level of the world. Tho perhaps there
was not any one Athenian or Roman equal to Theseus or Romulus in
courage and strength, yet they were not able to subdue many or if any
man should be so vain to think that each of them did at first subdue one
man, then two, and so proceeding by degrees conquered a whole people,
he cannot without madness ascribe the same to Numa, who being sent
for from a foreign country, was immediately made king of a fierce people,
that had already conquer'd many of their neighbours, and was grown too
boisterous even for Romulus himself. The like may be said of the first
Tarquin, and of Servius; they were strangers: and tho Tullus Hostilius
and Ancus Marcius were Romans, they had as little title to a dominion
over their fellow-citizens, or means of attaining to it, as if they had come
from the farthest parts of the earth. This must be in all places, unless
one man could prove by a perfect and uninterrupted genealogy that he
is the eldest son of the eldest line of Noah, and that line to have continued

perpetually in the government of the world: for if the power has been divided, it may be subdivided into infinity; if interrupted, the chain is broken, and can never be made whole. But if our author can perform this for the service of any man, I willingly surrender my arms, and yield up the cause I defend. If he fail, 'tis ridiculous to pretend a right that belongs to no man, or to go about to retrieve a right which for the space of four thousand years has lain dormant; and much more to create that which never had a subsistence. This leads us necessarily to a conclusion, that all kingdoms are at the first erected by the consent of nations, and given to whom they please; or else all are set up by force, or some by force and some by consent: If any are set up by the consent of nations, those kings do not confer liberties upon those nations, but receive all from them, and the general proposition is false. If our author therefore, or his followers, would confute me, they must prove that all the kingdoms of the world have their beginning from force, and that force doth always create a right; or if they recede from the general proposition, and attribute a peculiar right to one or more princes, who are so absolute lords of their people, that those under them have neither liberty, privilege, property or part in the government, but by their concessions, they must prove that those princes did by force gain the power they have, and that their right is derived from it. This force also must have been perpetually continued; for if that force be the root of the right that is pretended, another force by the same rule may overturn, extinguish or transfer it to another hand. If contracts have interven'd, the force ceases; and the right that afterwards doth accrue to the persons, must proceed from, and be regulated according to those contracts.

This may be sufficient to my purpose: For as it has been already proved, that the kingdoms of Israel, Judah, Rome, Sparta, France, Spain, England, and all that we are concerned in, or that deserve to be examples to us, did arise from the consent of the respective nations, and were frequently reduced to their first principles, when the princes have endeavour'd to transgress the laws of their institution; it could be nothing to us, tho Attila or Tamerlane had by force gained the dominions they possess'd. But I dare go a step further, and boldly assert, that there never was or can be a man in the world that did, or can subdue a nation; and that the right of one grounded upon force is a mere whimsey. It was not Agathocles, Dionysius, Nabis, Marius, Sulla or Caesar, but the mercenary soldiers, and other villains that joined with them, who subdued the Syracusans, Spartans or Romans: And as the work was not performed by those tyrants alone, if a right had been gained by the violence they used, it must have been common to all those that gained it; and he that commanded them could have had no more than they thought fit to confer upon him. When Miltiades desired leave to wear an olive garland, in commemoration of the victory obtained at Marathon, an Athenian did in my opinion rightly say, "If you alone did fight against the Persians, it is just that you only should be crowned; but if others did participate in the victory, they ought also to have a part in the honour."[1] And the principal difference that I have observ'd between the most regular proceedings of the wisest senates or assemblies of the people in their persons or delegates, and the fury of the most dissolute villains, has been, that the first seeking the publick good, do usually set up such a man, and invest him with such powers as seem most conducing to that good: whereas the others following the impulse of a bestial rage, and aiming at nothing but the satisfaction of their own lusts, always advance one from whom they expect the greatest advantages to themselves, and give him such powers as most conduce to the accomplishment of their own ends: but as to the person 'tis the same thing. Caesar and Nero did no more make themselves what they were, than Numa; and could no more confer any right, liberty or privilege upon the army, that gave them all they had, than the most regular magistrate can upon the senate or people that chose them.

This also is common to the worst as well as the best, that they who set up either, do, as into a publick treasury, confer upon the person they chuse, a power of distributing to particular men, or numbers of men, such honors, privileges and advantages, as they may seem, according to the principles of the government, to deserve. But there is this difference, that the ends of the one being good, and those of the other evil, the first do for the most part limit the powers, that something may remain to reward services done to the publick, in a manner proportion'd to the merit of everyone, placing other magistrates to see it really performed, so as they may not, by the weakness or vices of the governor, be turned to the publick detriment: the others think they never give enough, that the prince having all in his power, may be able to gratify their most exorbitant desires, if by any ways they can get his favour; and his infirmities and vices being most beneficial to them, they seldom allow to any other magistrate a power of opposing his will, or suffer those who for the publick good would assume it. The world affords many examples of both sorts, and every one of them have had their progress suitable to their constitution. The regular kingdoms of England, France, Spain, Poland, Bohemia, Denmark, Sweden, and others, whether elective or hereditary, have had high stewards, constables, mayors of the palace,

---

[1] Plut. in Vit. Cim. [Plutarch, *Life of Cimon*, ch. 8.]

reichshofmeisters, parliaments, diets, assemblies of estates, cortes, and the like, by which those have been admitted to succeed who seemed most fit for the publick service; the unworthy have been rejected; the infirmities of the weak supplied; the malice of the unjust restrained; and when necessity required, the crown transferr'd from one line or family to another. But in the furious tyrannies that have been set up by the violence of a corrupted soldiery, as in the ancient Roman empire, the kingdoms of the Moors and Arabians, the tyrannies of Ezzelino of Padua, those of the Visconti and Sforzeschi of Milan, Castruccio Castracani of Lucca, Cesare Borgia, and others, there was nothing of all this. The will of the prince was a law; all power was in him, and he kept it, till another stept up and took it from him, by the same means that he had gain'd it. This fell out so frequently, that tho all the Roman emperors endeavour'd to make their power hereditary, it hardly continued three generations in one line from Augustus to Augustulus, unless in that of Constantine, and that with extreme confusion and disorder. They who had madly set up a man to be their head, and exposed so much of the world as was under their power, to be destroy'd by him, did by the like fury throw him down, and never ceased till they had brought the empire to utter ruin.

But if this paternal sovereignty be a mere fiction that never had any effect; that no nation was ever commanded by God to make it their rule, nor any reproved for the neglect of it; none ever learnt it from the light of nature, nor were by wise men taught to regard it: The first fathers claimed no privilege from it when every man's genealogy was known; and if there were such a thing in nature, it could be of no use at this day, when the several races of men are so confused, that not one in the world can prove his own original; and that the first kingdoms, whether well or ill constituted, according to the command of God, or the inventions of men, were contrary to, and incompatible with it; There can have been no justice in any, if such a rule was to have been observed; the continuance of an unjust usurpation can never have created a right, but aggravated the injustice of overthrowing it: No man could ever by his own strength and courage subdue a multitude, nor gain any other right over them if he did, than they might have to tear it from him; whoever denies kingdoms or other magistracies to have been set up by men, according to their own will, and from an opinion of receiving benefit by them, accuses all the governments that are, or ever have been in the world, of that outrageous injustice in their foundation which can never be repair'd. If there be therefore, or ever was, any just government amongst men, it was constituted by them; and whether their proceedings were regular or violent, just or unjust, the powers annexed to it were their donation: The magistracies erected by them, whether in one or more men, temporary or perpetual, elective or hereditary, were their creatures; and receiving all from them, could confer nothing upon them.

SECTION 32

The Contracts made between Magistrates, and the Nations that created them, were real, solemn, and obligatory.

O UR author having with big words and little sense inveigh'd against popular and mix'd governments, proceeds as if he had proved they could not, or ought not to be. *If it be,* says he, *unnatural for the multitude to chuse their governors, or to govern, or to partake in the government; what can be thought of that damnable conclusion which is made by too many, that the multitude may correct or depose their princes if need be? Surely the unnaturalness and injustice of this position cannot sufficiently be expressed. For admit that a king make a contract or paction with his people originally in his ancestors, or personally at his coronation (for both these pactions some dream of, but cannot offer any proof of either) yet by no law of any nation can a contract be thought broken, except first a lawful trial be had by the ordinary judge of the breakers thereof; or else every man may be both party and judge in his own case, which is absurd once to be thought; for then it will lie in the hands of the headless multitude, when they please, to cast off the yoke of government that God hath laid upon them, and to judge and punish him, by whom they should be judged and punished themselves.*[1] To this I first answer briefly, that if it be natural for the multitude to chuse their governors, or to govern, or to participate of the government as best pleases themselves; or that there never was a government in the world that was not so set up by them, in pursuance of the power naturally inherent in themselves; what can be thought of that damnable conclusion, which has been made by fools or knaves, that the multitude may not, if need be, correct or depose their own magistrates? Surely the unnaturalness and injustice of such a position cannot be sufficiently expressed. If that were admitted, all the most solemn pacts and contracts made between nations and their magistrates, originally or personally, and confirmed by laws and mutual oaths, would be of no

---

[1] [*Patriarcha*, ch. 20, pp. 93–94.]

value. He that would break the most sacred bonds that can be amongst men, should by perjury and wickedness become judge of his own case, and by the worst of crimes procure impunity for all. It would be in his power by folly, wickedness and madness, to destroy the multitude which he was created and sworn to preserve, tho wise, virtuous and just, and headed by the wisest and justest of men; or to lay a yoke upon those who by the laws of God and nature ought to be free: He might in his own case judge that body by which he ought to be judged; and who in consideration of themselves and their own good, made him to be whatsoever he is more than every one of them: The governments instituted for the preservation of nations, would turn to their destruction: It would be impossible to check the fury of a corrupt and perfidious magistrate: The worst of men would be raised to a height that was never deserved by the best; and the assurance of indemnity would, by increasing their insolence, turn their other vices into madness, as has been too often seen in those who have had more power than they deserved, and were more hardly brought to account for their actions than ought to have been; tho I never heard of any who had so much as our author asserts to be in all, nor that any was absolutely assured he should not be question'd for the abuse of what he had.

Besides, if every people may govern, or constitute and chuse one or more governors, they may divide the powers between several men, or ranks of men, allotting to every one so much as they please, or retaining so much as they think fit. This has been practised in all the governments, which under several forms have flourished in Palestine, Greece, Italy, Germany, France, England, and the rest of the world. The laws of every place show what the power of the respective magistrate is, and by declaring how much is allowed to him, declare what is denied; for he has not that which he has not, and is to be accounted a magistrate whilst he exercises that which he has.

If any doubts do hereupon arise, I hope to remove them, proving in the first place, that several nations have plainly and explicitly made contracts with their magistrates.

2. That they are implicit, and to be understood, where they are not plainly expressed.

3. That they are not dreams, but real things, and perpetually obliging.

4. That judges are in many places appointed to decide the contests arising from the breach of these contracts; and where they are not, or the party offending is of such force or pride that he will not submit, nations have been obliged to take the extremest courses.

To the first: I suppose it will not be denied, that the annual magistrates of divers commonwealths are under some compact, and that there is a power of constraining them to perform the contents, or to punish them for the violation. The modest behaviour of the Roman consuls and dictators (as long as their laws were in force) might not probably proceed from their good nature. Tho the people had not been, as our author says, mad, foolish, and always desirous to chuse the worst men for being most like to themselves,[2] but admirably wise and virtuous, 'tis not to be imagined that in the space of three or four hundred years they should never have fallen upon one who would have transgressed, if he could have done it safely, tho they had used the utmost caution in their choice. But the power of the consuls being only for a year, that of the dictator for six months at most, and the commission that he should take care the commonwealth might suffer no damage,[3] show the end and condition upon which they were chosen; and tho their power is by some thought to have been absolute, yet the consuls were frequently opposed and brought into order by the senate, tribunes, or people, and sometimes the dictator himself. Camillus in his fourth dictatorship was threatened by the tribunes with a great fine, and by that means obliged to abdicate his magistracy.[4] I have already mention'd Marcus Fabius Maximus, who in the behalf of his son Quintus condemned to die by Papirius the dictator, appealed to the people:[5] And when the conduct of Fabius in the war against Hannibal was not approved, Naenius the tribune thought he made a very modest proposition, in that he did not desire his magistracy should be abrogated; but that the master of the horse should be made equal to him in power, which was done accordingly. 'Tis agreed by all, that the consuls were in the place of kings, and that the power of the dictator was at the least equal to what theirs had been. If they therefore were under such a rule, which they could not transgress, or might be reduced to order if they did, and forced to submit to the people as the kings had done, the kings were also made upon the same conditions, and equally obliged to perform them.

The Scripture is more clear in the case. The judges are said to have been in power equal to kings; and I may perhaps acknowledge it, with relation to the Deuteronomical king, or such as the people might have

---

[2] [*Patriarcha*, ch. 18, p. 90.]

[3] Ne quid detrimenti respubl. accipiat. [Livy, *History of Rome*, bk. 3, ch. 4.]

[4] Plut. Vit. Camil. [Plutarch, *Life of Camillus*, ch. 34.]

[5] Qui solus plus quam tua dictatura potest polletque cui et reges cessere, etc. T. Liv. l. 8. ["(The people,) who alone are more capable and powerful than your dictatorship; to them even kings yield, etc." See Section 13, note 5 above.]

chosen without offending God. The Gileadites made a covenant with Jephthah, that he should be their head and captain: He would not return to his country till they had done it. This was performed solemnly before the lord in Mizpeh, and all Israel followed them. They might therefore make a covenant with their kings, for the difference of name does not increase or diminish the right. Nay, they were in duty obliged to do it: The words of the 17th of Deuter. *He shall not multiply wives, &c. that his heart be not lifted up above his brethren,* can have no other signification, than that they should take care he did it not, or, as Josephus says, hinder him if he attempt it; for the law was not given to the king who was not, but to those who might make him if they thought fit.[6] In pursuance of this law—

[*The rest of this chapter is wanting in the original manuscript.*][7]

2dly. There was no absurdity in this, tho it was their own case; but to the contrary, because it was their own case: that is, concerning themselves only, and they had no superior.[8] They only were the competent judges, they decided their controversies, as every man in his own family doth, such as arise between him and his children, and his servants. This power hath no other restriction, than what is put upon it by the municipal law of the country, where any man [lives], and that hath no other force, than as he is understood to have consented unto it. Thus in England every man (in a degree) hath a right of chastising them; and in many places (even by the law of God) the master hath a power of life and death over his servant: It were a most absurd folly, to say, that a man might not put away, or in some places kill an adulterous wife, a disobedient son, or an unlawful servant, because he is party and judge; for the case doth admit of no other, unless he hath abridged his own right by entering into a society, where other rules are agreed upon, and a superiour-judge constituted, there being none such between king and people: That people must needs be the judge of things happening between

---

[6] [Deuteronomy 17:17, 20.]

[7] [This statement was inserted by the editor of the first edition of the *Discourses*. The rest of this chapter was probably the part of the *Discourses* seized by the government for evidence against Sidney at his trial. The passage printed here was read by the prosecution at Sidney's trial and is taken from *The Arraignment, Tryal, & Condemnation of Algernon Sidney* (London: Benj. Tooke, 1684), pp. 23–26. Judging from the many errors, it appears to be a verbal transcript taken down at the trial. There are probably quite a few pages missing after this passage, since Sidney's commentary on *Patriarcha*, ch. 21 ("No Tyrants in England since the Conquest"), pp. 94–95, is entirely lacking. The corrections in brackets are by the present editor, with the help of the 1763 edition of Sidney's *Discourses*, which contains a corrected printing of the trial.]

[8] [Sidney discusses Filmer's claim that it is absurd for the people to judge whether kings violate their contracts with the people, since that would make the people judges in their own case. *Patriarcha*, ch. 20, pp. 93–94.]

them and him whom they did not constitute that [he] might be great, glorious, and rich; but that [he] might judge them, and fight their battles; or otherwise do good unto them as they should direct. In this sense, he that is *singulis major*,[9] ought to be [obeyed] by every man, in his just and lawful commands tending to the publick good: And must be suffered to do nothing against it, nor in any respect more than the law doth allow.

For this reason Bracton saith, "that the king hath three superiors, to wit, *Deum legem, & parliament*";[10] that is, the power originally in the people of England, is delegated unto the parliament. He is subject unto the law of God as he is a man; to the people that makes him a king, in as much as he is a king: the law sets a measure unto that subjection, and the parliament judges of the particular cases thereupon arising: He must be content to submit his interest unto theirs, since he is no more than any one of them, in any other respect than that he is by the consent of all, raised above any other.

If he doth not like this condition, he may renounce the crown; but if he receive it upon that condition (as all magistrates do the power they receive), and swear to perform it, he must expect that the performance will be exacted, or revenge taken by those that he hath betrayed.

If this be not so, I desire to know of our author, how one or more men can come to be guilty of treason against the king, as *lex facit ut sit rex*.[11] No man can owe more unto him than unto any other, or he unto every other man by any rule but the law; and if he must not be judge in his own case, neither he nor any other by power received from him, would ever try any man for an offence against him, or the law.

If the king, or such as he appoints, cannot judge him, he cannot be judged by the ways ordinarily known amongst us. If he or other by authority from him may judge, he is judge in his own case, and we fall under that which he accounts the utmost of all absurdities: if a remedy be found for this, he must say that the king in his own case may judge the people, but the people must not judge the king, because it is theirs; that is to say, the servant entertained by the master may judge him, but the master must not judge the servant whom he took only for his own use. The magistrate is bound by no oath or contract to the people that created him, but the people is bound to its own creature, the magistrate.

---

9 [Greater than the individual (citizens). See Section 24, n. 13 above. The original text has the word "and" after this phrase and instead of "obeyed" has "obliged." Earlier in the sentence, where [he] is inserted, the text has "they."]

10 [God, law, and Parliament.]

11 ["The law makes him king." Henry Bracton, *On the Laws and Customs of England*, 4 vols., trans. Samuel E. Thorne (Cambridge: Harvard University Press, 1968), fol. 107, p. 306.]

This seems to be the ground of all our author's follies; he cannot comprehend that magistrates are for or by the people, but makes this conclusion, as if nations were created by or for the glory or pleasure of magistrates; and after such a piece of nonsense, it ought not to be thought strange if he[12] represent, as an absurd thing, that the headless multitude may shake off the yoke when they please. But I would know how the multitude comes under the yoke; it is a badge of slavery. He says that the power of kings is for the preservation of liberty and property. We may therefore change or take away kings without breaking any yoke, or that [is] made a yoke, which ought not to be one; the injury is therefore in making or imposing, and there can be none in breaking it.

That if there be not an injury, there may perhaps be an inconvenience; if the headless multitude may shake off the yoke.[13] I know not why the multitude should be concluded to be headless; it is not always so. Moses was head of the multitude that went out of Egypt; Othniel led them against the king of Mesopotamia; under the conduct of Phoebidas;[14] they obtain'd a victory against the Moabites; they had the like success under Shamgar, Barak, Gideon, Jephthah, Samuel, Samson, and others against Canaanites, Midianites, Philistines and others; the multitude that opposed Saul and Ishbosheth had David for its head: and the ten tribes that rejected Rehoboam chose unto themselves [Jeroboam]; the Athenians rising against the thirty tyrants had Thrasybulus; those that drave [Archias] from Thebes were conducted by Pelopidas: when the Romans drave out the Tarquins, they chose Brutus and Publicola, and they destroyed the decemviri under Horatius and Valerius. All the multitudes that afterwards revolted from them under Mauritius, Telerius, Spartanus, and others, were not headless; and we know of none that were, but all either found heads, or made them. The Germans set up Arminius; the Britains, and others in latter times; the Castilians, that rose against Peter the Cruel, had the Lord de Trastamara.

The French, when they grew weary of the corrupted races of Pharamond and Pepin, [had] the same Pepin and Hugh Capet: The Scots when they slew James the Third, had his son to be their head; and when they deposed and imprisoned Queen Mary, the earl of Murray and others supplied the want of age that was in her son: And in all the revolutions we have had in England, the people have been headed by the parliament, or the nobility and gentry that composed it; and when the kings failed of

---

[12] [The 1684 text reads "magistrates, and affect such a piece of nonsense;"]

[13] [*Patriarcha*, p. 94.]

[14] [Actually, Ehud.]

their duties, by their own authority called it. The multitude therefore is not ever headless, but doth either find or create heads unto itself, as occasion doth require; and whether it be one man, or a few, or more, for a short or a longer time, we see nothing more regular than its motions. *But they may*, saith our author, *shake off the yoke;*[15] and why may they not, if it prove uneasy or hurtful unto them? Why should not the Israelites shake off the yoke of Pharaoh, Jabin, Sisera, and others that oppressed them?

When pride had changed Nebuchadnezzar into a beast, what should persuade the Assyrians not to drive him out amongst beasts, until God had restored unto him the heart of a man? When Tarquin had turned the legal monarchy of Rome into a most abominable tyranny, why should they not abolish it? And when the Protestants of the Low-Countries were so grievously oppressed by the power of Spain, under the proud, cruel and savage conduct of the duke of Alva, why should they not make use of all the means that God had put into their hands for their deliverance? Let any man who sees the present state of the provinces that then united themselves, judge whether it is better for them to be as they are, or in the condition unto which his fury would have reduced them, unless they had, to please him, renounced God and their religion: Our author may say, they ought to have suffered: The king of Spain by their resistance lost those countries; and that they ought not to have been judges in their own case. To which I answer, That by resisting they laid the foundation of many churches, that have produced multitudes of men, eminent in gifts and graces; and established a most glorious and happy commonwealth, that hath been since its first beginning, the strongest pillar of the Protestant cause, now in the world, and a place of refuge unto those who in all parts of Europe have been oppressed for the name of Christ: Whereas they had slavishly, and, I think I may say, wickedly as well as foolishly, suffered themselves to be butchered, if they had left those empty provinces under the power of Antichrist, where the name of God is no otherwise known than to be blasphemed.

If the king of Spain desired to keep his subjects, he should have governed them with more justice and mercy; when contrary unto all laws both human and divine, he seeks to destroy those he ought to have preserved, he can blame none but himself, if they deliver themselves from his tyranny: and when the matter is brought to that, that he must not reign, or they over whom he would reign, must perish; the matter is

---

[15] [*Patriarcha*, p. 94.]

easily decided, as if the question had been asked in the time of Nero or Domitian, Whether they should be left at liberty to destroy the best part of the world, as they endeavoured to do, or it should be rescued by their destruction? And as for the peoples being judges in their own case, it is plain, they ought to be the only judges, because it is their own, and only concerns themselves.

CHAPTER
THREE

Kings not being fathers of their People,
nor excelling all others in Virtue, can have no other
just Power than what the Laws give; nor any title to
the privileges of the Lord's Anointed.

HAVING proved that the right of fathers is from nature, and incommunicable, it must follow, that every man doth perpetually owe all love, respect, service, and obedience to him that did beget, nourish, and educate him, and to no other under that name. No man therefore can claim the right of a father over any, except one that is so; no man can serve two masters; the extent and perpetuity of the duty which every man owes to his father, renders it impossible for him to owe the same to any other: This right of father cannot be devolved to the heir of the father, otherwise than as every son by the law of nature is heir to his father, and has the same right of commanding his children, as his father had of commanding him when he was a child: no man can owe to his brother that which he owed to his father, because he cannot receive that from him which he had from his father; but the utmost of all absurdities that can enter into the heart of man is, for one to exact the rights due to a father, who has no other title than force and usurpation, it being no less than to say, that I owe as much to one who has done me the greatest of all injuries, as to him who has conferred upon me the greatest benefits: or, which is yet worse, if possible, that as these usurpations cannot be made but by robbing, spoiling, imprisoning, or killing the person in possession; that duty, which by the eternal law of nature I owe to my father, should oblige me to pay the same veneration, obedience, and service to the man that has spoiled, imprison'd, or kill'd my father, as I owed to him; or that the same law, which obliged me to obey and defend my father, because he was so, should oblige me to obey and defend his enemy, because he has imprison'd or kill'd him; and not only to pass over the law of God, which makes me the avenger of my father's blood, but to reward his murderer with the rights that comprehend all that is most tender and sacred in nature, and to look upon one that has done me the greatest of all injustices and injuries, as upon him to whom I owe my birth and education. This being evident to all those who have any measure of common sense, I suppose it may be safely concluded, that what right soever a father may have over his family, it cannot relate to that which a king has over his people; unless he, like the man in the Island of Pines, mention'd before, be also the father of them all. That which is absolutely unlike in manner and substance, institution and exercise, must be unlike in all respects: and the conclusions, which have their strength from similitude and parity, can have none when there is not the least similitude of either. And tho it were true, that fathers are held by no contracts (which generally 'tis not; for when the son is of age, and does something for the father to which he is not obliged, or gives him that which he is not bound to give, suppose an inheritance received from a friend, goods of his own acquisition, or that he be emancipated, all good laws look upon those things as a valuable consideration, and give the same force to contracts thereupon made, as to those that pass between strangers), it could have no relation to our question concerning kings. One principal reason that renders it very little necessary by the laws of nations, to restrain the power of parents over their children is, because 'tis presumed they cannot abuse it: they are thought to have a law in their bowels, obliging them more strictly to seek their good, than all those that can be laid upon them by another power; and yet if they depart from it, so as inhumanly to abuse or kill their children, they are punished with as much rigour, and accounted more unpardonable than other men. Ignorance or wilful malice persuading our author to pass over all this, he boldly affirms, *That the father of a family governs it by no other law than his own will;* and from thence infers, that the condition of kings is the same. He would seem to soften the harshness of this proposition by saying,

That a king is always tied by the same law of nature to keep this general ground, that the safety of the kingdom is his chief law.[1] But he spoils it in the next page, by asserting, *That it is not right for kings to do injury, but it is right that they go unpunished by the people if they do; so that in this point it is all one, whether Samuel describe a king or a tyrant, for patient obedience is due unto both; no remedy in the text against tyrants, but crying and praying unto God in that day.*[2] In this our author, according to the custom of theaters, runs round in a circle, pretends to grant that which is true, and then by a lie endeavours to destroy all again. Kings by the law of nature are obliged to seek chiefly the good of the kingdom; but there is no remedy if they do it not; which is no less than to put all upon the conscience of those who manifestly have none. But if God has appointed that all other transgressions of the laws of nature, by which a private man receives damage, should be punished in this world, notwithstanding the right reserved to himself of a future punishment; I desire to know, why this alone, by which whole nations may be, and often are destroy'd, should escape the hands of justice? If he presume no law to be necessary in this case, because it cannot be thought that kings will transgress, as there was no law in Sparta against adultery, because it was not thought possible for men educated under that discipline to be guilty of such a crime; and as divers nations left a liberty to fathers to dispose of their children as they thought fit, because it could not be imagined that anyone would abuse that power, he ought to remember that the Spartans were mistaken, and for want of that law which they esteemed useless, adulteries became as common there as in any part of the world: and the other error being almost everywhere discovered, the laws of all civilized nations make it capital for a man to kill his children; and give redress to children if they suffer any other extreme injuries from their parents, as well as other persons. But tho this were not so, it would be nothing to our question, unless it could be supposed, that whoever gets the power of a nation into his hands, must be immediately filled with the same tenderness of affection to the people under him, as a father naturally has towards the children

---

[1] [Here begins Sidney's commentary on the third of the three chapters in the 1680 edition of Filmer, ch. 22–32 of the original manuscript (Laslett edition). This chapter begins: "Hitherto I have endeavoured to show *the natural institution of regal authority*, and to free it from subjection to an arbitrary election of the people. It is necessary also to inquire *whether human laws have a superiority over princes*, because those that maintain the acquisition of royal jurisdiction from the people do subject the exercise of it to human positive laws." *Patriarcha*, ch. 22 ("Regal Authority Not Subject to Human Laws. Kings before Laws. The Kings of Judah and Israel Not Tied to Laws"), pp. 95–96 (emphasis added).]

[2] [*Patriarcha*, ch. 23 ("Samuel's Description of a King. The Power Ascribed to Kings in the New Testament"), p. 97.]

he hath begotten. He that is of this opinion, may examine the lives of Herod, Tiberius, Caligula, and some later princes of like inclinations, and conclude it to be true, if he find that the whole course of their actions, in relation to the people under them, do well suit with the tender and sacred name of father; and altogether false, if he find the contrary. But as every man that considers what has been, or sees what is every day done in the world, must confess, that princes, or those who govern them, do most frequently so utterly reject all thoughts of tenderness and piety towards the nations under them, as rather to seek what can be drawn from them, than what should be done for them, and sometimes become their most bitter and publick enemies; 'tis ridiculous to make the safety of nations to depend upon a supposition, which by daily experience we find to be false; and impious, to prefer the lusts of a man who violates the most sacred laws of nature, by destroying those he is obliged to preserve, before the welfare of that people for whose good he is made to be what he is, if there be anything of justice in the power he exercises.

Our author foolishly thinks to cover the enormity of this nonsense, by turning *salutem populi* into *salutem regni*:[3] for tho *regnum* may be taken for the power of commanding, in which sense the preservation of it is the usual object of the care of princes; yet it does more rightly signify the body of that nation which is governed by a king. And therefore if the maxim be true, as he acknowledges it to be, then *salus populi est lex suprema;* and the first thing we are to inquire is, whether the government of this or that man do conduce to the accomplishment of that supreme law, or not; for otherwise it ought to have been said, *salus regis est lex suprema,*[4] which certainly never entered into the head of a wiser or better man than Filmer.

His reasons are as good as his doctrine: *No law,* says he, *can be imposed on kings, because there were kings before any laws were made.*[5] This would not follow, tho the proposition were true; for they, who imposed no laws upon the kings they at first made, from an opinion of their virtue, as in those called by the ancients *heroum regna,* might lay restrictions upon them, when they were found not to answer the expectation conceived of them, or that their successors degenerated from their virtue. Other nations also being instructed by the ill effects of an unlimited power given to some kings (if there was any such) might wisely avoid the rock upon which their neighbours had split, and justly moderate that power which

---

[3] [Welfare of the people . . . welfare of the kingdom. "Welfare" may also be translated "safety."]

[4] [The welfare of the king is the supreme law.]

[5] [*Patriarcha*, ch. 22, p. 96.]

had been pernicious to others. However a proposition of so great importance ought to be proved; but that being hard, and perhaps impossible, because the original of nations is almost wholly unknown to us, and their practice seems to have been so various, that what is true in one, is not so in another; he is pleased only to affirm it, without giving the least shadow of a reason to persuade us to believe him. This might justify me, if I should reject his assertion as a thing said *gratis*: but I may safely go a step farther, and affirm, that men lived under laws before there were any kings; which cannot be denied, if such a power necessarily belongs to kings as he ascribes to them. For Nimrod, who established his kingdom in Babel, is the first who by the Scripture is said to have been a mighty one in the earth. He was therefore the first king, or kings were not mighty; and he being the first king, mankind must have lived till his time without laws, or else laws were made before kings. To say that there was then no law, is in many respects most absurd; for the nature of man cannot be without it, and the violences committed by ill men before the Flood, could not have been blamed if there had been no law; for that which is not, cannot be transgressed. Cain could not have feared that every man who met him would slay him, if there had not been a law to slay him that had slain another. But in this case the Scripture is clear, at least from the time that Noah went out of the Ark; for God then gave him a law sufficient for the state of things at that time, if all violence was prohibited under the name of shedding blood, tho not under the same penalty as murder. But penal laws being in vain, if there be none to execute them, such as know God does nothing in vain, may conclude that he who gave this law, did appoint some way for its execution, tho unknown to us. There is therefore a law not given by kings, but laid upon such as should be kings, as well as on any other persons, by one who is above them; and perhaps I may say, that this law presseth most upon them, because they who have most power, do most frequently break out into acts of violence, and most of all disdain to have their will restrained: and he that will exempt kings from this law, must either find that they are excepted in the text, or that God who gave it has not a power over them.

Moreover, it has been proved at the beginning of this treatise, that the first kings were of the accursed race, and reigned over the accursed nations, whilst the holy seed had none. If therefore there was no law where there was no king, the accursed posterity of Ham had laws, when the blessed descendants of Shem had none, which is most absurd; the word *outlaw*, or *lawless*, being often given to the wicked, but never to the just and righteous.

The impious folly of such assertions goes farther than our author perhaps suspected: for if there be no law where there is no king, the Israelites had no law till Saul was made king, and then the law they had was from him. They had no king before, for they asked one. They could not have asked one of Samuel, if he had been a king. He had not been offended, and God had not imputed to them the sin of rejecting him, if they had asked that only which he had set over them. If Samuel were not king, Moses, Joshua, and the other judges were not kings; for they were no more than he. They had therefore no king, and consequently, if our author say true, no law. If they had no law till Saul was king, they never had any; for he gave them none; and the prophets were to blame for denouncing judgments against them for receding from, or breaking their law, if they had none. He cannot say that Samuel gave them a law; for that which he wrote in a book, and laid up before the Lord, was not a law to the people, but to the king.[6] If it had been a law to the people, it must have been made publick; but as it was only to the king, he laid it up before God, to testify against him if he should adventure to break it. Or if it was a law to the people, the matter is not mended; for it was given in the time of a king by one who was not king. But in truth it was the law of the kingdom by which he was king, and had been wholly impertinent, if it was not to bind him; for it was given to no other person, and to no other end.

Our author's assertion upon which all his doctrine is grounded, *That there is no nation that allows children any action or remedy for being unjustly governed,*[7] is as impudently false as any other proposed by him: for tho a child will not be heard that complains of the rod; yet our own law gives relief to children against their fathers, as well as against other persons that do them injuries, upon which we see many ill effects, and I do rather relate than commend the practice. In other places the law gives relief against the extravagancies of which fathers may be guilty in relation to their children, tho not to that excess as to bring them so near to an equality as in England: They cannot imprison, sell, or kill their children, without exposing themselves to the same punishments with other men; and if they take their estates from them, the law is open and gives relief against them: but on the other side, children are punished with death, if they strike or outrageously abuse their parents; which is not so with us.

Now, if the laws of nations take such care to preserve private men from being too hardly used by their true and natural fathers, who have such a love and tenderness for them in their own blood, that the most

---

[6] 1 Sam. 10.   [7] [*Patriarcha*, ch. 22, p. 96.]

wicked and barbarous do much more frequently commit crimes for them than against them; how much more necessary is it to restrain the fury that kings, who at the best are but phantastical fathers, may exercise to the destruction of the whole people? 'Tis a folly to say that David and some other kings have had, or that all should have a tenderness of affection towards their people as towards their children; for besides that even the first proposition is not acknowledged, and will be hardly verified in any one instance, there is a vast distance between what men ought to be, and what they are. Every man ought to be just, true, and charitable; and if they were so, laws would be of no use: but it were a madness to abolish them upon a supposition that they are so; or to leave them to a future punishment, which many do not believe, or not regard. I am not obliged to believe that David loved every Israelite as well as his son Absalom; but tho he had, I could not from thence infer that all kings do so, unless I were sure that all of them were as wise and virtuous as he.

But to come more close to the matter: Do we not know of many kings who have come to their power by the most wicked means that can enter into the heart of man, even by the most outrageous injuries done to the people, sometimes by a foreign aid? as kings were by the power of the Romans imposed upon the Britains, that they might waste the forces, and break the spirits of that fierce people. This Tacitus acknowledges, and says, *That amongst other instruments of enslaving nations, they imposed kings upon them.*[8] The Medicis were made masters of Florence by the force of Charles the Fifth's army. Sometimes by a corrupt party in their own country they have destroy'd the best men, and subdued the rest; as Agathocles, Dionysius, and Caesar did at Rome and Syracuse. Others taking upon them to defend a people, have turned the arms with which they were entrusted against their own masters; as Francesco Sforza, who being chosen by those of Milan to be their general against the Venetians, made peace with them, and by their assistance made himself prince, or, in our author's phrase, father of that great city. If these be acts of tenderness, love, justice, and charity, those who commit them may well think they have gained the affections of their people, and grow to love those from whom they fear nothing, and by whom they think they are loved. But if on the other hand they know they have attained to their greatness by the worst of all villainies, and that they are on that account become the object of the publick hatred, they can do no less than hate and fear those by whom they know themselves to be hated. The Italians ordinarily say that he who does an injury never pardons, because he

---

[8] Inter instrumenta servitutis reges habere.
Tacit. [Tacitus, *Agricola*, ch. 14.]

thinks he is never pardoned:[9] But he that enslaves and oppresses a people does an injury which can never be pardoned, and therefore fears it will be revenged.

Other princes who come to their thrones by better ways, and are not contented with the power that the law allows, draw the same hatred upon themselves when they endeavour by force or fraud to enlarge it; and must necessarily fear and hate their own people as much as he who by the ways beforemention'd has betray'd or subdued them. Our author makes nothing of this; but taking it for granted that it was all one whether Samuel spoke of a king or a tyrant, declares that the same patient obedience is due to both; but not being pleased to give any reason why we should believe him, I intend to offer some why we should not.

First, there is nothing in the nature or institution of monarchy that obliges nations to bear the exorbitances of it when it degenerates into tyranny.

In the second place, we have no precept for it.

Thirdly, we have many approved examples, and occasional particular commands to the contrary.

1. To the first: The point of paternity being explain'd; the duty of children to parents proved to proceed from the benefits received from them, and that the power over them, which at the first seems to have been left at large, because it was thought they would never abuse it, has long since been much restrain'd in all civilized nations, and particularly in our own; We may conclude that men are all made of the same paste, and that one owes no more to another than another to him, unless for some benefit received, or by virtue of some promise made. The duty arising from a benefit received must be proportionable to it: that which grows from a promise is determined by the promise or contract made, according to the true sense and meaning of it. He therefore that would know what the Babylonians, Hebrews, Athenians, or Romans did owe to Nimrod, Saul, Theseus or Romulus, must inquire what benefits were received from them, or what was promised to them. It cannot be said that anything was due to them for the sake of their parents; they could have no prerogative by birth: Nimrod was the sixth son of Cush the son of Ham, who was the youngest son of Noah: his kingdom was erected whilst Noah and his elder sons Shem and Japheth, as well as Ham, Cush, and his elder sons were still living. Saul was the son of Kish, a man of Benjamin, who was the youngest son of Jacob; and he was chosen in the

---

[9] Chi fa injuria non perdona mai.

most democratical way by lot amongst the whole people. Theseus according to the custom of the times pretended to be the son of Neptune; and Rhea was so well pleased with the soldier that had gotten her with child, that she resolved to think or say that Mars was the father of the children, that is to say they were bastards; and therefore whatever was due to them was upon their own personal account, without any regard to their progenitors. This must be measured according to what they did for those nations before they were kings, or by the manner of their advancement. Nothing can be pretended before they were kings: Nimrod rose up after the confusion of languages, and the people that understood the tongue he spoke, follow'd him; Saul was a young man unknown in Israel; Theseus and Romulus had nothing to recommend them before other Athenians and Romans, except the reputation of their valour; and the honours conferred upon them for that reason, must proceed from expectation or hope, and not from gratitude or obligation. It must therefore proceed from the manner by which they came to be kings. He that neither is nor has any title to be a king, can come to be so only by force or by consent. If by force, he does not confer a benefit upon the people, but injures them in the most outrageous manner. If it be possible therefore or reasonable to imagine that one man did ever subdue a multitude, he can no otherwise resemble a father than the worst of all enemies who does the greatest mischiefs, resembles the best of all friends who confers the most inestimable benefits, and consequently does as justly deserve the utmost effects of hatred, as the other does of love, respect, and service. If by consent, he who is raised from amongst the people, and placed above his brethren, receives great honours and advantages, but confers none. The obligations of gratitude are on his side, and whatsoever he does in acknowledgment to his benefactors for their love to him, is no more than his duty; and he can demand no more from them than what they think fit to add to the favours already received. If more be pretended, it must be by virtue of that contract, and can no otherwise be proved than by producing it to be examined, that the true sense, meaning, and intention of it may be known.

This contract must be in form and substance according to a general rule given to all mankind, or such as is left to the will of every nation. If a general one be pretended, it ought to be shown, that by enquiring into the contents, we may understand the force and extent of it. If this cannot be done, it may justly pass for a fiction, no conclusion can be drawn from it; and we may be sure, that what contracts soever have been made between nations and their kings, have been framed according to the will of those nations; and consequently how many soever they are, and whatsoever the sense of any or all of them may be, they can oblige no man, except those, or at the most the descendants of those that made them. Whoever therefore would persuade us, that one or more nations are, by virtue of those contracts, bound to bear all the insolences of tyrants, is obliged to show, that by those contracts they did forever indefinitely bind themselves so to do, how great soever they might be.

I may justly go a step farther, and affirm, that if any such should appear in the world, the folly and turpitude of the thing would be a sufficient evidence of the madness of those that made it, and utterly destroy the contents of it: but no such having been as yet produced, nor any reason given to persuade a wise man that there has ever been any such, at least among civilized nations (for whom only we are concerned), it may be concluded there never was any; or if there were, they do not at all relate to our subject; and consequently that nations still continue in their native liberty, and are no otherwise obliged to endure the insolence of tyrants, than they, or each of them may esteem them tolerable.

2. To the second: Tho the words of Samuel had implied a necessity incumbent upon the Hebrews to bear all the injuries that their kings should do to them, it could no way relate to us; for he does not speak of all kings, but of such as they had asked, even such as reigned over the slavish Asiaticks their neighbours, who are no less infamous in the world for their baseness and cowardice, than detestable for their idolatry and vices. It was not a plot or trick of Samuel to keep the government in himself and family: Such scurrilous expressions or thoughts are fit only for Filmer, Heylyn, and their disciples: but the prophet being troubled at the folly and wickedness of the people, who chose rather to subject themselves to the irregular will of a man, than to be governed by God and his law, did, by the immediate command of God, declare to them what would be the event of their fury; that since they would be like to their neighbours in sin and folly, he told them they should be like to them in shame and misery; since they desired to cast off the thing that was good, they should suffer evil as the product of their own counsels; and that when they should cry to the Lord from a sense of their miseries, he does not tell them, as our author falsely says, they should have no other remedy against tyrants but crying and praying, but that their cries and prayers should not be heard. It was just that when they had rejected God, he should reject them, and leave them under the weight of the calamities they had brought upon themselves. In all other cases God had ever said, that when his people returned to him, he would hear and save them. When they cried by reason of the oppressions they suffered under the Egyptians, Canaanites, Midianites, Philistines, and others, tho their

crimes had deserved them all, yet God heard and relieved them. But when they meditated this final defection from his law, and rejection of his government, God seemed to change his nature, and forget to be gracious; *When ye shall cry to me by reason of your king, I will not hear you.* This was the strongest dehortation from their wicked intention that can be imagined; but being not enough to reclaim them, they answered, *Nay, but we will have a king.*[10] They were like to their neighbours in folly and vice, and would be like to them in government; which brought all the calamities upon them that the others suffer'd. But I know not what conclusion can be drawn from hence in favour of our author's doctrine, unless all nations are obliged furiously to run into the same crimes with the Israelites, or to take upon themselves the same punishment, tho they do not commit the same crimes.

If this was not a precept to the Israelites, instructing them what they should do, but a denunciation of what they should suffer for the evil which they had committed, the Old Testament will afford none; and I hope in due time to answer such as he alleges from the New. Nay, we may conclude there can be none there, because being dictated by the same spirit, which is always uniform and constant to itself, it could not agree with the 17th of Deuteron. which so extremely restrains such a king as God allowed, as not to suffer him in any manner to raise his heart above his brethren; and was said in vain, if at the same time it gave him a power which might not be resisted, or forbade others to resist him if he would not obey the law.

3. To the third: Whatsoever was done by the command of God against Pharaoh king of Egypt, and against the kings of the Canaanites, Midianites, Moabites, Edomites, Amorites or Philistines, by Moses, Joshua, Ehud, Barak, Gideon, Samson, Jephthah, Samuel, and the rest of the judges, comes expressly under the particular precepts and examples promised by me, to show, that God had occasionally commanded, and his servants executed his commands in resisting and destroying the persons of kings, who were their own kings also, if possession was only to be regarded. And tho this be sufficient to overthrow our author's doctrine; *That we are not to examine the titles of kings, whether they be from usurpation, or any other means; but only to look upon the power:*[11] Yet they who seek truth, ought not to content themselves merely with victory; or to esteem that a victory, which is obtained by what the schools call *argumentum ad hominem,*[12]

---

[10] [1 Samuel 8:18–19.]

[11] [Not a quotation, but a summary of Filmer's doctrine on p. 62 and elsewhere.]

[12] [An argument (directed) to the man (with whom one is arguing).]

grounded upon a false proposition, and is of no force except against those who are so ill advised to advance it. Therefore laying aside the advantages that may be justly taken against Filmer, for the folly of asserting the same right to be in a usurper, as in a lawful prince; and confessing that tho such as have no title, may and ought to be suppressed as enemies and robbers, when respect and obedience is due to those who are rightly instituted; I say, that none can be claimed by a prince lawfully instituted, if he assume to himself a power which is not granted to him by the law of his institution, because, as Grotius says, *his legal power does not extend so far;*[13] or turn the power that is given him, to ends contrary to those for which it was given, because he thereby destroys it, and puts himself into the same condition as if it had never been. This is proved by the example of Saul; tho the people sinned grievously in asking a king, yet God assenting to their demand, no prince was ever more solemnly instituted than he. The people chose him by lot from amongst all the tribes, and he was placed in the throne by the general consent of the whole nation: But he turning his lawful power into tyranny, disobeying the word of the prophet, slaying the priests, sparing the Amalekites, and oppressing the innocent, overthrew his own right; and God declared the kingdom, which had been given him under a conditional promise of perpetuity, to be entirely abrogated. This did not only give a right to the whole people of opposing him, but to every particular man; and upon this account David did not only fly from his fury, but resisted it. He made himself head of all the discontented persons that would follow him: he had at first four, and afterwards six hundred men; he kept these in arms against Saul, and lived upon the country; and resolved to destroy Nabal with all his house, only for refusing to send provisions for his men. Finding himself weak and unsafe, he went to Achish the Philistine, and offer'd his service even against Israel. This was never reputed a sin in David, or in those that follow'd him, by any except the wicked court-flatterer Doeg the Edomite, and the drunken fool Nabal, who is said to have been a man of Belial.

If it be objected, that this was rather a flight than a war, in as much as he neither killed Saul nor his men, or that he made war as a king anointed by Samuel; I answer, that he who had six hundred men, and entertain'd as many as came to him, sufficiently shewed his intention rather to resist than to fly: And no other reason can be given why he did not farther pursue that intention, than that he had no greater power: and he who arms six hundred men against his prince, when he can have no

[13] Quia eatenus non habet imperium. *De jur. bel.* [Grotius, *De jure*, bk. 1, ch. 4, sec. 13.]

more, can no more be said to obey patiently, than if he had so many hundreds of thousands. This holds, tho he kill no man, for that is not the war, but the manner of making it: and 'twere as absurd to say David made no war, because he killed no men, as that Charles the eighth made no war in Italy, because Guicciardini says, he conquer'd Naples without breaking a lance. But as David's strength increased, he grew to be less sparing of blood. Those who say kings never die, but that the right is immediately transferr'd to the next heirs, cannot deny that Ishbosheth inherited the right of Saul, and that David had no other right of making war against him, than against Saul, unless it were conferred upon him by the tribe of Judah that made him king. If this be true, it must be confessed that not only a whole people, but a part of them, may at their own pleasure abrogate a kingdom, tho never so well established by common consent; for none was ever more solemnly instituted than that of Saul; and few subjects have more strongly obliged themselves to be obedient. If it be not true, the example of Nabal is to be follow'd; and David, tho guided by the Spirit of God, deserves to be condemned as a fellow that rose up against his master.

If to elude this it be said, that God instituted and abrogated Saul's kingdom, and that David to whom the right was transmitted, might therefore proceed against him and his heirs as private men: I answer, that if the obedience due to Saul proceeded from God's institution, it can extend to none but those who are so peculiarly instituted and anointed by his command, and the hand of his prophet, which will be of little advantage to the kings that can give no testimony of such an institution or unction; and an indisputable right will remain to every nation of abrogating the kingdoms which are instituted by and for themselves. But as David did resist the authority of Saul and Ishbosheth, without assuming the power of a king, tho designed by God, and anointed by the prophet, till he was made king of Judah by that tribe; or arrogating to himself a power over the other tribes till he was made king by them, and had enter'd into a covenant with them; 'tis much more certain that the persons and authority of ill kings, who have no title to the privileges due to Saul by virtue of his institution, may be justly resisted; which is as much as is necessary to my purpose.

Object. But David's heart smote him when he had cut off the skirt of Saul's garment, and he would not suffer Abishai to kill him.[14] This might be of some force, if it were pretended that every man was obliged to kill an ill king, whensoever he could do it, which I think no man ever did

---

[14] 1 Sam. 26.

say; and no man having ever affirmed it, no more can be concluded than is confessed by all. But how is it possible that a man of a generous spirit, like to David, could see a great and valiant king, chosen from amongst all the tribes of Israel, anointed by the command of God and the hand of the prophet, famous for victories obtained against the enemies of Israel, and a wonderful deliverance thereby purchased to that people, cast at his feet to receive life or death from the hand of one whom he had so furiously persecuted, and from whom he least deserved, and could least expect mercy, without extraordinary commotion of mind, most especially when Abishai, who saw all that he did, and thereby ought best to have known his thoughts, expressed so great a readiness to kill him? This could not but make him reflect upon the instability of all that seemed to be most glorious in men, and shew him that if Saul, who had been named even among the prophets, and assisted in an extraordinary manner to accomplish such great things, was so abandoned and given over to fury, misery and shame; he that seemed to be most firmly established ought to take care lest he should fall.

Surely these things are neither to be thought strange in relation to Saul, who was God's anointed, nor communicable to such as are not: Some may suppose he was king by virtue of God's unction (tho if that were true, he had never been chosen and made king by the people) but it were madness to think he became God's anointed by being king: for if that were so, the same right and title would belong to every king, even to those who by his command were accursed and destroyed by his servants Moses, Joshua and Samuel. The same men, at the same time, and in the same sense, would be both his anointed and accursed, loved and detested by him; and the most sacred privileges made to extend to the worst of his enemies.

Again; the war made by David was not upon the account of being king, as anointed by Samuel, but upon the common natural right of defending himself against the violence and fury of a wicked man; he trusted to the promise, *that he should be king*, but knew that as yet he was not so; and when Saul found he had spared his life, he said, *I now know well that thou shalt surely be king, and that the kingdom of Israel shall surely be established in thy hand;*[15] not that it was already. Nay David himself was so far from taking upon him to be king, till the tribe of Judah had chosen him, that he often acknowledged Saul to be his lord. When Baanah and Rechab brought the head of Ishbosheth to him, he commanded them to be slain; *Because they had killed a righteous man upon his bed, in his own house;*[16]

---

[15] 1 Sam. 24.   [16] 2 Sam. 4.

which he could not have said, if Ishbosheth had unjustly detained from him the ten tribes, and that he had a right to reign over them before they had chosen him. The word of God did not make him king, but only foretold that he should be king; and by such ways as he pleased prepared the hearts of the people to set him up; and till the time designed by God for that work was accomplished, he pretended to no other authority, than what the six hundred men who first followed him, afterwards the tribe of Judah, and at last all the rest of the people, conferred upon him.

I no way defend Absalom's revolt; he was wicked, and acted wickedly; but after his death no man was ever blamed or questioned for siding with him: and Amasa who commanded his army, is represented in Scripture as a good man, even David saying, that Joab, by slaying Abner and Amasa, had killed *two men who were better than himself;*[17] which could not have been unless the people had a right of looking into matters of government, and of redressing abuses: tho being deceived by Absalom, they so far erred, as to prefer him, who was in all respects wicked, before the man, who, except in the matter of Uriah, is said to be after God's own heart. This right was acknowledged by David himself, when he commanded Hushai to say to Absalom, *I will be thy servant O king;* and by Hushai in the following chapter, *Nay, but whom the Lord and his people, and all the men of Israel chuse, his will I be, and with him will I abide:*[18] which could have no sense in it, unless the people had a right of chusing, and that the choice in which they generally concurred, was esteemed to be from God.

But if Saul who was made king by the whole people, and anointed by the command of God, might be lawfully resisted when he departed from the law of his institution; it cannot be doubted that any other for the like reason may be resisted. If David, tho designed by God to be king, and anointed by the hand of the prophet, was not king till the people had chosen him, and he had made a covenant with them; it will, if I mistake not, be hard to find a man who can claim a right which is not originally from them. And if the people of Israel could erect and pull down, institute, abrogate, or transfer to other persons or families, kingdoms more firmly established than any we know, the same right cannot be denied to other nations.

---

[17] 2 Sam. 20. [Solomon actually says this, in 1 Kings 2:32.]

[18] 2 Kings. [2 Samuel 15:34; 16:18.]

Algernon Sidney

SECTION 2

The Kings of Israel and Judah were under a Law not safely to be transgress'd.

Our author might be pardon'd if he only vented his own follies; but he aggravates his own crime, by imputing them to men of more credit; and tho I cannot look upon Sir Walter Raleigh as a very good interpreter of Scripture, he had too much understanding to say, *That if practice declare the greatness of authority, even the best kings of Israel and Judah were not tied to any law, but they did whatsoever they pleased in the greatest matters;*[1] for there is no sense in those words. If practice declares the greatness of authority, even the best were tied to no law, signifies nothing, for practice cannot declare the greatness of authority. Peter the Cruel of Castile, and Christian the 2d of Denmark, kill'd whom they pleas'd; but no man ever thought they had therefore a right to do so: and if there was a law, all were tied by it, and the best were less likely to break it than the worst. But if Sir Walter Raleigh's opinion, which he calls a conjecture, be taken, there was so great a difference between the kings of Israel and Judah, that as to their general proceedings in point of power, hardly anything can be said which may rightly be applied to both; and he there endeavours to show, that the reason why the ten tribes did not return to the house of David, after the destruction of the houses of Jeroboam and Baasha, was, because they would not endure a power so absolute as that which was exercised by the house of David.[2] If he has therefore anywhere said that the kings did what they pleased, it must be in the sense that Moses Maimonides says, The kings of Israel committed many extravagancies, because they were *insolent, impious, and despisers of the law.*[3] But whatsoever Sir Walter Raleigh may say (for I do not remember his words, and have not leisure to seek whether any such are found in his books) 'tis most evident that they did not what they pleased. The tribes that did not submit to David, nor crown him till they thought fit, and then made a covenant with him, took care it might be observed whether he would or not. Absalom's rebellion follow'd by almost all Israel, was a terrible check to his will. That of Sheba, the son of Bichri, was like to have been

---

[1] [*Patriarcha*, ch. 22, p. 96. Filmer quotes Raleigh, *History of the World*, bk. 2, ch. 16.]

[2] 2 L. Hist. cap. 19. [Raleigh, *History of the World*, bk. 2, ch. 19, sec. 6.]

[3] Quia superbi erant corde, impii, & spre- tores legis. Mor. Nevoch. [Not found in *Guide of the Perplexed*; perhaps a paraphrase of *The Code of Maimonides, Book 14: The Book of Judges*, Treatise Five: Kings and Wars, ch. 3, p. 213.]

worse, if it had not been suppressed by Joab's diligence; and David often confessed the sons of Zeruiah were too hard for him. Solomon indeed overthrowing the law given by Moses, multiplying gold and silver, wives and horses, introducing idolatry, and lifting up his heart above his brethren, did what he pleased; but Rehoboam paid for all: the ten tribes revolted from him, by reason of the heavy burdens laid upon them; stoned Adoram who was sent to levy the tributes, and set up Jeroboam, who, as Sir Walter Raleigh says in the place before cited, had no other title than the courtesy of the people, and utterly rejected the house of David. If practice therefore declares a right, the practice of the people to avenge the injuries they suffered from their kings, as soon as they found a man fit to be their leader, shews they had a right of doing it.

'Tis true, the best of the kings, with Moses, Joshua and Samuel, may in one sense be said to have done what they pleased, because they desired to do that only which was good. But this will hardly be brought to confer a right upon all kings: And I deny that even the kings of Judah did what they pleased, or that it were anything to our question if they did. Zedekiah professed to the great men (that is, to the Sanhedrin) *that without them he could do nothing.*[4] When Amaziah, by his folly, had brought a great slaughter upon the tribe of Judah, they conspired against him in publick council: whereupon he fled to Lachish, and they pursuing him thither, killed him, avowed the fact, and it was neither question'd, nor blamed:[5] which examples agree with the paraphrase of Josephus on Deut. 17. *He shall do nothing without the consent of the Sanhedrin; and if he attempt it, they shall hinder him.*[6] This was the law of God, not to be abrogated by man; a law of liberty directly opposite to the necessity of submitting to the will of a man. This was a gift bestowed by God upon his children and people; whereas slavery was a great part of the curse denounced against Ham for his wickedness, and perpetually incumbent upon his posterity. The great Sanhedrin were constituted judges, as Grotius says, most particularly of such matters as concern'd their kings;[7] and Maimonides affirms, that the kings were judged by them: The distribution of the power to the inferior Sanhedrins, in every tribe and city, with the right of calling the people together in general assemblies as often as occasion required, were the foundations of their liberty; and being added to the law of the kingdom prescribed in the 17th of Deuteronomy (if they should think fit to have a king) established the freedom of that people upon a solid foundation. And tho they in their fury did in a great measure waive

---

[4] Jerem. 38.

[5] 2 Kings 14.

[6] Antiq. Jud. [Josephus, *Jewish Antiquities*, bk. 4, ch. 8.]

[7] [Grotius, *De jure*, bk. 1, ch. 3, sec. 20.]

the benefits God had bestowed upon them; yet there was enough left to restrain the lusts of their kings. Ahab did not treat with Naboth as with a servant, whose person and estate depended upon his will, and does not seem to have been so tender-hearted to grieve much for his refusal, if by virtue of his royal authority he could have taken away his vineyard and his life: But that failing, he had no other way of accomplishing his design, than by the fraud of his accursed wife, and the perfidious wretches she employed. And no better proof that it did fail, can reasonably be required, than that he was obliged to have recourse to such sordid, odious, and dangerous remedies: but we are furnished with one that is more unquestionable; *Hast thou killed, and also taken possession? In the place where dogs licked the blood of Naboth, shall they lick thy blood, even thine.*[8] This shews that the kings were not only under a law, but under a law of equality with the rest of the people, even that of retaliation. He had raised his heart above his brethren; but God brought him down, and made him to suffer what he had done; he was in all respects wicked, but the justice of this sentence consisted in the law he had broken, which could not have been, if he had been subject to none. But as this retaliation was the sum of all the judicial law given by God to his people, the sentence pronounced against Ahab in conformity to it, and the execution committed to Jehu, shews, that the kings were no less obliged to perform the law than other men, tho they were not so easily punished for transgressing it as others were; and if many of them did escape, it perfectly agrees with what had been foretold by Samuel.

SECTION 3

Samuel did not describe to the Israelites
the glory of a free Monarchy; but the Evils the People
should suffer, that he might divert them from
desiring a King.

THO no restraint had been put upon the lusts of the Hebrew kings, it could be no prejudice to any other nation. They deflected from the law of God; and rejecting him that he should reign over them no longer, they fell into that misery which could affect none but those who

---

[8] 1 Kings 21.

enjoy the same blessings, and with the same fury despise them. If their kings had more power than consisted with their welfare, they gave it, and God renounces the institution of such.[1] He gave them a law of liberty; and if they fell into the shame and misery that accompanies slavery, it was their own work. They were not obliged to have any king; and could not without a crime have any but one, who must not raise his heart above the rest of them. This was taught by Moses: And Samuel who spoke by the same spirit could not contradict him; and in telling the people what such a king as they desired would do when he should be established, he did announce to them the misery they would bring upon themselves, by chusing such a one as he had forbidden. This free monarchy, which our author thinks to be so majestically described, was not only displeasing to the prophet, but declared by God to be a rejection of him, and inconsistent with his reign over them. This might have been sufficient to divert any other people from their furious resolution; but the prophet farther enforcing his dissuasion, told them, that God (who had in all other cases been their helper) would not hear them when they should cry to him by reason of their king. This is the majestick description of that free monarchy with which our author is so much pleased: It was displeasing to the prophet, hateful to God, an aggravation of all the crimes they had committed since they came out of Egypt, and that which would bring (as it did) most certain and irreparable destruction upon themselves.

But it seems the regal majesty in that age was in its infancy, and little in comparison of that which we find described by Tacitus, Suetonius, and others in later times. He shall take your sons, says Samuel, and set them over his chariots, and your daughters to make them confectioners and cooks;[2] but the majesty of the Roman emperors was carried to a higher pitch of glory. Ahab could not, without employing treachery and fraud, get a small spot of ground for his money to make a garden of herbs: But Tiberius, Caligula and Nero killed whom they pleased, and took what they pleased of their estates. When they had satiated their cruelty and avarice by the murders and confiscations of the most eminent and best men, they commonly exposed their children to the lust of their slaves. If the power of doing evil be glorious, the utmost excess is its perfection; and 'tis pity that Samuel knew no more of the effects produced by unrestrained lust, that he might have made the description yet more majestick: and as nothing can be suffer'd by man beyond constupration,

[1] "Ye have chosen kings, but not by me; and princes, but I know them not." Hos. [Hosea 8:4.]

[2] [1 Samuel 8:13.]

torments and death, instead of such trifles as he mention'd, he might have shew'd them the effects of fury in its greatest exaltation.

If it be good for a nation to live under such a power, why did not God of his own goodness institute it? Did his wisdom and love to his people fail? Or if he himself had not set up the best government over them, could he be displeased with them for asking it? Did he separate that nation from the rest of mankind, to make their condition worse than that of others? Or can they be said to have sinned and rejected God, when they desir'd nothing but the government, which by a perpetual ordinance he had established over all the nations of the world? Is not the law of nature a rule which he has given to things? and the law of man's nature, which is reason, an emanation of the divine wisdom, or some footsteps of divine light remaining in us? Is it possible that this which is from God, can be contrary to his will; and can he be offended with those who desire to live in a conformity to that law? Or could it justly be said, the people had chosen that which is not good, if nothing in government be good but what they chose?

But as the worst men delight in the worst things, and fools are pleased with the most extreme absurdities, he not only gives the highest praises to that which bears so many marks of God's hatred; but after having said that Abraham, Isaac, Jacob, and Moses were kings, he goes on, and says, *The Israelites begged a king of Samuel;*[3] which had been impertinent, if the magistrates instituted by the law were kings: and tho it might be a folly in them to ask what they had already, it could be no sin to desire that which they enjoyed by the ordinance of God. If they were not kings, it follows that the only government set up by God amongst men wanted the principal part, even the head and foundation, from whence all the other parts have their action and being; that is, God's law is against God's law, and destroys itself.

But if God did neither by a general and perpetual ordinance establish over all nations the monarchy which Samuel describes, nor prescribe it to his own people by a particular command, it was purely the peoples' creature, the production of their own fancy, conceived in wickedness, and brought forth in iniquity, an idol set up by themselves to their own destruction, in imitation of their accursed neighbours; and their reward was no better than the concession of an impious petition, which is one of God's heaviest judgments. Samuel's words are acknowledged by all interpreters, who were not malicious or mad, to be a dissuasion from their wicked purpose; not a description of what a king might justly do

---

[3] [*Patriarcha*, ch. 15, pp. 84–85.]

by virtue of his office, but what those who should be set up against God and his law would do when they should have the power in their hands: And I leave such as have the understandings of men, and are not abandoned by God, to judge what influence this ought to have upon other nations, either as to obligation or imitation.

SECTION 4

*No People can be obliged to suffer from their Kings
what they have not a right to do.*

OUR author's next work is to tell us, That *the scope of Samuel was to teach the people a dutiful obedience to their king, even in the things that they think mischievous or inconvenient: For by telling them what the king would do, he indeed instructs them what a subject must suffer: Yet not so that it is right for kings to do injury, but it is right for them to go unpunished by the people if they do it; so that in this point it is all one whether Samuel describe a king or a tyrant.*[1] This is hard, but the conclusion is grounded upon nothing. There is no relation between a prediction that a thing shall be attempted or done to me, and a precept that I shall not defend myself, or punish the person that attempts or does it. If a prophet should say that a thief lay in the way to kill me, it might reasonably persuade me not to go, or to go in such a manner as to be able to defend myself; but can no way oblige me to submit to the violence that shall be offer'd, or my friends and children not to avenge my death if I fall; much less can other men be deprived of the natural right of defending themselves by my imprudence or obstinacy in not taking the warning given, whereby I might have preserved my life. For every man has a right of resisting some way or other that which ought not to be done to him; and tho human laws do not in all cases make men judges and avengers of the injuries offer'd to them, I think there is none that does not justify the man who kills another that offers violence to him, if it appear that the way prescribed by the law for the preservation of the innocent cannot be taken. This is not only true in the case of outrageous attempts to assassinate or rob upon the highway, but in divers others of less moment. I knew a man who being

[1] [*Patriarcha*, ch. 23, p. 97. This is Filmer's summary of part of James I's *True Law of Free Monarchy*; see *The Political Works of James* *I*, ed. Charles H. McIlwain (1918; repr. New York: Russell & Russell, 1965), pp. 56ff.]

appointed to keep his master's park, killed three men in one night that came to destroy his deer; and putting himself into the hands of the magistrate, and confessing the fact both in matter and manner, he was at the publick assizes not only acquitted, but commended for having done his duty; and this in a time when 'tis well known justice was severely administered, and little favour expected by him or his master. Nay, all laws must fall, human societies that subsist by them be dissolved, and all innocent persons be exposed to the violence of the most wicked, if men might not justly defend themselves against injustice by their own natural right, when the ways prescribed by publick authority cannot be taken.

Our author may perhaps say, this is true in all except the king: And I desire to know why, if it be true in all except the king, it should not be true in relation to him? Is it possible that he who is instituted for the obtaining of justice, should claim the liberty of doing injustice as a privilege? Were it not better for a people to be without law, than that a power should be established by law to commit all manner of violences with impunity? Did not David resist those of Saul? Did he not make himself head of the tribe of Judah, when they revolted against his son, and afterwards of the ten tribes, that rejected his posterity? Did not the Israelites stone Adoram who collected the taxes, revolt from the house of David, set up Jeroboam; and did not the prophet say it was from the Lord? If it was from the Lord, was it not good? If it was good then, is it not so forever? Did good proceed from one root then, and from another now? If God had avenged the blood of Naboth by fire from heaven, and destroyed the house of Ahab, as he did the two captains and their men who were sent to apprehend Elijah,[2] it might be said, he reserv'd that vengeance to himself; but he did it by the sword of Jehu and the army (which was the people who had set him up) for an example to others.

But 'tis good to examine what this *dutiful obedience* is that our author mentions. Men usually owe no more than they receive. 'Tis hard to know what the Israelites owed to Saul, David, Jeroboam, Ahab, or any other king, whether good or bad, till they were made kings: And the act of the people by which so great a dignity was conferr'd, seems to have laid a duty upon them, who did receive more than they had to give: so that something must be due from them unless it were releas'd by virtue of a covenant or promise made; and none could accrue to them from the people afterwards, unless from the merit of the person in rightly executing his office. If a covenant or promise be pretended, the nature and extent

[2] [1 Kings 1:10–12.]

of the obligation can only be known by the contents expressed, or the true intention of it. If there be a general form of covenant set and agreed upon, to which all nations must submit, it were good to know where it may be found, and by whose authority it is established, and then we may examine the sense of it. If no such do appear, we may rationally look upon those to be impostors who should go about from thence to derive a right: And as that which does not appear, is as if it were not, we may justly conclude there is no other, or none that can have any effect, but such as have been made by particular nations with their princes; which can be of no force or obligation to others, nor to themselves, any farther than according to the true intention of those that made them. There is no such thing therefore as a dutiful obedience, or duty of being obedient, incumbent upon all nations by virtue of any covenant; nor upon any particular nation, unless it be expressed by a covenant: and whoever pretends to a right of taking our sons and daughters, lands or goods, or to go unpunished if he do, must show that these things are expressed or intended by the covenant.

But tho nations for the most part owe nothing to kings, till they are kings, and that it can hardly be conceived, that any people did ever owe so much to a man, as might not be fully repaid by the honor and advantages of such an advancement; yet 'tis possible that when they are made kings, they may by their good government lay such obligations upon their subjects, as ought to be recompensed by obedience and service. There is no mortal creature that deserves so well from mankind, as a wise, valiant, diligent and just king, who as a father cherishes his people; as a shepherd feeds, defends, and is ready to lay down his life for his flock; who is a terror to evil doers, and a praise to those that do well. This is a glorious prerogative, and he who has it is happy. But before this can be adjudged to belong to all, it must be proved that all have the virtues that deserve it; and he that exacts the dutiful obedience that arises from them, must prove that they are in him. He that does this, need not plead for impunity when he does injuries; for if he do them, he is not the man we speak of: Not being so, he can have no title to the duty by human institution or covenant; nor by divine law, since, as is already proved, God has neither established kings over all nations by precept, nor recommended them by example, in setting them over his own people. He has not therefore done it at all; there is no such thing in nature; and nations can owe nothing to kings merely as kings, but what they owe by the contract made with them.

As these contracts are made voluntarily, without any previous obligation, 'tis evident men make them in consideration of their own good; and they can be of force no longer, than he with whom they are made perform his part in procuring it; and that if he turn the power which was given to him for the publick good, to the publick inconvenience and damage, he must necessarily lose the benefit he was to receive by it. The word *think* is foolishly and affectedly put in by our author; for those matters are very often so evident, that even the weakest know them. No great sagacity is requir'd to understand that lewd, slothful, ignorant, false, unjust, covetous and cruel princes bring inconveniences and mischiefs upon nations, and many of them are so evidently guilty of some or all these vices, that no man can be mistaken in imputing them; and the utmost calamities may rationally be expected from them, unless a remedy be applied.

But, says he, Samuel by telling them *what the king would do, instructs them what the subjects must suffer, and that 'tis right he should go unpunished:*[3] But, by his favour, Samuel says no such thing; neither is it to be concluded, that because a king will do wickedly, he must be suffer'd, any more than a private man, who should take the same resolution. But he told them, that *when they should cry to the Lord by reason of their king, he would not hear them.*[4] This was as much as to say, their ruin was unavoidable; and that, having put the power into the hands of those, who instead of protecting would oppress them; and thereby having provoked God against them, so as he would not hearken to their cries, they could have no relief. But this was no security to the authors of their calamity. The houses of Jeroboam, Baasha and Omri, escaped not unpunished, tho the people did not thereby recover their liberty. The kings had introduced a corruption that was inconsistent with it. But they who could not settle upon a right foundation to prevent future mischiefs, could avenge such as they had suffered, upon the heads of those who had caused them, and frequently did it most severely. The like befell the Romans, when by the violence of tyranny all good order was overthrown, good discipline extinguished, and the people corrupted. Ill princes could be cut in pieces, and mischiefs might be revenged, tho not prevented. But 'tis not so everywhere, nor at all times; and nothing is more irrational, than from one or a few examples to conclude a general necessity of future events. They alter according to circumstances: and as some nations by destroying tyrants could not destroy tyranny; others in removing the tyrant, have cut up tyranny by the roots. This variety has been seen in the same nation at different times: The Romans recovered their liberty by expelling Tarquin; but remained slaves notwithstanding the slaughter of Caesar. Whilst the body of the

[3] [*Patriarcha*, ch. 23, p. 97.]   [4] [1 Samuel 8:18.]

people was uncorrupted, they cured the evil wrought by the person, in taking him away. It was no hard matter to take the regal power that by one man had been enjoy'd for life, and to place it in the hands of two annual magistrates, whilst the nobility and people were, according to the condition of that age, strong and ready to maintain it. But when the mischief had taken deeper root; when the best part of the people had perished in the civil wars; when all their eminent men had fallen in battle, or by the proscriptions; when their discipline was lost, and virtue abolished, the poor remains of the distressed people were brought under the power of a mercenary soldiery, and found no relief. When they kill'd one tyrant, they often made room for a worse: It availed them nothing to cut off a rotten branch, whilst the accursed root remained, and sent forth new sprouts of the same nature to their destruction. Other generous nations have been subdued beyond a possibility of recovery; and those that are naturally base, slide into the like misery without the impulse of an exterior power. They are slaves by nature, and have neither the understanding nor courage that is required for the constitution and management of a government within themselves. They can no more subsist without a master, than a flock without a shepherd. They have no comprehension of liberty, and can neither desire the good they do not know, nor enjoy it if it were bestowed upon them. They bear all burdens; and whatever they suffer, they have no other remedy or refuge, than in the mercy of their Lord. But such nations as are naturally strong, stout, and of good understanding, whose vigour remains unbroken, manners uncorrupted, reputation unblemished, and increasing in numbers; who neither want men to make up such armies as may defend them against foreign or domestick enemies, nor leaders to head them, do ordinarily set limits to their patience. They know how to preserve their liberty, or to vindicate the violation of it; and the more patient they have been, the more inflexible they are when they resolve to be so no longer. Those who are so foolish to put them upon such courses, do to their cost find that there is a difference between lions and asses; and he is a fool who knows not that swords were given to men, that none might be slaves,[5] but such as know not how to use them.

---

[5] Ignoratque datos ne quisquam serviat enses. Lucan. [Lucan, *Pharsalia*, bk. 4, line 579.]

SECTION 5

The Mischiefs suffer'd from wicked Kings are such as render it both reasonable and just for all Nations that have virtue and Power to exert both in repelling them.

I F our author deserve credit, we need not examine whether nations have a right of resisting, or a reasonable hope of succeeding in their endeavours to prevent or avenge the mischiefs that are feared or suffered, for 'tis not worth their pains. *The inconveniences, says he, and miseries which are reckoned up by Samuel, as belonging unto kingly government, were not intolerable, but such as have been and are still born by the subjects' free consent from their princes. Nay at this day, and in this land, many tenants by their tenures are tied unto the same subjection, even unto subordinate and inferior lords.*[1] He is an excellent advocate for kingly government, that accounts inconveniences and miseries to be some of the essentials of it, which others esteem to be only incidents. Tho many princes are violent and wicked, yet some have been gentle and just: tho many have brought misery upon nations, some have been beneficial to them: and they who are esteemed most severe against monarchy, think the evils that are often suffer'd under that form of government, proceed from the corruption of it, or deviation from the principle of its institution; and that they are rather to be imputed to the vices of the person, than to the thing itself; but if our author speak truth, it is universally and eternally naught, inconvenience and misery belong to it.

He thinks to mend this by saying, they are not intolerable: but what is intolerable if inconveniences and miseries be not? For what end can he think governments to have been established, unless to prevent or remove inconveniences and miseries? or how can that be called a government which does not only permit, but cause them? What can incline nations to set up governments? Is it that they may suffer inconveniences, and be brought to misery? or if it be to enjoy happiness, how can that subsist under a government, which not by accident, deflection or corruption, but by a necessity inherent in itself, causes inconveniences and miseries? If it be pretended that no human constitution can be altogether free from inconveniences; I answer, that the best may to some degree fall into

[1] [*Patriarcha*, ch. 23, p. 97. Filmer quotes Raleigh, *History of the World*, in *Works*, vol. 4, p. 472.]

them, because they may be corrupted; but evil and misery can properly belong to none that is not evil in its own nature. If Samuel deserve credit, or may be thought to have spoken sense, he could not have enumerated the evils, which he foresaw the people should suffer from their kings, nor say, that they should cry to the Lord by reason of them, unless they were in themselves grievous, and in comparison greater than what they had suffer'd or known; since that would not have diverted them from their intention, but rather have confirmed them in it. And I leave it to our author to show, why any people should for the pleasure of one or a few men, erect or suffer that which brings more of evil with it than any others.

Moreover, there is a great difference between that which nations sometimes suffer under kings, and that which they willingly suffer; most especially if our author's maxim be received, That all laws are the mandates of kings, and the subjects' liberties and privileges no more than their gracious concessions; for how patient soever they are under the evils they suffer, it might reasonably be believ'd they are so because they know not how to help it: And this is certainly the case of too many places that are known to us. Whoever doubts of this, if he will not put himself to the trouble of going to Turkey or Morocco, let him pass only into Normandy, and ask the naked, barefooted and half-starved people whether they are willing to suffer the miseries under which they groan; and whether the magnificence of Versailles, and the pomp of their haughty master, do any way alleviate their calamities. If this also be a matter of too much pains, the wretches that come hither every day will inform him, that it is not by their own consent they are deprived of all honors and offices in the commonwealth, even of those, which by a corrupt custom that had gained the force of a law, they had dearly bought; prohibited to exercise any trade; exposed to the utmost effects of fraud and violence, if they refuse to adore their master's idols. They will tell him, that 'tis not willingly they leave their lands and estates to seek a shelter in the most remote parts of the world; but because they are under a force which they are not able to resist; and because one part of the nation, which is enriched with the spoils of the other, have foolishly contributed to lay a yoke upon them which they cannot break.

To what he says concerning tenures, I answer, No man in England owes any service to his lord, unless by virtue of a contract made by himself or his predecessors, under which he holds the land granted to him on that condition by the proprietor. There may be something of hardship, but nothing of injustice. 'Tis a voluntary act in the beginning and continuance; and all men know that what is done to one who is willing is no injury.[2] He who did not like the conditions, was not obliged to take the land; and he might leave it, if afterwards he came to dislike them. If any man say, the like may be done by anyone in the kingdom, I answer, That it is not always true; the Protestants now in France cannot without extreme hazard go out of that country, tho they are contented to lose their estates. 'Tis accounted a crime, for which they are condemned perpetually to the galleys, and such as are aiding to them to grievous fines. But before this be acknowledged to have any similitude or relation to our discourse concerning kings, it must be proved, that the present king, or those under whom he claims, is or were proprietors of all the lands in England, and granted the several parcels under the condition of suffering patiently such inconveniences and miseries as are above-mentioned: or that they who did confer the crown upon any of them, did also give a propriety in the land; which I do not find in any of the fifteen or sixteen titles that have been since the coming in of the Normans: and if it was not done to the first of every one, it cannot accrue to the others, unless by some new act to the same purpose, which will not easily be produced.

It will be no less difficult to prove that anything unworthy of freemen is by any tenures imposed in England, unless it be the offering up of the wives and daughters of tenants to the lust of abbots and monks; and they are so far from being willingly suffer'd, that since the dens and nurseries of those beasts were abolished, no man that succeeds them has had impudence sufficient to exact the performance; and tho the letter of the law may favour them, the turpitude of the thing has extinguished the usage.

But even the kings of Israel and Judah, who brought upon the people those evils that had been foretold by Samuel, did not think they had a right to the powers they exercised. If the law had given a right to Ahab to take the best of their vineyards, he might without ceremony have taken that of Naboth, and by the majestick power of an absolute monarch, have chastised the churlish clown, who refused to sell or change it for another: but for want of it, he was obliged to take a very different course.[3] If the lives of subjects had in the like manner depended upon the will of kings, David might without scruple have killed Uriah, rather than to place him in the front of the army that he might fall by his own courage. The malice and treachery of such proceedings argues a defect of power; and he that acts in such an oblique manner, shews that his actions are not warranted by the law, which is boldly executed in the face of the

---

[2] Volenti non sit injuria.   [3] [1 Kings 21.]

sun. This shews the interpretation put upon the words, *Against thee only have I sinned*,[4] by court-flatterers, to be false. If he had not sinned against Bathsheba whom he corrupted, Uriah whom he caused to be killed, the people that he scandalized, and the law which he violated, he had never endeavoured to cover his guilt by so vile a fraud. And as he did not thereby fly the sight of God, but of men, 'tis evident that he in that action feared men more than God.

If by the examples of Israel and Judah, we may judge whether the inconveniences and miseries brought upon nations by their kings be tolerable or intolerable, it will be enough to consider the madness of Saul's cruelty towards his subjects, and the slaughter brought upon them by the hand of the Philistines on Mount Gilboa, where he fell with the flower of all Israel; the civil wars that happened in the time of David, and the plague brought upon the people by his wickedness; the heavy burdens laid upon them by Solomon, and the idolatry favour'd by him; the wretched folly of Rehoboam, and the defection of the ten tribes caused by it; the idolatry established by Jeroboam and the kings of Israel, and that of many of those of Judah also; the frequent wars and unheard of slaughters ensuing thereupon between the tribes; the daily devastations of the country by all sorts of strangers; the murders of the prophets; the abolition of God's worship; the desolation of towns and provinces; the captivity of the ten tribes carried away into unknown countries; and in the end the abolition of both kingdoms, with the captivity of the tribe of Judah, and the utter destruction of the city. It cannot be said that these things were suffer'd under kings, and not from or by them; for the desolation of the cities, people and country is in many places of Scripture imputed to the kings that taught Israel to sin, as appears by what was denounced against Jeroboam, Jehu, Ahab, Manasseh, Zedekiah, and others. Nay the captivity of Babylon with the evils ensuing, were first announced to Hezekiah for his vanity; and Josiah by the like, brought a great slaughter upon himself and people.[5] But if mischiefs fell upon the people by the frailty of these, who after David were the best, nothing surely less than the utmost of all miseries could be expected from such as were set to do evil, and to make the nation like to themselves, in which they met with too great success.

If it be pretended that God's people living under an extraordinary dispensation can be no example to us, I desire other histories may be examined; for I confess I know no nation so great, happy and prosperous, nor any power so well established, that two or three ill kings immediately

---

[4] Psal. 51.   [5] 1 King. 14. 2 King. 21. 2 King. 20.

succeeding each other, have not been able to destroy and bring to such a condition, that it appeared the nations must perish, unless the senates, diets, and other assemblies of state had put a stop to the mischief, by restraining or deposing them; and tho this might be proved by innumerable testimonies, I shall content myself with that of the Roman empire, which perished by the vices, corruption, and baseness of their princes: the noble kingdom of the Goths in Spain overthrown by the tyranny of Witiza and Rodrigo: the present state of Spain now languishing and threatening ruin from the same causes: France brought to the last degree of misery and weakness by the degenerate races of Pharamond and Charles, preserved and restored by the virtues of Pepin and Capet; to which may be added those of our own country, which are so well known that I need not mention them.

SECTION 6

'Tis not good for such Nations as will have Kings, to suffer them to be glorious, powerful, or abounding in Riches.

OUR author having hitherto spoken of all nations, as born under a necessity of being subject to absolute monarchy, which he pretends to have been set up by the universal and indispensible law of God and nature, now seems to leave to their discretion, whether they will have a king or not; but says, that those *who will have a king, are bound to allow him royal maintenance, by providing revenues for the crown; since it is for the honour, profit and safety of the people to have their king glorious, powerful, and abounding in riches.*[1] If there be anything of sense in this clause, there is nothing of truth in the foundation or principle of his whole book. For as the right and being of a father is natural or inherent, and no ways depending upon the will of the child; that of a king is so also, if he be, and ought to enjoy the rights belonging to the father of the people: And 'tis not less ridiculous to say, *those who will have a king*, than it would be to say, *he that will have a father;* for everyone must have one whether he will or not. But if the king be a father, as our author from thence infers that all laws are from him, none can be imposed upon him; and whatsoever the subject enjoys is by his concessions: 'Tis absurd to speak of an obligation lying upon the people to allow him royal maintenance, by

[1] [*Patriarcha*, ch. 23, p. 97.]

providing revenues, since he has all in himself, and they have nothing that is not from him, and depending upon his will. For this reason a worthy gentleman of the house of commons in the year 1640 desired that the business of the judges, who in the Star-Chamber had given for their opinion concerning ship money, *That in cases of necessity the king might provide it by his own authority, and that he was judge of that necessity*, might be first examined, that they might know whether they had anything to give, before they should speak of giving. And as 'tis certain, that if the sentence of those perjur'd wretches had stood, the subjects of England by consequence would have been found to have nothing to give; 'tis no less sure, that if our author's principle concerning the paternal and absolute power of kings be true, it will by a more compendious way appear, that it is not left to the choice of any nation, whether they will have a king or not; for they must have him, and can have nothing to allow him, but must receive all from him.

But if those only who *will have a king*, are bound to have one, and to allow this *royal maintenance*, such as will not have a king, are by one and the same act delivered from the necessity of having one, and from providing maintenance for him; which utterly overthrows the magnificent fabrick of paternal monarchy; and the kings who were lately represented by our author, placed on the throne by God and nature, and endow'd with an absolute power over all, appear to be purely the creatures of the people, and to have nothing but what is received from them.

From hence it may be rationally inferred, that he who makes a thing to be, makes it to be only what he pleases.[2] This must hold in relation to kings as well as other magistrates; and as they who made consuls, dictators, and military tribunes, gave them only such power, and for such a time as best pleased themselves, 'tis impossible they should not have the same right in relation to kings, in making them what they please, as well as not to make them unless they please; except there be a charm belonging to the name, or the letters that compose it; which cannot belong to all nations, for they are different in every one according to the several languages.

But, says our author, 'tis *for the honor, profit, and safety of the people that the king should be glorious, powerful, and abounding in riches*. There is therefore no obligation upon them, and they are to judge whether it be so or not. The Scripture says plainly the contrary: *He shall not multiply silver and gold, wives and horses: he shall not lift up his heart above his brethren.*[3] He shall not therefore be glorious, powerful, or abounding in riches. Reason and

[2] Qui dat esse, dat modum esse. [He who gives being, gives the mode of being.] [3] Deut. 17.

experience teach us the same thing: If those nations that have been proud, luxurious and vicious, have desired by pomp and riches to foment the vices of their princes, thereby to cherish their own; such as have excelled in virtue and good discipline have abhorred it, and except the immediate exercise of their office have kept their supreme magistrates to a manner of living little different from that of private men: and it had been impossible to maintain that frugality, in which the integrity of their manners did chiefly consist, if they had set up an example directly contrary to it, in him who was to be an example to others; or to provide for their own safety, if they had overthrown that integrity of manners by which it could only be obtained and preserved. There is a necessity incumbent upon every nation that lives in the like principle, to put a stop to the entrance of those vices that arise from the superfluity of riches, by keeping their kings in that honest poverty, which is the mother and nurse of modesty, sobriety, and all manner of virtue: And no man can deny this to be well done, unless he will affirm that pride, luxury and vice is more profitable to a nation than the virtues that are upheld by frugality.

There is another reason of no less importance to those nations, who tho they think fit to have kings, yet desire to preserve their liberty, which obliges them to set limits to the glory, power and riches of their kings; and that is, that they can no otherwise be kept within the rules of the law. Men are naturally propense to corruption; and if he whose will and interest it is to corrupt them, be furnished with the means, he will never fail to do it. Power, honors, riches, and the pleasures that attend them, are the baits by which men are drawn to prefer a personal interest before the publick good; and the number of those who covet them is so great, that he who abounds in them will be able to gain so many to his service as shall be sufficient to subdue the rest. 'Tis hard to find a tyranny in the world that has not been introduced this way; for no man by his own strength could ever subdue a multitude; none could ever bring many to be subservient to his ill designs, but by the rewards they received or hoped. By this means Caesar accomplished his work, and overthrew the liberty of his country, and with it all that was then good in the world. They who were corrupted in their minds, desired to put all the power and riches into his hands, that he might distribute them to such as served him. And he who was nothing less than covetous in his own nature, desired riches, that he might gain followers; and by the plunder of Gaul he corrupted those that betray'd Rome to him. And tho I do not delight to speak of the affairs of our own time, I desire those who know the present state of France to tell me, whether it were possible for the king to keep that nation under servitude, if a vast revenue did not enable him to gain so many to his particular service as are sufficient to keep the rest in subjection: and if this be not enough, let them consider whether all the dangers that now threaten us at home, do not proceed from the madness of those who gave such a revenue, as is utterly unproportionable to the riches of the nation, unsuitable to the modest behaviour expected from our kings, and which in time will render parliaments unnecessary to them.

On the other hand, the poverty and simplicity of the Spartan kings was no less safe and profitable to the people, than truly glorious to them. Agesilaus denied that Artaxerxes was greater than he, unless he were more temperate or more valiant;[4] and he made good his words so well, that without any other assistance than what his wisdom and valour did afford, he struck such a terror into that great, rich, powerful and absolute monarch, that he did not think himself safe in Babylon or Ecbatana, till the poor Spartan was, by a captain of as great valour, and greater poverty, obliged to return from Asia to the defence of his own country. This was not peculiar to the severe Laconic discipline. When the Roman kings were expelled, a few carts were prepared to transport their goods: and their lands which were consecrated to Mars, and now go under the name of Campus Martius, hardly contain ten acres of ground. Nay the kings of Israel, who led such vast armies into the field (that is, were followed by all the people who were able to bear arms) seem to have possessed little. Ahab, one of the most powerful, was so fond of Naboth's vineyard (which being the inheritance of his fathers, according to their equal division of lands, could not be above two acres) that he grew sick when it was refused.

But if an allowance be to be made to every king, it must be either according to a universal rule or standard, or must depend upon the judgment of nations. If the first, they who have it, may do well to produce it; if the other, every nation proceeding according to the measure of their own discretion, is free from blame.

It may also be worth observation, whether the revenue given to a king be in such manner committed to his care, that he is obliged to employ it for the publick service without the power of alienation; or whether it be granted as a propriety, to be spent as he thinks fit. When some of the ancient Jews and Christians scrupled the payment of tribute to the emperors, the reasons alleged to persuade them to a compliance, seem to be grounded upon a supposition of the first: for, said they, the defence of the state lies upon them, which cannot be perform'd without armies

---

[4] [Plutarch, *Life of Agesilaus*, ch. 23.]

and garrisons; these cannot be maintained without pay, nor money raised to pay them without tributes and customs. This carries a face of reason with it, especially in those countries which are perpetually or frequently subject to invasions; but this will not content our author. He speaks of employing the revenue in keeping his house, and looks upon it as a propriety to be spent as he thinks convenient; which is no less than to cast it into a pit, of which no man ever knew the bottom. That which is given one day, is squandered away the next: The people is always oppress'd with impositions, to foment the vices of the court: These daily increasing, they grow insatiable, and the miserable nations are compelled to hard labour, in order to satiate those lusts that tend to their own ruin.

It may be consider'd that the virtuous pagans, by the light of nature, discovered the truth of this.[5] Poverty grew odious in Rome, when great men by desiring riches put a value upon them, and introduced that pomp and luxury which could not be borne by men of small fortunes. From thence all furies and mischiefs seem'd to break loose: The base, slavish, and so often subdued Asia, by the basest of men revenged the defeats they had received from the bravest; and by infusing into them a delight in pomp and luxury, in a short time rendered the strongest and bravest of nations the weakest and basest. I wish our own experience did not too plainly manifest, that these evils were never more prevalent than in our days, when the luxury, majestick pomp, and absolute power of a neighbouring king must be supported by an abundance of riches torn out of the bowels of his subjects, which renders them, in the best country of the world, and at a time when the crown most flourishes, the poorest and most miserable of all the nations under the sun. We too well know who are most apt to learn from them, and by what means and steps they endeavour to lead us into the like misery. But the bird is safe when the snare is discover'd; and if we are not abandoned by God to destruction, we shall never be brought to consent to the settling of that pomp, which is against the practice of all virtuous people, and has brought all the nations that have been taken with it into the ruin that is intended for us.

---

[5] Saevior armis / Luxuria incubuit, victumque ulciscitur orbem. / Nullum crimen abest, facinusque libidinis, ex quo / Paupertas Romana perit. Juvenal. ["Luxury more savage than arms settled upon and took vengeance upon a conquered world. No accusation and crime of lust were absent, from the time when Roman poverty perished." Juvenal, *Satire* 6, li. 292–295.]

SECTION 7

When the Israelites asked for such a King
as the Nations about them had, they asked for a Tyrant,
tho they did not call him so.

NOW *that Saul was no tyrant*, says our author, *note, that the people asked a king as all nations had: God answers, and bids Samuel to hear the voice of the people in all things which they spake, and appoint them a king. They did not ask a tyrant; and to give them a tyrant when they asked a king, had not been to hear their voice in all things, but rather when they asked an egg to have given them a scorpion; unless we will say that all nations had tyrants.*[1] But before he drew such a conclusion, he should have observed, that God did not give them a scorpion when they asked an egg, but told them that was a scorpion which they called an egg: They would have a king to judge them, to go out before them, and to fight their battles; but God in effect told them, he would overthrow all justice, and turn the power that was given him, to the ruin of them and their posterity. But since they would have it so, he commanded Samuel to hearken to their voice, and for the punishment of their sin and folly, to give them such a king as they asked, that is, one who would turn to his own profit and their misery, the power with which he should be entrusted; and this truly denominates a tyrant. Aristotle makes no other distinction between a king and a tyrant, than that the king governs for the good of the people, the tyrant for his own pleasure or profit:[2] and they who asked such a one, asked a tyrant, tho they called him a king. This is all could be done in their language: for as they who are skilled in the Oriental tongues assure me, there is no name for a tyrant in any of them, or any other way of expressing the thing than by circumlocution, and adding proud, insolent, lustful, cruel, violent, or the like epithets, to the word lord, or king. They did in effect ask a tyrant: They would not have such a king as God had ordain'd, but such a one as the nations had. Not that all nations had tyrants; but those who were round about them, of whom they had knowledge, and which in their manner of speaking went under the name of all, were blessed with such masters. This way of expression was used by Lot's daughters, who said, there was not a man in all the earth to come in to them;[3] because there was none in the neighborhood with whom it was thought fit they

---

[1] [*Patriarcha*, ch. 23, p. 98.]
[2] [Aristotle, *Politics*, bk. 5, 1311a.]
[3] [Genesis 19:31.]

should accompany. Now, that the Eastern nations were then, and are still under the government of those which all free people call tyrants, is evident to all men. God therefore in giving them a tyrant, or rather a government that would turn into tyranny, gave them what they asked under another name; and without any blemish to the mercy promised to their fathers, suffered them to bear the penalty of their wickedness and folly in rejecting him that he should not reign over them.

But tho the name of tyrant was unknown to them, yet in Greece, from whence the word comes, it signified no more than one who governed according to his own will, distinguished from kings that governed by law; and was not taken in an ill sense, till those who had been advanced for their justice, wisdom and valour, or their descendants, were found to depart from the ends of their institution, and to turn that power to the oppression of the people, which had been given for their protection: But by these means it grew odious, and that kind of government came to be thought only tolerable by the basest of men; and those who destroy'd it, were in all places esteemed to be the best.

If monarchy had been universally evil, God had not in the 17th of Deuteronomy given leave to the Israelites to set up a king; and if that kind of king had been asked, he had not been displeased: and they could not have been said to reject God, if they had not asked that which was evil; for nothing that is good is contrary, or inconsistent with a people's obedience to him. The monarchy they asked was displeasing to God, it was therefore evil. But a tyrant is no more than an evil or corrupted monarch: The king therefore that they demanded was a tyrant: God in granting one who would prove a tyrant, gave them what they asked; and that they might know what they did, and what he would be, he told them they rejected him, and should cry by reason of the king they desired.

This denotes him to be a tyrant: for as the government of a king ought to be gentle and easy, tending to the good of the people, resembling the tender care of a father to his family; if he who is set up to be a king, and to be like to that father, do lay a heavy yoke upon the people, and use them as slaves and not as children, he must renounce all resemblance of a father, and be accounted an enemy.

But, says our author, *whereas the people's crying argues some tyrannical oppression, we may remember that the people's cries are not always an argument of their living under a tyrant. No man will say Solomon was a tyrant, yet all the congregation complain'd that Solomon make their yoke grievous.*[4] 'Tis strange, that when children, nay when whelps cry, it should be accounted a mark

---

[4] [*Patriarcha*, ch. 23, p. 98.]

that they are troubled, and that the cry of the whole people should be none: Or that the government which is erected for their ease, should not be esteemed tyrannical if it prove grievous to those it should relieve. But as I know no example of a people that did generally complain without cause, our adversaries must allege some other than that of Solomon, before I believe it of any. We are to speak reverently of him: He was excellent in wisdom; he built the Temple, and God appeared twice to him: But it must be confess'd, that during a great part of his life he acted directly contrary to the law given by God to kings, and that his ways were evil and oppressive to the people, if those of God were good. Kings were forbidden to multiply horses, wives, silver and gold: But he brought together more silver and gold, and provided more horses, wives and concubines than any man is known to have had: And tho he did not actually return to Egypt, yet he introduced their abominable idolatry, and so far raised his heart above his brethren, that he made them subservient to his pomp and glory. The people might probably be pleased with a great part of this; but when the yoke became grievous, and his foolish son would not render it more easy, they threw it off; and the thing being from the Lord, it was good, unless he be evil.

But as just governments are established for the good of the governed, and the Israelites desir'd a king, that it might be well with them, not with him, who was not yet known to them; that which exalts one to the prejudice of those that made him, must always be evil, and the people that suffers the prejudice must needs know it better than any other. He that denies this, may think the state of France might have been best known from Bulion the late treasurer, who finding Lewis the Thirteenth to be troubled at the people's misery, told him they were too happy, since they were not reduced to eat grass. But if words are to be understood as they are ordinarily used, and we have no other than that of tyranny to express a monarchy that is either evil in the institution, or fallen into corruption, we may justly call that *tyranny* which the Scripture calls a *grievous yoke*, and which neither the old nor the new counsellors of Rehoboam could deny to be so: for tho the first advised him to promise amendment, and the others to do worse, yet all agreed that what the people said was true.

This yoke is always odious to such as are not by natural stupidity and baseness fitted for it; but those who are so, never complain. An ass will bear a multitude of blows patiently, but the least of them drives a lion into a rage. He that said, the rod is made for the back of fools, confessed that oppression will make a wise man mad. And the most unnatural of all oppressions is to use lions like asses, and to lay that yoke upon a generous nation, which only the basest can deserve; and for want of a better word we call this tyranny.

Our author is not contented to vindicate Solomon only, but extends his indulgence to Saul. His custom is to patronize all that is detestable, and no better testimony could be given of it. *It is true*, says he, *Saul lost his kingdom, but not for being too cruel or tyrannical unto his subjects, but for being too merciful unto his enemies:*[5] But he alleges no other reason, than that the slaughter of the priests is not blamed; not observing that the writers of the Scripture in relating those things that are known to be abominable by the light of nature, frequently say no more of them: And if this be not so, Lot's drunkenness and incest, Reuben's pollution of his father's bed, Abimelech's slaughter of his seventy brothers, and many of the most wicked acts that ever were committed, may pass for laudable and innocent.[6] But if Saul were not to be blamed for killing the priests, why was David blamed for the death of Uriah?[7] Why were the dogs to lick the blood of Ahab and Jezebel, if they did nothing more than kings might do without blame? Now if the slaughter of one man was so severely avenged upon the authors and their families, none but such as Filmer can think that of so many innocent men, with their wives and children, could escape unreproved or unpunished. But the whole series of the history of Saul shewing evidently that his life and reign were full of the most violent cruelty and madness, we are to seek no other reason for the ruin threatened and brought upon him and his family. And as those princes who are most barbarously savage against their own people, are usually most gentle to the enemies of their country, he could not give a more certain testimony of his hatred to those he ought to have protected, than by preserving those nations, who were their most irreconcilable enemies. This is proved by reason as well as by experience; for every man knows he cannot bear the hatred of all mankind: Such as know they have enemies abroad, endeavour to get friends at home: Those who command powerful nations, and are beloved by them, fear not to offend strangers. But if they have rendered their own people enemies to them, they cannot hope for help in a time of distress, nor so much as a place of retreat or refuge, unless from strangers, nor from them unless they deserve it, by favouring them to the prejudice of their own country. As no man can serve two masters, no man can pursue two contrary interests: Moses, Joshua, Gideon and Samuel, were severe to the Amorites, Midianites and Canaanites, but

---

5 [*Patriarcha*, ch. 23, p. 99.]

6 [Genesis 19:32–38; 35:22; Judges 9:1–6.]

7 Thou hast killed Uriah with the sword of the children of Ammon: Now therefore the sword shall never depart from thy house, 2 Sam. 12.

mild and gentle to the Hebrews. Saul, who was cruel to the Hebrews, spared the Amalekites, whose preservation was their destruction: and whilst he destroyed those he should have saved, and saved those that by a general and particular command of God he should have destroyed, he lost his ill-govern'd kingdom, and left an example to posterity of the end that may be expected from pride, folly and tyranny.

The matter would not be much alter'd, if I should confess, that in the time of Saul all nations were governed by tyrants (tho it is not true, for Greece did then flourish in liberty, and we have reason to believe that other nations did so also) for tho they might not think of a good government at the first, nothing can oblige men to continue under one that is bad, when they discover the evils of it, and know how to mend it. They who trusted men that appeared to have great virtues, with such a power as might easily be turned into tyranny, might justly retract, limit or abolish it, when they found it to be abused. And tho no condition had been reserved, the publick good, which is the end of all government,[8] had been sufficient to abrogate all that should tend to the contrary. As the malice of men and their inventions to do mischief increase daily, all would soon be brought under the power of the worst, if care were not taken, and opportunities embraced to find new ways of preventing it. He that should make war at this day as the best commanders did two hundred years past, would be beaten by the meanest soldier. The places then accounted impregnable are now slighted as indefensible; and if the arts of defending were not improved as well as those of assaulting, none would be able to hold out a day. Men were sent into the world rude and ignorant, and if they might not have used their natural faculties to find out that which is good for themselves, all must have been condemn'd to continue in the ignorance of our first fathers, and to make no use of their understanding to the ends for which it was given.

The bestial barbarity in which many nations, especially of Africa, America and Asia, do now live, shews what human nature is, if it be not improved by art and discipline; and if the first errors, committed through ignorance, might not be corrected, all would be obliged to continue in them, and for anything I know, we must return to the religion, manners and policy that were found in our country at Caesar's landing. To affirm this is no less than to destroy all that is commendable in the world, and to render the understanding given to men utterly useless. But if it be lawful for us by the use of that understanding to build houses, ships and forts better than our ancestors, to make such arms as are most fit for our

---

[8] Salus populi suprema lex.

defence, and to invent printing, with an infinite number of other arts beneficial to mankind, why have we not the same right in matters of government, upon which all others do almost absolutely depend? If men are not obliged to live in caves and hollow trees, to eat acorns, and to go naked, why should they be forever obliged to continue under the same form of government that their ancestors happened to set up in the time of their ignorance? Or if they were not so ignorant to set up one that was not good enough for the age in which they lived, why should it not be altered, when tricks are found out to turn that to the prejudice of nations, which was erected for their good? From whence should malice and wickedness gain a privilege of putting new inventions to do mischief every day into practice? and who is it that so far protects them, as to forbid good and innocent men to find new ways also of defending themselves from it? If there be any that do this, they must be such as live in the same principle; who whilst they pretend to exercise justice, provide only for the indemnity of their own crimes, and the advancement of unjust designs. They would have a right of attacking us with all the advantages of the arms now in use, and the arts which by the practice of so many ages have been wonderfully refined, whilst we should be obliged to employ no others in our just defence, than such as were known to our naked ancestors when Caesar invaded them, or to the Indians when they fell under the dominion of the Spaniards. This would be a compendious way of placing uncontroll'd iniquity in all the kingdoms of the world, and to overthrow all that deserves the name of good by the introduction of such accursed maxims. But if no man dares to acknowledge any such, except those whose acknowledgment is a discredit, we ought not to suffer them to be obliquely obtruded upon us, nor to think that God has so far abandoned us into the hands of our enemies, as not to leave us the liberty of using the same arms in our defence as they do to offend and injure us.

We shall be told, that prayers and tears were the only arms of the first Christians, and that Christ commanded his disciples to pray for those that persecuted them: But besides that those precepts of the most extreme lenity do ill suit with the violent practices of those who attempt to enslave nations, and who by alleging them do plainly shew either that they do not extend to all Christians, or that they themselves are none whilst they act contrary to them, they are to know, that those precepts were merely temporary, and directed to the persons of the apostles, who were armed only with the sword of the spirit; that the primitive Christians used prayers and tears only no longer than whilst they had no other arms. But knowing that by lifting themselves under the ensigns of Christianity they had not lost the rights belonging to all mankind, when nations came to be converted, they noway thought themselves obliged to give their enemies a certain opportunity of destroying them, when God had put means into their hands of defending themselves; and proceeded so far in this way, that the Christian valour soon became no less famous and remarkable than that of the pagans. They did with the utmost vigour defend both their civil and religious rights against all the powers of earth and hell, who by force and fraud endeavoured to destroy them.

SECTION 8

Under the name of Tribute
no more is understood than what the Law of each Nation
gives to the supreme Magistrate for the defraying of
publick Charges; to which the Customs of the Romans,
or sufferings of the Jews have no relation.

IF *any desire the directions of the New Testament*, says our author, *he may find our Saviour limiting and distinguishing royal power, by giving to Caesar those things that are Caesar's, and to God the things that are God's.*[1] But that will be of no advantage to him in this contest. We do not deny to any man that which is his due; but do not so well know who is Caesar, nor what it is that can truly be said to be due to him. I grant that when those words were spoken, the power of the Romans exercised by Tiberius was then expressed by the name of Caesar, which he without any title had assumed. The Jews amongst many other nations having been subdued, submitted to it; and being noway competent judges of the rights belonging to the senate or people of Rome, were obliged to acknowledge that power which their masters were under. They had no commonwealth of their own, nor any other government amongst themselves, that was not precarious. They thought Christ was to have restored their kingdom, and by them to have reigned over the nations; but he shewed them they were to be subject to the Gentiles, and that within few years their city and temple should be destroy'd. Their commonwealth must needs expire when all that was prefigured by it was accomplished. It was not for them at such a time to presume upon their abrogated privileges, nor the promises

---

[1] [*Patriarcha*, ch. 23, p. 99.]

made to them, which were then fulfilled. Nay, they had by their sins profaned themselves, and given to the Gentiles a right over them, which none could have had, if they had continued in their obedience to the law of God. This was the foundation of the Caesars' dominion over them, but can have no influence upon us. The first of the Caesars had not been set up by them: The series of them had not been continued by their consent: They had not interrupted the succession by placing or displacing such as they pleased: They had not brought in strangers or bastards, nor preferred the remotest in blood before the nearest: They had no part in making the laws by which they were governed, nor had the Caesars sworn to them: They had no Great Charter, acknowledging their liberties to be innate or inherent in them, confirmed by immemorial custom, and strengthen'd by thirty acts of their own general assemblies, with the assent of the Romans: The Caesar who then governed came not to the power by their consent: The question, *Will ye have this man to reign?* had never been asked; but he being imposed upon them, they were to submit to the laws by which he governed their masters. This can be nothing to us, whose case is in every respect most unlike to theirs. We have no dictatorian power over us; and neither we nor our fathers have rendered or owed obedience to any human laws but our own, nor to any other magistracy than what we have established. We have a king who reigns by law. His power is from the *law that makes him king:*[2] and we can know only from thence what he is to command, and what we are obliged to obey. We know the power of the Caesars was usurped, maintained and exercised with the most detestable violence, injustice and cruelty. But tho it had been established by the consent of the Romans from an opinion that it was good for them in that state of affairs, it were nothing to us: and we could be no more obliged to follow their example in that than to be governed by consuls, tribunes, and decemviri, or to constitute such a government as they set up when they expelled their kings. Their authority was as good at one time as at the other; or if a difference ought to be made, the preference is to be given to what they did when their manners were most pure, the people most free, and when virtue was most flourishing among them. But if we are not obliged to set up such a magistracy as they had, 'tis ridiculous to think that such an obedience is due to one who is not in being as they pay'd to him that was. And if I should confess that Caesar holding the senate and people of Rome under the power of the sword, imposed what tribute he pleased upon the provinces; and that

---

[2] Lex facit ut sit rex. Bracton. [Bracton, *On the Laws and Customs of England*, fol. 107, p. 306.]

the Jews, who had no part in the government, were obliged to submit to his will, our liberty of paying nothing, except what the parliament appoints, and yielding obedience to no laws but such as are made to be so by their authority, or by our own immemorial customs, could not be thereby infringed. But we may justly affirm, that the tribute imposed was not, as our author infers, *all their coin*,[3] nor a considerable part of it, nor more than what was understood to go for the defraying of the publick charges. Christ by asking whose image and superscription was stamped upon their money, and thereupon commanding them to give to Caesar that which was Caesar's, did not imply that all was his; but that Caesar's money being current amongst them, it was a continual and evident testimony, that they acknowledged themselves to be under his jurisdiction, and therefore could not refuse to pay the tribute laid upon them by the same authority, as other nations did.

It may also be observed, that Christ did not so much say this to determine the questions that might arise concerning Caesar's power; for he plainly says, that was not his work; but to put the Pharisees to silence who tempted him. According to the opinion of the Jews, that the Messiah would restore the kingdom of Israel, they thought his first work would be to throw off the Roman yoke; and not believing him to be the man, they would have brought him to avow the thing, that they might destroy him. But as that was not his business, and that his time was not yet come, it was not necessary to give them any other answer, than such as might disappoint their purpose. This shews that, without detracting from the honor due to Augustine, Ambrose or Tertullian, I may justly say, that the decision of such questions as arise concerning our government must be decided by our laws, and not by their writings. They were excellent men, but living in another time, under a very different government, and applying themselves to other matters, they had no knowledge at all of those that concern us. They knew what government they were under, and thereupon judged what a broken and dispersed people ow'd to that which had given law to the best part of the world before they were in being, under which they had been educated, and which after a most cruel persecution was become propitious to them. They knew that the word of the emperor was a law to the senate and people, who were under the power of that man that could get the best army; but perhaps had never heard of such mixed governments as ours, tho about that time they began to appear in the world. And it might be as reasonably concluded, that there ought to be no rule in the succession or election of

[3] [*Patriarcha*, pp. 99–100; but Filmer does not say "all their coin."]

[361]

princes, because the Roman emperors were set up by the violence of the soldiers, and for the most part by the slaughter of him who was in possession of the power, as that all other princes must be absolute when they have it, and do what they please, till another more strong and more happy, may by the like means wrest the same power from them.

I am much mistaken if this be not true; but without prejudice to our cause, we may take that which they say, according to their true meaning, in the utmost extent. And to begin with Tertullian: 'Tis good to consider the subject of his discourse, and to whom he wrote. The treatise cited by our author is the *Apologetick*, and tends to persuade the pagans, that civil magistrates might not intermeddle with religion; and that the laws made by them touching those matters, were of no value, as relating to things of which they had no cognizance. *'Tis not*, says he, *length of time, nor the dignity of the legislators, but equity only that can commend laws; and when any are found to be unjust, they are deservedly condemned.*⁴ By which words he denied that the magistratical power which the Romans acknowledged in Caesar, had anything to do in spiritual things. And little advantage can be taken by Christian princes from what he says concerning the Roman emperors; for he expressly declares, *That the Caesars would have believed in Christ, if they had either not been necessary to the secular government, or that Christians might have been Caesars.*⁵ This seems to have proceeded from an opinion received by Christians in the first ages, that the use of the civil as well as the military sword was equally accursed: That *Christians were to be sons of peace, enemies to no man; and that Christ by commanding Peter to put up his sword, did forever disarm all Christians.*⁶ He proceeds to say, *We cannot fight to defend our goods, having in our Baptism renounc'd the world, and all that is in it; nor to gain honors, accounting nothing more foreign to us than publick affairs, and acknowledging no other commonwealth than that of the whole world;*⁷ Nor to save our lives, because we account it a happiness to be killed. He dissuades the pagans from executing Christians, rather from charity to them in keeping them from the crime of slaughtering the innocent, than that they were unwilling to suffer: and

---

⁴ Leges non annorum numerus, nec conditorum dignitas, sed sola aequitas commendat, atque ideo si iniquae cognoscuntur merito damnantur. Tertul. Ap. [Tertullian, *Apology*, ch. 4, sec. 10.]

⁵ Sed & Caesares super Christo credidissent, si aut Caesares non essent saeculo necessarii, aut Christiani potuissent esse Caesares. Ibid. [Ibid., ch. 21, sec. 24.]

⁶ Filii pacis, nullius hostes; & Christus ex-armando Petrum, omnem Christianum militem in aeternum discinxit. Ibid. [Tertullian, *Letter to Scapula*, ch. 2, and *On Idolatry*, ch. 19.]

⁷ Nobis omnis gloriae & dignitatis ardore frigentibus, &c. Nec alia res est nobis magis aliena quam publica: unam nobis rempublicam mundum agnoscimus. [Tertullian, *Apology*, ch. 38, sec. 3.]

gives no other reasons of their prayers for the emperors, than that they were commanded to love their enemies, and to pray for those who persecuted them, except such as he drew from a mistake, that the world was shortly to finish with the dissolution of the empire. All his works, as well those that were written before he fell into Montanism, as those published afterwards, are full of the like opinions; and if Filmer acknowledges them to be true, he must confess, that princes are not fathers, but enemies:[8] and not only they, but all those who render themselves ministers of the powers they execute, in taking upon them the sword that Christ had cursed, do renounce him; and we may consider how to proceed with such as do so. If our author will not acknowledge this, then no man was ever guilty of a more vile prevarication than he, who alleges those words in favour of his cause, which have their only strength in opinions that he thinks false, and in the authority of a man whom in that very thing he condemns; and must do so, or overthrow all that he endeavours to support. But Tertullian's opinions concerning these matters have no relation to our present question. The design of his apology, and the treatise to Scapula almost upon the same subject, was to show, that the civil magistracy which he comprehends under the name of Caesar, had nothing to do with matters of religion; and that, as no man could be a Christian who would undertake the work of a magistrate, they who were jealous the publick offices might be taken out of their hands, had nothing to fear from Christians who resolved not to meddle with them. Whereas our question is only, whether that magistratical power, which by law or usurpation was then in Caesar, must necessarily in all times, and in all places, be in one man, or may be divided and balanced according to the laws of every country, concerning which he says nothing: Or whether we, who do not renounce the use of the civil or military sword, who have a part in the government, and think it our duty to apply ourselves to publick cares, should lay them aside because the ancient Christians every hour expecting death, did not trouble themselves with them.

If Ambrose after he was a bishop, employ'd the ferocity of a soldier which he still retained, rather in advancing the power of the clergy, than the good of mankind by restraining the rage of tyrants, it can be no prejudice to our cause, of which he had no cognisance. He spoke of the violent and despotical government, to which he had been a minister before his baptism, and seems to have had no knowledge of the Gothick polity, that within a few years grew famous by the overthrow of the

---

[8] Qui enim magis inimici Christianorum, quam de quorum majestate convenimur in crimen. Tertul. ib. ["For who could be greater enemies of Christians than those towards whom we are accused of treason?" Tertullian, *Apology*, ch. 31.]

Roman tyranny, and delivering the world from the yoke which it could no longer bear. And if Augustine might say, That *the emperor is subject to no laws, because he has a power of making laws,* I may as justly say, that our kings are subject to laws, because they can make no law, and have no power but what is given by the laws. If this be not the case, I desire to know who made the laws, to which they and their predecessors have sworn; and whether they can according to their own will abrogate those ancient laws by which they are made to be what they are, and by which we enjoy what we have; or whether they can make new laws by their own power? If no man but our author have impudence enough to assert any such thing; and if all the kings we ever had, except Richard the second, did renounce it, we may conclude that Augustine's words have no relation to our dispute; and that 'twere to no purpose to examine, whether the fathers mention any reservation of power to the laws of the land, or to the people, it being as lawful for all nations, if they think fit, to frame governments different from those that were then in being, as to build bastions, halfmoons, hornworks, ravelins or counterscarps, or to make use of muskets, cannon, mortars, carabines or pistols, which were unknown to them.

What Solomon says of the Hebrew kings, does as little concern us. We have already proved their power not to have been absolute, tho greater than that which the law allows to ours. It might upon occasion be a prudent advice to private persons living under such governments as were usual in the Eastern countries, *to keep the king's commandments, and not to say, What dost thou? because where the word of a king is, there is power, and all that he pleaseth he will do.*[9] But all these words are not his; and those that are, must not be taken in a general sense; for tho his son was a king, yet in his words there was no power: He could not do what he pleased, nor hinder others from doing what they pleased: He would have added weight to the yoke that lay upon the necks of the Israelites, but he could not;[10] and we do not find him to have been master of much more than his own tongue, to speak as many foolish things as he pleased. In other things, whether he had to deal with his own people, or with strangers, he was weak and impotent; and the wretches who flatter'd him in his follies, could be of no help to him. The like has befallen many others: Those who are wise, virtuous, valiant, just, and lovers of their people, have and ought to have power; but such as are lewd, vicious, foolish, and haters of their people, ought to have none, and are often deprived of all. This was well known to Solomon, who says, That *a wise child is better than an*

---

[9] [Ecclesiastes 8:2–4.]   [10] [1 Kings 12.]

old and foolish king that will not be advised.[11] When Nebuchadnezzar set himself in the place of God, his kingdom was taken from him, and he was driven from the society of men to herd with beasts.[12] There was power for a time in the word of Nero: he murdered many excellent men; but he was call'd to account, and the world abandon'd the monster it had too long endur'd. He found none to defend him, nor any better help, when he desir'd to die, than the hand of a slave. Besides this, some kings by their institution have little power; some have been deprived of what they had, for abusing, or rendering themselves unworthy of it; and histories afford us innumerable examples of both sorts.

But tho I shall confess that there is always power in the word of a king, it would be nothing to us who dispute concerning right, and have no regard to that power which is void of it. A thief or a pirate may have power; but that avails him not, when, as often befell the Caesars, he meets with one who has more, and is always unsafe, since having no effect upon the consciences of men, every one may destroy him that can: And I leave it to kings to consider how much they stand obliged to those, who placing their rights upon the same foot, expose their persons to the same dangers.

But if kings desire that in their word there should be power, let them take care that it be always accompanied with truth and justice. Let them seek the good of their people, and the hands of all good men will be with them. Let them not exalt themselves insolently, and everyone will desire to exalt them. Let them acknowledge themselves to be the servants of the publick, and all men will be theirs. Let such as are most addicted to them, talk no more of Caesars, nor the tributes due to them. We have nothing to do with the name of Caesar. They who at this day live under it, reject the prerogatives anciently usurped by those that had it, and are govern'd by no other laws than their own. We know no law to which we owe obedience, but that of God, and ourselves. Asiatick slaves usually pay such tributes as are imposed upon them; and whilst braver nations lay under the Roman tyranny, they were forced to submit to the same burdens. But even those tributes were paid for maintaining armies, fleets and garrisons, without which the poor and abject life they led could not have been preserved. We owe none but what we freely give. None is or can be imposed upon us, unless by ourselves. We measure our grants according to our own will, or the present occasions, for our own safety. Our ancestors were born free, and, as the best provision they could make for us, they left us that liberty entire, with the best laws they could

[11] [Ecclesiastes 4:13.] [12] [Daniel 4.]

devise to defend it. 'Tis no way impair'd by the opinions of the fathers. The words of Solomon do rather confirm it. The happiness of those who enjoy the like, and the shameful misery they lie under, who have suffer'd themselves to be forced or cheated out of it, may persuade, and the justice of the cause encourage us to think nothing too dear to be hazarded in the defence of it.

SECTION 9

Our own Laws confirm to us the enjoyment of our native Rights.

I f that which our author calls divinity did reach the things in dispute between us, or that the opinions of the fathers which he alleges, related to them, he might have spared the pains of examining our laws: for a municipal sanction were of little force to confirm a perpetual and universal law given by God to mankind, and of no value against it, since man cannot abrogate what God hath instituted, nor one nation free itself from a law that is given to all. But having abused the Scriptures, and the writings of the Fathers (whose opinions are to be valued only so far as they rightly interpret them), he seems desirous to try whether he can as well put a false sense upon our law, and has fully compassed his design. According to his custom he takes pieces of passages from good books, and turns them directly against the plain meaning of the authors, expressed in the whole scope and design of their writings. To show that he intends to spare none, he is not ashamed to cite Bracton, who of all our ancient law-writers is most opposite to his maxims. He lived, says he, in Henry the third's time, since parliaments were instituted:[1] as if there had been a time when England had wanted them; or that the establishment of our liberty had been made by the Normans, who, if we will believe our author, came in by force of arms, and oppressed us. But we have already proved the essence of parliaments to be as ancient as our nation, and that there was no time in which there were not such councils or assemblies of the people as had the power of the whole, and made or unmade such laws as best pleased themselves. We have indeed a French word from a people that came from France, but the power was always in ourselves; and the Norman kings were obliged to swear they would govern according

[1] [*Patriarcha*, ch. 23, p. 100.]

to the laws that had been made by those assemblies. It imports little whether Bracton lived before or after they came amongst us. His words are, *Omnes sub eo, & ipse sub nullo, sed tantum sub Deo; All are under him, and he under none but God only. If he offend, since no writ can go out against him, their remedy is by petitioning him to amend his faults; which if he will not do, it is punishment enough for him to expect God as an avenger. Let none presume to look into his deeds, much less to oppose him.* Here is a mixture of sense and nonsense, truth and falsehood, the words of Bracton with our author's foolish inferences from them.[2] Bracton spoke of the politick capacity of the king, when no law had forbidden him to divide it from his natural. He gave the name of king to the sovereign power of the nation, as Jacob called that of his descendants the scepter; which he said should not depart from Judah till Shiloh came, tho all men know that his race did not reign the third part of that time over his own tribe, nor full fourscore years over the whole nation. The same manner of speech is used in all parts of the world. Tertullian under the name of Caesar comprehended all magistratical power, and imputed to him the acts of which in his person he never had any knowledge. The French say, their king is always present, *sur son lit de justice*,[3] in all the sovereign courts of the kingdom, which are not easily numbered; and that maxim could have in it neither sense nor truth, if by it they meant a man, who can be but in one place at one time, and is always comprehended within the dimensions of his own skin. These things could not be unknown to Bracton, the like being in use amongst us; and he thought it no offence so far to follow the dictates of reason prohibited by no law, as to make a difference between the invisible and omnipresent king, who never dies, and the person that wears the crown, whom no man without the guilt of treason may endeavour to kill, since there is an act of parliament in the case. I will not determine whether he spoke properly or no as to England; but if he did not, all that he said being upon a false supposition, is nothing to our purpose. The same Bracton says, *the king doth no wrong*, in as much as he doth nothing but by law. *The power of the king is the power of the law, a power of right not of wrong.*[4] Again, *If the king does injustice, he is not king.*[5] In another place he has these words; *The king therefore ought to exercise the*

---

[2] [In fact, the words quoted are entirely Bracton's, *On the Laws and Customs of England*, fol. 5, p. 33. Sidney erred because in the 1680 edition of *Patriarcha* the Latin words are italicized while the rest of the quotation is not.]

[3] [On his bench of justice.]

[4] Potestas regis est potestas legis, potestas juris non injuriae. Bract. de Leg. Angl. [Bracton, *On the Laws and Customs of England*, fol. 107, p. 305.]

[5] Qui si facit injuriam, non est rex. Ibid.

power of the law, as becomes the vicar and minister of God upon earth, because that power is the power of God alone; but the power of doing wrong is the power of the Devil, and not of God. And the king is his minister whose work he does: Whilst he does justice, he is the vicar of the Eternal King; but if he deflect from it to act unjustly, he is the minister of the Devil.[6] He also says that the king is *singulis major, universis minor;*[7] and that he who is *in justitia exequenda omnibus major, in justitia recipienda cuilibet ex plebe fit aequalis.*[8] I shall not say Bracton is in the right when he speaks in this manner; but 'tis a strange impudence in Filmer to cite him as a patron of the absolute power of kings, who does so extremely depress them. But the grossest of his follies is yet more pardonable than his detestable fraud in falsifying Bracton's words, and leaving out such as are not for his purpose, which shew his meaning to be directly contrary to the sense put upon them. That this may appear, I shall set down the words as they are found in Bracton: *Ipse autem rex non debet esse sub homine, sed sub Deo, & sub lege, quia lex facit regem. Attribuat ergo rex legi quod lex attribuit ei, id est dominationem & potestatem: Non est enim rex ubi dominatur voluntas & non lex; & quod sub lege esse debeat, cum sit Dei vicarius, evidenter apparet.*[9] If Bracton therefore be a competent judge, the king is under the law; and he is not a king, nor God's vicegerent unless he be so; and we all know how to proceed with those who being under the law, offend against it. For the law is not made in vain. In this case something more is to be done than petitioning; and 'tis ridiculous to say, that if *he will not amend, 'tis punishment enough for him to expect God an avenger;* for the same may be said of all malefactors. God can sufficiently punish thieves and murderers: but the future judgment, of which perhaps they have no belief, is not sufficient to restrain them from committing more crimes, nor to deter others from following their example. God was always able to punish murderers, but yet by his law he commands man to shed the blood of him who should shed man's blood; and declares that the land cannot be purged of the guilt by any other means. He had judgments in store for Jeroboam, Ahab,

[6] Exercere igitur debet rex potestatem juris sicut Dei vicarius & minister in terra, quia illa potestas solius Dei est, potestas autem injuriae diaboli est non Dei; & cujus horum opera fecerit rex, ejus minister erit: igitur dum facit justitiam, vicarius est regis aeterni: minister autem diaboli dum declinet ad injuriam. Ibid. l. 3. [Fol. 107, p. 305.]

[7] ["Greater than the individual (citizens)" . . . "less than the whole (people)."]

[8] ["(He who is) greater than all in exacting justice, becomes equal to any of the common people in receiving justice." Fol. 107, p. 305.]

[9] ["The king himself, however, ought not to be subject to man but to God and to the law, since the law makes him king. Therefore, the king should bestow upon the law what the law bestows upon him, namely rule and power: for where mere will rules and not law, there is no king; and it is readily apparent that he ought to be under the law, since he is the vicar of God." Fol. 5, p. 33.]

and those that were like them; but yet he commanded that, according to that law, their houses should be destroy'd from the earth. The dogs lick'd up the blood of Ahab, where they had licked that of Naboth, and eat Jezebel who had contrived his murder. *But*, says our author, *we must not look into his deeds, much less oppose them.* Must not David look into Saul's deeds, nor oppose them? Why did he then bring together as many men as he could to oppose, and make foreign alliances against him, even with the Moabites and the accursed Philistines? Why did Jehu not only destroy Ahab's house, but kill the king of Judah and his forty brothers, only for going to visit his children?[10] Our author may perhaps say, because God commanded them. But if God commanded them to do so, he did not command them and all mankind not to do so; and if he did not forbid, they have nothing to restrain them from doing the like, unless they have made municipal laws of their own to the contrary, which our author and his followers may produce when they can find them.

His next work is to go back again to the tribute paid by Christ to Caesar, and judiciously to infer, that all nations must pay the same duty to their magistrates, as the Jews did to the Romans who had subdued them. *Christ did not*, says he, *ask what the law of the land was, nor inquire whether there was a statute against it, nor whether the tribute were given by the consent of the people, but upon sight of the superscription concluded, &c.*[11] It had been strange if Christ had inquired after their laws, statutes or consent, when he knew that their commonwealth, with all the laws by which it had subsisted, was abolished; and that Israel was become a servant to those who exercised a most violent domination over them; which being a peculiar punishment for their peculiar sins, can have no influence upon nations that are not under the same circumstances.

But of all that he says, nothing is more incomprehensible, than what he can mean by lawful kings to whom all is due that was due to the Roman usurpers. For lawful kings are kings by the law: In being kings by the law, they are such kings as the law makes them, and that law only must tell us what is due to them; or by a universal patriarchical right, to which no man can have a title, as is said before, till he prove himself to be the right heir of Noah. If neither of these are to be regarded, but that right follows possession, there is no such thing as a usurper; he who has the power has the right, as indeed Filmer says,[12] and his wisdom as well as his integrity is sufficiently declared by the assertion.

---

[10] [1 Samuel 22 and 27; 2 Kings 10.]   [12] [*Patriarcha*, pp. 100–101.]

[11] [*Patriarcha*, ch. 23, p. 100.]

This wicked extravagancy is followed by an attempt of as singular ignorance and stupidity, to shuffle together usurpers and conquerors, as if they were the same; whereas there have been many usurpers who were not conquerors, and conquerors that deserved not the name of usurpers. No wise man ever said that Agathocles or Dionysius conquer'd Syracuse; Tarquin, Galba or Otho, Rome; Cromwell, England; or that the magi, who seiz'd the government of Persia after the death of Cambyses, conquer'd that country. When Moses and Joshua had overthrown the kingdoms of the Amorites, Moabites and Canaanites; or when David subdued the Ammonites, Edomites, and others, none, as I suppose, but such divines as Filmer, will say they usurped a dominion over them. There is such a thing amongst men as just war, or else true valour would not be a virtue but a crime; and instead of glory, the utmost infamy would always be the companion of victory. There are, says Grotius, laws of war as well as of peace.[13] He who for a just cause, and by just means, carries on a just war, has as clear a right to what is acquired as can be enjoy'd by man, but all usurpation is detestable and abominable.

SECTION 10

The words of St. Paul enjoining obedience to higher Powers, favour all sorts of Governments no less than Monarchy.

OUR author's next quarrel is with St. Paul, *who did not*, as he says, *in enjoining subjection to the higher powers, signify the laws of the land, or mean the highest powers, as well aristocratical and democratical as regal, but a monarch that carries the sword*, &c.[1] But what if there be no monarch in the place? or what if he do not carry the sword? Had the Apostle spoken in vain, if the liberty of the Romans had not been overthrown by the fraud and violence of Caesar? Was no obedience to be exacted whilst that people enjoy'd the benefit of their own laws, and virtue flourished under the moderate government of a legal and just magistracy, established for the common good, by the common consent of all? Had God no minister amongst them till law and justice was overthrown, the best part of the

---

[13] Belli aeque ac pacis jura. *De jur. bel. &* *pac.* [Grotius, *De jure*, bk. 5, ch. 27.]

[1] [*Patriarcha*, ch. 23, pp. 100–101, commenting on Romans 13:1–4.]

people destroy'd by the fury of a corrupt mercenary soldiery, and the world subdued under the tyranny of the worst monsters that it had ever produced? Are these the ways of establishing God's vicegerents? and will he patronize no governors or governments but such as these? Does God uphold evil, and that only? If the world has been hitherto mistaken, in giving the name of evil to that which is good, and calling that good which is evil; I desire to know what can be call'd good amongst men, if the government of the Romans, till they entered Greece and Asia, and were corrupted by the luxury of both, do not deserve that name? or what is to be esteemed evil, if the establishment and exercise of the Caesar's power were not so? But says he, *Wilt thou not be afraid of the power?* [2] And was there no power in the governments that had no monarchs? Were the Carthaginians, Romans, Grecians, Gauls, Germans and Spaniards without power? Was there no sword in that nation and their magistrates, who overthrew the kingdoms of Armenia, Egypt, Numidia, Macedon, and many others, whom none of the monarchs were able to resist? Are the Venetians, Switzers, Grisons and Hollanders now left in the same weakness, and no obedience at all due to their magistrates? If this be so, how comes it to pass that justice is so well administered amongst them? Who is it that defends the Hollanders in such a manner, that the greatest monarchs with all their swords have had no great reason to boast of any advantages gained against them? at least till we (whom they could not resist when we had no monarch, tho we have been disgracefully beaten by them since we had one) by making leagues against them, and sowing divisions amongst them, instigated and assisted the greatest power now in the world to their destruction and our own. But our author is so accustom'd to fraud, that he never cites a passage of Scripture which he does not abuse or vitiate; and that he may do the same in this place, he leaves out the following words, *For there is no power but of God,* that he might entitle one sort only to his protection. If therefore the people and popular magistrates of Athens; the two kings, ephori and senate of Sparta; the Sanhedrin amongst the Hebrews; the consuls, tribunes, praetors and senate of Rome; the magistrates of Holland, Switzerland and Venice, have or had power, we may conclude that they also were ordained by God; and that according to the precept of the Apostle, the same obedience for the same reason is due to them as to any monarch.

The Apostle farther explaining himself, and shewing who may be accounted a magistrate, and what the duty of such a one is, informs us when we should fear, and on what account. *Rulers,* says he, *are not a*

[2] [Ibid., quoting Romans 13:3.]

terror to good works, but to the evil: Wilt thou then not be afraid of the power? do that which is good, and thou shalt have praise of the same; for he is the minister of God, a revenger to execute wrath upon him that doth evil.[3] He therefore is only the minister of God, who is not a terror to good works, but to evil; who executes wrath upon those that do evil, and is a praise to those that do well. And he who doth well, ought not to be afraid of the power, for he shall receive praise. Now if our author were alive, tho he was a man of a hard forehead, I would ask him, whether in his conscience he believed, that Tiberius, Caligula, Claudius, Nero, and the rabble of succeeding monsters, were a praise to those who did well, and a terror to those who did ill; and not the contrary, a praise to the worst, and a terror to the best men of the world? or for what reason Tacitus could say, that virtue brought men who lived under them to certain destruction,[4] and recite so many examples of the brave and good, who were murder'd by them for being so, unless they had endeavour'd to extinguish all that was good, and to tear up virtue by the roots?[5] Why did he call Domitian an enemy to virtue,[6] if he was a terror only to those that did evil? If the world has hitherto been misled in these things, and given the name of virtue to vice, and of vice to virtue, then Germanicus, Valerius Asiaticus, Corbulo, Helvidius Priscus, Thrasea, Soranus and others that resembled them, who fell under the rage of those beasts, nay Paul himself and his disciples were evil doers; and Macro, Narcissus, Pallas, Vinius, Laco and Tigellinus were virtuous and good men. If this be so, we are beholden to Filmer for admonishing mankind of the error in which they had so long continued. If not, those who persecuted and murder'd them for their virtues, were not a terror to such as did evil, and a praise to those who did well. The worst men had no need to fear them; but the best had, because they were the best. All princes therefore that have power are not to be esteemed equally the ministers of God. They that are so, must receive their dignity from a title that is not common to all, even from a just employment of their power to the encouragement of virtue, and to the discouragement of vice. He that pretends to the veneration and obedience due to the ministers of God, must by his actions manifest that he is so. And tho I am unwilling to advance a proposition that may sound harshly to tender ears, I am inclined to believe, that the same rule, which obliges us to yield obedience to the good magistrate who is the minister of God, and assures us that in obeying him we obey God, does equally

[3] [Romans 13:3–4.]

[4] Ob virtutes certissimum exitium. [Tacitus, *Histories*, bk. 1, ch. 2.]

[5] Ipsam excindere virtutem. [Tacitus, *Annals*, bk. 16, ch. 21.]

[6] Virtutibus infestum. [Tacitus, *Life of Agricola*, ch. 41.]

oblige us not to obey those who make themselves the ministers of the Devil, lest in obeying them we obey the Devil, whose works they do.

That none but such as are wilfully ignorant may mistake Paul's meaning, Peter who was directed by the same spirit, says distinctly, *Submit yourselves to every ordinance of man for the Lord's sake.*[7] If therefore there be several ordinances of men tending to the same end, that is, the obtaining of justice, by being a terror to the evil and a praise to the good, the like obedience is for conscience sake enjoined to all, and upon the same condition. But as no man dares to say, that Athens and Persia, Carthage and Egypt, Switzerland and France, Venice and Turkey were and are under the same government; the same obedience is due to the magistrate in every one of those places, and all others on the same account, whilst they continue to be the ministers of God.

If our author say, that Peter cannot comprehend kings under the name of human ordinances, since Paul says they are the ordinance of God, I may as well say that Paul cannot call that the ordinance of God, which Peter calls the ordinance of man. But as it was said of Moses and Samuel, that they who spoke by the same spirit could not contradict each other, Peter and Paul being full of wisdom and sanctity, and inspir'd by the same spirit, must needs say the same thing; and Grotius shews that they perfectly agree, tho the one calls kings, rulers and governors the ordinance of man, and the other the ordinance of God; inasmuch as God having from the beginning ordained that men should not live like wolves in woods, every man by himself, but together in civil societies, left to every one a liberty of joining with that society which best pleas'd him, and to every society to create such magistrates, and frame such laws as should seem most conducing to their own good, according to the measure of light and reason they might have. And every magistracy so instituted might rightly be called the ordinance of man, who was the instituter, and the ordinance of God, according to which it was instituted; *because,* says he, *God approved and ratified the salutary constitutions of government made by men.*[8]

But, says our author, Peter expounds his own words of the human ordinance to be the king, who is the *lex loquens;*[9] but he says no such thing, and I do not find that any such thought ever enter'd into the Apostle's mind. The words are often found in the works of Plato and Aristotle, but applied only to such a man as is a king by nature, who is

[7] [1 Peter 2:3.]

[8] Quia salubrem hominum constitutionem Deus probavit & sanxit. De jur. bel. & pac. [Grotius, *De jure*, bk. 1, ch. 4, sec. 7.]

[9] ["Speaking law." *Patriarcha*, ch. 23, p. 101.]

endow'd with all the virtues that tend to the good of human societies in a greater measure than any or all those that compose them; which character I think, will be ill applied to all kings. And that this may appear to be true, I desire to know whether it would well have agreed with Nero, Caligula, Domitian, or others like to them; and if not with them, then not with all, but only with those who are endow'd with such virtues. But if the king be made by man, he must be such as man makes him to be; and if the power of a law had been given by any human sanction to the word of a foolish, mad or wicked man (which I hardly believe) it would be destroy'd by its own iniquity and turpitude, and the people left under the obligation of rendering obedience to those, who so use the sword that the nations under them may live soberly, peaceably and honestly.

This obliges me a little to examine what is meant by the sword. The pope says there are two swords, the one temporal, the other spiritual, and that both of them were given to Peter and to his successors. Others more rightly understand the two swords to be that of war and that of justice, which according to several constitutions of governments have been committed to several hands, under several conditions and limitations. The sword of justice comprehends the legislative and the executive power: the one is exercised in making laws, the other in judging controversies according to such as are made. The military sword is used by those magistrates who have it, in making war or peace with whom they think fit, and sometimes by others who have it not, in pursuing such wars as are resolved upon by another power. The Jewish doctors generally agree that the kings of Judah could make no law, because there was a curse denounced against those who should add to, or detract from that which God had given by the hand of Moses; that they might sit in judgment with the high priest and Sanhedrin, but could not judge by themselves unless the Sanhedrin did plainly fail of performing their duty. Upon this account Maimonides excuses David for commanding Solomon not to suffer the grey hairs of Joab to go down to the grave in peace, and Solomon for appointing him to be kill'd at the foot of the altar:[10] for he having killed Abner and Amasa, and by those actions shed the blood of war in time of peace, the Sanhedrin should have punished him; but being protected by favour or power, and even David himself fearing him, Solomon was put in mind of his duty, which he performed, tho Joab laid hold upon the horns of the altar, which by the express words of the law gave no protection to wilful murderers.

[10] [1 Kings 2:28–34.]

The use of the military sword amongst them was also moderated. Their kings might make war upon the seven accursed nations that they were commanded to destroy, and so might any other man; for no peace was to be made with them: but not against any other nation, without the assent of the Sanhedrin. And when Amaziah contrary to that law had foolishly made war upon Joash king of Israel, and thereby brought a great slaughter upon Judah, the princes, that is the Sanhedrin, combined against him, pursued him to Lachish, and killed him there.[11]

The legislative power of Sparta was evidently in the people. The laws that go under the name of Lycurgus, were proposed by him to the general assembly of the people, and from them received their authority:[12] But the discipline they contained was of such efficacy for framing the minds of men to virtue, and by banishing silver and gold they so far banished all manner of crimes, that from the institution of those laws to the times of their corruption, which was more than eight hundred years, we hardly find that three men were put to death, of whom two were kings; so that it seems difficult to determine where the power of judging did reside, tho 'tis most probable, considering the nature of their government, that it was in the senate, and in cases extraordinary in the ephori, with a right of appealing to the people. Their kings therefore could have little to do with the sword of justice, neither the legislative nor the judicial power being any ways in them.

The military sword was not much more in their power, unless the excellency of their virtues gave them the credit of persuading, when the law denied the right of commanding. They were obliged to make war against those, and those only, who were declared enemies by the senate and ephori, and in the manner, place and time they directed: so that Agesilaus, tho carrying on a glorious war in Persia, no sooner received the parchment roll, wherein he was commanded by the ephori to come home for the defence of his own country, than he immediately returned, and is on that account called by no less a man than Xenophon, a good and faithful king rendering obedience to the laws of his country.[13]

By this it appears that there are kings who may be feared by those that do ill, and not by such as do well; for having no more power than what the law gives, and being obliged to execute it as the law directs, they cannot depart from the precept of the Apostle. My own actions therefore, or the sense of my own guilt arising from them, is to be the measure of my fear of that magistrate who is the minister of God, and not his power.

[11] [2 Kings 14:19.]

[12] Plut. vit. Lycur. [Plutarch, *Life of Lycurgus*, ch. 29.]

[13] De Reg. Agesil. [Xenophon, *Agesilaus*, in *Scripta Minora*.]

The like may be said of almost all the nations of the world, that have had anything of civil order amongst them. The supreme magistrate, under what name soever he was known, whether king, emperor, asymnetes, suffetes, consul, dictator, or archon, has usually a part assigned to him in the administration of justice and making war; but that he may know it to be assigned and not inherent, and so assigned as to be employ'd for the publick good, not to his own profit or pleasure, it is circumscribed by such rules as he cannot safely transgress. This is above all seen in the German nations, from whom we draw our original and government, and is so well described by Tacitus in his treatise of their customs and manners,[14] that I shall content myself to refer to it, and to what I have cited from him in the former part of this work. The Saxons coming into our country retain'd to themselves the same rights. They had no kings but such as were set up by themselves, and they abrogated their power when they pleased. Offa acknowledged *that he was chosen for the defence of their liberty, not from his own merit, but by their favour;*[15] and in the *Conventus Pananglicus*, at which all the chief men as well secular as ecclesiastical were present, it was decreed by the king, archbishops, bishops, abbots, dukes and senators, that the kings should be chosen by the priests, and by the elders of the people. In pursuance of which, Egbert, who had no right to the succession, was made king. Ethelwerd was chosen in the same manner by the consent of all.[16] Ethelwolf a monk, for want of a better, was advanced to the same honor. His son Alfred, tho crowned by the pope, and marrying without the consent of the nobility and kingdom against their customs and statutes,[17] acknowledged that he had received the crown from the bounty of the princes, elders and people; and in his will declared, that he left the people as he had found them, free as the inward thoughts of man. His son Edward was elected to be his successor.[18] Ethelstan, tho a bastard, and without all title, was elected by the consent of the nobility and people. Eadred by the same authority was elected and preferred before the sons of Edmond his predecessor. Edwin, tho rightly chosen, was deposed for his ill life, and Edgar elected

---

[14] De morib. Germ. [Tacitus, *Germania.*]

[15] Ad libertatis vestrae tuitionem non meis meritis, sed sola liberalitate vestra. [Matthew Paris, *Lives of the Two Offas* (c. 1250; London, 1640), p. 13.]

[16] Omnium consensu. [In Polydore Vergil, *History of England*, bk. 5, p. 189, the words apply to Egbert. Ethelwerd was a chronicler, not a king.]

[17] Contra morem & statuta. [In Bishop Asser's *Life of King Alfred* (c. 900 A.D.; Oxford, 1904, in Latin) and in Roger of Wendover's *Flowers of History*, vol. 1, p. 185, it was not Alfred but his father Ethelwulf who offended custom in this way.]

[18] Successor monarchiae electus. [*The Chronicle of Aethelweard* (written late 900s; London: Thomas Nelson, 1962), p. 51.]

king, by *the will of God, and consent of the people*.[19] But he also was deprived of the crown for the rape of a nun, and after seven years restored by the whole people, *coram omni multitudine populi Anglorum*.[20] Ethelred who is said to have been cruel in the beginning, wretched in the course, and infamous in the end of his reign,[21] was deposed by the same power that had advanced him. Canute made a contract with the princes and the whole people,[22] and thereupon was by general consent crown'd king over all England. After him Harold was chosen in the usual manner. He being dead, a message was sent to Hardicanute with an offer of the crown, which he accepted, and accordingly was received. Edward the Confessor was elected king with the consent of the clergy and people at London;[23] and Harold excused himself for not performing his oath to William the Norman, because he said he had made it unduly and presumptuously, without consulting the nobility and people, and without their authority.[24] William was received with great joy by the clergy and people, and saluted king by all, swearing to observe the ancient good and approved laws of England: and tho he did but ill perform his oath, yet before his death he seemed to repent of the ways he had taken, and only wishing his son might be king of England, he confessed in his last will made at Caen in Normandy, that he neither found nor left the kingdom as an inheritance.[25] If he possessed no right except what was conferred upon him, no more was conferred than had been enjoy'd by the ancient kings, according to the approved laws which he swore to observe. Those laws gave no power to any, till he was elected; and that which they did then give was so limited, that the nobility and people reserved to themselves the disposition of the greatest affairs, even to the deposition and expulsion of such as

---

[19] Et eligerunt Deo dictante Edgarum in regem annuente populo. [Roger of Wendover, *Flowers of History*, vol. 1, p. 258.]

[20] ["In the presence of the whole English people." John Capgrave, *Vita et Miracula Dunstani* ("Life and Miracles of Dunstan," 1516), in William Stubbs, ed., *Memorials of Saint Dunstan, Archbishop of Canterbury* (1874; repr. Wiesbaden: Kraus Reprint, 1965), p. 341.]

[21] Saevus in principio, miser in medio, turpis in exitu. [William of Malmesbury, *Chronicle of the Kings of England*, bk. 2, ch. 10, p. 165.]

[22] Canutus foedus cum principibus & omni populo, & illi cum ipso percusserunt. [Florence of Worcester, *Chronicle*, p. 133.]

[23] Annuente clero et populo Londini in re-

gem eligitur. [Roger of Wendover, *Flowers of History*, vol. 1, p. 306.]

[24] Absque generali senatus & populi conventu & edicto. Matth. Paris. Gul. Gemit. &c. [Found in both William of Malmesbury, pp. 271–272, and Roger of Wendover, *Flowers of History*, vol. 1, p. 328. Gulielmus Gemeticensis, *Historiae Normannorum* (1619), bk. 7, ch. 37.]

[25] Neminem Anglici regni constituo haeredem, non enim tantum decus haereditario jure possedi. Ibid. ["I appoint no one as heir to the kingdom of England, for I have not held this inestimable pearl by right of inheritance." *Fragmenta apud Anglicarum, Normannicarum, et Hibernicarum rerum scriptores*, ed. William Camden, p. 32.]

should not well perform the duty of their oaths and office. And I leave it to our author to prove, how they can be said to have had the sword and the power so as to be feared, otherwise than, as the Apostle says, by those that do evil; which we acknowledge to be not only in the king, but in the lowest officer of justice in the world.

If it be pretended that our later kings are more to be feared than William the Norman, or his predecessors, it must not be, as has been proved, either from the general right of kings, or from the doctrine of the Apostle, but from something else that is peculiar and subsequent, which I leave our author's disciples to prove, and an answer may be found in due time. But to show that our ancestors did not mistake the words of the Apostle, 'tis good to consider when, to whom, and upon what occasion he spoke. The Christian religion was then in its infancy: his discourses were addressed to the professors of it, who tho they soon grew to be considerable in number, were for the most part of the meanest sort of people, servants or inhabitants of the cities, rather than citizens and freemen; joined in no civil body or society, nor such as had or could have any part in the government. The occasion was to suppress the dangerous mistake of many converted Jews and others, who knowing themselves to be freed from the power of sin and the Devil, presumed they were also freed from the obligation of human laws. And if this error had not been cropp'd in the bud, it would have given occasion to their enemies (who desired nothing more), to destroy them all; and who knowing that such notions were stirring among them, would have been glad, that they who were not easily to be discovered, had by that means discovered themselves.

This induced a necessity of diverting a poor, mean, scatter'd people from such thoughts concerning the state; to convince them of the error into which they were fallen, that Christians did not owe the same obedience to civil laws and magistrates as other men, and to keep them from drawing destruction upon themselves by such ways, as not being warranted by God, had no promise of his protection. St. Paul's work was to preserve the professors of Christianity, as appears by his own words; *I exhort, that first of all, supplications, prayers, intercessions, and giving of thanks be made for all men: for kings, and for all that are in authority, that we may live a quiet and peaceable life in all godliness and honesty.*[26] *Put them in mind to be subject to principalities and powers, to obey magistrates, to be ready for every good work.*[27] St. Peter agrees with him fully in describing the magistrate and his duty; shewing the reasons why obedience should be

---

[26] 1 Tim. 2.   [27] Tit. 3.

pay'd to him, and teaching Christians to be humble and contented with their condition, as free, yet not using their liberty for a cover to malice; and not only to fear God and honor the king (of which conjunction of words such as Filmer are very proud) but to honor all men, as is said in the same verse.[28] This was in a peculiar manner the work of that time, in which those who were to preach and propagate the Gospel, were not to be diverted from that duty, by entangling themselves in the care of state-affairs; but it does in some sense agree with all times: for it can never be the duty of a good man to oppose such a magistrate as is the minister of God, in the exercise of his office, nor to deny to any man that which is his due.

But as the Christian law exempts no man from the duty he owes to his father, master, or the magistrate, it does not make him more a slave than he was before, nor deprive him of any natural or civil right; and if we are obliged to pay tribute, honor, or any other thing where it is not due, it must be by some precept very different from that which commands us to give to Caesar that which is Caesar's. If he define the magistrate to be the minister of God doing justice, and from thence draws the reasons he gives for rendering obedience to him, we are to inquire whose minister he is who overthrows it, and look for some other reason for rendering obedience to him than the words of the apostles. If David, who was willing to lay down his life for the people, who *hated iniquity*, and would not *suffer a liar to come into his presence*,[29] was the minister of God, I desire to know whose minister Caligula was who set up himself to be worshipped for a god, and would at once have destroyed all the people that he ought to have protected? Whose minister was Nero, who, besides the abominable impurities of his life, and hatred to all virtue, as contrary to his person and government, set fire to the great city? If it be true, that *contrariorum contraria est ratio*,[30] these questions are easily decided; and if the reasons of things are eternal, the same distinction grounded upon truth will be good forever. Every magistrate, and every man by his works, will forever declare whose minister he is, in what spirit he lives, and consequently what obedience is due to him according to the precept of the Apostle. If any man ask what I mean by justice, I answer, that the law of the land, as far as it is *sanctio recta, jubens honesta, prohibens contraria*,[31] declares what it is. But there have been and are laws that are neither just nor commendable. There was a law in Rome, that no god should be worshipped

---

[28] [1 Peter 2:13–17.]

[29] [Psalm 101.]

[30] [Contrary things have contrary causes.]

[31] Cicero. ["A right sanction, commanding honest deeds, forbidding the contrary." Perhaps a paraphrase of a line in *Second Philippic*, sec. 28, in Cicero, *Philippics* (Loeb, 1926).]

without the consent of the senate: Upon which Tertullian says scoffingly, *That God shall not be God unless he please man;*[32] and by virtue of this law the first Christians were exposed to all manner of cruelties; and some of the emperors (in other respects excellent men) most foully polluted themselves and their government with innocent blood. Antoninus Pius was taken in this snare; and Tertullian bitterly derides Trajan for glorying in his clemency, when he had commanded Pliny, who was proconsul in Asia, not to make any search for Christians, but only to punish them according to law when they should be brought before him.[33] No municipal law can be more firmly established by human authority, than that of the Inquisition in Spain, and other places: And those accursed tribunals, which have shed more Christian blood than all the pagans that ever were in the world, is commonly called *The Holy Office.* If a gentleman in Poland kill a peasant, he is by a law now in use free from punishment, if he lay a ducat upon the dead body. Evenus the third, king of Scotland, caused a law to pass, by which the wives and daughters of noblemen were exposed to his lust, and those of the commons to the lust of the nobility. These, and an infinite number of others like to them, were not right sanctions, but such as have produced unspeakable mischiefs and calamities. They were not therefore laws: The name of justice is abusively attributed to them: Those that govern by them cannot be the ministers of God: and the Apostle commanding our obedience to the minister of God for our good, commands us not to be obedient to the minister of the Devil to our hurt; for we cannot serve two masters.

SECTION I I

That which is not just, is not Law; and that which is not Law, ought not to be obeyed.

OUR author having for a long time pretended conscience, now pulls off his mask, and plainly tells us, that 'tis not on account of conscience, but for fear of punishment, or hopes of reward, that laws are to be obeyed. *That familiar distinction of the Schoolmen,* says he, *whereby they subject kings to the directive, but not to the coactive power of the law, is a confession, that kings are not bound by the positive laws of any nation, since the*

---

[32] Nisi homini Deus placuerit Deus non erit.   [33] [Ibid., ch. 2, sec. 7.]
[Tertullian, *Apology,* ch. 5, sec. 1.]

compulsory power of laws is that which properly makes laws to be laws.[1] Not troubling myself with this distinction of the Schoolmen, nor acknowledging any truth to be in it, or that they are competent judges of such matters, I say, that if it be true, our author's conclusion is altogether false; for the directive power of the law, which is certain, and grounded upon the inherent good and rectitude that is in it, is that alone which has a power over the conscience, whereas the coercive is merely contingent; and the most just powers commanding the most just things, have so often fallen under the violence of the most unjust men, commanding the most execrable villainies, that if they were therefore to be obeyed, the consciences of men must be regulated by the success of a battle or conspiracy, than which nothing can be affirmed more impious and absurd. By this rule David was not to be obeyed, when by the wickedness of his son he was driven from Jerusalem,[2] and deprived of all coercive power; and the conscientious obedience that had been due to him was transferr'd to Absalom who sought his life. And in St. Paul's time it was not from him who was guided only by the spirit of God, and had no manner of coercive power, that Christians were to learn their duty, but from Caligula, Claudius, and Nero, who had that power well established by the mercenary legions. If this were so, the governments of the world might be justly called *magna latrocinia;*[3] and men laying aside all considerations of reason or justice, ought only to follow those who can inflict the greatest punishments, or give the greatest rewards. But since the reception of such opinions would be the extirpation of all that can be called good, we must look for another rule of our obedience, and shall find that to be the law, which being, as I said before, *sanctio recta,* must be founded upon that eternal principle of reason and truth, from whence the rule of justice which is sacred and pure ought to be deduced, and not from the depraved will of man, which fluctuating according to the different interests, humors and passions that at several times reign in several nations, one day abrogates what had been enacted the other. The sanction therefore that deserves the name of a law, *which derives not its excellency from antiquity, or from the dignity of the legislators, but from an intrinsick equity and justice,*[4] ought to be made in pursuance of that universal reason to which all nations at all times owe an equal veneration and obedience. By this we may know whether he who has the power does justice or not:

---

[1] [*Patriarcha*, ch. 23, pp. 101–102.]

[2] [2 Samuel 15.]

[3] ["Robbery on a grand scale." Augustine, *City of God*, bk. 4, ch. 4.]

[4] Tertul. [Tertullian, *Apology*, ch. 4, sec. 10.]

Whether he be the minister of God to our good, a protector of good, and a terror to ill men; or the minister of the Devil to our hurt, by encouraging all manner of evil, and endeavouring by vice and corruption to make the people worse, that they may be miserable, and miserable that they may be worse. I dare not say I shall never fear such a man if he be armed with power: But I am sure I shall never esteem him to be the minister of God, and shall think I do ill if I fear him. If he has therefore a coercive power over me, 'tis through my weakness; *for he that will suffer himself to be compell'd, knows not how to die.*[5] If therefore he who does not follow the directive power of the law, be not the minister of God, he is not a king, at least not such a king as the Apostle commands us to obey: And if that sanction which is not just be not a law, and can have no obligation upon us, by what power soever it be established, it may well fall out, that the magistrate who will not follow the directive power of the law, may fall under the coercive, and then the fear is turned upon him, with this aggravation, that it is not only actual, but just. This was the case of Nero; the coercive power was no longer in him, but against him. He that was forced to fly and to hide himself, that was abandoned by all men, and condemned to die *according to ancient custom,*[6] did, as I suppose, fear, and was no way to be feared. The like may be said of Amaziah king of Judah, when he fled to Lachish;[7] of Nebuchadnezzar, when he was driven from the society of men;[8] and of many emperors and kings of the greatest nations in the world, who have been so utterly deprived of all power, that they have been imprisoned, deposed, confined to monasteries, kill'd, drawn through the streets, cut in pieces, thrown into rivers, and indeed suffer'd all that could be suffer'd by the vilest slaves.

If any man say these things ought not to have been done, an answer may be given in a proper place; though 'twere enough to say, that the justice of the world is not to be overthrown by a mere assertion without proof; but that is nothing to the present question: For if it was ill done to drive Nero to despair, or to throw Vitellius into the common shore, it was not because they were the ministers of God; for their lives were no way conformable to the character which the Apostle gives to those who deserve that sacred name. If those only are to be feared who have the power, there was a time when they were not to be feared, for they had none; and if those princes are not obliged by the law, who are not under the coercive power, it gave no exemption to those, for they fell

---

[5] Qui cogi potest nescit mori. [Seneca, *The Madness of Hercules*, li. 426.]

[6] More majorum. Sueton. [Suetonius, *Life of Nero*, ch. 49.]

[7] [2 Kings 14:19.]

[8] [Daniel 4:25–30.]

under it: and as we know not what will befall others who walk in their steps, till they are dead, we cannot till then know whether they are free from it or not.

SECTION 12

The Right and Power of a Magistrate depends upon his Institution, not upon his Name.

T IS usual with impostors to obtrude their deceits upon men, by putting false names upon things, by which they may perplex men's minds, and from thence deduce false conclusions. But the points above-mention'd being settled, it imports little whether the governors to whom Peter enjoins obedience, were only kings, and such as are employ'd by them, or all such magistrates as are the ministers of God; for he informs us of their works that we may know them, and accordingly yield obedience to them. This is that therefore which distinguishes the magistrate to whom obedience is due, from him to whom none is due, and not the name that he either assumes, or others put upon him. But if there be any virtue in the word king, and that the admirable prerogatives, of which our author dreams, were annexed to that name, they could not be applied to the Roman emperors, nor their substituted officers, for they had it not. 'Tis true, Mark Antony, in a drunken fit, at the celebration of the impure Lupercalia, did offer a diadem to Julius Caesar, which some flatterers pressed him to accept (as our great lawyers did Cromwell), but he durst not think of putting it upon his head. Caligula's affectation of that title, and the ensigns of royalty he wore, were taken for the most evident marks of his madness: and tho the greatest and bravest of their men had fallen by the wars or proscriptions; tho the best part of the senate had perished in Thessaly; tho the great city was exhausted, and Italy brought to desolation, yet they were not reduced so low as to endure a king. Piso was sufficiently addicted to Tiberius, yet he could not suffer that Germanicus should be treated as the son of a king; *Principis Romani non Parthorum regis filio has epulas dari.*[1] And whoever understands the Latin tongue, and the history of those times, will easily perceive that the word *princeps* signified no more than a principal or eminent man, as has

---

[1] Tacit. Ann. 2. ["(Piso said) that this feast was given for the son of a Roman *princeps*, not the son of a Parthian king." Tacitus, *Annals*, bk. 2, ch. 57.]

been already proved: and the words of Piso could have no other meaning, than that the son of a Roman ought not to be distinguished from others, as the sons of the Parthian kings were. This is verified by his letter to Tiberius, under the name of friend, and the answer of Tiberius promising to him *whatsoever one friend could do for another*.[2] Here was no mention of majesty or sovereign lord, nor the base subscriptions of servant, subject, or creature. And I fear, that as the last of those words was introduced amongst us by our bishops, the rest of them had been also invented by such Christians as were too much addicted to the Asiatick slavery. However, the name of king was never solemnly assumed by, nor conferred upon those emperors, and could have conferred no right, if it had. They exercised as they pleased, or as they durst, the power that had been gained by violence or fraud. The exorbitances they committed, could not have been justified by a title, any more than those of a pirate who should take the same. It was no otherwise given to them than by way of assimilation, when they were guilty of the greatest crimes: and Tacitus describing the detestable lust of Tiberius, says, *Quibus adeo indomitis exarserat, ut more regio pubem ingenuam stupris pollueret; nec formam tantum & decora corporis, sed in his modestam pueritiam, in aliis majorum imagines, incitamentum cupiditatis habebat.*[3] He also informs us that Nero took his time to put Barea Soranus to death, who was one of the most virtuous men of that age, when Tiridates king of Armenia was at Rome; *That he might shew the imperial grandeur by the slaughter of the most illustrious men, which he accounted a royal action.*[4] I leave it to the judgment of all wise men, whether it be probable that the apostles should distinguish such as these from other magistrates; and dignify those only with the title of God's ministers, who distinguished themselves by such ways; or that the succeeding emperors should be ennobled with the same prerogative, who had no other title to the name than by resembling those that had it in such things as these. If this be too absurd and abominable to enter into the heart of a man, it must be concluded, that their intention was only to divert the poor people to whom they preached, from involving themselves in the care of civil matters, to which they had no call. And the counsel would have been good (as things stood with them) if they

---

[2] Quod amicus amico praestare potest. [The letter, but not this answer, is in ibid., bk. 3, ch. 16.]

[3] Annal. l. 6. ["He was so aflame with these uncontrolled lusts that he defiled innocent youths, ravishing them as a king might do; and his desire was spurred not only by their features and fine bodies, but also by the boyish modesty of some and the resemblance of others to the busts of his ancestors." Ibid., bk. 6, ch. 1.]

[4] Ut magnitudinem imperatoriam caede insignium virorum quasi regio facinore ostentaret. An. l. 16. [Ibid., bk. 16, ch. 23.]

had been under the power of a pirate, or any other villain substituted by him.

But tho the apostles had looked upon the officers set over the provinces belonging to the Roman empire, as sent by kings, I desire to know whether it can be imagined, that they could think the subordinate governors to be sent by kings, in the countries that had no kings; or that obedience became due to the magistrates in Greece, Italy, or other provinces under the jurisdiction of Rome, only after they had emperors, and that none was due to them before? The Germans had then no king: The brave Arminius had been lately kill'd for aiming at a crown.[5] When he had blemish'd all his virtues by that attempt, they forgot his former services. They never consider'd how many Roman legions he had cut in pieces, nor how many thousands of their allies he had destroy'd. His valour was a crime deserving death, when he sought to make a prey of his country, which he had so bravely defended, and to enslave those who with him had fought for the publick liberty. But if the apostles were to be understood to give the name of God's ministers only to kings, and those who are employ'd by them, and that obedience is due to no other, a domestick tyrant had been their greatest benefactor. He had set up the only government that is authorized by God, and to which a conscientious obedience is due. Agathocles, Dionysius, Phalaris, Phaereus, Pisistratus, Nabis, Machanidas, and an infinite number of the most detestable villains that the world has ever produced, did confer the same benefits upon the countries they enslaved. But if this be equally false, sottish, absurd, and execrable, all those epithets belong to our author and his doctrine, for attempting to depress all modest and regular magistracies, and endeavouring to corrupt the Scripture to patronize the greatest of crimes. No man therefore who does not delight in error, can think that the Apostle designed precisely to determine such questions as might arise concerning any one man's right, or in the least degree to prefer any one form of government before another. In acknowledging the magistrate to be man's ordinance, he declares that man who makes him to be, may make him to be what he pleaseth; and tho there is found more prudence and virtue in one nation than in another, that magistracy which is established in any one ought to be obeyed, till they who made the establishment think fit to alter it. All therefore whilst they continue, are to be look'd upon with the same respect. Every nation acting freely, has an equal right to frame their own government, and to employ such officers as they please. The authority, right and power of these must be regulated by the judgment,

---

[5] [Ibid., bk. 2, ch. 88.]

right and power of those who appoint them, without any relation at all to the name that is given; for that is no way essential to the thing. The same name is frequently given to those, who differ exceedingly in right and power; and the same right and power is as often annexed to magistracies that differ in name. The same power which had been in the Roman kings, was given to the consuls; and that which had been legally in the dictators for a time not exceeding six months, was afterwards usurped by the Caesars, and made perpetual. The supreme power (which some pretend belongs to all kings) has been and is enjoy'd in the fullest extent by such as never had the name; and no magistracy was ever more restrain'd than those that had the name of kings in Sparta, Aragon, England, Poland and other places. They therefore that did thus institute, regulate and restrain, create magistracies, and give them names and powers as seemed best to them, could not but have in themselves the coercive as well as the directive over them: for the regulation and restriction is coercion; but most of all the institution, by which they could make them to be or not to be. As to the exterior force, 'tis sometimes on the side of the magistrate, and sometimes on that of the people; and as magistrates under several names have the same work incumbent upon them, and the same power to perform it, the same duty is to be exacted from them, and rendered to them: which being distinctly proportion'd by the laws of every country, I may conclude, that all magistratical power being the ordinance of man in pursuance of the ordinance of God, receives its being and measure from the legislative power of every nation. And whether the power be placed simply in one, a few, or many men; or in one body composed of the three simple species; whether the single person be called king, duke, marquess, emperor, sultan, mogul, or grand signor; or the number go under the name of senate, council, pregadi, diet, assembly of estates and the like, 'tis the same thing. The same obedience is equally due to all, whilst according to the precept of the Apostle, they do the work of God for our good: and if they depart from it, no one of them has a better title than the other to our obedience.

SECTION 13
*Laws were made to direct and
instruct Magistrates, and, if they will not be directed,
to restrain them.*

I KNOW not who they are that our author introduces to say, that *the first invention of laws was to bridle or moderate the overgreat power of kings;*[1] and unless they give some better proof of their judgment in other things, shall little esteem them. They should have considered, that there are laws in many places where there are no kings; that there were laws in many before there were kings, as in Israel the law was given three hundred years before they had any; but most especially, that as no man can be a rightful king except by law, nor have any just power but from the law, if that power be found to be overgreat, the law that gave it must have been before that which was to moderate or restrain it; for that could not be moderated which was not in being. Leaving therefore our author to fight with these adversaries if he please when he finds them, I shall proceed to examine his own positions. *The truth is,* says he, *the original of laws was for the keeping of the multitude in order. Popular estates could not subsist at all without laws, whereas kingdoms were govern'd many ages without them. The people of Athens as soon as they gave over kings, were forced to give power to Draco first, then to Solon to make them laws.* If we will believe him therefore, wheresoever there is a king, or a man who by having power in his hands, is in the place of a king, there is no need of law. He takes them all to be so wise, just, and good, that they are laws to themselves, *leges viventes.*[2] This was certainly verified by the whole succession of the Caesars, the ten last kings of Pharamond's race, all the successors of Charles the Great, and others that I am not willing to name; but referring myself to history, I desire all reasonable men to consider, whether the piety and tender care that was natural to Caligula, Nero or Domitian, was such a security to the nations that lived under them, as without law to be sufficient for their preservation: for if the contrary appear to be true, and that their government was a perpetual exercise of rage, malice and madness, by which the worst of men were armed with power to destroy the best, so that the empire could only be saved by their

[1] [*Patriarcha*, ch. 24 ("Laws Not First Found Out to Bridle Tyrants but the People. The Benefit of Laws. Kings Keep the Laws, though Not Bound by Them"), p. 102.]

[2] [Living laws.]

destruction, 'tis most certain, that mankind can never fall into a condition which stands more in need of laws to protect the innocent, than when such monsters reign who endeavour their extirpation, and are too well furnished with means to accomplish their detestable designs. Without any prejudice therefore to the cause that I defend, I might confess that all nations were at the first governed by kings, and that no laws were imposed upon those kings, till they, or the successors of those who had been advanced for their virtues, by falling into vice and corruption, did manifestly discover the inconveniences of depending upon their will. Besides these, there are also children, women and fools, that often come to the succession of kingdoms, whose weakness and ignorance stands in as great need of support and direction, as the desperate fury of the others can do of restriction. And if some nations had been so sottish, not to foresee the mischief of leaving them to their will, others, or the same in succeeding ages discovering them, could no more be obliged to continue in so pernicious a folly, than we are to live in that wretched barbarity in which the Romans found our ancestors, when they first entered this island.

If any man say, that Filmer does not speak of monsters, nor of children, women or fools, but of wise, just and good princes; I answer, that if there be a right inherent in kings, as kings, of doing what they please; and in those who are next in blood, to succeed them and inherit the same, it must belong to all kings, and such as upon title of blood would be kings. And as there is no family that may not, and does not often produce such as I mentioned, it must also be acknowledged in them; and that power which is left to the wise, just and good, upon a supposition that they will not make an ill use of it, must be devolved to those who will not or cannot make a good one; but will either maliciously turn it to the destruction of those they ought to protect, or through weakness suffer it to fall into the hands of those that govern them, who are found by experience to be for the most part the worst of all, most apt to use the basest arts, and to flatter the humors, and foment the vices that are most prevalent in weak and vicious princes. Germanicus, Corbulo, Valerius Asiaticus, Thrasea, Soranus, Helvidius Priscus, Julius Agricola, and other excellent men lived in the times of Tiberius, Caligula, Claudius and Nero; but the power was put into the hands of Sejanus, Macro, Tigellinus, and other villains like to them: and I wish there were not too many modern examples to shew that weak and vicious princes will never chuse such as shall preserve nations from the mischiefs that would ensue upon their own incapacity or malice; but that they must be imposed upon them by some other power, or nations be ruined for want of them. This imposition must be by law or by force. But as laws are made to keep things in good order without the necessity of having recourse to force, it would be a dangerous extravagance to arm that prince with force, which probably in a short time must be opposed by force; and those who have been guilty of this error, as the kingdoms of the East, and the ancient Roman empire, where no provision was made by law against ill-governing princes, have found no other remedy than to kill them, when by extreme sufferings they were driven beyond patience: and this fell out so often, that few of their princes were observed to die by a common death. But since the empire was transmitted to Germany, and the emperors restrain'd by laws, that nation has never been brought to the odious extremities of suffering all manner of indignities, or revenging them upon the heads of princes. And if the pope had not disturb'd them upon the account of religion, nor driven their princes to disturb others, they might have passed many ages without any civil dissension, and all their emperors might have lived happily, and died peaceably, as most of them have done.

This might be sufficient to my purpose: for if all princes without distinction, whether good or bad, wise or foolish, young or old, sober or mad, cannot be entrusted with an unlimited power; and if the power they have, ought to be limited by law, that nations may not, with danger to themselves as well as to the prince, have recourse to the last remedy, this law must be given to all, and the good can be no otherwise distinguished from the bad, and the wise from the foolish, than by the observation or violation of it. But I may justly go a step farther, and affirm, that this law which by restraining the lusts of the vicious and foolish, frequently preserves them from the destruction they would bring upon themselves or people, and sometimes upon both, is an assistance and direction to the wisest and best; so that they also as well as the nations under them are gainers by it. This will appear strange only to those who know not *how difficult and insupportable the government of great nations is*,[3] and how unable the best man is to bear it. And if it surpass the strength of the best, it may easily be determined how ordinary men will behave themselves under it, or what use the worst will make of it. I know there have been wise and good kings; but they had not an absolute power, nor would have accepted it, tho it had been offer'd: much less can I believe that any of them would have transmitted such a power to their posterity, when none of them could know any more than Solomon, whether his son would be a wise man or a fool. But if the best might have desired, and had been

---

[3] Quam grave & intolerandum sit cuncta regendi onus. Tacit. [Tacitus, *Annals*, bk. 1, ch. 11.]

able to bear it (tho Moses by his own confession was not) that could be no reason why it should be given to the worst and weakest, or those who probably will be so. Since the assurance that it will not be abused during the life of one man, is nothing to the constitution of a state which aims at perpetuity. And no man knowing what men will be, especially if they come to the power by succession, which may properly enough be called by chance, 'tis reasonably to be feared they will be bad, and consequently necessary so to limit their power, that if they prove to be so, the commonwealth may not be destroy'd, which they were instituted to preserve. The law provides for this in leaving to the king a full and ample power of doing as much good as his heart can wish, and in restraining his power so, that if he should depart from the duty of his office, the nation may not perish. This is a help to those who are wise and good, by directing them what they are to do, more certainly than any one man's personal judgment can do; and no prejudice at all, since no such man did ever complain he was not suffer'd to do the evil which he would abhor if it were in his power; and is a most necessary curb to the fury of bad princes, preventing them from bringing destruction upon the people. Men are so subject to vices and passions, that they stand in need of some restraint in every condition; but most especially when they are in power. The rage of a private man may be pernicious to one or a few of his neighbours; but the fury of an unlimited prince would drive whole nations into ruin: And those very men who have lived modestly when they had little power have often proved the most savage of all monsters, when they thought nothing able to resist their rage. 'Tis said of Caligula, that no man ever knew *a better servant, nor a worse master.*[4] The want of restraint made him a beast, who might have continued to be a man. And tho I cannot say, that our law necessarily admits the next in blood to the succession (for the contrary is proved) yet the facility of our ancestors, in receiving children, women, or such men as were not more able than themselves to bear the weight of a crown, convinces me fully, that they had so framed our laws, that even children, women, or ill men, might either perform as much as was necessarily required of them, or be brought to reason if they transgressed, and arrogated to themselves more than was allow'd. For 'tis not to be imagined, that a company of men should so far degenerate from their own nature, which is reason, to give up themselves and their posterity, with all their concernments in the world, to depend upon the will of a child, a woman, an ill man, or a fool.

[4] Nec meliorem servum, nec deteriorem dominum. [Ibid., bk. 6, ch. 20.]

If therefore laws are necessary to popular states, they are no less to monarchies; or rather, that is not a state or government which has them not: and 'tis no less impossible for any to subsist without them, than for the body of a man to be, and perform its functions without nerves or bones. And if any people had ever been so foolish to establish that which they called a government, without laws to support and regulate it, the impossibility of subsisting would evidence the madness of the constitution, and ought to deter all others from following their example.

'Tis no less incredible, that those nations which rejected kings, did put themselves into the power of one man, to prescribe to them such laws as he pleased. But the instances alleged by our author are evidently false. The Athenians were not without laws when they had kings: Aegeus was subject to the laws, and did nothing of importance without the consent of the people; and Theseus not being able to please them, died a banished man: Draco and Solon did not make, but propose laws, and they were of no force till they were established by the authority of the people.[5] The Spartans dealt in the same manner with Lycurgus; he invented their laws, but the people made them: and when the assembly of all the citizens had approved and sworn to observe them till his return from Crete, he resolved rather to die in a voluntary banishment, than by his return to absolve them from the oath they had taken.[6] The Romans also had laws during the government of their kings; but not finding in them that perfection they desired, the decemviri were chosen to frame others, which yet were of no value till they were passed by the people in the *comitia centuriata;*[7] and being so approved, they were established. But this sanction, to which every man, whether magistrate or private citizen, was subject, did no way bind the whole body of the people, who still retained in themselves the power of changing both the matter and the form of their government, as appears by their instituting and abrogating kings, consuls, dictators, tribunes with consular power, and decemviri, when they thought good for the commonwealth. And if they had this power, I leave our author to shew, why the like is not in other nations.

---

[5] Plut. vit. Solon. [Plutarch, *Life of Solon.*]

[6] [Plutarch, *Life of Lycurgus.*]

[7] Ingenti hominum consensu propositis decem tabulis populum ad concionem convocarunt, & quod bonum, faustum faelixque sit republicae, ipsis, liberisque eorum esset, ire & legere propositas jussere. T. Liv. l. 3.

["With the consent of the vast majority, when the ten tables had been proposed, they called the people to an assembly; and they ordered them to go and choose whichever of the proposed laws would be good, auspicious, and happy for the republic, themselves, and their children." Livy, *History of Rome*, bk. 3, ch. 34.]

SECTION 14

Laws are not made by Kings,
not because they are busied in greater matters than
doing Justice, but because Nations will be governed
by Rule, and not Arbitrarily.

O<small>UR</small> author pursuing the mistakes to which he seems perpetually condemned, says, that *when kings were either busied in war, or distracted with publick cares, so that every private man could not have access unto their persons, to learn their wills and pleasures, then of necessity were laws invented, that so every particular subject might find his prince's pleasure.*[1] I have often heard that governments were established for the obtaining of justice; and if that be true, 'tis hard to imagine what business a supreme magistrate can have to divert him from accomplishing the principal end of his institution. And 'tis as commonly said, that this distribution of justice to a people, is a work surpassing the strength of any one man. Jethro seems to have been a wise man, and 'tis probable he thought Moses to be so also; but he found the work of judging the people to be too heavy for him, and therefore advised him to leave the judgment of causes to others who should be chosen for that purpose; which advice Moses accepted, and God approved.[2] The governing power was as insupportable to him as the judicial. He desired rather to die than to bear so great a burden; and God neither accusing him of sloth or impatience, gave him seventy assistants. But if we may believe our author, the powers judicial and legislative, that of judging as well as that of governing, is not too much for any man, woman, or child whatsoever: and that he stands in no need, either of God's statutes to direct him, or man's counsel to assist him, unless it be when he is otherwise employ'd; and his will alone is sufficient for all. But what if he be not busied in greater matters, or distracted with publick cares; is every prince capable of this work? Tho Moses had not found it too great for him, or it should be granted that a man of excellent natural endowments, great wisdom, learning, experience, industry, and integrity might perform it, is it certain that all those who happen to be born in reigning families are so? If Moses had the law of God before his eyes, and could repair to God himself for the application or explanation of it; have all princes the same assistance? Do they all speak with God face to face, or can they do what he did, without the assistance he had?

---

[1] [*Patriarcha*, ch. 24, p. 102.]   [2] Exod. 18.

If all kings of mature years are of that perfection, are we assured that none shall die before his heir arrive to the same? Or shall he have the same ripeness of judgment in his infancy? If a child come to a crown, does that immediately infuse the most admirable endowments and graces? Have we any promise from heaven, that women shall enjoy the same prerogatives in those countries where they are made capable of the succession? Or does that law which renders them capable, defend them, not only against the frailty of their own nature, but confer the most sublime virtues upon them? But who knows not, that no families do more frequently produce weak or ill men, than the greatest? and that which is worse, their greatness is a snare to them; so that they who in a low condition might have passed unregarded, being advanced to the highest, have often appeared to be, or became the worst of all beasts; and they who advance them are like to them: For if the power be in the multitude, as our author is forced to confess (otherwise the Athenians and Romans could not have given all, as he says, nor a part, as I say, to Draco, Solon, or the decemviri) they must be beasts also, who should have given away their right and liberty, in hopes of receiving justice from such as probably will neither understand nor regard it, or protection from those who will not be able to help themselves, and expect such virtue, wisdom, and integrity should be, and forever remain in the family they set up as was never known to continue in any. If the power be not conferred upon them, they have it not; and if they have it not, their want of leisure to do justice, cannot have been the cause for which laws are made; and they cannot be the signification of their will, but are that to which the prince owes obedience, as well as the meanest subject. This is that which Bracton calls *esse sub lege*,[3] and says, that *rex in regno superiores habet Deum & legem*.[4] Fortescue says, The kings of England cannot change the laws:[5] and indeed, they are so far from having any such power, that the judges swear to have no regard to the king's letters or commands, but if they receive any, to proceed according to law, as if they had not been. And the breach of his oath does not only bring a blemish upon their reputation, but exposes them to capital punishments, as many of them have found. 'Tis not therefore the king that makes the law, but the law that makes the king. It gives the rule for succession, making kingdoms sometimes

---

[3] ["Being subject to the law." Bracton, *On the Laws and Customs of England*, bk. 1, ch. 8, fol. 5.]

[4] ["In his kingdom the king has these superiors, God and the law." Ibid., bk. 2, ch. 16, fol. 33.]

[5] De laud. leg. Angl. c. 9. [Sir John Fortescue, *De laudibus legum Angliae* (1545–46; Cambridge: Cambridge University Press, 1942), ch. 9, p. 25.]

hereditary, and sometimes elective, and (more often than either simply) hereditary under condition. In some places males only are capable of inheriting, in others females are admitted. Where the monarchy is regular, as in Germany, England, &c. the kings can neither make nor change laws: They are under the law, and the law is not under them; their letters or commands are not to be regarded: In the administration of justice, the question is not what pleases them, but what the law declares to be right, which must have its course, whether the king be busy or at leisure, whether he will or not. The king who never dies, is always present in the supreme courts, and neither knows nor regards the pleasure of the man that wears the crown. But lest he by his riches and power might have some influence upon judicial proceedings, the Great Charter that recapitulates and acknowledges our ancient inherent liberties, obliges him to swear, that he will neither sell, delay, nor deny justice to any man, according to the laws of the land:[6] which were ridiculous and absurd, if those laws were only the signification of his pleasure, or any way depended upon his will. This charter having been confirmed by more than thirty parliaments, all succeeding kings are under the obligation of the same oath, or must renounce the benefit they receive from our laws, which if they do, they will be found to be equal to every one of us.

Our author, according to his custom, having laid down a false proposition, goes about to justify it by false examples, as those of Draco, Solon, the decemviri, and Moses, of whom no one had the power he attributes to them, and it were nothing to us if they had. The Athenians and Romans, as was said before, were so far from resigning the absolute power without appeal to themselves, that nothing done by their magistrates was of any force, till it was enacted by the people. And the power given to the decemviri, *sine provocatione*,[7] was only in private cases, there being no superior magistrate then in being, to whom appeals could be made. They were vested with the same power the kings and dictators enjoy'd, from whom there lay no appeal, but to the people, and always to them; as appears by the case of Horatius in the time of Tullus Hostilius,[8] that of Marcus Fabius when Papirius Cursor was dictator,[9] and of Nenius the tribune during that of Q. Fabius Maximus,[10] all which I have cited already, and refer to them. There was therefore a reservation of the supreme power in the people, notwithstanding the creation of magistrates

---

[6] [*Magna Charta*, sec. 29.]

[7] [Not subject to appeal.]

[8] T. Liv. l. 1. [Livy, *History of Rome*, bk. 1, ch. 26.]

[9] L. 8. [Ibid., bk. 8, ch. 33.]

[10] [Ibid., bk. 22, ch. 25. Metellus, not Nenius, was tribune when Fabius Maximus was in the same office.]

without appeal; and as it was quietly exercised in making strangers, or whom they pleased kings, restraining the power of dictators to six months, and that of the decemviri to two years; when the last did, contrary to law, endeavour by force to continue their power, the people did by force destroy it and them.

The case of Moses is yet more clear: he was the most humble and gentle of all men: he never raised his heart above his brethren, and commanded kings to live in the same modesty: he never desired the people should depend upon his will: In giving laws to them he fulfill'd the will of God, not his own; and those laws were not the signification of his will, but of the will of God. They were the production of God's wisdom and goodness, not the invention of man; given to purify the people, not to advance the glory of their leader. He was not proud and insolent, nor pleas'd with that ostentation of pomp, to which fools give the name of majesty; and whoever so far exalts the power of a man, to make nations depend upon his pleasure, does not only lay a burden upon him, which neither Moses, nor any other could ever bear, and every wise man will always abhor; but with an impious fury, endeavours to set up a government contrary to the laws of God, presumes to accuse him of want of wisdom, or goodness to his own people, and to correct his errors, which is a work fit to be undertaken by such as our author.

From hence, as upon a solid foundation, he proceeds, and making use of King James's words, infers, that kings are above the laws, because he so teaches us.[11] But he might have remembered, that having affirmed the people could not judge of the disputes that might happen between them and kings, because they must not be judges in their own case, 'tis absurd to make a king judge of a case so nearly concerning himself, in the decision of which his own passions and interests may probably lead him into errors. And if it be pretended that I do the same, in giving the judgment of those matters to the people, the case is utterly different, both in the nature and consequences. The king's judgment is merely for himself; and if that were to take place, all the passions and vices that have most power upon men, would concur to corrupt it. He that is set up for the publick good, can have no contest with the whole people whose good he is to procure, unless he deflect from the end of his institution, and set up an interest of his own in opposition to it. This is in its nature the highest of all delinquencies; and if such a one may be judge of his own crimes, he is not only sure to avoid punishment, but to obtain all that he sought by them; and the worse he is, the more violent will his

---

[11] [*Patriarcha*, ch. 24, p. 103.]

desires be, to get all the power into his hands, that he may gratify his lusts, and execute his pernicious designs. On the other side, in a popular assembly, no man judges for himself, otherwise than as his good is comprehended in that of the publick: Nothing hurts him, but what is prejudicial to the commonwealth: such amongst them as may have received private injuries, are so far only considered by others, as their sufferings may have influence upon the publick; if they be few, and the matters not great, others will not suffer their quiet to be disturbed by them; if they are many and grievous, the tyranny thereby appears to be so cruel, that the nation cannot subsist, unless it be corrected or suppress'd. Corruption of judgment proceeds from private passions, which in these cases never govern: and tho a zeal for the publick good may possibly be misguided, yet till it be so, it can never be capable of excess. The last Tarquin, and his lewd son, exercised their fury and lust in the murders of the best men in Rome, and the rape of Lucretia. Appius Claudius was filled with the like madness. Caligula and Nero were so well established in the power of committing the worst of villainies, that we do not hear of any man that offer'd to defend himself, or woman that presumed to refuse them. If they had been judges in these cases, the utmost of all villainies and mischiefs had been established by law: but as long as the judgment of these matters was in the people, no private or corrupt passion could take place. Lucius Brutus, Valerius, Horatius and Virginius, with the people that followed them, did not by the expulsion of the kings, or the suppression of the decemviri, assume to themselves a power of committing rapes and murders, nor any advantages beyond what their equals might think they deserved by their virtues, and services to the commonwealth; nor had they more credit than others for any other reason, than that they shewed themselves most forward in procuring the publick good, and by their valour and conduct best able to promote it.

Whatsoever happen'd after the overthrow of their liberty, belongs not to my subject, for there was nothing of popularity in the judgments that were made. One tyrant destroy'd another; the same passions and vices for the most part reigned in both: The last was often as bad as his predecessor whom he had overthrown; and one was sometimes approved by the people for no other reason, than that it was thought impossible for him to be worse than he who was in possession of the power. But if one instance can be of force amongst an infinite number of various accidents, the words of Valerius Asiaticus, who by wishing he had been the man that had kill'd Caligula, did in a moment pacify the fury of the soldiers who were looking for those that had done it, shew, that as long as men retain anything of that reason which is truly their nature, they never fail of judging rightly of virtue and vice; whereas violent and ill princes have always done the contrary, and even the best do often deflect from the rules of justice, as appears not only by the examples of Edward the first and third, who were brought to confess it, but even those of David and Solomon.

Moreover to shew that the decision of these controversies cannot belong to any king, but to the people, we are only to consider, that as kings and all other magistrates, whether supreme or subordinate, are constituted only for the good of the people, the people only can be fit to judge whether the end be accomplished. A physician does not exercise his art for himself, but for his patients; and when I am, or think I shall be sick, I send for him of whom I have the best opinion, that he may help me to recover, or preserve my health; but I lay him aside if I find him to be negligent, ignorant, or unfaithful; and it would be ridiculous for him to say, I make myself judge in my own case, for I only, or such as I shall consult, am fit to be the judge of it. He may be treacherous, and through corruption or malice endeavour to poison me, or have other defects that render him unfit to be trusted: but I cannot by any corrupt passion be led wilfully to do him injustice, and if I mistake, 'tis only to my own hurt. The like may be said of lawyers, stewards, pilots, and generally of all that do not act for themselves, but for those who employ them. And if a company going to the Indies, should find that their pilot was mad, drunk, or treacherous, they whose lives and goods are concerned, can only be fit to judge, whether he ought to be trusted or not, since he cannot have a right to destroy those he was chosen to preserve; and they cannot be thought to judge perversely, because they have nothing to lead them but an opinion of truth, and cannot err but to their own prejudice. In the like manner, not only Solon and Draco, but Romulus, Numa, Hostilius, the consuls, dictators, and decemviri, were not distinguished from others, that it might be well with them, *sed ut bonum, faelix, faustumque sit populo Romano,*[12] but that the prosperity and happiness of the people might be procured; which being the thing always intended, it were absurd to refer the judgment of the performance to him who is suspected of a design to overthrow it, and whose passions, interests, and vices, if he has any, lead him that way. If King James said anything contrary to this, he might be answered with some of his own words; *I was,* says he, *sworn to maintain the laws of the land, and therefore had been perjured if I had broken them.*[13] It may also be presumed, he had not

[12] ["But in order that it might be good, happy, and auspicious for the Roman people." Livy, *History of Rome*, bk. 3, ch. 34.]

[13] Speech in Star-Chamber, 1616.

forgotten what his master Buchanan had taught in the books he wrote chiefly for his instruction, that the violation of the laws of Scotland could not have been so fatal to most of his predecessors, kings of that country (nor as he himself had made them to his mother) if kings as kings were above them.[14]

SECTION 15
A general presumption that Kings will govern well, is not a sufficient security to the People.

BUT says our author, *yet will they rule their subjects by the law; and a king governing in a settled kingdom, leaves to be a king, and degenerates into a tyrant, so soon as he ceases to rule according unto his laws: Yet where he sees them rigorous or doubtful, he may mitigate or interpret.*[1] This is therefore an effect of their goodness; they are above laws, but will rule by law, we have Filmer's word for it. But I know not how nations can be assured their princes will always be so good: Goodness is always accompanied with wisdom, and I do not find those admirable qualities to be generally inherent or entail'd upon supreme magistrates. They do not seem to be all alike, and we have not hitherto found them all to live in the same spirit and principle. I can see no resemblance between Moses and Caligula, Joshua and Claudius, Gideon and Nero, Samson and Vitellius, Samuel and Otho, David and Domitian; nor indeed between the best of these and their own children. If the sons of Moses and Joshua had been like to them in wisdom, valour and integrity, 'tis probable they had been chosen to succeed them; if they were not, the like is less to be presumed of others. No man has yet observed the moderation of Gideon to have been in Abimelech; the piety of Eli in Hophni and Phineas; the purity and integrity of Samuel in Joel and Abiah, nor the wisdom of Solomon in Rehoboam. And if there was so vast a difference between them and their children, who doubtless were instructed by those excellent men in the ways of wisdom and justice, as well by precept as example, were it not

---

[14] Hist. Scot. [*History of Scotland.*] De jure Reg. apud Scot. [*De jure regni apud Scotos, dialogus* (Edinburgh, 1579; trans. as *The Art and Science of Government among the Scots*; n.p.: William MacClelan, 1964).]

[1] [*Patriarcha*, ch. 24, p. 103, quoting James I,

The True Law of Free Monarchies (1598) and one sentence from his *Speech to the Lords and Commons* (1609), in *Political Works of James I*, pp. 63, 309. The 1680 edition of *Patriarcha* did not distinguish this quotation from Filmer's text.]

madness to be confident, that they who have neither precept nor good example to guide them, but on the contrary are educated in an utter ignorance or abhorrence of all virtue, will always be just and good; or to put the whole power into the hands of every man, woman, or child that shall be born in governing families upon a supposition, that a thing will happen, which never did; or that the weakest and worst will perform all that can be hoped, and was seldom accomplished by the wisest and best, exposing whole nations to be destroy'd without remedy, if they do it not? And if this be madness in all extremity, 'tis to be presumed that nations never intended any such thing, unless our author prove that all nations have been mad from the beginning, and must always continue to be so. To cure this, he says, *They degenerate into tyrants;* and if he meant as he speaks, it would be enough. For a king cannot degenerate into a tyrant by departing from that law, which is only the product of his own will. But if he do degenerate, it must be by departing from that which does not depend upon his will, and is a rule prescribed by a power that is above him. This indeed is the doctrine of Bracton, who having said that the power of the king is the power of the law, because the law makes him king, adds, *That if he do injustice, he ceases to be king, degenerates into a tyrant, and becomes the vicegerent of the Devil.*[2] But I hope this must be understood with temperament, and a due consideration of human frailty, so as to mean only those injuries that are extreme; for otherwise he would terribly shake all the crowns of the world.

But lest our author should be thought once in his life to have dealt sincerely, and spoken truth, the next lines shew the fraud of his last assertion, by giving to the prince a power of *mitigating or interpreting the laws that he sees to be rigorous or doubtful.* But as he cannot degenerate into a tyrant by departing from the law which proceeds from his own will, so he cannot mitigate or interpret that which proceeds from a superior power, unless the right of mitigating or interpreting be conferred upon him by the same. For as all wise men confess that *none can abrogate but those who may institute,*[3] and that all mitigation and interpretation varying from the true sense is an alteration, that alteration is an abrogation; for whatsoever is changed is dissolved,[4] and therefore the power of mitigating is inseparable from that of instituting. This is sufficiently evidenced by Henry the Eighth's answer to the speech made to him by the speaker of the House of Commons 1545, in which he, tho one of the most violent

---

[2] Quia si faciat injuriam definit esse rex, & degenerat in tyrannum, et sit vicarius diaboli. [Bracton, *On the Laws and Customs of England,* fol. 107, p. 305.]

[3] Cujus est instituere, ejus est abrogare.

[4] Quicquid mutatur dissolvitur, interit ergo.

princes we ever had, confesses the parliament to be the law-makers, and that an obligation lay upon him rightly to use the power with which he was entrusted. The right therefore of altering being inseparable from that of making laws, the one being in the parliament, the other must be so also. Fortescue says plainly, the king cannot change any law: *Magna Charta* casts all upon the laws of the land and customs of England:[5] but to say that the king can by his will make that to be a custom, or an ancient law, which is not, or that not to be so which is, is most absurd. He must therefore take the laws and customs as he finds them, and can neither detract from, nor add anything to them. The ways are prescribed as well as the end. Judgments are given by equals, *per pares*. The judges who may be assisting to those, are sworn to proceed according to law, and not to regard the king's letters or commands. The doubtful cases are reserved, and to be referred to the parliament, as in the statute of 35 Edw. 3d concerning treasons, but never to the king.[6] The law intending that these parliaments should be annual, and leaving to the king a power of calling them more often, if occasion require, takes away all pretence of a necessity that there should be any other power to interpret or mitigate laws. For 'tis not to be imagined that there should be such a pestilent evil in any ancient law, custom, or later act of parliament, which being on the sudden discover'd, may not without any great prejudice continue for forty days, till a parliament may be called; whereas the force and essence of all laws would be subverted, if under colour of mitigating and interpreting, the power of altering were allow'd to kings, who often want the inclination, and for the most part the capacity of doing it rightly. 'Tis not therefore upon the uncertain will or understanding of a prince, that the safety of a nation ought to depend. He is sometimes a child, and sometimes overburden'd with years. Some are weak, negligent, slothful, foolish or vicious: others, who may have something of rectitude in their intentions, and naturally are not incapable of doing well, are drawn out of the right way by the subtlety of ill men who gain credit with them. That rule must always be uncertain, and subject to be distorted, which depends upon the fancy of such a man. He always fluctuates, and every passion that arises in his mind, or is infused by others, disorders him. The good of a people ought to be established upon a more solid foundation. For this reason the law is established, which no passion can disturb. 'Tis void of desire and fear, lust and anger. 'Tis *mens sine affectu*,[7] written reason, retaining some measure of the divine perfection. It does not enjoin

---

[5] Leges terrae & consuetudines Angliae.　　　[7] [Mind without passion.]

[6] [Actually 25 Edward III.]

that which pleases a weak, frail man, but without any regard to persons commands that which is good, and punishes evil in all, whether rich or poor, high or low. 'Tis deaf, inexorable, inflexible.

By this means every man knows when he is safe or in danger, because he knows whether he has done good or evil. But if all depended upon the will of a man, the worst would be often the most safe, and the best in the greatest hazard: Slaves would be often advanced, the good and the brave scorn'd and neglected. The most generous nations have above all things sought to avoid this evil: and the virtue, wisdom and generosity of each may be discern'd by the right fixing of the rule that must be the guide of every man's life, and so constituting their magistracy that it may be duly observed. Such as have attained to this perfection, have always flourished in virtue and happiness: They are, as Aristotle says, governed by God, rather than by men, whilst those who subjected themselves to the will of a man were governed by a beast.

This being so, our author's next clause, that *tho a king do frame all his actions to be according unto law, yet he is not bound thereunto, but as his good will, and for good example, or so far forth as the general law for the safety of the commonwealth doth naturally bind him,*[8] is wholly impertinent. For if the king who governs not according to law, degenerates into a tyrant, he is obliged to frame his actions according to law, or not to be a king; for a tyrant is none, but as contrary to him, as the worst of men is to the best. But if these obligations were untied, we may easily guess what security our author's word can be to us, that the king of his own good will, and for a good example, will frame his actions according to the laws; when experience instructs us, that notwithstanding the strictest laws, and most exquisite constitutions, that men of the best abilities in the world could ever invent to restrain the irregular appetites of those in power, with the dreadful examples of vengeance taken against such as would not be restrained, they have frequently broken out; and the most powerful have for the most part no otherwise distinguished themselves from the rest of men, than by the enormity of their vices, and being the most forward in leading others to all manner of crimes by their example.

---

[8] [*Patriarcha*, p. 103, up to "example," quoted from James I, *The True Law* (see n. 1 above).]

SECTION 16

The observation of the Laws of Nature
is absurdly expected from Tyrants, who set themselves
up against all Laws: and he that subjects Kings to no
other Law than what is common to Tyrants,
destroys their being.

Our author's last clause acknowledging kings to be bound by a general law to provide for the safety of the people, would be sufficient for my purpose if it were sincere; for municipal laws do only shew how that should be performed: and if the king by departing from that rule degenerates, as he says, into a tyrant, 'tis easily determined what ought then to be done by the people. But his whole book being a heap of contradictions and frauds, we can rely upon nothing that he says: And his following words, which under the same law comprehend both kings and tyrants, shew that he intends kings should be no otherwise obliged than tyrants, which is, not at all. *By this means,* says he, *are all kings, even tyrants and conquerors, bound to preserve the lands, goods, liberties and lives of all their subjects, not by any municipal law of the land, so much as by the natural law of a father, which obligeth them to ratify the acts of their forefathers and predecessors in things necessary for the publick good of their subjects.*[1] If he be therefore in the right, tyrants and conquerors are kings and fathers. The words that have been always thought to comprehend the most irreconcileable contrariety, the one expressing the most tender love and care, evidently testified by the greatest obligations conferred upon those who are under it; the other the utmost of all injuries that can be offer'd to men, signify the same thing: There is no difference between a magistrate who is what he is by law, and a publick enemy, who by force or fraud sets himself up against all law: And what he said before, that kings degenerated into tyrants, signifies nothing, for tyrants also are kings.

His next words are no less incomprehensible; for neither king nor tyrant can be obliged to preserve the lands, goods and liberties of their subjects if they have none. But as liberty consists only in being subject to no man's will, and nothing denotes a slave but a dependence upon the will of another; if there be no other law in a kingdom than the will of a prince, there is no such thing as liberty. Property also is an appendage

---

[1] [*Patriarcha*, ch. 24, p. 103.]

to liberty; and 'tis as impossible for a man to have a right to lands or goods, if he has no liberty, and enjoys his life only at the pleasure of another, as it is to enjoy either when he is deprived of them. He therefore who says kings and tyrants are bound to preserve their subjects' lands, liberties, goods and lives, and yet lays for a foundation, that laws are no more than the significations of their pleasure, seeks to delude the world with words which signify nothing.

The vanity of these whimseys will farther appear, if it be considered, that as kings are kings by law, and tyrants are tyrants by overthrowing the law, they are most absurdly joined together; and 'tis not more ridiculous to set him above the law, who is what he is by the law, than to expect the observation of the laws that enjoin the preservation of the lands, liberties, goods and lives of the people, from one who by fraud or violence makes himself master of all, that he may be restrain'd by no law, and is what he is by subverting all law.

Besides, if the safety of the people be the supreme law, and this safety extend to, and consist in the preservation of their liberties, goods, lands and lives, that law must necessarily be the root and beginning, as well as the end and limit of all magistratical power, and all laws must be subservient and subordinate to it. The question will not then be what pleases the king, but what is good for the people; not what conduces to his profit or glory, but what best secures the liberties he is bound to preserve: he does not therefore reign for himself, but for the people; he is not the master, but the servant of the commonwealth; and the utmost extent of his prerogative is to be able to do more good than any private man. If this be his work and duty, 'tis easily seen whether he is to judge of his own performance, or they by whom and for whom he reigns; and whether in order to this he be to give laws, or to receive them. 'Tis ordinarily said in France, *il faut que chacun soit servi a sa mode;* Every man's business must be done according to his own mind: and if this be true in particular persons, 'tis more plainly so in whole nations. Many eyes see more than one: the collected wisdom of a people much surpasses that of a single person; and tho he should truly seek that which is best, 'tis not probable he would so easily find it, as the body of a nation, or the principal men chosen to represent the whole. This may be said with justice of the best and wisest princes that ever were; but another language is to be used when we speak of those who may succeed, and who very often through the defects of age, person, or sex, are neither fit to judge of other men's affairs, nor of their own; and are so far from being capable of the highest concernments relating to the safety of whole nations, that the most trivial cannot reasonably be referred to them.

There are few men (except such as are like Filmer, who by bidding defiance to the laws of God and man, seems to declare war against both) whom I would not trust to determine whether a people, that can never fall into nonage or dotage, and can never fail of having men of wisdom and virtue amongst them, be not more fit to judge in their own persons, or by representatives, what conduces to their own good, than one who at a venture may be born in a certain family, and who, besides his own infirmities, passions, vices, or interests, is continually surrounded by such as endeavour to divert him from the ways of truth and justice. And if no reasonable man dare prefer the latter before the former, we must rely upon the laws made by our forefathers, and interpreted by the nation, and not upon the will of a man.

'Tis in vain to say that a wise and good council may supply the defects, or correct the vices of a young, foolish, or ill disposed king. For Filmer denies that a king, whatever he be without exception (for he attributes profound wisdom to all), is obliged to follow the advice of his council; and even he would hardly have had the impudence to say, that good counsel given to a foolish or wicked prince were of any value, unless he were obliged to follow it. This council must be chosen by him, or imposed upon him: if it be imposed upon him, it must be by a power that is above him, which he says cannot be. If chosen by him who is weak, foolish, or wicked, it can never be good; because such virtue and wisdom is requir'd to discern and chuse a few good and wise men, from a multitude of foolish and bad, as he has not. And it will generally fall out, that he will take for his counsellors rather those he believes to be addicted to his person or interests, than such as are fitly qualified to perform the duty of their places. But if he should by chance, or contrary to his intentions, make choice of some good and wise men, the matter would not be much mended, for they will certainly differ in opinion from the worst. And tho the prince should intend well, of which there is no assurance; nor any reason to put so great a power into his hands if there be none, 'tis almost impossible for him to avoid the snares that will be laid to seduce him. I know not how to put a better face upon this matter; for if I examine rather what is probable than possible, foolish or ill princes will never chuse such as are wise and good; but favouring those who are most like to themselves, will prefer such as second their vices, humours, and personal interests, and by so doing will rather fortify and rivet the evils that are brought upon the nation through their defects, than cure them. This was evident in Rehoboam: he had good counsel, but he would not hearken to it. We know too many of the same sort; and tho it were not impossible (as Machiavelli says it is) for a weak prince to receive any benefit from a good council,[2] we may certainly conclude, that a people can never expect any good from a council chosen by one who is weak or vicious.

If a council be imposed upon him, and he be obliged to follow their advice, it must be imposed by a power that is above him; his will therefore is not a law, but must be regulated by the law: the monarchy is not above the law; and if we will believe our author, 'tis no monarchy, because the monarch has not his will, and perhaps he says true. For if that be not an aristocracy, where those that are, or are reputed to be the best do govern, then that is certainly a mixed state, in which the will of one man does not prevail. But if princes are not obliged by the law, all that is founded upon that supposition falls to the ground: They will always follow their own humours, or the suggestions of those who second them. Tiberius hearkened to none but Chaldeans,[3] or the ministers of his impurities and cruelties: Claudius was governed by slaves, and the profligate strumpets his wives. There were many wise and good men in the senate during the reigns of Caligula, Nero and Domitian; but instead of following their counsel, they endeavour'd to destroy them all, lest they should head the people against them; and such princes as resemble them will always follow the like courses.

If I often repeat these hateful names, 'tis not for want of fresher examples of the same nature; but I chuse such as mankind has universally condemn'd, against whom I can have no other cause of hatred than what is common to all those who have any love to virtue, and which can have no other relation to the controversies of later ages, than what may flow from the similitude of their causes, rather than such as are too well known to us, and which every man, according to the measure of his experience, may call to mind in reading these. I may also add, that as nothing is to be received as a general maxim, which is not generally true, I need no more to overthrow such as Filmer proposes, than to prove how frequently they have been found false, and what desperate mischiefs have been brought upon the world as often as they have been practiced, and excessive powers put into the hands of such as had neither inclination nor ability to make a good use of them.

1. But if the safety of nations be the end for which governments are instituted, such as take upon them to govern, by what title soever, are by the law of nature bound to procure it; and in order to this, to preserve the lives, lands, liberties and goods of every one of their subjects: and he

---

[2] [Machiavelli, *The Prince*, ch. 23.]

[3] [Tiberius believed in Chaldean astrology.
Tacitus, *Annals*, bk. 2, ch. 27.]

that upon any title whatsoever pretends, assumes, or exercises a power of disposing of them according to his will, violates the laws of nature in the highest degree.

2. If all princes are obliged by the law of nature to preserve the lands, goods, lives and liberties of their subjects, those subjects have by the law of nature a right to their liberties, lands, goods, &c. and cannot depend upon the will of any man, for that dependence destroys liberty, &c.

3. Ill men will not, and weak men cannot provide for the safety of the people; nay the work is of such extreme difficulty, that the greatest and wisest men that have been in the world are not able by themselves to perform it; and the assistance of counsel is of no use unless princes are obliged to follow it. There must be therefore a power in every state to restrain the ill, and to instruct weak princes by obliging them to follow the counsels given, else the ends of government cannot be accomplished, nor the rights of nations preserved.

All this being no more than is said by our author, or necessarily to be deduced from his propositions, one would think he were become as good a commonwealths-man as Cato; but the washed swine will return to the mire. He overthrows all by a preposterous conjunction of the rights of kings which are just and by law, with those of tyrants which are utterly against law; and gives the sacred and gentle name of father to those beasts, who by their actions declare themselves enemies not only to all law and justice, but to mankind that cannot subsist without them. This requires no other proof, than to examine whether Attila or Tamerlane did well deserve to be called fathers of the countries they destroy'd. The first of these was usually called the scourge of God, and he gloried in the name. The other being reproved for the detestable cruelties he exercised, made answer, *You speak to me as to a man; I am not a man, but the scourge of God and plague of mankind.*[4] This is certainly sweet and gentle language, savouring much of a fatherly tenderness: There is no doubt that those who use it will provide for the safety of the nations under them, and the preservation of the laws of nature is rightly referred to them; and 'tis very probable, that they who came to burn the countries, and destroy the nations that fell under their power, should make it their business to preserve them, and look upon the former governors *as their fathers, whose acts they were obliged to confirm,* tho they seldom attained to the dominion by any other means than the slaughter of them and their families.

But if the enmity be not against the nation, and the cause of the war

[4] Vit. Tamerl. Hist. Thuan. [Jacques-Auguste de Thou, *Life of Tamerlane.*]

[406]

be only for dominion against the ruling person or family, as that of Baasha against the house of Jeroboam, of Zimri against that of Baasha, of Omri against Zimri, and of Jehu against Jehoram, the prosecution of it is a strange way of becoming the son of the person destroyed. And Filmer alone is subtle enough to discover, that Jehu by extinguishing the house of Ahab, drew an obligation upon himself, of looking on him as his father, and confirming his acts. If this be true, Moses was obliged to confirm the acts of the kings of the Amalekites, Moabites and Amorites that he destroy'd; the same duty lay upon Joshua, in relation to the Canaanites: but 'tis not so easily decided, to which of them he did owe that deference; for the same could not be due to all, and 'tis hard to believe, that by killing above thirty kings, he should purchase to himself so many fathers; and the like may be said of divers others.

Moreover, there is a sort of tyrant who has no father, as Agathocles, Dionysius, Caesar, and generally all those who subvert the liberties of their own country. And if they stood obliged to look upon the former magistrates as their predecessors, and to confirm their acts, the first should have been to give impunity and reward to any that would kill them, it having been a fundamental maxim in those states, *that any man might kill a tyrant.*[5]

This being in all respects ridiculous and absurd, 'tis evident that our author, who by proposing such a false security to nations for their liberties, endeavours to betray them, is not less treacherous to kings, when under a pretence of defending their rights, he makes them to be the same with those of tyrants, who are known to have none (and are tyrants because they have none) and gives no other hopes to nations of being preserved by the kings they set up for that end, than what upon the same account may be expected from tyrants, whom all wise men have ever abhorr'd, and affirmed to have been *produced to bring destruction upon the world,*[6] and whose lives have verifi'd the sentence.

This is truly to depose and abolish kings, by abolishing that by which and for which they are so. The greatness of their power, riches, state, and the pleasures that accompany them cannot but create enemies. Some will envy that which is accounted happiness; others may dislike the use they make of their power: some may be unjustly exasperated by the best of their actions when they find themselves incommoded by them; others may be too severe judges of slight miscarriages. These things may reasonably temper the joys of those who delight most in the advantages of crowns. But the worst and most dangerous of all their enemies are

---

[5] Unicuique licere tyrannum occidere.   [6] In generis humani exitium natos.

these accursed sycophants, who by making those that ought to be the best of men, like to the worst, destroy their being; and by persuading the world they aim at the same things, and are bound to no other rule than is common to all tyrants, give a fair pretence to ill men to say, they are all of one kind. And if this should be received for truth, even they who think the miscarriages of their governors may be easily redressed, and desire no more, would be the most fierce in procuring the destruction of that which is naught in principle, and cannot be corrected.

SECTION 17

Kings cannot be the Interpreters of the Oaths they take.

OUR author's book is so full of absurdities and contradictions, that it would be a rope of sand, if a continued series of frauds did not, like a string of poisons running through the whole, give it some consistence with itself, and shew it to be the work of one and the same hand. After having endeavoured to subvert the laws of God, nature, and nations, most especially our own, by abusing the Scriptures, falsely alleging the authority of many good writers, and seeking to obtrude upon mankind a universal law, that would take from every nation the right of constituting such governments within themselves as seem most convenient for them, and giving rules for the administration of such as they had established, he gives us a full view of his religion and morals, by destroying the force of the oath taken by our kings at their coronation. *Others*, says he, *affirm that although laws of themselves do not bind kings, yet the oaths of kings at their coronation tie them to keep all the laws of their kingdoms. How far this is true, let us but examine the oath of the kings of England at their coronation, the words whereof are these. Art thou pleased to cause to be administered in all thy judgments, indifferent and upright justice, and to use discretion with mercy and verity? Art thou pleased that our upright laws and customs be observed, and dost thou promise that those shall be protected and maintained by thee?* &c. To which the king *answers in the affirmative, being first demanded by the archbishop of Canterbury, Pleaseth it you to confirm and observe the laws and customs of the ancient times, granted from God by just and devout kings unto the English nation, by oath unto the said people, especially the laws, liberties and customs granted unto the clergy and laity by the famous King Edward?* From this he infers, that the king *is not to observe all laws, but such as are upright, because he finds evil laws mention'd in the oath of Richard the 2d, which he swears to abolish: Now what laws are*

upright and what evil, who shall judge but the king? &c. So that in effect the
king doth swear to keep no laws but such as in his judgment are upright, &c.
And if he did strictly swear to observe all laws, he could not without perjury give
his consent to the repealing or abrogating of any statute by act of parliament, &c.
And again, But let it be supposed for truth, that kings do swear to observe all
laws of their kingdoms; yet no man can think it reason, that the kings should be
more bound by their voluntary oaths than common persons: Now if a private
person make a contract, either with oath or without oath, he is no farther bound
than the equity and justice of the contract ties him; for a man may have relief
against an unreasonable and unjust promise, if either deceit or error, force or fear
induced him thereunto; or if it be hurtful or grievous in the performance, since
the law in many cases gives the king a prerogative above common persons.[1] Lest
I should be thought to insist upon small advantages, I will not oblige any
man to shew where Filmer found this oath, nor observe the faults
committed in the translation; but notwithstanding his false representation,
I find enough for my purpose, and intend to take it in his own words.
But first I shall take leave to remark, that those who for private interests
addict themselves to the personal service of princes, tho to the ruin of
their country, find it impossible to persuade mankind that kings may
govern as they please, when all men know there are laws to direct and
restrain them, unless they can make men believe they have their power
from a universal and superior law; or that princes can attempt to dissolve
the obligations laid upon them by the laws, which they so solemnly swear
to observe, without rendering themselves detestable to God and man,
and subject to the revenging hands of both, unless they can invalidate
those oaths. Mr. Hobbes I think was the first, who very ingeniously
contrived a compendious way of justifying the most abominable perjuries,
and all the mischiefs ensuing thereupon, by pretending, that as the king's
oath is made to the people, the people may absolve him from the
obligation; and that the people having conferred upon him all the power
they had, he can do all that they could: he can therefore absolve himself,
and is actually free, since he is so when he pleases.[2] This is only false in
the minor: for the people not having conferred upon him all, but only a
part of their power, that of absolving him remains in themselves, otherwise
they would never have obliged him to take the oath. He cannot therefore
absolve himself. The pope finds a help for this, and as Christ's vicar
pretends the power of absolution to be in him, and exercised it in absolving

---

[1] [*Patriarcha*, ch. 25 ("Of the Oaths of Kings"), pp. 103–104. Robertson, the 1772 editor, reported that Filmer had transcribed these oaths with tolerable accuracy.]

[2] Lib. de Cive. [Hobbes, *On the Citizen*, ch. 6, sec. 14; ch. 7, sec. 11; ch. 12, sec. 4.]

King John. But our author despairing to impose either of these upon our age and nation, with more impudence and less wit, would enervate all coronation-oaths by subjecting them to the discretion of the taker; whereas all men have hitherto thought their force to consist in the declared sense of those who give them. This doctrine is so new, that it surpasses the subtlety of the Schoolmen, who, as an ingenious person said of them, had minced oaths so fine, that a million of them, as well as angels, may stand upon the point of a needle; and were never yet equalled but by the Jesuits, who have overthrown them by mental reservations, which is so clearly demonstrated from their books, that it cannot be denied, but so horrible, that even those of their own order who have the least spark of common honesty condemn the practice. And one of them, being a gentleman of a good family, told me, he would go the next day and take all the oaths that should be offer'd, if he could satisfy his conscience in using any manner of equivocation or mental reservation; or that he might put any other sense upon them, than he knew to be intended by those who offer'd them. And if our author's conscience were not more corrupted than that of the Jesuit, who had lived fifty years under the worst discipline that I think ever was in the world, I would ask him seriously, if he truly believe, that the nobility, clergy and commonalty of England, who have been always so zealous for their ancient laws, and so resolute in defending them, did mean no more by the oaths they so solemnly imposed, and upon which they laid so much weight, than that the king should swear to keep them, so far only as he should think fit. But *he swears only to observe those that are upright*, &c. How can that be understood otherwise, than that those who give the oath, do declare their laws and customs to be upright and good, and he by taking the oath affirms them to be so? Or how can they be more precisely specified than by the ensuing clause, *Granted from God by just and devout kings by oath, especially those of the famous King Edward?* But, says he, by the same oath *Richard the 2d was bound to abolish those that were evil*. If any such had crept in through error, or been obtruded by malice, the evil being discovered and declared by the nobility and commons who were concerned, he was not to take advantage of them, or by his refusal to evade the abolition, but to join with his people in annulling them, according to the general clause of assenting to those *quas vulgus elegerit*.[3]

Magna Charta being only an abridgment of our ancient laws and customs, the king that swears to it, swears to them all; and not being admitted to be the interpreter of it, or to determine what is good or evil,

---

[3] [Which the people shall have chosen.]

fit to be observed or annulled in it, can have no more power over the rest. This having been confirmed by more parliaments than we have had kings since that time, the same obligation must still lie upon them all, as upon John and Henry, in whose time that claim of right was compiled. The act was no less solemn than important; and the most dreadful curses that could be conceived in words, which were denounced against such as should any way infringe it, by the clergy in Westminster-Hall, in the presence and with the assent of K. Henry the 3d, many of the principal nobility, and all the estates of the kingdom, shew whether it was referred to the king's judgment or not; when 'tis evident they feared the violation from no other than himself, and such as he should employ. I confess the church (as they then called the clergy) was fallen into such corruption, that their arms were not much to be feared by one who had his conscience clear; but that could not be in the case of perjury: and our ancestors could do no better, than to employ the spiritual sword, reserving to themselves the use of the other in case that should be despised. Tho the pope's excommunications proved sometimes to be but *bruta fulmina*,[4] when a just cause was wanting, it may be easily judged what obedience a prince could expect from his subjects, when every man knew he had by perjury drawn the most heavy curses upon himself. King John was certainly wicked, but he durst not break these bonds till he had procured the pope's absolution for a cover; and when he had done so, he found himself unsafe under it, and could not make good what he had promised to the pope to obtain it, the parliament declaring that his grants to the pope were unjust, illegal, contrary to his coronation-oath, and that they would not be held by them. This went so far in that king's time, that writs were issued out to men of all conditions to oblige themselves by oath to keep the Great Charter; and if other means failed, *to compel the king to perform the conditions*.[5] 'Tis expressly said in his charter, "That the barons and commonalty of the land shall straighten and compel us by all means possible, as by seizing our towns, lands, and possessions, or any other way, till satisfaction be made according to their pleasure."[6] And in the charter of his son Henry, 'tis, upon the same supposition of not performing the agreement, said, "It shall be lawful for all men in our kingdom to rise up against us, and to do all things that may be grievous

---

[4] [Mere bluster.]

[5] Et quod ipsum regem per captionem distringerent & gravarent ad praefata exequenda. [Roger of Wendover, *Flowers of History*, vol. 2, p. 306.]

[6] Et ipsi barones cum communitate totius terrae distringent & gravabunt nos modis omnibus quibus poterunt, scilicet per captionem castrorum, terrarum, possessionem, & aliis modis quibus potuerint, donec emendatum fuerit secundum arbitrium eorum. [Ibid., p. 305.]

to us, as if they were absolutely free from any engagements to' our person."[7] These words seem to have been contrived to be so full and strong *propter duplicitatem regis*,[8] which was with too much reason suspected. And 'tis not, as I suppose, the language of slaves and villains begging something from their lord, but of noble and free men, who knew their lord was no more than what they made him, and had nothing but what they gave him: nor the language of a lord treating with such as enjoy'd their liberties by his favour, but with those whom he acknowledged to be the judges of his performing what had been stipulated; and equals the agreements made between the kings and people of Aragon, which I cited before from the *Relations* of Antonio Perez. This is as far as men can go; and the experience of all ages manifests, that princes performing their office, and observing these stipulations, have lived glorious, happy and beloved: and I can hardly find an example of any who have notoriously broken these oaths, and been adjudged to have incurred the penalties, who have not lived miserably, died shamefully, and left an abominable memory to posterity.

"But, says our author, kings cannot be more obliged by voluntary oaths than other men, and may be relieved from unjust and unreasonable promises, if they be induced by deceit, error, force or fear, or the performance be grievous."[9] Which is to say, that no oath is of any obligation: for there is none that is not voluntary or involuntary, and there never was any upon which some such thing may not be pretended, which would be the same if such as Filmer had the direction of their consciences who take the oaths, and of those who are to exact the performance. This would soon destroy all confidence between king and people, and not only unhinge the best established governments, but by a detestable practice of annihilating the force of oaths and most solemn contracts that can be made by men, overthrow all societies that subsist by them. I leave it to all reasonable men to judge how fit a work this would be for the supreme magistrate, who is advanced to the highest degree of human glory and happiness, that he may preserve them; and how that justice, for the obtaining of which governments are constituted, can be administered, if he who is to exact it from others, do in his own person utterly subvert it; and what they deserve, who by such base prevarications would teach them to pervert and abolish the most sacred

---

[7] Licet omnibus de regno nostro contra nos insurgere, & omnia facere quae gravamen nostrum respiciant, ac si nobis in nullo tenerentur. [*Annals of Waverly* (the year 1264), in Thomas Gale, *Historiae Anglicanae scriptores*

quinque or *Five Writers of English History* (Oxford, 1687).]

[8] [Because of the king's duplicity.]

[9] [*Patriarcha*, ch. 25, p. 104.]

of all contracts. A worthy person of our age was accustomed to say that contracts in writing were invented only to bind villains, who having no law, justice or truth within themselves, would not keep their words, unless such testimonies were given as might compel them. But if our author's doctrine were received, no contract would be of more value than a cobweb. Such as are not absolutely of a profligate conscience, so far reverence the religion of an oath, to think that even those which are most unjustly and violently imposed ought to be observed; and Julius Caesar, who I think was not over-scrupulous, when he was taken by pirates, and set at liberty upon his word, caused the ransom he had promised to be pay'd to them. We see the like is practiced every day by prisoners taken in unjust as well as just wars: And there is no honest man that would not abhor a person, who being taken by the pirates of Algiers should not pay what he had promised for his liberty. 'Twere in vain to say they had no right of exacting, or that the performance was grievous; he must return to the chains, or pay. And tho the people of Artois, Alsace, or Flanders, do perhaps with reason think the king of France has no right to impose oaths of allegiance upon them, no man doubts, that if they chuse rather to take those oaths, than to suffer what might ensue upon their refusal, they are as much bound to be faithful to him as his ancient subjects.

The like may be said of promises extorted by fraud; and no other example is necessary to prove they are to be performed than that of Joshua made to the Gibeonites.[10] They were an accursed nation, which he was commanded to destroy: They came to him with lies, and by deceit induced him to make a league with them, which he ought not to have done; but being made, it was to be performed; and on that account he did not only spare but defend them, and the action was approved by God. When Saul by a preposterous zeal violated that league, the anger of God for that breach of faith could no otherwise be appeased than by the death of seven of his children.[11] This case is so full, so precise, and of such undoubted authority, that I shall not trouble myself with any other. But if we believe our man of good morals, voluntary oaths and promises are of no more value than those gained by force or deceit, that is to say, none are of any. For voluntary signifying nothing but free, all human acts are either free or not free, that is, from the will of the person, or some impulse from without. If therefore there be no force in those that are free, nor in those that are not free, there is none in any.

No better use can be made of any *pretension of error*, or that the *performance was grievous*; for no man ought to be grieved at the performance

---

[10] [Joshua 9.]   [11] [2 Samuel 21:1–14.]

of his contract. David assures us, that a good man performs his agreement tho he lose by it;[12] and the lord chancellor Egerton told a gentleman, who desired relief against his own deed, upon an allegation that he knew not what he did when he signed it, that he did not sit to relieve fools.

But tho voluntary promises or oaths, when, to use the lawyers' language, there is not a valuable consideration, were of no obligation; or that men brought by force, fear or error, into such contracts as are grievous in the performance, might be relieved; this would not at all reach the cases of princes, in the contracts made between them and their subjects, and confirmed by their oaths, there being no colour of force or fraud, fear or error for them to allege; nor anything to be pretended that can be grievous to perform, otherwise than as it may be grievous to an ill man not to do the mischiefs he had conceived.

Nations according to their own will frame the laws by which they resolve to be governed; and if they do it not wisely, the damage is only to themselves: But 'tis hard to find an example of any people that did by force oblige a man to take upon him the government of them. Gideon was indeed much pressed by the Israelites to be their king;[13] and the army of Germanicus in a mutiny more fiercely urged him to be emperor; but both desisted when their offers were refused. If our kings have been more modest, and our ancestors more pertinacious in compelling them to accept the crowns they offer'd, I shall upon proof of the matter change my opinion. But till that do appear, I may be pardoned if I think there was no such thing. William the Norman was not by force brought into England, but came voluntarily, and desired to be king: The nobility, clergy, and commons proposed the conditions upon which they would receive him. These conditions were to govern according to their ancient laws, especially those that had been granted, or rather collected in the time of the famous king Edward. Here was neither force nor fraud; if he had disliked the terms, he might have retired as freely as he came. But he did like them; and tho he was not perhaps so modest, to say with the brave Saxon king Offa, *Ad libertatis vestrae tuitionem, non meis meritis, sed sola liberalitate vestra unanimiter me convocastis,*[14] he accepted the crown upon the conditions offer'd and swore upon the Evangelists to observe them. Not much valuing this, he pretended to govern according to his own will; but finding the people would not endure it, he renewed his

---

[12] [Psalm 15:5.]

[13] [Judges 8:22–23.]

[14] Addit. Mat. Par. ["You chose me unanimously for the defense of your liberty, not from my own merit, but by your generosity alone." Matthew Paris, *Additamenta* to the *Historia Major*, in *Lives of the Two Offas, Kings of Mercia, and of Twenty-three Abbots of St. Albans* (including *Auctarium Additamentorum*) (London, 1640; corrected text, 1684).]

oath upon the same Evangelists, and the relics of St. Alban, which he needed not to have done, but might have departed to his duchy of Normandy if he had not lik'd the conditions, or thought not fit to observe them. 'Tis probable he examined the contents of Edward's laws before he swore to them,[15] and could not imagine, that a free nation which never had any other kings than such as had been chosen by themselves for the preservation of their liberty, and from whose liberality the best of their kings acknowledged the crowns they wore, did intend to give up their persons, liberties and estates to him, who was a stranger, most especially when they would not receive him till he had sworn to the same laws by which the others had reigned, of which one was (as appears by the act of the *Conventus Pananglicus*) that *Reges à sacerdotibus & senioribus populi eligantur, the kings should be elected by the clergy and elders of the people.*[16] By these means he was advanced to the crown, to which he could have no title, unless they had the right of conferring it upon him. Here was therefore no force, deceit or error; and whatsoever equity there might be to relieve one that had been forced, frighted or circumvented, it was nothing to this case. We do not find that William the 2d, or Henry, were forced to be kings; no sword was put to their throats; and for anything we know, the English nation was not then so contemptible but men might have been found in the world, who would willingly have accepted the crown, and even their elder brother Robert would not have refused: but the nobility and commons trusting to their oaths and promises, thought fit to prefer them before him; and when he endeavoured to impose himself upon the nation by force, they so severely punished him, that no better proof can be required to shew that they were accustomed to have no other kings than such as they approved. And this was one of the customs that all their kings swore to maintain, it being as ancient, just, and well approved as any other.

Having already proved, that all the kings we have had since that time, have come in upon the same title; that the Saxon laws to which all have sworn, continue to be of force amongst us, and that the words pronounced four times on the four sides of the scaffold by the archbishop, *Will ye have this man to reign?* do testify it; I may spare the pains of a repetition, and justly conclude, that if there was neither force nor fraud, fear nor

---

[15] Bonas & approbatas antiquas regni leges, quas sancti & pii reges ejus antecessores, & maxime Edvardus statuit, inviolabiliter observare. ["(The king swore) strictly to observe the good and approved ancient laws of the realm, which his predecessors, holy and pious kings, especially Edward (the Confessor), had laid down." Matthew Paris, *Life of Frederick, Abbot of St. Albans*, sec. 13, p. 48.]

[16] [Sir Henry Spelman, *Concilia, decreta, leges, constitutiones in re ecclesiarum orbis Britannici*, p. 296.]

error, to be pretended by the first, there could be none in those that
followed.

But the *observation of this oath may be grievous*. If I received money the
last year upon bond, promise, or sale of a manor or farm, can it be
thought grievous to me to be compelled to repay, or to make over the
land according to my agreement? Or if I did not seal the bond till I had
the money, must not I perform the condition, or at the least restore what
I had received? If it be grievous to any king to preserve the liberties,
lives, and estates of his subjects, and to govern according to their laws,
let him resign the crown, and the people to whom the oath was made,
will probably release him. Others may possibly be found who will not
think it grievous: or if none will accept a crown unless they may do what
they please, the people must bear the misfortune of being obliged to
govern themselves, or to institute some other sort of magistracy that will
be satisfied with a less exorbitant power. Perhaps they may succeed as
well as some others have done, who without being brought to that
necessity, have voluntarily cast themselves into the misery of living
without the majestick splendor of a monarch: or if that fail, they may as
their last refuge, surrender up themselves to slavery. When that is done,
we will acknowledge that whatsoever we have is derived from the favour
of our master. But no such thing yet appearing amongst us, we may be
pardoned if we think we are free-men governed by our own laws, and
that no man has a power over us, which is not given and regulated by
them; nor that anything but a new law made by ourselves, can exempt
our kings from the obligation of performing their oaths taken, to govern
according to the old, in the true sense of the words, as they are understood
in our language by those who give them, and conducing to the ends for
which they are given, which can be no other than to defend us from all
manner of arbitrary power, and to fix a rule to which we are to conform
our actions, and from which, according to our deserts, we may expect
reward or punishment. And those who by prevarications, cavils or
equivocations, endeavour to dissolve these obligations, do either maliciously betray the cause of kings, by representing them to the world as
men who prefer the satisfaction of their irregular appetites before the
performance of their duty, and trample under foot the most sacred bonds
of human society; or from the grossest ignorance do not see, that by
teaching nations how little they can rely upon the oaths of their princes,
they instruct them as little to observe their own; and that not only because
men are generally inclined to follow the examples of those in power, but
from a most certain conclusion, that he who breaks his part of a contract
cannot without the utmost impudence and folly expect the performance

of the other; nothing being more known amongst men, than that all contracts are of such mutual obligation, that he who fails of his part discharges the other. If this be so between man and man, it must needs be so between one and many millions of men: If he were free, because he says he is, every man must be free also when he pleases; if a private man who receives no benefit, or perhaps prejudice from a contract, be obliged to perform the conditions, much more are kings who receive the greatest advantages the world can give. As they are not by themselves nor for themselves, so they are not different *in specie* from other men: they are born, live and die as we all do. The same law of truth and justice is given to all by God and nature, and perhaps I may say the performance of it is most rigorously exacted from the greatest of men. The liberty of perjury cannot be a privilege annexed to crowns; and 'tis absurd to think that the most venerable authority that can be conferred upon a man, is increased by a liberty to commit, or impunity in committing such crimes as are the greatest aggravations of infamy to the basest villains in the world.

SECTION 18

The next in blood to deceased Kings cannot generally be said to be Kings till they are crowned.

Tis hereupon usually objected, that kings do not come in by contract nor by oath, but are kings by, or according to proximity of blood, before they are crowned. Tho this be a bold proposition, I will not say 'tis universally false. 'Tis possible that in some places the rule of succession may be set down so precisely, that in some cases every man may be able to see and know the sense, as well as the person designed to be the successor: but before I acknowledge it to be universally true, I must desire to know what this rule of succession is, and from whence it draws its original.

I think I may be excused if I make these scruples, because I find the thing in dispute to be variously adjudged in several places, and have observed five different manners of disposing crowns esteemed hereditary, besides an infinite number of collateral controversies arising from them, of which we have divers examples; and if there be one universal rule appointed, one of these only can be right, and all the others must be vicious. The first gives the inheritance to the eldest male of the eldest legitimate line, as in France, according to that which they call the Salic Law. The second, to the eldest legitimate male of the reigning family, as anciently in Spain, according to which the brother of the deceased king has been often, if not always preferr'd before the son, if he were elder, as may appear by the dispute between Corbis and Orsua, cited before from Titus Livius; and in the same country during the reign of the Goths, the eldest male succeeded, whether legitimate or illegitimate. The fourth receives females or their descendants, without any other condition distinguishing them from males, except that the younger brother is preferr'd before the elder sister, but the daughter of the elder brother is preferr'd before the son of the younger. The fifth gives the inheritance to females under a condition, as in Sweden, where they inherit, unless they marry out of the country without the consent of the estates; according to which rule Charles Gustavus was chosen, as any stranger might have been, tho son to a sister of Gustavus Adolphus, who by marrying a German prince had forfeited her right. And by the same act of estates, by which her eldest son was chosen, and the crown entailed upon the heirs of his body, her second son the prince Adolphus was wholly excluded.

Till these questions are decided by a judge of such an undoubted authority, that all men may safely submit, 'tis hard for any man who really seeks the satisfaction of his conscience, to know whether the law of God and nature (tho he should believe there is one general law) do justify the customs of the ancient Medes and Sabeans, mentioned by the poet, who admitted females,[1] or those of France which totally exclude them as unfit to reign over men, and utterly unable to perform the duty of a supreme magistrate, as we see they are everywhere excluded from the exercise of all other offices in the commonwealth. If it be said that we ought to follow the customs of our own country, I answer, that those of our own country deserve to be observed, because they are of our own country: But they are no more to be called the laws of God and nature than those of France or Germany; and tho I do not believe that any general law is appointed, I wish I were sure that our customs in this point were not more repugnant to the light of nature, and prejudicial to ourselves, than those of some other nations: But if I should be so much an Englishman, to think the will of God to have been more particularly

---

[1] Medis levibusque Sabaeis / Imperat hic sexus, reginarumque sub armis / Barbariae pars magna jacet. Lucan. ["This sex rules the Medes and the light-armed Sabeans; and a great part of the barbarians is subjected to the arms of queens." Claudian, *Against Eutropius*, bk. 1, li. 322.]

revealed to our ancestors, than to any other nation, and that all of them ought to learn from us; yet it would be difficult to decide many questions that may arise. For tho the parliament in the 36th of Henry the sixth, made an act in favour of Richard duke of York, descended from a daughter of Mortimer, who married the daughter of the duke of Clarence, elder brother to John of Gaunt, they rather asserted their own power of giving the crown to whom they pleased, than determined the question. For if they had believed that the crown had belonged to him by a general and eternal law, they must immediately have rejected Henry as a usurper, and put Richard into the possession of his right, which they did not. And tho they did something like to this in the cases of Maud the empress in relation to King Stephen, and her son Henry the 2d; and of Henry the 7th in relation to the house of York, both before he had married a daughter of it, and after her death; they did the contrary in the cases of William the first and second, Henry the 1st, Stephen, John, Richard the 3d, Henry the 7th, Mary, Elizabeth, and others. So that, for anything I can yet find, 'tis equally difficult to discover the true sense of the law of nature that should be a guide to my conscience, whether I so far submit to the laws of my country, to think that England alone has produced men that rightly understand it, or examine the laws and practices of other nations.

Whilst this remains undecided, 'tis impossible for me to know to whom I owe the obedience that is exacted from me. If I were a French-man, I could not tell whether I ow'd allegiance to the king of Spain, duke of Lorraine, duke of Savoy, or many others descended from daughters of the house of Valois, one of whom ought to inherit, if the inheritance belongs to females; or to the house of Bourbon, whose only title is founded upon the exclusion of them. The like controversies will be in all places; and he that would put mankind upon such enquiries, goes about to subvert all the governments of the world, and arms every man to the destruction of his neighbour.

We ought to be informed when this right began: If we had the genealogy of every man from Noah, and the crowns of every nation had since his time continued in one line, we were only to inquire into how many kingdoms he appointed the world to be divided, and how well the division we see at this day agrees with the allotment made by him. But mankind having for many ages lain under such a vast confusion, that no man pretends to know his own original, except some Jews, and the princes of the house of Austria, we cannot so easily arrive at the end of our work; and the Scriptures making no other mention of this part of the world, than what may induce us to think it was given to the sons of Japheth, we have nothing that can lead us to guess how it was to be subdivided, nor to whom the several parcels were given: So that the difficulties are absolutely inextricable; and tho it were true, that some one man had a right to every parcel that is known to us, it could be of no use; for that right must necessarily perish which no man can prove, nor indeed claim. But as all natural rights by inheritance must be by descent, this descent not being proved, there can be no natural right; and all rights being either natural, created or acquired, this right to crowns not being natural, must be created or acquired, or none at all.

There being no general law common to all nations, creating a right to crowns (as has been proved by the several methods used by several nations in the disposal of them, according to which all those that we know are enjoy'd) we must seek the right concerning which we dispute, from the particular constitutions of every nation, or we shall be able to find none.

Acquir'd rights are obtained, as men say, either by fair means or by foul, that is, by force or by consent: such as are gained by force, may be recovered by force; and the extent of those that are enjoy'd by consent, can only be known by the reasons for which, or the conditions upon which that consent was obtain'd, that is to say, by the laws of every people. According to these laws it cannot be said that there is a king in every nation before he is crown'd. John Sobieski now reigning in Poland, had no relation in blood to the former kings, nor any title till he was chosen. The last king of Sweden[2] acknowledged he had none, but was freely elected; and the crown being conferred upon him and the heirs of his body, if the present king dies without issue, the right of electing a successor returns undoubtedly to the estates of the country. The crown of Denmark was elective till it was made hereditary by an act of the general diet, held at Copenhagen in the year 1660; and 'tis impossible that a right should otherwise accrue to a younger brother of the house of Holstein,[3] which is derived from a younger brother of the counts of Oldenburgh. The Roman empire having passed through the hands of many persons of different nations, no way relating to each other in blood, was by Constantine transferred to Constantinople; and after many revolutions coming to Theodosius, by birth a Spaniard, was divided between his two sons Arcadius and Honorius. From thence passing to such as could gain most credit with the soldiers, the Western empire being brought almost to nothing, was restored by Charles the Great of France; and continuing for some time in his descendants, came to the

---

[2] [Charles X (Gustavus). "The present king" was Charles XI.]   [3] [Christian V.]

Germans; who having created several emperors of the houses of Swabia, Saxony, Bavaria and others, as they pleased, about three hundred years past chose Rudolph of Austria: and tho since that time they have not had any emperor who was not of that family; yet such as were chosen had nothing to recommend them, but the merits of their ancestors, their own personal virtues, or such political considerations as might arise from the power of their hereditary countries, which being joined with those of the empire might enable them to make the better defence against the Turks. But in this line also they have had little regard to inheritance according to blood; for the elder branch of the family is that which reigns in Spain; and the empire continues in the descendants of Ferdinand younger brother to Charles the fifth, tho so unfix'd even to this time, that the present Emperor Leopold was in great danger of being rejected.

If it be said that these are elective kingdoms, and our author speaks of such as are hereditary; I answer, that if what he says be true, there can be no elective kingdom, and every nation has a natural lord to whom obedience is due. But if some are elective, all might have been so if they had pleased, unless it can be proved, that God created some under a necessity of subjection, and left to others the enjoyment of their liberty. If this be so, the nations that are born under that necessity may be said to have a natural lord, who has all the power in himself, before he is crowned, or any part conferred on him by the consent of the people; but it cannot extend to others. And he who pretends a right over any nation upon that account, stands obliged to shew when and how that nation came to be discriminated by God from others, and deprived of that liberty which he in goodness had granted to the rest of mankind. I confess I think there is no such right, and need no better proof than the various ways of disposing inheritances in several countries, which not being naturally or universally better or worse one than another, cannot spring from any other root, than the consent of the several nations where they are in force, and their opinions that such methods were best for them. But if God have made a discrimination of people, he that would thereupon ground a title to the dominion of any one, must prove that nation to be under the curse of slavery, which for anything I know, was only denounced against Ham: and 'tis as hard to determine whether the sense of it be temporal, spiritual, or both, as to tell precisely what nations by being only descended from him, fall under the penalties threatened.

If these therefore be either entirely false, or impossible to be proved true, there is no discrimination, or not known to us; and every people has a right of disposing of their government, as well as the Polanders, Danes, Swedes, Germans, and such as are or were under the Roman empire. And if any nation has a natural lord before he be admitted by their consent, it must be by a peculiar act of their own; as the crown of France by an act of that nation, which they call the Salic Law, is made hereditary to males in a direct line, or the nearest to the direct; and others in other places are otherwise disposed.

I might rest here with full assurance that no disciple of Filmer can prove this of any people in the world, nor give so much as the shadow of a reason to persuade us there is any such thing in any nation, or at least in those where we are concerned; and presume little regard will be had to what he has said, since he cannot prove of any that which he so boldly affirms of all. But because good men ought to have no other object than truth, which in matters of this importance can never be made too evident, I will venture to go farther and assert, that as the various ways by which several nations dispose of the succession to their respective crowns, shew they were subject to no other law than their own, which they might have made different, by the same right they made it to be what it is, even those who have the greatest veneration for the reigning families, and the highest regard for proximity of blood, have always preferr'd the safety of the commonwealth before the concernments of any person or family; and have not only laid aside the nearest in blood, when they were found to be notoriously vicious and wicked, but when they have thought it more convenient to take others: And to prove this I intend to make use of no other examples than those I find in the histories of Spain, France and England.

Whilst the Goths governed Spain, not above four persons in the space of three hundred years were the immediate successors of their fathers, but the brother, cousin german, or some other man of the families of the Balthi or Amalthi was preferred before the children of the deceased king: and if it be said, this was according to the law of that kingdom, I answer, that it was therefore in the power of that nation to make laws for themselves, and consequently others have the same right. One of their kings called Wamba was deposed and made a monk after he had reigned well many years;[4] but falling into a swoon, and his friends thinking him past recovery, cut off his hair, and put a monk's frock upon him, that, according to the superstition of those times, he might die in it; and the cutting off the hair being a most disgraceful thing amongst the Goths, they would not restore him to his authority.[5] Suintila another of their

---

[4] Saavedra Coron. Goth. [Saavedra, *Corona gothica, castellana, y austriaca* (the year 633).]

[5] Mar. Hist. l. 6. [Mariana, *General History of Spain*, bk. 6 (the year 680).]

kings being deprived of the crown for his ill government, his children and brothers were excluded, and Sisinandus crowned in his room.[6]

This kingdom being not long after overthrown by the Moors, a new one arose from its ashes in the person of Don Pelayo first king of the Asturias, which increasing by degrees at last came to comprehend all Spain, and so continues to this day: But not troubling myself with all the deviations from the common rule in the collateral lines of Navarre, Aragon and Portugal, I find that by fifteen several instances in that one series of kings in the Asturias and Leon (who afterwards came to be kings of Castile) it is fully proved, that what respect soever they shew'd to the next in blood, who by the law were to succeed, they preferred some other person, as often as the supreme law of *taking care that the nation might receive no detriment*, persuaded them to it.

Don Pelayo enjoy'd for his life the kingdom conferred upon him by the Spaniards, who with him retired into the mountains to defend themselves against the Moors, and was succeeded by his son Favila. But tho Favila left many sons when he died, Alfonso surnamed the Chaste was advanced to the crown, and they all laid aside. Fruela son to Alfonso the Catholick, was for his cruelty deposed, put to death, and his sons excluded. Aurelio his cousin german succeeded him; and at his death Silo, who married his wife's sister, was preferr'd before the males of the blood royal.[7] Alfonso, surnamed El Casto, was first violently dispossess'd of the crown by a bastard of the royal family; but he being dead, the nobility and people thinking Alfonso more fit to be a monk than a king, gave the crown to Bermudo called El Diacono; but Bermudo after several years resigning the kingdom, they conceived a better opinion of Alfonso, and made him king. Alfonso dying without issue, Don Ramiro son to Bermudo was preferred before the nephews of Alfonso. Don Ordoño, fourth from Ramiro, left four legitimate sons; but they being young, the estates laid them aside, and made his brother Fruela king. Fruela had many children, but the same estates gave the crown to Alfonso the fourth, who was his nephew. Alfonso turning monk, recommended his son Ordoño to the estates of the kingdom; but they refused him, and made his brother Ramiro king. Ordoño third son to Ramiro dying, left a son called Bermudo; but the estates took his brother Sancho, and advanced him to the throne. Henry the first being accidentally killed in his youth, left only two sisters, Blanche married to Lewis son to Philip Augustus king of France, and Berengaria married to Alfonso king of Leon. The estates made Ferdinand, son of Berengaria the youngest sister, king,

---

[6] Saaved. Cor. Goth.   [7] Mariana l. 13.

excluding Blanche, with her husband and children for being strangers, and Berengaria herself, because they thought not fit that her husband should have any part in the government.[8] Alfonso El Savio seems to have been a very good prince; but applying himself more to the study of astrology than to affairs of government, his eldest son Ferdinand de la Cerda dying, and leaving his sons Alfonso and Ferdinand very young, the nobility, clergy and people deposed him, excluded his grandchildren, and gave the crown to Don Sancho his younger son, surnamed El Bravo, thinking him more fit to command them against the Moors, than an old astrologer, or a child. Alfonso and Sancho being dead, Alfonso El Desheredado laid claim to the crown, but it was given to Ferdinand the Fourth, and Alfonso with his descendants the dukes de Medina Celi remain excluded to this day. Peter surnamed the Cruel was twice driven out of the kingdom, and at last killed by Bertrand de Guesclin constable of France, or Henry count of Trastamara his bastard-brother, who was made king without any regard to the daughters of Peter, or to the house of La Cerda. Henry the Fourth left a daughter called Joan, whom he declared his heir; but the estates gave the kingdom to Isabel his sister, and crowned her with Ferdinand of Aragon her husband. Joan daughter to this Ferdinand and Isabel falling mad, the estates committed the care of the government to her father Ferdinand, and after his death to Charles her son.[9]

But the French have taught us, that when a king dies, his next heir is really king before he take his oath, or be crowned. From them we learn that *le mort saisit le vif*.[10] And yet I know no history that proves more plainly than theirs, that there neither is nor can be in any man, a right to the government of a people, which does not receive its being, manner and measure from the law of that country; which I hope to justify by four reasons.

1. When a king of Pharamond's race died, the kingdom was divided into as many parcels as he had sons; which could not have been, if one certain heir had been assigned by nature, for he ought to have had the whole: and if the kingdom might be divided, they who inhabited the several parcels, could not know to whom they owed obedience, till the division was made, unless he who was to be king of Paris, Metz, Soissons or Orleans, had worn the name of his kingdom upon his forehead. But in truth, if there might be a division, the doctrine is false, and there was no

[8] Marian. l. 12. c. 7.

[9] Marian. l. 24. [The stories of the Spanish monarchy to which this paragraph refers are found in Mariana, bks. 7, 8, and 14. There are several errors of detail here, but they do not affect the argument.]

[10] ["The living seizes the dead."]

lord of the whole. This wound will not be healed by saying, the father appointed the division, and that by the law of nature every man may dispose of his own as he thinks fit; for we shall soon prove that the kingdom of France neither was, nor is disposable as a patrimony or chattel. Besides, if that act of kings had been then grounded upon the law of nature, they might do the like at this day. But the law, by which such divisions were made, having been abrogated by the assembly of estates in the time of Hugh Capet,[11] and never practised since, it follows that they were grounded upon a temporary law, and not upon the law of nature which is eternal. If this were not so, the pretended certainty could not be; for no man could know to whom the last king had bequeathed the whole kingdom, or parcels of it, till the will were opened; and that must be done before such witnesses as may deserve credit in a matter of this importance, and are able to judge whether the bequest be rightly made; for otherwise no man could know, whether the kingdom was to have one lord or many, nor who he or they were to be; which intermission must necessarily subvert their polity, and this doctrine. But the truth is, the most monarchical men among them are so far from acknowledging any such right to be in the king, of alienating, bequeathing or dividing the kingdom, that they do not allow him the right of making a will; and that of the last King Lewis the 13th touching the regency during the minority of his son was of no effect.[12]

2. This matter was made more clear under the second race.[13] If a lord had been assigned to them by nature, he must have been of the royal family: But Pepin had no other title to the crown except the merits of his father, and his own, approved by the nobility and people who made him king. He had three sons, the eldest was made king of Italy, and dying before him left a son called Bernard heir of that kingdom. The estates of France divided what remained between Charles the Great and Carloman.[14] The last of these dying in few years left many sons, but the nobility made Charles king of all France, and he dispossessed Bernard of the kingdom of Italy inherited from his father: so that he also was not king of the whole, before the expulsion of Bernard the son of his elder brother; nor of Aquitaine, which by inheritance should have belonged to the children of his younger brother, any otherwise than by the will of

[11] Hist. de Fr. en la Vie de Hugues Capet. [Serres, *General History of France* (chapter on Hugh Capet).]

[12] Mem. du Duc. de la Rochefocault. [François, Duc de Rochefoucauld, *Mémoires sur la régence d'Anne d'Autriche* (1662), bk. 1, ch. 2.]

[13] [The Carolingian dynasty.]

[14] Paul. Aemyl. Hist. Franc. [Aemilius Paulus, *De rebus gestis Francorum* (1555). There are some errors of detail here which do not affect the argument.]

the estates. Lewis the Debonair succeeded upon the same title, was deposed and put into a monastery by his three sons Lothair, Pepin and Lewis, whom he had by his first wife. But tho these left many sons, the kingdom came to Charles the Bald. The nobility and people disliking the eldest son of Charles, gave the kingdom to Lewis le Begue, who had a legitimate son called Charles le Simple; and two bastards, Lewis and Carloman, who were made kings. Carloman had a son called Lewis le Faineant; he was made king, but afterwards deposed for his vicious life. Charles le Gros succeeded him, but for his ill government was also deposed; and Eudes, who was a stranger to the royal blood, was made king. The same nobility that had made five kings since Lewis le Begue, now made Charles le Simple king, who according to his name, was entrapped at Peronne by Rudolph duke of Burgundy, and forced to resign his crown, leaving only a son called Lewis, who fled into England. Rudolph being dead; they took Lewis surnamed Outremer, and placed him in the throne: he had two sons, Lothair and Charles. Lothair succeeded him, and died without issue. Charles had as fair a title as could be by birth, and the estates confessed it; but their ambassadors told him, that he having by an unworthy life render'd himself unworthy of the crown, they, whose principal care was to have a good prince at the head of them, had chosen Hugh Capet; and the crown continues in his race to this day, tho not altogether without interruption. Robert son to Hugh Capet succeeded him. He left two sons Robert and Henry; but Henry the younger son appearing to the estates of the kingdom to be more fit to reign than his elder brother, they made him king, Robert and his descendants continuing dukes of Burgundy only for about ten generations, at which time his issue male failing, that duchy returned to the crown during the life of King John, who gave it to his second son Philip for an *apanage* still depending upon the crown. The same province of Burgundy was by the Treaty of Madrid granted to the emperor Charles the fifth, by Francis the first: but the people refused to be alienated, and the estates of the kingdom approved their refusal. By the same authority Charles the 6th was removed from the government, when he appeared to be mad; and other examples of a like nature may be alleged. From which we may safely conclude, that if the death of one king do really invest the next heir with the right and power, or that he who is so invested, be subject to no law but his own will, all matters relating to that kingdom must have been horribly confused during the reigns of 22 kings of Pharamond's race; they can have had no rightful king from the death of Chilperic to King John: and the succession since that time is very liable to be questioned, if not utterly overthrown by the house of Austria and others, who by the counts of Hapsburg derive their descent from Pharamond, and by the house of Lorraine claiming from Charles, who was excluded by Capet; all which is most absurd, and they who pretend it, bring as much confusion into their own laws, and upon the polity of their own nation, as shame and guilt upon the memory of their ancestors, who by the most extreme injustice have rejected their natural lord, or dispossessed those who had been in the most solemn manner placed in the government, and to whom they had generally sworn allegiance.

3. If the next heir be actually king, seized of the power by the death of his predecessor, so that there is no intermission; then all the solemnities and religious ceremonies, used at the coronations of their kings, with the oaths given and taken, are the most profane abuses of sacred things in contempt of God and man that can be imagined, most especially if the act be (as our author calls it) voluntary, and the king receiving nothing by it, be bound to keep it no longer than he pleases. The prince who is to be sworn, might spare the pains of watching all night in the church, fasting, praying, confessing, communicating, and swearing, *that he will to the utmost of his power defend the clergy, maintain the union of the church, obviate all excess, rapine, extortion and iniquity; take care that in all judgments justice may be observed, with equity and mercy,* &c. *or of invoking the assistance of the Holy Ghost for the better performance of his oath;*[15] and without ceremony tell the nobility and people, that he would do what he thought fit. 'Twere to as little purpose for the archbishop of Rheims to take the trouble of saying mass, delivering to him the crown, scepter, and other ensigns of royalty, explaining what is signified by them, anointing him with the oil which they say was deliver'd by an angel to St. Remigius,[16] blessing him, and praying to God to bless him if he rightly performed his oath to God and the people, and denouncing the contrary in case of failure on his part, if these things conferred nothing upon him but what he had before, and were of no obligation to him. Such ludifications of the most sacred things are too odious and impious to be imputed to nations that have any virtue, or profess Christianity. This cannot fall upon the French and Spaniards, who had certainly a great zeal to religion, whatever it was; and were so eminent for moral virtues as to be a reproach to us, who live in an age of more knowledge. But their meaning is so well declared by their most solemn acts, that none but those who are wilfully ignorant can mistake. One of the councils held at Toledo, declared by the clergy, nobility, and others assisting, *That no man should be placed in the royal seat*

[15] [John Selden, *Titles of Honour* (London: [16] [Ibid., p. 112.]
W. Stansby, 1614), pp. 177-181.]

till he had sworn to preserve the church, &c.[17] Another held in the same place, signified to Sisinandus, who was then newly crown'd, *That if he, or any of his successors should, contrary to their oaths, and the laws of their country, proudly and cruelly presume to exercise domination over them, he should be excommunicated, and separated from Christ and them to eternal judgment.*[18] The French laws, and their best writers asserting the same things, are confirmed by perpetual practice. Henry of Navarre, tho certainly according to their rules, and in their esteem a most accomplish'd prince, was by two general assemblies of the estates held at Blois, deprived of the succession for being a Protestant; and notwithstanding the greatness of his reputation, valour, victories, and affability, could never be admitted till he had made himself capable of the ceremonies of his coronation, by conforming to the religion which by the oath he was to defend.[19] Nay this present king,[20] tho haughty enough by nature, and elevated by many successes, has acknowledged, as he says, with joy, that he can do nothing contrary to law, and calls it a happy impotence; in pursuance of which, he has annulled many acts of his father and grandfather, alienating the demesnes of the crown, as things contrary to law and not within their power.

These things being confirmed by all the good authors of that nation, Filmer finds only the worst to be fit for his turn; and neither minding law nor history, takes his maxims from a vile flattering discourse of Belloy, calculated for the personal interest of Henry the fourth then king of Navarre in which he says, *That the heir apparent, tho furious, mad, a fool, vicious, and in all respects abominably wicked, must be admitted to the crown.*[21] But Belloy was so far from attaining the ends designed by his book, that by such doctrines, which filled all men with horror, he brought great prejudice to his master, and procured little favour from Henry, who desired rather to recommend himself to his people as the best man they could set up, than to impose a necessity upon them of taking him if he had been the worst. But our author not contented with what this sycophant says, in relation to such princes as are placed in the government by a law establishing the succession by inheritance, with an impudence peculiar to himself, asserts the same right to be in any man, who by any means gets into power; and imposes the same necessity of obedience upon the

[17] Concil. Tolet. 6. [Sixth Council of Toledo, the year 638, in Giovanni D. Mansi, *Sacrorum conciliorum, nova et amplissima collectio* (1901, repr. Graz: Akademische Druck- und Verlagsanstalt, 1960), pp. 659–672.]

[18] Concil. Tolet. 4. [Fourth Council of Toledo, the year 633, in Mansi, pp. 612–649.]

[19] Hist. Thuan. [de Thou, *History of His Time*, vol. 5, bk. 97ff.]

[20] [Louis XIV.]

[21] Apol. Cathol. [Pierre du Belloy, *Apologie Catholique contre les Libelles* (1585). Filmer does not quote this work directly.]

subject where there is no law, as Belloy does by virtue of one that is established.

4. In the last place. As Belloy acknowledges that the right belongs to princes only where 'tis established by law, I deny that there is, was, or ever can be any such. No people is known to have been so mad or wicked, as by their own consent, for their own good, and for the obtaining of justice, to give the power to beasts, under whom it could never be obtain'd: or if we could believe that any had been guilty of an act so full of folly, turpitude and wickedness, it could not have the force of a law, and could never be put in execution; for tho the rules, by which the proximity should be judged, be never so precise, it will still be doubted whose case suits best with them. Tho the law in some places gives private inheritances to the next heir, and in others makes allotments according to several proportions, no one knows to whom, or how far the benefit shall accrue to any man, till it be adjudged by a power to which the parties must submit. Contests will in the like manner arise concerning successions to crowns, how exactly soever they be disposed by law: For tho everyone will say that the next ought to succeed, yet no man knows who is the next; which is too much verified by the bloody decisions of such disputes in many parts of the world: and he that says the next in blood is actually king, makes all questions thereupon arising impossible to be otherwise determined than by the sword; the pretender to the right being placed above the judgment of man, and the subjects (for anything I know) obliged to believe, serve and obey him, if he says he has it. For otherwise, if either every man in particular, or all together have a right of judging his title, it can be of no value till it be adjudged.

I confess that the law of France by the utter exclusion of females and their descendants, does obviate many dangerous and inextricable difficulties; but others remain which are sufficient to subvert all the polity of that kingdom, if there be not a power of judging them; and there can be none if it be true that *le mort saisit le vif*. Not to trouble myself with feigned cases, that of legitimation alone will suffice. 'Tis not enough to say that the children born under marriage are to be reputed legitimate; for not only several children born of Joan daughter to the king of Portugal, wife to Henry the Fourth of Castile, during the time of their marriage, were utterly rejected, as begotten in adultery, but also her daughter Joan, whom the king during his life, and at the hour of his death acknowledged to have been begotten by him; and the only title that Isabel, who was married to Ferdinand of Aragon had to the crown of Spain, was derived from their rejection. It would be tedious, and might give offence to many great persons, if I should relate all the dubious cases, that have been, or still remain in the world, touching matters of this nature: but the lawyers of all nations will testify, that hardly any one point comes before them, which affords a greater number of difficult cases, than that of marriages, and the legitimation of children upon them; and nations must be involved in the most inextricable difficulties, if there be not a power somewhere to decide them; which cannot be, if there be no intermission, and that the next in blood (that is, he who says he is the next) be immediately invested with the right and power. But surely no people has been so careless of their most important concernments, to leave them in such uncertainty, and simply to depend upon the humour of a man, or the faith of women, who besides their other frailties, have been often accused of supposititious births: and men's passions are known to be so violent in relation to women they love or hate, that none can safely be trusted with those judgments. The virtue of the best would be exposed to a temptation, that flesh and blood can hardly resist; and such as are less perfect would follow no other rule than the blind impulse of the passion that for the present reigns in them. There must therefore be a judge of such disputes as may in these cases arise in every kingdom; and tho 'tis not my business to determine who is that judge in all places, yet I may justly say, that in England it is the Parliament. If no inferior authority could debar Ignotus son to the Lady Rosse, born under the protection, from the inheritance of a private family, none can certainly assume a power of disposing of the crown upon any occasion. No authority but that of the Parliament could legitimate the children of Catherine Swynford,[22] with a proviso, not to extend to the inheritance of the crown. Others might say, if they were lawfully begotten, they ought to inherit everything, and nothing if they were not: But the Parliament knew how to limit a particular favour, and prevent it from extending to a publick mischief. Henry the Eighth took an expeditious way of obviating part of the controversies that might arise from the multitude of his wives, by cutting off the heads of some, as soon as he was weary of them, or had a mind to take another; but having been hinder'd from dealing in the same manner with Catherine by the greatness of her birth and kindred, he left such as the Parliament only could resolve. And no less power would ever have thought of making Mary and Elizabeth capable of the succession, when, according to ordinary rules, one of them must have been a bastard; and it had been absurd to say, that both of them were immediately upon the death of their

---

[22] [Mistress and third wife of John of Gaunt, Duke of Lancaster. John's eldest son (by his first wife) became Henry IV, first of the Lancastrian kings. In the act legitimizing the children of John and Catherine, Parliament excluded Catherine's children and their descendants from the crown.]

predecessors possess'd of the crown, if an act of Parliament had not conferred the right upon them, which they could not have by birth. But the kings and princes of England have not been of a temper different from those of other nations: and many examples may be brought of the like occasions of dispute happening everywhere; and the like will probably be forever; which must necessarily introduce the most mischievous confusions, and expose the titles which (as is pretended) are to be esteemed most sacred, to be overthrown by violence and fraud, if there be not in all places a power of deciding the controversies that arise from the uncertainty of titles, according to the respective laws of every nation, upon which they are grounded: No man can be thought to have a just title, till it be so adjudged by that power: This judgment is the first step to the throne: The oath taken by the king obliges him to observe the laws of his country; and that concerning the succession being one of the principal, he is obliged to keep that part as well as any other.

SECTION 19

The greatest Enemy of a just Magistrate
is he who endeavours to invalidate the Contract between
him and the People, or to corrupt their Manners.

T is not only from religion, but from the law of nature, that we learn the necessity of standing to the agreements we make; and he who departs from the principle written in the hearts of men *pactis standum*,[1] seems to degenerate into a beast. Such as had virtue, tho without true religion, could tell us (as a brave and excellent Grecian did) that it was not necessary for him to live, but it was necessary to preserve his heart from deceit, and his tongue from falsehood. The Roman satirist carries the same notion to a great height, and affirms, that *tho the worst of tyrants should command a man to be false and perjur'd, and back his injunction with the utmost of torments, he ought to prefer his integrity before his life.*[2] And tho Filmer may be excused if he often mistake in matters of theology; yet his

---

[1] [One must stand by one's agreements.]

[2] Phalaris licet imperet ut sis / Falsus, & admoto dictet perjuria tauro, / Summum crede nefas animam praeferre pudori. Juvenal ["Though Phalaris commands you to be false, threatening the (torture of the) bull, and demands that you break your oath, you should believe that it is the greatest sacrilege to prefer life to honor." Juvenal, *Satire* 8, li. 81–83.]

[431]

inclinations to Rome which he prefers before Geneva, might have led him to the principles in which the honest Romans lived, if he had not observed that such principles as make men honest and generous, do also make them lovers of liberty, and constant in the defence of their country: which savouring too much of a republican spirit, he prefers the morals of that city, since they are become more refined by the pious and charitable Jesuits, before those that were remarkable in them, as long as they retained any shadow of their ancient integrity, which admitted of no equivocations and detested prevarications, by that means preserving innocence in the hearts of private men for their inward contentment, and in civil societies for the publick good; which if once extinguish'd, mankind must necessarily fall into the condition Hobbes rightly calls *bellum omnium contra omnes*,[3] wherein no man can promise to himself any other wife, children or goods, than he can procure by his own sword.

Some may perhaps think that the endeavours of our author to introduce such accursed principles, as tend to the ruin of mankind, proceed from his ignorance. But tho he appears to have had a great measure of that quality, I fear the evil proceeds from a deeper root; and that he attempts to promote the interests of ill magistrates, who make it their business to destroy all good principles in the people, with as much industry as the good endeavour to preserve them where they are, and teach them where they are wanting. Reason and experience instruct us, that every man acts according to the end he proposes to himself. The good magistrate seeks the good of the people committed to his care, that he may perform the end of his institution: and knowing that chiefly to consist in justice and virtue, he endeavours to plant and propagate them; and by doing this he procures his own good as well as that of the publick. He knows there is no safety where there is no strength, no strength without union, no union with[out] justice; no justice where faith and truth, in accomplishing publick and private contracts, is wanting. This he perpetually inculcates, and thinks it a great part of his duty, by precept and example, to educate the youth in a love of virtue and truth, that they may be seasoned with them, and filled with an abhorrence of vice and falsehood, before they attain that age which is exposed to the most violent temptations, and in which they may by their crimes bring the greatest mischiefs upon the publick. He would do all this, tho it were to his own prejudice. But as good actions always carry a reward with them, these contribute in a high measure to his advantage. By preferring the interest of the people before

[3] ["War of all against all." Hobbes, *Leviathan*, ch. 13.]

his own, he gains their affection, and all that is in their power comes with it; whilst he unites them to one another, he unites all to himself: In leading them to virtue, he increases their strength, and by that means provides for his own safety, glory and power.

On the other side, such as seek different ends must take different ways. When a magistrate fancies he is not made for the people, but the people for him; that he does not govern for them, but for himself; and that the people live only to increase his glory, or furnish matter for his pleasures, he does not inquire what he may do for them, but what he may draw from them. By this means he sets up an interest of profit, pleasure or pomp in himself, repugnant to the good of the publick for which he is made to be what he is. These contrary ends certainly divide the nation into parties; and whilst everyone endeavours to advance that to which he is addicted, occasions of hatred for injuries every day done, or thought to be done and received, must necessarily arise. This creates a most fierce and irreconcilable enmity, because the occasions are frequent, important and universal, and the causes thought to be most just. The people think it the greatest of all crimes, to convert that power to their hurt, which was instituted for their good; and that the injustice is aggravated by perjury and ingratitude, which comprehend all manner of ill; and the magistrate gives the name of sedition or rebellion to whatsoever they do for the preservation of themselves and their own rights. When men's spirits are thus prepared, a small matter sets them on fire; but if no accident happen to blow them into a flame, the course of justice is certainly interrupted, the publick affairs are neglected; and when any occasion whether foreign or domestick arises, in which the magistrate stands in need of the people's assistance, they, whose affections are alienated, not only shew an unwillingness to serve him with their persons and estates, but fear that by delivering him from his distress they strengthen their enemy, and enable him to oppress them: and he fancying his will to be unjustly opposed, or his due more unjustly denied, is filled with a dislike of what he sees, and a fear of worse for the future. Whilst he endeavours to ease himself of the one, and to provide against the other, he usually increases the evils of both, and jealousies are on both sides multiplied. Every man knows that the governed are in a great measure under the power of the governor; but as no man, or number of men, is willingly subject to those who seek their ruin, such as fall into so great a misfortune, continue no longer under it than force, fear, or necessity may be able to oblige them. But as such a necessity can hardly lie longer upon a great people, than till the evil be fully discovered and comprehended, and their virtue, strength and power be united to expel it; the ill magistrate looks upon all things that may conduce to that end, as so many preparatives to his ruin; and by the help of those who are of his party, will endeavour to prevent that union, and diminish that strength, virtue, power and courage, which he knows to be bent against him. And as truth, faithful dealing, due performance of contracts, and integrity of manners, are bonds of union, and helps to good, he will always by tricks, artifices, cavils, and all means possible endeavour to establish falsehood and dishonesty; whilst other emissaries and instruments of iniquity, by corrupting the youth, and seducing such as can be brought to lewdness and debauchery, bring the people to such a pass, that they may neither care nor dare to vindicate their rights, and that those who would do it, may so far suspect each other, as not to confer upon, much less to join in any action tending to the publick deliverance.

This distinguishes the good from the bad magistrate, the faithful from the unfaithful; and those who adhere to either, living in the same principle, must walk in the same ways. They who uphold the rightful power of a just magistracy, encourage virtue and justice, teach men what they ought to do, suffer, or expect from others; fix them upon principles of honesty, and generally advance everything that tends to the increase of the valour, strength, greatness and happiness of the nation, creating a good union among them, and bringing every man to an exact understanding of his own and the publick rights. On the other side, he that would introduce an ill magistrate; make one evil who was good, or preserve him in the exercise of injustice when he is corrupted, must always open the way for him by vitiating the people, corrupting their manners, destroying the validity of oaths and contracts, teaching such evasions, equivocations and frauds, as are inconsistent with the thoughts that become men of virtue and courage; and overthrowing the confidence they ought to have in each other, make it impossible for them to unite among themselves. The like arts must be used with the magistrate: He cannot be for their turn, till he is persuaded to believe he has no dependence upon, and owes no duty to the people; that he is of himself, and not by their institution; that no man ought to inquire into, nor be judge of his actions; that all obedience is due to him, whether he be good or bad, wise or foolish, a father or an enemy to his country. This being calculated for his personal interest, he must pursue the same designs, or his kingdom is divided within itself, and cannot subsist. By this means those who flatter his humour, come to be accounted his friends, and the only men that are thought worthy of great trusts, whilst such as are of another mind are exposed to all persecution. These are always such as excel in virtue, wisdom, and greatness of spirit: they have eyes, and they will always see the way they go; and leaving fools to be guided by implicit faith, will distinguish between good and evil, and chuse that which is best; they will judge of men by their actions, and by them discovering whose servant every man is, know whether he is to be obeyed or not. Those who are ignorant of all good, careless or enemies to it, take a more compendious way; their slavish, vicious and base natures inclining them to seek only private and present advantages, they easily slide into a blind dependence upon one who has wealth and power; and desiring only to know his will, care not what injustice they do, if they may be rewarded. They worship what they find in the temple, tho it be the vilest of idols, and always like that best which is worst, because it agrees with their inclinations and principles. When a party comes to be erected upon such a foundation, debauchery, lewdness and dishonesty are the true badges of it. Such as wear them are cherished; but the principal marks of favour are reserved for those who are the most industrious in mischief, either by seducing the people with the allurements of sensual pleasures, or corrupting their understandings by false and slavish doctrines. By this means a man who calls himself a philosopher or a divine, is often more useful than a great number of tapsters, cooks, buffoons, players, fiddlers whores or bawds. These are the Devil's ministers of a lower order; they seduce single persons, and such as fall into their snares are for the most part men of the simpler sort: but the principal supporters of his kingdom, are they, who by false doctrines poison the springs of religion and virtue, and by preaching or writing (if their falsehood and wickedness were not detected) would extinguish all principles of common honesty, and bring whole nations to be best satisfied with themselves, when their actions are most abominable. And as the means must always be suitable to the end proposed, the governments that are to be established or supported by such ways must needs be the worst of all, and comprehend all manner of evil.

SECTION 20

Unjust Commands are not to be obey'd;
and no man is obliged to suffer for not obeying
such as are against Law.

I N the next place our author gravely proposes a question, *Whether it be*
a sin to disobey the king, if he command anything contrary to law? and as
gravely determines, *that not only in human laws, but even in divine, a thing*
may be commanded contrary to law, and yet obedience to such a command is
necessary. The sanctifying of the Sabbath is a divine law, yet if a master command
his servant not to go to church upon a Sabbath day, the best divines teach us, the
servant must obey, &c. It is not fit to tie the master to acquaint the servant with
his secret counsel.[1] Tho he frequently contradicts in one line what he says
in another, this whole clause is uniform and suitable to the main design
of his book. He sets up the authority of man in opposition to the command
of God, gives it the preference, and says, the best divines instruct us so
to do. St. Paul then must have been one of the worst, for he knew that
the powers under which he lived, had under the severest penalties forbidden the publication of the Gospel; and yet he says, *Woe to me if I*
preach it not. St. Peter was no better than he, for he tells us, *That it is*
better to obey God than man: and they could not speak otherwise, unless
they had forgotten the words of their master, who told them, *They should*
not fear them that could only kill the body, but him who could kill and cast into
hell.[2] And if I must not fear him that can only kill the body, not only the
reason, but all excuse for obeying him is taken away.

To prove what he says, he cites a pertinent example from St. Luke,[3]
and very logically concludes, that because Christ reproved the hypocrisy
of the Pharisees (who generally adhered to the external and circumstantial
part of the law, neglecting the essential, and taking upon themselves to
be the interpreters of that which they did not understand), the law of
God is not to be obeyed: and as strongly proves, that because Christ
shewed them that the same law, which by their own confession permitted
them to pull an ass out of a pit on the sabbath day, could not but give a
liberty of healing the sick, therefore the commands of kings are to be
obeyed, tho they should be contrary to human and divine laws. But if

[1] [*Patriarcha*, ch. 25, pp. 104–105.]

[2] [1 Corinthians 9:16; Acts 5:29; Matthew
10:28.]

[3] Chap. 14.

perverseness had not blinded him, he might have seen, that this very text is wholly against his purpose; for the magistratical power was on the side of the Pharisees, otherwise they would not have sought an occasion to ensnare him; and that power having perverted the law of God by false glosses, and a superinduction of human traditions, prohibited the most necessary acts of charity to be done on the sabbath day, which Christ reproved, and restored the sick man to his health in their sight.

But I could wish our author had told us the names of those divines, who, he says, are the best, and who pretend to teach us these fine things. I know some who are thought good, that are of a contrary opinion, and say that God having required that day to be set apart for his service and worship, man cannot dispense with the obligation, unless he can abrogate the law of God. Perhaps, for want of other arguments to prove the contrary, I may be told, that this savours too much of Puritanism and Calvinism. But I shall take the reproach, till some better patrons than Laud and his creatures may be found for the other opinion. By the advice and instigation of these men, from about the year 1630, to 1640, sports and revelings, which ended for the most part in drunkenness and lewdness, were not only permitted on that day, but enjoined. And tho this did advance human authority in derogation to the divine, to a degree that may please such as are of our author's mind, yet others resolving rather to obey the laws of God than the commands of men, could not be brought to pass the Lord's day in that manner. Since that time no man except Filmer and Heylyn has been so wicked to conceive, or so impudent to assert such brutal absurdities. But leaving the farther consideration of the original of this abuse, I desire to know, whether the authority given to masters to command things contrary to the law of God, be peculiar in relation to the Sabbath, or to a few other points, or ought generally to extend to all God's laws; and whether he who may command his servant to act contrary to the law of God, have not a right in himself of doing the same. If peculiar, some authority or precept must be produced, by which it may appear that God has slighted his ordinance concerning that day, and suffer'd it to be contemned, whilst he exacts obedience to all others. If we have a liberty left to us of slighting others also, more or less in number, we ought to know how many, what they are, and how it comes to pass, that some are of obligation and others not. If the empire of the world is not only divided between God and Caesar, but every man also who can give five pounds a year to a servant, has so great a part in it, that in some cases his commands are to be obeyed preferably to those of God, it were fit to know the limits of each kingdom, lest we happen preposterously to obey man when we ought to obey God, or God when we are to follow the commands of men. If it be general, the law of God is of no effect, and we may safely put an end to all thoughts and discourses of religion: the word of God is nothing to us; we are not to enquire what he has commanded, but what pleases our master, how insolent, foolish, vile or wicked soever he may be. The apostles and prophets, who died for preferring the commands of God before those of men, fell like fools, and perished in their sins. But if every particular man that has a servant, can exempt him from the commands of God, he may also exempt himself, and the laws of God are at once abrogated throughout the world.

'Tis a folly to say there is a passive, as well as an active obedience, and that he who will not do what his master commands ought to suffer the punishment he inflicts: for if the master has a right of commanding, there is a duty incumbent on the servant of obeying. He that suffers for not doing that which he ought to do, draws upon himself both the guilt and the punishment. But no one can be obliged to suffer for that which he ought not to do, because he who pretends to command, has not so far an authority. However, our question is, whether the servant should forbear to do that which God commands, rather than whether the master should put away or beat him if he do not: for if the servant ought to obey his master rather than God, as our author says the best divines assert, he sins in disobeying, and that guilt cannot be expiated by his suffering. If it be thought I carry this point to an undue extremity, the limits ought to be demonstrated, by which it may appear that I exceed them, tho the nature of the case cannot be altered: for if the law of God may not be abrogated by the commands of men, a servant cannot be exempted from keeping the Sabbath according to the ordinance of God, at the will of his master. But if a power be given to man at his pleasure to annul the laws of God, the apostles ought not to have preached, when they were forbidden by the powers to which they were subject: The tortures and deaths they suffer'd for not obeying that command were in their own wrong, and their blood was upon their own heads.

His second instance concerning wars,[4] in which he says the subject is not to examine whether they are just or unjust, but must obey, is weak and frivolous, and very often false; whereas consequences can rightly be drawn from such things only as are certainly and universally true. Tho God may be merciful to a soldier, who by the wickedness of a magistrate whom he honestly trusts, is made a minister of injustice, 'tis nothing to this case. For if our author say true, that the word of a king can justify him in going against the command of God, he must do what is commanded

---

[4] [*Patriarcha*, ch. 25, p. 105.]

tho he think it evil: The Christian soldiers under the pagan emperors were obliged to destroy their brethren, and the best men in the world for being so: Such as now live under the Turk have the same obligation upon them of defending their master, and slaughtering those he reputes his enemies for adhering to Christianity: And the king of France may when he pleases, arm one part of his Protestant subjects to the destruction of the other; which is a godly doctrine, and worthy our author's invention.

But if this be so, I know not how the Israelites can be said to have sinned in following the examples of Jeroboam, Omri, Ahab, or other wicked kings: they could not have sinned in obeying, if it had been a sin to disobey their commands; and God would not have punished them so severely, if they had not sinned. 'Tis impertinent to say they were obliged to serve their kings in unjust wars, but not to serve idols; for tho God be jealous of his glory, yet he forbids rapine and murder as well as idolatry. If there be a law that forbids the subject to examine the commands tending to the one, it cannot but enjoin obedience to the other. The same authority which justifies murder, takes away the guilt of idolatry; and the wretches, both judges and witnesses, who put Naboth to death, could as little allege ignorance, as those that worshipped Jeroboam's calves; the same light of nature by which they should have known, that a ridiculous image was not to be adored as God, instructing them also, that an innocent man ought not under pretence of law to be murdered by perjury.

SECTION 21

It cannot be for the good of the People that the Magistrate have a power above the Law: and he is not a Magistrate who has not his power by Law.

THAT we may not be displeased, or think it dangerous and slavish to depend upon the will of a man, which perhaps may be irregular or extravagant in one who is subject to no law, our author very dexterously removes the scruples by telling us,

1. *That the prerogative of the king to be above the law, is only for the good of them that are under the law, and to preserve their liberties.*

2. *That there can be no laws without a supreme power to command or make them: In aristocracies the noblemen are above the law; in democracies the people: By the like reason in a monarchy, the king must of necessity be above the law.*

There can be no sovereign majesty in him that is under the law: that which gives the very being to a king, is the power to give laws. Without this power he is but an equivocal king. It skills not how he comes by this power, whether by election, donation, succession, or any other means.[1]

I am contented in some degree to follow our author, and to acknowledge that the king neither has nor can have any prerogative which is not for the good of the people, and the preservation of their liberties. This therefore is the foundation of magistratical power, and the only way of discerning whether the prerogative of making laws, of being above laws, or any other he may pretend, be justly due to him or not: and if it be doubted who is the fittest judge to determine that question, common sense will inform us, that if the magistrate receive his power by election or donation, they who elect, or give him that power, best know whether the good they sought be performed or not; if by succession, they who instituted the succession; if otherwise, that is, by fraud or violence, the point is decided, for he has no right at all, and none can be created by those means. This might be said, tho all princes were of ripe age, sober, wise, just and good; for even the best are subject to mistakes and passions, and therefore unfit to be judges of their own concernments, in which they may by various means be misguided: but it would be extreme madness to attribute the same to children, fools, or madmen, who are not able to judge of the least things concerning themselves or others; but most especially to those who, coming in by usurpation, declare their contempt of all human and divine laws, and are enemies to the people they oppress. None therefore can be judges of such cases but the people, for whom and by whom the constitutions are made; or their representatives and delegates, to whom they give the power of doing it.

But nothing can be more absurd than to say, that one man has an absolute power above law to govern according to his will, *for the people's good, and the preservation of their liberty:* For no liberty can subsist where there is such a power; and we have no other way of distinguishing between free nations and such as are not so, than that the free are governed by their own laws and magistrates according to their own mind, and that the others either have willingly subjected themselves, or are by force brought under the power of one or more men, to be ruled according to his or their pleasure. The same distinction holds in relation to particular persons. He is a free man who lives as best pleases himself, under laws made by his own consent; and the name of slave can belong to no man, unless to him who is either born in the house of a master, bought, taken,

[1] [*Patriarcha*, ch. 26 ("Of the King's Prerogative over Laws"), pp. 105–106.]

subdued, or willingly gives his ear to be nailed to the post, and subjects himself to the will of another. Thus were the Grecians said to be free in opposition to the Medes and Persians, as Artabanus acknowledged in his discourse to Themistocles.[2] In the same manner the Italians, Germans and Spaniards were distinguish'd from the Eastern nations, who for the most part were under the power of tyrants. Rome was said to have recovered liberty by the expulsion of the Tarquins; or as Tacitus expresses it, *Lucius Brutus established liberty and the consulate together*,[3] as if before that time they had never enjoyed any; and Julius Caesar is said to have overthrown the liberty of that people. But if Filmer deserve credit, the Romans were free under Tarquin, enslaved when he was driven away, and his prerogative extinguish'd, that was so necessarily required for the defence of their liberty; and were never restored to it, till Caesar assum'd all the power to himself. By the same rule the Switzers, Grisons, Venetians, Hollanders, and some other nations are now slaves; and Tuscany, the kingdom of Naples, the Ecclesiastical State, with such as live under a more gentle master on the other side of the water, I mean the Turk, are free nations. Nay the Florentines, who complain of slavery under the house of Medici, were made free by the power of a Spanish army who set up a prerogative in that gentle family, which for their good has destroyed all that could justly be called so in that country, and almost wholly dispeopled it. I, who esteem myself free, because I depend upon the will of no man, and hope to die in the liberty I inherit from my ancestors, am a slave; and the Moors or Turks, who may be beaten and kill'd whenever it pleases their insolent masters, are free men. But surely the world is not so much mistaken in the signification of words and things. The weight of chains, number of stripes, hardness of labour, and other effects of a master's cruelty, may make one servitude more miserable than another: but he is a slave who serves the best and gentlest man in the world, as well as he who serves the worst; and he does serve him if he must obey his commands, and depends upon his will. For this reason the poet ingeniously flattering a good emperor, said, that liberty was not more desirable, than to serve a gentle master;[4] but still acknowledged that it was a service, distinct from, and contrary to liberty: and it had not been a handsome compliment, unless the evil of servitude were so extreme, that nothing but the virtue and goodness of the master could any way compensate or alleviate it. Now tho it should be granted that

[2] Plut. Vit. Themist. [Plutarch, *Life of Themistocles*, ch. 27, sec. 3.]
[3] Libertatem & consulatum L. Brutus instituit. An. l. 1. [Tacitus, *Annals*, bk. 1, ch. 1.]

[4] ["No liberty was ever more welcome than servitude under a good king." Claudian, *Praise of Stilicho* (Loeb, 1922), vol. 1, lines 114–115.]

he had spoken more like to a philosopher than a poet; that we might take his words in the strictest sense, and think it possible to find such conveniences in a subjection to the will of a good and wise master, as may balance the loss of liberty, it would be nothing to the question; because that liberty is thereby acknowledged to be destroy'd by the prerogative, which is only instituted to preserve it. If it were true that no liberty were to be preferr'd before the service of a good master, it could be of no use to the perishing world, which Filmer and his disciples would by such arguments bring into a subjection to children, fools, mad or vicious men. These are not cases feigned upon a distant imaginary possibility, but so frequently found amongst men, that there are few examples of the contrary. And as 'tis folly to suppose that princes will always be wise, just and good, when we know that few have been able alone to bear the weight of a government, or to resist the temptations to ill, that accompany an unlimited power, it would be madness to presume they will for the future be free from infirmities and vices. And if they be not, the nations under them will not be in such a condition of servitude to a good master as the poet compares to liberty, but in a miserable and shameful subjection to the will of those who know not how to govern themselves, or to do good to others: Tho Moses, Joshua and Samuel had been able to bear the weight of an unrestrained power: though David and Solomon had never abused that which they had; what effect could this have upon a general proposition? Where are the families that always produce such as they were? When did God promise to assist all those who should attain to the sovereign power, as he did them whom he chose for the works he designed? Or what testimony can Filmer give us, that he has been present with all those who have hitherto reigned in the world? But if we know that no such thing either is, or has been; and can find no promise to assure us, nor reason to hope that it ever will be, 'tis as foolish to found the hopes of preserving a people upon that which never was, or is so likely to fail, nay rather which in a short time most certainly will fail, as to root up vines and fig trees in expectation of gathering grapes and figs from thistles and briars. This would be no less than to extinguish the light of common sense, to neglect the means that God has given us to provide for our security, and to impute to him a disposition of things utterly inconsistent with his wisdom and goodness. If he has not therefore order'd that thorns and thistles should produce figs and grapes, nor that the most important works in the world, which are not without the utmost difficulty, if at all, to be performed by the best and wisest of men, should be put into the hands of the weakest, most foolish and worst, he cannot have ordain'd that such men, women or children as happen to be born in reigning families, or get the power into their hands by fraud, treachery or murder (as very many have done) should have a right of disposing all things according to their will. And if men cannot be guilty of so great an absurdity to trust the weakest and worst with a power which usually subverts the wisdom and virtue of the best; or to expect such effects of virtue and wisdom from those who come by chance, as can hardly, if at all, be hoped from the most excellent, our author's proposition can neither be grounded upon the ordinance of God, nor the institution of man. Nay, if any such thing had been established by our first parents in their simplicity, the utter impossibility of attaining what they expected from it, must wholly have abrogated the establishment: Or rather, it had been void from the beginning, because it was not *a just sanction, commanding things good, and forbidding the contrary,*[5] but a foolish and perverse sanction, setting up the unruly appetite of one person to the subversion of all that is good in the world, by making the wisdom of the aged and experienc'd to depend upon the will of women, children and fools; by sending the strong and the brave to seek protection from the most weak and cowardly, and subjecting the most virtuous and best of men to be destroy'd by the most wicked and vicious. These being the effects of that unlimited prerogative, which our author says was only instituted for the good and defence of the people, it must necessarily fall to the ground, unless slavery, misery, infamy, destruction and desolation tend to the preservation of liberty, and are to be preferr'd before strength, glory, plenty, security and happiness. The state of the Roman empire after the usurpation of Caesar will set this matter in the clearest light; but having done it already in the former parts of this work, I content myself to refer to those places. And tho the calamities they suffer'd were a little allayed and moderated by the virtues of Antoninus and M. Aurelius, with one or two more, yet we have no example of the continuance of them in a family, nor of any nation great or small that has been under an absolute power, which does not too plainly manifest, that no man or succession of men is to be trusted with it.

But says our author, *there can be no law where there is not a supreme power,* and from thence very strongly concludes it must be in the king; for *otherwise there can be no sovereign majesty in him, and he is but an equivocal king.* This might have been of some force, if governments were establish'd, and laws made only to advance that sovereign majesty; but nothing at all to the purpose, if (as he confesses) the power which the prince has, be

---

[5] Sanctio recta, jubens honesta, prohibens contraria. Cicer. [See Section 10, n. 31.]

given for the good of the people, and for the defence of every private man's life, liberty, lands and goods: for that which is instituted, cannot be abrogated for want of that which was never intended in the institution. If the publick safety be provided, liberty and propriety secured, justice administered, virtue encouraged, vice suppressed, and the true interest of the nation advanced, the ends of government are accomplished; and the highest must be contented with such a proportion of glory and majesty as is consistent with the publick; since the magistracy is not instituted, nor any person placed in it for the increase of his majesty, but for the preservation of the whole people, and the defence of the liberty, life and estate of every private man, as our author himself is forced to acknowledge.

But what is this sovereign majesty, so inseparable from royalty, that one cannot subsist without the other? Caligula placed it in a power of doing what he pleased to all men:[6] Nimrod, Nebuchadnezzar and others, with an impious and barbarous insolence boasted of the greatness of their power. They thought it a glorious privilege to kill or spare whom they pleased. But such kings as by God's permission might have been set up over his people, were to have nothing of this. They were not to multiply gold, silver, wives or horses; they were not to govern by their own will, but according to the law; from which they might not recede, nor raise their hearts above their brethren.[7] Here were kings without that unlimited power, which makes up the sovereign majesty, that Filmer affirms to be so essential to kings, that without it they are only equivocal; which proving nothing but the incurable perverseness of his judgment, the malice of his heart, or malignity of his fate, always to oppose reason and truth, we are to esteem those to be kings who are described to be so by the Scriptures, and to give another name to those who endeavour to advance their own glory, contrary to the precept of God and the interest of mankind.

But unless the light of reason had been extinguished in him, he might have seen, that tho no law could be made without a supreme power, that supremacy may be in a body consisting of many men, and several orders of men. If it be true, which perhaps may be doubted, that there have been in the world simple monarchies, aristocracies or democracies legally established, 'tis certain that the most part of the governments of the world (and I think all that are or have been good) were mixed. Part of the power has been conferr'd upon the king, or the magistrate that represented him, and part upon the senate and people, as has been proved in relation to

[6] Omnia mihi in omnes licere. ["I can do all things to all men." Suetonius, *Caligula*, ch. 29.]   [7] Deut. 17.

the governments of the Hebrews, Spartans, Romans, Venetians, Germans, and all those who live under that which is usually called the Gothic polity. If the single person participating of this divided power dislike either the name he bears, or the authority he has, he may renounce it; but no reason can be from thence drawn to the prejudice of nations, who give so much as they think consistent with their own good, and reserve the rest to themselves, or to such other officers as they please to establish.

No man will deny that several nations have had a right of giving power to consuls, dictators, archons, suffetes, dukes and other magistrates, in such proportions as seemed most conducing to their own good; and there must be a right in every nation of allotting to kings so much as they please, as well as to the others, unless there be a charm in the word king, or in the letters that compose it. But this cannot be; for there is no similitude between king, rex, and basileus: they must therefore have a right of regulating the power of kings, as well as that of consuls or dictators; and it had not been more ridiculous in Fabius, Scipio, Camillus or Cincinnatus, to assert an absolute power in himself, under pretence of advancing his sovereign majesty against the law, than for any king to do the like. But as all nations give what form they please to their government, they are also judges of the name to be imposed upon each man who is to have a part in the power: and 'tis as lawful for us to call him king, who has a limited authority amongst us, as for the Medes or Arabs to give the same name to one who is more absolute. If this be not admitted, we are content to speak improperly, but utterly deny that when we give the name, we give anything more than we please; and had rather his majesty should change his name than to renounce our own rights and liberties which he is to preserve, and which we have received from God and nature.

But that the folly and wickedness of our author may not be capable of any farther aggravation, he says, *That it skills not how he come by the power.* Violence therefore or fraud, treachery or murder, are as good as election, donation or legal succession. 'Tis in vain to examine the laws of God or man; the rights of nature; whether children do inherit the dignities and magistracies of their fathers, as patrimonial lands and goods; whether regard ought to be had to the fitness of the person; whether all should go to one, or be divided amongst them; or by what rule we may know who is the right heir to the succession, and consequently what we are in conscience obliged to do. Our author tells us in short, it matters not how he that has the power comes by it.

It has been hitherto thought, that to kill a king (especially a good king) was a most abominable action. They who did it, were thought to be incited by the worst of passions that can enter into the hearts of men; and the severest punishments have been invented to deter them from such attempts, or to avenge their death upon those who should accomplish it: but if our author may be credited, it must be the most commendable and glorious act that can be performed by man: for besides the outward advantages that men so earnestly desire, he that does it, is presently invested with the sovereign majesty, and at the same time becomes God's vicegerent, and the father of his country, possessed of that government, which in exclusion to all other forms is only favoured by the laws of God and nature. The only inconvenience is, that all depends upon success, and he that is to be the minister of God, and father of his country if he succeed, is the worst of all villains if he fail; and at the best may be deprived of all by the same means he employ'd to gain it. Tho a prince should have the wisdom and virtues of Moses, the valour of Joshua, David and the Maccabees, with the gentleness and integrity of Samuel, the most foolish, vicious, base and detestable man in the world that kills him, and seizes the power, becomes his heir, and father of the people that he govern'd; it *skills* not how he did it, whether in open battle or by secret treachery, in the field or in the bed, by poison or by the sword: The vilest slave in Israel had become the Lord's anointed, if he could have kill'd David or Solomon, and found villains to place him in the throne. If this be right, the world has to this day lived in darkness, and the actions which have been thought to be the most detestable, are the most commendable and glorious. But not troubling myself at present to decide this question, I leave it to kings to consider how much they are beholden to Filmer and his disciples, who set such a price upon their heads, as would render it hard to preserve their lives one day, if the doctrines were received which they endeavour to infuse into the minds of the people; and concluding this point, only say, that we in England know no other king than he who is so by law, nor any power in that king except that which he has by law: and tho the Roman empire was held by the power of the sword; and Ulpian a corrupt lawyer undertakes to say, that *the prince is not obliged by the laws;*[8] yet Theodosius confessed, that it was the glory of a good emperor to acknowledge himself bound by them.[9]

---

[8] [Ulpian, *Ad legem Juliam et Papiam*, bk. 13.]

[9] [See *The Institutes of Justinian* (London: Longman, Green, 1948), proem, p. 1.]

SECTION 22

The rigour of the Law is to be temper'd by men of known integrity and judgment, and not by the Prince who may be ignorant or vicious.

Our author's next shift is to place the king above the law, that he may mitigate the rigour of it, without which he says, *The case of the subject would be desperately miserable.*[1] But this cure would prove worse than the disease. Such pious fathers of the people as Caligula, Nero or Domitian, were not like to mitigate the rigour; nor such as inherit crowns in their infancy (as the present kings of Spain, France and Sweden)[2] so well to understand the meaning of it as to decide extraordinary cases. The wisdom of nations has provided more assured helps; and none could have been so brutish and negligent of the publick concernments, to suffer the succession to fall to women, children, &c. if they had not reserved a power in themselves to prefer others before the nearest in blood, if reason require; and prescribed such rules as might preserve the publick from ruin, notwithstanding their infirmities and vices. These helps provided by our laws, are principally by grand and petty juries, who are not only judges of matters of fact, as whether a man be kill'd, but whether he be kill'd criminally. These men are upon their oaths, and may be indicted of perjury if they prevaricate: The judges are present, not only to be a check upon them, but to explain such points of the law as may seem difficult. And tho these judges may be said in some sense to be chosen by the king, he is not understood to do it otherwise than by the advice of his council, who cannot perform their duty, unless they propose such as in their consciences they think most worthy of the office, and most capable of performing the duty rightly; nor he accomplish the oath of his coronation, unless he admit those, who upon deliberation seem to be the best. The judges being thus chosen, are so far from depending upon the will of the king, that they swear faithfully to serve the people as well as the king, and to do justice to every man according to the law of the land, notwithstanding any writs, letters or commands received from him; and in default thereof they are to forfeit their bodies, lands and goods, as in cases of treason.[3] These laws have been so often, and so severely executed, that it concerns all judges well to consider them; and the cases of Tresilian,

[1] [*Patriarcha*, ch. 26, p. 105.]
[2] [Charles II, Louis XIV, and Charles XI.]
[3] 18 Edw. 3. cap. 1. [18 Edward III, statute 4 (1344).]

Empson, Dudley, and others shew, that neither the king's preceding command nor subsequent pardon could preserve them from the punishment they deserved. All men knew that what they did was agreeable to the king's pleasure, for Tresilian advanced the prerogative of Edward the 2d, and Empson brought great treasures into the coffers of Henry the 7th. Nevertheless they were charged with treason, for subverting the laws of the land, and executed as traitors. Tho England ought never to forget the happy reign of Q. Elizabeth, yet it must be acknowledged, that she as well as others had her failings. She was full of love to the people, just in her nature, sincere in her intentions; but could not so perfectly discover the snares that were laid for her, or resist the importunity of the persons she most trusted, as not sometimes to be brought to attempt things against law. She and her counsellors pressed the judges very hardly to obey the patent under her great seal, in the case of Cavendish: but they answered, *That both she and they had taken an oath to keep the law, and if they should obey her commands, the law would not warrant them*, &c. And besides the offence against God, their country, and the commonwealth, they alleged the example of Empson and Dudley, *whereby*, they said, *they were deterred from obeying her illegal commands*.[4] They who had sworn to keep the law notwithstanding the king's writs, knew that the law depended not upon his will; and the same oath that obliged them not to regard any command they should receive from him, shewed that they were not to expect indemnity by it, and not only that the king had neither the power of making, altering, mitigating or interpreting the law, but that he was not at all to be heard, in general or particular matters, otherwise than as he speaks in the common course of justice, by the courts legally established, which say the same thing, whether he be young or old, ignorant or wise, wicked or good: and nothing does better evidence the wisdom and care of our ancestors, in framing the laws and government we live under, than that the people did not suffer extremities by the vices or infirmities of kings, till an age more full of malice than those in which they lived, had found tricks to pervert the rule, and frustrate their honest intentions. It was not safe for the kings to violate their oaths by an undue interposition of their authority; but the ministers who served them in those violations, have seldom escaped punishment. This is to be understood when the deviations from justice are extreme and mischievous, for something must always be allow'd to human frailty: The best have their defects, and none could stand if a too exact scrutiny were made of all their actions. Edward the third, about the twentieth year of his reign, acknowledged his own

[4] Anderson's Rep. p. 155. [*Law Reports of Sir Edmund Anderson* (1605), ch. 201, p. 155.]

in parliament, and as well for the ease of his conscience, as the satisfaction of his people, promoted an act, *Commanding all judges to do justice, notwithstanding any writs, letters or commands from himself, and forbidding those that belonged to the king, queen and prince, to intermeddle in those matters.*[5] But if the best and wisest of our princes, in the strength and maturity of their years, had their failings, and every act proceeding from them that tended to the interruption of justice was a failing, how can it be said that the king in his personal capacity, directly or indirectly, may enter into the discussion of these matters, much less to determine them according to his will?

But, says our author, *the law is no better than a tyrant; general pardons at the coronation and in parliament, are but the bounty of the prerogative,* &c. *There may be hard cases;* and citing some perverted pieces from Aristotle's *Ethicks* and *Politicks,* adds, *That when something falls out besides the general rule, then it is fit that what the lawmaker hath omitted, or where he hath erred by speaking generally, it should be corrected and supplied, as if the lawmaker were present that ordained it. The governor, whether he be one man or more, ought to be lord of these things, whereof it was impossible that the law should speak exactly.*[6] These things are in part true; but our author makes use of them as the Devil does of Scripture, to subvert the truth. There may be something of rigour in the law that in some cases may be mitigated; and the law itself (in relation to England) does so far acknowledge it, as to refer much to the consciences of juries, and those who are appointed to assist them; and the most difficult cases are referred to the Parliament as the only judges that are able to determine them. Thus the statute of the 35 Edw. 3d, enumerating the crimes then declared to be treason, leaves to future parliaments to judge what other facts equivalent to them may deserve the same punishment: and 'tis a general rule in the law, which the judges are sworn to observe, that difficult cases should be reserved till the Parliament meet, who are only able to decide them: and if there be any inconvenience in this, 'tis because they do not meet so frequently as the law requires, or by sinister means are interrupted in their sitting. But nothing can be more absurd than to say, that because the king does not call parliaments as the law and his oath requires, that power should accrue to him, which the law and the consent of the nation has placed in them.

There is also such a thing in the law as a general or particular pardon, and the king may in some degree be entrusted with the power of giving

[5] [20 Edward III, ch. 1, 4.]

[6] [*Patriarcha,* ch. 26, p. 105. Aristotle is quoted on pp. 107 and 108.]

it, especially for such crimes as merely relate to himself, as every man may remit the injuries done to himself; but the confession of Edward the third, *That the oath of the crown had not been kept by reason of the grant of pardons contrary to statutes,* and a new act made, *that all such charters of pardon from henceforth granted against the oath of the crown and the said statutes, should be held for none,*[7] demonstrates that this power was not in himself, but granted by the nation, and to be executed according to such rules as the law prescribed, and the Parliament approved.

Moreover, there having been many, and sometimes bloody contests for the crown, upon which the nation was almost equally divided; and it being difficult for them to know, or even for us who have all the parties before us, to judge which was the better side, it was understood that he who came to be crown'd by the consent of the people, was acceptable to all: and the question being determined, it was no way fit that he should have a liberty to make use of the publick authority then in his hands, to revenge such personal injuries as he had, or might suppose to have received, which might raise new, and perhaps more dangerous troubles, if the authors of them were still kept in fear of being prosecuted; and nothing could be more unreasonable than that he should employ his power to the destruction of those who had consented to make him king. This made it a matter of course for a king, as soon as he was crown'd, to issue out a general pardon, which was no more than to declare, that being now what he was not before, he had no enemy upon any former account. For this reason Lewis the twelfth of France, when he was incited to revenge himself against those, who in the reign of his predecessor Charles the eighth, had caused him to be imprisoned with great danger of his life, made this answer, *That the king of France did not care to revenge the injuries done to the duke of Orleans:*[8] and the last king of Sweden seemed no otherwise to remember who had opposed the queen's abdication, and his election, than by conferring honours upon them; because he knew they were the best men of the nation, and such as would be his friends when they should see how he would govern, in which he was not deceived. But lest all those who might come to the crown of England, should not have the same prudence and generosity, the kings were obliged by a custom of no less force than a law, immediately to put an end to all disputes, and the inconveniences that might arise from them. This did not proceed from the bounty of the prerogative (which I think is nonsense,

---

[7] 14 Edw. 3.15. [14 Edward III, ch. 15.]

[8] [De Serres, *General History of France* (chapter on Louis XII).]

for tho he that enjoys the prerogative may have bounty, the prerogative can have none) but from common sense, from his obligation, and the care of his own safety; and could have no other effect in law, than what related to his person, as appears by the forementioned statute.

Pardons granted by act of Parliament are of another nature: For as the king who has no other power than by law, can no otherwise dispense with the crimes committed against the laws, than the law does enable him; the Parliament that has the power of making laws, may entirely abolish the crimes, and unquestionably remit the punishment as they please.

Tho some words of Aristotle's *Ethicks* are without any coherence shuffled together by our author, with others taken out of his *Politicks*, I do not much except against them. No law made by man can be perfect, and there must be in every nation a power of correcting such defects as in time may arise or be discovered. This power can never be so rightly placed as *in the same hand that has the right of making laws, whether in one person or in many.*[9] If Filmer therefore can tell us of a place, where one man, woman or child, however he or she be qualified, has the power of making laws, I will acknowledge that not only the *hard cases*, but as many others as he pleases, are referr'd to his or her judgment, and that they may give it, whether they have any understanding of what they do or not, whether they be drunk or sober, in their senses or stark mad. But as I know no such place, and should not be much concerned for the sufferings of a people that should bring such misery upon themselves, as must accompany an absolute dependence upon the unruly will of such a creature, I may leave him to seek it, and rest in a perfect assurance that he does not speak of England, which acknowledges no other law than its own; and instead of receiving any from kings, does to this day obey none, but such as have been made by our ancestors, or ourselves, and never admitted any king that did not swear to observe them. And if Aristotle deserve credit, the power of altering, mitigating, explaining or correcting the laws of England, is only in the Parliament, because none but the Parliament can make them.

[9] [*Patriarcha*, ch. 27, p. 108.]

SECTION 23

*Aristotle proves, that no man is to be entrusted
with an absolute Power, by shewing that no one knows
how to execute it, but such a man as is not
to be found.*

OUR author having falsely cited and perverted the sense of Aristotle,
now brings him in saying, *That a perfect kingdom is that wherein the
king rules all according to his own will.*[1] But tho I have read his books of
government with some attention, I can find no such thing in them, unless
the word which signifies *mere* or *absolute* may be justly translated into
perfect; which is so far from Aristotle's meaning, that he distinguishes the
absolute or despotical kingdoms from the legitimate; and commending
the latter, gives no better name than that of *barbarous* to the first, which
he says can agree only with the nature of such nations as are base and
stupid, little differing from beasts; and having no skill to govern, or
courage to defend themselves, must resign all to the will of one that will
take care of them. Yet even this cannot be done, unless he that should
take that care be wholly exempted from the vices which oblige the others
to stand in need of it; for otherwise 'tis no better than if a sheep should
undertake to govern sheep, or a hog to command swine; Aristotle plainly
saying, *That as men are by nature equal, if it were possible all should be
magistrates.* But that being repugnant to the nature of government, he
finds no other way of solving the difficulty, than by *obeying and commanding
alternately;* that they may do by turns that which they cannot do all
together, and to which no one man has more right than another, because
they are all by nature equal.[2] This might be composed by a more compendious way, if, according to our author's doctrine, possession could
give a right. But Aristotle speaking like a philosopher, and not like a
publick enemy of mankind, examines what is just, reasonable, and
beneficial to men, that is, what ought to be done, and which being done,
is to be accounted just, and therefore to be supported by good men. But
as *that which is unjust in the beginning, can never have the effect of justice;*[3] and
it being manifestly unjust for one or a few men to assume a power over

---

[1] [*Patriarcha*, ch. 26, p. 106, citing *Politics*,
bk. 3, 1287a.]

[2] Arist. Pol. l. 2. c. 1. [Aristotle, *Politics*,
bk. 2, 1261a end–1261b beginning.]

[3] Quod ab initio injustum est, nullum potest
habere juris effectum. Grot. de jur. bel &
pac. l. 3. [Grotius, *De jure.*]

those who by nature are equal to them, no such power can be just or beneficial to mankind; nor fit to be upheld by good men, if it be unjust and prejudicial. In the opinion of Aristotle, this natural equality continues till virtue makes the distinction, which must be either simply compleat and perfect in itself, so that he who is endued with it, is a god among men, or relatively, as far as concerns civil society, and the ends for which it is constituted, that is, defence, and the obtaining of justice. This requires a mind unbiased by passion, full of goodness and wisdom, firm against all the temptations to ill, that may arise from desire or fear; tending to all manner of good, through a perfect knowledge and affection to it; and this to such a degree, that he or they have more of these virtues and excellencies than all the rest of the society, tho computed together: Where such a man is found, he is by nature a king, and 'tis best for the nation where he is that he govern.[4] If a few men, tho equal and alike among themselves, have the same advantages above the rest of the people, nature for the same reason seems to establish an aristocracy in that place; and the power is more safely committed to them, than left in the hands of the multitude. But if this excellency of virtue do not appear in one, nor in a few men, the right and power is by nature equally lodged in all; and to assume or appropriate that power to one, or a few men, is unnatural and tyrannical, which in Aristotle's language comprehends all that is detestable and abominable.

If any man should think Aristotle a trifler, for speaking of such a man as can never be found, I answer, that he went as far as his way could be warranted by reason or nature, and was obliged to stop there by the defect of his subject. He could not say that the government of one was simply good, when he knew so many qualifications were required in the person to make it so; nor that it is good for a nation to be under the power of a fool, a coward, or a villain, because 'tis good to be under a man of admirable wisdom, valour, industry and goodness; or that the government of one should be continued in such as by chance succeed in a family, because it was given to the first who had all the virtues required, tho all the reasons for which the power was given fail in the successor; much less could he say that any government was good, which was not good for those whose good only it was constituted to promote.

Moreover, by shewing who only is fit to be a monarch, or may be made such, without violating the laws of nature and justice, he shews who cannot be one: and he who says that no such man is to be found, as according to the opinion of Aristotle can be a monarch, does most

[4] Arist. Pol. l. 2. [Aristotle, *Politics*, bk. 3, 1284a-b.]

ridiculously allege his authority in favour of monarchs, or the power which some amongst us would attribute to them. If anything therefore may be concluded from his words, 'tis this, that since no power ought to be admitted which is not just; that none can be just which is not good, profitable to the people, and conducing to the ends for which it is constituted; that no man can know how to direct the power to those ends, can deserve, or administer it, unless he do so far excel all those that are under him in wisdom, justice, valour and goodness, as to possess more of those virtues than all of them: I say, if no such man or succession of men be found, no such power is to be granted to any man, or succession of men. But if such power be granted, the laws of nature and reason are overthrown, and the ends for which societies are constituted, utterly perverted, which necessarily implies an annihilation of the grant. And if a grant so made by those who have a right of setting up a government among themselves, do perish through its own natural iniquity and perversity, I leave it to any man, whose understanding and manners are not so entirely corrupted as those of our author, to determine what name ought to be given to that person, who not excelling all others in civil and moral virtues, in the proportion requir'd by Aristotle, does usurp a power over a nation, and what obedience the people owe to such a one. But if his opinion deserve our regard, the king by having those virtues is *omnium optimus*, and the best guide to the people, *to lead them to happiness by the ways of virtue*.[5] And he who assumes the same power, without the qualifications requir'd, is *tyrannus omnium pessimus*,[6] leading the people to all manner of ill, and in consequence to destruction.

SECTION 24

The power of Augustus Caesar was not given, but usurped.

OUR author's next instance is ingeniously taken from the Romans, *Who*, he says, *tho they were a people greedy of liberty, freed Augustus from the necessity of laws*.[1] If it be true, as he affirms, that such a prerogative is instituted only for the preservation of liberty, they who are most greedy of it, ought to be most forward in establishing that which defends it best. But if the weight laid upon the words *greedy of liberty*, &c. render his

---

[5] Ad summum bonum secundum virtutem. Arist. Pol. [*Omnium optimus* means "the best of all."]

[6] [A tyrant, the worst of all.]

[1] [*Patriarcha*, ch. 26, p. 106.]

memory and judgment liable to censure, the unpardonable prevarication of citing any act done by the Romans in the time of Augustus, as done freely, shews him to be a man of no faith. *Omnium jura in se traxerat,* says Tacitus of Augustus;[2] nothing was conferred upon him, he took all to himself; there could be nothing of right in that which was wholly usurped. And neither the people or the senate could do anything freely, whilst they were under the power of a mad corrupted soldiery, who first betray'd, and then subdued them. The greatest part of the senate had fall'n at the battle of Pharsalia, others had been gleaned up in several places, the rest destroy'd by the proscriptions; and that which then retained the name of a senate, was made up chiefly of those who had been his ministers, in bringing the most miserable slavery upon their own country. The Roman liberty, and that bravery of spirit by which it had been maintained, was not only abolished, but almost forgotten. All consideration of law and right was trampled under foot; and none could dispute with him, who by the power of the sword had seiz'd the authority both of the senate and people. Nothing was so extravagant, that might not be extorted by the insolent violence of a conqueror, who had thirty mercenary legions to execute his commands. The uncorrupted part of the people that had escaped the sword of Julius, had either perished with Hirtius and Pansa, Brutus and Cassius, or been destroy'd by the detestable triumvirate. Those that remain'd could lose nothing by a verbal resignation of their liberty, which they had neither strength nor courage to defend. The magistracies were possess'd by the creatures of the tyrant; and the people was composed of such as were either born under slavery, and accustomed to obey, or remain'd under the terror of those arms that had consumed the assertors of their liberty. Our author standing in need of some Roman example was obliged to seek it in an age, when the laws were subverted, virtue extinguished, injustice placed in the throne, and such as would not be of the same spirit, exposed to the utmost cruelty. This was the time when the *sovereign majesty* shined in glory; and they who had raised it above the law, made it also the object of their religion, by adoring the statues of their oppressor. The corruption of this court spread itself over the best part of the world; and reduced the empire to that irrecoverable weakness in which it languished and perish'd. This is the state of things that pleases Filmer, and those that are like him, who for the introduction of the same among us, recommend such an elevation of the sovereign majesty, as is most contrary to the laws of God and men, abhorred by

[2] Annal. l. 1. ["He drew into himself the rights of everyone." Tacitus, *Annals,* bk. 1, ch. 2.]

all generous nations, and most especially by our ancestors, who thought nothing too dear to be hazarded in the defence of themselves and us from it.

SECTION 25

The Regal Power was not the first in this Nation; nor necessarily to be continued, tho it had been the first.

TRUTH being uniform in itself, those who desire to propagate it for the good of mankind, lay the foundations of their reasonings in such principles, as are either evident to common sense, or easily proved: but cheats and impostors delighting in obscurity, suppose things that are dubious or false, and think to build one falsehood upon another; and our author can find no better way to persuade us, that all our privileges and laws are from the king, than by saying, *That the first power was the kingly power, which was both in this and all other nations in the world, long before any laws or any other kind of government was thought of; from whence we must necessarily infer, that the common law, or common customs of this land were originally the laws and commands of the king.*[1] But denying both these points, I affirm,

1. First, that there was a power to make kings before there was any king.
2. Tho kings had been the first created magistrates in all places (as perhaps they were in some) it does not follow, that they must continue forever, or that laws are from them.

To the first; I think no man will deny, that there was a people at Babylon, before Nimrod was king of that place. This people had a power; for no number of men can be without it: Nay this people had a power of making Nimrod king, or he could never have been king. He could not be king by succession, for the Scripture shews him to have been the first. He was not king by the right of father, for he was not their father, Cush, Ham, with his elder brothers and father Noah being still living; and, which is worst of all, were not kings: for if they who lived in Nimrod's time, or before him, neither were kings, nor had kings, he that ought to

[1] [*Patriarcha*, ch. 27 ("The King Is Author, Interpreter and Corrector of the Common Law"), p. 107.]

[456]

have been king over all by the right of nature (if there had been any such thing in nature) was not king. Those who immediately succeeded him, and must have inherited his right, if he had any, did not inherit or pretend to it: and therefore he that shall now claim a right from nature, as father of a people, must ground it upon something more certain than Noah's right of reigning over his children, or it can have no strength in it.

Moreover, the nations who in and before the time of Nimrod had no kings, had power, or else they could have performed no act, nor constituted any other magistrate to this day, which is absurd. There was therefore a power in nations before there were kings, or there could never have been any; and Nimrod could never have been king, if the people of Babylon had not made him king, which they could not have done if they had not had a power of making him so. 'Tis ridiculous to say he made himself king, for tho he might be strong and valiant, he could not be stronger than a multitude of men. That which forces must be stronger than that which is forced; and if it be true, according to the ancient saying, that Hercules himself is not sufficient to encounter two, 'tis sure more impossible for one man to force a multitude, for that must be stronger than he. If he came in by persuasion, they who were persuaded, were persuaded to consent that he should be king. That consent therefore made him king. But, *Qui dat esse, dat modum esse:*[2] They who made him king, made him such a king as best pleased themselves. He had therefore nothing but what was given: his greatness and power must be from the multitude who gave it: and their laws and liberties could not be from him; but their liberties were naturally inherent in themselves, and their laws were the product of them.

There was a people that made Romulus king. He did not make or beget that people, nor, for anything we know, one man of them. He could not come in by inheritance, for he was a bastard, the son of an unknown man; and when he died, the right that had been conferred upon him reverted to the people, who according to that right, chose Numa, Hostilius, Marcius, Tarquinius Priscus, and Servius, all strangers, and without any other right than what was bestow'd upon them: and Tarquinius Superbus who invaded the throne *without the command of the people,*[3] was ejected, and the government of kings abolished by the same power that had created it.

We know not certainly by what law Moses and the judges created by the advice of Jethro, governed the Israelites; but may probably conjecture

---

[2] [Whoever gives something being, gives it its mode of being.]

[3] Sine jussu populi. T. Liv. l. 1. [Livy, *History of Rome*, bk. 1, ch. 49.]

it to have been by that law which God had written in the hearts of mankind; and the people submitted to the judgment of good and wise men, tho they were under no coercive power: but 'tis certain they had a law and a regular magistracy under which they lived, four hundred years before they had a king, for Saul was the first. This law was not therefore from the king, nor by the king; but the king was chosen and made by the people, according to the liberty they had by the law, tho they did not rightly follow the rules therein prescribed, and by that means brought destruction upon themselves.

The country in which we live lay long concealed under obscure barbarity, and we know nothing of the first inhabitants, but what is involved in fables that leave us still in the dark. Julius Caesar is the first who speaks distinctly of our affairs, and gives us no reason to believe there was any monarchy then established amongst us. Cassivellaunus was occasionally chosen by the nations that were most exposed to the violence of the Romans, for the management of those wars against them.[4] By others we hear of Boadicia, Arviragus, Galgacus, and many more set up afterwards when need required; but we find no footsteps of a regular succession either by inheritance or election. And as they had then no kings, or any other general magistrate, than can be said to be equivalent to a king, they might have had none at all unless they had thought fit. Tacitus mentions a sort of kings, used by the Romans to keep nations in servitude to them;[5] and tho it were true that there had been such a man as Lucius, and he one of this sort, he is to be accounted only as a Roman magistrate, and signifies no more to our dispute, than if he had been called proconsul, praetor, or by any other name. However there was no series of them: that which was temporary and occasional, depended upon the will of those, who thinking there was occasion, created such a magistrate, and omitted to do so, when the occasion ceased, or was thought to cease; and might have had none at all, if they had so pleased. The magistracy therefore was from them, and depended upon their will.

We have already mentioned the histories of the Saxons, Danes and Normans, from which nations, together with the Britains, we are descended, and finding that they were severe assertors of their liberties, acknowledged no human laws but their own, received no kings but such as swore to observe them, and deposed those who did not well perform their oaths and duty, 'tis evident that their kings were made by the people

---

[4] Jul. Caes. Comment. l. 5. [*Commentaries*, bk. 5, ch. 9, in Julius Caesar, *Gallic War* (Loeb, 1917).]

[5] Inter instrumenta servitutis reges habuere.

C. Tacit. ["They had kings among their instruments of (keeping others in) servitude." Tacitus, *Life of Agricola*, ch. 14.]

according to the law; and that the law, by which they became what they were, could not be from themselves. Our ancestors were so fully convinced that in the creation of kings they exercised their own right, and were only to consider what was good for themselves, that without regard to the memory of those who had gone before, they were accustomed to take such as seemed most like, wisely, justly and gently to perform their office; refused those that were suspected of pride, cruelty or any other vice that might bring prejudice upon the publick, what title soever they pretended; and removed such as had been placed in the throne if they did not answer the opinion conceived of their virtue; which I take to be a manner of proceeding that agrees better with the quality of masters, making laws and magistrates for themselves, than of slaves receiving such as were imposed upon them.

2. To the second. Tho it should be granted, that all nations had at the first been governed by kings, it were nothing to the question; for no man or number of men was ever obliged to continue in the errors of his predecessors. The authority of custom as well as of law (I mean in relation to the power that made it to be) consists only in its rectitude: And the same reason which may have induced one or more nations to create kings, when they knew no other form of government, may not only induce them to set up another, if that be found inconvenient to them, but proves that they may as justly do so, as remove a man who performs not what was expected from him. If there had been a rule given by God, and written in the minds of men by nature, it must have been from the beginning, universal and perpetual; or at least must have been observed by the wisest and best instructed nations: which not being in any measure (as I have proved already) there can be no reason, why a polite people should not relinquish the errors committed by their ancestors in the time of their barbarism and ignorance, and why they should not do it in matters of government, as well as in any other thing relating to life. Men are subject to errors, and 'tis the work of the best and wisest to discover and amend such as their ancestors may have committed, or to add perfection to those things which by them have been well invented. This is so certain, that whatsoever we enjoy beyond the misery in which our barbarous ancestors lived, is due only to the liberty of correcting what was amiss in their practice, or inventing that which they did not know: and I doubt whether it be more brutish to say we are obliged to continue in the idolatry of the Druids, with all the miseries and follies that accompany the most savage barbarity, or to confess that tho we have a right to depart from these, yet we are forever bound to continue the government they had established, whatever inconveniences might attend

it. Tertullian disputing with the pagans, who objected the novelty of the Christian religion, troubled not himself with refuting that error; but proving Christianity to be good and true, he thought he had sufficiently proved it to be ancient.[6] A wise architect may shew his skill, and deserve commendation for building a poor house of vile materials, when he can procure no better, but he no way ought to hinder others from erecting more glorious fabricks if they are furnished with the means required. Besides, such is the imperfection of all human constitutions, that they are subject to perpetual fluctuation, which never permits them to continue long in the same condition: Corruptions slide in insensibly; and the best orders are sometimes subverted by malice and violence; so that he who only regards what was done in such an age, often takes the corruption of the state for the institution, follows the worst example, thinks that to be the first, that is the most ancient he knows; and if a brave people seeing the original defects of their government, or the corruption into which it may be fallen, do either correct and reform what may be amended, or abolish that which was evil in the institution, or so perverted that it cannot be restor'd to integrity, these men impute it to sedition, and blame those actions, which of all that can be performed by men are the most glorious. We are not therefore so much to inquire after that which is most ancient, as that which is best, and most conducing to the good ends to which it was directed. As governments were instituted for the obtaining of justice, and (as our author says) the preservation of liberty,[7] we are not to seek what government was the first, but what best provides for the obtaining of justice, and preservation of liberty. For whatsoever the institution be, and how long soever it may have lasted, 'tis void, if it thwarts, or do not provide for the ends of its establishment. If such a law or custom therefore as is not good in itself, had in the beginning prevailed in all parts of the world (which in relation to absolute or any kind of monarchy is not true) it ought to be abolished; and if any man should shew himself wiser than others by proposing a law or government, more beneficial to mankind than any that had been formerly known, providing better for justice and liberty than all others had done, he would merit the highest veneration. If any man ask, who shall be judge of that rectitude or pravity which either authorises or destroys a law? I answer, that as this consists not in formalities and niceties, but in evident and substantial truths, there is no need of any other tribunal than that of

---

[6] Nullum tempus, nulla praescriptio occurrit veritati. Tertul. Id antiquius quod verius. Ibid. [No time, no prescription counteracts truth. The truer something is, the more ancient it is.]

[7] [*Patriarcha*, ch. 1, p. 55.]

common sense, and the light of nature, to determine the matter: and he that travels through France, Italy, Turkey, Germany and Switzerland without consulting Bartolus or Baldus, will easily understand whether the countries that are under the kings of France and Spain, the pope and the Great Turk, or such as are under the care of a well-regulated magistracy, do best enjoy the benefits of justice and liberty. 'Tis as easily determined, whether the Grecians when Athens and Thebes flourished were more free than the Medes; whether justice was better administered by Agathocles, Dionysius and Phalaris, than by the legal kings and regular magistrates of Sparta; or whether more care was taken that justice and liberty might be preserved by Tiberius, Caligula, Claudius, Nero and Vitellius, than by the senate and people of Rome whilst the laws were more powerful than the commands of men. The like may be said of particular laws, as those of Nebuchadnezzar and Caligula, for worshipping their statues; our acts of Parliament against hereticks and Lollards, with the statutes and orders of the Inquisition which is called the Holy Office. And if that only be a law which is *sanctio recta, jubens honesta, prohibens contraria*,[8] the meanest understanding, if free from passion, may certainly know that such as these cannot be laws, by what authority soever they were enacted, and that the use of them, and others like to them, ought to be abolished for their turpitude and iniquity. Infinite examples of the like nature might be alleged, as well concerning divine as human things. And if there be any laws which are evil, there cannot be an incontestable rectitude in all, and if not in all, it concerns us to examine where it is to be found. Laws and constitutions ought to be weighed, and whilst all due reverence is paid to such as are good, every nation may not only retain in itself a power of changing or abolishing all such as are not so, but ought to exercise that power according to the best of their understanding, and in the place of what was either at first mistaken or afterwards corrupted, to constitute that which is most conducing to the establishment of justice and liberty.

But such is the condition of mankind, that nothing can be so perfectly framed as not to give some testimony of human imbecility, and frequently to stand in need of reparations and amendments. Many things are unknown to the wisest, and the best men can never wholly divest themselves of passions and affections. By this means the best and wisest are sometimes led into error, and stand in need of successors like to themselves, who may find remedies for the faults they have committed, and nothing can or ought to be permanent but that which is perfect. No natural body was

[8] [See Section 10, n. 31.]

ever so well temper'd and organiz'd, as not to be subject to diseases, wounds or other accidents, and to need medicines and other occasional helps as well as nourishment and exercise; and he who under the name of innovation would deprive nations of the like, does, as much as lies in him, condemn them all to perish by the defects of their own foundations. Some men observing this, have proposed a necessity of reducing every state once in an age or two, to the integrity of its first principle:[9] but they ought to have examined, whether that principle be good or evil, or so good that nothing can be added to it, which none ever was; and this being so, those who will admit of no change would render errors perpetual, and depriving mankind of the benefits of wisdom, industry, experience, and the right use of reason, oblige all to continue in the miserable barbarity of their ancestors, which suits better with the name of a wolf than that of a man.

Those who are of better understanding, weigh all things, and often find reason to abrogate that which their fathers according to the measure of the knowledge they had, or the state of things among them had rightly instituted, or to restore that which they had abrogated; and there can be no greater mark of a most brutish stupidity, than for men to continue in an evil way, because their fathers had brought them into it. But if we ought not too strictly to adhere to our own constitutions, those of other nations are less to be regarded by us; for the laws that may be good for one people are not for all, and that which agrees with the manners of one age, is utterly abhorrent from those of another. It were absurd to think of restoring the laws of Lycurgus to the present inhabitants of Peloponnesus, who are accustomed to the most abject slavery. It may easily be imagined, how the Romans, Sabines and Latins, now under the tyranny of the pope, would relish such a discipline as flourished among them after the expulsion of the Tarquins; and it had been no less preposterous to give a liberty to the Parthians of governing themselves, or for them to assume it, than to impose an absolute monarch upon the German nation. Titus Livius having observed this, says, that if a popular government had been set up in Rome immediately upon the building of the city; and if that fierce people which was composed of unruly shepherds, herdsmen, fugitive slaves, and outlaw'd persons, who could not suffer the governments under which they were born, had come to be incited by turbulent orators, they would have brought all into confusion: whereas that boisterous humour being gradually temper'd by discipline under Romulus, or taught to vent its fury against foreign enemies, and soften'd by the

[9] Discors. di Machiav. lib. 2. [Machiavelli, *Discourses on Livy*, bk. 3, ch. 1.]

peaceable reign of Numa, a new race grew up, which being all of one blood, contracted a love to their country, and became capable of liberty, which the madness of their last king, and the lewdness of his son, gave them occasion to resume.[10] If this was commendable in them, it must be so in other nations. If the Germans might preserve their liberty, as well as the Parthians submit themselves to absolute monarchy, 'tis as lawful for the descendants of those Germans to continue in it, as for the Eastern nations to be slaves. If one nation may justly chuse the government that seems best to them, and continue or alter it according to the changes of times and things, the same right must belong to others. The great variety of laws that are or have been in the world, proceeds from this, and nothing can better shew the wisdom and virtue, or the vices and folly of nations, than the use they make of this right: they have been glorious or infamous, powerful or despicable, happy or miserable, as they have well or ill executed it.

If it be said that the law given by God to the Hebrews, proceeding from his wisdom and goodness, must needs be perfect and obligatory to all nations: I answer, that there is a simple and a relative perfection; the first is only in God, the other in the things he has created: *He saw that they were good*,[11] which can signify no more than that they were good in their kind, and suited to the end for which he designed them. For if the perfection were absolute, there could be no difference between an angel and a worm, and nothing could be subject to change or death, for that is imperfection. This relative perfection is seen also by his law given to mankind in the persons of Adam and Noah. It was good in the kind, fit for those times, but could never have been enlarged or altered, if the perfection had been simple; and no better evidence can be given to shew that it was not so, than that God did afterwards give one much more full and explicit to his people. This law also was peculiarly applicable to that people and season, for if it had been otherwise, the apostles would have obliged Christians to the entire observation of it, as well as to abstain from idolatry, fornication and blood. But if all this be not so, then their judicial law, and the form of their commonwealth must be received by all; no human law can be of any value; we are all brethren, no man has a prerogative above another; lands must be equally divided amongst all; inheritances cannot be alienated for above fifty years; no man can be raised above the rest unless he be called by God, and enabled by his spirit to conduct the people; when this man dies, he that has the same

---

[10] Hist. l. 2. [Livy, *History of Rome*, bk. 2, ch. 1.]   [11] Gen. 1.

spirit must succeed, as Joshua did to Moses, and his children can have
no title to his office: when such a man appears, a Sanhedrin of seventy
men chosen out of the whole people, are to judge such causes as relate
to themselves, whilst those of greater extent and importance are referred
to the general assemblies. Here is no mention of a king, and consequently,
if we must take this law for our pattern, we cannot have one: If the point
be driven to the utmost, and the precept of Deuteronomy, where God
permitted them to have a king, if they thought fit when they came into
the promised land, be understood to extend to all nations, every one of
them must have the same liberty of taking their own time, chusing him
in their own way, dividing the kingdom, having no king, and setting up
other governors when they please, as before the election of Saul, and
after the return from the Captivity: and even when they have a king, he
must be such a one as is describ'd in the same chapter, who no more
resembles the sovereign majesty that our author adores, and agrees as
little with his maxims, as a tribune of the Roman people.

We may therefore conclude, that if we are to follow the law of Moses,
we must take it with all the appendages; a king can be no more, and no
otherwise than he makes him: for whatever we read of the kings they
had, were extreme deviations from it. No nation can make any law, and
our lawyers burning their books may betake themselves to the study of
the Pentateuch, in which tho some of them may be well versed, yet
probably the profit arising from thence will not be very great.

But if we are not obliged to live in a conformity to the law of Moses,
every people may frame laws for themselves, and we cannot be denied
the right that is common to all. Our laws were not sent from heaven,
but made by our ancestors according to the light they had, and their
present occasions. We inherit the same right from them, and, as we may
without vanity say that we know a little more than they did, if we find
ourselves prejudic'd by any law that they made, we may repeal it. The
safety of the people was their supreme law, and is so to us: neither can
we be thought less fit to judge what conduces to that end, than they
were. If they in any age had been persuaded to put themselves under the
power, or in our author's phrase, under the sovereign majesty of a child,
a fool, a mad or desperately wicked person, and had annexed the right
conferred upon him to such as should succeed, it had not been a *just and
right sanction;* and having none of the qualities essentially belonging to a
law, could not have the effect of a law. It cannot be for the good of a
people to be governed by one, who by nature ought to be governed, or
by age or accident is rendered unable to govern himself. The publick
interests and the concernments of private men in their lands, goods,

liberties and lives (for the preservation of which our author says, that regal prerogative is only constituted) cannot be preserved by one who is transported by his own passions or follies, a slave to his lusts and vices; or, which is sometimes worse, governed by the vilest of men and women who flatter him in them, and push him on to do such things as even they would abhor, if they were in his place. The turpitude and impious madness of such an act must necessarily make it void, by overthrowing the ends for which it was made, since that justice which was sought cannot be obtain'd, nor the evils that were fear'd, prevented; and they for whose good it was intended must necessarily have a right of abolishing it. This might be sufficient for us, tho our ancestors had enslaved themselves. But, God be thanked, we are not put to that trouble: We have no reason to believe we are descended from such fools and beasts, as would willingly cast themselves and us into such an excess of misery and shame, or that they were so tame and cowardly to be subjected by force or fear. We know the value they set upon their liberties, and the courage with which they defended them: and we can have no better example to encourage us, never to suffer them to be violated or diminished.

SECTION 26

Tho the King may be entrusted with the power of chusing Judges, yet that by which they act is from the Law.

I CONFESS that no law can be so perfect, *to provide exactly for every case that may fall out, so as to leave nothing to the discretion of the judges,* who in some measure are to interpret them: But *that laws or customs are ever few, or that the paucity is the reason that they cannot give special rules, or that judges do resort to those principles or common law axioms, whereupon former judgments in cases something alike have been given by former judges, who all receive their authority from the king in his right to give sentence,*[1] I utterly deny; and affirm,

1. That in many places, and particularly in England, the laws are so many, that the number of them has introduced an uncertainty and confusion which is both dangerous and troublesome; and the infinite

---

[1] [*Patriarcha*, ch. 27, p. 107.]

variety of adjudged cases thwarting and contradicting each other, has render'd these difficulties inextricable. Tacitus imputes a great part of the miseries suffer'd by the Romans in his time to this abuse, and tells us, that *the laws grew to be innumerable in the worst and most corrupt state of things,*[2] and that justice was overthrown by them. By the same means in France, Italy, and other places, where the civil law is rendered municipal, judgments are in a manner arbitrary; and tho the intention of our laws be just and good, they are so numerous, and the volumes of our statutes with the interpretations and adjudged cases so vast, that hardly anything is so clear and fixed, but men of wit and learning may find what will serve for a pretence to justify almost any judgment they have a mind to give. Whereas the laws of Moses, as to the judicial part, being short and few, judgments were easy and certain; and in Switzerland, Sweden, and some parts of Denmark, the whole volume that contains them may be read in few hours, and by that means no injustice can be done which is not immediately made evident.

2. Axioms are not rightly grounded upon judged cases, but cases are to be judged according to axioms: the certain is not proved by the uncertain, but the uncertain by the certain; and everything is to be esteemed uncertain till it be proved to be certain. Axioms in law are, as in mathematicks, evident to common sense; and nothing is to be taken for an axiom, that is not so. Euclid does not prove his axioms by his propositions, but his propositions, which are abstruse, by such axioms as are evident to all. The axioms of our law do not receive their authority from Coke or Hales, but Coke and Hales deserve praise for giving judgment according to such as are undeniably true.

3. The judges receive their commissions from the king, and perhaps it may be said, that the custom of naming them is grounded upon a right with which he is entrusted; but their power is from the law, as that of the king also is. For he who has none originally in himself, can give none unless it be first conferred upon him. I know not how he can well perform his oath to govern according to law, unless he execute the power with which he is entrusted, in naming those men to be judges, whom in his conscience, and by the advice of his council, he thinks the best and ablest to perform that office: But both he and they are to learn their duty from that law, by which they are, and which allots to every one his proper work. As the law intends that men should be made judges for their integrity and knowledge in the law, and that it ought not to be imagined

---

[2] Et in corruptissima republica plurimae leges.
[Tacitus, *Annals*, bk. 3, ch. 27.]

that the king will break his trust by chusing such as are not so, till the violation be evident, nothing is more reasonable than to intend that the judges so qualified should instruct the king in matters of law. But that he who may be a child, over aged, or otherwise ignorant and incapable, should instruct the judges, is equally absurd, as for a blind man to be a guide to those who have the best eyes, and so abhorrent from the meaning of the law, that the judges (as I said before) are sworn to do justice according to the laws, without any regard to the king's words, letters or commands: If they are therefore to act according to a set rule, from which they may not depart what command soever they receive, they do not act by a power from him, but by one that is above both. This is commonly confess'd; and tho some judges have been found in several ages, who in hopes of reward and preferment have made little account of their oath, yet the success that many of them have had, may reasonably deter others from following their example; and if there are not more instances in this kind, no better reason can be given, than that nations do frequently fail, by being too remiss in asserting their own rights or punishing offenders, and hardly ever err on the severer side.[3]

4. Judgments are variously given in several states and kingdoms, but he who would find one where they lie in the breast of the king, must go at least as far as Morocco. Nay, the ambassador who was lately here from that place, denied that they were absolutely in him. However 'tis certain that in England, according to the Great Charter, *Judgments are passed by equals:*[4] no man can be imprison'd, disseiz'd of his freehold, depriv'd of life or limb, *unless by the sentence of his peers.*[5] The kings of Judah did *judge and were judged;*[6] and the judgments they gave were in and with the Sanhedrin. In England the kings do not judge, but are judged: and Bracton says, *That in receiving justice the king is equal to another man;*[7] which could not be, if judgments were given by him, and he were exempted from the judgment of all by that law, which has put all judgments into the hands of the people. This power is executed by them in grand or petty juries, and the judges are assistants to them in explaining the

---

[3] Jure igitur plectimur; nisi enim multorum impunita scelera tulissemus, nunquam ad unum tanta pervenisset licentia. Cicero. ["Thus we are justly punished; for such great license would never have come to one man had we not allowed the crimes of many others to go unpunished." Cicero, *De Officiis* (Loeb, 1913), bk. 2, sec. 28.]

[4] Judicia fiunt per pares. Mag. Chart. [*Magna Charta*, ch. 21.]

[5] Nisi per judicium parium suorum. Ibid. [Ch. 29.]

[6] Judicabant & judicabantur. Maimonid. [*The Code of Maimonides, Book 14: The Book of Judges*, Treatise One: Sanhedrin, ch. 2, p. 8.]

[7] In justitia recipienda rex cuilibet ex plebe aequalis est. [Bracton, *On the Laws and Customs of England*, fol. 107, p. 305.]

difficult points of the law, in which 'tis presumed they should be learned. The strength of every judgment consists in the verdict of these juries, which the judges do not give, but pronounce or declare: and the same law that makes good a verdict given contrary to the advice or direction of the judges, exposes them to the utmost penalties, if upon their own heads, or a command from the king, they should presume to give a sentence, without or contrary to a verdict; and no pretensions to a power of interpreting the law can exempt them if they break it. The power also with which the judges are entrusted, is but of a moderate extent, and to be executed *bona fide*. Prevarications are capital, as they proved to Tresilian, Empson, Dudley, and many others. Nay even in special verdicts, the judges are only assistants to the juries who find it specially, and the verdict is from them, tho the judges having heard the point argued, declare the sense of the law thereupon. Wherefore if I should grant that the king might personally assist in judgments, his work could only be to prevent frauds, and by the advice of the judges to see that the laws be duly executed, or perhaps to inspect their behaviour. If he has more than this, it must be by virtue of his politick capacity, in which he is understood to be always present in the principal courts, where justice is always done whether he who wears the crown be young or old, wise or ignorant, good or bad, or whether he like or dislike what is done.

Moreover, as governments are instituted for the obtaining of justice, and the king is in a great measure entrusted with the power of executing it, 'tis probable that the law would have required his presence in the distribution, if there had been but one court; that at the same time he could be present in more than one; that it were certain he would be guilty of no miscarriages; that all miscarriages were to be punished in him as well as in the judges; or that it were certain he should always be a man of such wisdom, industry, experience and integrity as to be an assistance to, and a watch over those who are appointed for the administration of justice. But there being many courts sitting at the same time of equal authority, in several places far distant from each other; impossible for the king to be present in all; no manner of assurance that the same or greater miscarriages may not be committed in his presence than in his absence, by himself than others; no opportunity of punishing every delict in him, without bringing the nation into such disorder, as may be of more prejudice to the publick than an injury done to a private man; the law which intends to obviate offences, or to punish such as cannot be obviated, has directed, that those men should be chosen who are most knowing in it, imposes an oath upon them, not to be diverted from the due course of justice by fear or favour, hopes or reward, particularly by any command from the king; and appoints the severest punishments for them if they prove false to God and their country.

If any man think that the words cited from Bracton by our author upon the question, *Quis primo & principaliter possit & debeat judicare*, &c. *Sciendum est quod rex & non alius, si solus ad haec sufficere possit; cum ad hoc per virtutem sacramenti teneatur,*[8] are contrary to what I have said, I desire the context may be considered, that his opinion may be truly understood, tho the words taken simply and nakedly may be enough for my purpose. For 'tis ridiculous to infer that the king has a right of doing anything, upon a supposition that 'tis impossible for him to do it. He therefore who says the king cannot do it, says it must be done by others, or not at all. But having already proved that the king, merely as king, has none of the qualities required for judging all or any cases, and that many kings have all the defects of age and person that render men most unable and unfit to give any sentence, we may conclude, without contradicting Bracton, that no king as king, has a power of judging, because some of them are utterly unable and unfit to do it; and if anyone has such a power, it must be conferr'd upon him by those who think him able and fit to perform that work. When Filmer finds such a man, we must inquire into the extent of that power which is given to him; but this would be nothing to his general proposition, for he himself would hardly have inferr'd, that because a power of judging in some cases was conferred upon one prince on account of his fitness and ability, therefore all of them, however unfit and unable, have a power of deciding all cases. Besides, if he believe Bracton, this power of judging is not inherent in the king, but incumbent upon him by virtue of his oath, which our author endeavours to enervate and annul. But as that oath is grounded upon the law, and the law cannot presume impossibilities and absurdities, it cannot intend, and the oath cannot require, that a man should do that which he is unable and unfit to do. Many kings are unfit to judge causes, the law cannot therefore intend they should do it. The context also shews, that this imagination of the king's judging all causes, if he could, is merely chimerical: for Bracton says in the same chapter, that *the power of the king is the power of the law;* that is, that he has no power but by the law. And the law that aims at justice, cannot make it to depend upon the uncertain humour of a child, a woman, or a foolish man; for by that means it would destroy itself. The law cannot therefore give any such power, and the king cannot have it.

[8] ["Who primarily and principally can and ought to judge? . . . Obviously the king and no other, if he alone is capable of this; since he is held to this by virtue of the sacrament." Ibid., cited in *Patriarcha*, ch. 28, p. 109.]

If it be said that all kings are not so; that some are of mature age, wise, just and good; or that the question is not what is good for the subject, but what is glorious to the king, and that he must not lose his right tho the people perish; I answer, first, that whatsoever belongs to kings as kings, belongs to all kings: this power of judging cannot belong to all for the reasons above mentioned: it cannot therefore belong to any as king, nor without madness be granted to any, till he has given testimony of such wisdom, experience, diligence and goodness, as is required for so great a work. It imports not what his ancestors were; virtues are not entail'd; and it were less improper for the heirs of Hales and Harvey, to pretend that the clients and patients of their ancestors should depend upon their advice in matters of law and physick, than for the heirs of a great and wise prince to pretend to powers given on account of virtue, if they have not the same talents for the performance of the works required.

Common sense declares, that governments are instituted, and judicatures erected for the obtaining of justice. The king's bench was not established that the chief justice should have a great office, but that the oppressed should be relieved, and right done. The honor and profit he receives, comes in as it were by accident, as the rewards of his service; if he rightly perform his duty: but he may as well pretend he is there for his own sake, as the king. God did not set up Moses or Joshua, that they might glory in having six hundred thousand men under their command, but that they might lead the people into the land they were to possess: that is, they were not for themselves but for the people; and the glory they acquir'd was by rightly performing the end of their institution. Even our author is obliged to confess this, when he says, that the king's prerogative is instituted for the good of those that are under it. 'Tis therefore for them that he enjoys it, and it can no otherwise subsist than in concurrence with that end. He also yields that *the safety of the people is the supreme law*.[9] The right therefore that the king has must be conformable and subordinate to it. If anyone therefore set up an interest in himself that is not so, he breaks this supreme law; he doth not live and reign for his people but for himself, and by departing from the end of his institution destroys it: and if Aristotle (to whom our author seems to have a great deference) deserves credit, such a one ceases to be a king, and becomes a tyrant; he who ought to have been the best of men is turned into the worst; and he who is recommended to us under the name of a father, becomes a publick enemy to the people.[10] The question therefore is not,

---

[9] [*Patriarcha*, ch. 24, p. 103.]
[10] Polit.l.1. [Aristotle, *Politics*, bk. 3, 1279a-b; bk. 4, 1295a.]

what is good for the king, but what is good for the people, and he can have no right repugnant to them.

Bracton is not more gentle. *The king,* says he, *is obliged by his oath, to the utmost of his power, to preserve the church, and the Christian world in peace; to hinder rapine, and all manner of iniquity; to cause justice and mercy to be observed: He has no power but from the law: that only is to be taken for law, quod recté fuerit definitum:*[11] he is therefore to cause justice to be done according to that rule, and not to pervert it for his own pleasure, profit or glory. He may chuse judges also, not such as will be subservient to his will, but *viros sapientes, timentes Deum, in quibus est veritas eloquiorum, & qui oderunt avaritiam.*[12] Which proves that kings and their officers do not possess their places for themselves, but for the people, and must be such as are fit and able to perform the duties they undertake. The mischievous fury of those who assume a power above their abilities is well represented by the known fable of Phaeton: they think they desire fine things for themselves when they seek their own ruin. In conformity to this the same Bracton says, that *If any man who is unskilful assume the seat of justice, he falls as from a precipice,* &c. *and 'tis the same thing as if a sword be put into the hand of a mad man;*[13] which cannot but affect the king as well as those who are chosen by him. If he neglect the functions of his office, *he does unjustly, and becomes the vicegerent of the Devil; for he is the minister of him whose works he does.*[14] This is Bracton's opinion, but desiring to be a more gentle interpreter of the law, I only wish, that princes would consider the end of their institution; endeavour to perform it; measure their own abilities; content themselves with that power which the laws allow, and abhor those wretches who by flattery and lies endeavour to work upon their frailest passions, by which means they draw upon them that hatred of the people, which frequently brings them to destruction.

Tho Ulpian's words, *princeps legibus non tenetur,*[15] be granted to have been true in fact, with relation to the Roman empire, in the time when he lived; yet they can conclude nothing against us. The liberty of Rome had been overthrown long before by the power of the sword, and the law render'd subservient to the will of the usurpers. They were not Englishmen, but Romans, who lost the battles of Pharsalia and Philippi: The carcasses of their senators, not ours, were exposed to the wolves and

[11] ["Which shall have been rightly defined." Bracton, *On the Laws and Customs of England,* fol. 107, p. 304.]

[12] Bract. l. 3. c. 10. ["Wise God-fearing men, whose eloquence is true, and who hate avarice." Ibid., fol. 108, p. 306.]

[13] Si quis minus sapiens & indoctus sedem judicandi & honestatem judicandi sibi praesumserit, exalto corruit, &c. & perinde erit ac si gladium poneret in manu furentis. Ibid. [p. 307.]

[14] [Ibid., fol. 107, p. 305.]

[15] ["The ruler is not bound by the laws." *Patriarcha,* ch. 26, p. 106.]

vultures: Pompeius, Scipio, Lentulus, Afranius, Petreius, Cato, Cassius and Brutus were defenders of the Roman, not the English liberty; and that of their country, not ours, could only be lost by their defeat. Those who were destroy'd by the proscriptions, left Rome, not England to be enslaved. If the best had gained the victory, it could have been no advantage to us, and their overthrow can be no prejudice. Every nation is to take care of their own laws; and whether any one has had the wisdom, virtue, fortune and power to defend them or not, concerns only themselves. The examples of great and good men acting freely deserve consideration, but they only perish by the ill success of their designs; and whatsoever is afterwards done by their subdued posterity ought to have no other effect upon the rest of the world, than to admonish them so to join in the defence of their liberties, as never to be brought under the necessity of acting by the command of one, to the prejudice of themselves and their country. If the Roman greatness persuade us to put an extraordinary value upon what passed among them, we ought rather to examine what they did, said, or thought when they enjoy'd that liberty which was the mother and nurse of their virtue, than what they suffer'd, or were forc'd to say, when they were fallen under that slavery which produced all manner of corruption, and made them the most base and miserable people of the world.

For what concerns us, the actions of our ancestors resemble those of the ancient rather than the later Romans: tho our government be not the same with theirs in form, yet it is in principle; and if we are not degenerated, we shall rather desire to imitate the Romans in the time of their virtue, glory, power and felicity, than what they were, in that of their slavery, vice, shame and misery. In the best times, when *the laws were more powerful than the commands of men*,[16] fraud was accounted a crime so detestable as not to be imputed to any but slaves; and he who had sought a power above the law under colour of interpreting it, would have been exposed to scorn, or greater punishments, if any can be greater than the just scorn of the best men. And as neither the Romans, nor any people of the world, have better defended their liberties than the English nation when any attempt has been made to oppress them by force, they ought to be no less careful to preserve them from the more dangerous efforts of fraud and falsehood.

Our ancestors were certainly in a low condition in the time of William the First: Many of their best men had perished in the civil wars or with Harold: their valour was great, but rough, and void of skill: The Normans

---

[16] [Livy, *History of Rome*, bk. 2, ch. 1.]

by frequent expeditions into France, Italy and Spain, had added subtlety to the boisterous violence of their native climate: William had engaged his faith, but broke it, and turned the power with which he was entrusted to the ruin of those that had trusted him. He destroy'd many worthy men, carried others into Normandy, and thought himself master of all. He was crafty, bold, and elated with victory; but the resolution of a brave people was invincible. When their laws and liberties were in danger, they resolved to die or to defend them, and made him see he could no otherwise preserve his crown and life than by the performance of his oath, and accomplishing the ends of his election. They neither took him to be the giver or interpreter of their laws, and would not suffer him to violate those of their ancestors. In this way they always continued; and tho perhaps they might want skill to fall upon the surest and easiest means of restraining the lusts of princes, yet they maintained their rights so well, that the wisest princes seldom invaded them; and the success of those who were so foolish to attempt it was such, as may justly deter others from following their unprosperous examples. We have had no king since William the First more hardy than Henry the 8th, and yet he so entirely acknowledged the power of making, changing and repealing laws to be in the parliament, as never to attempt any extraordinary thing otherwise than by their authority. It was not he, but the parliament, that dissolved the abbies: He did not take their lands to himself, but receiv'd what the parliament thought fit to give him: He did not reject the supremacy of the pope, nor assume any other power in spiritual matters, than the parliament conferred upon him. The intricacies of his marriages, and the legitimation of his children was settled by the same power: at least one of his daughters could not inherit the crown upon any other title; they who gave him a power to dispose of the crown by will might have given it to his groom; and he was too haughty to ask it from them, if he had it in himself, which he must have had, if the laws and judicatures had been in his hand.

This is farther evidenced by what passed in the Tower between Sir Thomas More and Rich the king's solicitor, who asking, if it would not be treason to oppose Richard Rich, if the parliament should make him king, More said that was *casus levis*;[17] for the parliament could make and depose kings as they thought fit; and then (as more conducing to his own case) asked Rich if the parliament should enact *that God should not be God*, whether such as did not submit should be esteemed traitors?[18] 'Tis evident

---

[17] [An easy case.]

[18] Herbert's Hen. 8. [Lord Edward Herbert, *Life and Reign of King Henry the Eighth* (London, 1649), (the year 1535).]

that a man of the acuteness and learning of Sir Tho. More would not have made use of such an argument to avoid the necessity of obeying what the parliament had ordained, by shewing his case to be of a nature far above the power of man, unless it had been confessed by all men that the parliament could do whatsoever lay within the reach of human power. This may be enough to prove that the king cannot have a power over the law; and if he has it not, the power of interpreting laws is absurdly attributed to him, since it is founded upon a supposition that he can make them, which is false.

SECTION 27

Magna Charta was not the Original, but a Declaration of the English Liberties. The King's Power is not restrained, but created by that and other Laws; and the Nation that made them can only correct the defects of them.

I AGREE with our author that *Magna Charta was not made to restrain the absolute authority;*[1] for no such thing was in being or pretended (the folly of such visions seeming to have been reserved to complete the misfortunes and ignominy of our age) but it was to assert the native and original liberties of our nation by the confession of the king then being, that neither he nor his successors should any way encroach upon them: and it cannot be said that the power of kings is diminished by that or any other law; for as they are kings only by law, the law may confer power upon one in particular, or upon him and his successors, but can take nothing from them, because they have nothing except what is given to them. But as that which the law gives, is given by those who make the law, they only are capable of judging, whether he to whom they gave it, do well or ill employ that power, and consequently are only fit to correct the defects that may be found in it. Therefore tho I should confess that faults may be found in many statutes, and that the whole body of them is greatly defective, it will not follow that the compendious way of referring all to the will of the king should be taken. But what defects

---

[1] [*Patriarcha*, ch. 28 ("The King Is Judge in All Causes. The King and His Council Anciently Determined Causes"), p. 110.]

soever may be in our law, the disease is not so great to require extreme remedies, and we may hope for a cheaper cure. Our law may possibly have given away too much from the people, and provided only insufficient defences of our liberties against the encroachments of bad princes; but none who are not in judgment and honesty like to our author, can propose for a remedy to the evils that proceed from the error of giving too much, the resignation of all the rest to them. Whatever he says, 'tis evident that he knows this to be true, when, tho he denies that the power of kings can be restrained by acts of parliament, he endeavours to take advantage of such clauses as were either fraudulently inserted by the king's officers, who till the days of Henry the fifth for the most part had the penning of the publick acts, or through negligence did not fully explain the intentions of the legislators; which would be to no purpose if all were put into the hands of the king by a general law from God, that no human power could diminish or enlarge; and as his last shift would obliquely put all into the power of the king by giving him a right of interpreting the law, and judging such cases as are not clearly decided; which would be equally impertinent, if he had openly and plainly a right of determining all things according to his will.

But what defects soever may be in any statutes, no great inconveniences could probably ensue, if that for annual parliaments was observed, as of right it ought to be. Nothing is more unlikely, than that a great assembly of eminent and chosen men should make a law evidently destructive to their own designs; and no mischief that might emerge upon the discovery of a mistake, could be so extreme that the cure might not be deferr'd till the meeting of the parliament, or at least forty days (in which time the king may call one) if that which the law has fixed seem to be too long. If he fail of this, he performs not his trust; and he that would reward such a breach of it with a vast and uncontrollable power, may be justly thought equal in madness to our author, who by forbidding us to examine the titles of kings, and enjoining an entire veneration of the power, by what means soever obtained,[2] encourages the worst of men to murder the best of princes, with an assurance that if they prosper they shall enjoy all the honors and advantages that this world can afford.

Princes are not much more beholden to him for the haughty language he puts into their mouths, it having been observed that the worst are always most ready to use it; and their extravagances having been often chastised by law, sufficiently proves, that their power is not derived from a higher original than the law of their own countries.

[2] [*Patriarcha*, ch. 26, p. 106.]

If it were true, that the answer sometimes given by kings to bills presented for their assent, did, as our author says, amount to a denial,[3] it could only shew that they have a negative voice upon that which is agreed by the parliament, and is far from a power of acting by themselves, being only a check upon the other parts of the government. But indeed it is no more than an elusion; and he that does by art obliquely elude, confesses he has not a right absolutely to refuse. 'Tis natural to kings, especially to the worst, to screw up their authority to the height; and nothing can more evidently prove the defect of it, than the necessity of having recourse to such pitiful evasions, when they are unwilling to do that which is required. But if I should grant that the words import a denial, and that (notwithstanding those of the coronation oath, *quas vulgus elegerit*[4]) they might deny; no more could be inferred from thence, than that they are entrusted with a power equal in that point, to that of either house, and cannot be supreme in our author's sense, unless there were in the same state at the same time three distinct supreme and absolute powers, which is absurd.

His cases relating to the proceedings of the Star-Chamber and Council-Table, do only prove that some kings have encroached upon the rights of the nation, and been suffer'd till their excesses growing to be extreme, they turn'd to the ruin of the ministers that advised them, and sometimes of the kings themselves. But the jurisdiction of the Council having been regulated by the statute of the 17 Car. I.[5] and the Star-Chamber more lately abolished, they are nothing to our dispute.

Such as our author usually impute to treason and rebellion the changes that upon such occasions have ensued; but all impartial men do not only justify them, but acknowledge that all the crowns of Europe are at this day enjoy'd by no other title than such acts solemnly performed by the respective nations, who either disliking the person that pretended to the crown (tho next in blood) or the government of the present possessor, have thought fit to prefer another person or family. They also say, that as no government can be so perfect but some defect may be originally in it, or afterwards introduced, none can subsist unless they be from time to time reduced to their first integrity, by such an exertion of the power of those for whose sake they were instituted, as may plainly shew them to be subject to no power under heaven, but may do whatever appears to be for their own good. And as the safety of all nations consists in

---

[3] [*Patriarcha*, ch. 31, pp. 119–120.]   [5] [Actually, 16 Charles I.]

[4] [(Laws) which the common people shall have chosen.]

rightly placing and measuring this power, such have been found always to prosper who have given it to those from whom usurpations were least to be feared, who have been least subject to be awed, cheated or corrupted; and who having the greatest interest in the nation, were most concerned to preserve its power, liberty and welfare. This is the greatest trust that can be reposed in men. This power was by the Spartans given to the ephori and the senate of twenty eight; in Venice to that which they call *Concilio de Pregadi;* in Germany, Spain, France, Sweden, Denmark, Poland, Hungary, Bohemia, Scotland, England, and generally all the nations that have lived under the Gothick polity, it has been in their general assemblies, under the names of diets, cortes, parliaments, senates, and the like. But in what hands soever it is, the power of making, abrogating, changing, correcting and interpreting laws, has been in the same; kings have been rejected or deposed; the succession of the crown settled, regulated, or changed: and I defy any man to shew me one king amongst all the nations abovementioned, that has any right to the crown he wears, unless such acts are good.

If this power be not well placed, or rightly proportioned to that which is given to other magistrates, the state must necessarily fall into great disorders, or the most violent and dangerous means must be frequently used to preserve their liberty. Sparta and Venice have rarely been put to that trouble, because the senates were so much above the kings and dukes in power, that they could without difficulty bring them to reason. The Gothick kings in Spain never ventur'd to dispute with the nobility; and Witiza and Rodrigo exposed the kingdom as a prey to the Moors, rather by weakening it through the neglect of military discipline, joined to their own ignorance and cowardice, and by evil example bringing the youth to resemble them in lewdness and baseness, than by establishing in themselves a power above the law. But in England our ancestors who seem to have had some such thing in their eye, as balancing the powers, by a fatal mistake placed usually so much in the hands of the king, that whensoever he happened to be bad, his extravagances could not be repress'd without great danger. And as this has in several ages cost the nation a vast proportion of generous blood, so 'tis the cause of our present difficulties, and threatens us with more, but can never deprive us of the rights we inherit from our fathers.

SECTION 28

The English Nation has always been governed by itself or its Representatives.

HAVING proved that the people of England have never acknowledged any other human law than their own, and that our parliaments having the power of making and abrogating laws, they only can interpret them and decide hard cases, it plainly appears there can be no truth in our author's assertion, that *the king is the author, corrector and moderator of both statute and common law:* and nothing can be more frivolous than what he adds, that *neither of them can be a diminution of that natural power which kings have over their people as fathers;*[1] in as much as the differences between paternal and monarchical power (as he asserts it) are vast and irreconcilable in principle and practice, as I have proved at large in the former parts of this work.

But lest we should be too proud of the honour he is pleased to do to our parliaments by making use of their authority, he says, *We are first to remember that till the conquest* (which name for the glory of our nation he gives to the coming in of the Normans) *there could be no parliament assembled of the general states, because we cannot learn that until those days it was entirely united in one.* Secondly he doubts, *Whether the parliament in the time of the Saxons were composed of the nobility and clergy, or whether the commons were also called;* but concludes, *there could be no knights of any shires, because there were no shires.* Thirdly, *That Henry the first caused the commons first to assemble knights and burgesses of their own chusing;* and would make this to be an act of grace and favour from that king: but adds, that *it had been more for the honour of parliaments, if a king whose title to the crown had been better, had been the author of the form of it.*[2]

In answer to the first, I do not think myself obliged to insist upon the name or form of the parliament; for the authority of a magistracy proceeds not from the number of years that it has continued, but the rectitude of the institution, and the authority of those that instituted it. The power of Saul, David and Jeroboam, was the same with that which belonged to the last kings of Israel and Judah. The authority of the Roman consuls, dictators, praetors and tribunes, was the same as soon as it was established; was as legal and just as that of the kings of Denmark, which is said to

---

[1] [*Patriarcha*, ch. 28, p. 113.]

[2] [*Patriarcha*, ch. 30 ("The People, When First Called to Parliament. The Liberties of Parliaments Not from Nature, but from the Grace of Princes"), pp. 114, 115, 118.]

have continued above three thousand years. For as time can make nothing lawful or just, that is not so of itself (tho men are unwilling to change that which has pleased their ancestors, unless they discover great inconveniences in it) that which a people does rightly establish for their own good, is of as much force the first day, as continuance can ever give to it: and therefore in matters of the greatest importance, wise and good men do not so much inquire what has been, as what is good and ought to be; for that which of itself is evil, by continuance is made worse, and upon the first opportunity is justly to be abolished. But if that liberty in which God created man, can receive any strength from continuance, and the rights of Englishmen can be render'd more unquestionable by prescription, I say that the nations whose rights we inherit, have ever enjoy'd the liberties we claim, and always exercised them in governing themselves popularly, or by such representatives as have been instituted by themselves, from the time they were first known in the world.

The Britains and Saxons lay so long hid in the obscurity that accompanies barbarism, that 'tis in vain to seek what was done by either in any writers more ancient than Caesar and Tacitus. The first describes the Britains to have been a fierce people zealous for liberty, and so obstinately valiant in the defence of it, that tho they wanted skill, and were overpower'd by the Romans, their country could no otherwise be subdued, than by the slaughter of all the inhabitants that were able to bear arms. He calls them a free people, in as much as they were not like the Gauls, governed by laws made by the great men, but by the people. In his time they chose Cassivellaunus, and afterwards Caratacus, Arviragus, Galgacus, and others to command them in their wars, but they retain'd the government in themselves. That no force might be put upon them, they met arm'd in their general assemblies; and tho the smaller matters were left to the determination of the chief men chosen by themselves for that purpose, they reserved the most important (amongst which the chusing of those men was one) to themselves. When the Romans had brought them low, they set up certain kings to govern such as were within their territories:[3] but those who defended themselves by the natural strength of their situation, or retired into the north, or the islands, were still governed by their own customs, and were never acquainted with domestick or foreign slavery. The Saxons, from whom we chiefly derive our original and manners, were no less lovers of liberty, and better understood the ways of defending it. They were certainly the

[3] Inter instrumenta servitutis reges habuere. C. Tacit. ["They had kings among their instruments of (keeping others in) servitude." Tacitus, *Life of Agricola*, ch. 14.]

most powerful and valiant people of Germany; and what the Germans performed under Ariovistus, Arminius and Maroboduus, shews both their force and their temper. If ever fear enter'd into the heart of Caesar, it seems to have been when he was to deal with Ariovistus. The advantages that the brave Germanicus obtained against Arminius, were at least thought equal to the greatest victories that had been gain'd by any Roman captain; because these nations fought not for riches, or any instruments of luxury and pleasure, which they despised, but for liberty. This was the principle in which they lived, as appears by their words and actions; so that Arminius when his brother Flavius, who served the Romans, boasted of the increase of his pay, and the marks of honour he had received, in scorn call'd them the *rewards of the vilest servitude;*[4] but when he himself endeavour'd to usurp a power over the liberty of his country which he had so bravely defended, he was killed by those he would have oppress'd. Tacitus farther describing the nature of the Germans, shews that the Romans had run greater hazards from them than from the Samnites, Carthaginians and Parthians, and attributes their bravery to the liberty they enjoyed;[5] for they are, says he, neither exhausted by tributes, nor vexed by publicans:[6] and lest this liberty should be violated, *the chief men consult about things of lesser moment; but the most important matters are determined by all.*[7] Whoever would know the opinion of that wise author concerning the German liberty, may read his excellent treatise concerning their manners and customs; but I presume this may be enough to prove that they lived free under such magistrates as they chose, regulated by such laws as they made, and retained the principal powers of the government in their general or particular councils. Their kings and princes had no other power than was conferred upon them by these assemblies, who having all in themselves could receive nothing from them, who had nothing to give.[8]

---

[4] Vilis servitii praemia. Tacit. [Tacitus, *Annals*, bk. 2, ch. 9.]

[5] Quippe gravior est Arsacis regno Germanorum libertas. ["The liberty of the Germans is stronger than the kingdom of an Arsaces." The Arsaces family ruled Parthia, Rome's strongest enemy in the Middle East. Tacitus contrasts Western freedom with Eastern despotism, *Germania*, ch. 37.]

[6] Exempti oneribus & collationibus, & tantum in usum praeliorum sepositi, velut tela & arma bellis reservantur. ["(The Batavians),

exempted from taxes and tributes, and set aside for use in battles only, are reserved for war, like weapons and arms." Ibid., ch. 29.]

[7] De minoribus principes consultant, de maioribus omnes. C. Tacit. de mor. Germ. [Ibid., ch. 11.]

[8] Ut turbae placuit considunt armati, silentium per sacerdotes, quibus tum coercendi jus est, imperatur. Mox rex vel princeps prout aetas cuique, prout nobilitas, prout decus bellorum, prout facundia est, audiuntur, auctoritate suadendi, magis quam ju-

'Tis as easily proved that the Saxons or Angles, from whom we descend, were eminent among those, whose power, virtue, and love to liberty the abovementioned historian so highly extols, in as much as besides what he says in general of the Saxons, he names the Angles; describes their habitation near the Elbe, and their religious worship of the goddess Erthum, or the earth, celebrated in an island lying in the mouth of that river, thought to be Heligoland; in resemblance of which a small one lying over against Berwick, is called Holy Island. If they were free in their own country, they must be so when they came hither. The manner of their coming shews they were more likely to impose, than submit to slavery; and if they had not the name of parliament, it was because they did not speak French; or, not being yet joined with the Normans, they had not thought fit to put their affairs into that method: but having the root of power and liberty in themselves, they could not but have a right of establishing the one in such a form as best pleased them, for the preservation of the other.

This being, as I suppose, undeniable, it imports not whether the assemblies in which the supreme power of each nation did reside, were frequent or rare; composed of many or few persons, sitting altogether in one place, or in more; what name they had; or whether every free man did meet and vote in his own person, or a few were delegated by many. For they who have a right inherent in themselves, may resign it to others; and they who can give a power to others, may exercise it themselves, unless they recede from it by their own act; for it is only matter of convenience, of which they alone can be the judges, because 'tis for themselves only that they judge. If this were not so, it would be very prejudicial to kings: for 'tis certain that Cassivellaunus, Caratacus, Arviragus, Galgacus, Hengist, Horsa, and others amongst the Britains and Saxons, what name soever may have been abusively given to them, were only temporary magistrates chosen upon occasion of present wars; but we know of no time in which the Britains had not their great council to determine their most important affairs: and the Saxons in their own country had their councils, where all were present, and in which Tacitus assures us they dispatched their greatest business. These were the same

---

bendi potestate. Si displicuit sententia, fremitu aspernantur; si placuit, frameas concutiunt, &c. Ibid. ["When the crowd resolves, they assemble, armed; silence is ordered by the priests, who then have the right to compel it. Next a king or leading man is heard, in order of age, nobility, glory in battle, or eloquence, with the authority that comes from his counsel, rather than from his power to order them. If they dislike the advice, they spurn it with a groan; if they like it, they clash their spears together."]

with the micklegemotes which they afterwards held here, and might have been called by the same name, if Tacitus had spoken Dutch.[9]

If a people therefore have not a power to create at any time a magistracy which they had not before, none could be created at all, for no magistracy is eternal: And if for the validity of the constitution it be necessary, that the beginning must be unknown, or that no other could have been before it, the monarchy amongst us cannot be established upon any right; for tho our ancestors had their councils and magistrates, as well here as in Germany, they had no monarchs. This appears plainly by the testimony of Caesar and Tacitus; and our later histories show, that as soon as the Saxons came into this country, they had their micklegemotes, which were general assemblies of the noble and free men, who had in themselves the power of the nation: and tho when they increased in numbers, they erected seven kingdoms, yet every one retained the same usage within itself. These assemblies were evidently the same in power with our parliaments; and tho they differ'd in name or form, it matters not, for they who could act in the one, could not but have a power of instituting the other; that is, the same people that could meet together in their own persons, and according to their own pleasure order all matters relating to themselves, whilst three or four counties only were under one government, and their numbers were not so great, or their habitation so far distant, that they might not meet altogether without inconvenience, with the same right might depute others to represent them, when being joined in one, no place was capable of receiving so great a multitude, and that the frontiers would have been exposed to the danger of foreign invasions, if any such thing had been practiced.

But if the authority of parliaments, for many ages representing the whole nation, were less to be valued (as our author insinuates) because they could not represent the whole, when it was not joined in one body, that of kings must come to nothing; for there could be no one king over all, when the nation was divided into seven distinct governments: And 'tis most absurd to think that the nation, which had seven great councils, or micklegemotes, at the same time they had seven kingdoms, could not as well unite the seven councils as the seven kingdoms into one. 'Tis to as little purpose to say, that the nation did not unite itself, but the several parcels came to be inherited by one; for that one could inherit no more from the others than what they had; and the seven being only magistrates set up by the micklegemotes, *&c.* the one must be so also. And 'tis neither reasonable to imagine, nor possible to prove, that a fierce nation,

[9] [That is, German.]

jealous of liberty, and who had obstinately defended it in Germany against all invaders, should conquer this country to enslave themselves, and purchase nothing by their valour but that servitude which they abhorred; or be less free when they were united into one state, than they had been when they were divided into seven; and least of all, that one man could first subdue his own people, and then all the rest, when by endeavouring to subdue his own, he had broken the trust reposed in him, and lost the right conferred upon him, and without them had not power to subdue any. But as it is my fate almost ever to dissent from our author, I affirm, that the variety of government, which is observed to have been amongst the Saxons, who in some ages were divided, in others united; sometimes under captains, in other times under kings; sometimes meeting personally in the micklegemotes, sometimes by their delegates in the witenagemotes, does evidently testify, that they ordered all things according to their own pleasure; which being the utmost act of liberty, it remained inviolable under all those changes, as we have already proved by the confession of Offa, Ine, Alfred, Canute, Edward, and other particular, as well as universal kings: And we may be sure those of the Norman race can have no more power, since they came in by the same way, and swore to govern by the same laws.

2. I am no way concerned in our author's doubt, *Whether parliaments did in those days consist of nobility and clergy; or whether the commons were also called.* For if it were true, as he asserts, that according to the eternal law of God and nature, there can be no government in the world but that of an absolute monarch, whose sovereign majesty can be diminished by no law or custom, there could be no parliaments, or other magistracies, that did not derive their power and being from his will. But having proved that the Saxons had their general councils and assemblies when they had no kings; that by them kings were made, and the greatest affairs determined, whether they had kings or not; it can be of no importance, whether in one or more ages the commons had a part in the government, or not. For the same power that instituted a parliament without them, might, when they thought fit, receive them into it: or rather, if they who had the government in their hands, did, for reasons known to themselves, recede from the exercise of it, they might resume it when they pleased.

Nevertheless it may be worth our pains to enquire, what our author means by nobility. If such, as at this day by means of patents obtained for money, or by favour, without any regard to merit in the persons or their ancestors, are called dukes, marquesses, *&c.* I give him leave to impute as late and base an original to them as he pleases, without fearing that the rights of our nation can thereby be impaired; and am content, that if the king do not think fit to support the dignity of his own creatures, they may fall to the ground. But if by noblemen we are to understand such as have been ennobled by the virtues of their ancestors, manifested in services done to their country, I say, that all nations, amongst whom virtue has been esteemed, have had a great regard to them and their posterity: And tho kings, when they were made, have been intrusted by the Saxons, and other nations, with a power of ennobling those who by services render'd to their country might deserve that honor; yet the body of the nobility was more ancient than such; for it had been equally impossible to take kings (according to Tacitus) out of the nobility if there had been no nobility, as to take captains for their virtue if there had been no virtue;[10] and princes could not, without breach of that trust, confer honors upon those that did not deserve them; which is so true, that this practice was objected as the greatest crime against Vortigern, the last and the worst of the British kings:[11] and tho he might pretend (according to such cavils as are usual in our time) that the judgment of those matters was referred to him; yet the world judged of his crimes, and when he had render'd himself odious to God and men by them, he perished in them, and brought destruction upon his country that had suffer'd them too long.

As among the Turks, and most of the Eastern tyrannies, there is no nobility, and no man has any considerable advantage above the common people, unless by the immediate favour of the prince; so in all the legal kingdoms of the North, the strength of the government has always been placed in the nobility; and no better defence has been found against the encroachments of ill kings, than by setting up an order of men, who by holding large territories, and having great numbers of tenants and dependents, might be able to restrain the exorbitances, that either the kings or the commons might run into. For this end Spain, Germany, France, Poland, Denmark, Sweden, Scotland and England, were almost wholly divided into lordships under several names, by which every

---

[10] Reges ex nobilitate, duces ex virtute sumere. [Tacitus, *Germania*, ch. 7.]

[11] Sublimato eo coepit lues omnium scelerum crescere: saeviebat scurrilis nequitia, odium veritatis, &c. ut vas omnium scelerum solus videretur Vortigernus; & quod maxime regiae honestati contrarium est, nobiles deprimens, & moribus & sanguine ignobiles extollens, Deo & hominibus efficitur odiosus. Mat. Westm. An. 446. ["When he had been raised (to the throne), the plague of all his crimes began to grow: there was such a raging of base worthlessness, hatred of the truth, etc., that Vortigern alone seemed the receptacle of all crimes; and what is most contrary to royal honor, namely, suppressing the nobles and exalting those who were ignoble both in manners and in birth, rendered him odious to God and men." Roger of Wendover, *Flowers of History* (the year 446).]

particular possessor owed allegiance (that is, such an obedience as the law requires) to the king, and he reciprocally swore to perform that which the same law exacted from him.

When these nations were converted to the Christian religion, they had a great veneration for the clergy; and not doubting that the men whom they esteemed holy, would be just, thought their liberties could not be better secured, than by joining those who had the direction of their consciences, to the noblemen who had the command of their forces. This succeeded so well (in relation to the defence of the publick rights) that in all the forementioned states, the bishops, abbots, &c. were no less zealous or bold in defending the publick liberty, than the best and greatest of the lords: And if it were true, that things being thus established, the commons did neither personally, nor by their representatives, enter into the general assemblies, it could be of no advantage to kings; for such a power as is above-mentioned, is equally inconsistent with the absolute sovereignty of kings, if placed in the nobility and clergy, as if the commons had a part. If the king has all, no other man, nor number of men can have any. If the nobility and clergy have the power, the commons may have their share also. But I affirm, that those whom we now call commons, have always had a part in the government, and their place in the councils that managed it; for if there was a distinction, it must have been by patent, birth, or tenure.

As for patents, we know they began long after the coming of the Normans, and those that now have them cannot pretend to any advantage on account of birth or tenure, beyond many of those who have them not. Nay, besides the several branches of the families that now enjoy the most ancient honors, which consequently are as noble as they, and some of them of the elder houses, we know many that are now called commoners, who in antiquity and eminency are no way inferior to the chief of the titular nobility: and nothing can be more absurd, than to give a prerogative of birth to Cr-v-n, T-ft-n, H-de, B-nn-t, Osb-rn,[12] and others, before the Cliftons, Hampdens, Courtneys, Pelhams, St. Johns, Baintons, Wilbrahams, Hungerfords, and many others.[13] And if the tenures of their estates be consider'd, they have the same, and as ancient as any of those who go under the names of duke, or marquess. I forbear to mention the

[12] [William, Earl of Craven; Laurence Hyde, Earl of Rochester; Henry Bennet, Earl of Arlington; and Sir Thomas Osborne, Earl of Danby, were leading ministers under Charles II. Nicholas Tufton, Earl of Thanet, supported Charles before the Restoration and was imprisoned for it in 1655.]

[13] [These were supporters of the rights of Parliament against royal prerogative during the Civil War and Commonwealth. The two most important were John Hampden and Oliver St. John, leading parliamentary opponents of Charles I.]

sordid ways of attaining to titles in our days; but whoever will take the pains to examine them, shall find that they rather defile than ennoble the possessors. And whereas men are truly ennobled only by virtue, and respect is due to such as are descended from those who have bravely serv'd their country, because it is presumed (till they shew the contrary) that they will resemble their ancestors, these modern courtiers, by their names and titles, frequently oblige us to call to mind such things as are not to be mentioned without blushing. Whatever the ancient noblemen of England were, we are sure they were not such as these. And tho it should be confess'd that no others than dukes, marquesses, earls, viscounts, and barons, had their places in the councils mentioned by Caesar and Tacitus, or in the great assemblies of the Saxons, it could be of no advantage to such as now are called by those names. They were the titles of offices conferred upon those, who did and could best conduct the people in time of war, give counsel to the king, administer justice, and perform other publick duties; but were never made hereditary except by abuse; much less were they sold for money, or given as recompences of the vilest services. If the ancient order be totally inverted, and the ends of its institution perverted, they who from thence pretend to be distinguished from other men, must build their claim upon something very different from antiquity.

This being sufficient (if I mistake not) to make it appear, that the ancient councils of our nation did not consist of such as we now call noblemen, it may be worth our pains to examine, of what sort of men they did consist: And tho I cannot much rely upon the credit of Camden, which he has forfeited by a great number of untruths, I will begin with him, because he is cited by our author.[14] If we will believe him, *That which the Saxons called witenagemote, we may justly name parliament, which has the supreme and most sacred authority of making, abrogating and interpreting laws, and generally of all things relating to the safety of the commonwealth.*[15] This witenagemote was, according to William of Malmesbury, *The general meeting of the senate and people;*[16] and Sir Harry Spelman calls it, *The general council of the clergy and people.*[17] In the assembly at Calchuth it was decreed

---

[14] [*Patriarcha*, ch. 29, p. 113.]

[15] Quod Saxones olim wittenagemot, parliamentum & pananglicum recte dici possit, summamque et sacrosanctam habet autoritatem in legibus ferendis, antiquandis, conformandis, interpretandis, & in omnibus quae ad reipublicae salutem spectant. Brit. fol. 63. [William Camden, *Britannia* (1586;

repub. 1806; repr. Adler's Foreign Books), vol. 1, p. cxcv.]

[16] Generalis senatus & populi conventus. Malms. [William of Malmesbury, *Chronicle of the Kings of England*, bk. 3, p. 271.]

[17] Commune concilium tam cleri quam populi. Spelm. [Spelman, *Concilia, decreta, leges, constitutiones in re ecclesiarum orbis Britannici* (the year 605, Council of Canterbury).]

by the archbishops, bishops, abbots, dukes, senators, and the people of the land (*populo terrae*) that *the kings should be elected by the priests and elders of the people.*[18] By these Offa, Ine, and others, were made kings; and Alfred in his will acknowledged his crown from them.[19] Edgar was elected by all the people, and not long after deposed by them, and again restored in a general assembly.[20] These things being sometimes said to be done by the assent of the barons of the kingdom, Camden says, that *under the name of the baronage, all the orders of the kingdom are in a manner comprehended;*[21] and it cannot be otherwise understood, if we consider that those called noblemen, or the nobility of England, are often by the historians said to be (*infinita multitudo*) an infinite multitude.

If any man ask how the nobility came to be so numerous; I answer, that the Northern nations, who were perpetually in arms, put a high esteem upon military valour; sought by conquest to acquire better countries than their own; valu'd themselves according to the numbers of men they could bring into the field; and to distinguish them from villains, called those noblemen, who nobly defended and enlarged their dominions by war; and for a reward of their services, in the division of lands gained by conquest, they distributed to them freeholds, under the obligation of continuing the same service to their country. This appears by the name of knight's service, a knight being no more than a soldier, and a knight's fee no more than was sufficient to maintain one. 'Tis plain, that knighthood was always esteemed nobility; so that no man, of what quality soever, thought a knight inferior to him, and those of the highest birth could not act as noblemen till they were knighted. Among the Goths in Spain, the cutting off the hair (which being long was the mark of knighthood) was accounted [as] degrading, and looked upon to be so great a mark of infamy, that he who had suffer'd it, could never bear any honor or office in the commonwealth; and there was no dignity so high, but every knight was capable of it. There was no distinction of men above it, and even to this day *baron*, or *varon*, in their language, signifies no more than *vir* in Latin, which is not properly given to any man unless he be free. The like was in France, till the coming in of the third race of kings, in which time the 12 peers (of whom 6 only were laymen) were raised to a higher

---

[18] Ut reges a sacerdotibus & senioribus populi eligantur. [Ibid., Council of Calchuth, 787.]

[19] Quam Deus & principes cum senioribus populi misericorditer & benigne dederunt. ["Which God and the chiefs and elders of the people have kindly and mercifully given." Asser, *Life of Alfred*.]

[20] Coram omni multitudine populi Anglorum. [Spelman, *Concilia* (the year 969).]

[21] Nomine Baronagii omnes quodam modo regni ordines continentur. Camd. [William Camden, *Britannia*, vol. 1, p. cxcv.]

dignity, and the commands annexed made hereditary; but the honour of knighthood was thereby no way diminished. Tho there were dukes, earls, marquesses and barons in the time of Froissart, yet he usually calls them knights: And Philippe de Comines, speaking of the most eminent men of his time, calls them good, wise or valiant knights. Even to this day the name of gentleman comprehends all that is raised above the common people; Henry the fourth usually called himself the first gentleman in France; and 'tis an ordinary phrase among them, when they speak of a gentleman of good birth, to say, *il est noble comme le roy; He is as noble as the king*. In their general assembly of estates, the Chamber of the Noblesse, which is one of three, is composed of the deputies sent by the gentry of every province; and in the inquiry made about the year 1668 concerning nobility, no notice was taken of such as had assumed the titles of earl, marquess, viscount, or baron, but only of those who called themselves gentlemen; and if they could prove that name to belong to them, they were left to use the other titles as they pleased. When duels were in fashion (as all know they were lately) no man except the princes of the blood, and marshals of France, could with honour refuse a challenge from any gentleman: The first, because it was thought unfit, that he who might be king, should fight with a subject to the danger of the commonwealth, which might by that means be deprived of its head: The others being by their office commanders of the nobility, and judges of all the controversies relating to honour that happen amongst them, cannot reasonably be brought into private contests with any. In Denmark, *nobleman* and *gentleman* is the same thing; and till the year 1660, they had the principal part of the government in their hands. When Charles Gustavus, king of Sweden, invaded Poland in the year 1655, 'tis said, that there were above three hundred thousand gentlemen in arms to resist him. This is the nobility of that country, kings are chosen by them: Every one of them will say, as in France, *He is noble as the king*. The last king was a private man among them, not thought to have had more than four hundred pounds a year.[22] He who now reigns was not at all above him in birth or estate, till he had raised himself by great services done for his country in many wars; and there was not one gentleman in the nation who might not have been chosen as well as he, if it had pleased the assembly that did it.

This being the nobility of the Northern nations, and the true baronage of England, 'tis no wonder that they were called *nobiles;* the most eminent

[22] [Michael (Korybut) Wisniowiecki (1669–73). "He who now reigns" in the sentence that follows was John III Sobieski.]

among them *magnates, principes, proceres;* and so numerous that they were esteemed to be *multitudo infinita.* One place was hardly able to contain them; and the inconveniences of calling them all together appeared to be so great, that they in time chose rather to meet by representatives, than every one in his own person. The power therefore remaining in them, it matters not what method they observed in the execution. They who had the substance in their hands, might give it what form they pleased. Our author sufficiently manifests his ignorance, in saying there could be no knights of the shires in the time of the Saxons, because there were no shires;[23] for the very word is Saxon, and we find the names of Berkshire, Wiltshire, Devonshire, Dorsetshire, and others most frequently in the writings of those times; and dukes, earls, thanes or aldermen, appointed to command the forces, and look to the distribution of justice in them. Selden cites Ingulph for saying, that *Alfred was the first that changed the provinces,* &c. *into counties:* but refutes him, and proves that the distinction of the land into shires or counties (for shire signified no more than the share or part committed to the care of the earl or *comes*) was far more ancient.[24] Whether the first divisions by the Saxons were greater or lesser than the shires or counties now are, is nothing to the question: they who made them to be as they were, could have made them greater or lesser as they pleased. And whether they did immediately, or some ages after that distinction, cease to come to their great assemblies, and rather chuse to send their deputies, or, whether such deputies were chosen by counties, cities and boroughs, as in our days, or in any other manner, can be of no advantage or prejudice to the cause that I maintain. If the power of the nation, when it was divided into seven kingdoms, or united under one, did reside in the micklegemotes or witenagemotes; if these consisted of the nobility and people, who were sometimes so numerous that no one place could well contain them; and if the preference given to the chief among them, was on account of the offices they executed, either in relation to war or justice, which no man can deny, I have as much as serves for my purpose. 'Tis indifferent to me, whether they were called earls, dukes, aldermen, herotoghs or thanes; for 'tis certain that the titular nobility now in mode amongst us has no resemblance to this ancient nobility of England. The novelty therefore is on the other side, and that of the worst sort; because by giving the name of noblemen (which anciently belonged to such as had the greatest interests in nations, and were the supporters of their liberty) to court-creatures, who often have

[23] [*Patriarcha,* ch. 30, p. 115.]

[24] Selden's Tit. of Hon. p. 2. c. 5. [Selden, *Titles of Honour,* pt. 2, ch. 5, p. 509.]

none, and either acquire their honours by money, or are preferr'd for servile and sometimes impure services render'd to the person that reigns, or else for mischiefs done to their country, the constitution has been wholly inverted, and the trust reposed in the kings (who in some measure had the disposal of offices and honours) misemploy'd. This is farther aggravated by appropriating the name of noblemen solely to them; whereas the nation having been anciently divided only into freemen or noblemen (who were the same) and villains; the first were, as Tacitus says of their ancestors the Germans, *exempted from burdens and contributions, and reserved like arms for the uses of war*,[25] whilst the others were little better than slaves, appointed to cultivate the lands, or to other servile offices. And I leave any reasonable man to judge, whether the latter condition be that of those we now call commoners. Nevertheless, he that will believe the title of noblemen still to belong to those only who are so by patent, may guess how well our wars would be managed if they were left solely to such as are so by that title. If this be approved, his majesty may do well with his hundred and fifty noblemen, eminent in valour and military experience as they are known to be, to make such wars as may fall upon him, and leave the despised commons under the name of villains, to provide for themselves if the success do not answer his expectations. But if the commons are as free as the nobles, many of them in birth equal to the patentees, in estate superior to most of them; and that it is not only expected they should assist him in wars with their persons and purses, but acknowledged by all, that the strength and virtue of the nation is in them, it must be confess'd, that they are true noblemen of England, and that all the privileges anciently enjoy'd by such, must necessarily belong to them, since they perform the offices to which they were annexed. This shews how the nobility were justly said to be almost infinite in number, so that no one place was able to contain them. The Saxon armies that came over into this country to a wholesome and generative climate, might well increase in four or five ages to those vast numbers, as the Franks, Goths and others had done in Spain, France, Italy, and other parts: and when they were grown so numerous, they found themselves necessarily obliged to put the power into the hands of representatives chosen by themselves, which they had before exercised in their own persons. But these two ways differing rather in form than essentially, the one tending to democracy, the other to aristocracy, they are equally opposite to the absolute dominion of one man reigning for himself, and governing the nation as his patrimony; and equally assert the rights of the people to put

---

[25] Exempti oneribus & collationibus, & tantum in usum praeliorum repositi, veluti tela & arma bellis reservantur. Corn. Tacit. de morib. Germ. [Tacitus, *Germania*, ch. 29.]

the government into such a form as best pleases themselves. This was suitable to what they had practised in their own country; *De minoribus consultant principes, de majoribus omnes.*[26] Nay, even these *smaller matters* cannot be said properly to relate to the king; for he is but one, and the word *principes* is in the plural number, and can only signify such principal men, as the same author says were chosen by the general assemblies to do justice, *&c.* and to each of them one hundred *comites* joined, not only to give advice, but authority to their actions.

The word *omnes* spoken by a Roman, must likewise be understood as it was used by them, and imports all the citizens, or such as made up the body of the commonwealth. If he had spoken of Rome or Athens whilst they remained free, he must have used the same word (because all those of whom the city consisted had votes) how great soever the number of slaves or strangers might have been. The Spartans are rightly said to have gained, lost and recovered the lordship or principality of Greece. They were all lords in relation to their helots, and so were the Dorians in relation to that sort of men, which under several names they kept, as the Saxons did their villains, for the performance of the offices which they thought too mean for those who were ennobled by liberty, and the use of arms, by which the commonwealth was defended and enlarged. Tho the Romans scorned to give the title of lord to those who had usurped a power over their lives and fortunes; yet every one of them was a lord in relation to his own servants, and altogether are often called *lords of the world:*[27] the like is seen almost everywhere. The government of Venice having continued for many ages in the same families, has ennobled them all. No phrase is more common in Switzerland, than *the lords of Bern,* or *the lords of Zurich* and other places, tho perhaps there is not a man amongst them who pretends to be a gentleman, according to the modern sense put upon that word. The states of the United Provinces are called high and mighty lords, and the same title is given to each of them in particular. Nay, the word *Herr,* which signifies lord both in high and low Dutch, is as common as *monsieur* in France, *signor* in Italy, or *señor* in Spain; and is given to everyone who is not of a sordid condition, but especially to soldiers: and tho a common soldier be now a much meaner thing than it was anciently, no man speaking to a company of soldiers in Italian, uses any other stile than *signori soldati*; and the like is done in other languages. 'Tis not therefore to be thought strange, if the

---

[26] Tacit. de mor. Germ. ["The chief men (*principes*) consult about smaller matters, the whole people about greater ones." Ibid., ch. 11.]

[27] Romanos rerum dominos. Virg. [Virgil, *Aeneid*, bk. 1, li. 282.]

Saxons, who in their own country had scorned any other employment than that of the sword, should think themselves farther ennobled, when by their arms they had acquired a great and rich country, and driven out or subdued the former inhabitants. They might well distinguish themselves from the villains they brought with them, or the Britains they had enslaved. They might well be called *magnates, proceres regni, nobiles, Angliae nobilitas, barones;* and the assemblies of them justly called *concilium regni generale, universitas totius Angliae nobilium, universitas baronagii,*[28] according to the variety of times and other occurrences. We have such footsteps remaining of the name of baron, as plainly shew the signification of it. The barons of London and the Cinque Ports are known to be only the freemen of those places. In the petty court-barons, every man who may be of a jury is a baron. These are noblemen; for there are noble nations as well as noble men in nations. The Mamelukes accounted themselves to be all noble, tho born slaves; and when they had ennobled themselves by the use of arms, they look'd upon the noblest of the Egyptians as their slaves. Tertullian writing, not to some eminent men, but to the whole people of Carthage, calls them *antiquitate nobiles, nobilitate felices.*[29] Such were the Saxons, ennobled by a perpetual application to those exercises that belong to noblemen, and an abhorrence to anything that is vile and sordid.

Lest this should seem far fetch'd, to those who please themselves with cavilling, they are to know, that the same general councils are expressed by other authors in other words. They are called *the general council of the bishops, noblemen, counts, all the wise men, elders, and people of the whole kingdom,*[30] in the time of Ine. In that of Edward the elder, *the great council of the bishops, abbots, noblemen and people.*[31] William of Malmesbury calls them, *the general senate and assembly of the people.*[32] Sometimes they are in short called *clergy and people;* but all express the same power, neither received from, nor limitable by kings, who are always said to be chosen or made, and sometimes deposed by them. William the Norman found,

---

[28] [Magnates, chiefs of the kingdom, nobles, nobility of England, barons . . . general council of the kingdom, the whole of the nobility of all England, the whole of the baronage.]

[29] ["Noble for antiquity, fortunate in nobility." *De Pallio*, ch. 1, in *Ante-Nicene Fathers*, vol. 4, pp. 5–12.]

[30] Commune concilium episcoporum, procerum, comitum & omnium sapientum, seniorum & populorum totius regni. Bed. Eccl.

Hist. [Actually in *Laws of King Edward*, ch. 35, in William Lambarde, *Archaionomia*. Published in 1644 in a volume with Bede's *Ecclesiastical History*.]

[31] Magnum concilium episcoporum, abbatum, fidelium, procerum & populorum. [Matthew Parker, *De antiquitate britannicae ecclesiae* (London, 1572), ch. 19.]

[32] Senatum generalem et populi conventum. [William of Malmesbury, *Chronicle of the Kings of England*, bk. 3, p. 272.]

and left the nation in this condition: Henry the second, John and Henry third, who had nothing but what was conferred upon them by the same clergy and people, did so too. *Magna Charta* could give nothing to the people, who in themselves had all; and only reduced into a small volume the rights which the nation was resolved to maintain; brought the king to confess, they were perpetually inherent, and time out of mind enjoyed, and to swear that he would no way violate them; if he did, he was *ipso facto* excommunicated; and being thereby declared to be an execrable perjur'd person, they knew how to deal with him. This act has been confirmed by thirty parliaments; and the proceedings with kings, who have violated their oaths, as well before as after the time of Henry the third, which have been already mentioned, are sufficient to shew, that England has always been governed by itself, and never acknowledged any other lord than such as they thought fit to set up.

SECTION 29

The King was never Master of the Soil.

THOSE who without regard to truth, resolve to insist upon such points as they think may serve their designs, when they find it cannot be denied that the powers before mentioned have been exercised by the English and other nations, say, that they were the concessions of kings, who being masters of the soil, might bestow parcels upon some persons with such conditions as they pleased, retaining to themselves the supreme dominion of the whole: and having already, as they think, made them the fountains of honour, they proceed to make them also the fountains of property; and for proof of this allege, that all lands, tho held of mean lords, do by their tenures at last result upon the king, as the head from whom they are enjoyed. This might be of force if it were true: but matters of the highest importance requiring a most evident proof, we are to examine, first, if it be possible; and in the next place, if it be true.

1. For the first; No man can give what he has not. Whoever therefore will pretend that the king has bestowed this propriety, must prove that he had it in himself. I confess, that the kings of Spain and Portugal obtained from the pope grants of the territories they possessed in the West-Indies; and this might be of some strength, if the pope as vicar of Christ had an absolute dominion over the whole earth; but if that fail, the whole falls to the ground, and he is ridiculously liberal of that which

no way belongs to him. My business is not to dispute that point; but before it can have any influence upon our affairs, our kings are to prove, that they are lords of England upon the same title, or some other equivalent to it. When that is done, we shall know upon whom they have a dependence, and may at leisure consider, whether we ought to acknowledge, and submit to such a power, or give reasons for our refusal. But there being no such thing in our present case, their property must be grounded upon something else, or we may justly conclude they have none.

In order to this 'tis hardly worth the pains to search into the obscure remains of the British histories: For when the Romans deserted our island, they did not confer the right they had (whether more or less) upon any man, but left the enjoyment of it to the poor remainders of the nation, and their own established colonies, who were grown to be one people with the natives. The Saxons came under the conduct of Hengist and Horsa, who seem to have been sturdy pirates; but did not (that I can learn) bear any characters in their persons of the so much admired sovereign majesty, that should give them an absolute dominion or propriety, either in their own country, or any other they should set their feet upon. They came with about a hundred men; and chusing rather to serve Vortigern, than to depend upon what they could get by rapine at sea, lived upon a small proportion of land by him allotted to them.[1] Tho this seems to be but a slender encouragement, yet it was enough to invite many others to follow their example and fortune; so that their number increasing, the county of Kent was given to them, under the obligation of serving the Britains in their wars. Not long after, lands in Northumberland were bestowed upon another company of them with the same condition. This was all the title they had to what they enjoyed, till they treacherously killed four hundred and sixty,[2] or, as William of Malmesbury says, three hundred principal men of the British nobility,[3] and made Vortigern prisoner, who had been so much their benefactor, that he seems never to have deserved well but from them, and to have incens'd the Britains by the favour he shew'd them, as much as by the worst of his vices. And certainly actions of this kind, composed of falsehood and cruelty, can never create a right, in the opinion of any better men than Filmer and his disciples, who think that the power only is to be regarded, and not the means by which it is obtained. But tho it should be granted

---

[1] Mat. Westm. Flor. Hist. [Roger of Wendover, *Flowers of History* (the year 449), vol. 1, p. 5.]

[2] Ibid. [The year 461.]

[3] [William of Malmesbury, *Chronicle of the Kings of England*, bk. 1, ch. 1.]

that a right had been thus acquired, it must accrue to the nation, not to Hengist and Horsa. If such an acquisition be called a conquest, the benefit must belong to those that conquer'd. This was not the work of two men; and those who had been free at home, can never be thought to have left their own country, to fight as slaves for the glory and profit of two men in another. It cannot be said that their wants compelled them, for their leaders suffer'd the same, and could not be relieved but by their assistance; and whether their enterprize was good or bad, just or unjust, it was the same to all: No one man could have any right peculiar to himself, unless they who gained it, did confer it upon him: and 'tis no way probable, that they who in their own country had kept their princes within very narrow limits, as has been proved, should resign themselves, and all they had, as soon as they came hither. But we have already shewn, that they always continued most obstinate defenders of their liberty, and the government to which they had been accustomed; that they managed it by themselves, and acknowledged no other laws than their own. Nay, if they had made such a resignation of their right, as was necessary to create one in their leaders, it would be enough to overthrow the proposition; for 'tis not then the leader that gives to the people, but the people to the leader. If the people had not a right to give what they did give, none was conferred upon the receiver: if they had a right, he that should pretend to derive a benefit from thence, must prove the grant, that the nature and intention of it may appear.

2. To the second: If it be said that records testify all grants to have been originally from the king; I answer, that tho it were confessed (which I absolutely deny, and affirm that our rights and liberties are innate, inherent, and enjoy'd time out of mind before we had kings), it could be nothing to the question, which is concerning reason and justice; and if they are wanting, the defect can never be supplied by any matter of fact, tho never so clearly proved. Or if a right be pretended to be grounded upon a matter of fact, the thing to be proved is, that the people did really confer such a right upon the first, or some other kings: And if no such thing do appear, the proceedings of one or more kings as if they had it, can be of no value. But in the present case, no such grant is pretended to have been made, either to the first, or to any of the following kings; the right they had not their successors could not inherit, and consequently cannot have it, or at most no better title to it than that of usurpation.

But as they who enquire for truth ought not to deny or conceal anything, I may grant that manors, *&c.* were enjoyed by tenure from kings; but that will no way prejudice the cause I defend, nor signify more, than that the countries which the Saxons had acquired, were to be divided among them; and to avoid the quarrels that might arise, if every man took upon him to seize what he could, a certain method of making the distribution was necessarily to be fixed; and it was fit, that every man should have something in his own hands to justify his title to what he possessed, according to which controversies should be determined. This must be testified by somebody, and no man could be so fit, or of so much credit as he who was chief among them; and this is no more than is usual in all the societies of the world. The mayor of every corporation, the speaker or clerk of the house of peers or house of commons, the first president of every parliament, or presidial in France; the consul, burgermaster, avoyer or bailiff in every free town of Holland, Germany or Switzerland, sign the publick acts that pass in those places. The dukes of Venice and Genoa do the like, tho they have no other power than what is conferred upon them, and of themselves can do little or nothing. The grants of our kings are of the same nature, tho the words *mero motu nostro*[4] seem to imply the contrary; for kings speak always in the plural number, to shew that they do not act for themselves, but for the societies over which they are placed; and all the veneration that is, or can be given to their acts, does not exalt them, but those from whom their authority is derived, and for whom they are to execute. The tyrants of the East and other barbarians whose power is most absolute, speak in the single number, as appears by the decrees of Nebuchadnezzar, Cyrus, Darius and Ahasuerus recited in Scripture, with others that we hear of daily from those parts: but wheresoever there is anything of civility or regularity in government, the prince uses the plural, to shew that he acts in a publick capacity. From hence, says Grotius, the rights of kings to send ambassadors, make leagues, *&c.* do arise: the confederacies made by them do not terminate with their lives, because they are not for themselves; they speak not in their own persons, but as representing their people; and *a king who is depriv'd of his kingdom loses the right of sending ambassadors,*[5] because he can no longer speak for those, who by their own consent, or by a foreign force, are cut off from him. The question is not whether such a one be justly or unjustly deprived (for that concerns only those who do it or suffer it) but whether he can oblige the people; and 'tis ridiculous for any nation to treat with a man that cannot perform what shall be agreed, or for him to stipulate that which can oblige, and will be made good only by himself.

But tho much may be left to the discretion of kings in the distribution

---

[4] [By our will alone.]

[5] Rex regno exutus, jus legandi amittit. Grot.

De jur. bell. [Grotius, *De jure*, bk. 2, ch. 18, sec. 2.]

of lands and the like, yet it no way diminishes the right of the people, nor confers any upon them otherwise to dispose of what belongs to the publick, than may tend to the common good, and the accomplishment of those ends for which they are entrusted. Nay, if it were true, that a conquered country did belong to the crown, the king could not dispose of it, because 'tis annexed to the office, and not alienable by the person. This is not only found in regular mixed monarchies (as in Sweden, where the grants made by the last kings have been lately rescinded by the general assembly of estates, as contrary to law) but even in the most absolute, as in France, where the present king, who has stretched his power to the utmost, has lately acknowledged that he cannot do it; and according to the known maxim of the state, that the demesnes of the crown, which are designed for the defraying of publick charges, cannot be alienated, all the grants made within the last fifteen years have been annulled; even those who had bought lands of the crown have been called to account, and the sums given being compared with the profits received, and a moderate interest allowed to the purchasers, so much of the principal as remained due to them has been repay'd, and the lands resumed.

SECTION 30

Henry the First was King of England by as good a Title
as any of his Predecessors or Successors.

HAVING made it appear, as I suppose, that the ancient nobility of England was composed of such men as had been ennobled by bearing arms in the defence or enlargement of the commonwealth; that the dukes, earls, &c. were those who commanded them; that they and their dependents received lands for such services, under an obligation of continuing to render the like, and according to their several degrees and proportions, to provide and maintain horses, arms and men for the same uses; it cannot be denied that they were such gentlemen and lords of manors, as we now call commoners, together with the freeholders, and such as in war were found most able to be their leaders. Of these the micklegemotes, witenagemotes, and other publick assemblies did consist; and nothing can be more absurd than to assign the names and rights of duke, earl and viscount, which were names of offices, to those who have not the offices, and are no way fit for them. If our author therefore had said, that such as these who had always composed the great councils of our nation, had in favour of Henry the First, bestowed the crown upon him, as they had done upon his father and brother, I should agree with him: but 'tis the utmost extravagance to say, that he who had neither title nor possession, should give the power to those who had always been in the possession of it, and exercised it in giving to him whatsoever he had. But I most wonder he should so far forget himself, to call this Henry a usurper,[1] and detract from the validity of his acts, because he had no title; whereas there neither is, was, or can be a usurper if there be any truth in his doctrine: for he plainly tells us, we are only to look to the power, and not at all to the means and ways by which it is obtained;[2] and making no difference between a king and a tyrant, enjoins an equal submission to the commands of both. If this were only a slip of his pen, and he did really take this Henry to be a usurper because he had not a good title, I should desire to know the marks by which a lawful king is distinguished from a usurper, and in what a just title does consist. If he place it in an hereditary succession, we ought to be informed, whether this right must be deduced from one universal lord of mankind, or from a particular lord of every people: If from the universal lord, the same descent that gives him a right to the dominion of any one country, enslaves the whole world to him: if from the particular lord of one place, proof must be given how he came to be so: for if there was a defect in the first, it can never be repaired, and the possession is no more than a continued usurpation. But having already proved the absurdity of any pretence to either, I shall forbear the repetition, and only say, that if the course of succession may never be justly interrupted, the family of Meroveus could not have had any right to the crown of France; Pepin was a usurper, if it must forever have continued in the descendants of Meroveus, and Hugh Capet could have no title, if the race of Pepin might not be dispossess'd. I leave our author to dispute this point with the king of France; and when he has so far convinced him that he is a usurper, as to persuade him to resign his crown to the house of Austria claiming from Pharamond, or to that of Lorraine as descended from Pepin, I can give him half a dozen more knots which will not be with less difficulty untied, and which instead of establishing the titles of such kings as are known to us, will overthrow them all, unless a right be given to usurpation, or the consent of a people do confer it.

But if there is such a thing as a usurper, and a rule by which men may judge of usurpation, 'tis not only lawful but necessary for us to examine

---

[1] [*Patriarcha*, ch. 30, p. 117.]   [2] [Ibid., ch. 26, p. 106.]

the titles of such as go under the name of kings, that we may know whether they are truly so or not, lest through ignorance we chance to give the veneration and obedience that is due to a king, to one who is not a king, and deny it to him, who by an uninterruptible line of descent is our natural lord, and thereby prefer the worst of men and our most bitter enemy before the person we ought to look upon as our father: and if this prove dangerous to one or more kings, 'tis our author's fault, not mine.

If there be no usurper, nor rule of distinguishing him from a lawful prince, Filmer is the worst of all triflers and impostors, who grounds his arguments in the most serious matters upon what he esteems to be false: but the truth is, he seems to have set himself against humanity and common sense, as much as against law and virtue; and if he who so frequently contradicts himself, can be said to mean anything, he would authorize rapine and murder, and persuade us to account those to be rightful kings, who by treachery and other unjust means overthrow the right of descent which he pretends to esteem sacred, as well as the liberties of nations, which by better judges are thought to be so, and gives the odious name of usurpation to the advancement of one who is made king by the consent of a willing people.

But if Henry the First were a usurper, I desire to know whether the same name belongs to all our kings, or which of them deserves a better, that we may understand whose acts ought to be reputed legal, and to whose descent we owe veneration, or whether we are wholly exempted from all: for I cannot see a possibility of fixing the guilt of usurpation upon Henry the First, without involving many, if not all our kings in the same.

If his title was not good because his brother Robert was still living, that of Rufus is by the same reason overthrown; and William their father being a bastard could have none. This fundamental defect could never be repair'd; for the successors could inherit no more than the right of the first, which was nothing. Stephen could deduce no title either from Norman or Saxon; whatsoever Henry the second pretended, must be from his mother Maud, and any other might have been preferred before her as well as he. If her title was from the Normans, it must be void, since they had none, and the story of Edgar Atheling is too impertinent to deserve mention. But however, it could be of no advantage to her; for David king of Scotland, brother to her mother from whom only her title could be derived, was then alive with his son Henry, who dying not long after, left three sons and three daughters, whose posterity being distributed into many families of Scotland, remains to this day; and if proximity of blood is to be consider'd, ought always to have been preferr'd before her and her descendants, unless there be a law that gives the preference to daughters before sons. What right soever Henry the second had, it must necessarily have perished with him, all his children having been begotten in manifest adultery on Eleanor of Gascony, during the life of Lewis king of France her first husband: and nothing could be alleged to colour the business, but a dispensation from the pope directly against the law of God, and the words of our Saviour, who says, *That a wife cannot be put away unless for adultery, and he that marrieth her that is put away committeth adultery.*[3] The pollution of this spring is not to be cured; but tho it should pass unregarded, no one part of the succession since that time has remained entire. John was preferred before Arthur his elder brother's son: Edward the third was made king by the deposition of his father: Henry the fourth by that of Richard the 2d. If the house of Mortimer or York had the right, Henry the 4th, 5th, and 6th, were not kings, and all who claim under them have no title. However, Richard the third could have none; for the children of his elder brother the duke of Clarence were then living. The children of Edward the fourth may be suspected of bastardy; and tho it may have been otherwise, yet that matter is not so clear as things of such importance ought to be, and the consequence may reach very far. But tho that scruple were removed, 'tis certain that Henry the 7th was not king in the right of his wife Elizabeth, for he reigned before and after her; and for his other titles, we may believe Philippe de Comines, who says, *He had neither cross nor pile.*[4] If Henry the eighth had a right in himself, or from his mother, he should have reigned immediately after her death, which he never pretended, nor to succeed till his father was dead, thereby acknowledging he had no right but from him, unless the parliament and people can give it. The like may be said of his children. Mary could have no title if she was a bastard, begotten in incest; but if her mother's marriage was good and she legitimate, Elizabeth could have none.

Yet all these were lawful kings and queens; their acts continue in force to this day to all intents and purposes: the parliament and people made them to be so, when they had no other title. The parliament and people therefore have the power of making kings: Those who are so made are not usurpers: We have had none but such for more than seven hundred years. They were therefore lawful kings, or this nation has had none in

[3] [Matthew 5:31.]

[4] Mem. de Commin. [Philippe de Comines, *Memoires*, bk. 6, ch. 9.]

all that time; and if our author like this conclusion, the account from whence it is drawn may without difficulty be carried as high as our English histories do reach.

This being built upon the steady foundation of law, history and reason, is not to be removed by any man's opinion; especially by one accompanied with such circumstances as Sir Walter Raleigh was in during the last years of his life: And there is something of baseness, as well as prevarication, in turning the words of an eminent person, reduced to great difficulties, to a sense no way agreeing with his former actions or writings, and no less tending to impair his reputation than to deceive others. Our author is highly guilty of both, in citing Sir Walter Raleigh to invalidate the Great Charter of our liberties, as *begun by usurpation, and shewed to the world by rebellion;*[5] whereas no such thing, nor anything like it in word or principle can be found in the works that deserve to go under his name. The dialogue in question, with some other small pieces published after his death, deserve to be esteemed spurious: Or if, from a desire of life, when he knew his head lay under the ax, he was brought to say things no way agreeing with what he had formerly profess'd, they ought rather to be buried in oblivion, than produced to blemish his memory. But that the publick cause may not suffer by his fault, 'tis convenient the world should be informed, that tho he was a well qualified gentleman, yet his morals were no way exact, as appears by his dealings with the brave Earl of Essex. And he was so well assisted in his *History of the World*, that an ordinary man with the same helps might have perform'd the same things. Neither ought it to be accounted strange, if that which he writ by himself had the tincture of another spirit, when he was deprived of that assistance, tho his life had not depended upon the will of the prince, and he had never said, that *the bonds of subjects to their kings should always be wrought out of iron, and those of kings to their subjects out of cobwebs.*[6]

---

[5] [*Patriarcha*, ch. 30, p. 117, citing Raleigh's *Dialogue on the Prerogative of Parliaments*, in *Works*, vol. 8, pp. 157–222.]

[6] See Sir W. Raleigh's Epistle to King James.

SECTION 31

Free Nations have a right of meeting, when and where they please, unless they deprive themselves of it.

APERVERTED judgment always leads men into a wrong way, and persuades them to believe that those things favour their cause, that utterly overthrow it. For a proof of this, I desire our author's words may be consider'd. *In the former parliaments*, says he, *instituted and continued since Henry the first his time, is not to be found the usage of any natural liberty of the people: For all those liberties that are claimed in parliament, are liberties of grace from the king, and not the liberties of nature to the people: For if the liberty were natural, it would give power unto the multitude to assemble themselves, when and where they pleased, to bestow the sovereignty, and by pactions to limit and direct the exercise of it.*[1] And I say that nations being naturally free may meet, when and where they please; may dispose of the sovereignty, and may direct or limit the exercise of it, unless by their own act they have deprived themselves of that right: and there could never have been a lawful assembly of any people in the world, if they had not had that power in themselves. It was proved in the preceding section, that all our kings having no title, were no more than what the nobility and people made them to be; that they could have no power but what was given to them, and could confer none except what they had received. If they can therefore call parliaments, the power of calling them must have been given to them, and could not be given by any who had it not in themselves. The Israelites met together, and chose Ehud, Gideon, Samson, Jephthah, and others, to be their leaders, whom they judged fit to deliver them from their enemies. By the same right they assembled at Mizpah to make war against the tribe of Benjamin, when justice was denied to be done against those who had villainously abused the Levite's concubine.[2] In the like manner they would have made Gideon king, but he refused. In the same place they met, and chose Saul to be their king. He being dead, the men of Judah assembled themselves, and anointed David: Not long after, all the tribes met at Hebron, made a contract with him, and received him as their king. In the same manner, tho by worse counsel, they made Absalom king. And the like was attempted in favour of Sheba the son of Bichri, tho they then had a king chosen by themselves. When they found themselves oppressed by the tributes that had been laid upon them by Solomon, they met at Shechem; and being displeased

[1] [*Patriarcha*, ch. 30, p. 118.]   [2] [Judges 19:1-21:25.]

with Rehoboam's answer to their complaints, ten of the tribes made Jeroboam king. Jehu, and all the other kings of Israel, whether good or bad, had no other title than was conferred upon them by the prevailing part of the people; which could not have given them any, unless they had met together; nor meet together without the consent, and against the will of those that reigned, unless the power had been in themselves.

Where governments are more exactly regulated, the power of judging when 'tis fit to call the senate or people together, is referr'd to one or more magistrates; as in Rome to the consuls or tribunes, in Athens to the archons, and in Thebes to the beotarchs: but none of them could have these powers, unless they had been given by those who advanced them to the magistracies to which they were annexed; nor could they have been so annexed, if those who created them had not had the right in themselves. If these officers neglected their duty of calling such assemblies when the publick affairs required, the people met by their own authority, and punished the person, or abrogated the magistracy, as appears in the case of the decemviri, and many others that might be alleged, if the thing were not so plain as to need no further proof. The reason of this is, that they who institute a magistracy, best know whether the end of the institution be rightly pursued or not: And all just magistracies being the same in essence, tho differing in form, the same right must perpetually belong to those who put the sovereign power into the hands of one, a few, or many men, which is what our author calls the disposal of the sovereignty. Thus the Romans did when they created kings, consuls, military tribunes, dictators, or decemviri: and it had been most ridiculous to say, that those officers gave authority to the people to meet and chuse them; for they who are chosen are the creatures of those who chuse, and are nothing more than others till they are chosen. The last king of Sweden, Charles Gustavus, told a gentleman who was ambassador there, that the Swedes having made him king, when he was poor and had nothing in the world, he had but one work to do, which was so to reign, that they might never repent the good opinion they had conceived of him. They might therefore meet, and did meet to confer the sovereignty upon him, or he could never have had it: For tho the kingdom be hereditary to males or females, and his mother was sister to the great Gustavus; yet having married a stranger without the consent of the estates, she performed not the condition upon which women are admitted to the succession; and thereby falling from her right, he pretended not to any. The act of his election declares he had none, and gives the crown to him and the heirs of his body, with this farther declaration, that the benefit of his election should no way extend to his brother Prince

Adolphus; and 'tis confessed by all the Swedish nation, that if the king now reigning should die without children, the estates would proceed to a new election.

'Tis rightly observ'd by our author, that if the people might meet and give the sovereign power, they might also direct and limit it; for they did meet in this and other countries, they did confer the sovereign power, they did limit and direct the exercise; and the laws of each people shew in what manner and measure it is everywhere done. This is as certain in relation to kings, as any other magistrates. The commission of the Roman dictators was, to take care *that the commonwealth might receive no detriment*.[3] The same was sometimes given to the consuls: King Offa's confession, that he was made king *to preserve the publick liberty*,[4] expresses the same thing: And Charles Gustavus, who said he had no other work, than to govern in such a manner, that they who had made him king might not repent, shew'd there was a rule which he stood obliged to follow, and an end which he was to procure, that he might merit and preserve their good opinion. This power of conferring the sovereignty was exercised in France by those who made Meroveus king, in the prejudice of the two grandchildren of Pharamond sons to Clodion; by those who excluded his race, and gave the crown to Pepin; by those who deposed Lewis le Debonair, and Charles le Gros; by those who brought in five kings, that were either bastards or strangers, between him and Charles le Simple; by those who rejected his race, and advanced Hugh Capet; by those who made Henry the first king, to the prejudice of Robert his elder brother, and continued the crown in the race of Henry for ten generations, whilst the descendants of Robert were only dukes of Burgundy. The like was done in Castile and Aragon, by frequently preferring the younger before the elder brother; the descendants of females before those of the male-line in the same degree; the more remote in blood before the nearest; and sometimes bastards before the legitimate issue. The same was done in England in relation to every king, since the coming in of the Normans, as I shewed in the last section, and other places of his work.

That they who gave the sovereignty, might also circumscribe and direct it, is manifest by the several ways of providing for the succession instituted by several nations. Some are merely elective, as the empire of Germany and the kingdom of Poland to this day; the kingdom of Denmark till the year 1660; that of Sweden till the time of Gustavus Ericson, who delivered

---

[3] Ne quid detrimenti respublica accipiat. T. Liv. [Livy, *History of Rome*, bk. 3, ch. 4.]

[4] In vestrae libertatis tuitionem. Mat. Par.

[Matthew Paris, *Chronica Majora*, section on Offa II.]

that nation from the oppression of Christian the second the cruel king of the Danes. In others the election was confined to one or more families, as the kingdom of the Goths in Spain to the Balthi and Amalthi. In some, the eldest man of the reigning family was preferr'd before the nearest, as in Scotland before the time of Kenneth. In other places the nearest in blood is preferr'd before the elder if more remote. In some, no regard is had to females, or their descendants, as in France and Turkey. In others, they or their descendants are admitted, either simply as well as males; or under a condition of marrying in the country, or with the consent of the estates, as in Sweden. And no other reason can be given for this almost infinite variety of constitutions, than that they who made them would have it so; which could not be, if God and nature had appointed one general rule for all nations. For in that case, the kingdom of France must be elective, as well as that of Poland and the Empire; or the empire and Poland hereditary, as that of France: Daughters must succeed in France, as well as in England, or be excluded in England as in France; and he that would establish one as the ordinance of God and nature, must necessarily overthrow all the rest.

A farther exercise of the natural liberty of nations is discovered in the several limitations put upon the sovereign power. Some kings, says Grotius, have the *summum imperium summo modo;* others, *modo non summo:*[5] and amongst those that are under limitations, the degrees, as to more or less, are almost infinite, as I have proved already by the example of Aragon, ancient Germany, the Saxon kings, the Normans, the kings of Castile, the present empire, with divers others. And I may safely say, that the ancient government of France was much of the same nature to the time of Charles the 7th, and Lewis the 11th; but the work of emancipating themselves, as they call it, begun by them, is now brought to perfection in a boundless elevation of the king's greatness and riches, to the unspeakable misery of the people.

'Twere a folly to think this variety proceeds from the concessions of kings, who naturally delight in power, and hate that which crosses their will. It might with more reason be imagined, that the Roman consuls, who were brought up in liberty, who had contracted a love to their country, and were contented to live upon an equal foot with their fellow citizens, should confine the power of their magistracy to a year; or that the dukes of Venice should be graciously pleased to give power to the Council of Ten to punish them capitally if they transgressed the laws,

---

[5] De jur. bell. et pac. ["The supreme power in the supreme manner" . . . "not in the supreme manner." Grotius, *De jure*, bk. 1, ch. 3, sec. 14.]

than that kings should put such fetters upon their power, which they so much abhor; or that they would suffer them, if they could be easily broken. If any one of them should prove so moderate, like Trajan, to command the prefect of the praetorian guard to use the sword for him if he governed well, and against him if he did not, it would soon be rescinded by his successor; the law which has no other strength than the act of one man, may be annulled by another. So that nothing does more certainly prove, that the laws made in several countries to restrain the power of kings, and variously to dispose of the succession, are not from them, than the frequent examples of their fury, who have exposed themselves to the greatest dangers, and brought infinite miseries upon the people, through the desire of breaking them. It must therefore be concluded, that nations have power of meeting together, and of conferring, limiting, and directing the sovereignty; or all must be grounded upon most manifest injustice and usurpation.

No man can have a power over a nation otherwise than *de jure*, or *de facto*. He who pretends to have a power *de jure*, must prove that it is originally inherent in him or his predecessor from whom he inherits; or that it was justly acquired by him. The vanity of any pretence to an original right appears sufficiently, I hope, from the proofs already given, that the first fathers of mankind had it not; or if they had, no man could now inherit the same, there being no man able to make good the genealogy that should give him a right to the succession. Besides, the facility we have of proving the beginnings of all the families that reign among us, makes it as absurd for any of them to pretend a perpetual right to dominion, as for any citizen of London, whose parents and birth we know, to say he is the very man Noah who lived in the time of the flood, and is now four or five thousand years old.

If the power were conferred on him or his predecessors, 'tis what we ask; for the collation can be of no value, unless it be made by those who had a right to do it; and the original right by descent failing, no one can have any over a free people but themselves, or those to whom they have given it.

If acquisition be pretended, 'tis the same thing; for there can be no right to that which is acquired, unless the right of invading be proved; and that being done, nothing can be acquired except what belonged to the person that was invaded, and that only by him who had the right of invading. No man ever did or could conquer a nation by his own strength; no man therefore could ever acquire a personal right over any; and if it was conferr'd upon him by those who made the conquest with him, they were the people that did it. He can no more be said to have the right originally in and from himself, than a magistrate of Rome or Athens immediately after his creation; and having no other at the beginning, he can have none to eternity; for the nature of it must refer to the original, and cannot be changed by time.

Whatsoever therefore proceeds not from the consent of the people, must be *de facto* only, that is, void of all right; and 'tis impossible there should not be a right of destroying that which is grounded upon none; and by the same rule that one man enjoys what he gained by violence, another may take it from him. Cyrus overthrew the Assyrians and Babylonians, Alexander the Medes and Persians; and if they had no right of making war upon those nations, the nations could not but have a right of recovering all that had been unjustly taken from them, and avenging the evils they had suffered. If the cause of the war was originally just, and not corrupted by an intemperate use of the victory, the conquer'd people was perhaps obliged to be quiet; but the conquering armies that had conferred upon their generals what they had taken from their enemies, might as justly expect an account of what they had given, and that it should be employ'd according to the intention of the givers, as the people of any city might do from their regularly created magistrates; because it was as impossible for Cyrus, Alexander or Caesar, to gain a power over the armies they led, without their consent, as for Pericles, Valerius, or any other disarmed citizen to gain more power in their respective cities than was voluntarily conferr'd upon them. And I know no other difference between kingdoms so constituted by conquering armies, and such as are established in the most orderly manner, than that the first usually incline more to war and violence, the latter to justice and peace. But there have not been wanting many of the first sort (especially the nations coming from the north) who were no less exact in ordaining that which tended to the preservation of liberty, nor less severe in seeing it punctually performed, than the most regular commonwealths that ever were in the world. And it can with no more reason be pretended, that the Goths received their privileges from Alan or Theodoric, the Franks from Pharamond or Meroveus, and the English from Ine or Ethelred, than that the liberty of Athens was the gift of Themistocles or Pericles, that the empire of Rome proceeded from the liberality of Brutus or Valerius, and that the commonwealth of Venice at this day subsists by the favour of the Contarini or Moresini: which must reduce us to matter of right, since that of fact void of right can signify nothing.

SECTION 32

The powers of Kings are so various according to the Constitutions of several States, that no consequence can be drawn to the prejudice or advantage of any one, merely from the name.

IN opposition to what is above said, some allege the name of king, as if there were a charm in the word; and our author seems to put more weight upon it, than in the reasons he brings to support his cause. But that we may see there is no efficacy in it, and that it conveys no other right than what particular nations may annex to it, we are to consider,

1. That the most absolute princes that are or have been in the world, never had the name of king; whereas it has been frequently given to those whose powers have been very much restrained. The Caesars were never called kings, till the sixth age of Christianity: the caliphs and sultan of Egypt and Babylon, the Great Turk, the khan of Tartary, or the Great Mogul never took that name, or any other of the same signification. The czar of Muscovy has it not, tho he is as absolute a monarch, and his people as miserable slaves as any in the world. On the other side, the chief magistrates of Rome and Athens for some time, those of Sparta, Aragon, Sweden, Denmark and England, *who could do nothing but by law*, have been called kings. This may be enough to shew, that a name being no way essential, what title soever is given to the chief magistrate, he can have no other power than the laws and customs of his country do give, or the people confer upon him.

2. The names of magistrates are often changed, tho the power continue to be the same; and the powers are sometimes alter'd tho the name remain. When Octavius Caesar by the force of a mad corrupted soldiery had overthrown all law and right, he took no other title in relation to military affairs than that of *imperator*, which in the time of liberty was by the armies often given to praetors and consuls: In civil matters he was, as he pretended, content with the power of tribune;[1] and the like was observed in his successor, who to new invented usurpations *gave old and approved names*.[2] On the other side, those titles which have been render'd odious and execrable by the violent exercise of an absolute power, are sometimes made popular by moderate limitations; as in Germany, where, tho the

[1] Tribunitia potestate contentus. C. Tacit.   [2] C. Tacit. [Ibid., bk. 4, ch. 19.]
[Tacitus, *Annals*, bk. 1, ch. 2. His successor
was Tiberius.]

monarchy seem to be as well temper'd as any, the princes retain the same names of *imperator*, Caesar and Augustus, as those had done, who by the excess of their rage and fury had desolated and corrupted the best part of [the] world.

Sometimes the name is changed, tho the power in all respects continue to be the same. The lords of Castile had for many ages no other title than that of count; and when the nobility and people thought good, they changed it to that of king, without any addition to the power.[3]

The sovereign magistrate in Poland was called duke till within the last two hundred years, when they gave the title of king to one of the Jagellan family; which title has continued to this day, tho without any change in the nature of the magistracy. And I presume, no wise man will think, that if the Venetians should give the name of king to their duke, it could confer any other power upon him than he has already, unless more should be conferr'd by the authority of the Great Council.

3. The same names which in some places denote the supreme magistracy, in others are subordinate or merely titular. In England, France and Spain, dukes and earls are subjects: in Germany the electors and princes who are called by those names are little less than sovereigns; and the dukes of Savoy, Tuscany, Muscovy and others, acknowledge no superior, as well as those of Poland and Castile had none, when they went under those titles. The same may be said of kings. Some are subject to a foreign power, as divers of them were subject to the Persian and Babylonian monarchs, who for that reason were called the kings of kings. Some also are tributaries; and when the Spaniards first landed in America, the great kings of Mexico and Peru had many others under them. Threescore and ten kings gathered up meat under the table of Adonibezek.[4] The Romans had many kings depending upon them. Herod and those of his race were of this number; and the dispute between him and his sons Aristobulus and Alexander was to be determined by them, neither durst he decide the matter till it was referred to him. But a right of appeal did still remain, as appears by the case of St. Paul when Agrippa was king. The kings of Mauritania from the time of Masinissa, were under the like dependence: Jugurtha went to Rome to justify himself for the death of Micipsa: Juba was commanded by the Roman magistrates Scipio, Petreius and Afranius: another Juba was made king of the same country by Augustus, and Tiridates of Armenia by Nero; and infinite examples of

---

[3] Saavedra, Mariana, Zurita. [Saavedra, *Corona Gotica*; Mariana, *General History of Spain*; Gerónimo Zurita y Castro, *Anales de la Corona* *de Aragón* (1610; repub. Zaragoza: Institución Fernando el Católico, 1976).]

[4] [Judges 1:7.]

this nature may be alleged. Moreover, their powers are variously regulated, according to the variety of tempers in nations and ages. Some have restrained the powers that by experience were found to be exorbitant; others have dissolved the bonds that were laid upon them: and laws relating to the institution, abrogation, enlargement or restriction of the regal power, would be utterly insignificant if this could not be done. But such laws are of no effect in any other country than where they are made. The lives of the Spartans did not depend upon the will of Agesilaus or Leonidas, because Nebuchadnezzar could kill or save whom he pleased: and tho the king of Morocco may stab his subjects, throw them to the lions, or hang them upon tenterhooks; yet a king of Poland would probably be called to a severe account, if he should unjustly kill a single man.

SECTION 33

The Liberty of a People is the gift of God and Nature.

I F any man ask how nations come to have the power of doing these things, I answer, that liberty being only an exemption from the dominion of another, the question ought not to be, how a nation can come to be free, but how a man comes to have a dominion over it; for till the right of dominion be proved and justified, liberty subsists as arising from the nature and being of a man. Tertullian speaking of the emperors says, *ab eo imperium a quo spiritus;*[1] and we taking man in his first condition may justly say, *ab eo libertas a quo spiritus;* for no man can owe more than he has received. The creature having nothing, and being nothing but what the creator makes him, must owe all to him, and nothing to anyone from whom he has received nothing. Man therefore must be naturally free, unless he be created by another power than we have yet heard of. The obedience due to parents arises from hence, in that they are the instruments of our generation; and we are instructed by the light of reason, that we ought to make great returns to those from whom under God we have received all. When they die we are their heirs, we enjoy the same rights, and devolve the same to our posterity. God only who confers this right upon us, can deprive us of it: and we can no way understand that he does so, unless he had so declared by express

---

[1] ["Dominion comes from the same source as one's spirit." Tertullian, *Apology*, ch. 30. The Latin phrase that follows substitutes "liberty" for "dominion."]

revelation, or had set some distinguishing marks of dominion and subjection upon men; and, as an ingenious person not long since said, caused some to be born with crowns upon their heads, and all others with saddles upon their backs.[2] This liberty therefore must continue, till it be either forfeited or willingly resigned. The forfeiture is hardly comprehensible in a multitude that is not entered into any society; for as they are all equal, and *equals can have no right over each other*,[3] no man can forfeit anything to one who can justly demand nothing, unless it may be by a personal injury, which is nothing to this case; because where there is no society, one man is not bound by the actions of another. All cannot join in the same act, because they are joined in none; or if they should, no man could recover, much less transmit the forfeiture; and not being transmitted, it perishes as if it had never been, and no man can claim anything from it.

'Twill be no less difficult to bring resignation to be subservient to our author's purpose; for men could not resign their liberty, unless they naturally had it in themselves. Resignation is a publick declaration of their assent to be governed by the person to whom they resign; that is, they do by that act constitute him to be their governor. This necessarily puts us upon the inquiry, why they do resign, how they will be governed, and proves the governor to be their creature; and the right of disposing the government must be in them, or they who receive it can have none. This is so evident to common sense, that it were impertinent to ask who made Carthage, Athens, Rome or Venice to be free cities. Their charters were not from men, but from God and nature. When a number of Phoenicians had found a port on the coast of Africa, they might perhaps agree with the inhabitants for a parcel of ground, but they brought their liberty with them. When a company of Latins, Sabines and Tuscans met together upon the banks of the Tiber, and chose rather to build a city for themselves, than to live in such as were adjacent, they carried their liberty in their own breasts, and had hands and swords to defend it. This was their charter; and Romulus could confer no more upon them, than Dido upon the Carthaginians. When a multitude of barbarous nations infested Italy, and no protection could be expected from the corrupted and perishing empire, such as agreed to seek a place of refuge in the scatter'd islands of the Adriatick gulf, had no need of any man's authority

---

[2] [Richard "Hannibal" Rumbold, like Sidney a politically active republican, was to say something similar when executed for treason in 1685—as did Thomas Jefferson in a famous letter to Roger Weightman, June 24, 1826.]

[3] Par in parem non habet imperium. [Bracton, *On the Laws and Customs of England*, fol. 5, p. 33.]

to ratify the institution of their government. They who were the formal part of the city, and had built the material, could not but have a right of governing it as they pleased, since if they did amiss, the hurt was only to themselves. 'Tis probable enough that some of the Roman emperors, as lords of the soil, might have pretended to a dominion over them, if there had been any colour for it: but nothing of that kind appearing in thirteen hundred years, we are not like to hear of any such cavils. 'Tis agreed by mankind, that subjection and protection are relative; and that he who cannot protect those that are under him, in vain pretends to a dominion over them. The only ends for which governments are constituted, and obedience render'd to them, are the obtaining of justice and protection; and they who cannot provide for both, give the people a right of taking such ways as best please themselves, in order to their own safety.

The matter is yet more clear in relation to those who never were in any society, as at the beginning, or renovation of the world after the Flood; or who upon the dissolution of the societies to which they did once belong, or by some other accident have been obliged to seek new habitations. Such were those who went from Babylon upon the confusion of tongues, those who escaped from Troy when it was burnt by the Grecians; almost all the nations of Europe, with many of Asia and Africa upon the dissolution of the Roman empire. To which may be added a multitude of Northern nations, who, when they had increased to such numbers that their countries could no longer nourish them, or because they wanted skill to improve their lands, were sent out to provide for themselves; and having done so, did erect many kingdoms and states, either by themselves, or in union and coalition with the ancient inhabitants.

'Tis in vain to say, that wheresoever they came, the land did belong to somebody, and that they who came to dwell there must be subject to the laws of those who were lords of the soil, for that is not always true in fact. Some come into desert countries that have no lord, others into such as are thinly peopled, by men who knowing not how to improve their land, do either grant part of it upon easy terms to the new comers, or grow into a union with them in the enjoyment of the whole; and histories furnish us with infinite examples of this nature.

If we will look into our own original, without troubling ourselves with the senseless stories of Samothes the son of Japheth and his magicians, or the giants begotten by spirits upon the thirty daughters of Danaus sent from Phoenicia in a boat without sail, oars or rudder, we shall find that when the Romans abandoned this island, the inhabitants were left to a full liberty of providing for themselves: and whether we deduce our original from them or the Saxons, or from both, our ancestors were perfectly free; and the Normans having inherited the same right when they came to be one nation with the former, we cannot but continue so still unless we have enslaved ourselves.

Nothing is more contrary to reason than to imagine this. When the fierce barbarity of the Saxons came to be softened by a more gentle climate, the arts and religion they learnt, taught them to reform their manners, and better enabled them to frame laws for the preservation of their liberty, but no way diminished their love to it: and tho the Normans might desire to get the lands of those who had joined with Harold, and of others into their hands; yet when they were settled in the country, and by marriages united to the ancient inhabitants, they became true Englishmen, and no less lovers of liberty and resolute defenders of it than the Saxons had been. There was then neither conquering Norman nor conquered Saxon, but a great and brave people composed of both, united in blood and interest in the defence of their common rights, which they so well maintained, that no prince since that time has too violently encroached upon them, who, as the reward of his folly, has not lived miserably and died shamefully.

Such actions of our ancestors do not, as I suppose, savour much of the submission which patrimonial slaves do usually render to the will of their lord. On the contrary, whatsoever they did was by a power inherent in themselves to defend that liberty in which they were born. All their kings were created upon the same condition, and for the same ends. Alfred acknowledged he found and left them perfectly free; and the confession of Offa, that they had not made him king for his own merits, but for the defence of their liberty, comprehends all that were before and after him. They well knew how great the honour was, to be made head of a great people, and rigorously exacted the performance of the ends for which such a one was elevated, severely punishing those who basely and wickedly betray'd the trust reposed in them, and violated all that is most sacred among men; which could not have been unless they were naturally free, for the liberty that has no being cannot be defended.

SECTION 34

No Veneration paid, or Honor conferr'd
upon a just and lawful Magistrate,
can diminish the Liberty of a Nation.

SOME have supposed, that tho the people be naturally free, and magistrates created by them, they do by such creations deprive themselves of that natural liberty; and that the names of king, sovereign lord, and dread sovereign, being no way consistent with liberty, they who give such titles do renounce it. Our author carries this very far, and lays great weight upon the submissive language used by the people, when they *humbly crave that his majesty would be pleased to grant their accustomed freedom of speech, and access to his person;* and *give the name of supplications and petitions to the addresses made to him:*[1] Whereas he answers in the haughty language of *le roy le veut, le roy s'avisera,*[2] and the like. But they who talk at this rate, shew, that they neither understand the nature of magistracy, nor the practice of nations. Those who have lived in the highest exercise of their liberty, and have been most tenacious of it, have thought no honor too great for such magistrates as were eminent in the defence of their rights, and were set up for that end. The name of dread sovereign might justly have been given to a Roman dictator, or consul, for they had the sovereign authority in their hands, and power sufficient for its execution. Whilst their magistracy continued, they were a terror to the same men, whose axes and rods had been a terror to them the year or month before, and might be so again the next. The Romans thought they could not be guilty of excess in carrying the power and veneration due to their dictator to the highest: And Livy tells us, that his *edicts were esteemed sacred.*[3] I have already shewn, that this haughty people, who might have commanded, condescended to join with their tribunes in a petition to the dictator Papirius, for the life of Quintus Fabius, who had fought a battle in his absence, and without his order, tho he had gained a great and memorable victory. The same Fabius, when consul, was commended by his father Q. Fabius Maximus, for obliging him by his lictors to dismount from his horse, and to pay him the same respect that was due from others. The tribunes of the people, who were instituted

---

[1] [*Patriarcha*, ch. 30, p. 118, and ch. 29 ("Of Parliaments"), p. 114.]

[2] [The king wishes it, the king will consider.]

[3] Edictum dictatoris pro numine observatum. Hist. l. 8 [Livy, *History of Rome*, bk. 8, ch. 34.]

for the preservation of liberty, were also esteemed sacred and inviolable, as appears by that phrase, *sacrosancta tribunorum potestas*,[4] so common in their ancient writers. No man, I presume, thinks any monarchy more limited, or more clearly derived from a delegated power, than that of the German emperors; and yet *sacra caesarea majestas*[5] is the publick style. Nay, the Hollanders at this day call their burgermasters, tho they see them selling herring or tar, *high and mighty lords*, as soon as they are advanced to be of the 36, 42 or 48 magistrates of a small town. 'Tis no wonder therefore, if a great nation should think it conducing to their own glory, to give magnificent titles, and use submissive language to that one man, whom they set up to be their head; most especially, if we consider that they came from a country where such titles and language were principally invented.

Among the Romans and Grecians we hear nothing of majesty, highness, serenity and excellence appropriated to a single person, but receive them from Germany and other Northern countries. We find *majestas populi Romani*, and *majestas imperii*,[6] in their best authors; but no man speaking to Julius or Augustus, or even to the vainest of their successors, ever used those empty titles, nor took upon themselves the name of servants, as we do to every fellow we meet in the streets. When such ways of speaking are once introduced, they must needs swell to a more than ordinary height in all transactions with princes. Most of them naturally delight in vanity, and courtiers never speak more truth, than when they most extol their masters, and assume to themselves the names that best express the most abject slavery. These being brought into mode, like all ill customs, increase by use; and then no man can omit them without bringing that hatred and danger upon himself, which few will undergo, except for something that is evidently of great importance. Matters of ceremony and title at the first seem not to be so; and being for some time neglected, they acquire such strength as not to be easily removed. From private usage they pass into publick acts; and those flatterers who gave a beginning to them, proposing them in publick councils, where too many of that sort have always insinuated themselves, gain credit enough to make them pass. This work was farther advanced by the church of Rome, according to their custom of favouring that most, which is most vain and corrupt; and it has been usual with the popes and their adherents, liberally to gratify princes for services render'd to the church, with titles that tended only to the prejudice of the people. These poisonous plants having

---

[4] [The sacrosanct power of the tribunes.]

[5] [Sacred Caesarean majesty.]

[6] [Majesty of the Roman people, majesty of the empire.]

taken root, grew up so fast, that the titles which, within the space of a hundred years, were thought sufficient for the kings and queens of England, have of late been given to Monk and his honourable duchess. New phrases have been invented to please princes, or the sense of the old perverted, as has happen'd to that of *le roy s'avisera:* And that which was no more than a liberty to consult with the lords upon a bill presented by the commons, is by some men now taken for a right inherent in the king of denying such bills as may be offer'd to him by the lords and commons; tho the coronation oath oblige him to hold, keep and defend the just laws and customs, *quas vulgus elegerit.*[7] And if a stop be not put to this exorbitant abuse, the words still remaining in acts of parliament, which shew that their acts are our laws, may perhaps be also abolished.

But tho this should come to pass, by the slackness of the lords and commons, it could neither create a new right in the king, nor diminish that of the people: But it might give a better colour to those who are enemies to their country, to render the power of the crown arbitrary, than anything that is yet among us.

SECTION 35

The Authority given by our Law
to the Acts performed by a King de facto,
detract nothing from the people's right of
creating whom they please.

THEY who have more regard to the prevailing power than to right, and lay great weight upon the statute of Henry the seventh, which authorizes the acts of a king *de facto*,[1] seem not to consider, that thereby they destroy all right of inheritance; that he only is king *de facto*, who is received by the people; and that this reception could neither be of any value in itself, nor be made valid by a statute, unless the people, and their representatives who make the statute, had in themselves the power of receiving, authorizing and creating whom they please. For he is not king *de facto* who calls himself so, as Perkin or Simnel, but he who by the consent of the nation is possess'd of the regal power. If there were such a thing in nature, as a natural lord over every country, and that the

[7] [Which the people shall have chosen.]   [1] [11 Henry VII, ch. 1.]

right must go by descent, it would be impossible for any other man to acquire it, or for the people to confer it upon him, and to give the authority to the acts of one, who neither is nor can be a king, which belongs only to him who has the right inherent in himself, and inseparable from him. Neither can it be denied, that the same power which gives the validity to such acts as are performed by one who is not a king, that belongs to those of a true king, may also make him king; for the essence of a king consists in the validity of his acts. And 'tis equally absurd for one to pretend to be a king, whose acts as king are not valid, as that his own can be valid if those of another are; for then the same indivisible right which our author, and those of his principles assert to be inseparable from the person, would be at the same time exercised and enjoyed by two distinct and contrary powers.

Moreover, it may be observed, that this statute was made after frequent and bloody wars concerning titles to the crown; and whether the cause were good or bad, those who were overcome, were not only subject to be killed in the field, but afterwards to be prosecuted as traitors under the colour of law. He who gained the victory, was always set up to be king by those of his party; and he never failed to proceed against his enemies as rebels. This introduced a horrid series of the most destructive mischiefs. The fortune of war varied often; and I think it may be said, that there were few, if any, great families in England, that were not either destroy'd, or at least so far shaken, as to lose their chiefs, and many considerable branches of them: And experience taught, that instead of gaining any advantage to the publick in point of government, he for whom they fought, seldom proved better than his enemy. They saw that the like might again happen, tho the title of the reigning king should be as clear as descent of blood could make it. This brought things into an uneasy posture; and 'tis not strange, that both the nobility and commonalty should be weary of it. No law could prevent the dangers of battle; for he that had followers, and would venture himself, might bring them to such a decision, as was only in the hand of God. But thinking no more could justly be required to the full performance of their duty to the king, than to expose themselves to the hazard of battle for him; and not being answerable for the success, they would not have that law which they endeavour'd to support, turned to their destruction by their enemies, who might come to be the interpreters of it. But as they could be exempted from this danger only by their own laws, which could authorize the acts of a king without a title, and justify them for acting under him, 'tis evident that the power of the law was in their hands, and that the acts of the person who enjoyed the crown, were of no value in themselves.

The law had been impertinent, if it could have been done without law; and the intervention of the parliament useless, if the kings *de facto* could have given authority to their own acts. But if the parliament could make that to have the effect of law, which was not law, and exempt those that acted according to it from the penalties of the law, and give the same force to the acts of one who is not king as of one who is, they cannot but have a power of making him to be king, who is not so; that is to say, all depends entirely upon their authority.

Besides, he is not king who assumes the title to himself, or is set up by a corrupt party; but he who according to the usages required in the case is made king. If these are wanting, he is neither *de facto* nor *de jure*, but *tyrannus sine titulo*. Nevertheless, this very man, if he comes to be received by the people, and placed in the throne, he is thereby made king *de facto*. His acts are valid in law; the same service is due to him as to any other: they who render it are in the same manner protected by the law; that is to say, he is truly king. If our author therefore do allow such to be kings, he must confess that power to be good which makes them so, when they have no right in themselves. If he deny it, he must not only deny that there is any such thing as a king *de facto*, which the statute acknowledges, but that we ever had any king in England; for we never had any other than such, as I have proved before.

By the same means he will so unravel all the law, that no man shall know what he has, or what he ought to do or avoid; and will find no remedy for this, unless he allow, that laws made without kings are as good as those made with them, which returns to my purpose: for they who have the power of making laws, may by law make a king as well as any other magistrate. And indeed the intention of this statute could be no other than to secure men's persons and possessions, and so far to declare the power of giving and taking away the crown to be in the parliament, as to remove all disputes concerning titles, and to make him to be a legal king, whom they acknowledge to be king.

SECTION 36
*The general revolt of a Nation cannot be
called a Rebellion.*

A s impostors seldom make lies to pass in the world, without putting false names upon things, such as our author endeavour to persuade the people they ought not to defend their liberties, by giving the name of rebellion to the most just and honourable actions that have been performed for the preservation of them; and to aggravate the matter, fear not to tell us that rebellion is like the sin of witchcraft. But those who seek after truth, will easily find, that there can be no such thing in the world as the rebellion of a nation against its own magistrates, and that rebellion is not always evil. That this may appear, it will not be amiss to consider the word, as well as the thing understood by it as it is used in an evil sense.

The word is taken from the Latin *rebellare*, which signifies no more than to renew a war. When a town or province had been subdued by the Romans, and brought under their dominion, if they violated their faith after the settlement of peace, and invaded their masters who had spared them, they were said to rebel. But it had been more absurd to apply that word to the people that rose against the decemviri, kings or other magistrates, than to the Parthians or any of those nations who had no dependence upon them; for all the circumstances that should make a rebellion were wanting, the word implying a superiority in them against whom it is, as well as the breach of an establish'd peace. But tho every private man singly taken be subject to the commands of the magistrate, the whole body of the people is not so; for he is by and for the people, and the people is neither by nor for him. The obedience due to him from private men is grounded upon, and measured by the general law; and that law regarding the welfare of the people, cannot set up the interest of one or a few men against the publick. The whole body therefore of a nation cannot be tied to any other obedience than is consistent with the common good, according to their own judgment: and having never been subdued or brought to terms of peace with their magistrates, they cannot be said to revolt or rebel against them to whom they owe no more than seems good to themselves, and who are nothing of or by themselves, more than other men.

Again, the thing signified by rebellion is not always evil; for tho every subdued nation must acknowledge a superiority in those who have subdued

[519]

them, and rebellion do imply a breach of the peace, yet that superiority is not infinite; the peace may be broken upon just grounds, and it may be neither a crime nor infamy to do it. The Privernates had been more than once subdued by the Romans, and had as often rebelled. Their city was at last taken by Plautius the consul, after their leader Vitruvius and great numbers of their senate and people had been kill'd: Being reduced to a low condition, they sent ambassadors to Rome to desire peace; where when a senator asked them what punishment they deserved, one of them answered, *The same which they deserve who think themselves worthy of liberty.* The consul then demanded, *what kind of peace might be expected from them, if the punishment should be remitted:* The ambassador answer'd, *If the terms you give be good, the peace will be observed by us faithfully and perpetually; if bad, it will soon be broken.*[1] And tho some were offended with the ferocity of the answer; yet the best part of the senate approved it as *worthy of a man and a freeman;*[2] and confessing that no man or nation would continue under an uneasy condition longer than they were compell'd by force, said, *They only were fit to be made Romans, who thought nothing valuable but liberty.*[3] Upon which they were all made citizens of Rome, and obtained whatsoever they had desired.

I know not how this matter can be carried to a greater height; for if it were possible, that a people resisting oppression, and vindicating their own liberty, could commit a crime, and incur either guilt or infamy, the Privernates did, who had been often subdued, and often pardoned; but even in the judgment of their conquerors whom they had offended, the resolution they professed of standing to no agreement imposed upon them by necessity, was accounted the highest testimony of such a virtue as rendered them worthy to be admitted into a society and equality with themselves, who were the most brave and virtuous people of the world.

But if the patience of a conquer'd people may have limits, and they who will not bear oppression from those who had spared their lives, may deserve praise and reward from their conquerors, it would be madness to think, that any nation can be obliged to bear whatsoever their own magistrates think fit to do against them. This may seem strange to those who talk so much of conquests made by kings; immunities, liberties and privileges granted to nations; oaths of allegiance taken, and wonderful benefits conferred upon them. But having already said as much as is needful concerning conquests, and that the magistrate who has nothing

---

[1] Si bonam dederitis, fidam & perpetuam; si malam, haud diuturnam. Liv. [Livy, *History of Rome,* bk. 8, ch. 21.]

[2] Viri & liberi vocem auditam. Ibid.

[3] Eos demum, qui nihil praeterquam de libertate cogitant, dignos esse, qui Romani fiant. Ibid.

except what is given to him, can only dispense out of the publick stock such franchises and privileges as he has received for the reward of services done to the country, and encouragement of virtue, I shall at present keep myself to the two last points.

Allegiance signifies no more (as the words, *ad legem* declare) than such an obedience as the law requires. But as the law can require nothing from the whole people, who are masters of it, allegiance can only relate to particulars, and not to the whole. No oath can bind any other than those who take it, and that only in the true sense and meaning of it: but single men only take this oath, and therefore single men are only obliged to keep it: the body of a people neither does, nor can perform any such act: Agreements and contracts have been made; as the tribe of Judah, and the rest of Israel afterward, made a covenant with David, upon which they made him king; but no wise man can think, that the nation did thereby make themselves the creature of their own creature.

The sense also of an oath ought to be considered. No man can by an oath be obliged to anything beyond, or contrary to the true meaning of it: private men who swear obedience *ad legem*, swear no obedience *extra* or *contra legem:* whatsoever they promise or swear, can detract nothing from the publick liberty, which the law principally intends to preserve. Tho many of them may be obliged in their several stations and capacities to render peculiar services to a prince, the people continue as free as the internal thoughts of a man, and cannot but have a right to preserve their liberty, or avenge the violation.

If matters are well examined, perhaps not many magistrates can pretend to much upon the title of merit, most especially if they or their progenitors have continued long in office. The conveniences annexed to the exercise of the sovereign power, may be thought sufficient to pay such scores as they grow due, even to the best: and as things of that nature are handled, I think it will hardly be found, that all princes can pretend to an irresistible power upon the account of beneficence to their people. When the family of Medici came to be masters of Tuscany, that country was without dispute, in men, money and arms, one of the most flourishing provinces in the world, as appears by Machiavelli's account, and the relation of what happened between Charles the eighth and the magistrates of Florence, which I have mentioned already from Guicciardini. Now whoever shall consider the strength of that country in those days, together with what it might have been in the space of a hundred and forty years, in which they have had no war, nor any other plague, than the extortion, fraud, rapine and cruelty of their princes, and compare it with their present desolate, wretched and contemptible condition, may, if he please, think that much veneration is due to the princes that govern them, but will never make any man believe that their title can be grounded upon beneficence. The like may be said of the duke of Savoy, who pretending (upon I know not what account) that every peasant in the duchy ought to pay him two crowns every half year, did in 1662 subtly find out, that in every year there were thirteen halves; so that a poor man who had nothing but what he gained by hard labour, was through his fatherly care and beneficence, forced to pay six and twenty crowns to his royal highness, to be employ'd in his discrete and virtuous pleasures at Turin.

The condition of the seventeen provinces of the Netherlands (and even of Spain itself) when they fell to the house of Austria, was of the same nature: and I will confess as much as can be required, if any other marks of their government do remain, than such as are manifest evidences of their pride, avarice, luxury and cruelty.

France in outward appearance makes a better show; but nothing in this world is more miserable, than that people under the fatherly care of their triumphant monarch. The best of their condition is like asses and mastiff-dogs, to work and fight, to be oppressed and kill'd for him; and those among them who have any understanding well know, that their industry, courage, and good success, is not only unprofitable, but destructive to them; and that by increasing the power of their master, they add weight to their own chains. And if any prince, or succession of princes, have made a more modest use of their power, or more faithfully discharged the trust reposed in them, it must be imputed peculiarly to them, as a testimony of their personal virtue, and can have no effect upon others.

The rights therefore of kings are not grounded upon conquest; the liberties of nations do not arise from the grants of their princes; the oath of allegiance binds no private man to more than the law directs, and has no influence upon the whole body of every nation: Many princes are known to their subjects only by the injuries, losses and mischiefs brought upon them; such as are good and just, ought to be rewarded for their personal virtue, but can confer no right upon those who no way resemble them; and whoever pretends to that merit, must prove it by his actions: Rebellion being nothing but a renewed war, can never be against a government that was not established by war, and of itself is neither good nor evil, more than any other war; but is just or unjust according to the cause or manner of it. Besides, that rebellion which by Samuel is compar'd to witchcraft, is not of private men, or a people against the prince, but of the prince against God:[4] The Israelites are often said to have rebelled

---

[4] 1 Sam. 15.23.

against the law, word, or command of God; but tho they frequently opposed their kings, I do not find rebellion imputed to them on that account, nor any ill character put upon such actions. We are told also of some kings who had been subdued, and afterwards rebelled against Chedorlaomer and other kings; but their cause is not blamed, and we have some reason to believe it good, because Abraham took part with those who had rebelled.[5] However it can be of no prejudice to the cause I defend: for tho it were true, that those subdued kings could not justly rise against the person who had subdued them; or that generally no king being once vanquished, could have a right of rebellion against his conqueror, it could have no relation to the actions of a people vindicating their own laws and liberties against a prince who violates them; for that war which never was, can never be renewed. And if it be true in any case, that hands and swords are given to men, that they only may be slaves who have no courage, it must be when liberty is overthrown by those, who of all men ought with the utmost industry and vigour to have defended it.

That this should be known, is not only necessary for the safety of nations, but advantageous to such kings as are wise and good. They who know the frailty of human nature, will always distrust their own; and desiring only to do what they ought, will be glad to be restrain'd from that which they ought not to do. Being taught by reason and experience, that nations delight in the peace and justice of a good government, they will never fear a general insurrection, whilst they take care it be rightly administered; and finding themselves by this means to be safe, will never be unwilling, that their children or successors should be obliged to tread in the same steps.

If it be said that this may sometimes cause disorders, I acknowledge it; but no human condition being perfect, such a one is to be chosen, which carries with it the most tolerable inconveniences: And it being much better that the irregularities and excesses of a prince should be restrained or suppressed, than that whole nations should perish by them, those constitutions that make the best provision against the greatest evils, are most to be commended. If governments were instituted to gratify the lusts of one man, those could not be good that set limits to them; but all reasonable men confessing that they are instituted for the good of nations, they only can deserve praise, who above all things endeavour to procure it, and appoint means proportioned to that end. The great variety of governments which we see in the world, is nothing but the effect of this

[5] [Genesis 14.]

care; and all nations have been, and are more or less happy, as they or their ancestors have had vigour of spirit, integrity of manners, and wisdom to invent and establish such orders, as have better or worse provided for this common good, which was sought by all. But as no rule can be so exact, to make provision against all contestations; and all disputes about right do naturally end in force when justice is denied (ill men never willingly submitting to any decision that is contrary to their passions and interests) the best constitutions are of no value, if there be not a power to support them. This power first exerts itself in the execution of justice by the ordinary officers: But no nation having been so happy, as not sometimes to produce such princes as Edward and Richard the Seconds, and such ministers as Gaveston, Spencer, and Tresilian, the ordinary officers of justice often want the will, and always the power to restrain them. So that the rights and liberties of a nation must be utterly subverted and abolished, if the power of the whole may not be employed to assert them, or punish the violation of them. But as it is the fundamental right of every nation to be governed by such laws, in such manner, and by such persons as they think most conducing to their own good, they cannot be accountable to any but themselves for what they do in that most important affair.

SECTION 37

The English Government was not ill constituted,
the defects more lately observed proceeding from the
change of manners, and corruption of the times.

I AM not ignorant that many honest and good men acknowledging these rights, and the care of our ancestors to preserve them, think they wanted wisdom rightly to proportionate the means to the end. 'Tis not enough, say they, for the general of an army to desire victory; he only can deserve praise, who has skill, industry, and courage to take the best measures of obtaining it. Neither is it enough for wise legislators to preserve liberty, and to erect such a government as may stand for a time; but to set such clear rules to those who are to put it in execution, that every man may know when they transgress; and appoint such means for restraining or punishing them, as may be used speedily, surely, and effectually, without danger to the publick. Sparta being thus constituted, we hardly find that, for more than eight hundred years, any king presumed to pass the limits prescribed by the law. If any Roman consul grew insolent, he might be reduced to order without blood, or danger to the publick; and no dictator ever usurped a power over liberty till the time of Sulla, when all things in the city were so changed, that the ancient foundations were become too narrow. In Venice the power of the duke is so circumscribed, that in 1300 years, no one except Falerio and Tiepoli, has dared to attempt anything against the laws: and they were immediately suppressed with little commotion in the city. On the other side, our law is so ambiguous, perplexed and intricate, that 'tis hard to know when 'tis broken. In all the publick contests we have had, men of good judgment and integrity have follow'd both parties. The means of transgressing and procuring partizans to make good by force the most notorious violations of liberty, have been so easy, that no prince who has endeavoured it, ever failed to get great numbers of followers, and to do infinite mischiefs before he could be removed. The nation has been brought to fight against those they had made to be what they were, upon the unequal terms of hazarding all against nothing. If they had success, they gained no more than was their own before, and which the law ought to have secured: whereas 'tis evident, that if at any one time the contrary had happened, the nation had been utterly enslaved; and no victory was ever gained without the loss of much noble and innocent blood.

To this I answer, that no right judgment can be given of human things, without a particular regard to the time in which they passed. We esteem Scipio, Hannibal, Pyrrhus, Alexander, Epaminondas and Caesar, to have been admirable commanders in war, because they had in a most eminent degree all the qualities that could make them so, and knew best how to employ the arms then in use according to the discipline of their times; and yet no man doubts, that if the most skilful of them could be raised from the grave, restored to the utmost vigour of mind and body, set at the head of the best armies he ever commanded, and placed upon the frontiers of France or Flanders, he would not know how to advance or retreat, nor by what means to take any of the places in those parts, as they are now fortified and defended; but would most certainly be beaten by any insignificant fellow with a small number of men, furnished with such arms as are now in use, and following the methods now practiced. Nay, the manner of marching, encamping, besieging, attacking, defending and fighting, is so much altered within the last threescore years, that no man observing the discipline that was then thought to be the best, could possibly defend himself against that which has been since found out, tho the terms are still the same. And if it be consider'd that political matters are subject to the same mutations (as certainly they are) it will be sufficient to excuse our ancestors, who suiting their government to the ages in which they lived, could neither foresee the changes that might happen in future generations, nor appoint remedies for the mischiefs they did not foresee.

They knew that the kings of several nations had been kept within the limits of the law, by the virtue and power of a great and brave nobility; and that no other way of supporting a mix'd monarchy had ever been known in the world, than by putting the balance into the hands of those who had the greatest interest in nations, and who by birth and estate enjoy'd greater advantages than kings could confer upon them for rewards of betraying their country. They knew that when the nobility was so great as not easily to be number'd, the little that was left to the king's disposal, was not sufficient to corrupt many; and if some might fall under the temptation, those who continued in their integrity, would easily be able to chastise them for deserting the publick cause, and by that means deter kings from endeavouring to seduce them from their duty. Whilst things continued in this posture, kings might safely be trusted (with the advice of their council) to confer the commands of the militia in towns and provinces upon the most eminent men in them: And whilst those kings were exercised in almost perpetual wars, and placed their glory in the greatness of the actions they achieved by the power and valour of their people, it was their interest always to chuse such as seemed best to deserve that honour. It was not to be imagined that through the weakness of some, and malice of others, those dignities should by degrees be turned into empty titles, and become the rewards of the greatest crimes, and the vilest services; or that the noblest of their descendants for want of them, should be brought under the name of commoners, and deprived of all privileges except such as were common to them with their grooms. Such a stupendous change being in process of time insensibly introduced, the foundations of that government which they had established, were removed, and the superstructure overthrown. The balance by which it subsisted was broken; and 'tis as impossible to restore it, as for most of those who at this day go under the name of noblemen, to perform the duties required from the ancient nobility of England. And tho there were a charm in the name, and those who have it, should be immediately filled with a spirit like to that which animated our ancestors, and endeavour to deserve the honors they possess, by such services to the country as they ought to have perform'd before they had them, they would not be able to accomplish it. They have neither the interest nor the estates required for so great a work. Those who have estates at a rack rent, have no dependents. Their tenants, when they have paid what is agreed, owe them nothing; and knowing they shall be turn'd out of their tenements, as soon as any other will give a little more, they look upon their lords as men who receive more from them than they confer upon them. This dependence being lost, the lords have only more money to spend or lay up than others, but no command of men; and can therefore neither protect the weak, nor curb the insolent. By this means all things have been brought into the hands of the king and the commoners, and there is nothing left to cement them, and to maintain the union. The perpetual jarrings we hear every day; the division of the nation into such factions as threaten us with ruin, and all the disorders that we see or fear, are the effects of this rupture. These things are not to be imputed to our original constitutions, but to those who have subverted them: And if they who by corrupting, changing, enervating and annihilating the nobility, which was the principal support of the ancient regular monarchy, have driven those who are truly noblemen into the same interest and name with the commons, and by that means increased a party which never was, and I think never can be united to the court, they are to answer for the consequences; and if they perish, their destruction is from themselves.

The inconveniences therefore proceed not from the institution, but from the innovation. The law was plain, but it has been industriously rendered perplex: They who were to have upheld it are overthrown. That which might have been easily performed when the people was armed, and had a great, strong, virtuous and powerful nobility to lead them, is made difficult, now they are disarmed, and that nobility abolished. Our ancestors may evidently appear, not only to have intended well, but to have taken a right course to accomplish what they intended. This had effect as long as the cause continued; and the only fault that can be ascribed to that which they established is, that it has not proved to be perpetual; which is no more than may be justly said of the best human constitutions that ever have been in the world. If we will be just to our ancestors, it will become us in our time rather to pursue what we know they intended, and by new constitutions to repair the breaches made upon the old, than to accuse them of the defects that will forever attend the actions of men. Taking our affairs at the worst, we shall soon find, that if we have the same spirit they had, we may easily restore our nation to its ancient liberty, dignity and happiness; and if we do not, the fault is owing to ourselves, and not to any want of virtue and wisdom in them.

SECTION 38

The Power of calling and dissolving
Parliaments is not simply in the King. The variety
of Customs in chusing Parliament men, and the Errors
a people may commit, neither prove that Kings
are or ought to be Absolute.

THE original of magistratical power, the intention of our ancestors in its creation, and the ways prescribed for the direction and limitation of it may, I presume, sufficiently appear by what has been said. But because our author, taking hold of every twig, pretends *that kings may call and dissolve parliaments at their pleasure*, and from thence infers *the power to be wholly in them;* alleges *the various customs in several parts of this nation used in the elections of parliament men, to proceed from the king's will;* and *because a people may commit errors*, thinks *all power ought to be put into the hands of the king:*[1]

I answer, 1. That the power of calling and dissolving parliaments is not simply in kings. They may call parliaments, if there be occasion, at times when the law does not exact it; they are placed as sentinels, and ought vigilantly to observe the motions of the enemy, and give notice of his approach: But if the sentinel fall asleep, neglect his duty, or maliciously endeavour to betray the city, those who are concern'd may make use of all other means to know their danger, and to preserve themselves. The ignorance, incapacity, negligence or luxury of a king, is a great calamity to a nation, and his malice is worse, but not an irreparable ruin. Remedies may be, and often have been found against the worst of their vices. The last French kings of the races of Meroveus and Pepin brought many mischiefs upon the kingdom, but the destruction was prevented. Edward and Richard the Seconds of England were not unlike them, and we know by what means the nation was preserved. The question was not who had the right, or who ought to call parliaments, but how the commonwealth might be saved from ruin. The consuls, or other chief magistrates in Rome, had certainly a right of assembling and dismissing the senate: But when Hannibal was at the gates, or any other imminent danger threatened them with destruction; if that magistrate had been drunk, mad, or gained by the enemy, no wise man can think that formalities were to have been observed. In such cases every man is a magistrate; and he who best knows

[1] [*Patriarcha*, ch. 30, pp. 118–119.]

the danger, and the means of preventing it, has a right of calling the senate or people to an assembly. The people would, and certainly ought to follow him, as they did Brutus and Valerius against Tarquin, or Horatius and Valerius against the decemviri; and whoever should do otherwise, might for sottishness be compared to the courtiers of the two last kings of Spain. The first of these, by name Philip the third, being indisposed in cold weather, · a *braziero* of coals was brought into his chamber, and placed so near to him, that he was cruelly scorched. A nobleman then present said to one who stood by him, *the king burns;* the other answered, it was true, but the page, whose office it was to bring and remove the *braziero*, was not there; and before he could be found, his majesty's legs and face were so burnt, that it caus'd an erysipelas, of which he died. Philip the fourth escaped not much better, who being surprised as he was hunting by a violent storm of rain and hail, and no man presuming to lend the king a cloak, he was so wet before the officer could be found who carried his own, that he took a cold, which cast him into a dangerous fever. If kings like the consequences of such a regularity, they may cause it to be observed in their own families; but nations looking in the first place to their own safety, would be guilty of the most extreme stupidity, if they should suffer themselves to be ruined for adhering to such ceremonies.

This is said upon a supposition, that the whole power of calling and dissolving parliaments, is by the law placed in the king: but I utterly deny that it is so; and to prove it, shall give the following reasons.

(1.) That the king can have no such power, unless it be given to him, for every man is originally free; and the same power that makes him king, gives him all that belongs to his being king. 'Tis not therefore an inherent, but a delegated power; and whoever receives it, is accountable to those that gave it; for, as our author is forced to confess, *they who give authority by commission, do always retain more than they grant.*[2]

(2.) The law for annual parliaments expressly declares it not to be in the king's power, as to the point of their meeting, nor consequently their continuance. For they meet to no purpose if they may not continue to do the work for which they meet; and it were absurd to give them a power of meeting, if they might not continue till it be done: For, as Grotius says, *Qui dat finem, dat media ad finem necessaria.*[3] The only reason why parliaments do meet, is to provide for the publick good; and they by law ought to meet for that end. They ought not therefore to be

---

[2] [*Patriarcha*, ch. 30, p. 118.]

[3] ["That [law] which provides an end, pro-vides the means necessary to the end." Gro-tius, *De jure*, bk. 2, ch. 7, sec. 4.]

dissolved, till it be accomplished. For this reason the opinion given by Tresilian, that kings might dissolve parliaments at their pleasure, was judged to be a principal part of his treason.

(3.) We have already proved, that Saxons, Danes, Normans, &c. who had no title to the crown, were made kings by micklegemotes, witenagemotes, and parliaments; that is, either by the whole people, or their representatives: Others have been by the same authority restrained, brought to order, or deposed. But as it is impossible that such as were not kings, and had no title to be kings, could by virtue of a kingly power call parliaments, when they had none; and absurd to think that such as were in the throne, who had not govern'd according to law, would suffer themselves to be restrain'd, imprisoned, or deposed by parliaments, called and sitting by themselves, and still depending upon their will to be or not to be; 'tis certain that parliaments have in themselves a power of sitting and acting for the publick good.

2. To the second. The various customs used in elections are nothing to this question. In the counties, which make up the body of the nation, all freeholders have their votes: these are properly *cives*, members of the commonwealth, in distinction from those who are only *incolae*, or inhabitants, villains, and such as being under their parents, are not yet *sui juris*. These in the beginning of the Saxons' reign in England, composed the micklegemotes; and when they grew to be so numerous that one place could not contain them, or so far dispersed, that without trouble and danger they could not leave their habitations, they deputed such as should represent them. When the nation came to be more polished, to inhabit cities and towns, and to set up several arts and trades; those who exercised them were thought to be as useful to the commonwealth, as the freeholders in the country, and to deserve the same privileges. But it not being reasonable that everyone should in this case do what he pleased, it was thought fit that the king with his council (which always consisted of the *proceres* and *magnates regni*[4]) should judge what numbers of men, and what places deserved to be made corporations or bodies politick, and to enjoy those privileges, by which he did not confer upon them anything that was his, but according to the trust reposed in him, did dispense out of the publick stock parcels of what he had received from the whole nation: And whether this was to be enjoy'd by all the inhabitants, as in Westminster; by the common hall, as in London; or by the mayor, aldermen, jurats and corporation, as in other places, 'tis the same thing: for in all these cases the king does only distribute, not give, and under

---

[4] [Nobles and great men of the kingdom.]

the same condition that he might call parliaments, that is, for the publick good. This indeed increases the honor of the person entrusted, and adds weight to the obligation incumbent upon him; but can never change the nature of the thing, so as to make that an inherent, which is only a delegated power. And as parliaments, when occasion required, have been assembled, have refus'd to be dissolved till their work was finished, have severely punished those who went about to persuade kings, that such matters depended absolutely upon their will, and made laws to the contrary: 'tis not to be imagined, that they would not also have interposed their authority in matters of charters, if it had been observed that any king had notoriously abused the trust reposed in ·him, and turned the power to his private advantage, with which he was entrusted for the publick good.

That which renders this most plain and safe, is, that men chosen in this manner to serve in parliament, do not act by themselves, but in conjunction with others who are sent thither by prescription; nor by a power derived from kings, but from those that chuse them. If it be true therefore that those who delegate powers, do always retain to themselves more than they give, they who send these men, do not give them an absolute power of doing whatsoever they please, but retain to themselves more than they confer upon their deputies: They must therefore be accountable to their principals, contrary to what our author asserts. This continues in force, tho he knows not, that *any knights and burgesses have ever been questioned by those that sent them;*[5] for it cannot be concluded they ought not, or may not be question'd, because none have been questioned. But in truth they are frequently questioned: The people do perpetually judge of the behaviour of their deputies. Whensoever any of them has the misfortune not to satisfy the major part of those that chose him, he is sure to be rejected with disgrace the next time he shall desire to be chosen. This is not only a sufficient punishment for such faults, as he who is but one of five hundred may probably commit, but as much as the greatest and freest people of the world did ever inflict upon their commanders that brought the greatest losses upon them. Appius Claudius, Pomponius, and Terentius Varro, survived the greatest defeats that ever the Romans suffer'd; and tho they had caused them by their folly and perverseness, were never punished. Yet I think no man doubts that the Romans had as much right over their own officers, as the Athenians and Carthaginians, who frequently put them to death. They thought the mind of a commander would be too much distracted, if at the same time

---

[5] [*Patriarcha*, ch. 30, p. 119.]

he should stand in fear both of the enemy and his own countrymen: And as they always endeavoured to chuse the best men, they would lay no other necessity upon them of performing their duty, than what was suggested by their own virtue and love to their country. 'Tis not therefore to be thought strange, if the people of England have follow'd the most generous and most prosperous examples. Besides, if anything has been defective in their usual proceedings with their delegates, the inconvenience has been repaired by the modesty of the best and wisest of them that were chosen. Many in all ages, and sometimes the whole body of the commons, have refused to give their opinion in some cases, till they had consulted with those that sent them: The houses have been often adjourned to give them time to do it; and if this were done more frequently, or that the towns, cities and counties, had on some occasions given instructions to their deputies, matters would probably have gone better in parliament than they have often done.

3. The question is not, whether the parliament be impeccable or infallible, but whether an assembly of nobility, with a house of commons composed of those who are best esteemed by their neighbors in all the towns and counties of England, are more or less subject to error or corruption, than such a man, woman or child, as happens to be next in blood to the last king. Many men do usually see more than one; and if we may believe the wisest king, *In the multitude of counsellors, there is safety.*[6] Such as are of mature age, good experience, and approved reputation for virtue and wisdom, will probably judge better than children or fools. Men are thought to be more fit for war than women; and those who are bred up in discipline, to understand it better than those who never knew anything of it. If some counties or cities fail to chuse such men as are eminently capable, all will hardly be so mistaken as to chuse those who have no more of wisdom or virtue, than is usually entail'd upon families. But Filmer at a venture admires the profound wisdom of the king; tho besides such as we have known, histories give us too many proofs, that all those who have been possessed of crowns, have not excelled that way. He speaks of kings in general, and makes no difference between Solomon and his foolish son. He distinguishes not our Edward the first from Edward the second; Edward the third from Richard the second; or Henry the fifth from Henry the sixth. And because all of them were kings, all of them, if he deserves credit, must needs have been endow'd with profound wisdom. David was wise as an angel of God; therefore the present kings of France, Spain and Sweden, must have been so also,

[6] Prov. 11.14.

when they were but five years old: Joan of Castile could not be mad, nor the two Joans of Naples infamous strumpets, or else all his arguments fall to the ground. For tho Solomon's wisdom surpassed that of all the people, yet men could not rely equally upon that of Rehoboam, unless it had been equal. And if they are all equal in wisdom when they come to be equally kings, Perseus of Macedon was as great a captain as Philip or Alexander; Commodus and Heliogabalus were as wise and virtuous as Marcus Aurelius and Antoninus Pius: nay, Christina of Sweden in her infancy was as fit to command an army as her valiant father. If this be most absurd and false, there can be neither reason nor sense in proposing, as our author does, that the power should be in the king, because the parliament is not infallible. *It is*, says he, *for the head to correct, and not to expect the consent of the members or parties peccant to be judges in their own cases; nor is it needful to confine the king*, &c.[7] Besides that this is directly contrary to his own fundamental maxim, that no man must be the judge of his own case, in as much as this would put the power into the king's hands, to decide the controversies between himself and the people, in which his own passions, private interest, and the corrupt counsels of ill ministers, will always lead him out of the way of justice, the inconveniences that may arise from a possibility that the parliament or people is not infallible, will be turned to the most certain and destructive mischiefs; as must have fallen out in Spain, if, upon a supposition that the estates of Castile might err, the correction of such errors had been left to the profound wisdom and exquisite judgment of Joan their queen and head, who was stark mad. And the like may be said of many other princes, who through natural or accidental infirmities, want of age, or dotage, have been utterly unable to judge of anything.

The matter will not be much mended, tho I pass from idiots and lunaticks, to such as know well enough how to clothe and feed themselves, and to perform the ordinary functions of life; and yet have been as uncapable of giving a right judgment concerning the weighty matters of government, as the weakest of children, or the most furious of madmen. Good manners forbid me to enumerate the examples of this kind, which Europe has produced even in this age: But I should commit a greater fault, if I did in silence pass over the extravagances of those, who being most weak in judgment, and irregular in their appetites, have been most impatient of any restraint upon their will. The brave Gustavus Adolphus, and his nephew Carolus Gustavus, who was not inferior to him in valour, wisdom, and love to his people, were content with the power that the

[7] [*Patriarcha*, ch. 30, p. 119.]

laws of their country gave to them: But Frederick the fourth of Denmark never rested till he had overthrown the liberty of that nation. Casimir by attempting the like in Poland, lost almost half of that kingdom; and flying from the other, left all to be ravaged by Swedes, Tartars, and Cossacks. The present emperor[8] who passed his time in setting songs in musick with a wretched Italian eunuch, when he ought to have been at the head of a brave army, raised to oppose the Turks in the year 1664, and which under good conduct might have overthown the Ottoman empire, as soon as he was delivered from the fear of that enemy, fell upon his own subjects with such cruelty, that they are now forced to fly to the Turks for protection; the Protestants especially, who find their condition more tolerable under those professed enemies to Christianity, than to be exposed to the pride, avarice, perfidiousness and violence of the Jesuits by whom he is governed. And the qualities of the king of Portugal[9] are so well known, together with the condition to which he would have brought his kingdom if he had not been sent to the Terceiras, that I need not speak particularly of him.

If kings therefore, by virtue of their office, are constituted judges over the body of their people, because the people, or parliaments representing them, are not infallible; those kings who are children, fools, disabled by age, or madmen, are so also; women have the same right where they are admitted to the succession; those men who, tho of ripe age and not superannuated, nor directly fools or madmen, yet absolutely uncapable of judging important affairs, or by their passions, interests, vices, or malice and wickedness of their ministers, servants and favorites, are set to oppress and ruin the people, enjoy the same privilege; than which nothing can be imagined more absurd and abominable, nor more directly tending to the corruption and destruction of the nations under them, for whose good and safety our author confesses they have their power.

[8] [Leopold I, ruler of the Holy Roman Empire. The subjects who called on the Turks for aid were the Hungarians.]   [9] [Alfonso VI.]

SECTION 39

*Those Kings only are heads of the People,
who are good, wise, and seek to advance no Interest
but that of the Publick.*

THE worst of men seldom arrive to such a degree of impudence, as plainly to propose the most mischievous follies and enormities. They who are enemies to virtue, and fear not God, are afraid of men, and dare not offer such things as the world will not bear, lest by that means they should overthrow their own designs. All poison must be disguised, and no man can be persuaded to eat arsenic, unless it be cover'd with something that appears to be harmless. Creusa would have abhorr'd Medea's present, if the pestilent venom had not been hidden by the exterior lustre of gold and gems. The garment that destroy'd Hercules appear'd beautiful;[1] and Eve had neither eaten of the forbidden tree, nor given the fruit to her husband, if it had not seemed to be good and pleasant, and she had not been induced to believe that by eating it they should both be as gods. The servants of the Devil have always followed the same method: their malice is carried on by fraud, and they have seldom destroy'd any, but such as they had first deceived. Truth can never conduce to mischief, and is best discovered by plain words; but nothing is more usual with ill men than to cover their mischievous designs with figurative phrases. It would be too ridiculous to say in plain terms, that all kings without distinction are better able to judge of all matters than any or all their people; they must therefore be called *the head*, that thereby they may be invested with all the preeminences which in a natural body belong to that part; and men must be made to believe the analogy between the natural and political body to be perfect. But the matter must be better examined before this mortal poison seem fit to be swallowed.

The word *head* is figuratively used both in Scripture and profane authors in several senses, in relation to places or persons, and always implies something of real or seeming preeminence in point of honor or jurisdiction. Thus Damascus is said to be the head of Syria; Samaria of Ephraim, and Ephraim of the ten tribes:[2] that is, Ephraim was the chief

---

[1] [Medea, divorced by Jason, sends to his new bride Creusa a magic robe that consumes her in fire. Similarly, Hercules' wife Deianira sends him a robe which she thinks will cause him to love her, but which in fact consumes him in fiery pain. See Seneca, *Medea* and *Hercules Oetaeus*.]

[2] [Isaiah 7:8–9.]

tribe; Samaria was the chief city of Ephraim, and Damascus of Syria; tho it be certain that Ephraim had no jurisdiction over the other tribes, nor Samaria over the other cities of Ephraim, but every one according to the law had an equal power within itself, or the territories belonging to it; and no privileges were granted to one above another, except to Jerusalem, in the matter of religion, because the Temple was placed there.

The words also head, prince, principal man, or captain, seem to be equivocal; and in this sense the same men are called heads of the tribes, princes in the houses of their fathers: and 'tis said, that two hundred heads of the tribe of Reuben were carried away captive by Tiglath-pileser,[3] and proportionably in the other tribes; which were a strange thing, if the word did imply that supreme, absolute and infinite power that our author attributes to it: and no man of less understanding than he, can comprehend how there should be two hundred or more sovereign unlimited powers in one tribe, most especially when 'tis certain that one series of kings had for many ages reigned over that tribe and nine more; and that every one of those tribes, as well as the particular cities, even from their first entrance into the promised land, had a full jurisdiction within itself. When the Gileadites came to Jephthah, he suspected them, and asked whether indeed they intended to make him their head? they answered, if he would lead them against the Ammonites, he should be their head.[4] In the like sense when Jul. Caesar in despair would have killed himself, one of his soldiers dissuaded him from that design, by telling him, *That the safety of so many nations that had made him their head, depending upon his life, it would be cruelty in him to take such a resolution.*[5] But for all that, when this head was taken off, the body did still subsist: upon which I observe many fundamental differences between the relation of this figurative head (even when the word is rightly applied) and that of the natural head to their respective bodies.

The figurative heads may be many, the natural but one.

The people makes or creates the figurative head, the natural is from itself, or connate with the body.

The natural body cannot change or subsist without the natural head; but a people may change and subsist very well without the artificial. Nay, if it had been true, that the world had chosen Caesar, as it was not

[3] 1 Chron. 5.

[4] Judg. 12.

[5] Cum tot ab hac anima populorum vita salusque/Pendeat, & tantus caput hoc sibi fecerit orbis,/Saevitia est voluisse mori. Lucan. [Lucan, *Pharsalia*, bk. 5, li. 685.]

(for he was chosen only by a factious mercenary army, and the soundest part so far opposed that election, that they brought him to think of killing himself) there could have been no truth in this flattering assertion, *That the safety of the whole depended upon his life:* for the world could not only subsist without him, but without any such head, as it had done, before he by the help of his corrupted soldiery had usurped the power; which also shews that a civil head may be a matter of convenience, but not of necessity. Many nations have had none; and if the expression be so far stretched, as to make it extend to the annual or temporary magistrates set up by the Athenians, Carthaginians, Romans, and other ancient commonwealths, or to those at this day in Venice, Holland, Switzerland, and other places, it must be confess'd that the people who made, deposed, abrogated, or abolished both the magistrates and magistracies, had the power of framing, directing and removing their heads, which our author will say is most absurd. Yet they did it without any prejudice to themselves, and very often much to their advantage.

In mentioning these vast and essential differences between the natural and political head, I no way intend to exclude others that may be of equal weight; but as all figurative expressions have their strength only from similitude, there can be little or none in this, which differs in so many important points, and can therefore be of no effect.

However, right proceeds from identity, and not from similitude. The right of a man over me is by being my father, and not by being like my father. If I had a brother so perfectly resembling me as to deceive our parents, which has sometimes happened to twins, it could give him no right to anything that is mine. If the power therefore of correcting the parties peccant, which our author attributes to kings, be grounded upon the name of head, and a resemblance between the heads of the body politick and body natural; if this resemblance be found to be exceedingly imperfect, uncertain, or perhaps no way relating to the matter in question; or tho it did, and were absolutely perfect, could confer no right; the allegation of it is impertinent and absurd.

This being cleared, 'tis time to examine, what the office of the head is in a natural body, that we may learn from thence why that name is sometimes given to those who are eminent in political bodies, and to whom it does belong.

Some men account the head to be so absolutely the seat of all the senses, as to derive even that of feeling, which is exercised in every part, from the brain: but I think 'tis not doubted that all the rest have both their seat and function in the head; and whatsoever is useful or hurtful to a man, is by them represented to the understanding; as Aristotle says, *Nihil est in intellectu, quod non sit prius in sensu.*[6] This is properly the part of every magistrate: He is the sentinel of the publick, and is to represent what he discovers beneficial or hurtful to the society; which office belongs not only to the supreme, but proportionably to the subordinate. In this sense were the chief men among the Israelites called *heads of their father's house, choice and mighty men of valour, chief of the princes.*[7] And in the following chapter mention is made of *nine hundred and fifty Benjaminites, chief men in the house of their fathers.*[8] These men exercised a charitable care over such as were inferior to them in power and valour, without any shadow of sovereignty, or possibility that there could be so many sovereigns: and such as were under their care are said to be their brethren; which is not a word of majesty and domination, but of dearness and equality. The name therefore of head may be given to a sovereign, but it implies nothing of sovereignty; and must be exercised with charity, which always terminates in the good of others. The head cannot correct or chastise; the proper work of that part is only to indicate, and he who takes upon him to do more, is not the head. A natural body is homogeneous, and cannot subsist if it be not so. We cannot take one part of a horse, another of a bear, and put upon them the head of a lion; for it would be a monster, that would have neither action nor life. The head must be of the same nature with the other members, or it cannot subsist. But the lord or master differs *in specie*[9] from his servants and slaves, he is not therefore properly their head.

Besides, the head cannot have a subsistence without the body, nor any interest contrary to that of the body; and 'tis impossible for anything to be good for the head, that is hurtful to the body. A prince therefore, or magistrate, who sets up an interest in himself distinct from, or repugnant to that of the people, renounces the title or quality of their head. Indeed, Moses was the head of the Israelites; for when God threatened to destroy that people, and promised to make him a great nation, he waived the particular advantages offer'd to himself, interceded for them, and procured their pardon. Yet he was not able to bear the weight of the government alone, but desired that some might be appointed to assist him. Gideon was the head of the same people, but he would not reign himself, nor suffer his sons to reign over them. Samuel was also their head; he took nothing from any man, defrauded none, took bribes from no man,

---

[6] ["Nothing is in the intellect which is not first in the senses." Aristotle, *On the Soul,* bk. 3, 432a.]

[7] 1 Chron. 7.40.

[8] [Actually in 9:9.]

[9] [In kind.]

oppressed none; God and the people were his witnesses: He blamed them for their rebellion against God in asking a king, but was no way concerned for himself or his family. David likewise had a right to that title; for he desired that God would spare the people, and turn the effect of his anger against himself, and the house of his father. But Rehoboam was not their head; for tho he acknowledged that his father had laid a heavy yoke upon them, yet he told them he would add to the weight; and that if his father had chastised them with whips, he would chastise them with scorpions. The head is no burden to the body, and can lay none upon it; the head cannot chastise any member; and he who does so, be it more or less, cannot be the head. Jeroboam was not the head of the revolting tribes; for the head takes care of the members, and to provide for the safety of the whole: But he through fear that the people going to Jerusalem to worship, should return to the house of David, by setting up idols to secure his own interests, drew guilt and destruction upon them. Tho it should be granted that Augustus by a gentle use of his power, had in a manner expiated the detestable villainies committed in the acquisition, and had truly deserved to be called the head of the Romans; yet that title could no way belong to Caligula, Claudius, Nero or Vitellius, who neither had the qualities requir'd in the head, nor the understanding or will to perform the office. Nay, if I should carry the matter farther, and acknowledge that Brutus, Cincinnatus, Fabius, Camillus, and others, who in the time of their annual or shorter magistracies, had by their vigilance, virtue and care to preserve the city in safety, and to provide for the publick good, performed the office of the head, and might deserve the name; I might justly deny it to the greatest princes that have been in the world, who having their power for life, and leaving it to descend to their children, have wanted the virtues requir'd for the performance of their duty: And I should less fear to be guilty of an absurdity in saying, that a nation might every year change its head, than that he can be the head, who cares not for the members, nor understands the things that conduce to their good, most especially if he set up an interest in himself against them. It cannot be said that these are imaginary cases, and that no prince does these things; for the proof is too easy, and the examples too numerous. Caligula could not have wished the Romans but one head, that he might cut it off at once, if he had been that head, and had advanced no interest contrary to that of the members. Nero had not burn'd the city of Rome, if his concernments had been inseparably united to those of the people. He who caused above three hundred thousand of his innocent unarmed subjects to be murder'd, and fill'd his whole kingdom with fire and blood, did set up a personal interest repugnant to that of the nation; and no better testimony can be requir'd to shew that he did so, than a letter written by his son, to take off the penalty due to one of the chief ministers of those cruelties, for this reason, that what he had done, was *by the command and for the service of his royal father.*[10] King John did not pursue the advantage of his people, when he endeavoured to subject them to the pope or the Moors. And whatever prince seeks assistance from foreign powers, or makes leagues with any stranger or enemy for his own advantage against his people, however secret the treaty may be, declares himself not to be the head, but an enemy to them. The head cannot stand in need of an exterior help against the body, nor subsist when divided from it. He therefore that courts such an assistance, divides himself from the body; and if he do subsist, it must be by a life he has in himself, distinct from that of the body, which the head cannot have.

But besides these enormities, that testify the most wicked rage and fury in the highest degree, there is another practice, which no man that knows the world can deny to be common with princes, and incompatible with the nature of a head. The head cannot desire to draw all the nourishment of the body to itself, nor more than a due proportion. If the rest of the parts are sick, weak or cold, the head suffers equally with them, and if they perish must perish also. Let this be compared with the actions of many princes we know, and we shall soon see which of them are heads of their people. If the gold brought from the Indies has been equally distributed by the kings of Spain to the body of that nation, I consent they may be called the heads. If the kings of France assume no more of the riches of that great kingdom than their due proportion, let them also wear that honourable name. But if the naked backs and empty bellies of their miserable subjects evince the contrary, it can by no means belong to them. If those great nations waste and languish; if nothing be so common in the best provinces belonging to them, as misery, famine, and all the effects of the most outrageous oppression, whilst their princes and favorites possess such treasures as the most wanton prodigality cannot exhaust; if that which is gained by the sweat of so many millions of men, be torn out of the mouths of their starving wives and children, to foment the vices of those luxurious courts, or reward the ministers of their lusts, the nourishment is not distributed equally to all the parts of the body; the economy of the whole is overthrown, and they who do these things, cannot be the heads, nor parts of the body, but something distinct from

[10] [Charles I is meant. The "minister of those cruelties" was the earl of Strafford. The "innocent unarmed subjects" were the English Protestants massacred in the Irish rebellion of 1641.]

and repugnant to it. 'Tis not therefore he who is found in, or advanced to the place of the head, who is truly the head: 'Tis not he who ought, but he who does perform the office of the head, that deserves the name and privileges belonging to the head. If our author therefore will persuade us that any king is head of his people, he must do it by arguments peculiarly relating to him, since those in general are found to be false. If he say that the king as king may direct or correct the people, and that the power of determining all controversies must be referred to him, because they may be mistaken, he must show that the king is infallible; for unless he do so, the wound is not cured. This also must be by some other way, than by saying he is their head; for such powers belong not to the office of the head, and we see that all kings do not deserve that name: Many of them want both understanding and will to perform the functions of the head; and many act directly contrary in the whole course of their government. If any therefore among them have merited the glorious name of heads of nations, it must have been by their personal virtues, by a vigilant care of the good of their people, by an inseparable conjunction of interests with them, by an ardent love to every member of the society, by a moderation of spirit affecting no undue superiority, or assuming any singular advantage which they are not willing to communicate to every part of the political body. He who finds this merit in himself, will scorn all the advantages that can be drawn from misapplied names: He that knows such honor to be peculiarly due to him for being the best of kings, will never glory in that which may be common to him with the worst. Nay, whoever pretends by such general discourses as these of our author, to advance the particular interests of any one king, does either know he is of no merit, and that nothing can be said for him which will not as well agree with the worst of men; or cares not what he says so he may do mischief, and is well enough contented, that he who is set up by such maxims as a publick plague, may fall in the ruin he brings upon the people.

SECTION 40

Good Laws prescribe easy and safe Remedies
against the Evils proceeding from the vices or
infirmities of the Magistrate; and when they fail,
they must be supplied.

THOSE who desire to advance the power of the magistrate above the law, would persuade us, that the difficulties and dangers of inquiring into his actions, or opposing his will when employ'd in violence and injustice, are so great, that the remedy is always worse than the disease; and that 'tis better to suffer all the evils that may proceed from his infirmities and vices, than to hazard the consequences of displeasing him. But on the contrary, I think and hope to prove,

1. That in well-constituted governments, the remedies against ill magistrates are easy and safe.

2. That 'tis good, as well for the magistrate as the people, so to constitute the government, that the remedies may be easy and safe.

3. That how dangerous and difficult soever they may be through the defects of the first constitution, they must be tried.

To the first; 'Tis most evident that in well-regulated governments these remedies have been found to be easy and safe. The kings of Sparta were not suffer'd in the least to deviate from the rule of the law: And Theopompus one of those kings, in whose time the ephori were created, and the regal power much restrained, doubted not to affirm, that it was by that means become more lasting and more secure. Pausanias had not the name of king, but commanded in the war against Xerxes with more than regal power; nevertheless being grown insolent, he was without any trouble to that state banished, and afterwards put to death. Leonidas father of Cleomenes, was in the like manner banished. The second Agis was most unjustly put to death by the ephori, for he was a brave and a good prince, but there was neither danger nor difficulty in the action.[1] Many of the Roman magistrates, after the expulsion of the kings, seem to have been desirous to extend their power beyond the bounds of the law; and perhaps some others as well as the decemviri, may have designed an absolute tyranny; but the first were restrained, and the others without

[1] Plutarch. [Lives of Aristides, Themistocles, and Agis.]

much difficulty suppressed. Nay, even the kings were so well kept in order, that no man ever pretended to the crown unless he were chosen, nor made any other use of his power than the law permitted, except the last Tarquin, who by his insolence, avarice and cruelty, brought ruin upon himself and his family. I have already mentioned one or two dukes of Venice who were not less ambitious, but their crimes returned upon their own heads, and they perished without any other danger to the state than what had passed before their treasons were discovered. Infinite examples of the like nature may be alleged; and if matters have not at all times, and in all places, succeeded in the same manner, it has been because the same courses were not everywhere taken; for all things do so far follow their causes, that being order'd in the same manner, they will always produce the same effects.

2. To the second; Such a regulation of the magistratical power is not at all grievous to a good magistrate. He who never desires to do anything but what he ought, cannot desire a power of doing what he ought not, nor be troubled to find he cannot do that which he would not do if he could. This inability is also advantageous to those who are evil or unwise; that since they cannot govern themselves, a law may be imposed upon them, lest by following their own irregular will, they bring destruction upon themselves, their families and people, as many have done. If Apollo in the fable had not been too indulgent to Phaethon, in granting his ill-conceiv'd request, the furious youth had not brought a necessity upon Jupiter, either of destroying him, or suffering the world to be destroy'd by him.

Besides, good and wise men know the weight of sovereign power, and misdoubt their own strength. Sacred and human histories furnish us with many examples of those who have feared the lustre of a crown. Men that find in themselves no delight in doing mischief, know not what thoughts may insinuate into their minds, when they are raised too much above their sphere. They who were able to bear adversity, have been precipitated into ruin by prosperity. When the prophet told Hazael the villainies he would commit, he answer'd, *Is thy servant a dog, that I should do these things?* but yet he did them.[2] I know not where to find an example of a man more excellently qualified than Alexander of Macedon; but he fell under the weight of his own fortune, and grew to exceed those in vice, whom he had conquer'd by his virtue. The nature of man can hardly suffer such violent changes without being disorder'd by them; and everyone ought to enter into a just diffidence of himself, and fear the temptations

---

[2] [2 Kings 8:7–15.]

that have destroy'd so many. If any man be so happily born, so carefully educated, so established in virtue, that no storm can shake him, nor any poison corrupt him, yet he will consider he is mortal; and knowing no more than Solomon, whether his son shall be a wise man or a fool, he will always fear to take upon him a power, which must prove a most pestilent evil both to the person that has it, and to those that are under it, as soon as it shall fall into the hands of one, who either knows not how to use it, or may be easily drawn to abuse it. Supreme magistrates always walk in obscure and slippery places: but when they are advanced so high, that no one is near enough to support, direct or restrain them, their fall is inevitable and mortal. And those nations that have wanted the prudence rightly to balance the powers of their magistrates, have been frequently obliged to have recourse to the most violent remedies, and with much difficulty, danger and blood, to punish the crimes which they might have prevented. On the other side, such as have been more wise in the constitution of their governments, have always had regard to the frailty of human nature, and the corruption reigning in the hearts of men; and being less liberal of the power over their lives and liberties, have reserved to themselves so much as might keep their magistrates within the limits of the law, and oblige them to perform the ends of their institution. And as the law which denounces severe penalties for crimes, is indeed merciful both to ill men, who are by that means deterred from committing them; and to the good, who otherwise would be destroy'd: so those nations that have kept the reins in their hands, have by the same act provided as well for the safety of their princes as for their own. They who know the law is well defended, seldom attempt to subvert it: they are not easily tempted to run into excesses, when such bounds are set, as may not safely be transgressed; and whilst they are by this means render'd more moderate in the exercise of their power, the people is exempted from the odious necessity of suffering all manner of indignities and miseries, or by their destruction to prevent or avenge them.

3. To the third: If these rules have not been well observed in the first constitution, or from the changes of times, corruption of manners, insensible encroachments, or violent usurpations of princes, have been render'd ineffectual, and the people exposed to all the calamities that may be brought upon them by the weakness, vices and malice of the prince, or those who govern him, I confess the remedies are more difficult and dangerous; but even in those cases they must be tried. Nothing can be fear'd that is worse than what is suffer'd, or must in a short time fall upon those who are in this condition. They who are already fallen into all that is odious, shameful and miserable, cannot justly fear. When things

are brought to such a pass, the boldest counsels are the most safe; and if they must perish who lie still, and they can but perish who are most active, the choice is easily made.[3] Let the danger be never so great, there is a possibility of safety whilst men have life, hands, arms, and courage to use them; but that people must certainly perish, who tamely suffer themselves to be oppress'd, either by the injustice, cruelty and malice of an ill magistrate, or by those who prevail upon the vices and infirmities of weak princes. 'Tis in vain to say, that this may give occasion to men of raising tumults or civil war; for tho these are evils, yet they are not the greatest of evils. Civil war in Machiavelli's account is a disease, but tyranny is the death of a state. Gentle ways are first to be used, and 'tis best if the work can be done by them; but it must not be left undone if they fail. 'Tis good to use supplications, advices and remonstrances; but those who have no regard to justice, and will not hearken to counsel, must be constrained. 'Tis folly to deal otherwise with a man who will not be guided by reason, and a magistrate who despises the law: or rather, to think him a man, who rejects the essential principle of a man; or to account him a magistrate who overthrows the law by which he is a magistrate. This is the last result; but those nations must come to it, which cannot otherwise be preserved. Nero's madness was not to be cured, nor the mischievous effects of it any otherwise to be suppressed than by his death. He who had spared such a monster when it was in his power to remove him, had brought destruction upon the whole empire; and by a foolish clemency made himself the author of his future villainies. This would have been yet more clear, if the world had then been in such a temper as to be capable of an entire liberty. But the ancient foundations had been overthrown, and nothing better could be built upon the new, than something that might in part resist that torrent of iniquity which had overflow'd the best part of the world, and give mankind a little time to breathe under a less barbarous master. Yet all the best men did join in the work that was then to be done, tho they knew it would prove but imperfect. The sacred history is not without examples of this kind: When Ahab had subverted the law, set up false witnesses and corrupt judges to destroy the innocent, killed the prophets, and established idolatry, his house must then be cut off, and his blood be licked up by dogs. When

---

[3] Moriendum victis, moriendum deditis: id solum interest, an inter cruciatus & ludibria, an pro virtutem expiremus. C. Tacit.

Quod si nocentes innocentesque idem exitus maneat, acrioris viri est meritò perire. Ibid. ["Death must come to the conquered, death to those who yield: the only difference is whether we die among tortures and mockery or through virtue." Tacitus, *Histories*, bk. 3, ch. 66. "But if the same death awaits the innocent and the guilty alike, it is the part of the bold man to perish worthily." Ibid., bk. 1, ch. 21.]

matters are brought to this pass, the decision is easy. The question is only, whether the punishment of crimes shall fall upon one or a few persons who are guilty of them, or upon a whole nation that is innocent. If the father may not die for the son, nor the son for the father, but everyone must bear the penalty of his own crimes, it would be most absurd to punish the people for the guilt of princes. When the earl of Morton was sent ambassador to Queen Elizabeth by the estates of Scotland, to justify their proceedings against Mary their queen, whom they had obliged to renounce the government; he alleged amongst other things the murder of her husband plainly proved against her; asserted the ancient right and custom of that kingdom, of examining the actions of their kings;[4] by which means, he said, many had been punished with death, imprisonment and exile;[5] confirmed their actions by the examples of other nations; and upon the whole matter concluded, that if she was still permitted to live, it was not on account of her innocence, or any exemption from the penalties of the law, but from the mercy and clemency of the people, who contenting themselves with a resignation of her right and power to her son, had spared her. This discourse, which is set down at large by the historian cited on the margin, being of such strength in itself as never to have been any otherwise answered than by railing, and no way disapproved by Queen Elizabeth or her council to whom it was made, either upon a general account of the pretensions of princes to be exempted from the penalties of the law, or any pretext that they had particularly misapplied them in relation to their queen, I may justly say, that when nations fall under such princes as are either utterly uncapable of making a right use of their power, or do maliciously abuse that authority with which they are entrusted, those nations stand obliged, by the duty

---

[4] Animadvertendi in reges. [Buchanan, *History of Scotland*, bk. 20.]

[5] Morte, vinculis & exilio puniti. Buchan. hist. Scot. l. 20. Qui tot reges regno exuerunt, exilio damnarunt, carceribus coercuerunt, supplicio denique affecerunt, nec unquam tamen de acerbitate legis minuenda mentio est facta, &c. Ibid. Facile apparet regnum nihil aliud esse, quam mutuam inter regem & populum stipulationem. Non de illarum sanctionum genere, quae mutationibus temporum sunt obnoxiae, sed in primo generis humani exortu, & mutuo prope omnium gentium consensu comprobatae, & una cum rerum natura infragiles & sempiternae perennent. Ibid. ["That they had been punished with death, imprisonment, and exile." Buchanan, *History of Scotland*, bk. 20. "Since they (the Scots' ancestors) stripped so many kings of their realm, condemned them to exile, forced them into prison, and, finally, executed them, there was not even any mention of lessening the severity of the law, etc." Ibid. "It is readily apparent that the kingship is nothing other than a mutual stipulation between the king and the people. This is not the sort of sanction that is exposed to the changes of the times, but existed in the first dawn of human kind and is approved by the mutual consensus of nearly all peoples; and may it endure as inviolate and sempiternal as the nature of things." Ibid.]

they owe to themselves and their posterity, to use the best of their endeavours to remove the evil, whatever danger or difficulties they may meet with in the performance. Pontius the Samnite said as truly as bravely to his countrymen, That *those arms were just and pious that were necessary, and necessary when there was no hope of safety by any other way.*[6] This is the voice of mankind, and is dislik'd only by those princes, who fear the deserved punishments may fall upon them; or by their servants and flatterers, who being for the most part the authors of their crimes, think they shall be involved in their ruin.

SECTION 41

*The People for whom and by whom
the Magistrate is created, can only judge whether he
rightly perform his Office or not.*

T IS commonly said, that no man ought to be the judge of his own case; and our author lays much weight upon it as a fundamental maxim, tho according to his ordinary inconstancy he overthrows it in the case of kings, where it ought to take place if in any; for it often falls out that no men are less capable of forming a right judgment than they. Their passions and interests are most powerful to disturb or pervert them. No men are so liable to be diverted from justice by the flatteries of corrupt servants. They never act as kings, except for those by whom and for whom they are created; and acting for others, the account of their actions cannot depend upon their own will. Nevertheless I am not afraid to say, that naturally and properly a man is the judge of his own concernments. No one is or can be deprived of this privilege, unless by his own consent, and for the good of that society into which he enters. This right therefore must necessarily belong to every man in all cases, except only such as relate to the good of the community, for whose sake he has divested himself of it. If I find myself afflicted with hunger, thirst, weariness, cold, heat, or sickness, 'tis a folly to tell me, I ought not to seek meat, drink, rest, shelter, refreshment, or physick, because I must not be the judge of my own case. The like may be said in relation to my house, land, or estate; I may do what I please with them, if I bring no damage

---

[6] Justa piaque sunt arma, quibus necessaria, & necessaria, quibus nulla nisi in armis spes   est salutis: *T. Liv.* lib. 8. [Livy, *History of Rome*, bk. 9, ch. 1.]

upon others. But I must not set fire to my house, by which my neighbour's house may be burnt. I may not erect forts upon my own lands, or deliver them to a foreign enemy, who may by that means infest my country. I may not cut the banks of the sea, or those of a river, lest my neighbour's ground be overflown, because the society into which I am incorporated, would by such means receive prejudice. My land is not simply my own, but upon condition that I shall not thereby bring damage upon the publick, by which I am protected in the peaceable enjoyment and innocent use of what I possess. But this society leaves me a liberty to take servants, and put them away at my pleasure. No man is to direct me, of what quality or number they shall be, or can tell me whether I am well or ill served by them. Nay, the state takes no other cognizance of what passes between me and them, than to oblige me to perform the contracts I make, and not to do that to them which the law forbids: that is to say, the power to which I have submitted myself, exercises that jurisdiction over me, which was established by my consent, and under which I enjoy all the benefits of life, which are of more advantage to me than my liberty could have been, if I had retained it wholly in myself. The nature also and measure of this submission must be determined by the reasons that induced me to it. The society in which I live cannot subsist unless by rule; the equality in which men are born is so perfect, that no man will suffer his natural liberty to be abridged, except others do the like: I cannot reasonably expect to be defended from wrong, unless I oblige myself to do none; or to suffer the punishment prescribed by the law, if I perform not my engagement. But without prejudice to the society into which I enter, I may and do retain to myself the liberty of doing what I please in all things relating peculiarly to myself, or in which I am to seek my own convenience.

Now if a private man is not subject to the judgment of any other, than those to whom he submits himself for his own safety and convenience; and notwithstanding that submission, still retains to himself the right of ordering according to his own will all things merely relating to himself, and of doing what he pleases in that which he does for his own sake; the same right must more certainly belong to whole nations. When a controversy happens between Caius and Seius in a matter of right, neither of them may determine the cause, but it must be referred to a judge superior to both; not because 'tis not fit that a man should be judge of his own case, but because they have both an equal right, and neither of them owes any subjection to the other. But if there be a contest between me and my servant concerning my service, I only am to decide it: He must serve me in my own way, or be gone if I think fit, tho he serve me never so well; and I do him no wrong in putting him away, if either I intend to keep no servant, or find that another will please me better. I cannot therefore stand in need of a judge, unless the contest be with one who lives upon an equal foot with me. No man can be my judge, unless he be my superior; and he cannot be my superior, who is not so by my consent, nor to any other purpose than I consent to. This cannot be the case of a nation, which can have no equal within itself. Controversies may arise with other nations, the decision of which may be left to judges chosen by mutual agreement; but this relates not to our question. A nation, and most especially one that is powerful, cannot recede from its own right, as a private man from the knowledge of his own weakness and inability to defend himself, must come under the protection of a greater power than his own. The strength of a nation is not in the magistrate, but the strength of the magistrate is in the nation. The wisdom, industry and valour of a prince may add to the glory and greatness of a nation, but the foundation and substance will always be in itself. If the magistrate and people were upon equal terms, as Caius and Seius, receiving equal and mutual advantages from each other, no man could be judge of their differences, but such as they should set up for that end. This has been done by many nations. The ancient Germans referred the decision of the most difficult matters to their priests: the Gauls and Britains to the Druids: the Mohammedans for some ages to the caliphs of Babylon: the Saxons in England, when they had embraced the Christian religion, to their clergy. Whilst all Europe lay under the popish superstition, the decision of such matters was frequently assumed by the pope; men often submitted to his judgment, and the princes that resisted were for the most part excommunicated, deposed and destroyed. All this was done for the same reasons. These men were accounted holy and inspired, and the sentence pronounced by them was usually reverenced as the judgment of God, who was thought to direct them; and all those who refused to submit, were esteemed execrable. But no man, or number of men, as I think, at the institution of a magistrate did ever say, if any difference happen between you or your successors and us, it shall be determined by yourself or by them, whether they be men, women, children, mad, foolish, or vicious. Nay if any such thing had been, the folly, turpitude and madness of such a sanction or stipulation must necessarily have destroy'd it. But if no such thing was ever known, or could have no effect if it had been in any place, 'tis most absurd to impose it upon all. The people therefore cannot be deprived of their natural rights upon a frivolous pretence to that which never was and never can be. They who create magistracies, and give to them such name, form and power as they think fit, do only know, whether the end for which they were created, be performed or not. They who give a being to the power which had none, can only judge whether it be employ'd to their welfare, or turned to their ruin. They do not set up one or a few men, that they and their posterity may live in splendor and greatness, but that justice may be administered, virtue established, and provision made for the publick safety. No wise man will think this can be done, if those who set themselves to overthrow the law, are to be their own judges. If Caligula, Nero, Vitellius, Domitian, or Heliogabalus, had been subject to no other judgment, they would have compleated the destruction of the empire. If the disputes between Durstus, Evenus the third, Dardannus, and other kings of Scotland, with the nobility and people, might have been determined by themselves, they had escaped the punishments they suffer'd, and ruined the nation as they designed. Other methods were taken; they perished by their madness; better princes were brought into their places, and their successors were by their example admonished to avoid the ways that had proved fatal to them. If Edward the second of England, with Gaveston and the Spencers, Richard the second with Tresilian and Vere, had been permitted to be the judges of their own cases, they who had murdered the best of the nobility would have pursued their designs to the destruction of such as remained, the enslaving of the nation, the subversion of the constitution, and the establishment of a mere tyranny in the place of a mixed monarchy. But our ancestors took better measures: They who had felt the smart of the vices and follies of their princes, knew what remedies were most fit to be applied, as well as the best time of applying them. They found the effects of extreme corruption in government to be so desperately pernicious, that nations must necessarily perish, unless it be corrected, and the state reduced to its first principle, or altered. Which being the case, it was as easy for them to judge whether the governor who had introduced that corruption should be brought to order, removed if he would not be reclaimed, or whether he should be suffer'd to ruin them and their posterity, as it is for me to judge, whether I should put away my servant, if I knew he intended to poison or murder me, and had a certain facility of accomplishing his design; or whether I should continue him in my service till he had performed it. Nay the matter is so much the more plain on the side of the nation, as the disproportion of merit between a whole people, and one or a few men entrusted with the power of governing them, is greater than between a private man and his servant. This is so fully confirmed by the general consent of mankind, that we know no government that has not frequently either been altered in form, or reduced to its original purity, by changing the families or persons who abused the power with which they had been entrusted. Those who have wanted wisdom and virtue rightly and seasonably to perform this, have been soon destroy'd; like the Goths in Spain, who by omitting to curb the fury of Witiza and Rodrigo in time, became a prey to the Moors.[1] Their kingdom by this means destroy'd was never restored, and the remainder of that nation joining with the Spaniards whom they had kept in subjection for three or four ages, could not in less than eight hundred years, expel those enemies they might have kept out, only by removing two base and vicious kings. Such nations as have been so corrupted, that when they have applied themselves to seek remedies to the evils they suffered by wicked magistrates, could not fall upon such as were proportionable to the disease, have only vented their passions in destroying the immediate instruments of their oppression, or for a while delay'd their utter ruin. But the root still remaining, it soon produced the same poisonous fruit, and either quite destroy'd, or made them languish in perpetual misery. The Roman empire was the most eminent example of the first; many of the monsters that had tyrannized over them were killed, but the greatest advantage gained by their death, was a respite from ruin; and the government which ought to have been established by good laws, depending only upon the virtue of one man, his life proved to be no more than a lucid interval, and at his death they relapsed into the depth of infamy and misery: and in this condition they continued till that empire was totally subverted.

All the kingdoms of the Arabians, Medes, Persians, Moors, and others of the East are of the other sort. Common sense instructs them, that barbarous pride, cruelty and madness grown to extremity, cannot be borne: but they have no other way than to kill the tyrant, and to do the like to his successor if he fall into the same crimes. Wanting that wisdom and valour which is requir'd for the institution of a good government, they languish in perpetual slavery, and propose to themselves nothing better than to live under a gentle master, which is but a precarious life, and little to be valued by men of bravery and spirit. But those nations that are more generous, who set a higher value upon liberty, and better understand the ways of preserving it, think it a small matter to destroy a tyrant, unless they can also destroy the tyranny. They endeavour to do the work thoroughly, either by changing the government entirely, or reforming it according to the first institution, and making such good laws as may preserve its integrity when reformed. This has been so frequent

[1] Mariana. [Mariana, *General History of Spain.*]

in all the nations (both ancient and modern) with whose actions we are best acquainted, as appears by the foregoing examples, and many others that might be alleged, if the case were not clear, that there is not one of them which will not furnish us with many instances; and no one magistracy now in being which does not owe its original to some judgment of this nature. So that they must either derive their right from such actions, or confess they have none at all, and leave the nations to their original liberty of setting up those magistracies which best please themselves, without any restriction or obligation to regard one person or family more than another.

SECTION 42
The Person that wears the Crown cannot determine the Affairs which the Law refers to the King.

OUR author, with the rest of the vulgar, seems to have been led into gross errors by the form of writs summoning persons to appear before the king.[1] The common style used in the trial of delinquents; the name of the king's witnesses given to those who accuse them; the verdicts brought in by juries, *coram domino rege*,[2] and the prosecution made in the king's name, seem to have caused this. And they who understand not these phrases, render the law a heap of the most gross absurdities, and the king an enemy to every one of his subjects, when he ought to be a father to them all; since without any particular consideration or examination of what any witness deposes in a court of justice, tending to the death, confiscation, or other punishment of any man, he is called the king's witness whether he speak the truth or a lie, and on that account favour'd. 'Tis not necessary to allege many instances in a case that is so plain; but it may not be amiss to insert two or three of the most important reasons to prove my assertion.

   1. If the law did intend that he or she who wears the crown, should in his or her person judge all causes, and determine the most difficult questions, it must like our author presume that they will always be of profound wisdom to comprehend all of them, and of perfect integrity always to act according to their understanding. Which is no less than to lay the foundation of the government upon a thing merely contingent,

---

[1] [*Patriarcha*, ch. 28, p. 112.]   [2] [In the presence of the lord king.]

that either never was, or very often fails, as is too much verified by experience, and the histories of all nations; or else to refer the decision of all to those who through the infirmities of age, sex, or person, are often uncapable of judging the least, or subject to such passions and vices as would divert them from justice tho they did understand it; both which seem to be almost equally preposterous.

2. The law must also presume that the prince is always present in all the places where his name is used. The king of France is (as I have said already) esteemed to be present *on the seat of justice*[3] in all the parliaments and sovereign courts of the kingdom: and if his corporeal presence were by that phrase to be understood, he must be in all those distinct and far distant places at the same time; which absurdity can hardly be parallel'd, unless by the popish opinion of *transubstantiation*. But indeed they are so far from being guilty of such monstrous absurdity, that he cannot in person be present at any trial, and no man can be judged if he be. This was plainly asserted to Lewis the 13th (who would have been at the trial of the duke of Candale)[4] by the president de Bellievre, who told him that as he could judge no man himself, so they could not judge any if he were present: upon which he retired.

3. The laws of most kingdoms giving to kings the confiscation of delinquents' estates, if they in their own persons might give judgment upon them, they would be constituted both judges and parties; which besides the foremention'd incapacities to which princes are as much subject as other men, would tempt them by their own personal interest to subvert all manner of justice.

This therefore not being the meaning of the law, we are to inquire what it is; and the thing is so plain that we cannot mistake, unless we do it wilfully. Some name must be used in all manner of transactions, and in matters of publick concernment none can be so fit as that of the principal magistrate. Thus are leagues made, not only with kings and emperors, but with the dukes of Venice and Genoa, the avoyer and senate of a canton in Switzerland, the burgermaster of an imperial town in Germany, and the states-general of the United Provinces. But no man thinking, I presume, these leagues would be of any value, if they could only oblige the persons whose names are used, 'tis plain that they do not stipulate only for themselves; and that their stipulations would be of no value if they were merely personal. And nothing can more certainly prove they are not so, than that we certainly know, these dukes, avoyers and

---

[3] Sur son lit de justice.

[4] [Sidney means Bernard de Nogaret, duke of LaValette. The duke of Candale was Henri de Nogaret.]

burgermasters can do nothing of themselves. The power of the states-general of the United Provinces is limited to the points mentioned in the Act of Union made at Utrecht. The empire is not obliged by any stipulation made by the emperor without their consent. Nothing is more common than for one king making a league with another, to exact a confirmation of their agreement, by the parliaments, diets or general estates; because, says Grotius, a prince does not stipulate for himself, but for the people under his government; and a king deprived of his kingdom, loses the right of sending an ambassador.[5] The powers of Europe shewed themselves to be of this opinion in the case of Portugal. When Philip the second had gained the possession, they treated with him concerning the affairs relating to that kingdom: Few regarded Don Antonio; and no man considered the dukes of Savoy, Parma or Braganza, who perhaps had the most plausible titles: But when his grandson Philip the fourth had lost that kingdom, and the people had set up the duke of Braganza, they all treated with him as king. And the English court, tho then in amity with Spain, and not a little influenced by a Spanish faction, gave example to others, by treating with him and not with Spain touching matters relating to that state. Nay, I have been informed by those who well understood the affairs of that time, that the Lord Cottington advising the late king[6] not to receive any persons sent from the duke of Braganza, rebel to his ally the king of Spain, in the quality of ambassadors; the king answered, that he must look upon that person to be king of Portugal, who was acknowledged by the nation. And I am mistaken if his majesty now reigning did not find all the princes and states of the world to be of the same mind, when he was out of his kingdom, and could oblige no man but himself and a few followers by any treaty he could make.

For the same reason the names of kings are used in treaties, when they are either children, or otherwise uncapable of knowing what alliances are fit to be made or rejected; and yet such treaties do equally oblige them, their successors and people, as if they were of mature age and fit for government. No man therefore ought to think it strange, if the king's name be used in domestick affairs, of which he neither ought nor can take any cognizance. In these cases he is perpetually a minor: He must suffer the law to take its due course; and the judges, tho nominated by him, are obliged by oath not to have any regard to his letters or personal commands. If a man be sued, he must appear; and a delinquent is to be tried *coram rege*, but no otherwise than *secundum legem terrae*, *according to*

---

[5] De jur. bell. l. 3. [Grotius, *De jure*, bk. 2, ch. 18, sec. 2.]   [6] [Charles I.]

the law of the land, not his personal will or opinion. And the judgments given must be executed, whether they please him or not, it being always understood that he can speak no otherwise than the law speaks, and is always present as far as the law requires. For this reason a noble lord who was irregularly detain'd in prison in 1681, being by *habeas corpus* brought to the bar of the king's bench, where he sued to be releas'd upon bail; and an ignorant judge telling him he must apply himself to the king, he replied, that he came thither for that end; that the king might eat, drink, or sleep where he pleased, but when he render'd justice he was always in that place. The king that renders justice is indeed always there: He never sleeps; he is subject to no infirmity; he never dies unless the nation be extinguished, or so dissipated as to have no government. No nation that has a sovereign power within itself, does ever want this king. He was in Athens and Rome, as well as at Babylon and Susa; and is as properly said to be now in Venice, Switzerland or Holland, as in France, Morocco or Turkey. This is he to whom we all owe a simple and unconditional obedience. This is he *who never does any wrong:* 'Tis before him we appear, when we demand justice, or render an account of our actions. All juries give their verdict in his sight: They are his commands that the judges are bound and sworn to obey, when they are not at all to consider such as they receive from the person that wears the crown. 'Twas for treason against him that Tresilian and others like to him in several ages were hanged. They gratified the lusts of the visible powers, but the invisible king would not be mock'd. He caused justice to be executed upon Empson and Dudley. He was injured when the perjur'd wretches who gave that accursed judgment in the case of ship money, were suffered to escape the like punishment by means of the ensuing troubles which they had chiefly raised. And I leave it to those who are concerned, to consider how many in our days may expect vengeance for the like crimes.

I should here conclude this point, if the power of granting a *noli prosequi: cesset processus*,[7] and pardons, which are said to be annexed to the person of the king, were not taken for a proof that all proceedings at law depend upon his will. But whoever would from hence draw a general conclusion, must first prove his proposition to be universally true. If it be wholly false, no true deduction can be made; and if it be true only in some cases, 'tis absurd to draw from thence a general conclusion; and to erect a vast fabrick upon a narrow foundation is impossible. As to the general proposition I utterly deny it. The king cannot stop any suit that I begin

---

[7] [Do not proceed; let the trial cease.]

in my own name, or invalidate any judgment I obtain upon it: He cannot release a debt of ten shillings due to me, nor a sentence for the like sum given upon an action of battery, assault, trespass, publick nuisance, or the like. He cannot pardon a man condemned upon an appeal, nor hinder the person injured from appealing. His power therefore is not universal: if it be not universal, it cannot be inherent, but conferred upon him, or entrusted by a superior power that limits it.

These limits are fixed by the law, the law therefore is above him. His proceedings must be regulated by the law, and not the law by his will. Besides, the extent of those limits can only be known by the intention of the law that sets them; and are so visible, that none but such as are wilfully blind can mistake. It cannot be imagined that the law, which does not give a power to the king of pardoning a man that breaks my hedge, can intend he should have power to pardon one who kills my father, breaks my house, robs me of my goods, abuses my children and servants, wounds me, and brings me in danger of my life. Whatever power he has in such cases, is founded upon a presumption, that he who has sworn not to deny or delay justice to any man, will not break his oath to interrupt it. And farther, as he does nothing but what he may rightly do, *cum magnatum & sapientum consilio;*[8] and that 'tis supposed, they will never advise him to do anything, but what ought to be done, in order to attain the great ends of the law, justice, and the publick safety; nevertheless lest this should not be sufficient to keep things in their due order, or that the king should forget his oath, not to delay or deny justice to any man, his counsellors are exposed to the severest punishments, if they advise him to do anything contrary to it, and the law upon which it is grounded. So that the utmost advantage the king can pretend to in this case, is no more than that of the Norman, who said he had gained his cause, because it depended upon a point that was to be decided by his oath; that is to say, if he will betray the trust reposed in him, and perjure himself, he may sometimes exempt a villain from the punishment he deserves, and take the guilt upon himself. I say sometimes; for appeals may be brought in some cases, and the waterman who had been pardoned by his majesty in the year 1680, for a murder he had committed, was condemned and hanged at the assizes upon an appeal. Nay, in cases of treason, which some men think relate most particularly to the person of the king, he cannot always do it. Gaveston, the two Spencers, Tresilian, Empson, Dudley, and others, have been executed as traitors for things done by the king's command; and 'tis not doubted they would have been

---

[8] [With the advice of the great and wise.]

saved, if the king's power had extended so far. I might add the cases of the earls of Strafford and Danby; for tho the king signed a warrant for the execution of the first, no man doubts he would have saved him, if it had been in his power. The other continues in prison notwithstanding his pardon; and for anything I know he may continue where he is, or come out in a way that will not be to his satisfaction unless he be found innocent, or something fall out more to his advantage than his majesty's approbation of what he has done. If therefore the king cannot interpose his authority to hinder the course of the law in contests between private men, nor remit the debts adjudged to be due, or the damages given to the persons aggriev'd, he can in his own person have no other power in things of this nature, than in some degree to mitigate the vindictive power of the law; and this also is to be exercised no other way than as he is entrusted. But if he acts even in this capacity by a delegated power, and in few cases, he must act according to the ends for which he is so entrusted, as the same law says, *cum magnatum & sapientum consilio*, and is not therein to pursue his own will and interests: If his oath farther oblige him not to do it; and his ministers are liable to punishment, if they advise him otherwise: If in matters of appeal he have no power; and if his pardons have been of no value, when contrary to his oath he has abused that with which he is entrusted, to the patronizing of crimes, and exempting such delinquents from punishment, as could not be pardoned without prejudice to the publick, I may justly conclude, that the king, before whom every man is bound to appear, who does perpetually and impartially distribute justice to the nation, is not the man or woman that wears the crown; and that he or she cannot determine those matters, which by the law are referr'd to the king. Whether therefore such matters are ordinary or extraordinary, the decision is and ought to be placed where there is most wisdom and stability, and where passion and private interest does least prevail to the obstruction of justice. This is the only way to obviate that confusion and mischief, which our author thinks it would introduce. In cases of the first sort, this is done in England by judges and juries: In the other by the parliament, which being the representative body of the people, and the collected wisdom of the nation, is least subject to error, most exempted from passion, and most free from corruption, their own good both publick and private depending upon the rectitude of their sanctions. They cannot do anything that is ill without damage to themselves and their posterity; which being all that can be done by human understanding, our lives, liberties and properties are by our laws directed to depend upon them.

SECTION 43
Proclamations are not Laws.

OUR author according to his usual method and integrity, lays great weight upon proclamations, as the significations of the king's pleasure, which in his opinion is our only law.[1] But neither law nor reason openly directing, nor by consequences insinuating, that such a power should be put into an uncertain or suspected hand, we may safely deny them to be laws, or in any sense to have the effect of laws. Nay, they cannot be so much as significations of his will; for as he is king, he can have no will but as the law directs. If he depart from the law, he is no longer king, and his will is nothing to us. Proclamations, at most, are but temporary, by the advice of council, in pursuance of the law. If they be not so, the subject is no way obliged to obey them, and the counsellors are to be punished for them. These laws are either immemorial customs, or statutes. The first have their beginning and continuance from the universal consent of the nation. The latter receive their authority and force of laws from parliaments, as is frequently expressed in the preambles. These are under God the best defence of our lives, liberties, and estates: they proceed not from the blind, corrupt, and fluctuating humor of a man, but from the mature deliberation of the choicest persons of the nation, and such as have the greatest interest in it. Our ancestors have always relied upon these laws; and 'tis to be hoped we shall not be so abandoned by God, so deprived of courage and common sense, to suffer ourselves to be cheated of the inheritance which they have so frequently, so bravely, and so constantly defended. Tho experience has too well taught us, that parliaments may have their failings, and that the vices, which are industriously spread amongst them, may be too prevalent; yet they are the best helps we have, and we may much more reasonably depend upon them, than upon those who propagate that corruption among them for which only they can deserve to be suspected. We hope they will take care of our concernments, since they are as other men so soon as a session is ended, and can do nothing to our prejudice that will not equally affect them and their posterity; besides the guilt of betraying their country, which can never be washed off. If some should prove false to their trust, 'tis probable that others would continue in their integrity: Or if the base arts, which are usually practised by those who endeavour

---

[1] [*Patriarcha*, ch. 32 ("The King Hath Governed Both Houses, either by Himself, or by His Council, or by His Judges").]

to delude, corrupt, enslave and ruin nations, should happen to prevail upon the youngest and weakest it may be reasonably hoped, that the wisest will see the snares, and instruct their companions to avoid them. But if all things were so put into the hands of one man, that his proclamations were to be esteemed laws, the nation would be exposed to ruin, as soon as it should chance to fall into an ill hand. 'Tis in vain to say we have a good king, who will not make an ill use of his power; for even the best are subject to be deceived by flatterers, and crown'd heads are almost ever encompassed by them. The principal art of a courtier is to observe his master's passions, and to attack him on that side where he seems to be most weak. It would be a strange thing to find a man impregnable in every part; and if he be not, 'tis impossible he should resist all the attempts that are made upon him. If his judgment come to be prepossess'd, he and all that depend on him are lost. Contradictions, tho never so just, are then unsafe, and no man will venture upon them, but he who dares sacrifice himself for the publick good. The nature of man is frail, and stands in need of assistance. Virtuous actions that are profitable to a commonwealth, ought to be made, as far as it is possible, safe, easy, and advantageous: and 'tis the utmost imprudence to tempt men to be enemies to the publick, by making the most pernicious actions to be the means of obtaining honour and favour, whilst no man can serve his country, but with the ruin of himself and his family.

However in this case the question is not concerning a person: the same counsels are to be follow'd when Moses or Samuel is in the throne, as if Caligula had invaded it. Laws ought to aim at perpetuity, but the virtues of a man die with him, and very often before him. Those who have deserved the highest praises for wisdom and integrity, have frequently left the honors they enjoyed to foolish and vicious children. If virtue may in any respect be said to outlive the person, it can only be when good men frame such laws and constitutions as by favouring it preserve themselves. This has never been done otherwise, than by balancing the powers in such a manner, that the corruption which one or a few men might fall into, should not be suffer'd to spread the contagion to the ruin of the whole. The long continuance of Lycurgus his laws is to be attributed to this: They restrained the lusts of kings, and reduced those to order who adventured to transgress them: Whereas the whole fabrick must have fallen to the ground in a short time, if the first that had a fancy to be absolute, had been able to effect his design. This has been the fate of all governments that were made to depend upon the virtue of a man, which never continues long in any family, and when that fails all is lost. The nations therefore that are so happy to have good kings, ought to make a right use of them, by establishing the good that may outlast their lives. Those of them that are good, will readily join in this work, and take care that their successors may be obliged in doing the like, to be equally beneficial to their own families, and the people they govern. If the rulers of nations be restrained, not only the people is by that means secured from the mischiefs of their vices and follies, but they themselves are preserved from the greatest temptations to ill, and the terrible effects of the vengeance that frequently ensues upon it. An unlimited prince might be justly compared to a weak ship exposed to a violent storm, with a vast sail and no rudder. We have an eminent example of this in the book of Esther.[2] A wicked villain having filled the ears of a foolish king with false stories of the Jews, he issues out a proclamation for their utter extirpation; and not long after being informed of the truth, he gave them leave by another proclamation to kill whom they pleased, which they executed upon seventy thousand men. The books of Ezra, Nehemiah and Daniel, manifestly discover the like fluctuation in all the counsels of Nebuchad-nezzar, Cyrus, Darius, and Artaxerxes. When good men had credit with them, they favour'd the Israelites; sent them back to their own country; restored the sacred vessels that had been taken away; gave them all things necessary for the rebuilding of the city, and advanced the chief of them to the highest employments. But if they fell into ill hands, three just men must be thrown into the burning furnace for refusing to worship an idol; Daniel must be cast to the lions; the holy city esteemed rebellious, and those who endeavoured to rebuild it, enemies to kings. Such was the state of things, when their proclamations passed for laws, and numbers of flattering slaves were ready to execute their commands, without examining whether they were just or unjust, good or bad. The life and death of the best men, together with the very being of nations, was exposed to chance, and they were either preserved or destroyed according to the humor of that man who spoke last to the king, or happened to have credit with him. If a frantick fancy come into the head of a drunken whore, Persepolis must be burnt, and the hand of Alexander is ready to execute her will.[3] If a dancing wench please Herod, the most venerable of all human heads must be offered in a dish for a sacrifice to the rage of her impure mother.[4] The nature of man is so frail, that wheresoever the word of a single person has had the force of a law, the innumerable extravagances and mischiefs it has produced have been so notorious, that

---

[2] Cap. 3.

[4] [Matthew 14:1–12.]

[3] [The Greek camp-follower Thais is said to have convinced Alexander to burn the palace of Xerxes in Persepolis.]

all nations who are not stupid, slavish and brutish, have always abominated it, and made it their principal care to find out remedies against it, by so dividing and balancing the powers of their government, that one or a few men might not be able to oppress and destroy those they ought to preserve and protect. This has always been as grateful to the best and wisest princes, as necessary to the weakest and worst, as I have proved already by the examples of Theopompus, Moses, and many others. These considerations have given beginning, growth and continuance to all the mixed governments that have been in the world; and I may justly say there never was a good one that was not mixed. If other proofs of their rectitude were wanting, our author's hatred would be enough to justify them. He is so bitter an enemy to mankind, as to be displeased with nothing but that which tends to their good, and so perverse in his judgment, that we have reason to believe that to be good which he most abhors. One would think he had taken the model of the government he proposes, from the monstrous tyranny of Ceylon an island in the East-Indies, where the king knows no other law than his own will. He kills, tears in pieces, impales, or throws to his elephants whomsoever he pleases: No man has anything that he can call his own: He seldom fails to destroy those who have been employ'd in his domestick service, or publick offices; and few obtain the favour of being put to death and thrown to the dogs without torments. His subjects approach him no otherwise, than on their knees, licking the dust, and dare assume to themselves no other name than that of dogs, or limbs of dogs. This is a true pattern of Filmer's *patriarchical monarch.* His majesty, as I suppose, is sufficiently exalted; for he does whatever he pleases. The exercise of his power is as gentle as can reasonably be expected from one who has all by the unquestionable right of usurpation; and knows the people will no longer suffer him, and the villains he hires to be the instruments of his cruelty, than they can be kept in such ignorance, weakness and baseness, as neither to know how to provide for themselves, or dare to resist him. We ought to esteem ourselves happy, if the like could be established among us; and are much obliged to our author for so kindly proposing an expedient that might terminate all our disputes. Let proclamations obtain the power of laws, and the business is done. They may be so ingeniously contrived, that the ancient laws, which we and our fathers have highly valued, shall be abolished, or made a snare to all those that dare remember they are Englishmen, and are guilty of the unpardonable crime of loving their country, or have the courage, conduct, and reputation requir'd to defend it. This is the sum of Filmer's philosophy, and this is the legacy he has left to testify his affection to the nation; which having for a long time

[561]

lain unregarded, has been lately brought into the light again, as an introduction of a popish successor,[5] who is to be established, as we ought to believe, for the security of the Protestant religion, and our English liberties. Both will undoubtedly flourish under a prince who is made to believe the kingdom is his patrimony; that his will is a law, and that he has a power which none may resist. If any man doubt whether he will make a good use of it, he may only examine the histories of what others in the same circumstances have done in all places where they have had power. The principles of that religion are so full of meekness and charity; the popes have always shew'd themselves so gentle towards those who would not submit to their authority; the Jesuits who may be accounted the soul that gives life to the whole body of that faction, are so well natur'd, faithful and exact in their morals; so full of innocence, justice and truth, that no violence is to be fear'd from such as are govern'd by them. The fatherly care shew'd to the Protestants of France, by the five last kings of the house of Valois; the mercy of Philip the second of Spain to his pagan subjects in the West-Indies, and the more hated Protestants in the Netherlands; the moderation of the dukes of Savoy towards the Vaudois in the marquisat of Saluzzo and the valleys of Piedmont; the gentleness and faith of the two Marys queens of England and Scotland; the kindness of the papists to the Protestants of Ireland in the year 1641; with what we have reason to believe they did and do still intend, if they can accomplish the ends of their conspiracy; In a word, the sweetness and apostolical meekness of the Inquisition, may sufficiently convince us that nothing is to be feared where that principle reigns. We may suffer the word of such a prince to be a law, and the people to be made to believe it ought to be so, when he is expected. Tho we should waive the bill of exclusion, and not only admit him to reign as other kings have done, but resign the whole power into his hands, it would neither bring inconvenience or danger on the present king. He can with patience expect that nature should take her course, and would neither anticipate nor secure his entrance into the possession of the power, by taking one day from the life of his brother. Tho the papists know that like a true son of their church, he would prefer the advancement of their religion before all other considerations; and that one stab with a dagger, or a dose of poison, would put all under his feet, not one man would be found among them to give it. The assassins were Mahometans, not pupils of the honest Jesuits, nor ever employ'd by them. These things being certain, all our concernments would be secure, if instead of the foolish statutes

[5] [The future James II, crowned in 1685.]

and antiquated customs, on which our ancestors and we have hitherto doted, we may be troubled with no law but the king's will, and a proclamation may be taken for a sufficient declaration of it. We shall by this means be delivered from that *liberty with a mischief*,[6] in which our mistaken nation seems so much to delight. This phrase is so new, and so peculiar to our author, that it deserves to be written upon his tomb. We have heard of *tyranny with a mischief, slavery and bondage with a mischief*; and they have been denounced by God against wicked and perverse nations, as mischiefs comprehending all that is most to be abhorr'd and dreaded in the world. But Filmer informs us that liberty, which all wise and good men have in all ages esteemed to be the most valuable and glorious privilege of mankind, is *a mischief*. If he deserve credit, Moses, Joshua, Gideon, Samson, and Samuel, with others like them, were enemies to their country, in depriving the people of the advantages they enjoy'd under the paternal care of Pharaoh, Adonibezek, Eglon, Jabin, and other kings of the neighbouring nations, and restoring them to that *liberty with a mischief* which he had promised to them. The Israelites were happy under the power of tyrants, whose proclamations were laws; and they ought to have been thankful to God for that condition, and not for the deliverances he wrought by the hands of his servants. Subjection to the will of a man is happiness, liberty is a *mischief*. But this is so abominably wicked and detestable, that it can deserve no answer.

SECTION 44

No People that is not free can substitute Delegates.

How full soever the power of any person or people may be, he or they are obliged to give only so much to their delegates, as seems convenient to themselves, or conducing to the ends they desire to attain; but the delegate can have none except what is conferred upon him by his principal. If therefore the knights, citizens and burgesses sent by the people of England to serve in parliament have a power, it must be more perfectly and fully in those that send them. But (as was proved in the last section) proclamations, and other significations of the king's pleasure,

---

[6] [The 1680 text of Filmer, which Sidney used, reads: "If the people had any such power over their burgesses [i.e., to call them to account for their misdeeds], then we might call it, the natural liberty of the people, with a mischief." Laslett's text omits the words "with a mischief" and adds, after "might," the words "have some colour to."]

are not laws to us. They are to be regulated by the law, not the law by them. They are to be considered only so far as they are conformable to the law from which they receive all the strength that is in them, and can confer none upon it. We know no laws but our own statutes, and those immemorial customs established by the consent of the nation; which may be, and often are changed by us. The legislative power therefore that is exercised by the parliament, cannot be conferred by the writ of summons, but must be essentially and radically in the people, from whom their delegates and representatives have all that they have. But, says our author, *They must only chuse, and trust those whom they chuse, to do what they list; and that is as much liberty as many of us deserve for our irregular elections of burgesses.*[1] This is ingeniously concluded: I take what servant I please, and when I have taken him I must suffer him to do what he pleases. But from whence should this necessity arise? Why may not I take one to be my groom, another to be my cook, and keep them both to the offices for which I took them? What law does herein restrain my right? And if I am free in my private capacity to regulate my particular affairs according to my own discretion, and to allot to each servant his proper work, why have not I with my associates the freemen of England the like liberty of directing and limiting the powers of the servants we employ in our publick affairs? Our author gives us reasons proportionable to his judgment: *This were liberty with a mischief; and that of chusing only is as much as many of us deserve.* I have already proved, that as far as our histories reach, we have had no princes or magistrates, but such as we have made, and they have had no other power than what we have conferred upon them. They cannot be the judges of our merit, who have no power but what we gave them, through an opinion they did or might deserve it. They may distribute in parcels to particulars that with which they are entrusted in the gross. But 'tis impossible that the publick should depend absolutely upon those who are nothing above other men, except what they are made to be, for, and by the publick. The restrictions therefore of the people's liberty must be from themselves, or there can be none.

Nevertheless I believe, that the powers of every county, city and borough of England, are regulated by the general law to which they have all consented, and by which they are all made members of one political body. This obliges them to proceed with their delegates in a manner different from that which is used in the United Netherlands, or in Switzerland. Amongst these every province, city or canton making a

---

[1] [*Patriarcha*, ch. 30, p. 119.]

distinct body independent from any other, and exercising the sovereign power within itself, looks upon the rest as allies, to whom they are bound only by such acts as they themselves have made; and when any new thing not comprehended in them happens to arise, they oblige their delegates to give them an account of it, and retain the power of determining those matters in themselves. 'Tis not so amongst us: Every county does not make a distinct body, having in itself a sovereign power, but is a member of that great body which comprehends the whole nation. 'Tis not therefore for Kent or Sussex, Lewis or Maidstone, but for the whole nation, that the members chosen in those places are sent to serve in parliament: and tho it be fit for them as friends and neighbours (so far as may be) to hearken to the opinions of the electors for the information of their judgments, and to the end that what they shall say may be of more weight, when everyone is known not to speak his own thoughts only, but those of a great number of men; yet they are not strictly and properly obliged to give account of their actions to any, unless the whole body of the nation for which they serve, and who are equally concerned in their resolutions, could be assembled. This being impracticable, the only punishment to which they are subject if they betray their trust, is scorn, infamy, hatred, and an assurance of being rejected, when they shall again seek the same honor. And tho this may seem a small matter to those who fear to do ill only from a sense of the pains inflicted; yet it is very terrible to men of ingenuous spirits, as they are supposed to be who are accounted fit to be entrusted with so great powers. But why should this be *liberty with a mischief* if it were otherwise? or how the liberty of particular societies would be greater, if they might do what they pleased, than whilst they send others to act for them, such wise men only as Filmer can tell us. For as no man, or number of men, can give a power which he or they have not, the Achaeans, Aetolians, Latins, Samnites and Tuscans, who transacted all things relating to their associations by delegates; and the Athenians, Carthaginians and Romans, who kept the power of the state in themselves, were all equally free. And in our days, the United Provinces of the Netherlands, the Switsers and Grisons, who are of the first sort, and the Venetians, Genoese, and Lucchesi, who are of the other, are so also. All men that have any degree of common sense, plainly see, that the liberty of those who act in their own persons, and of those who send delegates, is perfectly the same, and the exercise is, and can only be changed by their consent.

But whatever the law or custom of England be in this point, it cannot concern our question. The general proposition concerning a patriarchical power cannot be proved by a single example. If there be a general power everywhere, forbidding nations to give instructions to their delegates, they can do it nowhere. If there be no such thing, every people may do it, unless they have deprived themselves of their right, all being born under the same condition. 'Tis to no purpose to say that the nations before mentioned had not kings, and therefore might act as they did. For if the general thesis be true, they must have kings; and if it be not, none are obliged to have them, unless they think fit, and the kings they make are their creatures. But many of these nations had either kings, or other magistrates in power like to them. The provinces of the Netherlands had dukes, earls, or marquesses: Genoa and Venice have dukes. If any on account of the narrowness of their territories have abstained from the name, it does not alter the case; for our dispute is not concerning the name, but the right. If that one man, who is in the principal magistracy of every nation, must be reputed the father of that people, and has a power which may not be limited by any law, it imports not what he is called. But if in small territories he may be limited by laws, he may be so also in the greatest. The least of men is a man as well as a giant: And those in the West-Indies who have not above twenty or thirty subjects able to bear arms, are kings as well as Xerxes. Every nation may divide itself into small parcels as some have done, by the same law they have restrained or abolished their kings, joined to one another, or taken their hazard of subsisting by themselves; acted by delegation, or retaining the power in their own persons; given finite or indefinite powers; reserved to themselves a power of punishing those who should depart from their duty, or referred it to their general assemblies. And that liberty, for which we contend as the gift of God and nature, remains equally to them all.

If men who delight in cavilling should say, that great kingdoms are not to be regulated by the examples of small states, I desire to know when it was, that God ordained great nations should be slaves, and deprived of all right to dispose matters relating to their government; whilst he left to such as had, or should divide themselves into small parcels, a right of making such constitutions as were most convenient for them. When this is resolved, we ought to be informed, what extent of territory is required to deserve the name of a great kingdom. Spain and France are esteemed great, and yet the deputies or *procuradores* of the several parts of Castile did in the cortes held at Madrid, in the beginning of Charles the fifth's reign, excuse themselves from giving the supplies he desired, because they had received no orders in that particular from the towns that sent them; and afterwards receiving express orders not to do it, they gave his majesty a flat denial.[2] The like was frequently done during the reigns of that great prince, and of his son Philip the second. And generally those *procuradores* never granted anything of importance to either of them, without particular orders from their principals. The same way was taken in France, as long as there were any general assemblies of estates; and if it do not still continue, 'tis because there are none. For no man who understood the affairs of that kingdom, did ever deny, that the deputies were obliged to follow the orders of those who sent them. And perhaps, if men would examine by what means they came to be abolished, they might find, that the cardinals de Richelieu and Mazarin, with other ministers who have accomplished that work, were acted by some other principle than that of justice, or the establishment of the laws of God and nature. In the general assembly of estates held at Blois in the time of Henry the third, Bodin then deputy for the third estate of Vermandois, by their particular order, proposed so many things as took up a great part of their time. Other deputies alleged no other reason for many things said and done by them, highly contrary to the king's will, than that they were commanded so to do by their superiors.[3] These general assemblies being laid aside, the same custom is still used in the lesser assemblies of estates in Languedoc and Brittany. The deputies cannot without the infamy of betraying their trust, and fear of punishment, recede from the orders given by their principals; and yet we do not find that *liberty with a mischief* is much more predominant in France than amongst us. The same method is every day practised in the diets of Germany. The princes and great lords, who have their places in their own right, may do what they please; but the deputies of the cities must follow such orders as they receive. The histories of Denmark, Sweden, Poland and Bohemia, testify the same thing: and if this *liberty with a mischief* do not still continue entire in all those places, it has been diminished by such means as suit better with the manners of pirates, than the laws of God and nature. If England therefore do not still enjoy the same, we must have been deprived of it either by such unjustifiable means, or by our own consent. But thanks be to God, we know no people who have a better right to liberty, or have better defended it than our own nation. And if we do not degenerate from the virtue of our ancestors, we may hope to transmit it entire to our posterity. We always may, and often do give instructions to our delegates; but the less we fetter them,

[2] Vida de Carlos 5° de Sandoval. [Prudencio de Sandoval, *Historia de la Vida y Hechos del Emperador Carlos V* (1604–06; Pamplona: Bartholome Paris, 1614). Translated as *The His-* *tory of Charles the Vth, Emperor and King of Spain* (London: R. Smith, 1703).]

[3] Hist. Thuan. [De Thou, *History of His Time*, bk. 63.]

the more we manifest our own rights: for those who have only a limited power, must limit that which they give; but he that can give an unlimited power must necessarily have it in himself. The great treasurer Burleigh said, the parliament could do anything but turn a man into a woman. Sir Thomas More, when Rich solicitor to K. Henry the 8th asked him, if the parliament might not make R. Rich king, said, that was *casus levis*,[4] taking it for granted that they might make or unmake whom they pleased. The first part of this, which includes the other, is asserted by the statute of the 13th of Q. Elizabeth, denouncing the most grievous punishments against all such as should dare to contradict it. But if it be in the parliament, it must be in those who give to parliament-men the powers by which they act; for before they are chosen they have none, and can never have any if those that send them had it not in themselves. They cannot receive it from the magistrate, for that power which he has is derived from the same spring. The power of making and unmaking him cannot be from himself; for he that is not, can do nothing, and when he is made can have no other power than is conferred upon him by those that make him. He who departs from his duty desires to avoid the punishment, the power therefore of punishing him is not from himself. It cannot be from the house of peers as it is constituted, for they act for themselves, and are chosen by kings: and 'tis absurd to think that kings, who generally abhor all restriction of their power, should give that to others by which they might be unmade. If one or more princes relying upon their own virtue and resolutions to do good, had given such a power against themselves, as Trajan did, when he commanded the prefect to use the sword for him if he governed well, and against him if he governed ill, it would soon have been rescinded by their successors. If our Edward the first had made such a law, his lewd son would have abolished it, before he would have suffered himself to be imprisoned and deposed by it. He would never have acknowledged his unworthiness to reign, if he had been tied to no other law than his own will, for he could not transgress that; nor have owned the mercy of the parliament in sparing his life, if they had acted only by a power which he had conferred upon them. This power must therefore be in those who act by a delegated power, and none can give it to their delegates but they who have it in themselves. The most certain testimony that can be given of their unlimited power is, that they rely upon the wisdom and fidelity of their deputies, so as to lay no restrictions upon them: they may do what they please, if they take care *ne quid detrimenti respublica accipiat, that the commonwealth receive no*

---

[4] [An easy case.]

detriment. This is a commission fit to be granted by wise and good men, to those they chuse through an opinion that they are so also, and that they cannot bring any prejudice upon the nation, that will not fall upon themselves and their posterity. This is also fit to be received by those, who seeking nothing but that which is just in itself, and profitable to their country, cannot foresee what will be proposed when they are all together; much less resolve how to vote till they hear the reasons on both sides. The electors must necessarily be in the same ignorance; and the law which should oblige them to give particular orders to their knights and burgesses in relation to every vote, would make the decision of the most important affairs to depend upon the judgment of those who know nothing of the matters in question, and by that means cast the nation into the utmost danger of the most inextricable confusion. This can never be the intention of that law which is *sanctio recta*,[5] and seeks only the good of those that live under it. The foresight therefore of such a mischief can never impair the liberties of the nation, but establish them.

SECTION 45

The Legislative Power is always Arbitrary, and not to be trusted in the hands of any who are not bound to obey the Laws they make.

I F it be objected that I am a defender of arbitrary powers, I confess I cannot comprehend how any society can be established or subsist without them; for the establishment of government is an arbitrary act, wholly depending upon the will of men. The particular forms and constitutions, the whole series of the magistracy, together with the measure of power given to everyone, and the rules by which they are to exercise their charge, are so also. *Magna Charta*, which comprehends our ancient laws, and all the subsequent statutes were not sent from heaven, but made according to the will of men. If no men could have a power of making laws, none could ever have been made; for all that are or have been in the world, except those given by God to the Israelites, were made by them; that is, they have exercised an arbitrary power in making that to be law which was not, or annulling that which was. The various laws and governments, that are or have been in several ages and places,

---

[5] [A right sanction.]

are the product of various opinions in those who had the power of making them. This must necessarily be, unless a general rule be set to all; for the judgments of men will vary if they are left to their liberty, and the variety that is found among them, shews they are subject to no rule but that of their own reason, by which they see what is fit to be embraced or avoided, according to the several circumstances under which they live. The authority that judges of these circumstances is arbitrary, and the legislators shew themselves to be more or less wise and good, as they do rightly or not rightly exercise this power. The difference therefore between good and ill governments is not, that those of one sort have an arbitrary power which the others have not, for they all have it; but that those which are well constituted, place this power so as it may be beneficial to the people, and set such rules as are hardly to be transgressed; whilst those of the other sort fail in one or both these points. Some also through want of courage, fortune, or strength, may have been oppressed by the violence of strangers, or suffer'd a corrupt party to rise up within themselves, and by force or fraud to usurp a power of imposing what they pleased. Others being sottish, cowardly and base, have so far erred in the foundations, as to give up themselves to the will of one or few men, who turning all to their own profit or pleasure, have been just in nothing but in using such a people like beasts. Some have placed weak defences against the lusts of those they have advanced to the highest places, and given them opportunities of arrogating more power to themselves than the law allows. Where any of these errors are committed, the government may be easy for a while, or at least tolerable, whilst it continues uncorrupted, but it cannot be lasting. When the law may be easily or safely overthrown, it will be attempted. Whatever virtue may be in the first magistrates, many years will not pass before they come to be corrupted; and their successors deflecting from their integrity, will seize upon the ill-guarded prey. They will then not only govern by will, but by that irregular will, which turns the law, that was made for the publick good, to the private advantage of one or few men. 'Tis not my intention to enumerate the several ways that have been taken to effect this; or to shew what governments have deflected from the right, and how far. But I think I may justly say, that an arbitrary power was never well placed in any men and their successors, who were not obliged to obey the laws they should make. This was well understood by our Saxon ancestors: They made laws in their assemblies and councils of the nation; but all those who proposed or assented to those laws, as soon as the assembly was dissolved, were comprehended under the power of them as well as other men. They could do nothing to the prejudice of the nation, that would not be as hurtful to those who were present and their posterity, as to those who by many accidents might be absent. The Normans enter'd into, and continued in the same path. Our parliaments at this day are in the same condition. They may make prejudicial wars, ignominious treaties, and unjust laws: Yet when the session is ended, they must bear the burden as much as others; and when they die, *the teeth of their children will be set on edge with the sour grapes they have eaten.*[1] But 'tis hard to delude or corrupt so many: Men do not in matters of the highest importance yield to slight temptations. No man serves the Devil for nothing: Small wages will not content those who expose themselves to perpetual infamy, and the hatred of a nation for betraying their country. Our kings had not wherewithal to corrupt many till these last twenty years, and the treachery of a few was not enough to pass a law. The union of many was not easily wrought, and there was nothing to tempt them to endeavour it; for they could make little advantage during the session, and were to be lost in the mass of the people, and prejudiced by their own laws, as soon as it was ended. They could not in a short time reconcile their various interests or passions, so as to combine together against the publick; and the former kings never went about it. We are beholden to H-de, Cl-ff-rd and D-nby,[2] for all that has been done of that kind. They found a parliament full of lewd young men chosen by a furious people in spite to the Puritans, whose severity had distasted them. The weakest of all ministers had wit enough to understand that such as these might be easily deluded, corrupted, or bribed. Some were fond of their seats in parliament, and delighted to domineer over their neighbours by continuing in them: Others preferr'd the cajoleries of the court before the honour of performing their duty to the country that employ'd them. Some sought to relieve their ruined fortunes, and were most forward to give the king a vast revenue, that from thence they might receive pensions: others were glad of a temporary protection against their creditors. Many knew not what they did when they annulled the Triennial Act, voted the militia to be in the king, gave him the excise, customs and chimney-money, made the act for corporations, by which the greatest part of the nation was brought under the power of the worst men in it; drunk or sober pass'd the five mile act, and that for uniformity in the church.[3]

[1] [Jeremiah 31:29.]

[2] [Hyde, Clifford, Danby.]

[3] [The Triennial Act (1641) had stipulated that three years were not to pass without a parliament being summoned. The Act of Uniformity (1662) required the use of the Episcopal *Book of Common Prayer*. Clergymen who refused to comply lost their positions; and, by the Five Mile Act of 1665, they were forbidden to go within five miles of a place where they had held a church position.]

This embolden'd the court to think of making parliaments to be the instruments of our slavery, which had in all ages past been the firmest pillars of our liberty. There might have been perhaps a possibility of preventing this pernicious mischief in the constitution of our government. But our brave ancestors could never think their posterity would degenerate into such baseness to sell themselves and their country: but how great soever the danger may be, 'tis less than to put all into the hands of one man and his ministers: the hazard of being ruin'd by those who must perish with us, is not so much to be feared, as by one who may enrich and strengthen himself by our destruction. 'Tis better to depend upon those who are under a possibility of being again corrupted, than upon one who applies himself to corrupt them, because he cannot otherwise accomplish his designs. It were to be wished that our security were more certain; but this being, under God, the best anchor we have, it deserves to be preserved with all care, till one of a more unquestionable strength be framed by the consent of the nation.

SECTION 46

The coercive power of the Law proceeds from the Authority of Parliament.

HAVING proved that proclamations are not laws, and that the legislative power, which is arbitrary, is trusted only in the hands of those who are bound to obey the laws that are made, 'tis not hard to discover what it is that gives the power of law to the sanctions under which we live. Our author tells us, that *all statutes or laws are made properly by the king alone, at the rogation of the people, as his majesty King James of happy memory affirms in his* True Law of Free Monarchy; *and as Hooker teaches us, That laws do not take their constraining power from the quality of such as devise them, but from the power that giveth them the strength of law.*[1] But if the rogation of the people be necessary, that cannot be a law which proceeds not from their rogation: the power therefore is not alone in the king; for a most important part is confessed to be in the people. And as none could be in them, if our author's proposition, or the principles upon which it is grounded were true, the acknowledgment of such a part to be

---

[1] [*Patriarcha*, ch. 31 ("The King Alone Makes Laws in Parliament"), p. 119.]

in the people shews them to be false. For if the king had all in himself, none could participate with him: if any do participate, he hath not all; and 'tis from that law by which they do participate, that we are to know what part is left to him. The preambles of most acts of parliaments manifest this by the words, *Be it enacted by the Lords Spiritual and Temporal, and Commons in Parliament assembled, and by authority of the same.* But King James, says Filmer, *in his* Law of Free Monarchy *affirms the contrary;* and it may be so, yet that is nothing to us. No man doubts that he desired it might be so in England: but it does not from thence appear that it is so. The law of a free monarchy is nothing to us; for that monarchy is not free which is regulated by a law not to be broken without the guilt of perjury, as he himself confessed in relation to ours.[2] As to the words cited from Hooker, I can find no hurt in them. To draw up the form of a good law, is a matter of invention and judgment, but it receives the force of a law from the power that enacts it. We have no other reason for the payment of excise or customs, than that the parliament has granted those revenues to the king to defray the publick charges. Whatever therefore King James was pleased to say in his books, or in those written for him, we do not so much as know that the killing of a king is treason, or to be punished with death, otherwise than as it is enacted by parliament; and it was not always so: for in the time of Ethelstan, the estimates of lives were agreed in parliament, and that of a king valued at thirty thousand thrimsae.[3] And if that law had not been alter'd by the parliament, it must have been in force at this day. It had been in vain for a king to say he would have it otherwise; for he is not created to make laws, but to govern according to such as are made, and sworn to assent to *such as shall be proposed.*[4] He who thinks the crown not worth accepting on these conditions, may refuse it. The words *le roy le veult,*[5] are only a pattern of the French fashions, upon which some kings have laid great stress, and would no doubt have been glad to introduce *car tel est nostre plaisir;*[6] but that may prove a difficult matter. Nay in France itself, where that style, and all the ranting expressions that please the vainest of men, are in mode, no edict has the power of a law, till it be registered in parliament. This is not a mere ceremony as some pretend, but all that is essential to a law. Nothing has been more common than for those parliaments to

---

[2] Speech in Star-Chamber, 1616. [In *Political Works of James I.*]

[3] Leg. Aethelstani, fol. 71. [*Leges Aethelstani,* in Lambarde, *Archaionomia.* Thrimsa: an ancient English coin.]

[4] Quas vulgus elegerit.

[5] [*Patriarcha,* p. 119: " '*Le roi le veult*: the King will have it so' is the imperative phrase pronounced at the King's passing of every Act of Parliament."]

[6] [For such is our pleasure.]

refuse edicts sent to them by the king. When John Chastel had, at the instigation of the Jesuits, stabb'd Henry the fourth in the mouth, and that order had designed or executed many other execrable crimes, they were banished out of the kingdom by an arrest of the parliament of Paris. Some other parliaments registered the same; but those of Toulouse and Bordeaux absolutely refused, and notwithstanding all that the king could do, the Jesuits continued at Tournon and many other places within their precincts, till the arrest was revoked. These proceedings are so displeasing to the court, that the most violent ways have been often used to abolish them. About the year 1650, Seguier then chancellor of France was sent with a great number of soldiers to oblige the parliament of Paris to pass some edicts upon which they had hesitated: but he was so far from accomplishing his design, that the people rose against him, and he thought himself happy that he escaped with his life.[7] If the parliaments do not in all parts of the kingdom continue in the liberty of approving or rejecting all edicts, the law is not altered, but oppressed by the violence of the sword: And the prince of Condé who was principally employ'd to do that work, may, as I suppose, have had leisure to reflect upon those actions, and cannot but find reason to conclude, that his excellent valour and conduct was used in a most noble exploit, equally beneficial to his country and himself. However, those who are skilled in the laws of that nation do still affirm, that all publick acts which are not duly examined and registered, are void in themselves, and can be of no force longer than the miserable people lies under the violence of oppression; which is all that could reasonably be said, if a pirate had the same power over them. But whether the French have willingly offer'd their ears to be bor'd, or have been subdued by force, it concerns us not. Our liberties depend not upon their will, virtue, or fortune: how wretched and shameful soever their slavery may be, the evil is only to themselves. We are to consider no human laws but our own; and if we have the spirit of our ancestors we shall maintain them, and die as free as they left us. *Le roy le veult*, tho written in great letters, or pronounced in the most tragical manner, can signify no more than that the king in performance of his oath does assent to such laws as the lords and commons have agreed. Without prejudice to themselves and their liberties, a people may suffer the king to advise with his council upon what they propose. Two eyes see more than one, and human judgment is subject to errors. Tho the parliament consist of the most eminent men of the nation, yet when they intend good, they may be mistaken. They may safely put a check upon themselves, that

[7] Mem. de L. R. F. [*Memoires de Louis, Roi de France.*]

they may farther consider the most important matters, and correct the errors that may have been committed, if the king's council do discover them: but he can speak only by the advice of his council; and every man of them is with his head to answer for the advices he gives. If the parliament has not been satisfied with the reasons given against any law that they offer'd, it has frequently pass'd; and if they have been satisfied, 'twas not the king, but they that laid it aside. He that is of another opinion, may try whether *le roy le veult* can give the force of a law to anything conceived by the king, his council, or any other than the parliament. But if no wise man will affirm that he can do it, or deny that by his oath he is obliged to assent to those that come from them, he can neither have the legislative power in himself, nor any other part in it than what is necessarily to be performed by him, as the law prescribes.

I know not what our author means by saying, *le roy le veult is the interpretative*[8] *phrase pronounced at the passing of every act of parliament:* For if there be difficulty in any of them, those words do no way remove it. But the following part of the paragraph better deserves to be observed. *It was,* says he, *the ancient custom for a long time, until the days of Henry the fifth, for the kings when any bill was brought to them that had passed both houses, to take and pick out what they liked not; and so much as they chose was enacted as a law: But the custom of the latter kings hath been so gracious, as to allow always of the entire bill as it passed both houses.*[9] He judiciously observes when our kings began to be gracious, and we to be free. That king (excepting the persecution for religion in his time, which is rather to be imputed to the ignorance of that age, than to any evil in his own nature) governed well; and as all princes who have been virtuous and brave have always desired to preserve their subjects' liberty, which they knew to be the mother and nurse of their valour, fitting them for great and generous enterprises, his care was to please them, and to raise their spirits. But about the same time, those detestable arts by which the mixed monarchies in this part of the world have been everywhere terribly shaken, and in many places totally overthrown, began to be practised. Charles the seventh of France, under pretence of carrying on a war against him and his son, took upon him to raise money by his own authority, and we know how well that method has been pursued. The mischievous sagacity of his son Lewis the 11th, which is now called king-craft, was wholly exerted in the subversion of the laws of France, and the nobility that

---

[8] [Filmer wrote *imperative*, not *interpretative* (see note 5 above). The confusion arose because the 1680 edition of Filmer mistakenly printed "interpretative."]

[9] [*Patriarcha*, ch. 31, pp. 119–120.]

supported them. His successors, except only Lewis the 12th, followed his example; and in other nations, Ferdinand of Aragon, James the third of Scotland, and Henry the seventh of England, were thought to imitate him the most. Tho we have little reason to commend all the princes that preceded Henry the fifth; yet I am inclined to date the general impairing of our government from the death of that king, and his valiant brothers. His weak son[10] became a prey to a furious French woman, who brought the maxims of her own country into ours, and advanced the worst of villains to govern according to them. These measures were pursued by Edward the fourth, whose wants contracted by prodigality and debauchery, were to be supplied by fraud and rapine. The ambition, cruelty and perfidiousness of Richard the third; the covetousness and malicious subtlety of Henry the seventh; the violent lust, rage and pride of Henry the 8th, and the bigoted fury of Queen Mary, instigated by the craft and malice of Spain, persuaded me to believe that the English liberty did not receive birth or growth from the favour and goodness of their gracious princes. But it seems all this is mistaken; Henry the sixth was wise, valiant, and no way guided by his wife; Edward the fourth continent, sober, and contented with what the nation gave him; Richard the third mild, gentle and faithful; Henry the 7th sincere, and satisfied with his own; Henry the 8th humble, temperate and just; and Queen Mary a friend to our country and religion. No less praises sure can be due to those who were so gracious to recede from their own right of picking what they pleased out of our laws, and to leave them entirely to us as they passed both houses. We are beholden to our author for the discovery of these mysteries: but tho he seems to have taken an oath like that of the gypsies when they enter into that virtuous society, never to speak one word of truth, he is not so subtle in concealing his lies. All kings were trusted with the publication of the laws, but all kings did not falsify them. Such as were not wicked and vicious, or so weak as to be made subservient to the malice of their ministers and flatterers, could never be drawn into the guilt of so infamous a cheat, directly contrary to the oath of their coronation. They swear to pass such *laws as the people chuse;*[11] but if we will believe our author, they might have pick'd out whatever they pleased, and falsely imposed upon the nation, as a law made by the lords and commons, that which they had modeled according to their own will, and made to be different from, or contrary to the intention of the parliament. The king's part in this fraud (of which he boasts) was little more than might have been done by the speaker or his clerks. They might

---

[10] [Henry VI.] [11] Quas vulgus elegerit.

have falsified an act as well as the king, tho they could not so well preserve themselves from punishment. 'Tis no wonder if for a while no stop was put to such an abominable custom. 'Twas hard to think a king would be guilty of a fraud, that were infamous in a slave: But that proved to be a small security, when the worst of slaves came to govern them. Nevertheless 'tis probable they proceeded cautiously: the first alterations were perhaps innocent, or, it may be, for the best. But when they had once found out the way, they stuck at nothing that seemed for their purpose. This was like the plague of leprosy, that could not be cured; the house infected was to be demolished; the poisonous plant must be torn up by the root; the trust that had been broken was to be abolished; they who had perverted or frustrated the law, were no longer to be suffered to make the least alteration; and that brave prince readily joined with his people to extinguish the mischievous abuse that had been introduced by some of his worthless predecessors. The worst and basest of them had continual disputes with their parliaments, and thought that whatever they could detract from the liberty of the nation, would serve to advance their prerogative. They delighted in frauds, and would have no other ministers but such as would be the instruments of them. Since their word could not be made to pass for a law, they endeavoured to impose their own or their servants' inventions as acts of parliaments, upon the deluded people, and to make the best of them subservient to their corrupt ends and pernicious counsels. This, if it had continued, might have overthrown all our rights, and deprived us of all that men can call good in the world. But the providence of God furnished our ancestors with an opportunity of providing against so great, so universal a mischief. They had a wise and valiant prince, who scorned to encroach upon the liberties of his subjects, and abhorred the detestable arts by which they had been impair'd. He esteemed their courage, strength, and love, to be his greatest advantage, riches and glory. He aimed at the conquest of France, which was only to be effected by the bravery of a free and well-satisfied people. Slaves will always be cowards, and enemies to their master: By bringing his subjects into that condition, he must infallibly have ruined his own designs, and made them unfit to fight either for him or themselves. He desired not only that his people should be free during his time, but that his successors should not be able by oblique and fraudulent ways to enslave them. If it be a reproach to us that women have reigned over us, 'tis much more to the princes that succeeded our Henry, that none of them did so much imitate him in his government as Queen Elizabeth. She did not go about to mangle acts of parliament, and to pick out what might serve her turn, but frequently passed forty or fifty in a session, without reading one of them. She knew that she did not reign for herself, but for her people; that what was good for them, was either good for her, or that her good ought not to come into competition with that of the whole nation; and that she was by oath obliged to pass such laws as were presented to her on their behalf. This not only shews that there is no such thing as a legislative power placed in kings by the laws of God and nature, but that nations have it in themselves. It was not by law nor by right, but by usurpation, fraud and perjury that some kings took upon them to pick what they pleased out of the publick acts. Henry the fifth did not grant us the right of making our own laws; but with his approbation we abolished a detestable abuse that might have proved fatal to us. And if we examine our history we shall find, that every good and generous prince has sought to establish our liberties, as much as the most base and wicked to infringe them.

THE END.

INDEX

Aaron, 36, 228
Abel, 89
Abiah, 398
Abimelech, 228–229, 356, 398
Abishai, 331, 332
Abner, 333, 374
Abraham, 24–25, 27, 28, 29, 34–35, 57, 69, 71, 93, 98–99, 101, 104, 304, 338, 523
Abravanel, Isaac, 124
Absalom, 230, 325, 333, 334, 502
Absolute monarchy. *See also* Divine right of kings; Kingship; Limits upon monarchy; Mixed government
    ambition and, 238–239
    argument for, 287
    Bracton on, 368
    civil disorders under, 218, 228–229
    common good and, 270–279
    corruption and, 189, 194–195, 229–230
    cruelty under, 264–270
    English supporters of, 194–195
    factional strife under, 238
    flatterers and, 230
    justice and, 554–555
    law as a basis for power, 391, 439–446

liberty restrained under, 191–195
Magna Charta and, 474–477
mixed government compared with, 194
monarchy restrained by law, contrasted, 297
Parliament (England) and, 528–534
paternal rights not comparable to, 304
populace suffers under, 197
popular will and, 185
preservation of peace and, 195–202, 262
valour of people decreased under, 197–199
Absolute power
    Aristotle on, 452–454
    biblical case against, 26–27
    Hobbes on, 11n7
    justice, lack of, under, 58
Achilles, 47, 114
Achish the Philistine, 290, 330
Acts, 9n2, 436n2
Adam, 29, 30, 88–90, 93, 463
Ad legem Juliam et Papiam (Ulpian), 446n8
Adonibezek, 563
Adoram, 335, 340
Advertisements from Parnassus (Boccalini), 202n10, 288n6

Index

Aeacidae, 114
Aegeus, 391
Aemilius Paulus (Roman general), 154, 178, 179, 200, 211, 212, 253
Aemilius Paulus (historian), 425*n*13
Aeneid (Virgil), 199*n*6, 491*n*27
Afranius, Lucius, 472
Africa, 116
Against Apion (Josephus), 128*n*18
Against Eutropius (Claudian), 60, 255*n*5, 264*n*2, 418*n*1
Against Marcion (Tertullian), 261*n*3
Agatharchides, 115
Agathocles, 73, 169, 170, 187, 191, 193, 218, 306, 325, 370, 385, 407, 461
Agesilaus, 113, 142, 176, 177, 204, 283, 351, 375, 510
Agesilaus (Xenophon), 375*n*13
Agis II, 290, 542
Agricola, Julius, 388
Agricola, Germania, Dialogus (Tacitus), 103*n*11
Agrippa, Menenius, 217
Agrippa Posthumus, 87, 239
Agrippina, Vipsania, 149
Ahab, 185, 336, 337, 340, 346, 347, 351, 356, 368–369, 407, 439, 545
Ahala, Servilius, 182
Ahasuerus, 63, 138, 496
Alans, 147
Alaric, 240
Alcibiades, 212, 271
Alcibiades I, II (Plato), 86*n*12
Alexander of Epirus, 145, 213–214
Alexander of Macedon (the Great), 81, 139, 142–143, 146, 171, 177, 211, 214, 231, 507, 525, 534, 543, 560
Alexander VII (pope of Rome), 262
Alfonso II (k. of Castile), 168, 246
Alfonso VI (k. of Portugal), 534*n*9
Alfonso of Aragon (k. of Naples), 198, 215
Alfonso el Desheredado (k. of Castile), 168, 169, 246
Alfonso the Wise (k. of Castile), 59, 168
Alfred (k. of England), 17, 376, 483, 487, 489
Almohades, 116
Almoravides, 116
Alviano, General, 275
Amalekites, 330, 357
Amasa, 333, 374
Amaziah (k. of Judah), 231, 335, 375, 382
Ambition
cause of mischief under absolute monarchy, 238–239

as immoderate appetite, 234, 238
of Julius Caesar, 171, 186–187
Roman magistracy, 171, 175
wielding of power and, 188
Ambrose, Saint, 361, 363
Ammon, 34, 98, 120
Ammonites, 104, 135
Amulius, 48
Anabasis (Xenophon), 176*n*4
Anales de la Corona de Aragón (Zurita), 509*n*3
Anderson, Sir Edmund, 448*n*4
Angles, 481
Annals (Hoveden), 106*n*23, 107*n*25
Annals, The (Tacitus), 73*n*10–11, 87*n*15, 91*n*2, 148*n*6–8, 171*n*1, 181*n*9, 182*n*15, 242*n*30, 263*n*7, 267*n*11, 271*n*2, 282*n*3, 285*n*8, 295*n*25, 372*n*5, 383*n*1, 384*n*2–4, 389*n*3, 405*n*3, 441*n*3, 455*n*2, 466*n*2, 480*n*4, 508*n*1–2
Ante-Nicene Fathers (Tertullian), 261*n*3, 492*n*29
Antigonus, 171, 291
Antiochus, 73, 143, 145, 164, 200
Antoninus Pius, 185, 233, 252, 380, 443, 533
Antonius (Mark Anthony), 139, 140, 155, 174, 263, 383
Apollo, 202, 543
Apologia pro regibus (Blackwood), 11*n*6
Apologie Catholique contre les Libelles (Belloy), 428*n*20
Apology (Tertullian), 362*n*4–5, 362*n*7, 363*n*8, 380*n*32–33, 381*n*4, 510*n*1
Arabia, 17, 105
Arbaces, 137
Arbitrary power, in good and bad government, 569–572
Arcadius, 214, 233, 420
Archaionomia, sive, De priscis Anglorum legibus (Lambarde), 120*n*16
Arianism, 140
Ariovistus, 480
Aristides, 178, 212, 253
Aristippus, 253
Aristocracy, 87, 218. *See also* Mixed government
consent of the governed and, 99
creation of, as against absolute rule, 87, 490–491
democracy contrasted, 299
as element of good government, 31, 166–170
familial succession, 300–301
Israelite government as, 124–131

Aristocracy (*continued*)
  virtues of the select, 31
  well-being of the people in, 191
  Xenophon on, 175–178
Aristogiton, 15, 228
Aristotle, 9, 18, 49, 70, 110, 353*n*2, 373,
    401, 449, 451, 470, 538
  against absolute power, 452–454
  Alexander and, 81, 139
  attacks on, 78
  on governors, 79–80, 84, 87
  inclined to aristocracy, 191
  on kingship, 85, 287, 288
  on purposes of government, 91
  on restraints upon kings, 289–290
  on sorts of government, 81, 86, 123,
    132–134
  on tyranny, 94
Arlington, earl of. *See* Bennet, Henry
Arminius, 314, 385, 480
Ars Poetica (Horace), 64*n*3
Art and Science of Government among the Scots
    (MacClelan), 398*n*14
Artabanus, 441
Artaxerxes, 142, 218, 239, 351, 560
Arviragus (k. of Britain), 458, 479, 481
Assemblies. *See also* Parliament (England);
    Senates
  in the best governments, 166–167
  conducive to common good, 307, 396
  delegates to, 563–569
  in France, 425, 428, 573–576
  historical examples of, 102–103, 105
  Israelite, 127–128, 129, 166
  kings deposed by, 348
  kingship transferred by, 169
  law of nature and, 103–104
  of nobility, 497
  origins of, 482
  power of, 292, 296
  rights of, 502–507
  Roman, 149. *See also* Senate (Rome)
  sedition and, 220
  Spartan, 166
Asser, Bishop, 376*n*17, 487
Assyrians and Assyria, 17, 134, 137, 141,
    145, 211
Athaliah, 61, 120, 220, 231
Atheling, Edgar, 499
Athens, 30, 101, 161, 166, 169, 175, 177–
    178, 191, 201, 203, 221, 299, 387,
    391, 393, 394, 491, 503
Attila the Hun, 306, 406
Aubijoux, Count d', 294–295
Audley, Thomas, 66

Augustine, Saint, 134, 361, 364, 381*n*3
Augustulus, 308
Aurelius, Marcus, 140, 185, 233, 252, 443,
    533
Austria, 59, 117, 168, 215, 275, 522
Avarice. *See* Greed

Baanah, 332
Baasha, 45, 334, 342, 407
Babel, 27, 32, 323
Babylon, 29, 33, 42, 54, 55, 98, 137, 145,
    304, 456, 457
Balafré, Henry le, 245
Baldus, 461
Baliol, Edward de (k. of Scotland), 246
Barak, 228, 314, 329
Barclay, William, 11, 18*n*4
Bardanes, 218
Barea Soranus, 147, 267, 372, 384, 388
Barlotta, 222
Barneveldt, Jan van Olden, 207
Bartolus, 461
Bassompierre, General François de, 275
Bathsheba, 347
Belial, men of, 104
Bellarmine, Robert, 10, 11, 19, 20–21, 22,
    30, 77, 97
Belloy, Pierre du, 428–429
Belochus, 137
Belshazzar, 63, 137, 145, 211
Benemerini, 116
Benjamin, tribe of, 128–130, 538
Bennet, Henry, earl of Arlington, 194*n*4,
    258, 485
Bernard (k. of Italy), 243, 425
Bethuel, 28
Bianchi, 161
Bible and biblical evidence. *See also names of*
    biblical figures and books of the Bible
  covenant between people and ruler, 311–
    312
  election of kings, 102
  family of man in, 62
  "head" (preeminent), 535–536
  hereditary succession, 118, 119, 236,
    419–420
  kingship in, 39, 43, 109–112, 323, 329,
    456–457
  liberators seen as seditious, 228
  limits upon kingship, 287–289
  magistratical power, 70
  oaths of kings in, 408
  paternal authority, 28–30
  people's power, 22–23
  selection of governors, 79

Bible and biblical evidence *(continued)*
  wealth, vanity of, 67
  wisdom of kings, 64
Bichri, 334, 502
Bilain, Antoin, 294*n*23
Blackwood, Adam, 11
Blake, Admiral Robert, 278
Boadicia, 458
Boccalini, Trajano, 202, 288
Bodin, 567
Bohemia, 101, 167
Borgia, Cesare, 308
Bourbon kings, 60
Bracton, Henry, 313, 360*n*2, 366, 367,
  368, 393, 399, 467*n*7, 469, 471, 511*n*3
Braganza, duke of, 554
*Brevísima Relación de la Destrucción de las In-
  dias* (Las Casas), 52*n*7, 160*n*6
Brinvilliers, Marie, marchioness of, 16*n*2
Britains and Britain, 204, 478, 479, 481.
  See also England
Britannicus, 50
Brownlow, Richard, 66
Bruce (k. of Scotland), 246
Brunehaud (Frankish q.), 240, 241
Brutus, Lucius Junius, 15, 145, 180, 193,
  194, 211, 212, 225, 228, 256, 271,
  314, 396, 529, 539
Brutus, Marcus Junius, 15, 159, 187, 218–
  219, 228, 455, 472
Buchanan, George, 9*n*4, 11, 246*n*32, 292,
  398, 546*n*4–5
Bulion, 355
Burgesses. *See* Assembly and assemblies;
  Parliament (England)
Burleigh, 568
Busiris, 73

Caesar, Augustus (Octavius), 50, 155, 174,
  231, 232, 263, 308, 508, 539
  corrupt acts of, 139
  peace under, 159–160
  power usurped by, 454–456
Caesar, Julius, 50, 155, 159, 169, 170,
  182, 184, 218, 235, 263, 283, 306,
  307, 325, 357, 358, 383, 407, 413,
  455, 458, 479, 480, 482, 486, 507,
  525, 536
  ambition of, 186–187
  death of, 139, 342
  liberty under, 441
  Tarquin compared, 194
  usurpation by, 171
  wealth pursued by, 350
Cain, 89, 323

Caligula, 10, 11, 14, 19, 21, 41, 50, 63,
  65, 73, 139, 148, 158, 160, 184, 239,
  256, 264, 271, 284, 322, 337, 372,
  374, 379, 381, 383, 387, 388, 390,
  396, 398, 405, 444, 447, 461, 539,
  550, 559
  judge of, or judged by, the people, 225–
  226
  killed by his guards, 232
  as ruler justifiably deposed, 226–228
Caligula (Suetonius), 444*n*6
Callicratidas, 204
Callisthenes, 231
Calvin, John, 9*n*4, 10, 11, 124, 128
Calvinism, 294*n*22, 437
Cambyses, 221, 370
Camden, William, 486, 487
Camillus, 135, 154, 178, 179, 212, 256,
  271, 273, 311, 445, 539
Canaanites and Canaan, 98, 127–128
Candale, duke of, 553
Canute (k. of England), 106, 238, 377, 483
Capet, Hugh, 60, 114, 116, 118, 168, 172,
  244, 245, 295, 314, 348, 425, 426,
  427, 498, 504
Capgrave, John, 377*n*20
Capital punishment, 182–183, 223, 231,
  393, 556–557
Caracalla, 140
Caratacus (k. of Britain), 479, 481
Carloman, 242, 425
Carthaginians and Carthage, 17, 101, 152,
  161, 164, 203, 205, 215, 511
Casimir (k. of Poland), 534
Cassander, 231
Cassius Gaius, 15, 159, 187, 219, 228,
  286, 455, 472
Cassius, Spurius, 180, 218, 229
Cassivellaunus, 458, 479, 481
Castile, 168, 246
Castracani, Castruccio, 308
Catilinarian War (Sallust), 165*n*13, 182*n*10
Catiline, 50, 155, 165, 170, 174, 182, 184,
  191, 263
Cato, 15, 159, 187, 406, 472
Cavendish, 448
Cethegus, 182, 191
Ceylon, 561
Charlemagne (Charles the Great), 242–243,
  244, 281, 348, 387, 420, 425
Charles (k. of Rhaetia), 243
Charles I (k. of England), 11*n*7, 122*n*2,
  144*n*19, 476*n*5, 485*n*13, 540*n*10, 554
Charles II (k. of England), 165, 194–195,
  258*n*7, 485*n*12

Index

Charles II (k. of Spain), 447n2
Charles V (k. of Spain), 51, 325, 421, 566
Charles VI (k. of France), 293, 295, 426
Charles VII (k. of France), 245, 505, 575
Charles VIII (k. of France), 198, 215, 245, 261, 331, 450, 521
Charles IX (k. of France), 120, 141, 280
Charles X (k. of Sweden), 169, 420n2
Charles XI (k. of Sweden), 420n2, 447n2
Charles the Bald (k. of France), 426
Charles le Gros (k. of France), 243, 426, 504
Charles Gustavus (k. of Sweden), 116, 211, 418, 488, 503, 504, 533
Charles le Simple (k. of France), 243, 426, 504
Charles of Burgundy, 206–207, 292
Charles of Lorraine, 118, 120, 168
Charmides (Plato), 86n12
Chastel, John, 574
Chedorlaomer, 523
Chiffinch, William, 195
Chigi, Mario, 262
Child, Sir Josiah, 66
Childeric III (Frankish k.), 118
Children. *See also* Family
  heritability of paternal rights, 92–97
  independence of, 96–97
  as kings, 119, 447
  and patriarchy, analogy of, 96–97, 321, 324–325
Chilperic, 240, 426
Chilperic II (Frankish k.), 241
Christ (Jesus), 9, 68, 71, 93, 224, 267, 315, 358, 359, 361–363, 369, 409, 436, 437, 493
Christian (k. of Denmark), 73
Christian II (k. of Denmark), 334, 505
Christian V (k. of Denmark), 420n3
Christians and Christianity
  Bracton on kings and, 471
  conversion to, 485
  defenses against tyrants, 358–359
  observation of human law, 378–379, 436–439, 463
  Roman Empire and, 140, 362–363, 380
  Tertullian on, 460
Christina (q. of Sweden), 116, 211, 533
Chronica Majora (Paris), 504n4
Chronicle (Florence of Worcester), 106n23
Chronicle (Henry of Huntingdon), 106n20, 107n26
Chronicle of the Abbey of Croyland (Ingulf), 107n24, 107n27
Chronicle of the Kings of England (William of Malmesbury), 106n19, 377n21, 492n32, 494n3
I *Chronicles*, 536n3, 538n7
Cicero, 6, 49, 70, 191, 379n31, 443n5, 467n3
Cimon, 177
Cincinnatus, Lucius Quinctius, 180, 212, 253, 256, 271, 273, 445, 539
Cinna, Lucius Cornelius, 263
City of God (Augustine), 134n1, 381n3
Civil disorder and tumult. *See also* Rebellion
  causes of, 217
  commonwealths less afflicted than monarchies by, 248–249
  corruption of leaders resulting in a state of, 527
  Hebrew kings responsible for, 230–231
  justifiable, 220–228
  law, ineffectuality of, and, 219–220
  malice as root of, 228–229
  under popular government and monarchy (contrasted), 217–250
  rebellion of people not blamed as being, 523
  sedition defined, 220
  succession of kings leading to, 248
  tumult defined, 220
  violence of, 79
  Xenophon on, 175–184
Civil society
  civil disorder justified in, 227
  consent of freemen in, 97–108
  contract between people and governor in, 104–105, 432
  democracy in, 102
  entrance into, as voluntary, 35–36, 104
  family contrasted with, 89–90
  family heads, power of, in, 96
  government, purpose of, and, 91
  justice in, 82, 547–548
  king's power limited by law in, 288
  law to help attain happiness in, 83
  liberty of individual diminished in, 30–31
  natural advancement in, 84
  nature as guide in organization of, 83–84
Civil war
  England, 485, 517
  Israel, 347
  Machiavelli on, 545
  under monarchy in general, 248
  Rome, 151, 154–156
  under unrestrained, violent kings, 244
  valour in freeing a country from, 276
  under weak kings, 241–242

Civil War, The (Lucan). See *Pharsalia* (Lucan)

Claudian, 60*n*3, 264*n*2, 418*n*1, 441*n*4

Claudius, 14, 50, 65, 73, 139, 148, 160, 232, 255, 256, 271, 284, 372, 381, 388, 398, 405, 461, 539

Claudius, Appius, 149, 155, 180, 182, 203, 249, 396, 531

Cleanthes, 253

Clearchus, 176

Cleomenes, 161, 291, 542

Cleonymus of Sparta, 264, 290

Cleorestes, 238

Clifford, Sir Thomas, 194–195, 571

Clitus, 231

Clodion, 504

Clothaire, 240

Clovis (Frankish k.), 240

Code of Maimonides, The (Mishneh Torah), Book 14: The Book of Judges (Maimonides), 290*n*12–13, 334*n*3

Coke, Sir Edward, 466

Comines, Philippe de, 207, 247, 292, 488, 500

Commentary on the Prior Prophets (Abravanel), 124*n*3

Commerce. See Trade

Commodus, 14, 140, 233, 271, 533

Common good. See Public good

Common sense, 13, 41–42, 52, 300, 440

Commonwealth(s). See also Mixed government; Popular government

civil disturbances in, 248–249

consent of multitude in forming, 105

corruption natural to monarchies seldom found in, 184–191

Filmer's general argument concerning, 6

liberty necessarily limited in, 30

peace and war under the various types of, 202–208

Plato on, 82

sedition impossible before creation of, 104

selection of governors according to law in, 79

superiority to monarchy in waging war, 213

Compact. See Contract between people and governors

Competency

conferral of rights according to, 66

government, administration of, by those having, 49

heritability of, unreasonability of expecting, 94

implicit faith dependent upon, 13

inequality according to, 80

of kings in all professions, unlikelihood of, 13–14

mixed government and, 199

natural law in allotting responsibilities according to, 83–84

reason used in advancement according to, 51

Concilia, decreta, leges, constitutiones, in re ecclesiarum orbis Britannici (Spelman), 106*n*18, 415*n*16, 487*n*20

Condé, prince of, 277, 278, 574

Conference about the Next Succession to the Crowne of Ingland, A (Doleman), 9*n*4

Confiscation, laws of, against kings as judges, 552–553

Conquest, 32, 94, 108, 154–155, 157–158, 210, 327, 406–407, 507, 519, 522. See also Force; War

Consent of the governed

versus force as source of power to command, 32–33

of freemen in framing societies, 49, 97–108

and governor's rights, 108–112

Hobbes on magistrates lacking title and, 221

kingship derived from nations', 306

kingship derived from people's, 107, 287–288, 298

in mixed government, 169

Constantine (the Great), 114, 233, 239, 301, 308, 420

Constitution(s). See also Law

corruption undermining effectiveness of, 524–525

French, 295

hereditary dominion rights unalterable by, 58

kingship succession in, and universal law, 61

kings' infirmity safeguarded against in, 542

king's powers under various, 508–510

limits upon king's power, 289, 293–294, 296, 299

peace and war under various, 202–208

reforms in, 173, 461–462

variety among, 202, 204, 505

Consuls (Rome), 109, 114, 311, 528–529

Contract(s) between people and governors

civil society and, 104–105

kingship derived from, 327–328, 341–342, 345–346

law and, 295, 548

Contract(s) between people and governors
(*continued*)
oaths and, 225, 412–413, 416–417
obligatory nature of, 295, 309–316
observance of, by magistrate and people,
431–435
paternal rights and obligations and, 320
Corbis, 59, 115, 238, 418
Corbulo, 146, 180, 272, 372, 388
I *Corinthians*, 436*n*2
Coriolanus, 145, 178
Cornelii, 148
Corona gothica, castellana, y austriaca (Saavedra), 115*n*6, 422*n*4, 509*n*3
Corruption, 135, 138, 139, 186, 229, 252,
350, 434, 544, 550
civil disorders and, 527
commonwealths, seldom found in, 184–
191
in England, 524–527
equality as preventer of, 229
of governors in Indies under Charles V,
51–52
of Hebrew kings, 138–139
law and, 375, 395, 396, 466
liberty and, 252–253
limits upon monarchy and, 302–303
luxury and, 165, 254–258, 350
monarchy and, 123, 137, 161–162, 189,
194–195, 229–230, 251–258, 344–348
office holders and, 276–277
Parliament (England) and, 571
reform and, 150, 460
in Rome, 148, 172, 337, 342–343, 455
Schoolmen and, 8
war and, 214–215
Corvinus, 212
Cottington, Lord, 554
Council of Ten, 505
Councils
in Israel (Sanhedrin), 127–128
in mixed governments, 526
Counsellors, 404, 405, 558. *See also* Ministers
Courtiers, 140–141, 266, 559
Courts. *See also* Absolute monarchy; Kingship and monarchy
corruption natural to, 184–191, 251–258
limited monarchy and, 296
valour rendered ridiculous by, 277
Covenants, 119, 130–131, 341. *See also*
Constitution(s); Contract(s) between
people and governors
between Israelites and their kings, 119,
130–131

rights of king expressed by, 341
Crassus, 159, 174
Craven, William, earl of, 485
Crequi, marechal de, 277–278
Creusa, 535
Cromwell, Oliver, 370, 383
Cueva, La, 206
Cum magnatum & sapientum consilio, 556,
557
Curio, 187
Curius, 253
Cush, 26, 42, 43, 326, 456
Cushan-Rishathaim, 125
Cyrus, 66, 142, 145, 176, 211, 218, 496,
507, 560

Danaus, 512
Danby, earl of. *See* Osborne, Sir Thomas
Daniel, 137, 138, 141, 365*n*12, 560
Daniel, 382*n*8
Daniel, Roger, 120*n*16
Dardannus (k. of Scotland), 550
Darius, 138, 239, 496, 560
Dashwood, 66
David, 37, 45, 61, 102, 106, 110, 118,
119, 128, 185, 220, 228, 230, 290,
297, 305, 314, 325, 330, 331, 332,
333, 334, 335, 340, 346, 347, 356,
369, 370, 374, 379, 381, 396, 398,
414, 442, 446, 478, 521, 532, 539
David (k. of Scotland), 499
Davila, Enrico Caterino, 292
De antiquitate britannicae ecclesiae (Parker),
492*n*31
Decemviri, 171, 218
assembly rights under, 503, 529
power given to, 394
Decii, 148
De facto power, 516–518
*Defense of the People of England Against Sal-
masius* (Milton), 122*n*2
De Hoveden, Roger, 106*n*23, 107*n*25
De jure belli ac pacis libri tres (Grotius),
33*n*2, 115*n*2, 119*n*12, 222*n*7, 222*n*9,
223*n*10, 265*n*8, 296*n*26–27, 330*n*13,
335*n*7, 370*n*13, 373*n*8, 452*n*3, 496*n*5,
505*n*5, 529*n*3, 554*n*5
De jure regni apud Scotos (Buchanan), 9*n*4
De Laicis (Bellarmine), 10*n*5
Democracy, 87. *See also* Commonwealth(s);
Mixed government; Popular government
civil disorders under, 218
in civil society, 102
consent of governed in forming, 99

Democracy *(continued)*
  God as author of, 20, 129
  of Israelites, 127, 128
  laws made under, 439
  liberty, restraint of, under, 31, 192
  mixed government and, 166–170, 298–299
  origins of, 490–491
  Peloponnesian War and, 299
  precedents for, biblical and historical, 102–103
  pure, 189
  Xenophon on, 175–184
Denmark, 101, 167, 420, 466, 488, 504
De officiis (Cicero), 467n3
De origine et moribus Germanorum (Tacitus). *See Germania* (Tacitus)
De regno et regali potestate (Barclay), 11n6
De Serres, Jean, 240n29, 425n10, 450n8
De Thou, Jacques-Auguste, 207, 207n5, 222, 222n8, 245, 292, 406n4, 428n18, 567n3
Detur digniori, 51, 80
Deuteronomy, 23, 61, 109, 125, 287, 288–289, 290, 311–312, 329, 335, 349, 354, 444, 464
De Witt, Jan, 207
Dialogue Concerning the Rights of Her Most Christian Majesty, A (Bilain), 294n23
Dictatorship, 273, 311. *See also* Absolute monarchy; Tyrants and tyranny
Diocletian, 251
Diogenes, 267
Diogenes Laërtius, 253n3
Dion, 193, 228, 283
Dionysius, 19, 41, 73, 91, 169, 170, 187, 191, 193, 218, 263, 267, 283, 297, 306, 325, 370, 385, 407, 461
Discourses on Livy (Machiavelli), 135n2, 283n5, 462n9
Divine right of kings, 6–7, 10–11, 17, 34, 100, 161–162, 319, 333. *See also* Absolute monarchy
Division of power, 6, 33–36. *See also* Mixed government
Doeg the Edomite, 330
Doleman, R. (Robert Parsons), 9n4
Dominion. *See also* Conquest; Force
  hereditary right of, 44–45, 57–61, 79
  paternal right and, 39–44
  peace under, 160
Domitian, 14, 15, 139, 181, 225–226, 233, 263, 264, 271, 316, 372, 374, 387, 398, 405, 447, 550
Donaldson, James, 261n3

Don Pelayo (k. of the Asturias), 423
Don Sancho the Brave, 168
Dorians, 177, 491
Draco, 387, 391, 393, 394, 397
Drummond, William, 246n32
Dudley, Edmund, 448, 468, 555, 556
Duppa, Bishop Brian, 66
Durstus (k. of Scotland), 550

Eadred (k. of England), 376
Ebroïn, 242
Ecclesiastes, 38, 64, 84, 94, 364–365
Edgar (k. of England), 106, 487
Edward I (k. of England), 211, 397, 408, 410, 414, 415, 532, 568
Edward II (k. of England), 244, 247, 280, 297, 448, 524, 528, 532, 550
Edward III (k. of England), 59, 211, 237, 244–245, 247, 396, 400, 447n3, 448–449, 450, 500, 532
Edward IV (k. of England), 237, 239, 292, 500, 576
Edward V (k. of England), 120, 280
Edward VI (k. of England), 120, 248, 280
Edward the Confessor (k. of England), 107, 377, 483
Edwin (k. of England), 106
Egbert (k. of England), 106, 376
Egerton (lord chancellor of England), 414
Eglon, 73, 125, 563
Egyptians and Egypt, 17, 137, 141, 197
Ehud, 71, 125, 228, 329, 502
Elah, 45
Eleanor of Gascony, 500
Election
  consent of multitude in, 107
  in mixed government, 167
  to Parliament (England), 530, 531, 565
  of princes, 101
  proxies in, 105
Eleutherius (bishop of Rome), 120
Eliezer of Damascus, 24, 35
Eligere, 109, 110
Elijah, 340
Elizabeth I (q. of England), 185, 248, 430, 448, 546, 568, 577–578
Empson, Richard, 448, 468, 555, 556
England. *See also* Parliament (England)
  absolute monarchy supported in, 194–195, 194n4
  civil war in, 246–247, 517
  corruption in, 524–527
  election of kings in, 106–107
  laws in, 393, 451, 465–468
  leaders before start of kingship, 458

England *(continued)*
liberty in, 481
limits by law to monarchy in, 295–296,
299, 313
Magna Charta, 474–477
mixed government in, 167
nobility in, 489–490, 492, 526–527
origins of, 478–483
Rome and, 160, 472, 479
sovereignty in, 376–377, 565
succession in, 114, 236, 237–238, 430–
431
wealth of kings in, 349
wisdom of kings in, 280
witenagemote for electing early kings of,
486–487
English History (Polydorus Vergilius),
106*n*21
Epaminondas, 15, 204, 212, 221, 228, 253,
271, 525
Ephesians, 60*n*1
Ephraim, 93
Epicides, 193
Epictetus, 67
Epistles (Horace), 64*n*3
Epodes (Horace), 163*n*10
Equality. *See also* Natural equality
competency and, 80, 81, 94
corruption prevented by, 229
and God's gift of power to the people,
22
heritability of paternal rights and, 93
human nature and, 452–453
liberty and, 511
monarchy and, 184
in pre-civil state, 30
Errors of learned men, 18
Esau, 28, 29, 34, 35, 98
Esther, 138, 141
Esther, 560
Ethelred (k. of England), 377
Ethelstan (k. of England), 106, 376, 573
Ethelwerd (supposed k. of England), 106,
376
Ethelwolf (k. of England), 106, 376
Ethics (Aristotle), 449, 451
Euclid, 8, 466
Euclidas, 161
Eudes (k. of France), 426
Eumenes, 171, 231
Eutropius, 255
Eve, 535
Evenus III (k. of Scotland), 380, 550
Evil. *See* Good and evil
Excommunication, 411, 493, 549

Executions. *See* Capital punishment
Exodus, 36, 138, 392*n*2
Ezra, 560
Ezzelino of Padua, 308

Faber, Johannes, 19
Fabius (Marcus Fabius Maximus), 311, 394
Fabius (Quintus Fabius Maximus), 65,
135, 151–152, 182, 212, 256, 271,
273, 394, 445, 514, 539
Fabricius, 253
Faith, implicit, 12–16
Falerio, 525
Family, 22, 32, 62, 95. *See also* Children;
Paternal right, authority
Biblical transmissions of power, 24–29
granting of powers by succession in,
300–301
hereditary kingship and, 115
household authority and, 88–90
of Israelites, 129–130
law and, 321–322, 324–325
paternal power, 27–30
poverty and, 261
Farnese, Luigi (duke of Parma), 264
Ferdinand (k. of Naples), 198, 215
Ferdinand (k. of Portugal), 169
Ferdinand of Aragon, 429, 576
Five Mile Act (1665), 571*n*3
Flaccus (Quintus Fulvius Flaccus), 155
Flaminius (Quintus Flaminius), 143
Flatterers and flattery, 162, 230, 234, 251,
253, 266, 434, 547, 559
Flavius, 480
Florence, 161, 325
Florence of Worcester, 106*n*23
Flowers of History (Roger of Wendover),
106*n*17, 107*n*28, 265*n*6, 376*n*17,
377*n*19, 411*n*5, 484*n*11, 494*n*1
Foedus inequale, 119
Fontrailles, 245
Force. *See also* Conquest
government gained by, 32–33
kingship gained by, 306, 327
law and, 209–210, 381, 388–389
of law, and parliaments, 574–575
oaths gained by, 413–414
in rebellion, use of, 524
usurpation by, 320
Fortescue, Sir John, 393, 400
Fox, Sir Stephen, 66, 195
France, 17, 66, 95, 197, 216, 355, 403,
413, 522
absolute monarchy in, 58, 287, 299
assemblies in, 222, 566, 567, 573–576

France *(continued)*
  civil disorders in, 218, 219, 240–241
  corruption in, 257–258, 345
  division of, 172–173, 295, 424
  England and, 278
  kingship in, 40, 141, 348, 553
  law in, 295, 466, 553, 573
  limits upon monarchy in, 292–293, 294
  mixed government in, 167–169
  nobility in, 487–488
  Protestants in, 346, 439, 562
  public good in, 274–276
  reform of government in, 168
  sovereignty of, 504, 505
  succession of kings in, 60, 61, 114, 116,
    117, 236, 237, 240–241, 418, 422,
    424–427, 429, 505
  Switzerland and, 206–207
  valour in, 277–278
  war in, 197–198
  wealth in, 350–351, 540
  wise kings of, 280, 281
Francis I (k. of France), 141
Francis I (k. of Spain), 293
Francis II (k. of France), 141, 280
Francogallia (Hotman), 293*n*20, 295*n*24
Franks, 102, 204
Fratricide, 94–95, 225
Fredegarius, 240*n*28
Fredegonde, 240, 241
Frederick IV (k. of Denmark), 534
Freedom. *See* Liberty
Froissart, Jean, 488

Gad, 127
Galba, 50, 65, 139, 148, 155, 160, 175,
    232, 235, 271, 370
Gale, Thomas, 412*n*7
Galgacus, 458, 479, 481
Gallic War (Caesar), 458*n*4
Gauls, 17, 148, 204, 214, 479
Gaveston, Piers, 524, 550, 556
General Chronological History of France, A
    (Mézeray and de Serres), 240*n*29,
    292*n*17
General History of France (De Serres),
    240*n*29, 425*n*11, 450*n*8
General History of Spain (Mariana), 302*n*33,
    422*n*5, 509*n*3, 551*n*1
Genesis, 24–25, 26, 123*n*3, 137, 353*n*3,
    356*n*6, 463*n*11, 523*n*5
Genoa, 161, 166, 206, 224
Gentius, 164, 200
Geographical History of Africa, A (Leo),
    105*n*16

Germania (Tacitus), 103*n*11, 291*n*14,
    480*n*5–8, 484*n*10, 490*n*25, 491*n*26
Germanicus, 146, 180, 239, 272, 372, 383,
    388, 414, 480
Germans and Germany, 17, 102–103, 167,
    169, 214, 291, 376, 421, 462, 463,
    480, 490, 504, 508–509, 515
Ghibellines, 161, 206
Gibeonites, 138
Gideon, 37, 61, 71, 91, 125, 126, 127,
    228, 314, 329, 356, 398, 414, 502,
    538, 563
Gillon, 240
Giustiniano, 222
God. *See also* Divine right of kings; God,
    law(s) of; God, liberty as gift of
  in Aristotle's view of favorable monarch,
    132–134
  as author of democracy, 129
  as author of nature, 123, 273, 291, 459
  good and evil, distinguishing of, and,
    38, 371
  and government framed by man, 20–23,
    53–57, 100
  government instituted by (monarchical
    vs. aristocratic), 124–131
  hereditary succession as contrary to, 57–
    61, 421, 427
  kingship and, 36, 44, 81, 100, 109, 110,
    118–119, 121–126, 188–189, 230, 283,
    331, 333, 335, 336–339, 341, 347,
    367–368, 538–539
  kingship restrained by, 289, 313
  knowledge of, in civil society, 82
  leaders chosen by, for common good,
    470
  magistratical power and, 69–74, 268
  natural man's enmity to, 123
  nature of, 329
  obedience to, 372–373, 385, 436, 437–
    438
  paternal rights and, 28–29, 36–39, 93
  Plato on communion with, 86
  power of, as supreme, 323, 371, 442–
    443
  providence of, 163
  rebellion among Israelites and, 522–523
  rulers endowed by, 39, 81
  tribute of the Jews to Caesar and, 359–
    360
  tyrants not ordained by, 353–359
  virtue rewarded by, 134, 135, 145
  virtuous rule and, 44–45
  wisdom and, 131

God, law(s) of, 9, 28, 37, 50, 52, 54, 60, 61, 82, 109, 112, 121, 123, 178, 192, 219, 220, 226, 228, 230, 231, 236, 253, 266, 267, 290, 291, 293, 308, 312, 313, 320, 323, 328, 335–338, 365, 366, 392, 395, 404, 436–439, 445, 455, 458, 463, 475
God, liberty as gift of, 8, 20, 25, 30, 49, 57, 100, 121, 130, 189, 303, 335, 337, 445, 479, 510–513, 566
Good and evil. *See also* Virtue
  distinguishing of, 38, 371
  in kings, 64
Gothic polity, 363, 477
Goths, 59, 101, 102, 115, 147, 204, 210, 214, 215, 224, 277, 348, 418, 422, 477, 487, 490, 505, 551
  Rome and, 214
  Spain and, 204, 422
Government. *See also* Absolute monarchy; Commonwealth(s); Kingship; Limits upon monarchy; Mixed government
  in ancient Greece, 177
  Aristotle on, 81, 132–134, 453–454
  best form of, 31, 166–170
  choice of form of, 20–23
  consent of men and, 30–33, 49, 97–108
  ends of, 268, 357, 395, 405–407, 432, 434, 444, 454, 460, 465, 468, 470, 512, 529, 550, 556
  establishing of, 78–79, 490–491
  fitness to perform duties of, 49, 51
  God and, 20–23, 53–57, 100, 124–131
  good and evil in, 38
  hereditary title to, 58
  of Israelites, 124–131
  lawmaking, power of, and, 111
  nature, voice of, in constituting, 192
  paternal power in analogy for, 41, 42
  peace under popular or mixed, 196
  Plato on, 82
  power of, as proceeding from God, 371
  reform in well-founded, 170–175
  society, entering into, and, 30–31
  for benefit of supreme lord, 52–53
  variety of, 112
  war, provisions for, and, 209–216
Governors. *See* Magistrates
Gracchi, 151, 153, 181, 200
Granada, 302
Greece, 17, 47, 108, 141–142, 145, 164, 178, 204, 259, 273, 297, 354, 441
  Xenophon on, 176–178
Greed, 66–67, 150, 176, 228–229
Griffon, 242

Grimbauld, 242
Grimoald, 242
Grisons, 17, 371, 441
Grotius, Hugo, 33, 77*n*1, 115, 119, 222, 223, 265, 296, 330, 335*n*7, 370, 373, 452*n*3, 496, 505, 529, 554
Guelphs, 161, 206
Guicciardini, Francesco, 198, 215, 261*n*4, 331, 521
Guide of the Perplexed, The (Maimonides), 124*n*4, 290*n*12
Guise, Cardinal de, 245
Gustavus I (k. of Sweden), 101
Gustavus II Adolphus (k. of Sweden), 418, 533
Gustavus Ericson, 504

Habeas corpus, 555
Hales, 466, 470
Ham, 26, 30, 41, 42, 43, 90, 323, 326, 335, 421, 456
Haman, 138, 141
Hamilcar Barca, 161, 212, 271
Hammer against the Lutheran Heresy (Faber), 19*n*6
Hampden, John, 485
Hannibal, 65, 135, 154, 161, 164, 168, 179, 200, 212, 214, 260, 262, 271, 311, 525
Hanseatick Society, 207
Hardicanute (k. of England), 377
Harmodius, 15, 228
Harold (k. of England), 377
Harvey, 470
Hasdrubal, 161, 212
Hayward, John, 11
Hazael, 543
Hebert (earl of Vermandois), 243
Hebrews. *See* Israelites
Heliogabalus, 14, 140, 233, 271, 533, 550
Helvidius Priscus, 73, 147, 181, 372, 388
Hengist, 481, 494, 495
Henry I (k. of England), 59, 114, 237, 415, 419, 478, 497–501, 502
Henry I (k. of France), 116, 118, 504
Henry II (k. of England), 61, 114, 237, 239*n*27, 246, 280, 419, 493, 499, 500
Henry II (k. of France), 141
Henry III (k. of England), 247, 366, 411, 493
Henry III (k. of France), 141, 245, 294, 567
Henry IV (k. of England), 237, 239, 247, 430*n*21, 500

Henry IV (k. of France), 116, 117, 120, 141, 211, 294, 428, 488, 574
Henry V (k. of England), 211, 245, 247, 293, 475, 532, 575, 576, 578
Henry VI (k. of England), 120, 280, 419, 532, 576
Henry VII (k. of England), 61, 237, 239*n*27, 247*n*34, 282, 419, 448, 500, 516, 576
Henry VIII (k. of England), 248, 399–400, 430, 473, 500, 568, 576
Henry of Huntingdon, 106*n*20
Henry of Navarre. *See* Henry IV (k. of France)
Henry of Saxony, 243–244
Heraclidae, 47, 114, 298
Herbert, Edward, 473*n*18
Hercules, 47, 114, 457, 535
Hercules Oetaeus (Seneca), 535*n*1
Hereditary right, power
    Aristotle's doubts about, 79
    coronation, necessity of, and, 417–431
    as derived from God, 34
    disputes in, 236
    of dominion, 44–45, 57–61, 69
    escheat and, 53
    impossibility of proof in, 39–44, 54–55, 59
    kingship and, 36, 45–47, 54, 108–113, 304, 331
    limits to (Salic Law), 293
    mixed government and, 167
    nobility and, 486, 488
    origins of heredity as basis for, 114
    paternity, analogy of, refuted, 33–34, 56–57, 92–97
    regicide as means to, 45–46
    in Rome, 308
    succession and, 235–238
    valour not transmitted with, 211
Hermingrade, 243
Herminius, 145
Hermolaus, 231
Herod, 73, 127, 239, 322, 560
Herodotus, 63*n*2, 238*n*26
Heylyn, Peter, 11, 12, 24, 46, 55, 66, 67, 123, 134, 284, 328, 437
Hezekiah, 120, 185, 347
Hiero, 176*n*2
Hieronymus, 193
Hippocrates, 193
Hirtius, 455
Historiae Anglicanae scriptores quinque (Gale), 412*n*7

Historiae Francorum (Fredegarius), 240*n*28
Historia General de España (Mariana), 116*n*7
Histories (Herodotus), 63*n*2, 238*n*26
Histories (Tacitus), 73*n*10, 146*n*2, 147*n*4, 160*n*5, 162*n*7–8, 165*n*13, 197*n*3, 232*n*20, 267*n*11, 271*n*2, 372*n*4, 545*n*3
History of Charles the Vth, Emperor and King of Spain (Sandoval), 567*n*2
History of England (Vergil), 376
History of Florence (Guicciardini), 261*n*4
History of Florence (Machiavelli), 261*n*5
History of His Time (De Thou), 207*n*5, 222*n*8, 223*n*11, 292*n*19, 428*n*18, 567*n*3
History of Italy (Guicciardini), 198*n*4, 215*n*3, 261*n*4, 275*n*6
History of Rome (Livy), 6*n*2, 17*n*2, 48*n*3, 65*n*6, 65*n*8, 95*n*4, 101*n*5, 115*n*5, 152*n*4–6, 154*n*4–5, 157*n*2, 179*n*8, 182*n*12–14, 183*n*16, 193*n*3, 203*n*1, 215*n*4–5, 218*n*1, 229*n*17, 238*n*26, 249*n*35, 273*n*5, 311*n*3, 391*n*7, 394*n*8, 397*n*12, 457*n*3, 463*n*10, 472*n*16, 504*n*3, 514*n*3, 520*n*1, 547*n*6
History of Scotland, The (Buchanan), 246*n*32, 292*n*16, 546*n*4
History of Scotland from the Year 1423 until the Year 1542, The (Drummond), 246*n*32
History of the Civil Wars of France, The (Davila), 292*n*18
History of the World (Raleigh), 43*n*2, 334*n*1–2, 344*n*1
Hobbes, Thomas, 11, 49, 55–56, 221, 409, 432
Hocquincourt, 245
Holland. *See* Netherlands
Homicide, 94–95, 139, 144–145, 174, 239, 320, 337, 339–340, 407, 510
Honorius, Flavius, 214, 233, 420
Hooker, Richard, 18, 110–111, 112, 118, 572, 573
Hophni, 398
Horace, 54, 64*n*3, 163*n*10
Horatii, 148
Horatius, 145, 152, 182, 218, 228, 314, 394, 396, 529
Horsa, 481, 494, 495
Hosea, 126, 337*n*1
Hostilius, Tullus, 154
Hotman, François, 292–293, 295
Household government, 88–90
Hoveden, Roger de. *See* De Hoveden, Roger
Huguenots, Wars of the, 172

Human nature, 49, 54, 58, 60, 67, 78, 80, 83, 85, 110, 136, 158, 164, 187–189, 191–193, 234, 235, 253, 266, 338, 350, 357, 390, 396, 400, 401, 431, 432, 452, 453, 461, 523, 535–541, 543–545, 559, 560, 574
Hundred Years War, 293
Hungary, 101, 167, 534n8
Hushai, 333
Hyde, Laurence, earl of Rochester, 194–195, 258, 485, 571

Icetus, 181
Ignotus, 430
Illegitimacy, and succession, 117, 168–169, 237, 327, 418, 429–430, 499, 500, 504
Indians, American, 358
Ine (k. of England), 483, 487, 492
Inequality, 81, 84–85. *See also* Equality
Ingulf, Abbot, 107n24, 489
Injustice. *See* Justice
Inquisition, 380, 461, 562
Institutes (Calvin), 10n5
Ionians, 177
Ireland, 116, 143, 265, 562
Irish Rebellion of 1641, 540n10
Ironside (k. of England), 238
Isaac, 24–25, 28, 29, 34, 57, 69, 93, 98, 101, 104, 304, 338
Isabel (q. of Spain), 429
Isabel of Portugal, 117
Ishbosheth, 102, 118, 314, 331, 332–333
Ishmael, 28, 35, 98, 104
Isle of Pines, The (Neville), 96n6
Israelites and Israel
    arbitrary legislative power of, 569
    aristocratical government of, 124–131, 299
    assembly rights of, 502–503
    Benjaminites and, 538
    child kings of, 119–120
    corruption of, 138–139
    covenants of, 312, 521
    election of kings by, 102, 106
    government of, fitted for war, 205
    justice and, 374
    kingship and, 60–61, 109, 118, 125, 128–129, 138, 230–231, 297, 305, 328–333
    law and, 324, 387, 457–458, 463–464
    liberty and, 336–339
    limits upon monarchy, 287–289, 290, 297, 334–336
    mixed government of, 166

    obedience of, to wicked kings, 439
    patriarchical power among, 36–39, 45
    proclamations and, 560
    rebellions of, 522–523
    succession of kingship, excluding females, 60, 61
    tribute to Caesar by, 359, 361, 369
    tyranny and, 353–359
Istoria Veneziana (Guicciardini), 275n6
Italy, 95, 466. *See also entries under names of cities*

Jabesh-Gilead, 130
Jabin, 563
Jacob, 25, 28, 29, 34, 35, 36, 45, 57, 69, 93, 94, 101, 304, 326, 338
James I (k. of England), 65n5, 263, 265–266, 296, 339n1, 395, 397, 398n1, 401n8, 573
James II (k. of England), 265n7, 562n5
James III (k. of Scotland), 282, 292, 314, 576
Janizaries, 155
Japheth, 26, 30, 42, 43, 90, 326, 419, 512
Jason, 176, 535n1
Jefferson, Thomas, 511n2
Jehoiada, 119, 228, 231
Jehoram, 407
Jehu, 45, 61, 71, 228, 336, 340, 347, 369, 407, 503
Jenkins, Sir Leoline, 195, 258
Jephthah, 125, 228, 312, 314, 329, 502, 536
Jeremiah, 289n9, 335n4, 571n1
Jeroboam, 37, 45, 61, 71, 102, 106, 110, 185, 230, 297, 334, 335, 340, 342, 347, 368–369, 439, 478, 503, 539
Jerusalem, 137
Jesuits and Jesuitism, 9n4, 19, 88, 206, 207, 410, 432, 534, 562, 574
Jesus Christ. *See* Christ; Christians and Christianity
Jethro, 392, 457
Jewish Antiquities (Josephus), 124n2, 128n19, 228n15, 284n6, 289n8, 299n31, 335n6
Jews. *See* Israel
Jezebel, 220, 356, 369
Joab, 333, 335, 374
Joash (k. of Israel), 119, 120, 231, 375
Joel, 398
John (k. of England), 265, 293, 410, 411, 426, 540
John II (k. of Portugal), 292

John III (k. of Castile), 117, 169
John III Sobieski (k. of Poland), 420, 488*n*22
John of Gaunt, 419, 430*n*22
Jonathan (son of Saul), 138
Joseph, 93, 138, 141
Josephus, 124, 128, 284*n*6, 289, 299*n*31, 312, 335
Joshua, 37, 39, 71, 86, 125, 127, 135, 300, 324, 329, 332, 335, 356, 370, 398, 407, 413, 442, 446, 464, 470, 563
Joshua, 413*n*10
Josiah, 119, 120, 347
Jotham, 91–92
Judah, 25, 127, 305
Judaism. *See* Israelites and Israel
Judges, 92, 229*n*16, 356*n*6, 414*n*13, 502*n*2, 536*n*4
Judges. *See also* Magistrates and magistracy
  assembly rights and, 503
  biblical, 37, 125, 126
  contracts and, 310, 312–313
  kings as, 395
  power from law, not king who appoints, 393, 465–474
  rigour of law tempered by, 447–451
  Sanhedrin, 335
  selection of, 447
Judgments
  in England, 467–468
  by king, 392, 552–557
  by parliaments (England), 400
  by the people, 397, 440, 547–552
Jugurtha, 164
Julius II (pope of Rome), 275
Junii, 148
Jupiter, 543
Juries, 467–468
Justice. *See also* Law
  absolute power and, 58, 452–453
  civil society and, 82, 547–548
  corruption in governments and, 257–258
  equal justice and, 178–184
  James I (k. of England) and, 266
  judges and, 470
  killing, acquittal for, and, 339–340
  law and, 380–383
  liberty and, 30–31, 460
  peace and, 21, 160–161
  power in word of a king accompanied by, 365
  rebellion and, 522–523, 524
  seditions, tumults, and war and, 219–220, 226–227
  sword of, 374

unjust commands not to be obeyed, 436–439
  virtue and, 178–179
Juvenal, 47*n*2, 91, 147*n*5, 165*n*12, 254, 264*n*4, 352*n*5, 431*n*2

Kéroualle, Louise Renée de, duchess of Portsmouth, 195
Keturah, 28, 35, 104
I *Kings*, 138, 139*n*12, 333*n*17, 336*n*8, 340*n*2, 346*n*3, 347*n*5
II *Kings*, 102, 220, 333*n*18, 335*n*5, 347*n*5, 369*n*10, 375*n*11, 382*n*7, 543*n*2
Kingship and monarchy. *See also* Absolute monarchy; Limits upon monarchy; Mixed government
  Abraham and, 24–25
  Aristotle on, 81, 85, 86, 132–134, 453–454
  childhood succession, 119–120, 280. *See also* Succession
  civil disorders and, 217–250
  civil war and, 248
  conquest establishing, 325
  consent of governed in forming, 99, 108–112, 287–288, 298
  constitutional variability and, 508–510
  contract between people and governor and, 309, 345–346
  coronation required for, 417–431
  corruption and, 184–191, 251–258
  de facto powers and, 516–518
  in France, example of arbitrary government, 216
  God and, 102, 124, 188–189, 336–339, 538–539
  government, ends of, and, 91
  head of body, figurative for, 535–541
  heritability of, 39–44, 46–47, 54, 113. *See also* Succession
  illegitimacy and, 168–169
  implicit faith and, 13–14
  among Israelites, 36–37, 125, 128–129, 138, 230–231, 336–339
  judges, selection of, and, 465–474
  law and, 110–111, 319–333, 345, 387, 447–451, 467–468, 474, 526
  law, limits to, 287–303, 542–547
  laws not made by kings, 392–398
  law supreme to, 439–446, 556
  leadership and, 185
  liberty and, 17–19, 303–309, 502, 514–516
  mixed government and, 166–170
  national rights and, 16

Kingship and monarchy *(continued)*
natural propensity to, denied, 121–123
Nimrod, 26–28
oaths and, 408–417
obedience to, 436–439, 485
origins of, 482–487
pardons and, 556
Parliaments (England) and, 528–534
paternal rights and, 39–46, 62–69, 95–96
Paul, Saint and, 370–380
people and, 10–11, 19, 117, 119, 322, 339–343
Plato on, 85–86
power and, 113, 188, 223, 287, 296, 456–465, 469
proclamations and, 558–563
public good, 51–52, 464–465, 538–541
punishment and, 321, 339, 342, 468–469
right to depose and, 10–11, 314–315, 339–348, 407–408, 457
in Rome, 151–153, 157–166, 172, 180, 184
royal maintenance and, 348–352
succession of. *See* Succession
treason and, 556–557
usurpation and, 100, 498–499. *See also* Usurpation
virtue and, 47–53, 126, 135, 137, 398–401
war and, 213
wisdom and, 63–64, 532–533
Xenophon on, 175–184
Kish, 326

Laban, 25, 28
Laco, 149, 181, 372
Lambarde, William, 120
Landry, 241
Larcius, 145
Las Casas, Bartolomé de, 51–52, 160n6
Laud, William, 11
Laudibus legum Angliae, De (Fortescue), 393n5
Law
assemblies and, 477, 563–569
axioms in, 466
civil society and, 83
contract(s) and, 548. *See also* Contract(s) between people and governors
cum magnatum & sapientum consilio, 556, 557
de facto power of king, 516–518
defects in, 474–475
dictatorship under, 273

of England, regarding judgments, 467–468
fathers' rights under, 321–322, 324–325
force for defence and, 209–210, 388–389
of France, 294–295, 553, 573
of God. *See* God, law(s) of
habeas corpus, 555
hereditary kingship, among various forms of government according to particular, 167, 236
of Israelites, 334–336, 457–458
judges and, 447–451, 464–465
justice and, 178, 380–383
kingship and, 110–111, 140, 322–323, 345, 367–368, 387, 392–398, 474, 526
king subject to, 334–336, 339–343, 398, 556
leagues and, 553–554
legislative power, arbitrariness of, and, 569–572
liberty restrained by, 193–194, 336–339
limits upon monarchy and, 287–303, 313, 542–547
magistratical power and, 113–121, 310, 387–391, 439–446
noli prosequi: cesset processus, 555
oaths and, 408–409, 415
obedience to, 436–439
Plato on, 82
power and, 222–223, 225, 443–444
proclamations contrasted to, 558–563
reforms of, 461–462
of Rome, 149–156, 171, 379–380
seditions, tumults, wars and, 219–220
treason and, 182
tyrants and, 221, 284, 403
usurpation and, 221, 284, 455
of war, 370
writs and intention of, 552–557
Law(s) of God. *See* God, law(s) of
Law(s) of God and nature. *See* Nature, law(s) of God and
Law(s) of nature. *See* Nature, law(s) of
Law of War and Peace, The (Grotius), 33n2
Laws (Plato), 82n7, 83n8, 288n4
League of the Public Weal, 172
Leagues (alliances)
consent of people and, 553–554
foedus inequale and, 119
Swiss cantons, as superior example of, 206–207
Legislation. *See* Assembly and assemblies; Law; Parliament (England)
Legitimacy. *See* Illegitimacy
Lentulus, 182, 191, 472

Leo Africanus, 105
Leonidas, 290, 510, 542
Leopold I (Holy Roman Emperor), 421, 534*n*8
Lepidus, 174
Leslie, Alexander (earl of Leven), 278
Letter to Scapula (Tertullian), 363
Levi and Levites, 25, 37
Leviathan (Hobbes), 55–56, 432*n*3
Lewis (k. of Bavaria), 243
Lewis I (le Debonair; the Gentle; k. of France), 243, 426, 504
Lewis II (the Stutterer; le Begue; k. of France), 243, 426
Lewis IV (Outremer; k. of France), 244
Lewis XI (k. of France), 245, 282, 291, 292, 293, 505, 575
Lewis XII (k. of France), 198, 275, 450, 576
Lewis XIII (k. of France), 120, 141, 172, 211, 245, 275, 355, 425, 553
Lewis XIV (k. of France), 120, 447*n*2
Liberty. *See also* God, liberty as gift of; Natural liberty; Nature, liberty as gift of
  absolute monarchy and, 191
  absolute power of one man and, 440–441
  Anglo-Saxons and, 481
  civil society and, 78, 548
  corruption and, 252–253
  equality and, 80
  of Germans, fighting Roman empire, 480
  of Israelites, 336–339
  magistracy and, 514–516
  Magna Charta and, 474
  "with a mischief" (Filmer), 563, 564, 567
  monarchy and, 17–19, 132, 191, 440
  Parliament (England) and, 574
  property an appendage to, 402–403
  public and personal, 18
  reason and, 191–195
  rebellion and, 519, 520
  Rome and, 144–149, 262–263, 455, 471–472
  sedition and, 104
  society, entrance into, diminishes, 30–31
  universal, 34
  virtue and, 134–144, 161, 177, 181, 273
Life, The, Against Apion (Josephus), 128*n*18
Life and Miracles of Dunstan (Capgrave), 377*n*20
Life and Reign of King Henry the Eighth (Herbert), 473*n*18
Life of Agesilaus (Plutarch), 351*n*4

Life of Agis, 542*n*1
Life of Agricola (Tacitus), 160*n*5, 264*n*3, 325*n*8, 372*n*6, 458*n*5, 479*n*3
Life of Alexander (Plutarch), 139*n*13, 231*n*18
Life of Aristides (Plutarch), 542*n*1
Life of Artaxerxes (Plutarch), 142*n*16
Life of Caligula (Suetonius), 63*n*2, 158*n*3
Life of Camillus (Plutarch), 311*n*4
Life of Cimon (Plutarch), 307*n*1
Life of Frederick, Abbot of St. Albans (Paris), 415*n*15
Life of King Alfred (Asser), 376*n*17, 487*n*19
Life of Lucullus (Plutarch), 143*n*18
Life of Lycurgus (Plutarch), 291*n*15, 375*n*12, 391*n*6
Life of Nero (Suetonius), 63*n*2, 382*n*6
Life of Pyrrhus (Plutarch), 232*n*21, 265*n*5
Life of Quintus Flaminius (Plutarch), 143*n*17
Life of Solon (Plutarch), 391*n*5
Life of Tamerlane (De Thou), 406*n*4
Life of Themistocles (Plutarch), 178*n*7, 252*n*2, 441*n*2, 542*n*1
Life of Timoleon (Plutarch), 297*n*28
Limits upon monarchy. *See also* Absolute monarchy; Commonwealth(s); Kingship; Mixed government
  democracy contrasted to, 298–299
  in England, 313
  in Germany, 515
  in Israel, 334–336
  preferable to absolute monarchy, 287–303
  in Rome, 542–543
Lives of Eminent Philosophers (Diogenes Laertius), 253*n*3
Lives of the Caesars (Suetonius), 63*n*2
Lives of the Two Offas (Paris), 376*n*15, 414
Livy, 6*n*2, 17*n*2, 48, 65*n*8, 95*n*4, 101*n*5, 115*n*5, 151–152, 154, 157*n*2, 179*n*8, 182, 183, 191, 193*n*3, 203*n*1, 215, 218, 229, 238*n*26, 249*n*35, 273, 283*n*5, 311*n*3, 311*n*5, 391*n*7, 394*n*8, 397*n*12, 418, 457*n*3, 462, 463*n*10, 472*n*16, 504*n*3, 514, 520*n*1, 547*n*6
Locusta, 50
Lot, 24, 28, 34, 35, 98, 99, 104, 353, 356
Lothair (k. of France), 118, 243, 244, 426
Louis. *See entries under* Lewis
Loyalty. *See* Oaths; Obedience
Lucan, 28*n*4, 60*n*3, 72*n*9, 154*n*1, 165, 186, 187, 210*n*1, 235, 343*n*5, 418*n*1, 536*n*5
Lucius, 458
Lucretia, 396
Lucullus, 143
Luke, 9*n*2

Luke, Saint, 436
Luxury, 165, 176, 184, 254–258. *See also*
    Wealth
Lycurgus, 217, 219, 375, 391, 462, 559
Lysander, 178, 204

Maccabees, 228
MacClelan, William, 398n14
Macedonia, 171–172, 211, 240
Machanidas, 73, 291, 385
Machiavelli, Niccolo, 96n6, 135, 261, 283,
    404–405, 462n9, 521, 545
Macro, 148, 160, 181, 194, 372, 388
Madness of Hercules, The (Seneca), 382n5
Maelius, Spurius, 180, 182, 218, 229, 286
Magistrates and magistracy. *See also* Judges
    changes in, 149–153
    consent of governed and, 108–112, 221
    contract between governed and, 309–
        316, 431–435
    election of, 77–87, 101, 102
    fitness of, 49, 51, 80
    of Israelites, 127
    law and, 113–121, 219–220, 387–391,
        439–446
    liberty not diminished by power of,
        514–516
    limits upon, 223–224, 307
    ministers, 14–15
    as ministers of God, 70–72, 170, 268,
        370–386, 446
    mixed government and, 167
    parliaments (England) and, 528–534
    the people and, 69–74, 190, 547–552
    power of institution, under various
        names, 383–386
    punishment of, 544, 546
    rebellion and, 521–522
Magna Charta (Great Charter)
    freedom of will and, 17–18
    judicial proceedings, influence of king
        upon, and, 394
    laws, king unable to make changes in,
        under, 400
    legislative power and, 569
    liberty and, 360, 474–475
    oath sworn upon by king, 410–411
    usurpation, as source of, 501
    violation of people's rights by king, pun-
        ishment for, and, 493
Mahomet (Mohammed), 105
Mahomet II, 241
Mahometan (Mohammedans), 562
Maimonides, Moses, 124–125, 290, 334,
    335, 374

Malleus in Haeresin Lutheranam (Faber),
    19n6
Mamelukes, 155, 197, 492
Mamercus, 178, 179, 212, 273
Manasseh, 93, 119, 127, 347
Manlii, 148
Manlius Capitolinus, Marcus, 135, 148,
    151, 178, 180, 182, 212, 218, 229, 286
Manlius (Gnaeus Manlius), 170, 184
Manlius (Titus Manlius), 182
Mansi, Giovanni D., 428n17
Manwaring, Roger, 11
Marcellus, 200
Marcius (Martius), Ancus, 48, 70, 299,
    305, 457
Marguerite of Valois, 117
Mariana, Juan de, 302n33, 422n5, 423n7–
    424n9, 509n3, 551n1
Marius, 50, 155, 170, 171, 181, 184, 263,
    301, 306
Mark, 231n19
Maroboduus, 480
Mars, 48, 351
Martel, Charles, 116, 242, 281
Martius. *See* Marcius, Ancus
Mary (q. of England), 246, 430, 562, 576
Mary (q. of Scotland), 314, 546, 562
Matthew, 123n3, 436n2, 500n3, 560n4
Maud (Holy Roman empress), 419
Mauritius, 314
Maxentius, 233
Maximilian, 275
Mazarin, Cardinal Jules, 66, 245, 257–258,
    294–295, 567
McIlwain, Charles H., 339n1
Medea, 535
Medea (Seneca), 535n1
Media and Medes, 17, 137
Medici, Catherine de, 141, 180
Medici family, 143, 261, 325, 521
Melville, Sir James, of Hal-Hill, 246n32
Memoires (Comines), 207n4, 247n33
Memoires de Louis, Roi de France, 574n7
Memoires du Mareschal de Bassompierre, 275n7
Memoires of Sir James Melville of Hal-Hill,
    246n32
Mémoires sur la régence d'Anne d'Autriche
    (Rochefoucauld), 425n12
Memorials of Saint Dunstan (Stubbs), 377n20
Mercenaries, 198, 200, 210, 229, 455
Meroveus and Merovingian kings, 60, 114,
    116, 118, 168, 172, 199n5, 219, 240,
    281, 293, 294, 295, 498, 528
Mesopotamia, 28
Messalina, 73, 149

Metellus, Lucius Caecilius, 152, 200,
    394*n*10
Mezentius, 167
Mézeray, François Eudes de, 240*n*29, 292
Micklegemotes, 482, 483, 489, 497, 530
Midianites, 125, 135
Miltiades, 307
Milton, John, 122*n*2
Ministers, 14–15. *See also* Counsellors;
    Magistrates and magistracy
Mithridates, 143, 164, 282
Mixed government
    absolute monarchy compared to, 194
    advantages of, 166–170
    consent of governed in forming, 99
    corruption not profitable in, 185
    democracy contrasted with, 298–299
    nobility in, 526
    peace and war and, 195–202
    power in, 444–445
    virtue and, 186
Moab, 34, 98
Mohammed. *See* Mahomet
Montanism, 363
Montmorency, 245
Moors, 105, 116, 215, 265, 302, 477, 551
Moralia (Plutarch), 267*n*12
Mordecai, 141
More, Sir Thomas, 473–474, 568
Morocco, 467
Morodach, 137
Mortimer, 419
Morton, earl of, 546
Moses, 36, 37, 38–39, 66, 71, 86, 87, 131,
    135, 174, 228, 288–289, 300, 301,
    314, 324, 329, 332, 335, 337, 338,
    356, 370, 373, 374, 390, 394, 398,
    407, 442, 446, 457, 464, 470, 538,
    559, 561, 563
    kingship and, 91, 125
    laws of, 392, 395, 466
    mixed government and, 288–289
    Sanhedrin instituted by, 127
    sedition, tumult, and war and, 228
    war and, 205
Murder. *See* Homicide
Mysteries of state, 12, 13

Nabal, 330, 331
Nabis, 41, 169, 283, 291, 306, 385
Naboth, 336, 340, 346, 351, 369, 439
Nadab, 45
Naenius, 311
Naples, 108, 156
Narcissus, 149, 181, 372

Naturâ regem, 81
Natural equality, 30, 32, 35, 78, 86, 99,
    304, 385, 452, 453, 511, 548
Natural liberty, 8, 18, 19, 31, 34, 35, 61,
    78, 97–99, 103, 104, 131, 304, 328,
    360, 365, 457, 495, 502, 510–514,
    548, 552
Natural right(s), 53, 64, 112, 319, 339,
    340, 359, 379, 420, 445, 457, 547, 549
Natural slavery, 9, 44, 84, 94, 116, 133,
    136–140, 343
Nature
    civil society and, 83–84
    competency and, 51, 80
    contract between people and governed
        and, 105
    human. *See* Human nature
    kingship and, 38, 44, 85, 110, 121–123,
        321
    light of, 38, 291, 444, 510
    paternal authority and, 63, 68–69
    slavery. *See* Natural slavery
    tyranny and, 402–408
    voice of, 80, 96, 192
Nature, human. *See* Human nature
Nature, law(s) of, 51, 57, 60, 61, 68, 84,
    94, 103–105, 110, 111, 192, 273, 319–
    322
    assemblies, power of, and, 103–104
    hereditary rights and, 57–61, 93–94, 96–
    97, 117
Nature, law(s) of God and, 28, 30, 33, 36,
    43, 44, 57–59, 61, 93, 95, 97, 102,
    105, 112, 119, 131, 162–164, 166,
    177, 196, 235, 310, 348, 408, 417,
    418, 483, 505, 567, 578
Nature, liberty as gift of, 8–12, 49, 57,
    130, 303–309, 445, 510–513, 566
Nebuchadnezzar, 63, 73, 137, 211, 315,
    365, 382, 444, 461, 496, 510, 560
Nehemiah, 560
Nenius, 394
Neri, 161
Nero (e. of Rome), 10, 11, 14, 15, 19, 21,
    41, 50, 63, 65, 73, 139, 148, 155, 160,
    181, 182, 185, 226, 232, 235, 239,
    256, 264, 267, 271, 301, 307, 316,
    337, 365, 372, 374, 379, 381, 382,
    384, 387, 388, 396, 398, 405, 447,
    461, 539, 545, 550
Nerva, 140
Netherlands, 17, 105, 143–144, 207,
    277*n*8, 294, 371, 522, 553–554, 562,
    564
Neville, Henry, 96*n*6

Nicomachean Ethics (Aristotle), 132*n*1
Nimrod, 25–29, 32, 33, 34, 41, 42, 43, 54,
   55, 57, 62, 92, 112, 118, 137, 304,
   323, 326, 327, 444, 456, 457
Ninus, 41, 42, 92, 137
Noah, 26, 27, 29–30, 33, 34, 40, 41, 42,
   43, 44, 53, 55, 69, 89, 93, 98, 101,
   304, 305, 323, 326, 369, 456, 463
Nobility
   defined, 483–484
   in Denmark, 488
   in England, 299, 489–490, 526–527
   in France, 487–488
   in Germany, 490
   kings and, 287
   limits upon monarchy and, 299, 526
   modern courtiers compared to ancestors,
      486
   origins of, 491–492, 497
   in Rome, 491
   valour and, 487
Nogaret, Bernard de, 553*n*4
Noli prosequi: cesset processus, 555
Normans, 366, 478, 483, 513, 571
Numa, 48, 70, 159, 203, 297, 299, 305,
   307, 397, 457, 463
Numitor, 48

Oaths, 225, 408–417, 427, 447, 448, 466,
   469, 521, 554
Obedience
   Aristotle on, 454
   Christian law and, 379
   covenants, 341
   due only to ministers of God, 372–373,
      383
   law and, 380–383
   oaths of allegiance and, 521
   of private men and rebellion, 519
   secrets of government and, 15
   succession of kings and, 419, 428–429
   unconditional, to nation, called the king
      in legal proceedings, 555
   unjust commands and, 436–439
Odes (Horace), 54
Oedipus, 66
Offa (k. of England), 375, 414, 483, 487,
   504, 513
Of the Laws of Ecclesiastical Polity (Hooker),
   111*n*7
Omri, 45, 342, 407, 439
On the Citizen (Hobbes), 49, 221*n*5, 409*n*2
On the Laws and Customs of England (Bracton), 313*n*11, 360*n*2, 367*n*2, 393*n*3,
   399*n*2, 467*n*7, 471*n*11, 511*n*3

On the Soul (Aristotle), 538*n*6
On Tyranny (Strauss), 176*n*2
Oppius, 249
Oppression, 520. *See also* Tyrants and tyr-
   anny
Orange, Prince of (later k. William of En-
   gland), 277
Order, 134–144, 149–153. *See also* Civil
   disorder
Orsua, 59, 115, 238, 418
Osborne, Sir Thomas, 194–195, 258, 485,
   557, 571
Othniel, 125, 228, 314
Otho, 50, 139, 148, 155, 160–161, 165*n*13,
   175, 232, 235, 370, 398
Otto of Saxony, 243–244
Ottoman Empire, 534

Pallas, 149, 181, 372
Pansa, 455
Papacy. *See* Popes of Rome
Papirius Cursor, 151, 152, 182, 256, 271,
   273, 311, 394, 514
Pardons, 449–451, 555–556
Paris, Matthew, 106*n*17, 376*n*15, 414*n*14,
   415*n*15, 504*n*4
Parker, Matthew, 492*n*31
Parliament(s). *See also* Assemblies
   in the election of kings, 107
   historical examples of, 102–103
   sharing power with king, 296
Parliament (England), 144*n*19. *See also*
   Micklegemotes, Witenagemotes
   coercive power of law and, 572–578
   Commons, House of, 349, 399–400
   corruption of, 571
   delegates to, 563–569
   existence of, prior to Norman conquest,
      482, 486–487
   king's *de facto* power and, 518
   kingship and, 483, 528–534
   lawmaking by, 394, 399–400, 449–450,
      473, 572–578
   liberty and, 502
   Magna Charta and, 411, 493
   origin of, according to Filmer, 478
   pardons by, 451
   reforms of, in opposition to king, 65*n*5
   succession of kings and, 419, 430–431
   superior to king, 313
Parliament (France), 173, 222
Parliament (Scotland), 34
Parmenio, 231
Parsons, Robert, 9*n*4

Paternal right, authority
  biblical examples in Filmer disputed,
    28–30
  contracts and, 320
  divisibility vs. indivisibility of, 33–36
  freedom from domination and, 32
  full-grown heirs and, 88
  incommunicability of, 62–69
  inheritance and, 56–57, 92–97
  in the kingdom of Israel, 36–39, 45
  kingship vs., 24–25, 39–46, 73, 78, 319–
    321
  in Rome, 47–48, 50
  usurpation and, 62–63, 100–101
Pater patriae, 40, 73
*Patriarcha: A Defence of the Natural Power of
  Kings against the Unnatural Liberty of the
  People* (Filmer), 5*n*1, 77*n*1
Patriarcha and Other Political Works (Laslett,
  ed.), 5*n*1
Patricians, 217–218
Paul, Saint, 370–380, 381, 436
Paul V (pope of Rome), 223
Pausanias, 290, 542
Peace. *See also* War
  civil disorders and, 218
  commonwealths, when disposed toward,
    202–208
  forms of government and, compared,
    195–202
  justice and, 21, 160–161
  monarchy and, 262
  poverty and, 260–261
  valour contrasted with, 259–260
  warfare contrasted with, 158–160
Pelopidas, 15, 212, 221, 228, 314
Peloponnesian War, 299
Peloponnesian War (Thucydides), 201*n*8
People
  contract between magistrates and, 431–
    435
  corruption of, 343
  delegates to assemblies and, 563–569
  in England in time of Romans, 479
  government form chosen by, 56
  hereditary kingship by will of, 114
  as judge, 397
  kingship and, 19, 28, 287, 298
  king's responsibility to, 322
  law and, 387, 476–477
  liberty of, 502
  magistracy and, 69–74, 190, 225–227,
    431–435, 547–552
  Magna Charta and, 493

  power to change government and, 20, 21
  right of to resist kings, 339–343
  degradation of, in ancient Rome, 147
  sovereignty and, 504
Pepin (Frankish k.), 60, 114, 116, 118,
    120, 168, 172, 173, 219, 242, 243,
    244, 245, 293, 294, 295, 314, 348,
    425, 498, 504, 528
Perez, Antonio, 101, 412
Periander, 238
Pericles, 212, 271, 507
Perseus of Macedon, 145, 164, 200, 533
Persia, 113, 138, 141–142, 145, 178, 211,
    221, 290
Peru, 234
I *Peter*, 373*n*7, 379*n*28
Peter, Saint, 373, 378, 383, 436
Peter the Cruel (k. of Castile), 73, 169,
    265, 314, 334
Petreius, 472
Phaereus, 176, 385
Phaethon, 543
Phalaris, 41, 73, 169, 176, 191, 283, 385,
    461
Pharamond (Frankish k.), 60, 118, 168,
    240, 293, 314, 348, 387, 424, 426,
    498, 504
Pharaoh, 36, 63, 73, 92, 137–138, 329, 563
Pharasmenes (k. of Iberia), 282
Pharnabazus, 142, 176
Pharsalia (Lucan), 28*n*4, 60*n*3, 72*n*9, 154*n*1,
    186*n*2, 187*n*3, 210*n*1, 235*n*23, 343*n*5,
    536*n*5
Philip II (k. of Spain), 73, 101, 239, 261,
    554, 562, 567
Philip III (k. of Spain), 529
Philip IV (k. of Portugal), 554
Philip IV (k. of Spain), 239, 529
Philip of Macedon, 143, 164, 533
Philippics (Cicero), 379*n*31
Philistines, 125, 135, 347
Philo, 124
Philopoemen, 15, 161, 271
Philotas, 231
Phineas, 127, 398
Phocion, 178, 212, 253
Phoebidas, 314
Phoenicia, 203
Phoenissae (Seneca). See *Thebaid* (Seneca)
Phraates, 218
Pisa, 161
Pisistratus, 186, 218, 385
Piso, 383, 384
Plantagenets, 239*n*27

Plato, 18, 49, 67, 70, 78, 110, 176, 373
  aristocracy, inclination to, 191
  on king distinguished from tyrant, 91,
    287, 288
  on the selection of magistrates, 82–86
  on virtue and advancement, 126
Plautius, 520
Pliny, 380
Plutarch, 18, 113, 139, 142*n*16, 143*n*17–
    18, 231*n*18, 232*n*21, 252*n*2, 264,
    265*n*5, 267*n*12, 291*n*15, 297, 307*n*1,
    311*n*4, 351*n*4, 375*n*12, 391*n*5–6,
    441*n*2, 542*n*1
Poland, 101, 167, 224, 420, 488, 504, 505,
    534
Political Works of James I (McIlwain, ed.),
    339*n*1, 398*n*1
Politics (Aristotle), 9*n*3, 79*n*3, 81*n*4–5,
    84*n*10, 87*n*14, 133*n*2, 288*n*4, 290*n*10,
    353*n*2, 449, 451, 452*n*1–2, 453,
    470*n*10
Polybius, 18
Polydorus Vergilius, 106*n*19–20, 376*n*16
Polynices, 219, 238
Polyperchon, 178
Pompey, 155, 159, 174, 263, 295, 472
Pomponius Laetus, 251*n*1, 531
Pontius the Samnite, 547
Popes of Rome. *See also* Roman Catholic
    Church
  excommunication of king for perjury re-
    garding *Magna Charta*, 411, 493
  implicit faith and, 12–13
  judgments by, 549
  justice and war, swords of, 374
  oaths, absolving King John from, 409–
    410
  superiority to secular magistrates denied,
    223
Poppaea, 73, 149
Popular consent. *See* Consent of the gov-
    erned
Popular government. *See also* Common-
    wealths; Democracy
  Aristotle's caution about, 132–134
  civil disorders and, vs. monarchies, 217–
    250
  corruption in, vs. evils of courts, 251–
    258
  cruelty under, 263–264
  preservation of common good in, vs. ab-
    solute monarchy, 270–279
  in Rome, 151, 152–156, 157
Porsenna Lars, 65, 95

Portugal, 169, 275, 493, 554
Poverty, 261, 345, 351–352, 355
Power. *See also* Conquest; Force
  arbitrariness of, 569–572
  Aristotle on, 452–454
  as burdensome, 91–92
  corruption and, 138, 139, 140, 252
  de facto, 516–518
  de jure, 506–507
  of delegates to assemblies, 563–569
  division of, 99–100, 306, 310
  election of princes by people and, 101
  extrajudicial, and overthrow of, 227
  God and, 371, 442–443
  in governments without monarchs, 371
  granting of, by consent, 99
  heritability of, 96
  of judges, derived from law, not from
    kings, 466, 468
  justice and, 365
  of kings, law, and, 188, 287, 296, 322–
    324, 367–368, 443–444, 469
  of kings, the people and, 456–465
  of kings, unlawfully attained, 325–326,
    329–330
  of kings, variety of, according to consti-
    tutions of different states, 113, 508–
    510
  law and, 225
  law of nature and, 103–104, 321–322
  liberty and, 440–441
  limits upon, 222–224
  of magistrates, 69–74, 113–121, 383–
    386, 439–446, 514–516
  merit and, 94
  overreaching and, 222–223
  parliaments (England) and, 475, 476,
    528–534, 568, 572–578
  in ancient Rome, 151–153, 454–456
  submission to, however acquired, 220–
    221
  usurpation and, 67, 100
  virtue and, 81
Praise of Stilicho (Claudian), 441*n*4
Precepts of Statecraft (Plutarch), 267*n*12
Primogeniture, 25, 37
Prince, The (Machiavelli), 405*n*2
Princes
  election of, 101–103, 105–108
  paternal care of people by, 73–74
  paternal right of, 65
Privernates, 520
Proculus, Julius, 203

Property
  civil society and, 548
  kingship and, 493–497
  land grants, 493–497
  liberty and, 402–403
Protestants and Protestantism, 534
  in France, 346, 428, 439, 562
  Irish rebellion of 1641 and, 265, 540*n*10
Proverbs, 85, 532*n*6
Prusias, 145
Psalms, 123*n*3, 347*n*4, 379*n*29, 414*n*12
Ptolemy, 145, 164, 200
Public good (common good)
  assemblies and, 307
  deposing kings and, 226
  government, ends of, and, 49, 91, 92
  government reform and, 174
  kingship and, 51–52, 321–322, 341, 342,
    395–396, 440, 464–465, 470–471, 535–
    542
  magistrates and, 432–433
  mixed government and, 199, 270–279,
    526
  parliaments (England) and, 531
  power to change government and, 21
  proclamations and, 559
  rebellion and, 523–524
  in ancient Rome, 174, 504
  society and, 35–36
  virtue and, 80–81, 136
Publicola (Publius Valerius Poplicola), 15,
  145, 180, 193, 212, 217, 218, 228,
  271, 314, 507, 529
Punishment
  in civil society, 548
  by God, not sufficient to deter crimes,
    368–369
  of kings, 321, 339, 341, 342, 468–469
  by law, 219–220, 380, 448
  magistrates, 544, 546
  pardons granted by Parliament and, 451
  in Rome, 531–532
  for virtue, 372
Puritans and Puritanism, 9, 10, 437, 571
Pyrrhus, 168, 214, 232, 264–265, 525

Quintii, 148
Quintius, 178, 200
Quintus, 311

Ragnacaire, 240
Raleigh, Sir Walter, 33, 43, 334, 335,
  344*n*1, 501
Raoul (d. of Burgundy), 243

Rationality, reason
  detur digniori, as expression of, 80
  equality and, 30
  good and evil distinguished by, 38
  government, form of, and, 121, 123
  of Grecians regarding government, 47
  human nature and, 60
  implicit faith contrasted, 13
  law and, 461
  liberty and, 191–195
  light of, 38, 47, 291, 444, 510
  pater patriae concept and, 41–42
Rebellion
  contracts and, 521
  defined, 519
  general revolt compared, 519–524
  justice of, 522–523
  Plato and, 82
Rebus gestis Francorum, De (Aemilius Pau-
    lus), 425*n*14
Rechab, 332
Reform
  of constitutions, 461–462
  contracts between magistrates and na-
    tions and, 309–310
  of government superstructures, 170–175
  kingship abolished under, 459–460
  of law, cannot be made by kings, 393–
    394
Reformation, 8–10, 19*n*6. *See also* Protes-
    tants and Protestantism
Regicide
  legitimacy conferred by, 45–46, 50, 445–
    446
  unrestrained monarchy and, 302, 551
Rehoboam, 37, 45, 63, 102, 128, 138, 280,
  314, 335, 347, 355, 398, 404, 503,
  533, 539
Relaciones de Antonio Pérez, 298*n*30, 412
Religion. *See* Christians and Christianity;
    God
Remigius, Saint, 427
Remus, 47–48
Representation, 102, 105. *See also* Assem-
    blies
Republic (Plato), 82*n*7
Rerum Anglicarum scriptores post Bedam (Sa-
    vile), 107*n*28
*Rerum Scoticarum historia. See History of Scot-
    land, The* (Buchanan)
Reuben, 25, 104, 127, 356, 536
Revolt, distinguished from rebellion, 519–
  524. *See also* Civil disorders
Rhadamistus, 282
Rhea, 327

Rich, Richard, 473, 568
Richard II (k. of England), 59, 236, 237, 280, 297, 364, 408, 410, 500, 524, 528, 550
Richard III (k. of England), 239*n*27, 292, 576
Richard (Plantagenet), duke of York, 247, 419
Richelieu, Cardinal, 141, 275, 567
Riches. *See* Wealth
Right of assembly. *See* Assemblies
Rights, native, confirmed by law, 366–370
Right(s), natural. *See* Natural right(s)
Rimmon, 118
Robert (d. of Anjou), 243
Robert (k. of France), 118
Robert of Burgundy, 118, 120
Roberts, Alexander, 261*n*3
Robert the Norman, 118, 120
Rochefoucault, François, Duc de, 425*n*12
Rochelle, 275
Rodrigo (k. of Spain), 215, 277, 348, 477, 551
Roger of Wendover, 106*n*17, 106*n*22, 107*n*28, 376*n*17, 377*n*19, 411*n*5, 484*n*11, 494*n*1
Romanae historiae compendium (Laetus), 251*n*1
Roman Catholic Church. *See also* Popes of Rome
   governments instituted by, 51, 52
   implicit faith doctrine, 12–13
   liberty and, 9–10
Romans, 57, 93, 370*n*1, 371*n*2, 372*n*3
Rome (ancient), 30, 101
   assemblies, people's, in, 503
   best form of government in, 166–169
   capital punishment in, 182–183
   civil disorders in, 217–218, 219, 225–226, 229, 231–232, 233, 240, 249–250
   civil wars, 154–156, 180
   common good, government for, in, 174, 270–273, 277, 397, 504
   consent of the governed in, 104, 109
   contract between people and governors in, 311, 314, 431–432
   corruption in, 139–140, 153, 174–175, 183–184, 253, 256, 337, 342–343, 350
   councils, disregard of, in, 405
   dictators, elevation of, 127, 514
   disaffection of people in, 197
   elections in, 101–102, 106, 109
   England and, 472, 479, 512
   fall of, 140, 146, 148–149, 157–166
   founding of, 48, 98

Gauls and, 214
Germany and, 214, 480
government reform in, 170–171, 174
hereditary power in, 308
judging of officials by the people in, 531–532
law(s) of, 262–263, 379–380, 391, 394, 466, 542–543
liberty in, 144–149, 193, 462–463, 471–472, 511
magistracy in, 69–70, 73, 149–153, 180, 314, 383–386, 394, 503, 542, 551
monarchy in, 10, 47–48, 109, 153, 167, 172, 180, 297, 299, 348
peace by subjection and injustice in, 160
people as source of power in, 394
power in, 222, 361–362, 446, 454–456, 525
rebellion of subjects of, 519, 520
restraints upon governors in, 301, 505, 542–543
riches in, 156, 350
Senate of. *See* Senate (Rome)
Spain and, 215
and Sparta compared, 205
strong defenses of, 211–212
succession in, 420–421
titles in, 539
tribute paid to, 351–352, 359–366
valour in, 253, 260
virtue, flourishing of, in, 180, 253
war and, 143, 153, 197, 199–200, 203, 204
Romulus, 47–48, 66, 69, 152, 154, 203, 297, 298, 299, 305, 326, 327, 397, 457, 462, 511
Royal Charter, 6
Royal Commentaries of the Incas (Vega), 234*n*22
Royal Defense of Charles I (Salmasius), 122*n*2
Rufus, William, 114
Rullus, 212, 271
Rumbold, Richard "Hannibal," 511*n*2
Russia, 224

Saavedra y Fajardo, Diego de, 115*n*6, 422*n*4, 509*n*3
Sabaeans, 115
Sabines, 157, 203
Sacrorum conciliorum, nova et amplissima collectio (Mansi), 428*n*17
Safety. *See* Security
St. John, Oliver, 485*n*13
Salic Law, 293, 295, 418, 422
Salinator, Marcus Livius, 154, 178, 179

Sallust, 165, 182*n*10
Salmasius, Claudius, 122, 122*n*2
Samnites, 154
Samothes, 512
Samson, 15, 125, 314, 329, 398, 502, 563
Samuel, 37, 60, 63, 71, 86, 87, 102, 104,
    119, 126, 128, 130, 131, 135, 228,
    289, 300, 321, 324, 326, 328, 329,
    330, 332, 335, 336–339, 342, 344,
    345, 346, 353, 356, 373, 398, 442,
    446, 522, 538, 559, 563
I *Samuel*, 105*n*13, 130, 138, 324*n*6, 329*n*10,
    331*n*14, 332*n*15, 332*n*16, 337*n*2,
    342*n*4, 369*n*10, 522*n*4
II *Samuel*, 119*n*11, 138, 333*n*17, 356*n*7,
    381*n*2, 413*n*11
Sancho the Brave (k. of Castile), 59
Sandoval, Prudencio de, 567*n*2
Sanhedrin, 127, 128, 166, 289, 335, 371,
    374, 375, 464, 467
Sarah, 28
Sardanapalus, 145
Satires (Juvenal), 47*n*2, 91*n*1, 147*n*5,
    165*n*12, 254*n*4, 264*n*4, 352*n*5, 431*n*2
Satires, Epistles, and Ars Poetica (Horace),
    64*n*3
Satraps, 176
Saul, 37, 45, 61, 63, 104, 129, 230, 297,
    298, 305, 314, 326, 327, 330, 331,
    332, 333, 340, 347, 353, 356, 357,
    369, 413, 458, 478, 502
    abolition of aristocracy by, 124
    election of, 102, 110, 128, 464
    as lawgiver, 324
    instability under, 138
Savile, Henry, 107*n*28
Saxons, 102, 103, 106, 114, 120, 204, 376–
    377, 415, 458, 479, 484, 486, 489,
    490, 494, 495–496, 513, 530, 549, 570
Scaevola, Gaius Mucius, 65, 95
Schoolmen (Scholastics), 8–12, 18, 77–78,
    380–381, 410
Scipio Africanus, 59, 115, 135, 161, 179,
    200, 212, 256, 271, 283, 445, 472, 525
Scipio Nasica, 200, 212
Scotland, 143, 246, 265, 278, 398, 505,
    546
Security (national defense, safety)
    as the ends of government, 405–406
    force as means to, 209–210
    law at the root of public's safety, 403
    rulers set up for public's safety, 470, 550
    tyranny and, 407
    war preparedness of a good government,
    209–216

Sedition. *See also* Civil disorder
    defined, 220, 227
    opposition to legally chosen rule, 104
    orderly reform of government vs., 168
    "popular," as disobedience to tyrants, 15
    Roman wealth and, 153–156
    usury and, 149, 150
    virtue, reliance on, vs., 141–142
Seguier, Pierre, 574
Seius, 548, 549
Sejanus, 148, 160, 181, 194, 388
Selden, John, 77*n*1, 427*n*15, 489
Selim, 197
Selim II, 241
Sempronius, Tiberius, 65
Senate(s), 299
Senate (Rome), 151, 157, 273, 455, 528–
    529
Senate (Sparta), 166, 477
Seneca, 46, 68*n*11, 180, 188, 382*n*5, 535*n*1
Servilius, 200
Servitude, 89, 103, 312, 436, 438, 548,
    549
Servius Tullius, 48, 70, 305, 457
Severus, Lucius Septimius, 233, 241
Sforza, Francesco, 325
Sforza, Lodovico (k. of Milan), 198
Shallum, 45
Shamgar, 125, 314
Sheba, 230, 334, 502
Shem, 26, 27, 28, 29, 30, 33, 41, 42, 43,
    53, 90, 101, 304, 323, 326
Sicily, 156, 178
Sigebert, 240
Sigismond of Metz, 240
Sigismund (k. of Sweden), 169
Simeon, 25, 104, 127
Simnel, Lambert, 248, 516
Simonides, 176*n*2
Sin, 9, 378, 439
    kingdom given to Hebrews as punish-
        ment for, 125
    kingdom of Hebrews imputed to, 39,
        124
Sine jussu populi, 101
Sisinandus (k. of the Goths), 423, 428
Slavery. *See also* Natural slavery
    flattery the worst effect of, 162
    gladiatorian wars versus civil wars, 154
    monarchy and, 17–19, 325, 326
    of subjects in Nimrod's kingdom, 32
    vice and, 84, 137–142
    wisdom, uselessness of, under, 31
    Xenophon on tyranny and, 176
Smith, Dog, 66

Sobieski, John. *See* John III Sobieski (k. of Poland)
Society. *See* Civil society
Socrates, 67, 178
Soissons, count de, 245
Solomon, 14, 37, 38, 45, 63, 64, 67, 84, 85, 94, 110, 119, 120, 230, 280, 335, 347, 354, 356, 364–365, 366, 374, 389, 396, 442, 446, 502, 532, 533, 544
  after death of, abrogation of kingdom, 128
  oppression of Hebrews by, 138
Solon, 387, 391, 393, 394, 397
Soranus, 147
Sovereignty
  assemblies and, 502
  division of, 297
  in England, 565
  limitations on, 505
  people and, 504
  of Roman people, rather than their magistrates, 152–153
  sovereign power, 115, 222–223, 296, 505
  in Sparta, 375
Spain, 40, 95, 101, 115, 160, 169, 204, 215, 246, 265, 277, 294, 302, 315, 348, 380, 421–424, 477, 493, 533, 540, 551, 566–567, 576
Sparta, 47, 113, 114, 142, 161, 166, 167, 177, 203–205, 217, 221, 290, 291, 297–298, 299, 301, 321, 351, 375, 391, 477, 524–525, 542
Spartacus, 164, 314
Spelman, Sir Henry, 106*n*18, 415*n*16, 486, 487*n*20
Spencer, 524, 550, 556
Spencer, Robert, earl of Sunderland, 258*n*7
Sporus, 73
Star-Chamber (England), 476, 573*n*2
Stephen (k. of England), 419
Strafford, Sir Thomas, earl of, 540*n*10, 557
Strauss, Leo, 176*n*2
Straw, Jack, 235*n*25, 237
Stuart dynasty, 246
Stubbs, William, 377*n*20
Suarez, Francisco, 77, 88–89, 96, 97
Succession
  children and, 119, 280, 393, 447
  civil wars over, 248, 517
  coronation creates kings, not heredity, in, 417–431
  hereditary kingship, variety of forms in, 236–237, 417–418

heredity, difficulty deciding in, 235
  restraints upon kings due to uncertainty of, 390
  Salic Law and, 293
  usurpation and, 499–500
  virtue and, 136–137
  women and. *See* Women
Suetonius, 63*n*2, 158*n*3, 337, 382*n*6, 444*n*6
Sueves, 147
Suintila (k. of the Goths), 422–423
Sulla, Lucius Cornelius, 50, 155, 181, 262, 306, 525
Sweden, 101, 116, 167, 169, 237, 418, 466, 503–505
Switzerland, 17, 105, 143, 206–207, 224, 466, 491, 564–565
Swynford, Catherine, 430
Sybthorpe, Robert, 11, 11*n*7
Syphax, 145, 164, 200
Syracuse, 19, 193

Tacitus, 17*n*2, 73, 87*n*15, 91, 103*n*11, 146, 147, 148, 160*n*5, 162, 165*n*13, 171*n*1, 180, 182*n*15, 191, 197, 228, 232*n*20, 242*n*30, 263*n*7, 264, 266–267, 271, 282, 285, 291, 295*n*25, 325, 372*n*4–6, 376, 383*n*1, 384, 384*n*2–4, 389*n*3, 405*n*3, 441, 455, 458, 466, 479, 480, 481–482, 484, 486, 490, 491*n*26, 508*n*1–2, 545*n*3
Tamerlane, 306, 406
Tanistry law, 59, 116
Tarquin (the first), 48, 305
Tarquin(s), 144, 148, 151, 174, 193, 217, 286, 301, 314, 441
Tarquinius Priscus, 48, 70, 203, 299, 457
Tarquinius Superbus ("the Proud"), 19, 48, 101, 106, 144, 157, 167–170, 174, 186, 194, 225, 238, 249, 342, 370, 396, 457, 529, 543
Tatius, 203
Taxation, 260, 348. *See also* Tribute
Tears of the Indians (Las Casas), 106*n*6
Telerius, 314
Telesinus, 154
Term of office
  expired, defiance of a cause of disorders, 220, 221–222
  in Rome, not detrimental to leadership, 271
Tertullian, 261, 285, 361, 362, 363, 367, 380, 460, 492, 510
Thais, 560*n*3
Thebaid (Seneca), 46, 68*n*11
Thebes, 221, 503

Index

Themistocles, 177, 201, 212, 252, 271, 441
Theocracy, 128
Theodorus, 193
Theodosius, 233, 420, 446
Theopompus, 113, 291, 542, 561
Theorestes, 219
Theseus, 305, 326, 327, 391
Thirty Years War, 279
Thorne, Samuel E., 313*n*11
Thrasea, Paetus, 73, 147, 181, 267, 372, 388
Thrasybulus, 15, 221, 228, 314
Thucydides, 18, 177, 191, 195, 201
Thyestes (Seneca), 68*n*11, 188*n*4
Tiberius, 50, 65, 139, 148, 155, 185, 232, 239, 271, 272*n*4, 322, 337, 359, 372, 383, 384, 388, 405, 461
Tiepoli, 525
Tigellinus, Gaius, 148, 181, 194, 372, 388
Tiglathpileser, 536
Tigranes, 143, 145, 200
Timoleon, 193, 228, 283
Timothy, 70
Tiridates, 384
Tissaphernes, 142, 176
Titles
 dominion not signified by, in Rome, Italy, and Spain, 95
 empty, to swell the importance of princes, 515–516
 variety in, and extent of power, 508–509
Titles of Honour (Selden), 427*n*14, 489*n*24
Titus, 139, 233
Titus Livius. *See* Livy
Torquatus, Titus Manlius, 182, 212
Tractatus de Legibus (Suarez), 88*n*2
Trade, 83, 203–205, 209
Trajan, 140, 157, 158, 181, 185, 380, 506, 568
Treason
 impossible if king is above the law, 313
 king's command as, 448, 556
 law of (*lex perduellionis*), 182
 pardon for, not always in king's power to obtain, 556–557
 subversion of laws and, 448
Treaties
 prince's name in, stipulating whole nation, 553–554
 secret, for advantage of prince against the people, 540
Trepanners, 146
Tresilian, Robert, 447, 448, 468, 524, 550, 555, 556

Tribunes (Rome)
 created for publick good, 171
 power of, over dictators, 311
 power of, for preservation of liberty, 514–515
Tribute, 351–352, 359–361, 365–366, 369, 379, 502. *See also* Taxation
Triennial Act of 1641 (England), 571, 571*n*3
Trivultio, Marquess, 159
Tromp, Admiral Martin, 278*n*10
True Law of Free Monarchies, The (James I of England), 398*n*1, 401*n*8, 572–573
Tudor, Owen, 239*n*27
Tudor dynasty, 247*n*34
Tufton, Nicholas, 485*n*12
Tullus Hostilius, 48, 69, 152*n*4, 297, 299, 305, 394, 397, 457
Tumult. *See* Civil disorder and tumult
Turenne, Vicomte Henri de, 275, 278
Turks and Turkey, 17, 34, 58, 94–95, 116, 197, 236, 534
Tuscany, 108, 143, 167
Tyler, Wat, 237, 237*n*25
Tyrants and tyranny
 Aristotle on degeneration of kings into, 94
 Aristotle on distinction between king and, 353, 452–454
 civil war and, 545
 common good and, 51–52, 91
 corruption of subjects under, 186, 229
 cruelties of, 263–270
 degeneration of kings into tyrants, 398–399
 deliverance from, 15–16
 flattery and, 253
 God's law, ironically imputed to, 20
 in Greece, signification of name, 354
 Israelites and, 330, 353–359
 killing of, 221, 224–225, 228, 407, 551
 law, overthrowing, and, 403
 laws of nature and, 193, 402–408
 punishment of, 321, 342
 sedition obviated through obedience to, 15
 violence and wrong springing from, 79
 virtue and, 135
 wealth of, 350
 wisdom of, 282–284

Ulpian, 446*n*8, 471
Unions. *See* Leagues
United Provinces. *See* Netherlands

[604]

Uriah, 346, 347, 356
Usurpation, usurped power, 67, 72, 285.
 See also Nimrod
 of Augustus Caesar, 454–456
 Henry I (k. of England), 498
 hereditary succession and, 43, 54, 100–
  101, 498
 kingship, lawful, vs., 108, 329–330,
  369–370, 498–499
 law, vs. usurper's claim to rights, 32–33,
  55, 220–221, 284
 in Macedonia, 171–172
 patriarchal rights not owed to usurpers,
  62–63, 319–320
 people's legal defenses against, 226–227
 regicide and, 45–46, 445–446
 in Rome, 48, 50, 69, 171, 369
Usury, 149, 150, 171

Valerius Asiaticus, 180, 227–228, 372,
 388, 396
Valerius, Publius. *See* Publicola
Valour, 47, 161, 211
 under absolute monarchy, 197–199
 Christianity and, 358–359
 in civil wars, 276
 common good, advance of, promotes,
  272, 276
 courtly subversion of, 277
 of England, 278, 483
 of France, 277–278
 of Germany, 480
 military, and enlargement of the nobility, 487
 in mixed monarchies, 526
 peace and, 205, 259–260
 in Rome, 153, 200, 455
 virtue and, 211–212
 war and, 142, 160, 259–260
Vandals, 102, 147
Varro, Gaius Terentius, 531
Vega, Garcilaso de la (El Inca), 234*n*22
Venice, 17, 143, 166, 205–206, 224, 274,
 325, 477, 491, 505, 525, 543
Vere, 550
Vergil, Polydore. *See* Polydorus Vergilius
Vespasian, 50, 114, 139, 155, 175, 235,
 271
Vice. *See also* Sin
 instability as effect of, 136–140
 inviting to kings, 45–46
 of slaves by nature, 84
Villiers, Barbara, duchess of Cleveland,
 195*n*5

Vinius, 149, 181, 372
Virgil, 491*n*27
Virginius, 396
Virtue
 aristocracy's excellence in, 31
 Aristotle on, 454
 civil society best instituted through, 84–
  85
 and frugality of kings, 350
 in Greece, 164, 273
 hatred of, 266–267
 human frailty and, 178
 human nature and, 253
 inequality of, in men, 81
 justice, and veneration of, 179
 kingship and, 46–53, 85, 132–133, 279–
  286, 398–401
 liberty as "nurse" of, 142, 161, 177, 273
 liberty as result of, in rulers, 17, 134–
  144
 liberty in Rome and, 144–149, 151, 181
 in ministers, vs. princes, 14–15
 mixed governments upheld by, 186
 necessity of, for liberty, 134–144, 302
 noblemen and, 484
 not inherited, 93
 Plato on, 126
 public good promoted by ruler's, 80–81,
  272
 punishment for, 372
 reform of government and, 302
 as requirement of a good governor, 6,
  135
 right to overthrow kings and, 344–348
 rulers set up because endowed with, 74,
  79, 80, 81, 87
 sedition and, 141–142
 upholding of contract between people
  and governor, 431
 valour and, 211–212
 wisdom of kings as consistent with, 282–
  283
Vitellius, 14, 50, 139, 148, 155, 175, 232,
 235, 271, 382, 398, 461, 539, 550
Vitruvius, 520
Vortigern the Britain, 265, 484, 494

Wamba (k. of the Goths), 422
War(s)
 for attaining dominion, 406–407
 common good and, 199, 277–278
 commonwealths' constitution for, 79,
  202–208
 of conquest and, 210. *See also* Conquest

War(s) *(continued)*
    cruel monarchs as provokers of, 264–265
    effects of corruption, 214–215
    forms of government in, compared, 195–202
    governments best that provide for, 209–216
    Israel, 127–128, 129–130, 375
    just, 370
    kingship and, 296, 332
    law and, 370
    mercenaries in, 204–205
    peace contrasted with, 158–160
    popes of Rome and, 374
    public's willingness to fight, 199–200, 201, 209, 213
    renewal of, as rebellion, 519
    Rome, 145, 147–148, 153, 170
    of succession of kings, 517
    valour and, 142, 160, 199–202, 259–260
Warbeck, Perkin, 237, 237n25, 248, 516
Wars of the Roses, 247n34, 250n36
Wealth, 67, 150, 153–156. *See also* Luxury
    of king, as people's obligation, 348–351
    prodigal, evils of, 540
    subjection of nations, 352
West-Indies, 160, 493, 540, 562, 566
Westminster, Matthew, 106n22, 265n6
William I (William the Norman, k. of England), 107, 114, 237, 246, 377, 378, 414, 419, 472–473, 492–493
William II (k. of England), 237, 415, 419. *See also* Orange, Prince of
William of Malmesbury, 106n19, 106n21, 377n21, 377n24, 486, 492, 494

Will of man
    fallibility of, 403–404, 406
    forms of government proceed from, 31, 53–57
Wisdom, 31, 134, 271
    of aristocracy, 31
    divine, in Plato, 85
    God's, subject to no error, 131
    kingship and, 47, 63–64, 279–286, 532–533, 535–542
    required of fit governors, 80, 85–86, 135
Wisniowiecki, Michael (Korybut), 488n22
Witenagemotes, 483, 486, 489, 497, 530
Witiza (k. of Spain), 215, 348, 477, 551
Women
    nature of, 60
    Spartan, 201
    succession to crown and, 59–61, 116, 117, 168, 237, 418, 429, 447, 504, 505, 534
    war and, 532

Xenophon, 18, 113, 142, 175–184, 191, 195, 375
Xerxes, 63, 201, 542, 560n3, 566

Zechariah, 45
Zedekiah, 289, 335, 347
Zeruiah, 335
Zimri, 45, 407
Zoroaster, 41
Zurita y Castro, Gerónimo, 509n3

This book is set in Janson, a typeface long thought to be based on a design by the Dutch typefounder Anton Janson, who worked in Leipzig in the latter half of the seventeenth century. More recent scholarship attributes the original design to his slightly older contemporary, the Hungarian Nicolas Kis.

Printed on paper that is acid-free and meets the requirements of the American National Standard for Permanence of Paper for Printed Library Materials, z39.48-1992. ∞

Book Design by
Betty Binns, Binns & Lubin
New York, New York

Editorial Services and Index by
Harkavy Publishing Service
New York, New York

Typography by
Monotype Composition Company
Baltimore, Maryland

Printing and Binding by
Sheridan Books, Inc.
Chelsea, Michigan